Communications in Computer and Information Science 976

Commenced Publication in 2007
Founding and Former Series Editors:
Phoebe Chen, Alfredo Cuzzocrea, Xiaoyong Du, Orhun Kara, Ting Liu,
Krishna M. Sivalingam, Dominik Ślęzak, and Xiaokang Yang

More information about this series at http://www.springer.com/series/7899

Ana Fred · David Aveiro ·
Jan L. G. Dietz · Kecheng Liu ·
Jorge Bernardino · Ana Salgado ·
Joaquim Filipe (Eds.)

Knowledge Discovery, Knowledge Engineering and Knowledge Management

9th International Joint Conference, IC3K 2017
Funchal, Madeira, Portugal, November 1–3, 2017
Revised Selected Papers

Springer

Editors
Ana Fred
Instituto de Telecomunicações
Lisbon, Portugal

Jan L. G. Dietz
Delft University of Technology
Delft, The Netherlands

Jorge Bernardino
University of Coimbra
Coimbra, Portugal

Joaquim Filipe
INSTICC and Instituto Politecnico
de Setúbal
Setúbal, Portugal

David Aveiro (iD)
University of Madeira
Funchal, Portugal

Madeira Interactive Technologies Institute
Funchal, Portugal

Kecheng Liu
Henley Business School
University of Reading
Reading, UK

Ana Salgado
Federal University of Pernambuco
Recife, Brazil

ISSN 1865-0929   ISSN 1865-0937 (electronic)
Communications in Computer and Information Science
ISBN 978-3-030-15639-8   ISBN 978-3-030-15640-4 (eBook)
https://doi.org/10.1007/978-3-030-15640-4

Library of Congress Control Number: 2019934199

This Springer imprint is published by the registered company Springer Nature Switzerland AG
The registered company address is: Gewerbestrasse 11, 6330 Cham, Switzerland

Preface

The present book includes extended and revised versions of a set of selected papers from the 9th International Joint Conference on Knowledge Discovery, Knowledge Engineering and Knowledge Management (IC3K 2017), held in Funchal, Madeira, Portugal, during November 1–3, 2017.

The purpose of IC3K is to bring together researchers, engineers, and practitioners in the areas of knowledge discovery, knowledge engineering, and knowledge management. IC3K is composed of three co-located conferences, each specialized in one of the aforementioned main knowledge areas: KDIR (International Conference on Knowledge Discovery and Information Retrieval), KEOD (International Conference on Knowledge Engineering and Ontology Development) and KMIS (International Conference on Knowledge Management and Information Sharing). For IC3K 2017, we received 157 paper submissions from 47 countries, of which 12% are included in this book. These papers were selected, after their presentation at the conference, by the Program Chairs. The selection process was based on a number of criteria that included the classifications and comments provided by the Program Committee members, the session chairs' assessment of the presentation and discussion, and finally the program chairs' global view of all papers included in the technical program. The authors of selected papers were then invited to submit a revised and extended version of their papers having at least 30% of innovative material and incorporating the comments received at the conference venue.

The papers selected to be included in this book contribute to the understanding of relevant trends of current research on knowledge discovery, knowledge engineering, and knowledge management. There were ten selected papers from KDIR, six from KEOD, and three from KMIS. The collection of papers from KDIR focused mainly on innovative aspects of research on machine learning, including the papers authored by Andrea Pagliarani et al., Abdullah Alshehri et al., and Sreekanth Madisetty et al.; data and text mining, including the papers authored by Piyush Lakhawat et al., Andrey Timofeyev et al., and Giacomo Domeniconi et al.; and information extraction and data analytics, including the papers authored by Liqun Shao et al., Khaled Nagi, and Stephen Bradshaw et al. From KEOD, we selected papers focusing on ontology engineering, authored by Matthias Frank et al., Adrian Horzyk, and Marzieh Talebpour et al.; decision support systems, including the papers authored by Gianluca Torta et al. and Ahmed Sadik et al., and also one paper focusing on natural language processing and knowledge acquisition, authored by Fumiyo Fukumoto et al. From KMIS, we selected three papers, offering insights on best practices, information sharing, impact measurement of knowledge management, and resilience aspects of information systems, authored by Nabil Badr, Rauno Pirinen, and Christian Riera et al., respectively. We would like to thank all the authors for their contributions and also the reviewers who helped ensure the quality of this publication.

November 2017

Ana Fred
David Aveiro
Jan Dietz
Kecheng Liu
Jorge Bernardino
Ana Salgado
Joaquim Filipe

Organization

IC3K Conference Chair

Joaquim Filipe   Polytechnic Institute of Setúbal/INSTICC, Portugal

Program Co-chairs

KDIR

Ana Fred   Instituto de Telecomunicações and Instituto Superior
                                Técnico, Lisbon University, Portugal

KEOD

David Aveiro   University of Madeira/Madeira-ITI, Portugal
Jan Dietz   Delft University of Technology, The Netherlands

KMIS

Kecheng Liu   University of Reading, UK
Jorge Bernardino   Polytechnic Institute of Coimbra, ISEC, Portugal
Ana Salgado   Federal University of Pernambuco, Brazil

KDIR Program Committee

Davide Moroni   Institute of Information Science and Technologies
                                (Isti)-CNR, Italy
Luigi Pontieri   National Research Council (CNR), Italy
Muhammad Abulaish   South Asian University, India
Amir Ahmad   United Arab Emirates University, UAE
Mayer Aladjem   Ben-Gurion University of the Negev, Israel
Sabeur Aridhi   LORIA France, France
Eva Armengol   IIIA CSIC, Spain
Zeyar Aung   Masdar Institute of Science and Technology, UAE
Kerstin Bach   Norwegian University of Science and Technology
                                (NTNU), Norway
Vladimir Bartik   Brno University of Technology, Czech Republic
Márcio Basgalupp   Universidade Federal de São Paulo, Brazil
Amel Borgi   Université de Tunis El Manar, Institut Supérieur
                                d'Informatique, LIPAH, Tunisia
Jesús Carrasco-Ochoa   INAOE, Mexico
André Carvalho   University of São Paulo, Brazil
Arnaud Castelltort   LIRMM, France
Sunandan Chakraborty   New York University, USA

Keith Chan	The Hong Kong Polytechnic University, SAR China
Lijun Chang	UNSW, Australia
Zhiyuan Chen	University of Maryland Baltimore County, USA
Patrick Ciarelli	Universidade Federal do Espírito Santo, Brazil
Paulo Cortez	University of Minho, Portugal
Ingemar Cox	University of Copenhagen, Denmark
Fabio Crestani	University of Lugano, Switzerland
Luis M. de Campos	University of Granada, Spain
Alessandro Di Bucchianico	Eindhoven University of Technology, The Netherlands
Emanuele Di Buccio	University of Padua, Italy
Thanh-Nghi Do	College of Information Technology, Can Tho University, Vietnam
Antoine Doucet	University of La Rochelle, France
Markus Endres	University of Augsburg, Germany
Iaakov Exman	The Jerusalem College of Engineering Azrieli, Israel
Dan Feldman	MIT, Israel
Elisabetta Fersini	University of Milano-Bicocca, Italy
Alvis Fong	Auckland University of Technology, New Zealand
Philippe Fournier-Viger	University of Moncton, Canada
Ana Fred	Instituto de Telecomunicações and Instituto Superior Técnico, Lisbon University, Portugal
Ingo Frommholz	University of Bedfordshire, UK
Michael Gashler	University of Arkansas, USA
Angelo Genovese	Università degli Studi di Milano, Italy
Rosario Girardi	Ufma, Brazil
Nuno Gonçalves	Superior School of Technology, Polytechnic Institute of Setúbal, Portugal
Francesco Gullo	UniCredit R&D, Italy
Yaakov Hacohen-Kerner	Jerusalem College of Technology (Machon Lev), Israel
Jennifer Harding	Loughborough University, UK
Lynette Hirschman	The MITRE Corporation, USA
Roberto Interdonato	DIMES, Unversità della Calabria, Italy
Abdeslam Jafjaf	Sorbonne University of Paris 1, France
Szymon Jaroszewicz	Polish Academy of Sciences, Poland
Mouna Kamel	IRIT, France
Mehmed Kantardzic	University of Louisville, USA
Ron Kenett	Samuel Neaman Institute, Technion, Israel
Margita Kon-Popovska	Ss Cyril and Methodius University, Macedonia, The Former Yugoslav Republic of
Ralf Krestel	Hasso-Plattner-Institut, Germany
Anne Laurent	Lirmm, Montpellier University, France
Carson Leung	University of Manitoba, Canada
Chun Li	Hong Kong Baptist University, SAR China
Chun-Wei Lin	Western Norway University of Applied Sciences, Norway
Xia Lin	Drexel University, USA

Berenike Litz	Attensity Corporation, USA
Giovanni Livraga	Università degli Studi di Milano, Italy
Jose Macedo	Federal University of Ceara, Brazil
Juan Manuel Corchado	University of Salamanca, Spain
Devignes Marie-Dominique	LORIA, CNRS, France
J. Martínez-Trinidad	Instituto Nacional de Astrofísica, Óptica y Electrónica, Puebla, Mexico
Sérgio Matos	University of Aveiro, Portugal
Misael Mongiovi	Università di Catania, Italy
Stefania Montani	Piemonte Orientale University, Italy
Manuel Montes y Gómez	INAOE, Mexico
Eduardo Morales	INAOE, Mexico
Yashar Moshfeghi	University of Strathclyde, UK
Wolfgang Nejdl	L3S and University of Hannover, Germany
Engelbert Nguifo	LIMOS, Université Clermont Auvergne, France
Mitsunori Ogihara	University of Miami, USA
Elias Oliveira	Universidade Federal do Espirito Santo, Brazil
José Oliveira	Universidade de Aveiro, Portugal
Márcia Oliveira	Universidade Federal do Espírito Santo, Brazil
Fabrício Olivetti de França	Universidade Federal do ABC, Brazil
Colm O'Riordan	NUI, Galway, Ireland
Sarala Padi	National Institute of Standards and Technology, USA
Rui Pedro Paiva	University of Coimbra, Portugal
Krzysztof Pancerz	University of Rzeszow, Poland
NhatHai Phan	University of Oregon, USA
Alberto Pinto	LIAAD INESC TEC, University of Porto, Portugal
Gianvito Pio	Università degli Studi di Bari Aldo Moro, Italy
Giovanni Ponti	ENEA, DTE-ICT-HPC, Portici Research Center, Italy
Alfredo Pulvirenti	University of Catania, Italy
Marcos Quiles	Federal University of Sao Paulo, UNIFESP, Brazil
Antonio Rinaldi	University of Naples Federico II, Italy
Ovidio Salvetti	National Research Council of Italy, CNR, Italy
Vasilis Samoladas	Technical University of Crete, Greece
Milos Savic	University of Novi Sad, Serbia
Filippo Sciarrone	Roma Tre University, Italy
Fabricio Silva	FIOCRUZ, Fundação Oswaldo Cruz, Brazil
Minseok Song	Pohang University of Science and Technology, Korea, Republic of
Marcin Sydow	IPI PAN (and PJIIT), Warsaw, Poland
Andrea Tagarelli	University of Calabria, Italy
Ulrich Thiel	Fraunhofer Gesellschaft, Germany
Kar Toh	Yonsei University, Korea, Republic of
Juan-Manuel Torres-Moreno	Ecole Polytechnique de Montréal, Canada
Predrag Tosic	Washington State University, USA
Alicia Troncoso Lora	Pablo de Olavide University of Seville, Spain

Domenico Ursino	Università Politecnica delle Marche, Italy
Nina Wacholder	Rutgers University, USA
Bingsheng Wang	Google, USA
Jiabing Wang	South China University of Technology, China
Yanghua Xiao	Fudan University, China
Yi Zhang	University of Technology Sydney, Australia

KDIR Additional Reviewers

Alessia Amelio	DIMES University of Calabria, Italy
Enrico Caldarola	Università di Napoli, Italy
Bilel Moulahi	LIRMM, University of Montpellier, France
Cristiano Russo	Université Paris-est, France

KEOD Program Committee

Rocío Abascal-Mena	Col. Santa Fe Cuajimalpa, Delegación Cuajimalpa de Morelos, Mexico
Alia Abdelmoty	Cardiff University, UK
Mamoun Abu Helou	Al-Istiqlal University, Palestinian Territory, Occupied
Alessandro Adamou	Knowledge Media Institute, The Open University, UK
Raian Ali	Bournemouth University, UK
Francisco Antunes	Institute of Computer and Systems Engineering of Coimbra and Beira Interior University, Portugal
Petra Bago	University of Zagreb, Croatia
Claudio Baptista	Universidade Federal de Campina Grande, Brazil
Jean-Paul Barthes	Université de Technologie de Compiègne, France
Ines Ben Messaoud	Laboratory Mir@cl, Tunisia
Giacomo Bucci	Università degli Studi di Firenze, Italy
Vladimír Bureš	University of Hradec Kralove, Czech Republic
Radek Burget	Brno University of Technology, Faculty of Information Technology, Czech Republic
Jin Chen	University of Kentucky, USA
Davide Ciucci	Università degli Studi di Milano Bicocca, Italy
João Costa	Institute of Computer and Systems Engineering of Coimbra, Portugal
Christophe Cruz	Laboratoire Le2i - FRE 2005 CNRS, France
Ananya Dass	New Jersey Institute of Technology, USA
Valeria De Antonellis	Università degli Studi di Brescia, Italy
Erdogan Dogdu	TOBB University of Economics and Technology, Turkey
John Edwards	Aston University, UK
Henrik Eriksson	Linköping University, Sweden
Ricardo Falbo	Federal University of Espírito Santo, UFES, Brazil
Catherine Faron-Zucker	University of Nice Sophia Antipolis, France
Dieter Fensel	University of Innsbruck, Austria

Orazio Tomarchio	University of Catania, Italy
Evangelos Triantaphyllou	Louisiana State University, USA
Petr Tucnik	University of Hradec Kralove, Czech Republic
Manolis Tzagarakis	University of Patras, Greece
Rafael Valencia-Garcia	Universidad de Murcia, Spain
Yue Xu	Queensland University of Technology, Australia
Gian Zarri	Sorbonne University, France
Jinglan Zhang	Queensland University of Technology, Australia
Ying Zhao	Naval Postgraduate School, USA
Qiang Zhu	The University of Michigan, Dearborn, USA

KEOD Additional Reviewers

Zaenal Akbar	Semantic Technology Institute (STI) Innsbruck, Austria
Sergio Angelastro	Università degli studi di Bari, Italy
Bogart Marquez	Baja California Autonomous University, Mexico
Umutcan Simsek	University of Innsbruck, Austria

KMIS Program Committee

Marie-Helene Abel	HEUDIASYC CNRS UMR, University of Compiègne, France
Miriam Alves	Institute of Aeronautics and Space, Brazil
Ana Azevedo	CEOS.PP-ISCAP/IPP, Portugal
Jorge Bernardino	Polytechnic Institute of Coimbra, ISEC, Portugal
Kelly Braghetto	University of São Paulo, Brazil
Frada Burstein	Monash University, Australia
Uwe Cantner	University of Jena, Germany
Byron Choi	Hong Kong Baptist University, SAR China
Ritesh Chugh	Central Queensland University, Australia
Silvia Dallavalle de Pádua	Universidade de São Paulo, Brazil
Júlio Duarte	University of Minho, Portugal
Alan Eardley	Staffordshire University, UK
Nour El Mawas	Université de Lille, France
Michael Fellmann	Universität Rostock, Germany
Joao Ferreira	ISEL, Portugal
Joan-Francesc Fondevila-Gascón	CECABLE (Centre d'Estudis sobre el Cable), UPF, URL, UdG (EU Mediterrani) and UOC, Spain
Yiwei Gong	Wuhan University, China
Anna Goy	University of Turin, Italy
Tan Guan	Universiti Malaysia Kelantan, Malaysia
Teresa Guarda	Universidad de las Fuerzas Armadas, ESPE, Sangolqui, Ecuador/Portugal
Renata Guizzardi	Universidade Federal do Espírito Santo, UFES, Brazil
Anne Håkansson	KTH, Sweden
Jennifer Harding	Loughborough University, UK

Mounira Harzallah	LS2N, Polytech Nantes, University of Nantes, France
Maria-Eugenia Iacob	University of Twente, The Netherlands
Cirano Iochpe	Universidade Federal do Rio Grande do Sul, Brazil
Anca Ionita	University Politehnica of Bucharest, Romania
Abdeslam Jafjaf	Sorbonne University of Paris 1, France
Nikos Karacapilidis	University of Patras and CTI, Greece
Radoslaw Katarzyniak	Wroclaw University of Science and Technology, Poland
Katarzyna Kuzmicz	Bialystok University of Technology, Poland
Inaya Lahoud	Galatasaray University, Turkey
Dominique Laurent	CNRS UMR 8051 - Cergy-Pontoise University, ENSEA, France
Michael Leyer	University of Rostock, Germany
Antonio Lieto	University of Turin and ICAR-CNR, Italy
Kecheng Liu	University of Reading, UK
Lin Liu	Tsinghua University, China
Xiaoyue Ma	University of Xidian, China
Carlos Malcher Bastos	Universidade Federal Fluminense, Brazil
Nada Matta	University of Technology of Troyes, France
Christine Michel	INSA-Lyon, France
Michele Missikoff	ISTC-CNR, Italy
Jean-Henry Morin	University of Geneva, Switzerland
Normen Müller	Safeplace at Protection One GmbH, Germany
Fabio Nonino	Università degli Studi di Roma la Sapienza, Italy
Wilma Penzo	University of Bologna, Italy
Erwin Pesch	University Siegen, Germany
Filipe Portela	Centro ALGORITMI, University of Minho, Portugal
Arkalgud Ramaprasad	University of Illinois at Chicago, USA
Edie Rasmussen	University of British Columbia, Canada
Marina Ribaudo	Università di Genova, Italy
Colette Rolland	Université de Paris 1 Panthèon Sorbonne, France
Ana Roxin	University of Burgundy, France
Ana Salgado	Federal University of Pernambuco, Brazil
Masaki Samejima	Osaka University, Japan
Christian Seel	University of Applied Sciences Landshut, Germany
Mukhammad Setiawan	Universitas Islam Indonesia, Indonesia
Conrad Shayo	California State University, USA
Tijs Slaats	University of Copenhagen, Denmark
Malgorzata Sterna	Poznan University of Technology, Poland
Martin Wessner	Darmstadt University of Applied Sciences, Germany
Uffe Wiil	University of Southern Denmark, Denmark
Rafal Wojciechowski	Poznan University of Economics, Poland
Qiang Zhu	The University of Michigan, Dearborn, USA

KMIS Additional Reviewer

Paulo Lemos   Unicamp, Brazil

Invited Speakers

Linda Terlouw   ICRIS Consultancy, Antwerp Management School,
                                   Avans University of Applied Sciences, Nyenrode
                                   Business University, The Netherlands
Slinger Jansen   Utrecht University, The Netherlands
Jonathan Garibaldi   University of Nottingham, UK
Paulo Novais   Universidade do Minho, Portugal

Contents

Knowledge Discovery and Information Retrieval

Transfer Learning in Sentiment Classification with Deep Neural Networks

Andrea Pagliarani[1], Gianluca Moro[1(✉)], Roberto Pasolini[1],
and Giacomo Domeniconi[2]

[1] Department of Computer Science and Engineering, University of Bologna,
Via Cesare Pavese, 47522 Cesena, Italy
{andrea.pagliarani12,gianluca.moro,roberto.pasolini}@unibo.it
[2] IBM - Watson Research Center, 1101 Kitchawan Road,
Yorktown Heights, NY 10598, USA
giacomo.domeniconi1@ibm.com

Abstract. Cross-domain sentiment classifiers aim to predict the polarity (i.e. sentiment orientation) of target text documents, by reusing a knowledge model learnt from a different source domain. Distinct domains are typically heterogeneous in language, so that transfer learning techniques are advisable to support knowledge transfer from source to target. Deep neural networks have recently reached the state-of-the-art in many NLP tasks, including in-domain sentiment classification, but few of them involve transfer learning and cross-domain sentiment solutions. This paper moves forward the investigation started in a previous work [1], where an unsupervised deep approach for text mining, called Paragraph Vector (PV), achieved cross-domain accuracy equivalent to a method based on Markov Chain (MC), developed ad hoc for cross-domain sentiment classification. In this work, Gated Recurrent Unit (GRU) is included into the previous investigation, showing that memory units are beneficial for cross-domain when enough training data are available. Moreover, the knowledge models learnt from the source domain are tuned on small samples of target instances to foster transfer learning. PV is almost unaffected by fine-tuning, because it is already able to capture word semantics without supervision. On the other hand, fine-tuning boosts the cross-domain performance of GRU. The smaller is the training set used, the greater is the improvement of accuracy.

Keywords: Transfer learning · Cross-domain · Deep learning ·
Fine-tuning · Sentiment analysis · Big Data

This work was partially supported by the project "Toreador", funded by the European Union's Horizon 2020 research and innovation programme under grant agreement No. 688797. We thank NVIDIA Corporation for the donated Titan GPU used in this work.

© Springer Nature Switzerland AG 2019
A. Fred et al. (Eds.): IC3K 2017, CCIS 976, pp. 3–25, 2019.
https://doi.org/10.1007/978-3-030-15640-4_1

1   Introduction

Sentiment analysis deals with the computational treatment of opinion, appraisals, attitudes, and emotions toward entities, individuals, issues, events, topics and their attributes (a survey is in [2]). The task is technically challenging but very useful in practice. For instance, companies always want to know customer opinions about their products and services.

When an understanding of plain text document polarity (e.g. positive, negative or neutral orientation) is required, sentiment classification is involved. This supervised approach aims to learn a model from a labelled training set of documents, then to apply it to an unlabelled test set, whose sentiment orientation has to be found. The typical approach to sentiment classification assumes that both the training set and the test set deal with the same topic. For example, a model is learnt on a set of board game reviews and applied to a distinct set of reviews, but always about board games. This modus operandi, known as in-domain sentiment classification, guarantees optimal performance provided that documents from the same domain are semantically similar. Unluckily, this approach is often inapplicable in practice, given that most documents are normally unlabelled. Tweets, blogs, fora, chats, emails, public repositories, social networks could bear opinions, and have been proved to support complex tasks, such as stock market prediction [3], job recommendation [4] and genomics [5]. However, no information is available on whether such opinions are positive, negative or neutral. Text categorisation by human experts is the only way to deal with such a problem in order to learn an in-domain sentiment classifier. This method becomes infeasible as soon as very large text sets are required to be labelled, like for instance in big data scenarios.

Transfer learning addresses exactly these limitations, paving the way for model reuse [6]. While these methods are used in image matching [7], genomic prediction [8–10] and many other contexts, their most common application is perhaps in text document categorisation. Basically, a knowledge model, once learnt on a source domain, can be applied to classify document polarity in a distinct target domain. For instance, a model built on a set of labelled documents about board games (i.e. source domain) could be employed for the categorisation of a set of unlabelled documents about electrical appliances (i.e. target domain). The practical implications of model reuse made cross-domain learning a hot research thread. The biggest obstacle to learning an effective cross-domain sentiment classifier is the language heterogeneity in documents of different domains. Just think that a board game can be *engaging* or *dull*, whereas an electrical appliance can be *working* or *broken*. In such cases, transfer learning (or knowledge transfer) techniques may help solving the problem, so that the knowledge extracted from the source is available to classify the target.

To the best of our knowledge, transfer learning has rarely been applied to sentiment classification with deep learning techniques, despite their success in other research areas. Several works [11–14] motivate such an investigation, pointing out the ability of deep approaches to learn semantic-bearing word representation, typically without supervision, independently of domains.

Our previous work [1] has begun the study by comparing a well-known unsupervised deep learning technique, namely Paragraph Vector [12], with a Markov Chain approach [15,16], tailored to cross-domain sentiment classification. When enough data are available for training, Paragraph Vector achieves accuracy comparable with Markov Chain, despite no explicit transfer learning mechanism. The outcome suggested that cross-domain solutions could be dramatically improved by combining deep learning with transfer learning techniques. The multi-source approach, proposed to validate this intuition, boosted the cross-domain accuracy from 2% to 3% depending on the configuration.

This paper carries on with the investigation on deep learning in cross-domain sentiment classification, by including Gated Recurrent Unit (GRU) [17] in the comparison. GRU is a deep architecture, evolution of LSTM, able to adaptively capture dependencies of different time scales. Similarly to Paragraph Vector, GRU does not provide any explicit transfer learning mechanism. Apart from supporting the outcome of our previous work with the inclusion of another outstanding deep learning technique, this paper also shows the impact of fine-tuning on cross-domain sentiment classification. Fine-tuning is an explicit transfer learning mechanism, where a small sample of target instances is used to tune the parameters of a model learnt from the source domain.

Experiments have been carried out to compare GRU with both PV and MC in cross-domain sentiment classification. The same benchmark text sets have been used to assess 2-classes (i.e. positive and negative) performance. GRU performs worse than PV and MC with small and medium-scale data sets, whereas it outperforms both when trained on large-scale data. The outcome suggests that GRU memory units are beneficial for cross-domain, but require large-scale data in order to learn accurate word relationships. When tuned with samples of target data, GRU achieves accuracy comparable with the other methods with small and medium-scale data as well, proving that fine-tuning helps transfer learning across domains.

The rest of the paper is organized as follows. Section 2 reviews the literature about transfer learning, cross-domain sentiment classification and deep learning. The main features of the methods compared are outlined in Sect. 3. Section 4 describes, shows and discusses the experiments performed. Finally, Sect. 5 draws conclusions and paves the way for future work.

2   Related Work

Transfer learning techniques are usually advisable to effectively map knowledge extracted from a *source* domain into a *target* domain. This is particularly useful in *cross-domain* methods, also known as *domain adaptation* methods [18], where labelled instances are only available in a source domain but a different target domain is required to be classified. Basically, two knowledge transfer modes have been identified in [19], namely *instance transfer* and *feature representation transfer*. In order to bridge the inter-domain gap, the former adapts source instances to the target domain, whereas the latter maps source and target features into a different space.

Before the advent of Deep Learning, many approaches have already been attempted to address transfer learning in cross-domain sentiment classification, mostly supervised. Aue and Gamon tried several approaches to adapt a classifier to a target domain: training on a mixture of labelled data from other domains where such data is available, possibly considering just the features observed in the target domain; using multiple classifiers trained on labelled data from different domains; a semi-supervised approach, where few labelled data from the target are included [20]. Blitzer et al. discovered a measure of domain similarity supporting domain adaptation [21]. Pan et al. advanced a spectral feature alignment to map words from different domains into same clusters, by means of domain-independent terms. These clusters form a latent space that can be used to enhance accuracy on the target domain in a cross-domain sentiment classification problem [22]. Furthermore, He et al. extended the joint sentiment-topic model by adding prior words sentiment; then, feature and document enrichment were performed by including polarity-bearing topics to align domains [23]. Bollegala et al. recommended the adoption of a thesaurus containing labelled data from the source domain and unlabelled data from both the source and the target domains [24]. Zhang et al. proposed an algorithm that transfers the polarity of features from the source domain to the target domain with the independent features as a bridge [25]. Their approach focuses not only on the feature divergence issue, namely different features are used to express similar sentiment in different domains, but also on the polarity divergence problem, where the same feature is used to express different sentiment in different domains. Franco et al. used the BabelNet multilingual semantic network to generate features derived from word sense disambiguation and vocabulary expansion that can help both in-domain and cross-domain tasks [26]. Bollegala et al. modelled cross-domain sentiment classification as embedding learning, using objective functions that capture domain-independent features, label constraints in the source documents and some geometric properties derived from both domains without supervision [27].

On the other hand, the advent of Deep Learning, whose a review can be found in [28], brought to a dramatic improvement in sentiment classification. Socher et al. introduced the Recursive Neural Tensor Networks to foster single sentence sentiment classification [11]. Apart from the high accuracy achieved in classification, these networks are able to capture sentiment negations in sentences due to their recursive structure. Dos Santos et al. proposed a Deep Convolutional Neural

Network that jointly uses character-level, word-level and sentence-level representations to perform sentiment analysis of short texts [29]. Kumar et al. presented the Dynamic Memory Network (DMN), a neural network architecture that processes input sequences and questions, forms episodic memories, and generates relevant answers [30]. The ability of DMN in naturally capturing position and temporality allows this architecture achieving the state-of-the-art performance in single sentence sentiment classification over the Stanford Sentiment Treebank proposed in [11]. Tang et al. introduced Gated Recurrent Neural Networks to learn vector-based document representation, showing that the underlying model outperforms the standard Recurrent Neural Networks in document modeling for sentiment classification [14]. Zhang and LeCun applied temporal convolutional networks to large-scale data sets, showing that they can perform well without the knowledge of words or any other syntactic or semantic structures [13]. Wang et al. combined Convolutional Neural Networks (CNN) and Recurrent Neural Networks (RNN) for sentiment analysis of short texts, taking advantage of the coarse-grained local features generated by CNN and long-distance dependencies learnt via RNN [31]. Chen et al. proposed a three-steps approach to learn a sentiment classifier for product reviews. First, they learnt a distributed representation of each review by a one-dimensional CNN. Then, they employed a RNN with gated recurrent units to learn distributed representations of users and products. Finally, they learnt a sentiment classifier from user, product and review representations [32].

Despite the recent success of Deep Learning in in-domain sentiment classification tasks, few attempts have been made in cross-domain problems. Glorot et al. used the Stacked Denoising Autoencoder introduced in [33] to extract domain-independent features in an unsupervised fashion, which can help transferring the knowledge extracted from a source domain to a target domain [34]. However, they relied only on the most frequent 5000 terms of the vocabulary for computational reasons. Although this constraint is often acceptable with small or medium data sets, it could be a strong limitation in big data scenarios, where very large data sets are required to be analysed.

3   Methods Description

This Section firstly outlines the features of the methods used for the investigation. Then fine-tuning is described, along with the reason why it can be beneficial for transfer learning and cross-domain sentiment classification. The techniques compared in our previous work [1] were Paragraph Vector (referred as PV hereinafter), proposed in [12], and a Markov Chain (referred as MC hereinafter) based algorithm introduced in [15] and extended in [16], whereas Gated Recurrent Unit (GRU) [17] is added to the investigation in this work.

Careful readers can find further details on the approaches described below in [12, 15–17].

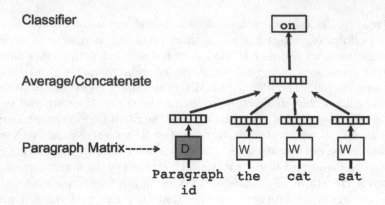

Fig. 1. The figure [12] shows a framework for learning the Distributed Memory Model of Paragraph Vector (PV-DM). With respect to word vectors, an additional paragraph token is mapped to a vector via matrix D. In this model, the concatenation or average of this vector with a context of three words is used to predict the fourth word. The paragraph vector represents the missing information from the current context and can act as a memory of the topic of the paragraph.

3.1   Paragraph Vector

PV is an unsupervised Deep Learning technique that aims to solve the weaknesses of the bag-of-words model. Alike bag-of-words, PV learns fixed-length feature representation from variable length chunks of text, such as sentences, paragraphs, and documents. However, bag-of-words features lose the ordering of the words and do not capture their semantics. For example, "good", "robust" and "town" are equally distant in the feature space, despite "good" should be closer to "robust" than "town" from the semantic point of view. The same holds for the bag-of-n-grams model, because it suffers from data sparsity and high dimensionality, although it considers the word order in short context. On the other hand, PV intrinsically handles the word order by representing each document by a dense vector, which is trained to predict words in the document itself. More precisely, the paragraph vector is concatenated with some word vectors from the same document to predict the following word in a given context. The paragraph token can be thought of as another word that acts as a memory that remembers what is missing from the current context. For this reason, this model, represented in Fig. 1, is called the Distributed Memory Model of Paragraph Vector (PV-DM).

Another way to learn the paragraph vector is to ignore the context words in the input, but force the model to predict words randomly sampled from the paragraph in the output. Actually this means that at each iteration of stochastic gradient descent, a text window is sampled, then a random word is sampled from the text window and a classification task is formed given the paragraph vector. This version of Paragraph Vector, shown in Fig. 2, is called the Distributed Bag of Words version (PV-DBOW).

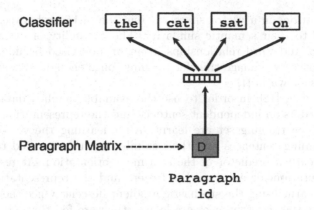

Fig. 2. The figure [12] shows the Distributed Bag of Words version of Paragraph Vector (PV-DBOW). The paragraph vector is trained to predict the words in a small window.

Both word vectors and paragraph vectors are trained by means of the stochastic gradient descent and backpropagation [35].

Sentiment classification requires sequential data to be handled, because document semantics is typically affected by word order. PV is shown to be able to learn vector representation for such sequential data, becoming a candidate technique for sentiment classification. We have already stated the PV learns fixed-length feature representation from variable-length chunks of text, dealing with any kind of plain text, from sentences to paragraphs, to whole documents. Though, this aspect is just as relevant as exactly knowing how many of these features are actually required to learn accurate models. The feature vectors have dimensions in the order of hundreds, much less than bag-of-words based representations, where there is one dimension for each word in a dictionary. The consequence is that either the bag-of-words models cannot be used for representing very large data sets due to the huge number of features or a feature selection is needed to reduce dimensionality. Feature selection entails information loss, beyond requiring parameter tuning to choose the right number of features to be selected. The fact that PV is not affected by the curse of dimensionality suggests that the underlying method is not only scalable just like an algorithm should be when dealing with large data sets, but it also entirely preserves information by increasing the data set size.

Le and Mikolov [12] showed that Paragraph Vector achieves brilliant in-domain sentiment classification results, but no cross-domain experiment has been conducted. Nevertheless, some characteristics of PV make it appropriate for cross-domain sentiment classification, where language is usually heterogeneous across domains. PV is very powerful in modelling syntactic as well as hidden relationships in plain text without any kind of supervision. Moreover, words are mapped to positions in a vector space wherein the distance between vectors is closely related to their semantic similarity. The capability of extracting both word semantics and word relationships in an unsupervised fashion makes PV able to automatically manage transfer learning, once enough data are available for training, as shown in [1].

As described in [12], in order to use the available labelled data, each subphrase is treated as an independent sentence and the representations for all the subphrases in the training set are learnt. After learning the vector representations for training sentences and their subphrases, they are fed to a logistic regression to learn a predictor of the sentiment orientation. At test time, the vector representation for each word is frozen, and the representations for the sentences are learnt using the stochastic gradient descent. Once the vector representations for the test sentences are learnt, they are fed through the logistic regression to predict the final label.

3.2 Markov Chain

Alike PV, MC can handle sentences, paragraphs and documents, but it is much more affected by the curse of dimensionality, because it is based on a dense bag-of-words model. Feature selection is often advisable to mitigate this issue, or even necessary with very large data sets, typically containing million or billion words. Basically, only the k most significant terms according to a given scoring function are kept. The basic idea of the MC based approach consists in modelling term co-occurrences: the more terms co-occur in documents the more their connection will be stronger. The same strategy could be followed to model the polarity of a given term: the more terms are contained in positive (negative) documents the more they will tend to be positive (negative). Following this idea, terms and classes are represented as states of a Markov Chain, whereas term-term and term-class relationships are modelled as transitions between these states. Thanks to this representation, MC is able to perform both sentiment classification and transfer learning. It is pretty easy to see that MC can be used as a classifier, because classes are reachable from terms at each state transition in the Markov Chain, since each edge models a term-class relationship. Instead, it is less straightforward to understand why it is also able to perform transfer learning. The assumption the method relies on is that there exists a subset of common terms between the source and target domains that act as a bridge between domain specific terms, allowing and supporting transfer learning. Dealing with this assumption, at each state transition in the Markov Chain, sentiment information can flow from the source-specific to the target-specific terms passing through the layer of shared terms (Fig. 3). The information flow is possible by exploiting the edges in the Markov Chain that, as previously stated, represent term-term relationships.

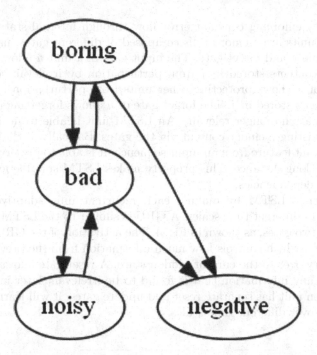

Fig. 3. The figure [15] shows transfer learning in Markov Chain from a book specific term like *boring* to an electrical appliance specific term like *noisy* through a common term like *bad*.

Actually, the classification process usually works in the opposite direction, i.e. from the target-specific to the source-specific terms, and goes on while the class states are eventually reached. For instance, say that a review from the target domain only contains target-specific terms. None of these terms is connected to the classes, but they are connected to some terms within the shared terms, which in turn are connected to some source-specific terms. Finally, both the shared and source-specific terms are connected to the classes. Therefore, starting from some target-specific terms, Markov Chain before performs transfer learning and then sentiment classification. It is important to remark that the transfer learning mechanism is not an additional step to be added in cross-domain tasks; on the contrary, it is intrinsic to the Markov Chain algorithm.

3.3 Gated Recurrent Unit

Gated Recurrent Unit (GRU), proposed by Cho et al. [17], is an evolution of Long Short-Term Memory (LSTM), presented by Hochreiter and Schmidhuber [36]. LSTM is a deep architecture that has been introduced to overcome the vanishing (or blowing up) gradient problem [37] that affects recurrent nets when signals are backpropagated through long time sequences. Indeed, LSTM can learn to bridge time intervals in excess of 1000 discrete time steps without loss of short time lag capabilities, by enforcing constant error flow through internal states of special units. LSTM units are memory cells composed of different gates, namely input gate, output gate, and forget gate. The input gate of a unit u allows protecting the memory contents stored in j from perturbation by irrelevant inputs. The output gate of u allows protecting other units from perturbation by irrelevant memory contents stored in j. The forget gate of u allows forgetting the memory contents that are no longer relevant. An LSTM unit is able to decide whether to keep the existing memory content via the gates. Basically, if the LSTM unit detects a relevant feature from an input sequence, it is able to preserve this information over a long distance. This property makes LSTM suitable for capturing long-distance dependencies.

GRU extends LSTM by making each recurrent unit adaptively capture dependencies of different time scales. A GRU is similar to the LSTM unit, but it only presents two gates, as shown in Fig. 4. The activation of the GRU is ruled by an update gate, which controls how much information from the previous hidden state will carry over to the current hidden state. A reset gate allows the hidden state to drop any information that is found to be irrelevant later in the future. As each hidden unit has separate reset and update gates, it will learn to capture dependencies over different time scales.

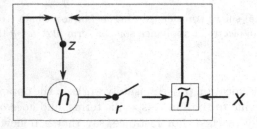

Fig. 4. The figure [17] shows a GRU. The update gate z selects whether the hidden state is to be updated with a new hidden state $\tilde{h}$. The reset gate r decides whether the hidden state is ignored.

LSTM based schemes have already been proved to work well in sentiment classification [14]. In this work, GRU is applied to cross-domain sentiment classification, to assess whether it is able to automatically bridge the semantic gap between the source and the target domain. Alike PV, GRU is a deep architecture and does not rely on a transfer learning mechanism. However, GRU gates, which allow each unit working as a memory wherein relevant information can be stored and preserved, make GRU suitable for cross-domain problems. Important domain-independent information can be automatically extracted by GRU if trained with an appropriate amount of data.

3.4   Fine-Tuning in Cross-domain

Fine-tuning consists in using a labelled sample of target instances to refine a model previously learnt on the source domain. The sample should be reasonably small for both theoretical and practical reasons. From a theoretical point of view, the cross-domain task would be converted into an in-domain problem if the sample used for fine-tuning was too large. Moreover, cross-domain would be no longer needed if an appropriate amount of labelled target instances were available. An in-domain model could be easily learnt in that case. On the other hand, readers already know that cross-domain learning is essential from a practical point of view, since most real-world data are unlabelled. Finding a large labelled sample is challenging in practice, and manually labelling it is even infeasible. Therefore, using a large sample would not be a viable alternative for tuning a pre-trained model. On the other hand, if the sample was small, categorisation by human experts would become a good option to increase cross-domain efficacy.

Beyond being a good trade-off between its cost and the improvement of performance that guarantees, fine-tuning could be even critical for techniques that do not rely on explicit transfer learning mechanisms. In particular, this work assesses whether fine-tuning of deep neural networks can bring to an improvement of ad-hoc cross-domain solutions.

4   Experiments

This Section shows some experiments to assess whether GRU, alike PV, is automatically able to handle language heterogeneity in cross-domain tasks, in relation to the amount of training data available. The effect of fine-tuning on deep architectures is also discussed, showing that it can help improving cross-domain performance, especially with small-scale data sets. Markov Chain has been implemented in a custom Java-based framework. Paragraph Vector relies on 0.12.4 *gensim* release [38], a Python-based open sourced and freely available framework[1]. For Gated Recurrent Unit (GRU) we used the Python-based implementation provided by Keras[2], choosing TensorFlow as back-end.

4.1   Setup

A common benchmark text set has been used to compare results with our previous work [1], that is a collection of Amazon reviews[3] about Books (B), Movies (M), Electronics (E) and Clothing-Shoes-Jewelry (J). Each domain contains plain English reviews along with their labels, namely a score from 1 (i.e. very negative) to 5 (i.e. very positive). The reviews whose scores were 1 and 2 have been mapped to the negative category, those whose scores were 4 and 5 to the positive one, whereas we discarded those whose score was 3 because they were likely to

---

[1] http://nlp.fi.muni.cz/projekty/gensim/.
[2] https://keras.io/layers/recurrent/.
[3] http://jmcauley.ucsd.edu/data/amazon/.

express a neutral sentiment orientation. To assess to what extent the amount of training data affects performance, source-target partitions with three orders of magnitude have been tested, preserving 80%–20% as source-target ratio, and balancing positive and negative examples. The small-scale data set has 1600 instances as the training set and 400 as the test set; the medium-scale 16000 and 4000 respectively; and the large-scale 80000 and 20000 respectively. Accuracy (i.e. the percentage of correctly classified instances) has been measured for each source-target configuration, averaging results on 10 different training-test partitions to reduce the variance, that is, the sensitivity to small fluctuations in the training set.

The same configurations of our previous work [1] have been used for Paragraph Vector and Markov Chain. The Distributed Bag of Words version (PV-DBOW) [12] has been chosen for PV, selecting 100-dimensional feature vectors, considering 10 words in the window size, ignoring words occurring in just one document and applying negative sampling with 5 negative samples. The initial learning rate has been set to 0.025, letting it linearly decade to 0.001 in 30 epochs. Readers can refer to [12,39] for details on the parameters. A logistic classifier, whose regression coefficients have been estimated through the Newton-Raphson method, has been used to perform sentiment classification.

In conformity with the previous work [1], we relied on the Markov Chain algorithm introduced in [15]. The relative frequency of terms in documents has been chosen as the term weighting measure [40]. Feature selection by means of χ^2 scoring function has been carried out to mitigate the curse of dimensionality that inherently affects dense bag-of-words models. 750, 10000 and 25000 terms have been chosen for the small-scale, medium-scale, and large-scale data sets respectively. Readers can refer to [15,16] for further details on the method.

For the GRU-based architecture, 3 main layers have been chosen: the first two are GRU layers, and the last one is a dense layer, fully-connected to the classes. Each GRU layer consists of 128 units as the output space dimensionality, whereas Glorot uniform initialisation [41] has been performed for the kernel weights matrix. 10% of the inputs to the second GRU layer have been discarded via dropout, in order to improve network robustness to noise. Adam optimizer [42] has been used to perform stochastic gradient descent, with binary cross-entropy as the loss function to optimize. Default values have been kept for the other parameters. Readers can refer to Keras documentation for further details.

The analysis below mainly focuses on cross-domain sentiment classification, where transfer learning is typically required to bridge the semantic gap between distinct domains. In-domain experiments have been shown just to have a baseline for the cross-domain comparison between GRU and the techniques already examined in the previous work [1]. The impact of fine-tuning on the deep architectures is finally addressed, assessing whether tuning allows increasing their cross-domain performance, since PV and GRU do not provide explicit transfer learning mechanisms.

4.2   In-domain Experiments

In-domain results are presented for a matter of comparison with the previous work [1]. They act as a baseline for cross-domain comparison. Table 1 shows the results over the 4 domains of the Amazon reviews dataset, namely Books (B), Movies (M), Electronics (E) and Clothing-Shoes-Jewelry (J).

Table 1. In-domain comparison among the three techniques used in this paper. Nk-Mk means that the experiment has been performed by using N * 1000 instances as the training set and M * 1000 instances as the test set. $X \rightarrow X$ means that the model has been learnt on reviews from a domain X and then applied to different reviews from the same domain. Values have been rounded to one decimal place for space reason.

Domain(s)	1.6k-0.4k			16k-4k			80k-20k		
	PV	*MC*	*GRU*	*PV*	*MC*	*GRU*	*PV*	*MC*	*GRU*
In-domain experiments									
$B \rightarrow B$	67.3%	79.3%	83.5%	75.4%	81.9%	73.8%	84.7%	83.8%	89.6%
$M \rightarrow M$	79.8%	91.2%	76.8%	74.9%	82.4%	78.9%	84.1%	80.2%	79.5%
$E \rightarrow E$	79.3%	92.0%	80.8%	80.2%	80.7%	82.5%	85.6%	84.4%	85.2%
$J \rightarrow J$	75.5%	72.0%	82.3%	80.1%	83.8%	85.0%	85.3%	87.0%	84.4%
Average	**75.4%**	**83.6%**	**80.8%**	**77.6%**	**82.2%**	**80.0%**	**84.9%**	**83.9%**	**84.7%**

GRU achieves performance comparable with the other techniques. The outcome is not surprising for many reasons. Firstly, GRU has a recurrent architecture, suitable for modelling sequences of terms. Secondly, GRU is able to capture dependencies of different time scales. Relationships among terms arise independently of how much they are distant. Finally, GRU can store relevant information through time, working as a memory. Readers can find further discussion on PV and MC in the previous paper [1].

4.3   Cross-domain Experiments

The following experiment aims to compare the performance of GRU with PV and MC in cross-domain sentiment classification. The goal is to assess whether the memory mechanism of GRU, which allows preserving relevant information through time, makes it suitable for cross-domain learning. This comparison also strengthens our earlier investigation [1] on deep learning in cross-domain sentiment classification.

The analysis involves all source-target configurations of the four domains, namely $B \rightarrow E$, $B \rightarrow M$, $B \rightarrow J$, $E \rightarrow B$, $E \rightarrow M$, $E \rightarrow J$, $M \rightarrow B$, $M \rightarrow E$, $M \rightarrow J$, $J \rightarrow B$, $J \rightarrow E$, $J \rightarrow M$. The detailed results are shown in Table 2, whereas the average trend across domains is represented in Fig. 5.

Table 2. Comparison between GRU, PV and MC in cross-domain sentiment classification. Nk-Mk means that the experiment has been performed by using N*1000 instances as the training set and M*1000 instances as the test set. $X \rightarrow Y$ means that the model has been learnt on reviews from the source domain X and then applied to reviews from the target domain Y. Values have been rounded to one decimal place for space reason.

Domain(s)	1.6k-0.4k			16k-4k			80k-20k		
	PV	*MC*	*GRU*	*PV*	*MC*	*GRU*	*PV*	*MC*	*GRU*
Cross-domain experiments (*source → target*)									
$B \rightarrow E$	70.8%	69.3%	64.0%	67.3%	71.2%	73.2%	73.2%	74.1%	78.2%
$B \rightarrow M$	66.8%	70.9%	65.0%	80.3%	79.3%	77.8%	82.0%	79.0%	83.3%
$B \rightarrow J$	73.3%	79.7%	69.5%	70.6%	71.8%	78.0%	74.9%	76.0%	82.7%
$E \rightarrow B$	74.0%	54.0%	65.8%	78.8%	80.1%	69.5%	76.9%	79.2%	77.0%
$E \rightarrow M$	71.5%	56.8%	64.7%	76.2%	76.2%	73.4%	76.9%	77.2%	79.3%
$E \rightarrow J$	82.8%	74.3%	69.2%	79.5%	80.5%	82.0%	80.8%	81.9%	85.7%
$M \rightarrow B$	74.8%	65.8%	59.0%	85.6%	86.1%	71.7%	85.2%	83.8%	81.2%
$M \rightarrow E$	71.8%	68.2%	69.5%	75.3%	77.1%	74.7%	74.8%	72.9%	79.5%
$M \rightarrow J$	82.3%	82.0%	68.0%	73.5%	74.9%	77.0%	77.0%	78.6%	82.3%
$J \rightarrow B$	66.3%	75.3%	60.5%	69.6%	80.6%	68.2%	76.5%	78.6%	77.2%
$J \rightarrow E$	76.5%	80.6%	77.0%	78.6%	79.8%	78.4%	80.1%	81.8%	82.2%
$J \rightarrow M$	74.3%	81.3%	63.5%	70.8%	74.3%	72.7%	76.1%	77.9%	77.6%
Average	**73.7%**	**71.5%**	**66.3%**	**75.5%**	**77.7%**	**74.7%**	**77.9%**	**78.4%**	**80.5%**

The average trend is pretty clear: the more data GRU relies on, the more it performs well. Indeed, GRU underperforms the other techniques with small-scale data. Increasing the number of training instances, GRU experienced a dramatic growth in accuracy, becoming comparable with both PV and MC with medium-scale data and even outperforming them with large-scale data. A reasonable explanation for this behaviour is that the memory mechanism of GRU needs an appropriate amount of data in order to learn what is actually relevant within a review. Somebody might argue that, looking at in-domain results in Table 1, GRU achieves good performance even with small data sets. This means that GRU needs few data to capture intra-domain term relationships, whereas few facts are not enough to capture inter-domain dependencies in absence of some explicit transfer learning mechanism. This is rational. Just think that in a single domain identifying the polarity-bearing terms could be enough to understand the overall sentiment orientation of the review, whereas the same does not hold between distinct domains, because of language heterogeneity. The polarity-bearing terms of the source domain generally differ from those of the target domain. In order to support the knowledge transfer from source to target, cross-domain makes it necessary to identify relevant hidden concepts rather than important terms. Careful readers could argue that PV, similarly to GRU, does not provide for a transfer learning phase, achieving good performance with small-scale data anyway. This is true, but it should not be forgotten that PV is able to capture word semantics without supervision [12]. This feature makes PV suitable for bridging the inter-domain semantic gap, as shown in [1].

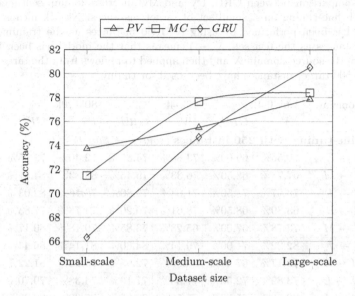

Fig. 5. Average accuracy achieved by the compared methods in cross-domain sentiment classification. The number of instances respectively used for small-scale, medium-scale and large-scale are reported in Sect. 4.1.

The outcome of cross-domain experiments suggests that gated recurrent units are automatically able to decide which information is better to preserve even across heterogeneous domains. However, GRU needs a large-scale training set in order to perform well in cross-domain tasks. Since GRU does not rely on explicit transfer learning mechanisms, it requires more data in order to extract hidden relevant concepts to bridge the semantic gap between distinct domains.

4.4   Experiments with Fine-Tuning

The experiments illustrated below assess the effectiveness of fine-tuning in supporting deep learning techniques in cross-domain sentiment classification. As explained in Sect. 3.4, fine-tuning of a pre-trained model can be useful in practice only if the labelled sample of the target domain is reasonably small. If it was too large, cross-domain would lose its benefits and, at the same time, in-domain approaches would be both feasible and preferable. For this purpose, 250 and 500 target examples have been used to assess the potentiality of fine-tuning as transfer learning mechanism. The detailed cross-domain results with fine-tuning are shown in Table 3, whereas the average trend is plotted in Fig. 6 and compared with the accuracy that PV and GRU obtained without tuning on target instances.

Table 3. Comparison between GRU, PV and MC in cross-domain sentiment classification with fine-tuning on a small set of target instances. Nk-Mk means that the experiment has been performed by using N * 1000 instances as the training set and M * 1000 instances as the test set. $X \rightarrow Y$ means that the model has been learnt on reviews from the source domain X and then applied to reviews from the target domain Y. 250 and 500 target instances have been used for tuning.

Domain(s)	1.6k-0.4k		16k-4k		80k-20k	
	PV	*GRU*	*PV*	*GRU*	*PV*	*GRU*
Fine-tuning with 250 instances (*source → target*)						
$B \rightarrow E$	70.56%	69.00%	73.86%	74.85%	72.40%	79.05%
$B \rightarrow M$	67.78%	68.50%	76.33%	79.45%	83.83%	84.51%
$B \rightarrow J$	76.67%	71.50%	71.03%	79.80%	75.16%	82.03%
$E \rightarrow B$	63.89%	68.50%	78.61%	70.20%	74.73%	77.83%
$E \rightarrow M$	73.78%	67.00%	65.28%	73.85%	79.18%	80.17%
$E \rightarrow J$	82.22%	71.00%	79.14%	84.60%	81.14%	86.44%
$M \rightarrow B$	79.17%	67.50%	80.08%	72.95%	81.22%	81.22%
$M \rightarrow E$	73.89%	72.50%	77.33%	77.10%	74.38%	79.70%
$M \rightarrow J$	82.50%	75.50%	75.58%	78.85%	77.92%	82.83%
$J \rightarrow B$	64.17%	67.50%	74.81%	70.30%	75.22%	78.78%
$J \rightarrow E$	73.89%	77.50%	83.11%	78.50%	80.70%	82.51%
$J \rightarrow M$	70.83%	68.00%	62.53%	75.25%	78.25%	79.19%
Average	**73.28%**	**70.33%**	**74.81%**	**76.31%**	**77.84%**	**81.19%**
Fine-tuning with 500 instances (*source → target*)						
$B \rightarrow E$	70.72%	70.50%	73.54%	73.95%	72.24%	78.56%
$B \rightarrow M$	67.56%	68.00%	76.28%	79.55%	83.66%	84.07%
$B \rightarrow J$	76.17%	78.00%	70.53%	80.50%	74.89%	82.30%
$E \rightarrow B$	66.83%	69.00%	78.21%	71.85%	74.97%	77.39%
$E \rightarrow M$	73.03%	72.50%	64.99%	76.65%	79.23%	80.82%
$E \rightarrow J$	81.33%	76.50%	79.02%	82.15%	81.15%	85.19%
$M \rightarrow B$	79.33%	69.00%	80.94%	76.55%	81.35%	81.78%
$M \rightarrow E$	74.61%	72.50%	77.55%	77.25%	74.34%	79.91%
$M \rightarrow J$	84.17%	77.50%	74.65%	79.25%	77.70%	82.33%
$J \rightarrow B$	66.06%	70.00%	74.42%	71.85%	75.62%	78.52%
$J \rightarrow E$	74.83%	78.00%	82.84%	79.55%	80.28%	83.66%
$J \rightarrow M$	71.66%	68.50%	62.33%	76.60%	78.04%	79.59%
Average	**73.86%**	**72.50%**	**74.61%**	**77.14%**	**77.79%**	**81.18%**

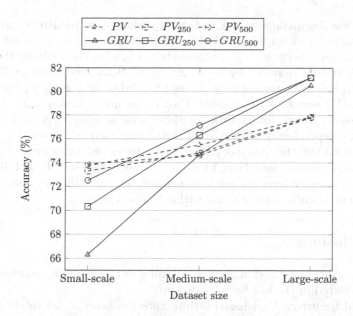

Fig. 6. Average accuracy achieved by the compared methods when fine-tuning on small samples of target instances is performed to foster cross-domain sentiment classification. The number of instances respectively used for small-scale, medium-scale and large-scale are reported in Sect. 4.1. The subscripts 250 and 500 are referred to the number of instances sampled from the target domain in order to perform fine-tuning.

The first outcome that catches the eye is that PV is almost unaffected by fine-tuning, regardless of the data set size. This behaviour is explained by the ability of PV to capture word semantics without supervision. PV automatically handles language heterogeneity by discovering hidden relationships between semantically similar words [12]. On the other hand, the benefits of fine-tuning dramatically affect GRU, which is not inherently able to align domains without supervision. The improvement is particularly evident with small-scale data, and decreases by growing the amount of source data employed to pre-train the model. The reason is pretty obvious. When few training data are available, GRU cannot capture inter-domain dependencies, and even a small sample of target data leads to a significant boost of performance. The impact is a bit reduced with medium-scale data, mainly for two factors. The first factor is the increased capability of GRU in bridging the inter-domain semantic gap without fine-tuning, as already shown in Sect. 4.3. The second factor is that 250 and 500 instances are two orders of magnitude less than the dataset size considered, whereas the small-scale data were just one order of magnitude more than the amount used for tuning. It is obviously challenging to increase the performance of a model pre-trained on a set of medium-scale data, by using only such a small sample for tuning. The same two factors also affect performance improvement when large-scale data are taken into account.

Despite the few instances used, fine-tuning is beneficial to GRU on average in all the considered configurations. With small-scale data, the sample of 250 target instances improves accuracy by approximately 4%, whereas doubling the tuning instances, accuracy increases by about 2% more. With medium-scale data, the smaller sample boosts accuracy by about 1.6%, whereas the bigger one by less than 1% with respect to the smaller. Finally, accuracy increases by less than 1% with respect to the configuration without tuning when large-scale data are considered, independently of the size of the tuning sample.

The outcome of the analysis proves that fine-tuning on a small sample of labelled target data is beneficial to deep architectures that do not have neither explicit transfer learning mechanisms nor the capability of automatically detecting semantically similar terms without supervision.

5   Conclusions

In this work, the investigation on deep learning in cross-domain sentiment classification, started in [1], has been carried on.

A Gated Recurrent Unit based architecture has been added to the previous comparison, which already took into account Paragraph Vector, an unsupervised deep learning technique not designed for cross-domain purposes, and a Markov Chain based method tailored to transfer learning and cross-domain sentiment classification. Moreover, fine-tuning of a pre-trained model has been attempted to assess its impact on cross-domain as explicit transfer learning mechanism. The model pre-trained on the source domain was tuned on a small sample of labelled target instances. The sample should be small in order for human experts to manually label data without too much effort. Moreover, if a large amount of labelled data was available, in-domain approaches would be preferable, as they are generally more effective than cross-domain ones.

The cross-domain experiments without fine-tuning show that GRU needs many instances in order to learn bridging the semantic gap between the source and the target domain. Indeed, GRU performs poorly with small-scale data (e.g. 2000 examples), achieves accuracy comparable with the other techniques with medium-scale data (e.g. 20000 examples), and even outperforms both with large-scale data (e.g. 100000). The outcome also means that, once enough data are available for training, GRU is able to bridge the inter-domain semantic gap without explicit transfer learning mechanisms. This ability is supposedly due to GRU gates, which allow each unit working as a memory wherein relevant information can be stored and preserved.

The deep architectures analysed manifest different behaviours in the experiments with fine-tuning. PV does not take advantage of fine-tuning, since it is able to capture word semantics as well as word relationships without supervision. On the other hand, fine-tuning is beneficial to GRU, because it acts as a transfer learning mechanism. The less training examples have been used to pre-train the model on the source domain, the higher impact fine-tuning has had on performance. As expected, a greater amount of tuning data (e.g. 500 reviews rather than 250) brings to better performance with small-scale data. The impact of this factor decreases by augmenting the dataset cardinality, and completely vanishes with large-scale data.

The analysis carried out in this work confirms that deep architectures are promising for cross-domain sentiment classification, although the techniques used in this investigation do not explicitly incorporate transfer learning mechanisms. Some features make deep nets suitable for bridging the inter-domain semantic gap, like the capability of PV to learn word semantics and relationships without supervision, and the memory mechanism of GRU that allows preserving relevant information through time. When combined with explicit transfer learning mechanisms as fine-tuning, deep learning techniques achieve accuracy comparable with or better than ad-hoc cross-domain solutions. Moreover, the fact that deep learning algorithms are able to take advantage of large-scale data is extremely important in nowadays big data scenarios, where scalability always is a requirement.

Future work will focus on combining different deep learning approaches, in order to take advantage of the respective benefits. We argue that this study is a start point to overcome ad-hoc solutions for cross-domain sentiment classification. A possibility is to combine deep approaches to learn semantic-bearing word representation - like Paragraph Vector, Glove [43], ELMo [44], etc. - with deep architectures with some memory mechanism, such as Gated Recurrent Unit, Differentiable Neural Computer [45], Dynamic Memory Network, etc. (see in [46] for an extensive treatment in transfer learning). Moreover this study can be extended to cope with other emerging text classification problems where large data sets are unlabelled, such as in thread of conversational messages of social networks and discussion forums [47,48].

References

1. Domeniconi, G., Moro, G., Pagliarani, A., Pasolini, R.: On deep learning in cross-domain sentiment classification. In: Proceedings of the 9th International Joint Conference on Knowledge Discovery, Knowledge Engineering and Knowledge Management: KDIR, INSTICC, vol. 1, pp. 50–60. SciTePress (2017)
2. Liu, B., Zhang, L.: A survey of opinion mining and sentiment analysis. In: Aggarwal, C., Zhai, C. (eds.) Mining Text Data, pp. 415–463. Springer, Boston (2012). https://doi.org/10.1007/978-1-4614-3223-4_13
3. Domeniconi, G., Moro, G., Pagliarani, A., Pasolini, R.: Learning to predict the stock market Dow Jones index detecting and mining relevant tweets. In: Fred, A.L.N., Filipe, J. (eds.) Proceedings of the 9th International Joint Conference on Knowledge Discovery, Knowledge Engineering and Knowledge Management, Funchal, Madeira, Portugal, 1–3 November 2017, vol. 1, pp. 165–172. SciTePress (2017)
4. Domeniconi, G., Moro, G., Pagliarani, A., Pasini, K., Pasolini, R.: Job recommendation from semantic similarity of Linkedin users' skills. In: Proceedings of the 5th International Conference on Pattern Recognition Applications and Methods: ICPRAM, INSTICC, vol. 1, pp. 270–277. SciTePress (2016)

5. Lena, P.D., Domeniconi, G., Margara, L., Moro, G.: GOTA: GO term annotation of biomedical literature. BMC Bioinform. **16**, 346 (2015)
6. Domeniconi, G., Moro, G., Pasolini, R., Sartori, C.: Iterative refining of category profiles for nearest centroid cross-domain text classification. In: Fred, A., Dietz, J.L.G., Aveiro, D., Liu, K., Filipe, J. (eds.) IC3K 2014. CCIS, vol. 553, pp. 50–67. Springer, Cham (2015). https://doi.org/10.1007/978-3-319-25840-9_4
7. Shrivastava, A., Malisiewicz, T., Gupta, A., Efros, A.A.: Data-driven visual similarity for cross-domain image matching. ACM Trans. Graph. **30**, 154:1–154:10 (2011)
8. Domeniconi, G., Masseroli, M., Moro, G., Pinoli, P.: Cross-organism learning method to discover new gene functionalities. Comput. Meth. Progr. Biomed. **126**, 20–34 (2016)
9. Domeniconi, G., Masseroli, M., Moro, G., Pinoli, P.: Random perturbations of term weighted gene ontology annotations for discovering gene unknown functionalities. In: Fred, A., Dietz, J.L.G., Aveiro, D., Liu, K., Filipe, J. (eds.) IC3K 2014. CCIS, vol. 553, pp. 181–197. Springer, Cham (2015). https://doi.org/10.1007/978-3-319-25840-9_12
10. Domeniconi, G., Masseroli, M., Moro, G., Pinoli, P.: Discovering new gene functionalities from random perturbations of known gene ontological annotations. In: KDIR 2014 - Proceedings of the International Conference on Knowledge Discovery and Information Retrieval, Rome, Italy, 21–24 October 2014, pp. 107–116. SciTePress (2014)
11. Socher, R., et al.: Recursive deep models for semantic compositionality over a sentiment TreeBank. In: Proceedings of the 2013 Conference on Empirical Methods in Natural Language Processing, pp. 1631–1642. Association for Computational Linguistics, Stroudsburg (2013)
12. Le, Q., Mikolov, T.: Distributed representations of sentences and documents. In: Proceedings of the 31st International Conference on Machine Learning, ICML 2014, vol. 32, pp. II-1188–II-1196. JMLR.org (2014)
13. Zhang, X., LeCun, Y.: Text understanding from scratch. CoRR abs/1502.01710 (2015)
14. Tang, D., Qin, B., Liu, T.: Document modeling with gated recurrent neural network for sentiment classification. In: EMNLP, pp. 1422–1432. The Association for Computational Linguistics (2015)
15. Domeniconi, G., Moro, G., Pagliarani, A., Pasolini, R.: Markov chain based method for in-domain and cross-domain sentiment classification. In: Fred, A.L.N., Dietz, J.L.G., Aveiro, D., Liu, K., Filipe, J. (eds.) KDIR 2015 - Proceedings of the International Conference on Knowledge Discovery and Information Retrieval, part of the 7th International Joint Conference on Knowledge Discovery, Knowledge Engineering and Knowledge Management (IC3K 2015), Lisbon, Portugal, 12–14 November 2015, vol. 1, pp. 127–137. SciTePress (2015)
16. Domeniconi, G., Moro, G., Pagliarani, A., Pasolini, R.: Cross-domain sentiment classification via polarity-driven state transitions in a Markov model. In: Fred, A., Dietz, J.L.G., Aveiro, D., Liu, K., Filipe, J. (eds.) IC3K 2015. CCIS, vol. 631, pp. 118–138. Springer, Cham (2016). https://doi.org/10.1007/978-3-319-52758-1_8
17. Cho, K., et al.: Learning phrase representations using RNN encoder-decoder for statistical machine translation. In: Proceedings of the 2014 Conference on Empirical Methods in Natural Language Processing (EMNLP), Doha, Qatar, pp. 1724–1734. Association for Computational Linguistics (2014)
18. Daumé III, H., Marcu, D.: Domain adaptation for statistical classifiers. J. Artif. Intell. Res. **26**, 101–126 (2006)

19. Pan, S.J., Yang, Q.: A survey on transfer learning. IEEE Trans. Knowl. Data Eng. **22**, 1345–1359 (2010)
20. Aue, A., Gamon, M.: Customizing sentiment classifiers to new domains: a case study. In: Proceedings of Recent Advances in Natural Language Processing (RANLP) (2005)
21. Blitzer, J., Dredze, M., Pereira, F.: Biographies, bollywood, boom-boxes and blenders: domain adaptation for sentiment classification. In: Carroll, J.A., van den Bosch, A., Zaenen, A. (eds.) ACL 2007, Proceedings of the 45th Annual Meeting of the Association for Computational Linguistics, Prague, Czech Republic, 23–30 June 2007, pp. 440–447. The Association for Computational Linguistics (2007)
22. Pan, S.J., Ni, X., Sun, J., Yang, Q., Chen, Z.: Cross-domain sentiment classification via spectral feature alignment. In: Rappa, M., Jones, P., Freire, J., Chakrabarti, S. (eds.) Proceedings of the 19th International Conference on World Wide Web, WWW 2010, Raleigh, North Carolina, USA, 26–30 April 2010, pp. 751–760. ACM (2010)
23. He, Y., Lin, C., Alani, H.: Automatically extracting polarity-bearing topics for cross-domain sentiment classification. In: Lin, D., Matsumoto, Y., Mihalcea, R. (eds.) The 49th Annual Meeting of the Association for Computational Linguistics: Human Language Technologies, Proceedings of the Conference, 19–24 June 2011, Portland, Oregon, USA, pp. 123–131. The Association for Computer Linguistics (2011)
24. Bollegala, D., Weir, D.J., Carroll, J.A.: Cross-domain sentiment classification using a sentiment sensitive thesaurus. IEEE Trans. Knowl. Data Eng. **25**, 1719–1731 (2013)
25. Zhang, Y., Hu, X., Li, P., Li, L., Wu, X.: Cross-domain sentiment classification-feature divergence, polarity divergence or both? Pattern Recogn. Lett. **65**, 44–50 (2015)
26. Franco-Salvador, M., Cruz, F.L., Troyano, J.A., Rosso, P.: Cross-domain polarity classification using a knowledge-enhanced meta-classifier. Knowl.-Based Syst. **86**, 46–56 (2015)
27. Bollegala, D., Mu, T., Goulermas, J.Y.: Cross-domain sentiment classification using sentiment sensitive embeddings. IEEE Trans. Knowl. Data Eng. **28**, 398–410 (2016)
28. LeCun, Y., Bengio, Y., Hinton, G.E.: Deep learning. Nature **521**, 436–444 (2015)
29. dos Santos, C.N., Gatti, M.: Deep convolutional neural networks for sentiment analysis of short texts. In: Hajic, J., Tsujii, J. (eds.) COLING 2014, 25th International Conference on Computational Linguistics, Proceedings of the Conference: Technical Papers, 23–29 August 2014, Dublin, Ireland, pp. 69–78. ACL (2014)
30. Kumar, A., et al.: Ask me anything: dynamic memory networks for natural language processing. In: Balcan, M., Weinberger, K.Q. (eds.) Proceedings of the 33rd International Conference on Machine Learning, ICML 2016, New York City, NY, USA, 19–24 June 2016. JMLR Workshop and Conference Proceedings, vol. 48, pp. 1378–1387. JMLR.org (2016)
31. Wang, X., Jiang, W., Luo, Z.: Combination of convolutional and recurrent neural network for sentiment analysis of short texts. In: Calzolari, N., Matsumoto, Y., Prasad, R. (eds.) COLING 2016, 26th International Conference on Computational Linguistics, Proceedings of the Conference: Technical Papers, Osaka, Japan, 11–16 December 2016, pp. 2428–2437. ACL (2016)
32. Chen, T., Xu, R., He, Y., Xia, Y., Wang, X.: Learning user and product distributed representations using a sequence model for sentiment analysis. IEEE Comp. Int. Mag. **11**, 34–44 (2016)

33. Vincent, P., Larochelle, H., Lajoie, I., Bengio, Y., Manzagol, P.: Stacked denoising autoencoders: learning useful representations in a deep network with a local denoising criterion. J. Mach. Learn. Res. **11**, 3371–3408 (2010)
34. Glorot, X., Bordes, A., Bengio, Y.: Domain adaptation for large-scale sentiment classification: a deep learning approach. In: Getoor, L., Scheffer, T. (eds.) Proceedings of the 28th International Conference on Machine Learning, ICML 2011, Bellevue, Washington, USA, 28 June–2 July 2011, pp. 513–520. Omnipress (2011)
35. Rumelhart, D.E., Hinton, G.E., Williams, R.J.: Learning representations by back-propagating errors. Nature **323**, 533–536 (1986)
36. Hochreiter, S., Schmidhuber, J.: Long short-term memory. Neural Comput. **9**, 1735–1780 (1997)
37. Hochreiter, S.: The vanishing gradient problem during learning recurrent neural nets and problem solutions. Int. J. Uncertain. Fuzziness Knowl.-Based Syst. **6**, 107–116 (1998)
38. Řehůřek, R., Sojka, P.: Software framework for topic modelling with large corpora. In: Proceedings of the LREC 2010 Workshop on New Challenges for NLP Frameworks, Valletta, Malta, pp. 45–50. ELRA (2010). http://is.muni.cz/publication/884893/en
39. Mikolov, T., Sutskever, I., Chen, K., Corrado, G.S., Dean, J.: Distributed representations of words and phrases and their compositionality. In: Burges, C.J.C., Bottou, L., Ghahramani, Z., Weinberger, K.Q. (eds.) Advances in Neural Information Processing Systems: 27th Annual Conference on Neural Information Processing Systems 2013, 5–8 December 2013, Lake Tahoe, Nevada, United States, vo. 26, pp. 3111–3119 (2013)
40. Domeniconi, G., Moro, G., Pasolini, R., Sartori, C.: A comparison of term weighting schemes for text classification and sentiment analysis with a supervised variant of tf.idf. In: Helfert, M., Holzinger, A., Belo, O., Francalanci, C. (eds.) DATA 2015. CCIS, vol. 584, pp. 39–58. Springer, Cham (2016). https://doi.org/10.1007/978-3-319-30162-4_4
41. Glorot, X., Bengio, Y.: Understanding the difficulty of training deep feedforward neural networks. In: Teh, Y.W., Titterington, D.M. (eds.) Proceedings of the Thirteenth International Conference on Artificial Intelligence and Statistics, AISTATS 2010, Chia Laguna Resort, Sardinia, Italy, 13–15 May 2010. JMLR Proceedings, vol. 9, pp. 249–256. JMLR.org (2010)
42. Kingma, D.P., Ba, J.: Adam: a method for stochastic optimization. CoRR abs/1412.6980 (2014)
43. Pennington, J., Socher, R., Manning, C.D.: Glove: global vectors for word representation. In: Moschitti, A., Pang, B., Daelemans, W. (eds.) Proceedings of the 2014 Conference on Empirical Methods in Natural Language Processing, EMNLP 2014, 25–29 October 2014, Doha, Qatar, A Meeting of SIGDAT, a Special Interest Group of the ACL, pp. 1532–1543. ACL (2014)
44. Peters, M.E., et al.: Deep contextualized word representations. In: Walker, M.A., Ji, H., Stent, A. (eds.) Proceedings of the 2018 Conference of the North American Chapter of the Association for Computational Linguistics: Human Language Technologies, NAACL-HLT 2018 (Long Papers), New Orleans, Louisiana, USA, 1–6 June 2018, vol. 1, pp. 2227–2237. Association for Computational Linguistics (2018)
45. Graves, A., et al.: Hybrid computing using a neural network with dynamic external memory. Nature **538**, 471–476 (2016)

46. Moro, G., Pagliarani, A., Pasolini, R., Sartori, C.: Cross-domain & in-domain sentiment analysis with memory-based deep neural networks. In: Proceedings of the 10th International Joint Conference on Knowledge Discovery, Knowledge Engineering and Knowledge Management: KDIR, INSTICC, vol. 1. SciTePress (2018)
47. Domeniconi, G., Semertzidis, K., Moro, G., Lopez, V., Kotoulas, S., Daly, E.M.: Identifying conversational message threads by integrating classification and data clustering. In: Francalanci, C., Helfert, M. (eds.) DATA 2016. CCIS, vol. 737, pp. 25–46. Springer, Cham (2017). https://doi.org/10.1007/978-3-319-62911-7_2
48. Domeniconi, G., Semertzidis, K., López, V., Daly, E.M., Kotoulas, S., Moro, G.: A novel method for unsupervised and supervised conversational message thread detection. In: DATA, pp. 43–54. SciTePress (2016)

Prediction and Trading of Dow Jones from Twitter: A Boosting Text Mining Method with Relevant Tweets Identification

Gianluca Moro[1], Roberto Pasolini[1], Giacomo Domeniconi[2(✉)],
Andrea Pagliarani[1], and Andrea Roli[1]

[1] Department of Computer Science and Engineering, University of Bologna,
Via dell'Università, 47522 Cesena, Italy
{gianluca.moro,roberto.pasolini,andrea.pagliarani12,andrea.roli}@unibo.it
[2] IBM TJ Watson Research Center, 1101 Kitchawan Road,
Yorktown Heights, NY 10598, USA
giacomo.domeniconi1@ibm.com

Abstract. Previous studies claim that financial news influence the movements of stock prices almost instantaneously, however the poor foreseeability of news limits their possibility of predicting the stock price changes and trading actions. Recently complex sentiment analysis techniques have also showed that large amount of social network posts can predict the price movements of the Dow Jones Industrial Average (DJIA) within a less stringent timescale. From the idea that the contents of social posts can forecast the future stock trading actions, in this paper we present a simpler text mining method than the sentiment analysis approaches, which extracts the predictive knowledge of the DJIA movements from a large dataset of tweets, boosting also the prediction accuracy by identifying and filtering out irrelevant/noisy tweets. The noise detection technique we introduced improves the initial effectiveness of more than 10%. We tested our method on 10 millions twitter posts spanning one year, achieving an accuracy of 88.9% in the Dow Jones daily predictions, which, to the best of our knowledge, improves the best literature result based on social networks. Finally we have used the prediction method to drive the DJIA buy/sell actions of a trading protocol; the achieved return on investments (ROI) outperforms the state-of-the-art.

Keywords: Stock market prediction · Trading · Dow Jones ·
Machine learning · Text mining · Noise detection · Twitter ·
Return on investment

This work was partially supported by the project "Toreador", funded by the European Union's Horizon 2020 research and innovation programme under grant agreement No. 688797. We thank NVIDIA Corporation for the donated Titan GPU used in this work. G. Domeniconi—Contribution done during the affiliation at the University of Bologna.

A. Fred et al. (Eds.): IC3K 2017, CCIS 976, pp. 26–42, 2019.
https://doi.org/10.1007/978-3-030-15640-4_2

1   Introduction

Online posts from social networks, micro blogging and comment sections on news enable people to share opinions and moods, creating big data sets constantly updated of textual corpora. Sentiment analysis techniques aim at extracting emotional states and/or opinions' polarity orientation expressed in unstructured text in order to create a collective social emotional state.

Recent studies claims that the trend of social emotional state predict the macroscopic evolution of global events such as some economic indicators. In particular, [1] using a Probabilistic Latent Semantic Analysis (pLSA) model extracts sentiment indicators on blogs that predict future sales, [2] shows how through assessments of blog sentiments can predict the movie sales; similarly [3] shows how public sentiments on movies expressed on Twitter can actually predict box office receipts. [4] tests the predictability of books sales using online chat activities. But all that glitters ain't gold: [5] criticises some literature on this topic, showing results that are in fact unpredictable, for instance the prediction of election. Of course analyses of tweets can help to understand the political popularity, but can not consistently predict the results so far.

In this work we experimented the prediction of the Dow Jones Industrial Average (DJIA) from Twitter messages, moreover we assessed the return on investments (ROI) achieved by trading it according to such a forecast capability. For obvious reasons, the ability to predict the stock market trends has historically attracted interest from shareholders as well as academia. Efficient Market Hypothesis (EHM) proposed in [6] states that prices of financial assets are managed by rational investors who rely on new information, i.e. *news*, and not by present or past prices; since news are not predictable, neither is the stock market, which, according to past studies [7,8], follows in general a random walk trend. However, [9] confutes the EMH, providing evidences that market prices reflect all the available information. Moreover, several studies show that the trend of the stock market does not follow a random walk model and can be predicted in some way [10,11], including, for example, with mining techniques applied to market news [12,13] or to past prices [14] or even to financial reports [15].

Recently several works have studied the correlation between sentiments extracted from Twitter and socio-cultural phenomena [16,17], such as the popularity of brands [18], and also the correlation between public mood in Twitter and the DJIA trend [19].

Differently from previous works that predict DJIA by computing people sentiments or moods from their twitter opinions, we introduce a simpler method based on NLP techniques for the characterisation and detection of relevant tweets with respect to increments or decrements of DJIA. In particular, as far as the selection of tweets is concerned, our method includes a noise detection approach in short textual messages in order to filter out irrelevant tweets in predicting DJIA. As discusses in Sect. 6, there is a large literature regarding the detection of noise in data mining and especially in data clustering; various methods have also been applied to text mining, generally for the recognition of noisy features [20] or for novelty detection [21], i.e. the discovery of unknown data that a machine learning system has not been trained with.

In this work we employed the same dataset[1] of ten millions tweets posted in 2008 used by [19], but with a much smaller training set in order to assess our method more reliably with a wider test set. Intuitively, our method is based on training an intermediate classifier on five millions tweets posted in the first seven months of the 2008. By analysing the results of this classification, we create a pruning scheme based on four goodness groups of tweets, namely true and false positives and true and false negatives, depending on the outcome of the classification. We subsequently transform the training set by removing irrelevant tweets considered noise. This technique has been applied at two level: both to individual tweets and to aggregations of them, which correspond to actual instances of the training set. The method achieves on average a daily prediction accuracy of 79.9% and 88.9% without and with noise removal respectively.

Moreover we have extended our previous work [22] by adding a trading protocol in order to perform buy/sell operations on the basis of our prediction method mentioned above. The trading experiments show that the total return on investments (ROI) from the initial capital are 56% and 84% with and without noise removal respectively. The two ROIs have been accumulated in the test period of three months, therefore to get their correspondent values on a yearly basis, they should be multiplied by four.

The paper is organized as follows. Section 2 draws a short background of the precedent literature about the predictive mood of Twitter for several social-economic phenomenons. Section 3 explains the data considered, the Vector Space Model construction and the noise detection technique. Section 4 illustrates the trading protocol. Section 5.1 describes and compares DJIA prediction experiments with other works showing our results improves the best existing outcomes based on social network approaches. Section 5.2 reports the DJIA trading results showing that the achieved ROI outperforms the state-of-the-art, even with respect to advanced deep learning approaches. Section 6 illustrates literature about stock market prediction based on news, social network analysis and noise detection methods. Finally, Sect. 7 sums results up and outlines future work.

2   Background

Twitter represents a humongous knowledge base providing information about almost every topics. It can also be argued that this knowledge base can provide an indication on the public mood. In fact the emotional state, as the prerogative of a single human being, propagates to social status as a feature of all of the individuals. This phenomenon is studied by [16]: authors find that events in the social, political, cultural and economic sphere do have a significant, immediate and highly specific effect on the various dimensions of public mood extracted from Twitter. They speculate that large scale mood analysis can provide a solid platform to model collective emotive trends in terms of their predictive value with regards to existing social as well as economic indicators. This predictive

---

[1] https://bit.ly/2x0WsVD.

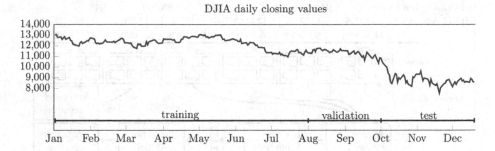

Fig. 1. Daily closing values of the DJIA prices and split of the benchmark set. Based from [22].

feature of Twitter mood has been used for forecasting different phenomenons, like the sales of a movie [3], the public opinion on a particular brand [18] and so on.

Precedent literature proposed to use Several approaches proposed in past years apply *sentiment analysis* techniques to tweets to create forecast models. [19] measure collective mood states (positive, negative, calm, alert, sure, vital, kind and happy) through sentiment analysis applied to more than 9 million tweets posted in 2008. Tweets are filtered by some generic sentiment expressions (e.g. "I'm feeling") not directly related to stock market. They analyse tweets by two mood tracking tools: Opinion Finder (OF, [23]) that classifies tweets as positive or negative, and Google-Profile of Mood States (GPOMS) that measure mood in the other 6 dimensions.

They found that the *calm* mood profile yields the best prediction result for Dow Jones Industrial Average (DJIA) with an accuracy of 86.7% in the prediction of the daily directions in the month of December, moreover they also show how a tweet aggregation in a 3-day period ensures better prediction on the daily DJIA.

Unlike the latter work, the proposal of this paper is a boosting text mining method with the capacity of recognizing and filtering out irrelevant tweets that negatively affect the accuracy prediction of the DJIA price movements. Moreover the paper introduces a trading protocol with buy/sell actions driven by this prediction method and shows the return on investments achieved.

3 Methodology

3.1 Benchmark Text Set

To obtain a comparative evaluation than the well-known work of [19], we use the same collection of tweets: that is about 10 million tweets posted from January 1th to December 19th of 2008, by approximately 2.7M users. Following the pre-processing applied by Bollen et al., only tweets in English language that contain explicit statements of the author's mood state are taken into consideration, i.e. those that contains one of this expressions "i fell", "i am feeling", "i'm feeling",

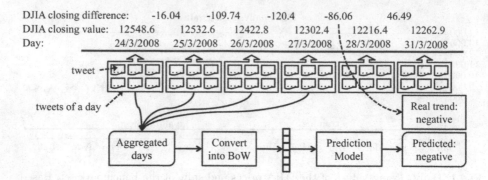

Fig. 2. Diagram of the DJIA prediction process through tweets aggregation. In this example the system predicts the DJIA trend for 28/03/2008 using the aggregated tweets posted in the previous four days ($l = 0$ and $a = 3$). Based from [22].

"i dont feel", "I'm", "Im", "I am", and "makes me". Tweets that contain links or that address the tweet content to another user are removed. All tweets are tokenized in single words and, as done by [24], also the emoticons are considered into our model using three different tokens.

Figure 1 shows the daily closing values of DJIA of 2008. To properly evaluate the models' ability in the prediction of DJIA prices, we split the benchmark set into (i) a training set with the first seven months of the year (from January 2 to July 31) to create the prediction models; (ii) a validation set with two months, August and September, with which we tune the models and apply the noise detection; (iii) finally a test set with the latest three months, from October 1st to December 19th, larger than the work of Bollen et al., which refers to only 19 days of December and consequently to only 15 days of opening stock market.

3.2 Vector Space Model Construction and DJIA Prediction

Tweets are grouped according to the publication date and will provide the information base to generate future predictions on the stock market. As shown by the experiments of Bollen et al., the higher correlation between social mood and the DJIA is obtained by grouping tweets of several days and shifting the prediction for a certain time lag. Thus it becomes interesting to evaluate the accuracy of the predictions considering these two parameters in the forecasting model:

- Lag (l): temporal translation from the forecast date, $l = 0$ means the day before the prediction.
- Aggregation (a): number of days to be aggregated to make a prediction, $a = 0$ means only one day.

As a simple example, assume that we consider $l = 1$ and $a = 2$, to make the prediction on day t will be considered tweets published in the days $t - 2$, $t - 3$ and $t - 4$. The range of days considered for the prediction of day t will be: $[t - 1 - l - a, t - 1 - l]$.

According to the two previous parameters, all the tweets related to the prediction of a day (in the previous example, all tweets of $t-2$, $t-3$ and $t-4$) are collected in a single *Bag-of-Words* (BoW). Given the high number of tweets available, a dimensionality reduction is required. Once selected the tweets, stop-words are removed and a stemming process is performed, each term is then weighted using the common *tf.idf* [25]. Finally, a number n_f of them, with greater weight, are selected.

At the end of each day d, the method predicts from the mentioned aggregation of tweets, the sign of the difference between the unknown closing price at day $d+1$ and the known closing prices at day d of DJIA. The prediction process is summarised in Fig. 2 and its accuracy refers to the forecast of whether the above difference is negative or positive. Section 4 explains how this sign prediction determines the trading actions.

3.3   Detection of Relevant and Noisy Tweets

Twitter provides a great deal of information, but is necessary to understand what is useful for a given analysis and what is not. Considering this, we propose a noise detection method to define what tweets to use in the DJIA prediction model. Our idea can be summarised in few steps:

1. Once created the representation of the data, as described in the previous section, we train a classification model and we apply it on the validation set.
2. We create four prototypes, one for each possible outcome of the classification, i.e. true positive (TP), predicted days, true negative (TN), false positive (FP) and false negative (FN). Each prototype is a BoW merging all the instances of the validation set, i.e. all the tweets of the a days before each prediction.
3. We use prototypes to discover the noisy tweets in the dataset. We propose to apply this method at two different levels: (i) a tweet level: removing from the dataset all the tweets with cosine similarity less than a threshold τ_g with respect to the good prototypes (TP and TN) or greater then a threshold τ_b with respect to the bad prototypes (FP and FN); (ii) a instance level: removing from the training set instances similar to the bad prototypes.
4. With the cleaned data set we train a new prediction model using the training and validation set and we use it to classify the test set.

4   Trading Protocol Driven by the Prediction Method

The accuracy of a predictive regression model is usually measured with RMSE or in this case evaluating the error in Dow Jones points, or also, as we performed, using the sign of the difference among consecutive closing prices, as illustrated in Subsect. 3.2. In fact, what is ultimately important to measure the effectiveness of a prediction model is its capability of correctly driving trading actions to buy/sell shares. If the market is predicted to rise, the trading protocol receives from the prediction model a signal to buy, while a sell signal occurs when it is predicted a drop; sell/buy actions are performed without any predefined rise/drop threshold.

In our simple trading protocol each buy/sell trade is conducted at the market opening value of each day d and the forecast of the DJIA movements consists on the prediction of the sign of the difference between the unknown closing price, $closing_{unknown}^{(d)}$ of the day d, and $closing_{known}^{(d-1)}$ the known closing price of the previous day as follows:

$$action\_at\_opening^{(d)} = \begin{cases} buy & \text{if } closing_{unknown}^{(d)} - closing_{known}^{(d-1)} > 0 \\ sell & \text{otherwise} \end{cases} \qquad (1)$$

The trading protocol performs at most one action a day according to 1 and it spends in each buy action the full capital available, including the possibly achieved gains (i.e. all in). At the first buy signal from the prediction model, the full initial capital is invested and any new subsequent buy signal is treated as a hold command.

When a sell signal is received, all investment held is sold (all out) and subsequent sell signals are ignored, until another buy is emitted iterating in this manner the protocol. When the trading protocol stops, it performs a sell action sailing all the shares acquired, independently on the sign predicted.

To measure gain/loss performances, we adopted the standard *Return On Investment* (ROI) [26], which is defined as

$$ROI = \frac{Gain\ from\ Investment - Cost\ of\ Investment}{Cost\ of\ Investment} \qquad (2)$$

where the *Cost of Investment* is the value of the initial capital before the first trading action and the *Gain from Investment* is the proceeds achieved from the sale of the investment. For instance, a cost of investment 1 at the opening value of the day d, means we have bought shares spending 1 (no matter the currency) and if we sail at the first sell signal the shares for 1.1, which is the gain from investment, the ROI is $\frac{1.1-1}{1} = 0.1$, that is 10% of profit. The sum of each ROI over the trading period is the percentage gain in investment capital.

5   Experiments: Prediction and Trading

5.1   Predictions of Positive/Negative Dow Jones Movements

We tested the effectiveness of the prediction varying (i) the classification algorithm, we tested two different supervised models using the *Weka*[2] implementation: *Decision tree* (the J48 C4.5) and *SVM* (the SMO algorithm), (ii) the number n_f of features (i.e. words) selected in the dataset, (iii) the aggregation a and (iv) the lag l parameters on the data cited above.

Before the application of the noise detection method, we tested a simple prediction model based on the VSM built as described in Sect. 3.2, varying the parameters in order to discover the best tuning of them. Tables 1 and 2 show

---

[2] www.cs.waikato.ac.nz/ml/weka/.

Table 1. Results obtained in tuning the decision tree algorithm.

Aggr	Lag	n_f feat	fMeasure
3	0	500	0.799
3	1	2000	0.736
3	0	1000	0.700
0	2	500	0.668
0	2	2000	0.660
2	2	500	0.657
3	2	2000	0.653

Table 2. Results obtained in tuning the SVM algorithm.

Aggr	Lag	n_f feat	fMeasure
2	1	1000	0.682
1	2	2000	0.668
3	2	1000	0.649
2	1	2000	0.649
1	3	2000	0.643
0	2	2000	0.642
2	1	500	0.642

Table 3. Comparison with cosine similarities between instances (aggregated tweets) belonging to the different four groups. Each cell of the table is calculated as average value of the comparison of all the related couples of instances.

	TP	TN	FP	FN
TP	0.819	0.828	0.779	0.772
TP	0.823	0.914	0.776	0.738
FP	0.779	0.776	0.848	0.770
FN	0.772	0.738	0.77	0.912

the best results obtained by the two supervised algorithms with the related parameters combination.

A first noteworthy aspect is the aggregation parameter, that gives best results with three days gathered, this confirms the analysis done by Bollen et al. in their work, in which authors obtain the same consideration. This means that there is a strong correlation between the information extracted in a couple of days before and the outcome of a market trading day. In other words, the stock market seems to be affected to the information, and thus event or moods and so on, of the previous days.

Moreover, it is evident the best accuracy obtained by the decision tree model, that with few features required (just 500), achieves a f-Measure almost of 80%. From now on, every test is performed using the best combination of parameters shown in Tables 1 and 2.

Once defined the best model, we applied the noise detection method in order to clean the dataset. The idea is to analyze the predictions made on the validation set in order to define four groups of predictions and use those to find only the useful tweets, or aggregations of tweets, in the dataset.

First, we divided the validation set instances based on the outcome of the predictions. Among all the tested instances, we selected only the predictions with the probability given by the classifier greater than 90%, in order to pull out only the *surest* among them. These selected instances are then grouped based on the outcome (i.e. TP, TN, FP, FN). In order to assess the assumptions and the quality of the groupings made, we calculated the cosine similarity between both instances of the same group and belonging to different groups; we expected that the instances belonging to the same group should have a high similarity, while should appear dissimilarities comparing instances of different groups. These comparisons are shown in the Table 3; the main diagonal contains the comparisons between instances belonging to the same group, noteworthy is that these similarities are significantly greater than the other comparisons and this supports our hypothesis underlying the noise detection method.

The first noise detection experiment has been made comparing all the single tweets in the dataset (both training and test sets) with the four prototypes created aggregating the instances of the four groups of predictions analyzed above. We conducted a double experiment: (i) keeping only the tweets similar to the two *good* prototypes, i.e. tweets whose cosine similarity with respect to TP or TN overcomes a threshold τ_g; (ii) discarding all the tweets similar to the *bad* prototypes, i.e. tweets whose cosine similarity with respect to FP or FN overcomes a threshold τ_b. Figure 3 shows the obtained results in both experiments, varying the thresholds. Unfortunately, the results do not show an improving trend by using this noise detection technique.

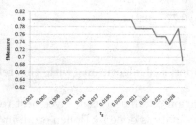 

(a) Mantaining tweets similar to the *good* prototypes. Based from [22].   (b) Discarding tweets similar to the *bad* prototypes.

Fig. 3. Tweets level noise detection experiments. Based from [22].

A further proposal to detect and remove noise is based on idea of that some training instances could compromise the accuracy of the prediction model, as outliers or simply containing noisy tweets. In this experiment, we remove in the training set of the final classification model all the instances that are similar to the bad prototypes and thus could negatively affect the model. Figure 4 shows the results obtained with the best tuning using both a decision tree and a SVM algorithm, varying the threshold τ in the noise detection algorithm. Results show a noteworthy improvement using the noise detection method. In particular, using the Decision tree algorithm, we achieve a $fMeasure = 0.889$ that is an improvement of 10% with respect to the results obtained in tests without the training set cleaning techniques. Similar considerations can be done when using

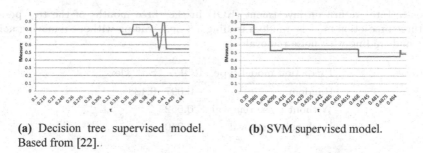

(a) Decision tree supervised model. Based from [22].   **(b)** SVM supervised model.

Fig. 4. Instance level noise detection experiments. Based from [22].

a SVM classifier; in this case the improvement is even greater, since we started from a $fMeasure = 0.682$ and, with an improvement of 27%, we obtain a maximum of $fMeasure = 0.867$ when using the noise detection algorithm.

By analyzing the results obtained by the best model, we found a $fMeasure$ related to the prediction of the positive market day of 0.848 and to the negative day of 0.912. The precision of the predictions in the test set is 88.9%, that is higher than the precision obtained by Bollen et al. in their work, i.e. 86.7%.

A real comparison with the work of Bollen et al. can be done considering the same test set of their works, i.e. considering the 19 trading days in December 2008. Using this test set and training our method with the first 11 months of the year, we obtain a perfect classification (100%) of the 19 trading days, showing a sharp improvement with respect to the 86.7% obtained by Bollen et al.

5.2 Trading Results

We have performed the trading actions according to the protocol described in Sect. 4 and the experiments have been conducted comparing three prediction models: a random predictor of the DJIA rise/drop and our two best prediction models illustrated in previous Section without and with the removal of noisy tweets, with $fMeasure$ 79.9% and 88.9% respectively. The trading period coincides with the prediction test period from October to December 2008.

The three experiments have been compared according to the return on investment (ROI) described in Sect. 4. Table 4 reports the total ROI achieved by the above mentioned prediction models over the three months of test.

The random predictor model, which conducts buy/sell trading actions completely random, has been executed 10000 times, changing in each the random generator seed. It achieves on average a loss of 10% with a standard deviation of 14%.

Our first best prediction model, trained without removing noisy tweets, gains 56%, while the second one, which is trained removing noisy tweets from the training, gains 84% with the noise detection technique described in the previous subsection. The two latter results do not have a standard deviation as there are not random choices for which repeating the experiments. As far as we know, both

Table 4. Total return on investment (ROI) in the three months of the test period with three prediction models: random trading actions, trading without removing noisy tweets and trading with noise removal.

Prediction model type	ROI	Std. Dev.
Random	−0.097	0.138
Without noise removal	0.562	
With noise removal	0.840	

results outperform the state-of-the-art in trading with the DJIA [26], even with respect to more recent advanced approaches based on deep learning and recurrent neural networks [27,28]. To get the *annual* ROI, the gains above mentioned should be multiplied by four as they have been accumulated in a period of just three months.

Figure 5 reports the ROIs time series produced by the three models over the test period of the last three months of 2008. The ROI time series of random prediction model (the bottom one) is always negative and in some days the loss is more than 10%. The ROI time series of the prediction model without noise removal (the one in the middle) has initially a slight loss and then is increasing almost constantly. The top time series, which is the trend of the ROI of the prediction model with noise removal, in the first week does not produce gains, then it grows with a larger and larger difference with respect to the two previous models.

6   Related Work

Stock market analysis and prediction has always received great interest by the academic world: several possible approaches have been proposed, from time series prediction to textual news analysis, until arriving to the social networks analysis. In this section we review the literature starting from classic stock market prediction approaches, then we summarize the most recent works using social network information to forecast the market prices. Finally, we analyze the most known noise detection methods proposed in literature.

In the beginning, the scientific researches were based on the Efficient Market Hypothesis [6] according to which prices of traded assets reflect all relevant information available at any time. In such financial market model, neither technical prediction analysis of future prices based on the study of past prices, nor fundamental analysis studying the evolution of the business value, allows an investor to achieve higher profits than those that another investor would get with a portfolio of stocks selected randomly, with the same degree of risk. However, in the last decades a great amount of works refused the unpredictability hypothesis [9,29] showing that stock price series follow the random walk theory only in a short period of time and consequently arguing that in general they could be predicted.

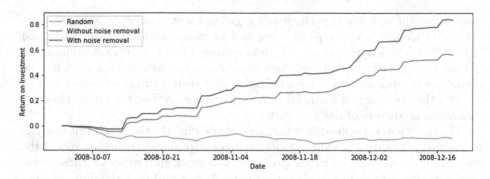

Fig. 5. Time series of the return on investments (ROI) of the three prediction models in the test of three months: random, without noise removal, with noise removal.

Two major approaches to stock market prediction exist: using features derived from technical analysis based on the history of stock index prices and using related news and textual information to predict trends. Surveys about the two approaches are given in [30] and [31] respectively. Other researches employ blog posts to predict stock market behaviour by determining correlation between activities in Internet message boards and stock volatility and trading volumes [32]. [33] create an index of the US national mood, called Anxiety Index, by exploiting over 20 million posts from the LiveJournal website: when this index increased significantly, the S&P 500 ended the day marginally lower than expected. A comparative survey of artificial intelligence applications in finance is reported in [34].

Several studies in the literature have proposed the use of information from twitter to analyze and predict the trend of the stock prices. Similarly to the work of Bollen et al. [19], already described in Sect. 2, authors in [35] use the calm score of tweets extracts from June and December 2009, achieving an accuracy of 75% in 20-day test of prediction of Dow Diamonds ETF (DIA). They increase the accuracy up to 80% by adding a quantitative feature related to the previous value of the DIA. [36] uses in a multi-class classification, considering only *calm*, *happy*, *alert* and *kind* mood dimensions. Furthermore, 4 different learning algorithms (i.e. Linear Regression, Logistic Regression, SVMs and SOFNN) are used to learn and exploit the actual predictions; SOFNN based model performed best among all other algorithms, giving nearly 76% of accuracy. A comparison of six different and popular sentiment analysis lexical resources (Harvard General Inquirer, Opinion Lexicon, Macquarie Semantic Orientation Lexicon, MPQA Subjectivity Lexicon, SentiWordNet, Emoticons) to evaluate the usefulness of each resource in stock prediction is done by [24]. [37] uses sentiment analysis on stock related tweets collected during a 6-month period. To reduce noise, they selected tweets containing *cashtags* ($) of S&P 100 companies. Each message is classified by a Naïve Bayes method trained with a set of 2500 tweets. Results show that sentiment indicators are associated with abnormal returns and message volume is correlated to the trading volume. Similarly, [38] associates a polarity to each day considering the number of positive and negative tweets via *sentiment140*[3], testing the DJIA and NASDAQ-100 index in a 13-month period between 2010 and 2011. [39] surveys a variety of web data sources (Twitter, news headlines and Google search queries) and tests two sentiment analysis methods used for the prediction of stock market behavior, finding that their Twitter sentiment indicator and the frequency of financial terms occurrence on Twitter are statistically significant predictors of daily market returns.

There are several approaches that do not use directly the sentiment analysis to make predictions. For example [40] analyses with linear regression model the correlation between the Twitter predictor and stock indicators at three levels (stock market, sector and single company level) and find that the daily number of tweets that mention S&P 500 stocks is significantly correlated with S&P 500 daily closing price. They obtain in a 19-day test an accuracy of 68% for Stock Market and sector level prediction and of 52% for company stock. [41] creates different types of features: to a "basic" data set corresponding to the tweets BoW of the previous day, they add features regarding the number of tweets containing the words "worry", "hope" or "fear" (Basic&HWF), or the words "happy", "loving", "calm", "energetic", "fearful", "angry", "tired" and "sad" (Basic&8emo), training a SVM with these datasets relating at 7 months of 2013. They get a maximum baseline accuracy of 65.17% for the DJIA, 57% for the S&P 500 and 50.67% for NASDAQ. In a different way, [42] extracts two types of features, one concerning the overall activity in twitter and one measure the properties of an induced interaction graph. They found a correlation between these features and changes in S&P 500 price and volume traded. [43] found a high negative correlation (0.726, significant at level $p < 0.01$) between the Dow Jones index and the presence of the words hope, fear, and worry in tweets.

A quantitative analysis is made by [44]: using Twitter volume spikes in a 15-month period (from February 2012 to May 2013) they train a Bayesian classifier to assist S&P 500 stock trading and they show that it can provide substantial profit. [45] through extensive testing shows that adding Twitter-related data (either in term of volume or public sentiment) to in non-linear time series (SVMs or neural networks) will improve the predictions of stocks or indexes.

Noise detection is a topic of interest since the dawn of information retrieval. In the Vector Space Model representation, the noise removal can be addressed at two levels. At *feature level* useless and non-informative words are removed: normally this problem is addressed with a lists of stopwords and feature selection schemes [46,47]. At *instance level* are instead removed non-informative documents, which could be source of confusion for the classification model. Here can be ideally used the various noise detection techniques proposed in IR, without considering the textual nature of the single features. There exist in literature a large amount of proposed methods, for example using K-nearest neighbors approach, neural networks, decision trees, SVM or Bayesian networks. In-depth descriptions of all of these techniques have been reported in surveys as [21,48].

---

[3] http://help.sentiment140.com/.

7   Conclusion

In this paper, we have developed a prediction method of the DJIA trend based on text mining knowledge extracted from ten millions of tweets emitted in a year. Moreover the method recognises and filters out irrelevant tweets that represent noise and would negatively affect the prediction accuracy. The current stock price prediction depends from the contents of tweets posted in the previous days. This correlation was already shown in some works in literature that use complex techniques to try to understand the semantic content of the textual documents in order to predict the stock market trends.

The aim of our work was to use a simple method, based on the well-known Vector Space Model representation and a supervised classifier. We have also introduced a noise detection technique, both at tweets and at instances level of the learning model (i.e. aggregation of tweets), we have used to filter out from the data the large irrelevant corpus of tweets retrieved. We have tested and compared the method on the same tweets dataset and DJIA trends in the whole 2008 used by [19]. Results shows that even a simple classification model based on the VSM achieves a high accuracy of 80%.

This work have also demonstrated that our noise detection technique is able to distinguish the irrelevant tweets and instances, thus noise, in the training data, leading the accuracy to 88.9%, outperforming both our base classifier and the best prediction method based on social network posts illustrated in [19].

Moreover we have added a trading protocol whose buy/sell operations are driven by our prediction method. The return on investments (ROI) we achieved, using the two prediction models mentioned above, are 56% and 84% and they have been accumulated only in the test period of three months. These two ROIs outperform previous DJIA trading approaches, both stock market methods based only on the historical time series of DJIA prices [26] and recent advanced deep learning proposals [27,28].

As future works we plan to further investigate possible correlations among different market indexes and stock options expanding the analysis to other sources of unstructured text streams. In this context the heterogeneity of multi-domain text sources could be dealt and leveraged with novel cross domain [49–51] and transfer learning methods [52–54].

References

1. Liu, Y., Huang, X., An, A., Yu, X.: ARSA: a sentiment-aware model for predicting sales performance using blogs. In: Proceedings of the 30th Annual International ACM SIGIR Conference on Research and Development in Information Retrieval, pp. 607–614. ACM (2007)
2. Mishne, G., de Rijke, M.: Capturing global mood levels using blog posts. In: AAAI Spring Symposium: Computational Approaches to Analyzing Weblogs 2006, pp. 145–152 (2006)
3. Asur, S., Huberman, B.A.: Predicting the future with social media. In: 2010 IEEE/WIC/ACM International Conference on Web Intelligence and Intelligent Agent Technology (WI-IAT), vol. 1, pp. 492–499. IEEE (2010)

4. Gruhl, D., Guha, R., Kumar, R., Novak, J., Tomkins, A.: The predictive power of online chatter. In: Proceedings of the Eleventh ACM SIGKDD International Conference on Knowledge Discovery in Data Mining, pp. 78–87. ACM (2005)
5. Gayo-Avello, D.: "I wanted to predict elections with Twitter and all I got was this lousy paper"–a balanced survey on election prediction using Twitter data. arXiv preprint arXiv:1204.6441 (2012)
6. Fama, E.F.: The behavior of stock-market prices. J. Bus. **38**, 34–105 (1965)
7. Kimoto, T., Asakawa, K., Yoda, M., Takeoka, M.: Stock market prediction system with modular neural networks. In: 1990 IJCNN International Joint Conference on Neural Networks, pp. 1–6. IEEE (1990)
8. Fama, E.F.: Efficient capital markets: II. J. Financ. **46**, 1575–1617 (1991)
9. Malkiel, B.G.: The efficient market hypothesis and its critics. J. Econ. Perspect. **17**, 59–82 (2003)
10. Lo, A.W., MacKinlay, A.C.: Stock market prices do not follow random walks: evidence from a simple specification test. Rev. Financ. Stud. **1**, 41–66 (1988)
11. Butler, K.C., Malaikah, S.: Efficiency and inefficiency in thinly traded stock markets: Kuwait and Saudi Arabia. J. Bank. Financ. **16**, 197–210 (1992)
12. Gidófalvi, G., Elkan, C.: Using news articles to predict stock price movements. Department of Computer Science and Engineering, University of California, San Diego (2001)
13. Schumaker, R.P., Chen, H.: Textual analysis of stock market prediction using financial news. In: Americas Conference on Information Systems (2006)
14. Li, X., Wang, C., Dong, J., Wang, F., Deng, X., Zhu, S.: Improving stock market prediction by integrating both market news and stock prices. In: Hameurlain, A., Liddle, S.W., Schewe, K.-D., Zhou, X. (eds.) DEXA 2011. LNCS, vol. 6861, pp. 279–293. Springer, Heidelberg (2011). https://doi.org/10.1007/978-3-642-23091-2_24
15. Lin, M.C., Lee, A.J.T., Kao, R.T., Chen, K.T.: Stock price movement prediction using representative prototypes of financial reports. ACM Trans. Manag. Inf. Syst. **2**, 19:1–19:18 (2008)
16. Bollen, J., Mao, H., Pepe, A.: Modeling public mood and emotion: Twitter sentiment and socio-economic phenomena. In: ICWSM (2011)
17. Si, J., Mukherjee, A., Liu, B., Pan, S.J., Li, Q., Li, H.: Exploiting social relations and sentiment for stock prediction. In: Proceedings of the 2014 Conference on Empirical Methods in Natural Language Processing, EMNLP 2014, 25–29 October 2014, Doha, Qatar, A Meeting of SIGDAT, a Special Interest Group of the ACL, pp. 1139–1145. ACL (2014)
18. Ghiassi, M., Skinner, J., Zimbra, D.: Twitter brand sentiment analysis: a hybrid system using n-gram analysis and dynamic artificial neural network. Expert Syst. Appl. **40**, 6266–6282 (2013)
19. Bollen, J., Mao, H., Zeng, X.: Twitter mood predicts the stock market. J. Comput. Sci. **2**, 1–8 (2011)
20. Samant, R.M., Rao, S.: The effect of noise in automatic text classification. In: Proceedings of the International Conference & #38; Workshop on Emerging Trends in Technology, ICWET 2011, pp. 557–558. ACM, New York (2011)
21. Markou, M., Singh, S.: Novelty detection: a review? Part 1: statistical approaches. Sig. Process. **83**, 2481–2497 (2003)
22. Domeniconi, G., Moro, G., Pagliarani, A., Pasolini, R.: Learning to predict the stock market Dow Jones index detecting and mining relevant tweets. In: Proceedings of the 9th International Joint Conference on Knowledge Discovery, Knowledge Engineering and Knowledge Management, Funchal, Madeira, Portugal, 1–3 November 2017, vol. 1, pp. 165–172. SciTePress (2017)

23. Wilson, T., et al.: OpinionFinder: a system for subjectivity analysis. In: Proceedings of HLT/EMNLP on Interactive Demonstrations, pp. 34–35. Association for Computational Linguistics (2005)

24. Oliveira, N., Cortez, P., Areal, N.: Some experiments on modeling stock market behavior using investor sentiment analysis and posting volume from Twitter. In: Proceedings of the 3rd International Conference on Web Intelligence, Mining and Semantics, WIMS 2013, pp. 31:1–31:8. ACM, New York (2013)

25. Domeniconi, G., Moro, G., Pasolini, R., Sartori, C.: A comparison of term weighting schemes for text classification and sentiment analysis with a supervised variant of tf.idf. In: Helfert, M., Holzinger, A., Belo, O., Francalanci, C. (eds.) DATA 2015. CCIS, vol. 584, pp. 39–58. Springer, Cham (2016). https://doi.org/10.1007/978-3-319-30162-4_4

26. O'Connor, N., Madden, M.G.: A neural network approach to predicting stock exchange movements using external factors. Knowl. Based Syst. **19**, 371–378 (2006)

27. Fabbri, M., Moro, G.: Dow Jones trading with deep learning: the unreasonable effectiveness of recurrent neural networks. In: Proceedings of the 7th International Conference on Data Science, Technology and Applications: DATA, INSTICC, vol. 1, pp. 142–153. SciTePress (2018)

28. Bao, W., Yue, J., Rao, Y.: A deep learning framework for financial time series using stacked autoencoders and long-short term memory. PLOS ONE **7**, (2017)

29. Qian, B., Rasheed, K.: Stock market prediction with multiple classifiers. Appl. Intell. **26**, 25–33 (2007)

30. Atsalakis, G.S., Valavanis, K.P.: Surveying stock market forecasting techniques-part ii: soft computing methods. Expert Syst. Appl. **36**, 5932–5941 (2009)

31. Mittermayer, M.A., Knolmayer, G.: Text mining systems for market response to news: a survey. Institut für Wirtschaftsinformatik der Universität Bern (2006)

32. Antweiler, W., Frank, M.Z.: Is all that talk just noise? The information content of internet stock message boards. J. Financ. **59**, 1259–1294 (2004)

33. Gilbert, E., Karahalios, K.: Widespread worry and the stock market. In: ICWSM, pp. 59–65 (2010)

34. Bahrammirzaee, A.: A comparative survey of artificial intelligence applications in finance: artificial neural networks, expert system and hybrid intelligent systems. Neural Comput. Appl. **19**, 1165–1195 (2010)

35. Chyan A, Lengerich C, Hsieh T.: A stock-purchasing agent from sentiment analysis of Twitter (2012)

36. Mittal, A., Goel, A.: Stock prediction using Twitter sentiment analysis (2012)

37. Sprenger, T.O., Tumasjan, A., Sandner, P.G., Welpe, I.M.: Tweets and trades: the information content of stock microblogs. Eur. Financ. Manag. **20**, 926–957 (2013)

38. Rao, T., Srivastava, S.: Twitter sentiment analysis: how to hedge your bets in the stock markets. CoRR abs/1212.1107 (2012)

39. Mao, H., Counts, S., Bollen, J.: Predicting financial markets: comparing survey, news, Twitter and search engine data. arXiv preprint arXiv:1112.1051 (2011)

40. Mao, Y., Wei, W., Wang, B., Liu, B.: Correlating S&P 500 stocks with Twitter data. In: Proceedings of the First ACM International Workshop on Hot Topics on Interdisciplinary Social Networks Research, HotSocial 2012, pp. 69–72. ACM, New York (2012)

41. Porshnev, A., Redkin, I., Shevchenko, A.: Improving prediction of stock market indices by analyzing the psychological states of Twitter users. In: HSE Working Papers WP BRP 22/FE/2013. National Research University Higher School of Economics (2013)

42. Ruiz, E.J., Hristidis, V., Castillo, C., Gionis, A., Jaimes, A.: Correlating financial time series with micro-blogging activity. In: Proceedings of the Fifth ACM International Conference on Web Search and Data Mining, WSDM 2012, pp. 513–522. ACM, New York (2012)
43. Zhang, X., Fuehres, H., Gloor, P.A.: Predicting stock market indicators through Twitter "I hope it is not as bad as I fear". Proc. Soc. Behav. Sci. **26**, 55–62 (2011)
44. Mao, Y., Wei, W., Wang, B.: Twitter volume spikes: analysis and application in stock trading. In: Proceedings of the 7th Workshop on Social Network Mining and Analysis, p. 4. ACM (2013)
45. Arias, M., Arratia, A., Xuriguera, R.: Forecasting with Twitter data. ACM Trans. Intell. Syst. Technol. **5**, 8:1–8:24 (2014)
46. Yang, Y.: Noise reduction in a statistical approach to text categorization. In: Proceedings of the 18th Annual International ACM SIGIR Conference on Research and Development in Information Retrieval, pp. 256–263. ACM (1995)
47. Gabrilovich, E., Markovitch, S.: Text categorization with many redundant features: using aggressive feature selection to make SVMs competitive with C4. 5. In: Proceedings of the Twenty-First International Conference on Machine Learning, p. 41. ACM (2004)
48. Chandola, V., Banerjee, A., Kumar, V.: Anomaly detection: a survey. ACM Comput. Surv. **41**, 15:1–15:58 (2009)
49. Domeniconi, G., Moro, G., Pasolini, R., Sartori, C.: Iterative refining of category profiles for nearest centroid cross-domain text classification. In: Fred, A., Dietz, J.L.G., Aveiro, D., Liu, K., Filipe, J. (eds.) IC3K 2014. CCIS, vol. 553, pp. 50–67. Springer, Cham (2015). https://doi.org/10.1007/978-3-319-25840-9_4
50. Domeniconi, G., Moro, G., Pagliarani, A., Pasolini, R.: Markov chain based method for in-domain and cross-domain sentiment classification. In: KDIR 2015 - Proceedings of the International Conference on Knowledge Discovery and Information Retrieval, part of the 7th International Joint Conference on Knowledge Discovery, Knowledge Engineering and Knowledge Management (IC3K 2015), Lisbon, Portugal, vol. 1, pp. 127–137. SciTePress (2015)
51. Domeniconi, G., Masseroli, M., Moro, G., Pinoli, P.: Cross-organism learning method to discover new gene functionalities. Comput. Meth. Progr. Biomed. **126**, 20–34 (2016)
52. Moro, G., Pagliarani, A., Pasolini, R., Sartori, C.: Cross-domain & in-domain sentiment analysis with memory-based deep neural networks. In: Proceedings of the 10th International Joint Conference on Knowledge Discovery, Knowledge Engineering and Knowledge Management, Seville, Spain, 18–20 September 2018. SciTePress (2018)
53. Domeniconi, G., Moro, G., Pagliarani, A., Pasolini, R.: On deep learning in cross-domain sentiment classification. In: Proceedings of the 9th International Joint Conference on Knowledge Discovery, Knowledge Engineering and Knowledge Management, KDIR, Funchal, Madeira, Portugal, 1–3 November 2017, vol. 1, pp. 50–60. INSTICC, SciTePress (2017). https://doi.org/10.5220/0006488100500060. ISBN: 978-989-758-271-4
54. Pagliarani, A., Moro, G., Pasolini, R., Domeniconi, G.: Transfer learning in sentiment classification with deep neural networks. In: International Joint Conference on Knowledge Discovery, Knowledge Engineering, and Knowledge Management, Springer, Heidelberg (2017)

Behavioural Biometric Continuous User Authentication Using Multivariate Keystroke Streams in the Spectral Domain

Abdullah Alshehri[1(✉)], Frans Coenen[2], and Danushka Bollegala[2]

[1] Department of Information Technology, Albaha University, Albaha, Saudi Arabia
[2] Department of Computer Science, University of Liverpool, Liverpool, UK
aashehri@bu.edu.sa, {coenen,danushka.bollegala}@liverpool.ac.uk

Abstract. Continuous authentication is significant with respect to many online applications where it is desirable to monitor a user's identity throughout an entire session; not just at the beginning of the session. One example application domain, where this is a requirement, is in relation to Massive Open Online Courses (MOOCs) when users wish to obtain some kind of certification as evidence that they have successfully competed a course. Such continuous authentication can best be realised using some forms of biometric checking; traditional user credential checking methods, for example username and password checking, only provide for "entry" authentication. In this paper, we introduce a novel method for the continuous authentication of computer users founded on keystroke dynamics (keyboard behaviour patterns); a form of behavioural biometric. The proposed method conceptualises keyboard dynamics in terms of a Multivariate-Keystroke Time Series which in turn can be transformed into the spectral domain. The time series can then be monitored dynamically for typing patterns that are indicative of a claimed user. Two transforms are considered, the Discrete Fourier Transform and the Discrete Wavelet Transform. The proposed method is fully described and evaluated, in the context of impersonation detection, using real keystroke datasets. The reported results indicate that the proposed time series mechanism produced an excellent performance, outperforming the comparator approaches by a significant margin.

Keywords: Biometrics · Continuous authentication ·
Keystroke dynamics · Keystroke time series

1 Introduction

Recent decades have seen a considerable increase in the popularity of digital learning. Digital learning, also referred to as online education and eLearning, refers to internet facilitated education, as opposed to traditional face-to-face

© Springer Nature Switzerland AG 2019
A. Fred et al. (Eds.): IC3K 2017, CCIS 976, pp. 43–66, 2019.
https://doi.org/10.1007/978-3-030-15640-4_3

classroom-style education. A current example is the prevalence of MOOCs (Massive Open Online Courses) where students learn at their own pace and withdraw openly and freely [7]. The increasing popularity of digital learning, whatever form this might take, has resulted in an increasing number of people who wish to attain some kind of certification as evidence of successful completion of (say) an online programme. One mechanism for doing this is in the form online assessments and exams which students take remotely. Consequently, user authentication has become an issue [14, 25, 28]; certification providers need systems in place to confirm that the person taking an online assessment/exam is who they say they are.

Today, the vast majority of digital learning systems depend on traditional (*log-in*) credentials, such as passwords and usernames, for authentication. However, this means that the identity of students is only authenticated at the start of an eLearning assessment. The utilisation of this form of authentication is obviously inadequate with respect to what is known as "insider attacks". The form of insider attack most relevant to eLearning is impersonation, where an imposter poses as the real user when performing some kind of remote assessment. Therefore, a major issue with respect to digital learning systems is how to continuously confirm that a student taking an assessment is who they say they are. This means, not only that students need to be authenticated at the start of each assessment, but throughout the course of the assessment; continuous authentication of student identity is thus required.

Continuous authentication can best be realised using some forms of Biometric checking system [36], because such systems operate using features that are inherent to the user [33]. Moreover, Biometrics can produce strong authentication solutions comparing to other forms of authentication [4]. Biometrics, in general, can be categorised as follows:

1. **Physiological Biometrics:** Physiological biometrics are the organic characteristics of an individual. Well known examples include: (i) iris recognition [40], (ii) face recognition [32] and (iii) fingerprint recognition [26].
2. **Behavioural Biometrics:** Behavioural biometrics are concerned with the manner in which individuals perform certain tasks. Examples include: (i) keystroke dynamics (typing patterns) [30], (ii) mouse movement usage [1], (iii) voice recognition [20], (iv) handwriting recognition [38] and (v) gait (walking style) recognition [27].

Typically, the use of physiological biometrics requires specialised equipment to operate, such as iris, face or fingerprint recognition devices. However, in the context of the digital learning domain, it seems unreasonable to expect online students to purchase such equipment for authentication reasons. Furthermore, physiological biometrics are impractical for continuous authentication in that students need to re-conduct the biometric authentication periodically. In contrast, behavioural biometrics, seem well suited to continuous user authentication in the eLearning context, because they do not require dedicated devices which in turn make their deployment relatively straightforward. The most obvious behavioural biometric to be used in the context of digital learning is keystroke dynamics (typing patterns).

Keystroke dynamics is a promising behavioural biometric recognition mechanism that can provide the desired continuous authentication [6]. It offers the advantage that no special equipment is required such as in the case of continuous iris or fingerprint recognition. The intuition behind the use of keystroke dynamics is that individuals use keyboards in different manners regardless of what they are typing [16]. Thus such "typing rhythms", captured using keystroke dynamics, can be effectively used to authenticate keyboard users. In this context, typing behaviour can be expressed in the form of patterns made up of the keystroke timing attribute-values associated with: (i) flight times ($\mathcal{F}^t$) and (ii) key-hold times ($\mathcal{KH}^t$) [16]. The first is the time from the first key press to the last key release of n-grams; the second is the duration of holding down a key. An n-grams in this context is a sequence of n keyboard characters.

Keystroke dynamics have been studied, as a biometric technology, in the context of Keystroke Static Authentication (KSA) and in the context of Keystroke Continuous Authentication (KCA). The first, as the name implies, is directed at user authentication with respect to static (fixed) texts such as passwords, usernames, and pin numbers. Whilst KCA is directed at authentication in the context of free (arbitrary) text.

The most common existing mechanism for learning typing patterns, regardless of whether KSA or KCA is being considered, is founded on the feature vector representation where individual feature vectors describe individual typing templates [5,22,30,41]. In this context, the feature vectors typically comprise statistical values representing keystroke timing data specific to certain n-grams. For instance, the mean and standard deviation of the flight time for certain di-grams. Authentication is then conducted by determining the similarity between stored feature vectors representing reference templates (profiles) which are known to belong to a specific user, and a previously unseen current profile that is claimed to belong to the same specific user. If the similarity falls below some predefined threshold, the user is declared to be who they say they are; otherwise the user will be "flagged up" as a potential imposter.

The feature vector representation has met with some success, particularly in the context of KSA. However, in the context of KCA, the construction of typing templates, and the consequent learning of typing patterns, has been found to be more challenging. This is because, by definition, the text to be considered is free and unstructured. This, in turn, means that typing templates need to be much more generic than in the case of KSA (where we know what is going to be typed), and consequently more sophisticated. One approach is to generate feature vector templates by identifying statistical details concerning the most frequently occurring n-grams [11,17,29]. However, a criticism that can be directed at this mechanism is that the generated typing templates (profiles) might not feature the same frequently occurring n grams as the sample to be authenticated, which in turn can lead to poor authentication rates. A suggested solution is to increase the number of training n-grams considered; however, this means that users need to be asked to provide a lot of samples. An obvious question is how many n-grams do we require to ensure that a typing template is sufficiently robust? Whatever the answer, the number of n-grams, and hence the number of required samples, is significant. Furthermore, feature vectors comprised of very large numbers of features raises efficiency concerns, particularly when the intention is to conduct continuous authentication, as required in the case of the online assessments and examinations frequently used in digital learning. Thus, a robust, accurate and more efficient continuous authentication mechanism, founded on keystroke dynamics, is desirable.

In this paper, a novel method for KCA is proposed using time series analysis to recognise typing patterns from free text in a manner suited to the continuous authentication required with respect to digital learning. The proposed method operates using, simultaneously, the $\mathcal{F}^t$ and $\mathcal{KH}^t$ keystroke timing features associated with all keystrokes, not just specific n-grams. More specifically, the proposed approach operates by considering typing behaviour in terms of Multivariate-Keystroke Time Series (M-KTS) subsequences of length ω. The idea is that these subsequences are extracted from a continuous keyboard dynamic stream, $\mathcal{K}_{ts} = \{p_1, p_2, \dots\}$, where each point p_i is a keystroke event represented in terms of $\mathcal{F}^t$ and $\mathcal{KH}^t$ values. The collected M-KTS subsequence are then transformed form the temporal domain to the spectral domain using either: (i) the Discrete Fourier Transformation (DFT) or (ii) the Discrete Wavelet Transform (DWT). In this manner, a spectral M-KTS can be obtained. KCA is then performed by comparing the most recent spectral M-KTS subsequence with the previous extracted spectral M-KTS subsequence (in a given typing session). On start-up the subject's identity will be initially confirmed in a "traditional" manner with reference to stored typing templates. The time series comparison is conducted using Dynamic Time Warping (DTW); a well-known similarity comparison method for time series.

The work presented in this paper is founded on previous work presented in [2] and [3]. In [2] KCA was accomplished using M-KTS but in the temporal domain, whilst in [3] KCA was realised using the spectral domain but only in the context of for Univariate Keystroke Time Series (U-KTS). The central intuition of the work presented in this paper was firstly that better KCA results could be obtained using M-KTS than were obtained using U-KTS (regardless of whether the time series are considered in the temporal or spectral domain). Secondly that usage of the spectral domain would be better suited to KCA because with respect to other time series applications, such as time series indexing [13] and time series pattern extraction [35], it had been demonstrated that usage of the spectral domain could significantly improve analysis in terms of both speed and accuracy.

The remainder of this paper is structured as follows. Section 2 reviews the pertinent previous work concerning KCA. Section 3 presents some preliminaries for the multivariate keystroke time series representation. The framework for the proposed KCA method, using spectral M-KTS, is then presented in Sect. 4. Next the evaluation of the proposed approach is reported in Sect. 5. Finally, the work is summarised and concluded in Sect. 6.

2   Previous Work

As noted in the introduction to this paper, there has been significant previous work directed at KCA, although directed at the use of statistical measurements to define feature vectors with respect to sets of n-grams. One of the earliest reported studies can be found in [29] where typing templates were constructed using feature vectors comprised of $\mathcal{F}^t$ mean values for all di-grams that featured in a training set. KCA was performed by repeatedly generating "test" feature vectors for a given user, one every minute, and comparing these with stored templates. If a statistically similar match was found this was considered to be a correct authentication. A criticism of this approach is the size of the feature vectors to be constructed because of the large number of di-grams that were needed, and thus the search complexity was expensive. To minimise the search complexity, the authors proposed a clustering mechanism, so only the most relevant cluster had to be searched in detail. However, this then meant that re-clustering was required every time a new user was added. Furthermore, a reported accuracy of only 23% was reported.

In [11], $\mathcal{F}^t$ was also used for the construction of feature vectors. Each feature vector was generated by considering the first 500 di-grams and tri-grams in the input typing sample, and the most frequently occurring 2000 keywords in the English language. Valid $\mathcal{F}^t$ values were required to be within the range 10 ms to 750 ms. The mean and Standard Deviation (SD) of each di-gram, tri-gram and keyword were extracted and n-grams with SD values in the top and bottom 10% pruned so as to remove n-grams that had very large or very small SDs. During KCA, potential imposter samples were compared with a stored template and an "alert criterion" adjusted accordingly. A deviation (threshold) value was used to identify imposters. For evaluation purposes, a simulated environment was used. The metric used to measure the performance of the system was the False Match Rate (FMR). Experiments were conducted using di-grams, tri-grams and keywords; independently and in combination. Best results were obtained using di-grams. The reason that tri-grams and keywords did not perform well was that the tri-grams did not appear as frequently as di-grams; many of the identified keywords did not appear at all in the test data.

The study presented in [17] utilised the average $\mathcal{F}^t$ values for shared di-grams and tri-grams between two given typing samples. The similarity between two typing samples, determined for KCA purposes, was performed as follows. The $\mathcal{F}^t$ average values of all shared n-grams in the two samples were extracted, and ordered, in ascending order, in two arrays. The similarity was then computed by finding the differences between the order numbering of each n-grams in each array and summing them to give a "degree of disorder" value. The smaller the degree of disorder the more similar the two typing samples. Thus, authenticating a new typing sample required comparison with all stored typing samples (reference profiles); a computationally expensive process. In the reported evaluation, 600 reference profiles were considered (generated from 40 users, each with 15 samples); the time taken for a single match, in this case, was 140 s (using a Pentium IV, 2.5 GHz).

The work presented in [2] and [3] first considered the use of time series analysis in the context of KCA; the first using M-KTS but in the temporal domain, the second in the spectral domain but using U-KTS. In [2] and [3] it was conclusively demonstrated that time series-based approaches outperformed feature vector-based approaches. The work presented in this paper was motivated by the desire to improve on the work of [2] and [3], and by extension the feature vector based approach.

3   Preliminaries

The generic concept of time series is well defined in the literature (see for example [39]); however, this section presents the application of the concept to keystroke time series, more specifically M-KTS. The section commences with a formal description of what a keystroke time series is and then goes on to define the keystroke timing features used.

Definition 1. *A keystroke time series, $\mathcal{K}_{ts}$, is an ordering of keyboard events $\{p_1, p_2, \ldots, p_n\}$ where $n \in \mathbb{N}$ is the length of the series.*

Definition 2. *A dimensional keyboard event (keystroke) $p_i \in \mathcal{K}_{ts}$ is parametrised as a tuple of the form $\langle t_i, k_i \rangle$, where t_i is an identifying index and k_i is a collection of multivariate keystroke timing features.*

The keystroke timing features used in the proposed representation are flight time ($\mathcal{F}^t$) and key-hold time ($\mathcal{KH}^t$). That is, each event $p_i \in \mathcal{K}_{ts}$ can be given as:

$$p_i \rightarrow \langle t_i, k_i \rangle \mid t = [0, n), k = \{\mathcal{F}^t, \mathcal{KH}^t\}$$

such that a keystroke time series can be formulated as an M-KTS of the form

$$\{\langle t_1, \mathcal{F}_1^t, \mathcal{KH}_1^t \rangle, \langle t_2, \mathcal{F}_2^t, \mathcal{KH}_2^t \rangle, \ldots\}$$

Because the identifying index t can be inferred from the ordering of points in the time series, the M-KTS can be simply conceptualised as a series of dimensional points such that:

$$\{\langle \mathcal{F}_1^t, \mathcal{KH}_1^t \rangle, \langle \mathcal{F}_2^t, \mathcal{KH}_2^t \rangle, \ldots\}$$

Given a keystroke time series $\mathcal{K}_{ts_i}$ (in the form of M-KTS) of length n, it can be divided in to $\frac{n}{\omega}$ subsequences where $\omega \in \mathbb{N}$ and $1 < \omega \leq n$ is the length of the derived subsequences.

Definition 3. *A keystroke time series subsequence (s), of length ω, is a subsequence of $\mathcal{K}_{ts}$ that starts at the point p_i within $\mathcal{K}_{ts}$ and ends at point $p_{i+\omega-1}$, thus:*

$$s = \{p_i, p_{i+1}, \ldots, p_{i+\omega-1}\}$$

4   Framework of the Proposed KCA Method

The proposed KCA method operates, at a high-level, in a similar manner to other biometric pattern recognition mechanisms in that it features two central components, enrolment and verification, as shown in Fig. 1. Enrolment is the process whereby an enrolment database, a database of typing templates for legitimate users, is built up. The enrolment stage also involves the generation of individual threshold values (σ values) for each subject. Verification is then the process whereby subjects are authenticated. The first precedes the second.

In more detail, the fundamental components of the proposed KCA method can be subdivided into the following parts:

1. M-KTS Extraction.
2. Noise Reduction.
3. Transformation.
4. Similarity Comparison.
5. Template Construction.
6. Authentication.

Each of these is considered in further detail in the following sub-sections.

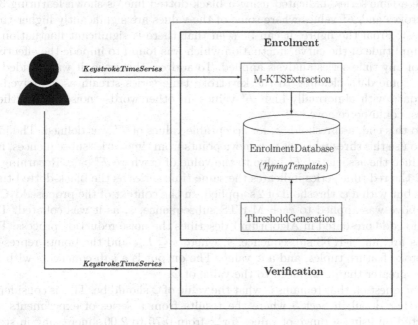

Fig. 1. The proposed KCA operational framework.

4.1 M-KTS Extraction

A key aspect of the proposed KCA method, with respect to both enrolment and verification, is the usage of M-KTS subsequences. The idea is that M-KTS subsequences are periodically extracted from the input data stream using a sliding window of length ω, where ω is user-defined. More formally, given a keystroke time series $\mathcal{K}_{ts_i} = \{p_1, p_2, \ldots, p_n\}$, where p_i represents a typing event in the form of a $\mathcal{F}^t$ and $\mathcal{KH}^t$ pair, an M-KTS subsequence, s, of length ω, is periodically extracted such that $s = \{p_i, \ldots, p_{i+\omega-1}\}$. In this manner, an ordered collection of M-KTS subsequences is produced, $\{s_1, s_2, \ldots, s_k\}$. The extracted M-KTS subsequence can then be used either as user typing templates or for authenticate purposes. It was anticipated that a small ω value would provide efficiency gains, desirable in the context of KCA; whilst a larger value would provide for accuracy gains. A trade-off between efficiency and accuracy was therefore anticipated.

4.2 Noise Reduction

An issue with keystroke time series represented using $\mathcal{F}^t$ values is that these capture significant pauses in keyboard activity and, on occasion, "away from keyboard" events. It was found that such pauses could adversely affect the extraction of typing patterns from keystroke time series. The problem is illustrated in Fig. 2 where a time series, indicated using a black-dotted line, is shown featuring 300 keystrokes and $\mathcal{F}^t$ values where some of the values are significantly higher than the rest. From the figure, it can be seen that there is significant fluctuation in the amplitude of the curve, fluctuation which was found to impede the effectiveness of any time series analysis applied. To address this issue, it was decided to apply some data cleaning to the keystroke time series stream as it arrived so that data with abnormally high $\mathcal{F}^t$ values, in other words "noise" or "outlier" values, could be removed.

To this end, a threshold, φ, for acceptable values of $\mathcal{F}^t$ was defined. The idea was to use this threshold, not to remove points from time series subsequences, but to reduce the associated $\mathcal{F}^t$ value to the value of φ where $\mathcal{F}^t > \varphi$. Returning to Fig. 2 the red time series indicates the same time series as the black-dotted time series but with a φ threshold of 2 s applied. In the context of the proposed KCA, the above was applied to each M-KTS subsequence, s, as it was collated. The pseudo code presented in Algorithm 1 describes the noise reduction process. The inputs are: an M-KTS subsequence, s, where $s \subseteq \mathcal{K}_{ts}$ and the points represent keystroke feature tuples; and a φ value. The output is a subsequence $\hat{s}$ with $\mathcal{F}^t$ values greater than φ reduced to the value of φ.

The question that remains is what the value of φ should be. This is considered in further detail in Sect. 5 where the results from a series of experiments are reported on using a range of values for φ from 0.75 to 2.00 s increasing in steps of 0.25 s ($\{0.75, 1.00, 1.25, 1.50, 1.75, 2.00\}$).

It should also be noted that key-hold time, $\mathcal{KH}^t$, is normally no longer than 1 s. Inspection of the datasets used in this thesis indicated that the highest recorded value of $\mathcal{KH}^t$ was 950 ms. Consequently, it was felt that no threshold needed to be applied to $\mathcal{KH}^t$ values as in the case of $\mathcal{F}^t$ values.

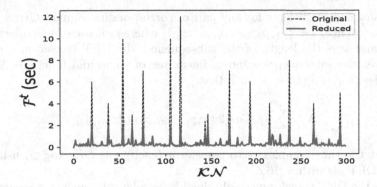

Fig. 2. The effect of applying a threshold φ to a keystroke time series stream $\mathcal{K}_{ts}$ so as to limit the $\mathcal{F}^t$ values, $\varphi = 2$ (sec). (Color figure online)

Algorithm 1. Reducing Outlier Values of $\mathcal{F}^t$.

Input: $s \leftarrow$ subsequence of $\mathcal{K}_{ts}$, $\varphi \leftarrow \mathcal{F}^t$ limit.
Output: $\widehat{s} \leftarrow$ subsequence with reduced $\mathcal{F}^t$.
1: $s \leftarrow (p_1, p_2, \ldots, p_i, \ldots, p_l)$
2: $l \leftarrow$ length of s
3: **for** $i = 1$ to $i = l$ **do**
4:     $p_i \leftarrow \langle \mathcal{F}_i^t \rangle$ $\triangleright$ Return $\mathcal{F}^t$ value from ρ (a tuple point).
5:     **if** $p_i > \varphi$: **then**
6:         $p_i == \varphi$
7:         Update(s)
8:     **end if**
9: **end for**
10: **Return** $\widehat{s}$

4.3 Transformation

The next component of the proposed KCA method was the transformation of the extracted M-KTS sequences from the temporal domain to the spectral domain. As noted in the introduction to this paper, two spectral transforms were considered: (i) Discrete Fourier Transformation (DFT) and (ii) Discrete Wavelet Transform (DWT). Both are considered in further details in the following two sub-sections (see also considered in [3]).

The Discrete Fourier Transform for Keystroke Streams. The fundamental idea of the DFT is to transform a given M-KTS subsequence from the temporal domain into the frequency domain. The resulting frequency-domain representation shows how much of a given signal lies within each given frequency band over a range of frequencies. The fundamental benefit is that the DFT serves to compact the data without loosing any salient information [21].

Compression is conducted by first representing the time series as a linear combination of sinusoidal coefficients, and then computing the similarity between the transformed coefficients for any pair of corresponding signals. Given an M-KTS subsequence, $s = \{p_1, p_2, \ldots, p_i, \ldots, p_\omega\}$, where p_i is some keystroke timing feature, and ω is the length of the subsequence, the DFT transform typically compresses the subsequence s into a linear set of sinusoidal functions X with amplitudes p, q and phase w, such that:

$$X = \sum_{i=1}^{\omega} (p_i Cos(2\pi w_i p_i) + q_i Sin(2\pi w_i p_i)) \tag{1}$$

Note that the time complexity to transform (each) s is $\mathcal{O}(\omega \log \omega)$ using the Radix 2 DFT algorithm [10, 21].

Using the DFT transform the obtained keystroke subsequence s is composed of a new magnitude (the amplitude of the discrete coefficients) and phase spectral shape, which can be compared with other transformed keystroke time series subsequences.

Figures 3 and 4 illustrate the intuition behind the DFT as applied to M-KTS, within the context of the proposed KCA method, for typing samples associated with two subjects; Fig. 3 for subject **A** and Fig. 4 for subject **B**. Typing samples were taken from the ACB evaluation dataset presented in Sect. 5. Each figure comprises two subfigures: (a) $\mathcal{F}^t$ subsequences, and (b) $\mathcal{KH}^t$ subsequences. In each subfigure, two free text typing samples are shown, on the left-hand side the raw time series, and on the right-hand side the DFT equivalent time series. Form the figures, it can be seen that the DFT signals describe distinctive patterns of typing behaviour for the same subject.

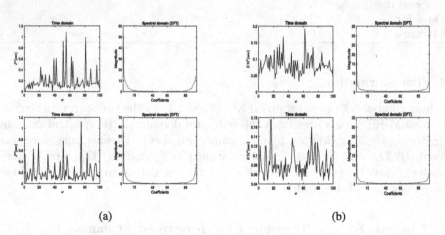

(a)   (b)

Fig. 3. Examples of the application of DFT for subject **A**; (a) $\mathcal{F}^t$ keystroke subsequences, (b) $\mathcal{KH}^t$ keystroke subsequences.

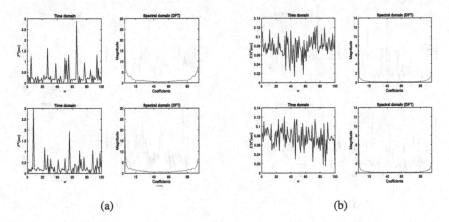

(a)   (b)

Fig. 4. Example of the application of DFT for subject **B**; (a) $\mathcal{F}^t$ keystroke subsequences, (b) $\mathcal{KH}^t$ keystroke subsequences.

The Discrete Wavelet Transform for Keystroke Streams. The Discrete Wavelet Transform (DWT) is an alternative form of time series representation that considers time series according to the frequencies that are present. DWT is sometimes claimed to provide a better transformation than DFT in that it retains more information [9]. DWT can be applied to time series according to different scales, orthogonal [18] and non-orthogonal [15]. For the work presented in this chapter the orthogonal scale was used, more specifically the well known Haar transform [18] as described in [9]. Fundamentally a Haar Wavelet is simply a sequence of functions which together form a wavelet comprised of a series of square shapes. The Haar transform is considered to be the simplest form of DWT; however, it has been shown to offer advantages with respect to time series analysis where the time series features sudden changes. The transformation is usually defined as shown in Eq. 2 where, in the context of this thesis, x is a keystroke timing feature.

$$\phi(x) = \begin{cases} 1, & \text{if } 0 < t < \frac{1}{2} \\ -1, & \text{if } \frac{1}{2} < t < 1 \\ 0, & \text{otherwise} \end{cases} \tag{2}$$

The time complexity for the Haar transform is $\mathcal{O}(n)$ for each $\mathcal{K}_{ts}$. Note that in the context of the Haar transform, the length of a given time series should be an integral power of 2 [23], thus 2, 4, 8, 16 and so on. For further detail concerning the DWT interested readers are to referred to [8] and [12].

The principle of DWT, as adopted with respect to the proposed KCA method, is illustrated in Figs. 5 and 6 (in a manner similar to Figs. 3 and 4). The figures show the DWT coefficients for keystroke subsequences obtained from two subjects, **A** and **B**; the same keystroke subsequences as given in Figs. 3 and 4. The figures clearly show that DWT coefficients are distinctive in the context of keystroke data from the same subjects.

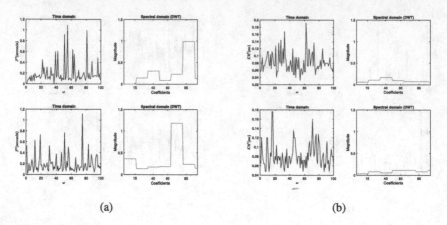

(a)   (b)

Fig. 5. Example of the application of DWT for subject **A**; (a) $\mathcal{F}^t$ keystroke subsequences, (b) $\mathcal{KH}^t$ keystroke subsequences.

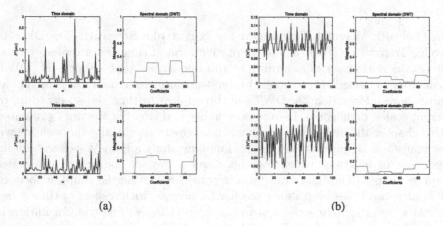

(a)   (b)

Fig. 6. Example of the application of DWT for subject **B**; (a) $\mathcal{F}^t$ keystroke subsequences, (b) $\mathcal{KH}^t$ keystroke subsequences.

4.4   Similarity Comparison

Dynamic Time Warping (DTW), a well-established method for time series similarity checking, was adopted for the proposed KCA method. A great advantage of DTW is that it serves to warp the linearity of sequences (even of different lengths) so that any phase shifting can be taken into consideration. This is done by calculating what is referred to as a *warping path*. The length, Θ, of this warping path (the minimum warping distance) is then treated as a similarity measure; if the length is zero the two time series under consideration are identical. Thus, it can be usefully adopted to find similarity in shape between two corresponding time series signals.

The method for determining Θ, using DTW, adopted with respect to the work presented in this paper, directed at M-KTS, is to calculate two warping paths. This could be achieved using two DTW matrices. However, it is more efficient to use a single matrix with two values stored in each cell. An alternative approach would have been to store 3-D distances at each cell. Although much less storage would be required to store such 3-D distances the calculation of 3-D distances would be equivalent to calculating two 2-D distances. The main advantage offered by the proposed two 2-D distances approach is simplicity.

Thus given two M-KTS sequences, such that $s_1 = \{p_1, p_2, \ldots, p_i, \ldots, p_x\}$ and $s_2 = \{q_1, q_2, \ldots, q_j, \ldots, q_y\}$, where x and y are the lengths of the two series respectively, and the values represented by each point $p_i \in s_1$ and each point $q_j \in s_2$ comprise a tuple of the form $\langle \mathcal{F}^t, \mathcal{KH}^t \rangle$, Θ is calculated as follows. First a DTW matrix M of size $(x-1) \times (y-1)$ is constructed. Each cell $m_{i,j} \in M$ then holds two distance values, the difference between the $\mathcal{F}^t$ value for point $p_i \in s_1$ and that for point $q_j \in s_2$; and the difference between the $\mathcal{KH}^t$ value for point $p_i \in s_1$ and that for point $q_j \in s_2$.

The matrix M is used to find two minimum warping distance (Θ) associated with two minimum warping paths, $\mathbb{P}_{\mathcal{F}^t}$ and $\mathbb{P}_{\mathcal{KH}^t}$. Each warping path is determined as a sequence of cell locations, $\mathbb{P} = \{k_1, k_2, \ldots\}$, such that given $k_n = m_{i,j}$ the follow on location k_{n+1} is either $m_{i+1,j}$, $m_{i,j+1}$ or $m_{i+1,j+1}$. The value for a single Θ associated with a particular $\mathbb{P}$ is then the sum of the values held at the locations in $\mathbb{P}$:

$$\Theta = \sum_{n=1}^{|\mathbb{P}|} k_n \in \mathbb{P} \tag{3}$$

Consequently, two minimum warping distances are then determined, $\Theta_{\mathcal{F}^t}$ and $\Theta_{\mathcal{KH}^t}$. The final value for Θ is then the average of these two values:

$$\Theta = \frac{1}{2}(\Theta_{\mathcal{F}^t} + \Theta_{\mathcal{KH}^t}) \tag{4}$$

4.5   Template Construction

As previously indicated, the proposed KCA method operates using an enrolment database, a "bank" of subject (user) typing templates (profiles), one per subject. A user typing template $\mathcal{U}^T$ is therefore a set of m spectral M-KTS subsequences such that $\mathcal{U}^T = \{s_1, s_2, \ldots, s_m\}$. Note that the total length of the time series from which templates are generated must be substantially greater than the window size ω so that a significant number of M-KTS subsequences can be extracted. Figure 7 illustrates the process whereby a profile $\mathcal{U}^T$ is generated. In the example, the windows are non-overlapping and abutting, this does not have to be the case, but this was the mechanism adopted with respect to the proposed KCA method evaluation presented later in this paper. The templates stored in the enrolment databases, as noted above, are also used to derive a bespoke similarity threshold, σ, for each user. This is calculated by comparing all spectral

M-KTS subsequences within a template $\mathcal{U}^T$, using the DTW method described above, and obtaining an average warping distance $\bar{\Theta}$ which is then used as the value for σ:

$$\sigma = \bar{\Theta} = \frac{1}{|\mathcal{U}^T|} \sum_{i=2}^{|\mathcal{U}^T|} dtw(s_{i-1}, s_i) \tag{5}$$

It has been shown that averaging the warping distances associated with a set of time series can lead to an effective and more accurate classification of streaming data than if only one warping distance is considered [31].

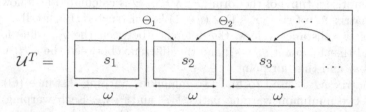

Fig. 7. A schematic illustrating the process of constructing a user typing profile $\mathcal{U}^T$ for a single subject.

4.6   Authentication

The actual KCA, in the context of the proposed time series-based method, is conducted by comparing the most recent spectral M-KTS subsequence with the immediately preceding spectral M-KTS subsequence (extracted during the typing session). At the beginning of the session, the subject's identity is first confirmed; in other words, it is confirmed that the subject is who (s)he says (s)he is. This initial process is called "start-up" authentication. In this context, the start-up authentication is done by comparing, using DTW, the first spectral M-KTS subsequence collected, s_1, with the relevant user template profiles in $\mathcal{U}^T$ (stored in the enrolment database) and obtaining an average similarity value (minimum warping distance). If the average similarity value is less than or equal to σ, the validation process proceeds accordingly. Each subsequent spectral M-KTS subsequence s_k (where $k > 1$) is then compared with the preceding, previously collected, subsequence s_{k-1}, again utilising DTW. In this manner, changes in typing behaviour can be detected.

The operation of the proposed KCA process is presented, more formally, in the form of pseudo code in Algorithm 2. The algorithm takes as input: (i) the M-KTS subsequence (window) size ω, (ii) the similarity threshold σ (derived as described above in Sub-sect. 4.5) and (iii) a φ threshold for limiting the $\mathcal{F}^t$ feature. The process operates continuously, following a loop, until the typing

---

Algorithm 2. The proposed KCA algorithm.

Input: ω, σ, φ.
Output: Continuous authentication commentary.
 1: $counter = 0$
 2: $\mathcal{K}_{ts} = \emptyset$
 3: **loop**
 4:     **if** terminated signal received **then**
 5:        break
 6:     **end if**
 7:     $p =$ keystroke features (e.g. $\mathcal{F}^t$ and $\mathcal{KH}^t$)
 8:     **if** $(\mathcal{F}^t \in p) > \varphi$ **then**
 9:        $p = \varphi$ $\triangleright$ Noise reduction.
10:     **end if**
11:     $\mathcal{K}_{ts} = \mathcal{K}_{ts} \cup \langle counter, k \rangle$
12:     $counter + +$
13:     **if** $REM(counter/\omega) == 0$ **then**
14:        $s_i =$ M-KTS subsequence $\{\mathcal{K}_{ts_{counter-\omega}} \cdots \mathcal{K}_{ts_{counter}}\}$
15:        **if** $counter = \omega$ **then** $\triangleright$ Start-up situation
16:           $Transform(s)$ $\triangleright$ Transform s to (DFT)/(DWT)
17:           Start-up: authenticate s_i w.r.t $\mathcal{U}^T$ and σ, and report
18:        **else**
19:           Authenticate s_i w.r.t. s_{i-1} and σ, and report
20:        **end if**
21:     **end if**
22: **end loop**

---

session is terminated (the user completes the assessment, times out or logs-out) (lines 4–6). Values for p are recorded as soon as the typing session starts (line 7). Note that in the case of flight time the value will be checked, and if necessary reduced according to φ (lines 8 to 10). The p value is then appended to the time series $\mathcal{K}_{ts}$. The *counter* is monitored and M-KTS subsequences are extracted whenever ω keystrokes have been obtained. Each extracted subsequence s is then transformed into DFT or DWT as required. The first transformed time series subsequence ($s_1 \in \mathcal{K}_{ts}$), the start-up time series, is compared with the stored profile for the subject in question; while each subsequent subsequence s_i is compared, using DTW, with the previous s_{i-1} subsequence.

5 Evaluation

This section presents a review of the evaluation conducted with respect to the proposed KCA using spectral M-KTS. The central objectives of the evaluation were:

1. **Typing Template Construction Efficiency:** To determine the efficiency of constructing the typing templates (enrolment database) using the proposed KCA approach.

2. **Authentication Performance:** To evaluate the effectiveness of the proposed KCA, in terms of impersonation detection, using different values for ω (the sampling window size) and φ (the noise reduction threshold value).

Note that the proposed method was evaluated using different values for ω and φ to determine the effect of these parameters on the KCA. As indicated in Subsect. 4.3, the DWT transform can only support time series data whose length is defined as an integral power of 2, thus for the evaluation the range of ω values considered was $\{16, 32, 64, 128, 256, 512\}$, where the range of φ values considered was $\{0.750, 1.00, 1.25, 1.50, 2.00\}$ s.

The evaluation was also aimed, in the context of the above objectives, at providing a comparison with the approaches to KCA as proposed in the study presented in [2] and [3]. Recall that in [2] KCA was accomplished using M-KTS in the temporal domain and in [3] using the spectral domain but in the context of U-KTS. For ease of presentation, the following terminology is used in the remainder of this section:

1. M-KTS: KCA using the temporal domain applied to M-KTS as proposed in [2].
2. U-KTS+DFT: KCA using DFT applied to U-KTS as proposed in [3].
3. U-KTS+DWT: KCA using DWT applied to U-KTS as proposed in [3].
4. **M-KTS+DFT**: KCA using DFT applied to M-KTS as proposed in this paper.
5. **M-KTS+DWT**: KCA using DWT applied to M-KTS as proposed in this paper.

For the evaluation two datasets were used, as described in [2], namely the ACB and VHHS datasets. Each dataset consisted of typing samples collected from real subjects typing free (unstructured) text. Table 1 presents a summary of the characteristics of the two datasets; the table is based from [2]. The table lists the number of subjects, the environment setting where typing samples were collected, the language used to type samples, and the average and standard deviation of the keystroke time series with respect to each entire data set. Also, for the evaluation, the records associated with each subject in the datasets were divided into two so that one-half could be used for enrolment (typing template generation) and the other for authentication (typing stream simulation). Thus, two-fold cross-validation was conducted, hence results presented below are average results from two cross-validations. The metrics used for the evaluation were: (i) Authentication accuracy (Acc.), (ii) False Match Rate (FMR) and (iii) False Non-Match Rate (FNMR). FMR and FNMR are the standard metrics used to measure the performance of Biometric systems [37], although some researchers, in the literature, have used the terms FMR (False Acceptance Rate) and FRR (False Rejection Rate) instead.

The results obtained with respect to the two evaluation objectives are discussed below in further detail, Sub-sects. 5.1 and 5.2 respectively.

Table 1. Summary of evaluation datasets [2].

Dataset	# Subject	Environment	Language used	Average size	Standard deviation
ACB	30	Free	English	4625	1207
VHHS	39	Lab.	English	4853	1021

Table 2. Typing template generation complexity (seconds) for spectral M-KTS applied to KCA.

ω	DFT		DWT	
	ACB	VHHS	ACB	VHHS
16	0.013	0.012	0.021	0.022
32	0.022	0.023	0.042	0.043
64	0.051	0.035	0.071	0.052
128	0.076	0.065	0.098	0.071
256	0.095	0.089	0.122	0.094
512	0.102	0.099	0.132	0.105

5.1   Typing Template Construction Efficiency

The first evaluation objective was to analyse the processing time required to generate the enrolment databases, including the associated individual σ threshold value calculation. Table 2 presents the average run-time complexity (seconds) results obtained for the construction of the typing template for each subject (the average time required to create the typing template for a single subject). From the table, it can be seen that the time complexity increases as ω increases. This was to be expected, as noted in Sub-sect. 4.1, because the time complexity to compute the DTW increases as the value for ω increases. Nonetheless, the results presented in Table 2 demonstrate that the constructing of typing templates was extremly efficiency; the worst run-time was less than one second.

Figure 8 gives the run-time (seconds) results obtained with respect to the proposed KCA using spectral M-KTS compared with the results obtained using the KCA variations given in [2] and [3]. Figure 8(a) shows the reported run-time results for the ACB dataset, whilst Fig. 8(b) shows the run-time results for the VHHS dataset. From the figure, it can be seen that, regardless of which KCA variation was used, in all cases, the run-time increased as ω increased. As noted earlier, this was to be anticipated because the DTW computation time increases as the ω value increases. Overall the template construction efficiency results indicated that when using the proposed KCA approach (with spectral M-KTS) efficiency gains were made over the other approaches, except in the case of U-KTS+DFT which produced the best run time. Nevertheless, with respect to the proposed KCA approach, it can be observed from the figure that M-KTS+DFT produced better run-time results than M-KTS+DWT; thus M-KTS+DFT was more efficient than M-KTS+DWT.

5.2   Authentication Performance

For each dataset, the continuous typing process was simulated by presenting the keystroke dynamics for each subject in the form of a data stream. In each case, the data stream was appended with a randomly selected second data stream from another user. The idea being to simulate one subject being impersonated by another half way through a typing session. For every comparison of a subsequence s_i with a subsequence s_{i-1}, it was recorded as to whether this was a True Positive (TP), False Positive (FP), False Negative (FN) or True Negative (TN). In this manner a *confusion matrix* was built up from which accuracy (Acc.), FAR and FRR could be calculated (using Eqs. 6, 7 and 8).

$$Acc = \frac{TP + TN}{TP + FP + FN + TN} \tag{6}$$

$$FAR = \frac{FP}{FP + TN} \tag{7}$$

$$FRR = \frac{FN}{FN + TP} \tag{8}$$

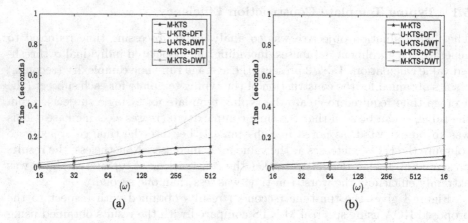

Fig. 8. Template construction run-time (seconds) comparison using variations of KCA: (a) ACB dataset, (b) VHHS dataset.

The obtained accuracy results are given in the form of 3D bar charts in Figs. 9 and 10 for the ACB and VHHS datasets respectively. In each figure, the vertical axis indicates accuracy, while the horizontal axises represent the window size (ω) and the limit value (φ). Each figure includes two such charts, with DFT on the left (a) and DWT on the right (b). From the figures, it can be observed that, in the context of M-KTS+DFT, best accuracy results were obtained when using $\omega = 64$ (with respect to both datasets); the red bars in the figure shows the best results with $\omega = 64$ across a range of φ values. However, in the context of M-KTS+DWT, best results were recorded at $\omega = 32$ across φ values. This means that good authentication accuracy can be gained using short time series subsequences. In other words, an accurate authentication can be obtained using only a small portion of the keystroke data stream; an important advantage for the form KCA desirable in the context of the online assessments frequently used with respect to digital learning. It can also be observed that when the value for ω increases beyond 64 the effect on accuracy is marginal. With respect to the φ parameter, the best recorded performance was obtained using $\varphi = 1.25$ s, although, it can be noted that the φ setting had less effect on authentication performance than the ω setting.

The accuracy (Acc.), FMR and FNMR results obtained, in the context of KCA coupled with spectral M-KTS, are summarised in tabular form in Table 3.

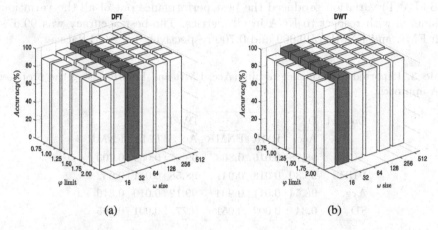

Fig. 9. The effect of ω and φ parameter settings on accuracy using the proposed KCA with **ACB** dataset.

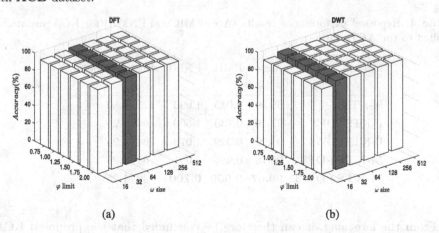

Fig. 10. The effect of ω and φ parameter settings on accuracy using the proposed KCA with **VHHS** dataset.

Note that in the context of DFT the reported results are shown when using $\omega = 64$ and $\varphi = 1.25$, whereas in the context of DWT the results are presented when $\omega = 32$ and $\varphi = 1.25$; the parameter values that produced the best results in each case. The table also gives the overall average values and the associated Standard Deviation (SD) in each case. The table clearly shows that DWT produced the best performance, with an average accuracy of 99.12% (and an associated SD of 0.77). For FMR and FNMR, the best obtained results were 0.010 and 0.816, again using DWT.

For completeness, Tables 4 and 5 summarise the results obtained using the KCA variations in terms of accuracy, FMR and FNMR; Table 4 considers the ACB dataset, whilst Table 5 considers the VHHS dataset. In each case, the best performing ω and φ parameters wee used (also listed in the table). From the tables, it can be observed that the proposed spectral M-KTS with DWT (M-KTS+DWT) variation produced the best performance out of all the variations considered with respect to KCA in all metrics. The best accuracy was 99.67% with FMR and FNMR of 0.009 and 0.700 respectively for ACB dataset.

Table 3. Reported performance results (Acc, FMR and FNMR) using the proposed KCA approach.

Dataset	DFT			DWT		
	Acc.	FMR	FNMR	Acc.	FMR	FNMR
ACB	98.78	0.016	0.868	99.67	0.009	0.700
VHHS	98.30	0.018	0.941	98.58	0.011	0.932
Avg.	98.54	0.017	0.904	99.12	0.010	0.816
SD	0.34	0.002	0.051	0.77	0.001	0.165

Table 4. Reported performance results (Acc, FMR and FNMR) for KCA variations applied to the **ACB** dataset.

Method	Acc.	FMR	FNMR	Best parameters	
				ω	φ
M-KTS	98.39	0.045	1.093	125	1.50
U-KTS+DFT	97.43	0.130	1.500	64	1.25
U-KTS+DWT	99.22	0.029	1.070	64	1.25
M-KTS+DFT	98.78	0.036	1.091	64	1.25
M-KTS+DWT	**99.67**	**0.009**	**0.700**	32	1.25

From the foregoing, it can therefore be concluded that the proposed KCA method, using spectral M-KTS, provides a significant KCA improvement with respect to earlier time series-based KCA approaches.

Table 5. Reported performance results (Acc, FMR and FNMR) for KCA variations applied to the **VHHS** dataset.

Method	Acc.	FMR	FNMR	Best parameters	
				ω	φ
M-KTS	97.32	0.057	1.095	125	1.50
U-KTS+DFT	97.42	0.045	1.085	64	1.25
U-KTS+DWT	97.09	0.059	1.098	64	1.25
M-KTS+DFT	98.30	0.018	0.941	64	1.25
M-KTS+DWT	**98.58**	**0.011**	**0.932**	32	1.25

6   Conclusion

In this paper, a novel method for Keystroke Continuous Authentication (KCA) has been presented. The idea was to use subsequences of keystroke streams in the form of Multivariate-Keystroke Time Series (M-KTS) of length ω. These subsequences incorporated both flight time $\mathcal{F}^t$ and key-hold time $\mathcal{KH}^t$ values. The idea was then to transform these subsequences from the temporal domain to the spectral domain. Two spectral transforms were experimented with: (i) Discrete Fourier Transform (DFT), and (ii) Discrete Wavelet Transform (DWT). The intuition was that such time series transformations would provide for efficiency gains and improved performance. Using the proposed KCA method, on start-up, the first spectral M-KTS subsequence extracted, s_1, for a given subject, is compared to a reference typing template. Then, the subsequence s_i^- ($i > 1$) will be compared to the immediate predecessor subsequence s_{i-1}, and so on. In this manner, continuous user authentication can take place. The comparison between transformed keystroke signals was conducted using Dynamic Time Warping (DTW) due to the advantages that DTW offered with respect to capturing time shifting (offsets) between corresponding subsequences.

The proposed KCA method was evaluated so as to establish its effectiveness and efficiency in the context of KCA. The evaluation also considered the effect of different parameter settings for the window size (ω) and the noise reduction limit (φ). The experimental results indicated that the proposed KCA, in the context of spectral M-KTS, coupled with the DWT spectral transform, outperformed KCA coupled with the DFT transform in terms of authentication performance; a best overall accuracy of 99.12% (with FMR = 0.010 and FNMR = 816) was recorded. In this context, the best result was obtained using $\omega = 32$ keystrokes, and $\varphi = 1.5$ s. However, the proposed KCA coupled with DFT was found to be the most efficient. Furthermore, it was observed that the proposed KCA method produced superior performance, in terms of authentication and efficiency, than the earlier KCA approaches presented in [2] and [3], and by extension the feature vector based approach from the literature.

For future work, the authors intend to investigate the performance of different time series transformations with respect to KCA. This is motivated by the observation that, in the proposed approach, a drawback of the Haar DWT transform is that the keystroke time series must have a length which is an integral power of two. An alternative is Piecewise Aggregate Approximation (PAA) [24] which operates using any time series length using an approximation of the DWT representation [23]. Consequently, the use of alternative time series transformations for the proposed KCA method is seen as a fruitfully topic for further research. Moreover, the time complexity of DTW, in the context of the proposed keystroke time series representation, remains an open research topic. From the literature a number of DTW mitigation techniques have been proposed (such as [19,34]) which can provide for additional efficiency gains, these have yet to be investigated in the context of time series-based KCA.

References

1. Ahmed, A.A.E., Traore, I.: A new biometric technology based on mouse dynamics. IEEE Trans. Dependable Secure Comput. **4**(3), 165–179 (2007)
2. Alshehri, A., Coenen, F., Bollegala, D.: Accurate continuous and non-intrusive user authentication with multivariate keystroke streaming. In: Proceedings of the 9th International Joint Conference on Knowledge Discovery, Knowledge Engineering and Knowledge Management - Volume 1: KDIR, pp. 61–70. SciTePress, INSTICC (2017). https://doi.org/10.5220/0006497200610070
3. Alshehri, A., Coenen, F., Bollegala, D.: Spectral analysis of keystroke streams: towards effective real-time continuous user authentication. In: Proceedings of the 4th International Conference on Information Systems Security and Privacy - Volume 1: ICISSP, pp. 62–73. SciTePress, INSTICC (2018). https://doi.org/10.5220/0006606100620073
4. Asha, S., Chellappan, C.: Authentication of e-learners using multimodal biometric technology. In: International Symposium on Biometrics and Security Technologies, 2008, ISBAST 2008, pp. 1–6. IEEE (2008)
5. Bergadano, F., Gunetti, D., Picardi, C.: User authentication through keystroke dynamics. ACM Trans. Inf. Syst. Secur. (TISSEC) **5**(4), 367–397 (2002)
6. Bours, P.: Continuous keystroke dynamics: a different perspective towards biometric evaluation. Inf. Secur. Tech. Rep. **17**(1), 36–43 (2012)
7. Breslow, L., Pritchard, D.E., DeBoer, J., Stump, G.S., Ho, A.D., Seaton, D.T.: Studying learning in the worldwide classroom: Research into edx's first MOOC. Res. Pract. Assess. **8**, 13–25 (2013)
8. Burrus, C.S., Gopinath, R.A., Guo, H.: Introduction to Wavelets and Wavelet Transforms: A Primer. Prentice-Hall Inc., Englewood Cliffs (1997)
9. Chan, K.P., Fu, A.W.C.: Efficient time series matching by wavelets. In: Proceedings of 15th International Conference on Data Engineering, 1999, pp. 126–133. IEEE (1999)
10. Cooley, J.W., Tukey, J.W.: An algorithm for the machine calculation of complex fourier series. Math. Comput. **19**(90), 297–301 (1965)
11. Dowland, P.S., Furnell, S.M.: A long-term trial of keystroke profiling using digraph, trigraph and keyword latencies. In: Deswarte, Y., Cuppens, F., Jajodia, S., Wang, L. (eds.) SEC 2004. ITIFIP, vol. 147, pp. 275–289. Springer, Boston, MA (2004). https://doi.org/10.1007/1-4020-8143-X_18
12. Edwards, T.: Discrete wavelet transforms: theory and implementation. Universidad de (1991)

13. Faloutsos, C., Ranganathan, M., Manolopoulos, Y.: Fast subsequence matching in time-series databases. vol. 23. ACM (1994)
14. Furnell, S., Karweni, T.: Security issues in online distance learning. Vine **31**(2), 28–35 (2001)
15. Gabor, D.: Theory of communication. part 1: the analysis of information. J. Inst. Electr. Eng.-Part III: Radio Commun. Eng. **93**(26), 429–441 (1946)
16. Gaines, R.S., Lisowski, W., Press, S.J., Shapiro, N.: Authentication by keystroke timing: some preliminary results. Technical report, DTIC Document (1980)
17. Gunetti, D., Picardi, C.: Keystroke analysis of free text. ACM Trans. Inf. Syst. Secur. (TISSEC) **8**(3), 312–347 (2005)
18. Haar, A.: Zur theorie der orthogonalen funktionensysteme. Math. Ann. **69**(3), 331–371 (1910)
19. Itakura, F.: Minimum prediction residual principle applied to speech recognition. IEEE Trans. Acoust. Speech Signal Process. **23**, 52–72 (1975)
20. Jain, A., Hong, L., Pankanti, S.: Biometric identification. Commun. ACM **43**(2), 90–98 (2000)
21. Janacek, G.J., Bagnall, A.J., Powell, M.: A likelihood ratio distance measure for the similarity between the fourier transform of time series. In: Ho, T.B., Cheung, D., Liu, H. (eds.) PAKDD 2005. LNCS (LNAI), vol. 3518, pp. 737–743. Springer, Heidelberg (2005). https://doi.org/10.1007/11430919_85
22. Janakiraman, R., Sim, T.: Keystroke dynamics in a general setting. In: Lee, S.-W., Li, S.Z. (eds.) ICB 2007. LNCS, vol. 4642, pp. 584–593. Springer, Heidelberg (2007). https://doi.org/10.1007/978-3-540-74549-5_62
23. Keogh, E., Chakrabarti, K., Pazzani, M., Mehrotra, S.: Dimensionality reduction for fast similarity search in large time series databases. Knowl. Inf. Syst. **3**(3), 263–286 (2001)
24. Keogh, E., Chakrabarti, K., Pazzani, M., Mehrotra, S.: Locally adaptive dimensionality reduction for indexing large time series databases. ACM Sigmod Rec. **30**(2), 151–162 (2001)
25. Maas, A., Heather, C., Do, C.T., Brandman, R., Koller, D., Ng, A.: Offering verified credentials in massive open online courses: MOOCs and technology to advance learning and learning research (ubiquity symposium). Ubiquity **2014**(May), 2 (2014)
26. Maltoni, D., Maio, D., Jain, A., Prabhakar, S.: Handbook of Fingerprint Recognition. Springer, Heidelberg (2009)
27. Mantyjarvi, J., Lindholm, M., Vildjiounaite, E., Makela, S.M., Ailisto, H.: Identifying users of portable devices from gait pattern with accelerometers. In: Proceedings of IEEE International Conference on Acoustics, Speech, and Signal Processing, 2005, (ICASSP'05), vol. 2, pp. ii–973. IEEE (2005)
28. Moini, A., Madni, A.M.: Leveraging biometrics for user authentication in online learning: a systems perspective. IEEE Syst. J. **3**(4), 469–476 (2009)
29. Monrose, F., Rubin, A.: Authentication via keystroke dynamics. In: Proceedings of the 4th ACM Conference on Computer and Communications Security, pp. 48–56. ACM (1997)
30. Monrose, F., Rubin, A.D.: Keystroke dynamics as a biometric for authentication. Future Gener. Comput. Syst. **16**(4), 351–359 (2000)
31. Niennattrakul, V., Ratanamahatana, C.A.: Shape averaging under time warping In: 6th International Conference on Electrical Engineering/Electronics, Computer, Telecommunications and Information Technology, 2009, ECTI-CON 2009, vol. 2, pp. 626–629. IEEE (2009)

32. Phillips, P.J., Moon, H., Rizvi, S.A., Rauss, P.J.: The feret evaluation methodology for face-recognition algorithms. IEEE Trans. Pattern Anal. Mach. Intell. **22**(10), 1090–1104 (2000)
33. Revett, K.: A bioinformatics based approach to user authentication via keystroke dynamics. Int. J. Control Autom. Syst. **7**(1), 7–15 (2009)
34. Sakoe, H., Chiba, S.: Dynamic programming algorithm optimization fro spoken word recognition. IEEE Trans. Acoust. Speech Signal Process. **26**, 43–49 (1978)
35. Staszewski, W.J., Worden, K., Tomlinson, G.R.: Time-frequency analysis in gearbox fault detection using the wigner-ville distribution and pattern recognition. Mech. Syst. Signal Process. **11**(5), 673–692 (1997)
36. Traore, I.: Continuous Authentication Using Biometrics: Data, Models, and Metrics: Data, Models, and Metrics. IGI Global, Hershey (2011)
37. Unar, J., Seng, W.C., Abbasi, A.: A review of biometric technology along with trends and prospects. Pattern Recogn. **47**(8), 2673–2688 (2014)
38. Vielhauer, C., Steinmetz, R.: Handwriting: feature correlation analysis for biometric hashes. EURASIP J. Appl. Signal Process. **2004**, 542–558 (2004)
39. Wang, X., Mueen, A., Ding, H., Trajcevski, G., Scheuermann, P., Keogh, E.: Experimental comparison of representation methods and distance measures for time series data. Data Min. Knowl. Disc. **26**(2), 275–309 (2013)
40. Wildes, R.P.: Iris recognition: an emerging biometric technology. Proc. IEEE **85**(9), 1348–1363 (1997)
41. Wu, P.Y., Fang, C.C., Chang, J.M., Gilbert, S.B., Kung, S.: Cost-effective kernel ridge regression implementation for keystroke-based active authentication system. In: 2014 IEEE International Conference on Acoustics, Speech and Signal Processing (ICASSP), pp. 6028–6032. IEEE (2014)

Constructing Language Models from Online Forms to Aid Better Document Representation for More Effective Clustering

Stephen Bradshaw[1]([✉]), Colm O'Riordan[1], and Daragh Bradshaw[2]

[1] National University of Galway, College Road, Galway, Ireland
s.bradshaw1@nuigalway.ie
[2] National University of Limerick, Castletroy, Limerick, Ireland

Abstract. Clustering is the practice of finding tacit patterns in datasets by grouping the corpus by similarity. When clustering documents this is achieved by converting the corpus into a numeric format and applying clustering techniques to this new format. Values are assigned to terms based on their frequency within a particular document, against their general occurrence in the corpus. One obstacle in achieving this aim is as a result of the polysemic nature of terms. That is words having multiple meanings; each intended meaning only being discernible when examining the context in which they are used. Thus, disambiguating the intended meaning of a term can greatly improve the efficacy of a clustering algorithm. One approach to achieve this end has been done through the creation of an ontology - Wordnet, which can act as a look-up as to the intended meaning of a term. Wordnet however, is a static source and does not keep pace with the changing nature of language. The aim of this paper is to show that while Wordnet can be affective, however it is static in nature and thus does not capture some contemporary usage of terms. Particularly when the dataset is taken from online conversation forums, who would not be structured in a standard document format. Our proposed solution involves using Reddit as a contemporary source which moves with new trends in word usage. To better illustrate this point we cluster comments found in online threads such as Reddit and compare the efficacy of different representations of these document sets.

Keywords: Document Clustering · Graph theory · WordNet · Classification · Word Sense Disambiguation · Data mining

1 Introduction

Social media has shown itself in recent times to have a huge impact on social events [2]. Examples of which include the use of twitter during the Arab Spring [3]; the Green Movement in Iran [4]. The most notable political impact could

© Springer Nature Switzerland AG 2019
A. Fred et al. (Eds.): IC3K 2017, CCIS 976, pp. 67–81, 2019.
https://doi.org/10.1007/978-3-030-15640-4_4

be said to be the recent American Presidential race [5]. Reddit is an online chat forum that has seen a huge surge of use of late. Reddit is often referred to as the *front page of the internet* and found within are a huge range of opinions around many spheres of interest [6]. Since its founding in 2005 Reddit has drawn an ever expanding group of participants with diverse backgrounds and far ranging interests. Section 2 will contain a more indepth look at this datasource.

Table 1. List of all threads and sizes after processing [20].

Thread_A	Thread_B	Thread_A_Size	Thread_B_Size	Total comments
Rugbyunion	Quadcopters	926	672	1598
LearnPython	Worldnews	904	513	1417
Movies	Politics	422	963	1385
Music	Boardgames	448	942	1390
England	Ireland	743	935	1678

Clustering is a long established unsupervised approach in machine learning that entails grouping things that are similar in nature together. Clusters can be created as either disjointed or overlapping. Disjointed clustering is where each cluster contains only one instance of an item, while overlapping allows for one item to be a member of a number of different clusters. Clustering is deemed unsupervised because there is no a priori knowledge of what category an item is a member of. This paper uses K-means clustering which Is a *partition* based approach. The process typically involves determining for each item which cluster it is most similar to in an iterative fashion. Over the iterations an item may be re-assigned to a different cluster group many times before an equilibrium is achieved [7].

K-means is a long standing clustering approach which was first introduced in 1955. It has been used as the basis for creating many similar approaches; this and the longevity of this approach are a testament to its effectiveness. K-means, like many clustering approaches is susceptible to a number of factors that can hamper effective implementation. Issues associated with it include; knowing in advance how many clusters are present in a dataset, the Curse of Dimensionality (CoD), how best to represent an input vector and specifically related to the clustering of documents; the problem of creating strong clusters when faced with such high dimensional vectors as would be created from a large document set [7]. The presence of synonymy and polysemy in words means that a direct mapping of document to document may not accurately return documents of similar nature which use different terms to capture a concept. This phenomenon is noted by [8] who use statistical methods to improve recall in document queries. Previous work to offset this issue has been the creation of an ontology that can be used as reference to reduce the number of terms. In the case of synonymy this would involve selecting on synonym to represent all potential instances of that meaning, or with hypernym resolving all words to their hyponym.

A notable feature of Reddit is that there are many sub-domains similar in nature. This paper proposes using identified related domains as a source of evidence, and using graph principles to construct a bespoke ontology that can be used to better augment comments leading to more precise clustering of the original collection. Our graph approach allows for the creation of clusters that are not reliant on directly mapping terms with terms in documents, but instead will allow for concepts to be represented by a number of closely related terms. Our results show that such an approach considerably improves performance. Using a bespoke ontology is beneficial over a relatively general and static ontology such as Wordnet as better expansion candidate are provided. Upon clustering user comments, using a graph representation of the ontology reduces the ambiguity in the original comments through polysemy resolution. These two factors; a better ontology and a graph model, benefit the clustering through better document representation.

The paper outline is as follows: in the next section, we discuss Reddit, the source of data for our clustering experiments. In Sect. 3, we outline our methodology before discussing related work in the subsequent section.

2 Related Work

The original authors of Wordnet [9] show that document clusters can be improved with the addition of background material. They use synonyms and hypernyms to augment their document vectors [9]. They investigated three approaches; firstly **All Concepts** which involves taking all of the related terms and using these to augment the document. Secondly, **First Concept** which entails replacing the term in the document with the identified related term. Finally they used a **Disambiguation by Context Approach**, which involved using the definition of the term in question and measuring the similarity with the words found in the document.

There have been many subsequent papers that have shown how Wordnet can be used to improve clusters. Baghel et al. [10] propose an algorithm (**Frequent Concept Based Document Clustering (FCBDC)**) which identifies frequently occurring concepts. They define concepts as words that have the same meaning and use WordNet to identify when words have a similar meaning. They subsequently appoint each concept as a kernel and cluster the documents around them. Their approach involves using *first concept* so the initial words are replaced with their synonyms.

Wang et al. [11] investigate if the use of semantic relatedness can be used to cluster using Word Sense Disambiguation (WSD) principles. They define semantic relatedness as *a criterion to scale the relatedness of two senses in a semantic network* [11]. They used a Part of Speech Tagger (POS) to identify the grammatical use of each word. Each document was converted this way so that the words in the vector space model were converted into tuples of the term and the POS of the term. The POS were then used as the intended context of the word. They applied this approach to a corpus of 1600 abstracts of 200 words each.

These abstracts were further divided into 8 different categories. They found that through this approach they were able to improve upon results however, the small scale of their experiment meant that results were hindered through lack of sufficient distinguishing features for each category.

Mahajan et al. [12] use an approach similar in nature to the work of Wang et al. [11]. They investigate ways in which one can improve upon cluster results. They investigate changing the number of clusters, the use and stop word removal and lemmatisation. In addition, they engaged with Wordnet to augment the document vectors with their respective synonyms. Using a POS tagger to identify if a word is a noun, verb, adjective they augmented the vectors with the most closely identified one. Their approach was applied to a Reuters document corpus and they achieved an improvement of 11% for purity and 29% for entropy in the 20 news group and additionally they got an improvement of 18% and 38% respectively on the Reuters corpus.

Another approach which utilises Wordnet to improve upon traditional clustering is the work of Hung et al. [13]. They endeavour to better classify news articles as found in the Reuters text corpus. They take 200,000 articles with over 50 classifications. They use Wordnet to identify if a hypernymy exists for a given word. They use a replace policy to reduce dimensionality (**First Concept**), whereby the hyponym will be replaced with its hypernym. Their approach allows for multiple classifications. Similar to how Latent Dirchlet Allocation (LDA) works they count the words in the document as well as per topic [14]. As documents allow for multiple topics, words can be used to indicate the presence of different topics. As well as hosting hypernyms and synonyms, Wordnet contains a definition of each potential meaning of the target word as well as an example of usage. This is similar to the approach *Disambiguation by Context Approach* used by the original authors to disambiguate the intended meaning for the word used [9].

The premise of the approach of Zheng et al. [16] is that documents are made up of concepts and that different terms are often used to describe a concept. By resolving the various terms to their concepts one can improve upon information retrieval. The authors focus on noun phrases and the semantic patterns inherent in documents. Stemming and stopword removal are important preprocessing steps in achieving this end. They define a **noun phrase** as *a grammatical category (or phrase) which normally contains a noun as its head and which can be modified in many ways* [16]. The authors propose using syntactical analysis to identify the noun phrases. Partial parsing is used, which means that the appropriate noun phrases are analysed rather than the document as a whole. They analyse noun phrases by considering the synonyms of the adjective. Then the relationship between the noun phrases are explored. Synsets are a useful tool here as the first synset is the most common for of the term. Additionally WordNet is used to identify the hypernyms, hyponyms, meronyms and holonyms which are resolved to one representative concept. The authors find the use of hypernyms to be most effective; they speculated that the use of hypernyms is most effective because *document categorization tends to more naturally on the more-general terms rather than more-specific terms* [16].

The approach of this paper of mapping semantic similarity by considering re-occurring proximity of terms is similar in nature to the approach proposed by Lund and Burgess [17]. They construct a dataset from Usenet and map the strength of the proximity of terms. They use a sliding window of 10 and store the terms in a matrix. The proceeding terms are stored row-wise and the preceding terms as stored in a column-wise fashion. They use multi-dimensional scaling to draw inferences on the associations of the target terms. They conduct three experiments and make the following conclusions. First, the euclidean distance of the associative matrices of terms show that proximity is related to the frequent co-occurrence of terms. Second, categorical relationships can be ascertained through this approach. More concretely they show that hyponym terms can be grouped with their corresponding hypernyms. Third, that automatically determined semantic distance between terms are comparable with human judgment of the same.

Other work that embodies the Hyperspace Analogue to Language (HAL) approach is that of Song and Bruza [18]. They aim to model the information flow that is created when two terms are located adjacent to one another. The concept those two terms represent is the sum of their associate terms. Applying HAL, they create a matrix of associative terms. Each concept they propose is the sum of those associative terms. They normailise those matrices values by taking the strength of the re-occurring terms and dividing it by all the terms, after the terms that have fallen below a quality threshold have been removed. $w_{c_i p_j} = \frac{w_{c_i p_j}}{\sqrt{\sum_k w_{c_i p_k^2}}}$. To find the strength of the common terms between two concepts they apply the formula $w_{c_1 p_i} = l_1 + \frac{l_1 * w_{c_1 p_i}}{\max_k (w_{c_1 p_k})}$, where l_1 represents a weight that reflects that this particular concept is more dominant than the second concept. They make no statistical evaluation of their approach other than to discuss the relatedness of the vectors produced by this process.

3   Dataset

To conduct our investigation, data from Reddit was utilised. Social platforms like Reddit are forums where users create and curate the comments found at the site. The quality of the content is appraised through a voting system. Reddit has been described as a *Web-democracy* because everyone has a voice and can express their opinion [19]. Social media platforms mark a divergence from traditional media outlets where there are a handful of curators who dictate the conversation. Instead, everyone is free to suggest a topic and the impact of that suggestion is felt in the number of people who engage with the narrative. The hierarchical structure of the conversation threads allows for divergences in topics. The structure of Reddit is as follows:

- **Subreddits:** These are sub domains of a common theme. They comprise users who have an interest in that theme. Related topics to that general theme are submitted by users and people then engage with those topics through making comments on the original posts. All subreddits have at least one moderator who ensures that the rules of that thread are upheld and that relevance is maintained.

- **Posts:** are the initial comment submissions made in a subreddit. It can be in the form of text, image or links. It is an invitation to other users to engage in a discourse or express their opinion on an issue through up-voting or down-voting.
- **Comments:** are user submissions to an initial post. They can be new comments (referred below as parent comments) which mark a new perspective on the post or they can be comments on existing comment threads (child comments), this indicates that the point is related to that branch of conversation.
- **Parent Comments:** refers to the original comment made to a post. Child comments are all of the subsequent comments posted to that comment thread. One post can have many parent comments and each parent comment can have a number of children comments.
- **Voting:** allows for each user to express their opinion on a post or comment. It is in the form of an upvote or a downvote. There is an algorithm that ranks the votes which informs where that post is placed in the thread hierarchy. A particular popular post can make it to the front page of Reddit which is not topic specific and will garner increased attention through increased visibility.
- **Karma:** represents the overall feedback that a user has on the user's collective posts. Each upvote is an additional karma point and each downvote takes from the users overall accrued karma points.

Table 2. List of all threads and their related thread [20].

Thread	Related thread
Rugbyunion	NRL
LearnPython	Python
Movies	Fullmoviesonyoutube
Music	popheads
England	London
Quadcopters	Quadcopter
Worldnews	News
Politics	ukpolitics
Boardgames	Risk
Ireland	Dublin

A user has the option to *subscribe* to a thread. Typically a user will be subscribed to a number of different threads, and the most popular posts in these are shown on the user's personal wall. In addition there is a universal wall which displays the most commented upon or upvoted posts and can come from any thread.

4   Methodology

4.1   Introduction

To perform our experiments in improving clustering of documents from social media forums and improving performance of said clustering, we first created a document collection. We selected 10 threads for the purpose of running our experiments and a further 10 threads for the creation of relevant ontologies; the threads used are listed in Table 2. As a baseline experiment, we apply K-means clustering to the content of the 10 threads. We then re-apply that clustering approach on the same documents using augmented versions of the documents. We analyse a number of document expansion techniques from the literature and finally our own approach. We now discuss how the dataset was constructed and processed, the baseline approach, how WordNet was used to augment the document set, and finally, we describe in detail our own proposed approach.

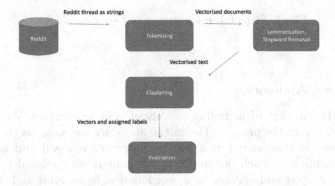

Fig. 1. Steps taken for standard approach [20].

4.2   Baseline Approach

First we tokenise the text; this involves removing stopwords, lemmatising and vectorising. We use a K-means as implemented in Sklearn [15] to cluster the documents. For the basic approach we clustered the document set in it's vectorised form, and recorded the results. See Fig. 1 for a graphical representation of the process.

Table 1 contains the names and sizes of each of our threads. To test the robustness of our approach we took each thread in Thread_A and combined it with each of the threads found in the Thread_B column. This produced a result set of 25 collections; we then attempt to cluster the documents back into the two original clusters. The results of this are discussed in the results section. We selected threads that were similar in nature, because we were attempting to capture the nuanced speech associated with a thread. We felt that if we could single out threads that would have common members, we would better be able to model the language used. All approaches discussed below were evaluated in the same manner. Each document representation was augmented in a different way according to the approach being investigated.

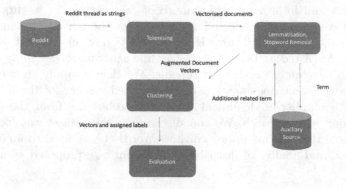

Fig. 2. Steps taken for augmented approach [20].

4.3 Wordnet Approach

To measure the impact of including synonyms and hypernyms, Wordnet was used. Figure 2 shows the process. The initial steps are the same as the baseline. Each document is represented as a vector. Stopword removal and lemmatisation was then applied. Each document is augmented with related hypernyms. We took the corpus and checked if a word had a hypernym, and if so, that hypernym was added to the document vector. Wordnet is represented by the data source titles *Auxiliary Source* in Fig. 2. So for each term t in a document d if the term has a hypernym, we retrieved it and added it to the document representation. So our documents now contain each term and its hypernym $d = <t_1, t_2, \ldots t_n, h_1, h_2, \ldots h_k)>$. We then applied K-means to the document sets and recorded the results. The same procedure was performed on the synonym dataset. However rather than adding hypernyms, synonyms were instead included in the documents.

4.4 Graph Approach

For each of our main threads, we identified a thread dealing with a similar topic that would hopefully use the same, or similar, terminology. This is important for constructing a related ontology, e.g the thread *rugbyunion* is seen to be a related thread to *Australian Rugby League (NRL)*. Table 2 contains a list of the initial threads and the related threads from which we constructed our ontology. Our external ontology is represented by the data source titles *Auxiliary Source* in Fig. 2.

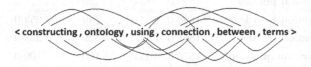

< constructing , ontology , using , connection , between , terms >

Fig. 3. Recording the connection between terms [20].

To construct the ontology, we processed the related threads. As above, lemmatisation and stopword removal was applied to the document vectors. Next we constructed a graph where each word is represented as a node and the weight on the edge represents the number of times two words occurred in close proximity. We used a window size parameter to define the notion of proximity. In this work we use a window size of two, i.e., the nearest two preceding and proceeding words for each word are considered as occurring in close proximity and their corresponding nodes are linked. Figure 3 illustrates how two words can be connected. Our ontology comprises of the term t and all of the occurrences of the surrounding terms t_r and their frequency, $t = \{tr_1 : score, tr_2 : score, ...tr_n : score_n\}$. Next, we augmented the vectors representing the original document by augmenting the document vector with its highest correlated word. The resulting documents were stored as follows: $d = <t_1, tr_1, t_2, tr_2...t_n, tr_n>$. We applied the K-means clustering algorithm to the resulting corpus and recorded the results.

4.5 Process

Ten social media conversation threads were randomly selected from the social media platform Reddit. Threads were allocated into two groups of 5 threads called Thread A and Thread B (see Table 1). Threads from the first group were then paired with threads from the second group using a round-robin approach. This resulted in the creation of 25 document sets containing two separate threads each. In order to measure prediction performance, documents were subjected to four independent prediction processes: *Standard* which serves as the baseline (standard clustering), *Synonym* (document augmentation with synonyms), *Hypernym* (augmentation with Hypernyms), and finally *Graph*, our approach which augments the documents with the strongest correlates according to our graph measure over the bespoke ontology. Prediction performance was measured by the number of errors in identification of separate threads within a document. Lower levels indicated greater prediction performance.

Table 3. Results for each algorithm or each combination of threads from the first and second group respectively [20].

Index	Name	Size	Standard	Synonym	Hypernym	Graph
0	rugbyunion_quadcopter	1598.0	215.0	215.0	226.0	43.0
1	rugbyunion_Worldnews	1439.0	373.0	201.0	123.0	22.0
2	rugbyunion_politics	1889.0	372.0	438.0	414.0	1.0
3	rugbyunion_boardgames	1868.0	283.0	289.0	253.0	48.0
4	rugbyunion_Ireland	1861.0	337.0	329.0	333.0	31.0
5	learnpython_quadcopter	1576.0	105.0	100.0	109.0	23.0
6	learnpython_Worldnews	1417.0	178.0	124.0	114.0	4.0
7	learnpython_politics	1867.0	373.0	446.0	411.0	0.0
8	learnpython_boardgames	1846.0	220.0	219.0	201.0	19.0
9	learnpython_Ireland	1839.0	235.0	219.0	211.0	19.0
10	Movies_quadcopter	1094.0	126.0	122.0	132.0	39.0
11	Movies_Worldnews	935.0	376.0	131.0	127.0	23.0
12	Movies_politics	1385.0	454.0	527.0	515.0	20.0
13	Movies_boardgames	1364.0	258.0	262.0	231.0	21.0
14	Movies_Ireland	1357.0	153.0	151.0	150.0	32.0
15	music_quadcopter	1120.0	156.0	138.0	132.0	51.0
16	music_Worldnews	961.0	153.0	134.0	124.0	27.0
17	music_politics	1411.0	445.0	521.0	503.0	2.0
18	music_boardgames	1390.0	109.0	103.0	91.0	16.0
19	music_Ireland	1383.0	154.0	136.0	133.0	39.0
20	England_quadcopter	1415.0	320.0	251.0	219.0	84.0
21	England_Worldnews	1256.0	378.0	380.0	378.0	81.0
22	England_politics	1706.0	426.0	491.0	470.0	2.0
23	England_boardgames	1685.0	294.0	286.0	283.0	67.0
24	England_Ireland	1678.0	666.0	668.0	667.0	226.0

5   Results

Table 3 presents the results from each individual clustering task. It contains the name of the two threads being investigated; the number of documents being clustered in that case, and the number of errors for each approach. We used precision as a metric for evaluating the success of each approach. We found that adding synonyms and hypernyms improves upon the baseline case. Echoing findings in previous work, we found that hypernyms are more effective than synonyms. Finally, we note that using our graph approach is six times more effective than using any of the other approaches. The combination of using a bespoke ontology and a graph mechanism to identify correlates for expansion works extremely well.

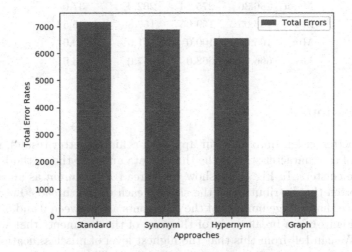

Fig. 4. Combined error rate over all tests [20].

5.1   Statistical Analysis

A non-parametric Kruskil-Walis (Cohen 1988) test was conducted to explore whether using a Graph analysis approach would improve prediction performance of the presence of separate threads in a body of text when compared with three commonly used approaches. This paper makes the hypothesis that using the graph approach will result in lower prediction errors. No hypothesis is made between prediction levels of the three commonly used techniques when compared to each other. Analysis was conducted using the computer software package SPSS (Fig. 4).

Results indicate that Graph approach reported fewer errors in identification (M = 4.72, SD = 9.14) to Approach Standard (M = 35.97, SD = 38.48), Approach Synonym (M = 34.58, SD = 36.90) and Approach Hypernym (M = 32.91, SD = 35.94).

A Kuskal-Wallis test revealed a statistical difference in prediction performance across the four prediction approaches $H(3) = 95.19, p < .001$. Pairwise comparisons with adjusted p values showed there was a significant difference between the graph approach and the standard approach ($p < .001, r = .4$) the synonym approach, ($p < .001, r = .4$) the hypernym approach, ($p < .001, r = .4$), indicating medium to strong effect sizes. The standard, synonym and hypernym approaches did not differ significantly from each other ($P > .05$) (Table 4).

Table 4. Data facts [20].

	Standard	Synonym	Hypernym	Graph
Count	25.0	25.0	25.0	25.0
Mean	286.36	275.24	262.0	37.6
Std	136.05	159.65	157.88	45.52
Min	105.0	100.0	91.0	0.0
Max	666.0	668.0	667.0	226.0

6   Discussion

To gain a better insight into why our approach achieves better results, we analysed some of the characteristics of the thread data and how the methods applied
affected the clusters. In Fig. 5, we show the thread *Rugbyunion* as an example;
we first plotted the distribution of the sizes of each of the threads. From this it
is clear to see that a large number of the comments are between 0 and 500 words
in length. Figure 6 is a break down of the sizes of the comments that were misclassified. We can tell from this that the highest level of misclassification comes
from documents that are 30 words or less in length. This makes intuitive sense
when one considers that the less evidence the classifying agent has, the poorer
the end result will be. Our graph approach helps to offset this issue, by incorporating words that are more indicative of the document class thus producing
significantly more accurate classifications. The sum total of words added for each
method were Synonym - 285,321; Hypernym - 220,935 and Graph 304, 997. Of
these additional words the number of unique words added were 9435, 3584 and
4023 respectively. While the Hypernym had the least number of unique terms

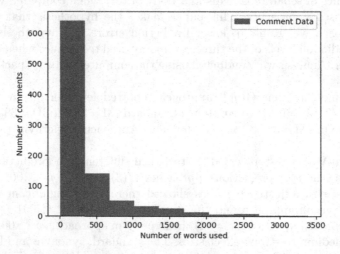

Fig. 5. Break down of comment lengths [20].

it also had markedly less terms added compared to the other two approaches. The Synonym approach had a large number of additional terms, although there were a little less than the Graph approach which had the most terms added, but a relatively low unique word count. This leads us to conclude that the terms returned were more closely correlated in this approach, which resulted in the higher precision counts.

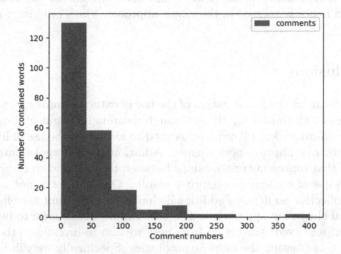

Fig. 6. Break down of comment lengths from misclassified comments [20].

Figure 7 offers some more insight into performance of the various algorithms across the different clustering cases. The graph approach is clearly superior to the other approaches with a much lower median number of errors but also a

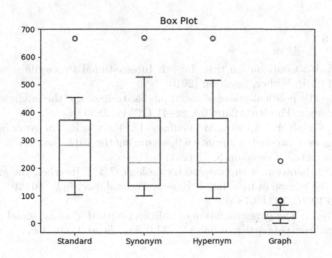

Fig. 7. A box plot of all of the errors [20]. (Color figure online)

much smaller deviation. The orange line represents the median line, and interestingly it is higher in the standard approach. This means that in over half of the clusters, the hypernym and synonym approach are superior. The whiskers are higher in both of these approaches suggesting that there is a large variation in a small number of results. This suggests that while the addition of hypernym and synonym did, on average, improve the results, there are a minority of instances where they added noise to the dataset and skewed some of the results. This phenomenon is not witnessed in the graph approach which only improved upon results.

7   Conclusions

This paper discusses the investigation of the use of external ontologies to improve performance of a clustering algorithm through meaningful augmentation of documents. A standard package Wordnet was used to identify if the use of hypernyms and synonyms can improve performance. Additionally a bespoke ontology was constructed that represents relationships between terms based on co-occurrence, to see if the use of context can improve results. Our dataset is not a standard document collection so it poses additional challenges that limit the effectiveness of traditional clustering approaches. The best results were shown to be achieved when context was used. Moving on from here we aim to investigate the parameters used in constructing the bespoke ontologies. Specifically we will investigate using a weighting system for the terms based on proximity which incorporates a decay factor allowing for the fact that some terms are further way from the target term than others.

Future work will involve increasing the level of difficulty in the clustering. This can be achieved by increasing the number of sub domains which need to be clustered.

References

1. Author, A.-B.: Contribution title. In: 9th International Proceedings on Proceedings, pp. 1–2. Publisher, Location (2010)
2. Shirky, C.: The political power of social media: technology, the public sphere, and political change. Foreign Affairs **90**, 28–41 (2011). JSTOR
3. Lotan, G., Graeff, E., Ananny, M., Gaffney, D., Pearce, I.: The Arab Spring—the revolutions were tweeted: information flows during the 2011 Tunisian and Egyptian revolutions. Int. J. Commun. **5**, 31 (2011)
4. Golkar, S.: Liberation or suppression technologies? The Internet, the green movement and the regime in Iran. Int. J. Emerg. Technol. Soc. **9**(1), 50 (2011). https://doi.org/10.10007/1234567890
5. Bennett, W.L.: The personalization of politics political identity, social media, and changing patterns of participation. ANNALS Am. Acad. Polit. Soc. Sci. **644**, 20–39 (2012)

6. Singer, P., Flöck, F., Meinhart, C., Zeitfogel, E., Strohmaier, M.: Evolution of reddit: from the front page of the internet to a self-referential community? In: Proceedings of the 23rd International Conference on World Wide Web, pp. 1–13. ACM (2014)
7. Shah, N., Mahajan, S.: Document clustering: a detailed review. Int. J. Appl. Inf. Syst. **4**, 30–38 (2016)
8. Deerwester, S., Dumais, S.T., Furnas, G.W., Landauer, T.K., Harshman, R.: Indexing by latent semantic analysis. J. Am. Soc. Inf. Sci. **41**, 391 (1990)
9. Hotho, A., Staab, S., Stumme, G.: Ontologies improve text document clustering. In: Third IEEE International Conference on Data Mining, ICDM 2003, pp. 541–544 (2003)
10. Baghel, R., Dhir, R.: A frequent concepts based document clustering algorithm. Int. J. Comput. Appl. **4**, 6–12 (2010)
11. Wang, Y., Hodges, J.: Document clustering with semantic analysis. In: Proceedings of the 39th Annual Hawaii International Conference on System Sciences, vol. 3, pp. 54. IEEE (2006)
12. Mahajan, S., Shah, N.: Efficient pre-processing for enhanced semantics based distributed document clustering. In: 3rd International Conference on Computing for Sustainable Global Development (INDIACom), pp. 338–343. IEEE (2016)
13. Hung, C., Wermter, S., Smith, P.: Hybrid neural document clustering using guided self-organization and wordnet. IEEE Intell. Syst. **19**, 68–77 (2004)
14. Blei, D.M., Ng, A.Y., Jordan, M.I.: Latent dirichlet allocation. In: Advances in Neural Information Processing Systems, vol. 1, pp. 601–608. MIT (2002)
15. Pedregosa, F., et al.: Scikit-learn: machine learning in Python. J. Mach. Learn. Res. **12**, 2825–2830 (2011)
16. Zheng, H.-T., Kang, B.-Y., Kim, H.-G.: Exploiting noun phrases and semantic relationships for text document clustering. Inf. Sci. **179**, 2249–2262 (2009)
17. Lund, K., Burgess, C.: Producing high-dimensional semantic spaces from lexical co-occurrence. Behav. Res. Methods Instrum. Comput. **28**, 203–208 (1996)
18. Bruza, P., Song, D.: Discovering information flow using a high dimensional conceptual space. In: Proceedings of the 24th ACM SIGIR Conference on Research and Development in Information Retrieval (2001)
19. Weninger, T., Zhu, X.A., Han, J.: An exploration of discussion threads in social news sites: a case study of the reddit community. In: Proceedings of the 2013 IEEE/ACM International Conference on Advances in Social Networks Analysis and Mining, pp. 579–583. ACM (2013)
20. Stephen, B., Colm O., Daragh B.: Improving document clustering performance: the use of an automatically generated ontology to augment document representations. In: Proceedings of the 9th International Joint Conference on Knowledge Discovery, Knowledge Engineering and Knowledge Management - Volume 1: KDIR, pp. 215–223. SciTePress, INSTICC (2017). https://doi.org/10.10007/1234567890

Identification of Relevant Hashtags for Planned Events Using Learning to Rank

Sreekanth Madisetty[(✉)] and Maunendra Sankar Desarkar

Department of Computer Science and Engineering,
Indian Institute of Technology Hyderabad, Hyderabad, India
{cs15resch11006,maunendra}@iith.ac.in

Abstract. Lots of planned events (e.g. concerts, sports matches, festivals, etc.) keep happening across the world every day. In various applications like event recommendation, event reporting, etc. it might be useful to find user discussions related to such events from social media. Identification of event related hashtags can be useful for this purpose. In this paper, we focus on identifying the top hashtags related to a given event. We define a set of features for (event, hashtag) pairs, and discuss ways to obtain these feature scores. A linear aggregation of these scores is used to finally output a ranked list of top hashtags for the event. The aggregation weights of the features are obtained using a learning to rank algorithm. We establish the superiority of our method by performing detailed experiments on a large dataset containing multiple categories of events and related tweets.

Keywords: Social media · Information Retrieval · Learning to rank ·
Hashtags · Twitter

1 Introduction

Every day, lots of planned events keep happening across the world. A "planned event" is defined by a real world occurrence or incident which is pre-planned, takes place at a certain location, certain time or duration and is of interest to several people. Examples of such events are festivals, concerts, shows, conferences, sports events, movie launches, etc.

Nowadays, people actively participate in various social media platforms such as Twitter, Facebook to discuss their expectations, anticipations, feedbacks about multiple topics. It has been observed that people discuss about various events also, like the ones mentioned above. If such user discussions related to an event can be retrieved from social media, then it can be useful in various applications like event reporting, event recommendation, etc. Since such social media posts are very short, the context of the post is often difficult to identify in an automated way. In Twitter, people can use hashtags to express some context of the tweet. If relevant hashtags for a given event can be identified, then many tweets related to the same event can be confidently retrieved. For example,

© Springer Nature Switzerland AG 2019
A. Fred et al. (Eds.): IC3K 2017, CCIS 976, pp. 82–99, 2019.
https://doi.org/10.1007/978-3-030-15640-4_5

the hashtag "#Race3" may relate to the movie release Race3 starring Salman Khan, "#FIFAWorldCup2018", "#FIFAWC2018","#FIFA2018" are related to the FIFA World Cup 2018, "#InternationalYogaDay2018" may be related to the celebrations for International Yoga Day 2018. By specifying these hashtags, tweets related to the corresponding events may be retrieved from Twitter. However, manual selection of these hashtags is not a scalable approach. In this work, we focus on the problem of *automated identification of high-precision hashtags for given planned events*. Our main contributions towards this task as follows:

1. We identify a set of features that describe relatedness of a hashtag to an event.
2. We propose a method for determining scores for these features and aggregating the scores.
3. We perform detailed evaluation involving a large dataset and analyze the performance of the proposed method, and present a thorough analysis of the experimental results.

Rest of the paper is organized as follows. Related literature for current work is described in Sect. 2. Next in Sect. 3, problem statement of our work is defined. Details of the proposed method are presented in Sect. 4. Experimental evaluation of the method is described in Sect. 5. We conclude the work by providing directions for future research in Sect. 6.

2   Related Work

Use of social media in the context of planned events is gaining interest among the researchers recently. [1–3] work on detecting details about planned events from social media streams. [2] presents a method to identify live news events using Twitter. A technique to identify events and sub-events related to that event is discussed in [3]. A method to discover breaking events using hashtags using the instability for temporal analysis, Twitter memes possibility to distinguish social events from virtual topics or memes and author entropy is presented in [4]. Ozdikis et al. [5] present an event detection method in Twitter based on clustering of hashtags and introduce an enhancement technique by using the semantic similarities between the hashtags. Although our problem is different from planned event detection problem, some clues regarding the interplay between events, social media posts, and hashtags can be obtained from these works.

There are several works in literature that recommend hashtags to users [6,7]. The recommendations are based on usage analysis, user-to-user similarities in collaborative filtering framework, tweet-similarity, etc. Methods for content based hashtag recommendation for tweets are discussed in [8,9]. These methods consider the semantics of the tweets by using topic models and use that for scoring the hashtags to be recommended. [9] proposed a supervised topic model for hashtag recommendation on Twitter in which they treat hashtags as labels of topics and discovered the relationship among words, hashtags, and topics of tweets. However, these methods take user preferences for recommending hashtags. Recommending hashtags for hyperlinked tweets is proposed in [10]. They showed that functions of hashtags can be extended to the linked documents from hyperlinked tweets. They select the candidate hashtags by exploiting the content of the tweets, the linked document, and domain of the rank. Then, using learning to rank models, candidate hashtags are ranked. However, this method works only for hyperlinked tweets whereas less fraction of the tweets actually contain hyperlinks. Moreover, in none of these approaches, the relevance of a hashtag with respect to an external context is determined.

Real-time hashtag recommendation for streaming news (external context) is proposed in [11]. The semantic similarity of the hashtag to existing news articles is obtained by comparing the similarity of the article with the tweet bag of the hashtags. The performance would degrade if the tweet bags of the hashtags are not known or are small in size. Moreover, the news articles are generally large, whereas most of the event metadata obtained from event aggregators are shorter in size.

[12] proposed an adaptive crawling model that identifies emerging popular hashtags, and monitors them to retrieve larger amounts of associated content for an event. This model analyses the patterns of hashtags collected from the live stream to update subsequent collection queries. [13] proposed an approach for hashtag recommendation in Twitter by using Naive Bayes approach. The authors considered the hashtag as a class and words in the tweet are features. Both these methods heavily rely on the frequency aspect of the hashtags. The focus on hashtag semantics for short contexts like events is limited in the existing work in literature. Metadata features are defined to identify the hashtags in [14].

[15] proposed a cognitive-inspired hashtag recommendation approach for recommending the hashtags. The authors found that temporal effects play an important role for both individual and social hashtag reuse in hashtag recommendation. A word embedding based method for hashtag recommendation on Twitter is developed in [16]. To recommend the hashtags for the given post, the authors calculated the similarity scores between the word embeddings of the post and hashtags. Then hashtags are ranked based on their similarity scores. A method for phrase-based hashtag recommendation for microblog posts is described in [17]. The authors have used bag-of-phrases model to better capture the underlying topics of posted microblogs. Hidden topic model for content-based hashtag recommendation is proposed in [18]. A set of candidate hashtags was selected by ranking the occurrence probability of hashtags of a given topic. An extended spreading activation technique for hashtag recommendation in Twitter is proposed in [19]. This approach first annotates the tweets and hashtags semantically then it constructs semantic network using DBPedia. By using an extended version of the spreading activation function technique, the authors have calculated the similarities between the tweets and hashtags and recommend top k hashtags. An Empirical analysis of factors influencing Twitter Hashtag recommendation on detected communities is presented in [20].

A method is proposed for hashtag recommendation based on content and user characteristics [21]. The authors have used personal profiles of the Twitter users to find the relevant hashtags. Hashtags are ranked based on their popularity. A sentence-level attention model for hashtag recommendation by utilizing temporal factors is developed in [22]. An approach is proposed for hashtag recommendation in Twitter using word embeddings in [23].

3   Problem Definition

Here we briefly define the problem addressed in this paper: *Given metadata of an event E, find a list of hashtags relevant for the event E.* Event metadata comprises of context features of the event such as title, venue, time, location, participants or performers of the event. Event metadata can be obtained from several event aggregation sites (e.g., Eventbrite[1], Eventful[2], last.fm[3], etc.). The following are the examples of event metadata in JSON format.

```
{
"title": "Euro Cup 2016 final between
          Portugal and France",
"venue": "Stade de France",
"location": "Saint-Denis",
"performers":{
    "performer 1": "Portugal",
    "performer 2": "France"
             },
"date": "10th July 2016",
"duration-type": "fixed time period"
}

{
"title": "Sultan (2016 film)",
"venue":
"location": "India",
"performers":{
    "performer 1": "Salman Khan",
    "performer 2": "Anushka Sharma",
             },
"date": "6th July 2016",
"duration-type": "After specified date"
}

{
"title": "Janmashtami",
"venue":
```

[1] https://www.eventbrite.com/.
[2] https://eventful.com/.
[3] https://www.last.fm/.

```
"location": "India",
"performers":
"date": "25 August 2016",
"duration-type": "Whole Day"
}
```

For few events, some of the metadata entries are missing. Here, duration-type attribute indicates whether the event is a whole day event, or happens at a specific time period on the mentioned date or it is available for attending on or after the specified date. However, we do not consider date and duration-type features in the current version of our work.

Table 1. Example precision queries for the "Euro Cup 2016 final between Portugal and France" event.

Strategy	Example
["title"+"city"]	["Euro Cup final between Portugal and France" "Saint-Denis"]
[title+"city"]	[Euro Cup final between Portugal and France "Saint-Denis"]
[title-stopwords+"city"]	[Euro Cup final Portugal France "Saint-Denis"]
["title"+"venue"]	["Euro Cup final between Portugal and France" "Stade de France"]
[title+"venue"]	[Euro Cup final between Portugal and France "Stade de France"]
["title"]	["Euro Cup final between Portugal and France"]
[title]	[Euro Cup final between Portugal and France]
[title-stopwords]	[Euro Cup final Portugal France]

4   Methodology

We use a two-phase approach for identifying relevant hashtags for a given event. In the first phase, we retrieve a set of candidate hashtags for an event from Twitter. This phase is described in Sect. 4.1. In the second phase, we rank the hashtags from this candidate set according to their relevances with the event. The method for finding relevance scores is presented in Sect. 4.2.

4.1   Identifying Candidate Hashtags

In this phase, given metadata of an event, we first identify a set of tweets for the event from Twitter. We use the *precision query* approach presented in [24] for retrieving the tweets for the event. The method first prepares few *precision queries* from the event metadata. *Precision queries* are queries which retrieve highly relevant results for the specific information need. For *precision queries*, different combinations of context features, namely, title, and location, of each event are used. Some example precision queries for an event in our dataset are shown in Table 1. Such precision queries are submitted to the Twitter search API. Hashtags that appear in the tweet collection returned by Twitter for this call are added to the candidate set. As the keywords of the precision query come from the event title, venue, etc. the retrieved tweets generally match well with the event under consideration. However, we observe the presence of many noisy tweets and hashtags in the result set. The candidate set thus generated contains a huge number of hashtags. Many of them are not related to the event. Details about the size of candidate hashtag set are presented in Sect. 5.

4.2   Assigning Scores to Candidate Hashtags

Once we have the candidate hashtags for an event, we wish to assign a relevance score to each of those hashtags. We identify a set of features that we consider important for measuring this relevance for an (event, hashtag) pair. These feature scores are linearly combined to get the final score of the hashtag for that event. In the following discussion, we use EM to denote event metadata and HT to denote the hashtag. EM includes context features of an event like its title, location, performer. We now describe the features in more detail.

Features.

- **Frequency of Hashtag (f_1):** This is the frequency of the hashtag in tweet corpus of the event E. Tweet corpus is different for different events. Let the raw frequency of hashtag HT in tweet corpus for event E be $freq_{HT,E}$.

$$f_1 = \begin{cases} 1 + log(freq_{HT,E}) & \text{if } freq_{HT,E} > 0 \\ 0 & \text{otherwise} \end{cases}$$

  We have used log frequency of the hashtag.
- **Bigram Feature (f_2):** This feature computes the number of common character-level bigrams present in the hashtag HT and event metadata EM. If HT_B is a set of Hashtag Bigrams and EM_B is a set of Event Metadata Bigrams then the value of this feature is computed as

$$f_2 = |HT_B \cap EM_B|$$

  For example, Bigrams for hashtag #Euro2016 are #E, Eu, ur, ro, o2, 20, 01, 16. For the event metadata EM we find the set of bigrams for the available event metadata component (e.g. title, performer, location.) and take the union of these sets to get EM_B.
- **Trigram Feature (f_3):** This feature counts the number of common character-level trigrams present in the hashtag HT and event metadata EM. If HT_T is a set of hashtag trigrams and EM_T is a set of event metadata trigrams then the value of this feature is computed as

$$f_3 = |HT_T \cap EM_T|$$

  For example, trigrams for hashtag #Eurocup are #Eu, Eur, uro, roc, ocu, cup.

- **Bigrams of Abbreviated Title (f_4):** Let T, abbreviated title of the event, be the concatenation of first letters of tokenized words (in sequence) of event title. This feature enumerates the number of common character-level bigrams in the hashtag HT and T. If HT_B is a set of hashtag bigrams and T_B is a set of bigrams of T then the value of this feature is computed as

$$f_4 = |HT_B \cap T_B|$$

- **Trigrams of Abbreviated Title (f_5):** This feature counts the number of common character-level trigrams in the hashtag HT and T. If HT_T is a set of hashtag trigrams and T_T is a set of trigrams of T then this feature is computed as

$$f_5 = |HT_T \cap T_T|$$

- **Bigrams of Top-K trigrams (f_6):** Let S be the set of Top-K word-level trigrams of an event. S_{KB} is the union of character-level bigrams obtained from the elements of S. Score according to this feature is computed as

$$f_6 = |HT_B \cap S_{KB}|$$

This feature specifies the number of bigrams that are common in both hashtag HT and Top-K trigrams of tweet corpus of an event. We set $K=30$ in our algorithm.

- **Subsequence Feature (f_7):** This feature checks whether hashtag HT is a subsequence of event metadata EM or not. String A is a subsequence of string B if and only if A is obtained by deleting some elements from B without changing the order of remaining elements. For example, if "FRANCE vs. PORTUGAL" is event metadata EM then FRAPOR is a subsequence.

$$f_7 = \begin{cases} 1 & \text{if } HT \text{ is a subsequence of } EM \\ 0 & \text{otherwise} \end{cases}$$

- **Substring (f_8):** This feature tests whether hashtag HT is a substring of event metadata EM or not. This feature value is equal to 1 if it is a substring of event metadata EM, otherwise equal to 0.

$$f_8 = \begin{cases} 1 & \text{if } HT \text{ is a substring of } EM \\ 0 & \text{otherwise} \end{cases}$$

Combining Feature Scores. Given an (event, hashtag) pair, the different feature scores can be found by following the descriptions given above. Next, we want to find a weighted combination of these individual feature scores to determine a single score for each (event, hashtag) pair. If w is a weight vector where w_i denotes the weight of the ith feature, and s_i is the score of the (event, hashtag) pair for the ith feature, then the final score can be computed as $score = \sum_i w_i s_i$. Given an event, hashtags with the highest values of this $score$ can be output as the relevant hashtags for the event. A brief outline of the proposed method is given in Algorithm 1.

A baseline method may consider the w_i, i.e., the weight of the feature i, to be 1 for all i and treat all features equally. We use a machine learning algorithm for learning the weights of the features. We employ a learning to rank algorithm for determining these weights. We use SVM^{rank}, which is a pairwise learning to rank method for our purpose. Details of SVM^{rank} can be found in [25]. The results obtained with SVM^{rank} were promising, and we did not try any other learning to rank method. However, it should be noted that any learning to rank algorithm can be applied for determining the combination weights.

Algorithm 1. Top K hashtags for event E.
___

1: *Input* : Event Metadata, Tweet corpus of event E, K, w
2: *Output* : Top K hashtags
3: Dictionary $d=\{\}$, F is set of features
4: $HT_{list}=$ list of hashtags in the tweet corpus of an event
5: **for** each hashtag HT in HT_{list} **do**
6:    compute value of feature f_i for each $f_i \in F$
7:    $Score_{HT} = \sum_{f_i \in F} w_i f_i$
8:    Add (HT, $Score_{HT}$) to the dictionary d
9: **end for**
10: Sort the d in decreasing order of $Score_{HT}$
11: return *Top K* hashtags from d

---

5 Experiments

In this section, we evaluate the performance of the proposed method. First, we describe the dataset that we used for experiments. Detailed comparative evaluation against other alternative approaches is presented next.

5.1 Data

The data for the experiment was collected using Twitter streaming API. The dataset is divided into six categories: Birthdays, Euro Cup, Festivals, International Days, Movies, Politics and Governance.

Birthdays: This category contains tweets about the celebrity birthdays that occurred between August and October 2016. Here, a celebrity may be leading movie actor or actress, singer, political leader, etc. We have searched for celebrities in Wikipedia and selected the people whose birthdays fall inside the above mentioned timeline. There are ten events in this category. Tweet Volume for this category is 0.97 million.

Euro Cup: This category contains the tweets about Euro Cup 2016 Soccer Competition. It was held in France from 10th June to 10th July 2016. The schedule is posted on Euro Cup website. Events are collected from that site. Each football match played by two different countries is considered as a separate event. For example, a match played between Wales and Belgium in this competition is an event. Similarly, Germany vs Italy, France vs Iceland matches played in the competition are some other events. There are 51 events in this dataset. We collected the tweets using Twitter streaming API from 10 June to 19 July 2016. Tweet volume of this Euro Cup category is 14.4 million.

Festivals: This category contains the data about Indian festivals which occurred between July and September 2016. These events are collected from Wikipedia holidays list. It contains five events. Tweet Volume for this category is 1.62 million.

International Days: This category contains the tweets about national and international days in the history that occurred between July and September 2016. These international observances are collected from Wikipedia. There are eleven events in this category. Tweet Volume for this category is 2.58 million.

Movies: This category contains the tweets about movie launches like Indian movie releases which happened between July and September 2016. Events are collected from Internet Movie Database (IMDb). There are thirteen events in this category. Tweet volume for this category is 1.70 million.

Politics and Governance: This category contains the tweets about political events. These events are identified manually at the time of happening. There are four events in this category. Tweet volume for this category is 62K.

In summary, there are 94 events in our experiment and total tweet volume is 21.37 million. Total count of distinct hashtags for all the events is 0.66 million and with repetitions, the count is 37.6 million. The average number of distinct hashtags for each event is 7.13 K and with repetitions, the count is 0.40 million.

A pooling exercise was performed for generating a labeled dataset for evaluation. Different unsupervised algorithms described in Sect. 5.2 were used to retrieve a set of 100 hashtags for each event. All the hashtags thus retrieved were given to 5 volunteers for relevance judgments. Volunteers were asked to choose from three relevance labels: 2 being highly relevant to the event, 1 being moderately relevant to the event, 0 being irrelevant to the event. For each (event, hashtag) pair, a median of labels entered by the volunteers for that pair was used as the final label. If the label given by k volunteers are $r_1, r_2, ..., r_k$ (without loss of generality, assuming, $r_1 \leq r_2 \leq ... \leq r_k$) then $r_{\lfloor k/2 \rfloor}$th label is considered to be the label for given (event, hashtag) pair. However, for around 98% of the (event, hashtag) pairs, there was an agreement among the volunteers regarding the relevance labels.

5.2 Methods Compared

We compare the proposed method with the methods mentioned below. Two of these methods, namely, FreqPearson [12], Naive Bayes method [13] are taken from literature, whereas the other methods are obtained by using different subsets of the features mentioned in Sect. 4.2.

FreqPearson [12]: Each hashtag is represented by a vector. The vector is calculated by dividing the time frame into several time slots, and value at one particular field of the vector is the frequency count of the hashtag in the corresponding time slot. Similarly, seed hashtag vector is calculated. Then, the correlation between carefully selected seed hashtags and hashtags in tweets is computed. Details of the method can be found in [12].

Naive Bayes [13]: In this method, a hashtag is considered as a class, and words in the tweet are features. By using Bayes theorem, the probability of a hashtag given a set of words in a tweet corpus for an event is calculated. It is done for all the hashtags in the event, and the top hashtags are those which are having highest probability. This method is unsupervised in the sense that it does not use relevance information of the hashtags.

AlldiffW: This is the combination of all features with the weights determined by the SVM^{Rank} algorithm. We used 10-fold cross-validation to split the training and test sets. This is our proposed method for retrieving relevant hashtags for an event.

AllequalW: This is the combination of all features with equal weights given to all features. This is a standard baseline for our algorithm.

Next, we use different combinations of the features mentioned in Sect. 4.2. The scores of the features in the combination are added to get the final score of each hashtag for the event. We experimented with different feature combinations. For brevity, here we include for discussion top four feature combinations that give the best performance. The selected feature combinations are as follows.

- **Frequency:** The score of the hashtag is calculated by the frequency of the hashtag. Hashtags are sorted in descending order based on their frequencies. Then top hashtags are recommended.
- **FrTg:** This is the combination of frequency feature and trigrams feature.
- **FrTgSeq:** This is the combination of three features namely, frequency, trigrams, and subsequence.
- **FrTgBgtSeq:** This is the combination of four features namely, frequency, trigrams, bigrams of T, and subsequence.

All the above methods (except AlldiffW) use equal weights for the features and are unsupervised. The AlldiffW method uses different weights for the features and is supervised.

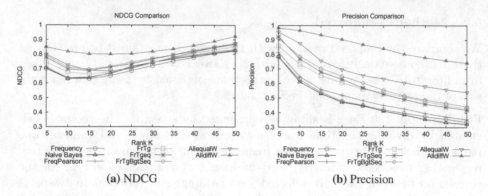

(a) NDCG   (b) Precision

Fig. 1. Comparing our proposed method with other alternative approaches and with feature combinations for top-k hashtags.

5.3   Evaluation Metrics

The performance of our method was evaluated using the evaluation metrics NDCG, Precision. These metrics are widely used in Information Retrieval literature. For both these measures, higher values indicate better performance.

5.4   Results and Discussions

Comparison with Other Methods. We compare our proposed method with the other methods listed in Sect. 5.2. The comparison is presented in Fig. 1. The NDCG values are compared in Fig. 1a and precision values are compared in Fig. 1b. It is clear that the performance of the proposed method is significantly better than the other methods used for comparison. This is because the frequency of the hashtags play a significant role in the algorithms [12,13] taken from literature. Hence, they are more biased towards frequency. However, along with frequency, we consider various other features that attempt to measure the semantic relatedness between the event and hashtag. The other methods fail to capture semantic relatedness and hence keep retrieving the hashtags that are more frequent but unrelated to the event. It can be observed that even our baseline method or different feature combinations achieve high scores than *FreqPearson* and *Naive Bayes*. This signifies the usefulness of the semantic features described in this work. The performance of *AlldiffW* (weights are learned) is better than *AllequalW* (uniform weights). This indicates the importance of supervision along with semantic features.

NDCG comparison with methods in the literature and baseline method for each category, Birthdays, Eurocup, Festivals, International Days, Movies, and Politics and Governance is presented in Tables 2, 3, 4, 5, 6, and 7 respectively. Metric values for the est performing method are put in bold. For all the categories except Eurocup, our proposed method outperforms the methods in the literature and baseline method. However, for Eurocup category for $K = 5$ to $K = 15$ and

Table 2. NDCG of Birthdays.

Rank K	FreqPearson	Naive Bayes	AlleqW	AlldiffW
5	0.616	0.594	0.724	**0.911**
10	0.552	0.568	0.653	**0.838**
15	0.570	0.559	0.621	**0.803**
20	0.596	0.599	0.645	**0.804**
25	0.631	0.633	0.693	**0.799**
30	0.689	0.675	0.735	**0.819**
35	0.732	0.711	0.758	**0.848**
40	0.751	0.737	0.801	**0.870**
45	0.766	0.772	0.836	**0.898**
50	0.795	0.786	0.858	**0.933**

Table 3. NDCG of Euro Cup.

Rank K	FreqPearson	Naive Bayes	AlleqW	AlldiffW
5	0.782	0.780	**0.820**	0.730
10	0.721	0.703	**0.736**	0.717
15	0.720	0.701	**0.741**	0.728
20	0.729	0.731	0.740	**0.752**
25	0.757	0.752	0.758	**0.767**
30	0.794	0.774	0.779	**0.781**
35	**0.817**	0.801	0.810	0.806
40	0.834	0.819	**0.840**	0.836
45	0.850	0.833	**0.865**	0.857
50	0.867	0.857	**0.887**	0.882

Table 4. NDCG of Festivals.

Rank K	FreqPearson	Naive Bayes	AlleqW	AlldiffW
5	0.870	0.878	0.983	**0.983**
10	0.708	0.698	0.878	**0.951**
15	0.652	0.697	0.790	**0.924**
20	0.674	0.718	0.743	**0.894**
25	0.726	0.800	0.748	**0.879**
30	0.753	0.834	0.787	**0.861**
35	0.799	0.861	0.821	**0.864**
40	0.819	0.870	0.851	**0.887**
45	0.854	0.872	0.900	**0.928**
50	0.873	0.887	0.931	**0.970**

Table 5. NDCG of International Days.

Rank K	FreqPearson	Naive Bayes	AlleqW	AlldiffW
5	0.707	0.687	0.816	**0.843**
10	0.647	0.640	0.748	**0.821**
15	0.664	0.668	0.702	**0.804**
20	0.683	0.708	0.686	**0.791**
25	0.702	0.747	0.693	**0.796**
30	0.743	0.774	0.740	**0.807**
35	0.764	0.801	0.776	**0.828**
40	0.796	0.813	0.818	**0.850**
45	0.815	0.825	0.839	**0.881**
50	0.828	0.831	0.876	**0.922**

$K = 40$ to $K = 50$ *AllequalW* performs better, for $K = 20$ to $K = 30$ our method performance is better than other methods, and for $K = 35$ only our method is underperforming with a very small difference.

Precision comparison with methods in the literature and baseline method for each category, Birthdays, Eurocup, Festivals, International Days, Movies, and Politics and Governance is presented in Tables 8, 9, 10, 11, 12, and 13 respectively. It can be observed that for all the categories our method is performing better than other methods. For some categories (Festivals, and Politics and Governance) *Precision@10* is 1. This means all the top 10 hashtags for all the events in these categories are relevant. For Movies category *Precision@5* is 1 i.e. all the top five hashtags for each event in this category are relevant.

Analyzing the Retrieved Hashtags. In this section, we analyze the quality of retrieved hashtags in each category. Table 14 shows the set of top ten hashtags for six events from six different categories, namely, Birthday of Indian P.M. Narendra Modi (Category: Birthdays), Euro Cup match between Wales and Slovakia (Category: Euro Cup), Raksha Bandhan (Category: Festivals), International Yoga Day (Category: International Days), Sultan (Category: Movies), and GSTBill (Category: Politics and Governance). The hashtags presented here

Table 6. NDCG of Movies.

Rank K	FreqPearson	Naive Bayes	AlleqW	AlldiffW
5	0.609	0.590	0.634	**0.652**
10	0.571	0.585	0.583	**0.651**
15	0.586	0.598	0.573	**0.669**
20	0.620	0.655	0.594	**0.709**
25	0.678	0.686	0.626	**0.733**
30	0.720	0.712	0.655	**0.753**
35	0.757	0.738	0.719	**0.776**
40	0.767	0.762	0.756	**0.800**
45	0.784	0.771	0.794	**0.833**
50	0.798	0.792	0.824	**0.874**

Table 7. NDCG of Politics & Governance.

Rank K	FreqPearson	Naive Bayes	AlleqW	AlldiffW
5	0.691	0.699	0.816	**0.976**
10	0.613	0.595	0.748	**0.925**
15	0.647	0.599	0.702	**0.875**
20	0.694	0.597	0.686	**0.846**
25	0.734	0.658	0.693	**0.835**
30	0.759	0.685	0.740	**0.882**
35	0.785	0.700	0.776	**0.894**
40	0.796	0.721	0.818	**0.910**
45	0.820	0.766	0.839	**0.932**
50	0.837	0.809	0.876	**0.958**

Table 8. Precision of Birthdays category.

Rank K	FreqPearson	Naive Bayes	AlleqW	AlldiffW
5	0.756	0.733	0.867	**0.978**
10	0.667	0.644	0.800	**0.922**
15	0.578	0.541	0.696	**0.896**
20	0.556	0.483	0.689	**0.867**
25	0.511	0.453	0.684	**0.813**
30	0.489	0.437	0.667	**0.759**
35	0.460	0.419	0.616	**0.730**
40	0.428	0.394	0.600	**0.703**
45	0.400	0.378	0.580	**0.681**
50	0.382	0.351	0.556	**0.664**

Table 9. Precision of Euro Cup category.

Rank K	FreqPearson	Naive Bayes	AlleqW	AlldiffW
5	0.914	0.876	0.984	**0.988**
10	0.710	0.642	0.945	**0.947**
15	0.639	0.584	0.818	**0.905**
20	0.581	0.545	0.722	**0.854**
25	0.538	0.494	0.667	**0.805**
30	0.501	0.450	0.610	**0.756**
35	0.467	0.419	0.577	**0.710**
40	0.431	0.392	0.543	**0.672**
45	0.405	0.364	0.515	**0.636**
50	0.382	0.350	0.488	**0.607**

are obtained by FreqPearson, Naive Bayes, and the proposed method respectively. The events are selected based on their tweet volume in each category. The hashtags showed in italics and red color indicate that they are not relevant to the event. The hashtags which are only retrieved by the proposed method are presented in the last column. We observe that the proposed method is able to retrieve many relevant hashtags that are not retrieved by other methods. We also observe that proposed method retrieves very few italic hashtags, and other methods retrieve more number of italic hashtags. This indicates that our method retrieves more number of relevant hashtags (relevance label 1 or 2) whereas many irrelevant hashtags are picked up by other methods.

Category-wise Analysis of the Proposed Method. We now evaluate the performance of the proposed method. Figure 2a shows NDCG values for different categories for rank positions (K values) 1 to 50. It can be observed that, for all categories, the NDCG value initially is very close to 1. It indicates that the proposed method is able to put highly relevant hashtags at the top of the hashtag list for most of the events. After that, the NDCG value decreases slightly for almost all the categories. It happens because, after few rank positions, the method retrieves few less relevant or irrelevant hashtags. However, very soon,

Table 10. Precision of Festivals category.

Rank K	FreqPearson	Naive Bayes	AlleqW	AlldiffW
5	0.880	0.900	1.000	1.000
10	0.680	0.650	0.920	1.000
15	0.560	0.550	0.827	0.987
20	0.530	0.463	0.770	0.980
25	0.496	0.470	0.728	0.968
30	0.440	0.425	0.727	0.967
35	0.429	0.393	0.697	0.937
40	0.405	0.350	0.660	0.930
45	0.387	0.317	0.649	0.933
50	0.368	0.310	0.632	0.924

Table 11. Precision of International Days category.

Rank K	FreqPearson	Naive Bayes	AlleqW	AlldiffW
5	0.733	0.740	0.950	0.933
10	0.542	0.540	0.867	0.942
15	0.467	0.453	0.717	0.928
20	0.404	0.415	0.646	0.896
25	0.357	0.380	0.587	0.867
30	0.342	0.343	0.567	0.828
35	0.314	0.317	0.543	0.790
40	0.306	0.293	0.523	0.758
45	0.293	0.273	0.500	0.743
50	0.275	0.252	0.488	0.730

Table 12. Precision of Movies category.

Rank K	FreqPearson	Naive Bayes	AlleqW	AlldiffW
5	0.700	0.667	0.980	1.000
10	0.580	0.611	0.860	0.980
15	0.493	0.533	0.760	0.953
20	0.460	0.489	0.700	0.950
25	0.440	0.444	0.680	0.916
30	0.417	0.400	0.650	0.887
35	0.403	0.378	0.649	0.854
40	0.363	0.344	0.630	0.835
45	0.342	0.316	0.609	0.831
50	0.322	0.300	0.586	0.816

Table 13. Precision of Politics and Governance category.

Rank K	FreqPearson	Naive Bayes	AlleqW	AlldiffW
5	0.900	0.800	0.950	1.000
10	0.700	0.575	0.867	1.000
15	0.617	0.517	0.717	0.933
20	0.588	0.438	0.646	0.875
25	0.550	0.440	0.587	0.840
30	0.508	0.408	0.567	0.842
35	0.486	0.386	0.543	0.786
40	0.444	0.356	0.523	0.769
45	0.411	0.361	0.500	0.728
50	0.395	0.370	0.488	0.705

the NDCG value again picks up, indicating that it is able to include those missed hashtags in later part of the ranked list.

We observe that NDCG values for movies category are low because names of movie artists also come in hashtags. Many of those hashtags also appear in tweets that are not related to the particular movie under consideration. Hence those hashtags are not fully relevant to the event. Similarly for Euro Cup, sometimes the hashtags denote the country for a team involved in the match, the same hashtag is also found in tweets mentioned in other events from that country.

Figure 2b shows Precision values for different categories. We observe that the top hashtags for each category are all relevant (relevance label 1 or 2) to the events, as the precision values are close to 1. After that, some irrelevant hashtags are also retrieved and precision decreases. Still, the overall precision value is reasonably good. For example, except three categories (Birthdays, Euro Cup, Movies), all other categories have Precision@5 as 1. Which means that all the top-5 hashtags are relevant to the event. Moreover, for those three categories, the Precision@5 values are .970, .988 and .933, which are quite high.

Table 14. Comparing top ten hashtags identified by our proposed method with the hashtags identified by other alternative approaches. Hashtags in italic form and in red colour represent they are not relevant (relevance label 0) to the event under conideration. Hashtags in normal form represent they are relevant (relevance label 1 or 2) to the event.

Event	FreqPearson	Naive Bayes	Proposed Method	Hashtags retrieved by our method but missed by other methods
Narendra Modi (Birthdays)	#happybdaypmmodi, #hbdpradhansewak, #sevadiwas, #sewadiwas, *#mindrocks16*, *#happybdayp*, #narendramodi, *#india*, #happybdaypm, *#modi*	#happybdaypmmodi, #hbdpradhansewak, #sevadiwas, *#thestage2*, *#sewadiwas*, *#mindrocks16*, *#fliptech*, *#msglionheartmusic*, *#karachibakery*, *#filmin50hours*	#happybirthdaynarendramodi, #happybdaypmmodi, #narendramodi, #happybirthdaypmmodi, #happybirthdaynamo, #happybirthdaypm, *#happybirthday*, #happybirthdaynarend, #happybdaypm, #hbdnarendramodi	#happybirthdaynarendramodi, #happybirthdaypmmodi, #happybirthdaynamo, #happybirthdaynarend, #hbdnarendramodi
Wales vs Slovakia (Euro Cup)	#walsvk, #euro2016, #wal, #svk, *#ripchristina*, *#amjoy*, *#shapethefuturein5words*, *#thingsifindheartwarming*, *#togetherstronger*, #wales	#walsvk, #euro2016, *#ripchristina*, *#amjoy*, *#shapethefuturein5words*, *#thingsifindheartwarmingH*, #wal, #svk, *#engrus*, *#albsui*	#walesvslovakia, #walesvsslovakia, #walesslovakia, #walsvk, #stadedebordeaux, #euro2016, #bordeaux, #slovakia, #uefaeuro2016, #wal	#walesvslovakia, #walesvsslovakia, #walesslovakia
Raksha Bandhan (Festivals)	#rakhi, #happyrakshabandhan, #rakshabandhan, *#msgwishes*, #happyrakhi, *#sakshimalik*, *#msglovessewadars*, *#love*, *#safetyinyourhands*, *#sakhshimalik*	#rakhi, #rakshabandhan, #happyrakshabandhan, #happyrakhi, *#msgwishes*, *#love*, *#sister*, #rakshabandan, *#sakshimalik*, *#safetyinyourhands*	#happyrakshabandhan, #rakshabandhan, #happyrakshabandan, #happyrakhi, #happyrakshabandhanindia, #rakshabandan, #happyrakshabandha, #sabkarakshabandhan, #happyrakhshabandhan, #happyrakshabandh	#happyrakshabandhanindia, #sabkarakshabandhan, #happyrakshabandh
International Yoga Day (International Days)	#yogaday, #yoga, #idy2016, #internationalyogaday, #iyd2016, #internationaldayofyoga, #worldyogaday, #yoga4sdgs, #yogaday2016, *#health*	#yogaday, #yoga, #internationalyogaday, *#workout*, #idy2016, *#fitness*, *#health*, *#nationalselfieday*, *#weightloss*, #meditation	#internationalyogaday, #internationaldayofyoga, #internationalyogaday2016, #internationaldayofyoga2016, #yogaday, #internatioanlyogaday, #idy2016, #happyinternationalyogaday, #yogainternationalday, #internationalyogadaycelebrat	#internationalyogaday2016, #internationaldayofyoga2016, #happyinternationalyogaday, #yogainternationalday, #internationalyogadaycelebrat
Sultan (Movies)	#sultan, #salmankhan, *#bajrangibhaijaan*, #sultanday, #salman, *#eidmubarak*, #anushkasharma, *#eid*, *#boxoffice*, *#prdp*	#sultan, #salmankhan, *#review*, *#bollywood*, #anushkasharma, #salman, #sultanday, #salmankhan's, *#eidmubarak*, *#boxoffice*	#anushkasharma, #salmankhan, #sultan, #sultansalmankhan, #anushkasharma's, #anushkasharm, #salmankhan's, #salmankhanfilms, #megastarsalmankhan, #sultan10th100crfilmofsalman	#sultansalmankhan, #sultan10th100crfilmofsalman
GST Bill (Politics and Governance)	#gst, #gstbill, #transformingindia, *#raghuramrajan*, *#rajanslastpolicy*, *#diljumlajumlahogaya*, *#fdi*, *#rbi*, *#aadhaar*, *#foodsecurity*	#gst, #gstbill, *#india*, #transformingindia, #tax, *#modi*, *#raghuramrajan*, *#rajanslastpolicy*, #gstcleared, #loksabha	#goodsandservicestax, #gstbill, #goodandservicesbill, #constitutionalamendmentbill, #goodsandservicetax, *#constitution*, #goodsandservice, #evilandservicesbill, #gst, #onenononetax	#goodsandservicestax, #goodandservicesbill, #constitutionalamendmentbill, #goodsandservicetax, #onenationonetax

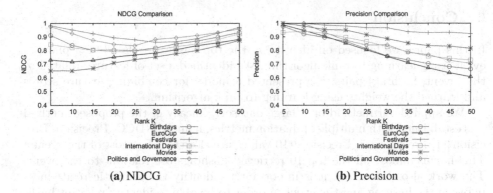

(a) NDCG   **(b)** Precision

Fig. 2. Category-wise comparison of NDCG and precision of top-k hashtags for six different categories using our method.

Table 15. Top features (first feature with highest importance, last feature with lowest importance) identified by training category-wise (2nd to 7th columns) and by training entire dataset (8th column).

S.No.	Birthdays	EuroCup	Festivals	International Days	Movies	Politics and Governance	All categories
1.	Trigrams	Trigrams	Trigrams	Trigrams	Trigrams	Trigrams	Trigrams
2.	Bigrams of T	Subsequence	Bigrams of T	Trigrams of T	Bigrams	Bigrams of T	Bigrams
3.	Frequency of Hashtag	Frequency of Hashtag	Frequency of Hashtag	Frequency of Hashtag	Frequency of Hashtag	Subsequence	Frequency of Hashtag
4.	Subsequence	Bigrams of T	Subsequence	Subsequence	Subsequence	Frequency of Hashtag	Bigrams of T
5.	Substring	Trigrams of T	Substring	Bigrams of T	Bigrams of T	Trigrams of T	Subsequence
6.	Bigrams	Bigrams	Trigrams of T	Substring	Substring	Substring	Trigrams of T
7.	Bigrams of topk Trigrams	Bigrams of topk Trigrams	Bigrams	Bigrams	Trigrams of T	Bigrams	Substring
8.	Trigrams of T	Substring	Bigrams of topk Trigrams	Bigrams of topk Trigrams	Bigrams of topk Trigrams	Bigrams of topk Trigrams	Bigrams of topk Trigrams

Feature Analysis. In this section, we analyze the performance of features in each category. The last column in Table 15 shows the most important features that were obtained by applying SVM^{Rank} across all categories. A similar exercise is done where training is done separately for each category. This exercise allows us to get the most important features for each category. We observe that trigrams feature, subsequence feature, frequency feature, and bigrams of T are present in all the categories in top positions. It happens because the number of common trigrams between event metadata and the hashtag is a good indicator of semantic similarity between the event and the hashtag. The same is true for bigrams of T and subsequence feature also. Frequency feature is also very important feature as hashtags that are relevant to event tend to be used more frequently in the tweets related to the event.

6   Conclusion

In this paper, we focused on identifying the top hashtags related to a planned event using learning to rank algorithm. We identified a set of features related to the (event, hashtag) pairs. We presented a model for combining feature scores and learned the weights using learning to rank algorithm.

We applied our method on a large dataset. Efficacy of the proposed method was established with multiple evaluation metrics, namely, NDCG, Precision. Precision@1, Precision@5, Precision@10 values are close to 1 for most of the events. This means almost all the top 10 retrieved hashtags are relevant to the event. The work also shows that it is important to identify the semantic relatedness between the hashtag and the event in order to be able to identify relevant hashtags for the event. As an extension to this work, we want to identify additional features for (event, hashtag) pairs. For future work, we want to combine word embedding features along with the features identified in this paper to find the relevant hashtags.

References

1. Hürriyetoglu, A., Oostdijk, N., van den Bosch, A.: Estimating time to event from tweets using temporal expressions (2014)
2. Jackoway, A., Samet, H., Sankaranarayanan, J.: Identification of live news events using Twitter. In: Proceedings of the 3rd ACM SIGSPATIAL International Workshop on Location-Based Social Networks, pp. 25–32. ACM (2011)
3. Khurdiya, A., Dey, L., Mahajan, D., Verma, I.: Extraction and compilation of events and sub-events from twitter. In: Proceedings of the 2012 IEEE/WIC/ACM International Joint Conferences on Web Intelligence and Intelligent Agent Technology, vol. 1, pp. 504–508. IEEE Computer Society (2012)
4. Cui, A., Zhang, M., Liu, Y., Ma, S., Zhang, K.: Discover breaking events with popular hashtags in Twitter. In: Proceedings of the 21st ACM international conference on Information and Knowledge Management, pp. 1794–1798. ACM (2012)
5. Ozdikis, O., Senkul, P., Oguztuzun, H.: Semantic expansion of hashtags for enhanced event detection in Twitter. In: Proceedings of the 1st International Workshop on Online Social Systems. Citeseer (2012)
6. Kywe, S.M., Hoang, T.-A., Lim, E.-P., Zhu, F.: On recommending hashtags in Twitter networks. In: Aberer, K., Flache, A., Jager, W., Liu, L., Tang, J., Guéret, C. (eds.) SocInfo 2012. LNCS, vol. 7710, pp. 337–350. Springer, Heidelberg (2012). https://doi.org/10.1007/978-3-642-35386-4_25
7. Zangerle, E., Gassler, W., Specht, G.: Recommending#-tags in Twitter. In: Proceedings of the Workshop on Semantic Adaptive Social Web (SASWeb 2011), CEUR Workshop Proceedings, vol. 730, pp. 67–78 (2011)
8. Godin, F., Slavkovikj, V., De Neve, W., Schrauwen, B., Van de Walle, R.: Using topic models for Twitter hashtag recommendation. In: Proceedings of the 22nd International Conference on World Wide Web, pp. 593–596. ACM (2013)
9. She, J., Chen, L.: Tomoha: Topic model-based hashtag recommendation on twitter. In: Proceedings of the 23rd International Conference on World Wide Web, pp. 371–372. ACM (2014)

10. Sedhai, S., Sun, A.: Hashtag recommendation for hyperlinked tweets. In: Proceedings of the 37th International ACM SIGIR Conference on Research & Development in Information Retrieval, pp. 831–834. ACM (2014)
11. Shi, B., Ifrim, G., Hurley, N.: Learning-to-rank for real-time high-precision Hashtag recommendation for streaming news. In: Proceedings of the 25th International Conference on World Wide Web, International World Wide Web Conferences Steering Committee, pp. 1191–1202 (2016)
12. Wang, X., Tokarchuk, L., Cuadrado, F., Poslad, S.: Exploiting hashtags for adaptive microblog crawling. In: Proceedings of the 2013 IEEE/ACM International Conference on Advances in Social Networks Analysis and Mining, pp. 311–315. ACM (2013)
13. Dovgopol, R., Nohelty, M.: Twitter hash tag recommendation. arXiv preprint arXiv:1502.00094 (2015)
14. Madisetty, S., Desarkar, M.S.: Exploiting meta attributes for identifying event related Hashtags. In: Proceedings of the 9th International Joint Conference on Knowledge Discovery, Knowledge Engineering and Knowledge Management - (Volume 1: KDIR), 1–3 November 2017, Funchal, Madeira, Portugal, pp. 238–245 (2017)
15. Kowald, D., Pujari, S.C., Lex, E.: Temporal effects on Hashtag reuse in twitter: a cognitive-inspired Hashtag recommendation approach. In: Proceedings of the 26th International Conference on World Wide Web, International World Wide Web Conferences Steering Committee, pp. 1401–1410 (2017)
16. Dey, K., Shrivastava, R., Kaushik, S., Subramaniam, L.V.: Emtagger: a word embedding based novel method for Hashtag recommendation on Twitter. arXiv preprint arXiv:1712.01562 (2017)
17. Gong, Y., Zhang, Q., Han, X., Huang, X.: Phrase-based hashtag recommendation for microblog posts. Sci. China Inf. Sci. **60**, 012109 (2017)
18. Cheung, K.C., Cheung, T.K.Y.: Recommendation of hashtags in social twitter network. Int. J. Data Anal. Tech. Strat. **9**, 222–236 (2017)
19. Ben-Lhachemi, N., Nfaoui, E.H.: An extended spreading activation technique for hashtag recommendation in microblogging platforms. In: Proceedings of the 7th International Conference on Web Intelligence, Mining and Semantics, p. 16. ACM (2017)
20. Alsini, A., Datta, A., Li, J., Huynh, D.: Empirical analysis of factors influencing twitter hashtag recommendation on detected communities. In: Cong, G., Peng, W.-C., Zhang, W.E., Li, C., Sun, A. (eds.) ADMA 2017. LNCS (LNAI), vol. 10604, pp. 119–131. Springer, Cham (2017). https://doi.org/10.1007/978-3-319-69179-4_9
21. Tran, V.C., Hwang, D., Nguyen, N.T.: Hashtag recommendation approach based on content and user characteristics. Cybern. Syst. **49**(5–6), 368–383 (2018)
22. Ma, J., Feng, C., Shi, G., Shi, X., Huang, H.: Temporal enhanced sentence-level attention model for hashtag recommendation. CAAI Trans. Intell. Technol. **3**, 95–100 (2018)
23. Ben-Lhachemi, N., Nfaoui, E.H.: Using tweets embeddings for hashtag recommendation in Twitter. Proc. Comput. Sci. **127**, 7–15 (2018)
24. Becker, H., Iter, D., Naaman, M., Gravano, L.: Identifying content for planned events across social media sites. In: Proceedings of the fifth ACM International Conference on Web Search and Data Mining, pp. 533–542. ACM (2012)
25. Joachims, T.: Training linear SVMs in linear time. In: Proceedings of the 12th ACM SIGKDD International Conference on Knowledge Discovery and Data Mining, pp. 217–226. ACM (2006)

Investigation of Passage Based Ranking Models to Improve Document Retrieval

Ghulam Sarwar[1]([⊠]), Colm O'Riordan[1], and John Newell[2]

[1] Department of Information Technology, National University of Ireland, Galway, Ireland
{g.sarwar1,colm.oriordan}@nuigalway.ie
[2] School of Mathematics, Statistics and Applied Mathematics, National University of Ireland, Galway, Ireland
john.newell@nuigalway.ie

Abstract. Passage retrieval deals with identifying and retrieving small but explanatory portions of a document that answers a user's query. In this paper, we focus on improving the document ranking by using different passage based evidence. Several similarity measures were evaluated and a more in-depth analysis was undertaken into the effect of varying specific. We have also explored the notion of query difficulty to understand whether the best performing passage-based approach helps to improve, or not, the performance of certain queries. Experimental results indicate that for the passage level technique, the worst-performing queries are damaged slightly and the those that perform well are boosted for the WebAp collection. However, our rank-based similarity function boosted the performance of the difficult queries in the Ohsumed collection.

Keywords: Document retrieval · Passage-based document retrieval · Passage similarity functions · Inverse rank · Query difficulty

1 Introduction

Information Retrieval (IR) deals with the organization, representation, and the retrieval of information from a large set of text documents. The retrieval of relevant information from large collections is a difficult problem; search queries and documents are typically expressed in natural language which introduces many problems such as ambiguity caused by the presence of synonyms and abbreviations, and issues arising from the *vocabulary difference problem* which occurs when the user expresses their information need with terms different to those used to express the same concept in the document collection.

Several models have been shown to be very effective in ranking documents in terms of their relevance to a user's query. The user formulates the query by expressing their information need in natural language. Approaches include different mathematical frameworks (vector space model, probabilistic models)

© Springer Nature Switzerland AG 2019
A. Fred et al. (Eds.): IC3K 2017, CCIS 976, pp. 100–117, 2019.
https://doi.org/10.1007/978-3-030-15640-4_6

to represent documents and queries and to formulate a comparison approach. The BM25 weighting scheme [1] derived within a probabilistic framework is a well-known effective one in estimating the relevance of a document to a query. The main goal of an IR system is to estimate the relevance of a document to a query; this notion of 'relevance' is often interpreted as measuring the level of similarity between a document to a query.

In IR, the traditional approaches consider the document as a single entity. However, some researchers choose to split the document into a separate passages given the intuition that a highly relevant passage may exist in a larger document which itself will be considered as non relevant. If a passage is indexed as an individual *pseudo-document*, the number of documents stored and indexed will increase significantly and in a result, it will effect the speed and cost of retrieval [2]. However, one may now retrieve relevant passages that occur in documents deemed not very relevant. Moreover, if the document returned as relevant is too long, it can be difficult for the users to find the appropriate relevant passages in the document. In other words, returning a large relevant document, while useful, still, puts an onus on the user to find the relevant passages. Therefore, we opt for the passage level retrieval approach to finding the relevant passage and aim to use that to improve the document ranking. The intuition behind our approach is that by identifying very relevant passages in a document we can better estimate the relevance of the overall document.

One can imagine the passages themselves as documents at indexing time. The division of these passages can be done in a number of ways. For example, either via some textual identifier e.g. paragraph markings ($<p>$), new line feed ($/n$) etc. or it can be defined by a number of words. A passage could be a sentence, a number of sentences or a paragraph itself. The passages can be considered as discrete passages with no intersection or can be viewed as overlapping passages.

In this paper, we extend our previous work [3] in which we utilised the inverse rank of a passage as a measure and compared it with the other passage based approaches. We recap some of our previous findings including the passage based equations and several figures and a table (Figures 1, 2(a), (b), Table 1 etc.) to support our new approaches and analysis undertaken in this paper. Our main goal is to generate new document rankings by computing the passage similarity and using this score (or its combination with document level similarity score) as a means to rank the overall document. In this extended work, we present a more extensive analysis of the SF2 approach (explained in Sect. 3) and also highlight the impact of difficult queries on the overall performance by analysing the ranking functions we used in our previous paper.

The main focus of our work is to see how effectively the passage level evidence affected the document retrieval. Furthermore, we extend our focus by doing a more in-depth analysis of the passage based functions based on different parameters and examining whether the difficult queries damages the passage based results or improves it. Factors such as different means to define passage boundaries are not of huge concern to us as present.

We have used the WebAp (Web Answer Passage)[1] test collection which is obtained from the 2004 TREC Terabyte Track Gov2 collection and the Ohsumed test collection [4] which comprises titles and/or abstracts from 270 Medline reference medical journals. The results show that different similarity functions behave differently across the two test collections. Furthermore, difficult queries have different characteristics and the impact on the overall performance.

The paper outline is as follows: Section 2 presents a brief overview of the previous work in passage level retrieval and some work done in query difficulty area. Section 3 gives an overview of the methodology employed, outlining the details of different similarity functions, the passage boundary approach, and the evaluation measures adopted in the experiments. Section 4 presents a brief explanation of the test collections used in the experiments and the assumptions made for them. Section 5 discusses different experimental results obtained. In Sect. 5.1, further analysis for the SF2 approach is presented. A discussion on the impact of difficult queries by using the passage level measures is presented in Sect. 5.2. Finally, Sect. 6 provides a summary of the main conclusions and outlines future work.

2   Related Work

In previous research, passage level retrieval has been studied in information retrieval from different perspectives. For defining the passage boundaries, several approaches have been used. Bounded passages, overlapping window size, text-tiling, usage of language models and arbitrary passages [5–9] are among the few main techniques. Window size approaches consider the word count to separate the passages from each other, irrespective of the written structure of the document. Overlapping window size is shown to be more effective and useful for the document retrieval [5]. Similarly, a variant of the same approach was used by Croft [10].

Jong [11] proposed an approach which involved considering the score of passages generated from an evaluation function to effectively retrieve documents in a Question Answering system. Their evaluation function calculates the proximity of the different terms used in the query with different passages and takes the maximum proximity score for the document ranking.

Callan [5] demonstrated that ordering documents based on the score of the best passage may be up to 20% more effective than standard document ranking. Similarly, for certain test collections, it was concluded that combining the document score with the best passage score gives improved results [12]. Buckley et al. also use the combination of both scores in a more complex manner, to generate scores for ranking [13]. Moreover, Hearst et al. [14] showed that instead of only using the best passage with the maximum score, adding other passages gives better overall ranking as compare to the ad-hoc document ranking approach.

Salton [15] discussed another idea to calculate the similarity of the passage to the query. They re-ranked and filtered out the documents that has a low passage

---

[1]   https://ciir.cs.umass.edu/downloads/WebAP/.

score associated with it. They included all the passages that have a higher score than its overall document score, and then used these scores to raise, or lower, the final document rank. In this way, the document that has a lower score to the document level score but a higher score at passage level for certain passages, will get a better ranking score in the end.

Different language modelling approaches at passage level and document level have been used in the past to improve the document ranking [10,16]. A similar approach has been used by Bendersky et al. [7], where they used the measure of the document homogeneity and heterogeneity to combine the document and passage similarity with the query to retrieve the best documents. To use the passage level evidence, their scoring method used the maximum query-similarity score that is assigned to any passage in the document ranking. As for their passage based language model, they used the simple unigram based standard to estimate the probabilities at passage and document level. Moreover, Krikon and Kurland [17,18] used a different language modeling approach where they tried to improve the initial ranking of the documents by considering the centrality of the documents and the passages by building their respective graphs. The edges denote the inter-term similarities and the centrality is computed using the page rank approach. They reported that their approach performed better than the normal maximum passage approach and some variation of interpolation score of maximum passage score with document score.

Due to the recent improvements in the learning based models, researcher are using neural networks for passage evidences that could improve the Ad-hoc Document retrieval. Ai and Croft [19] developed a passage based neural model that uses the evidences given from the passages for the document retrieval. They used a learning based approach to weights the passages of different sizes and granularities and did not adopt the usual single window for passage extraction. They introduced a fusion framework that aggregates the passage score based on the its document properties and relation with the query characteristics. They compared their results with the work done by Liu et al. and Ponte et al. [10,20] and showed that their neural passage model out performed the previous passage based retrieval models. Similarly, Galko et al. [21] used the neural network based approach to improve the passage retrieval for the Question Answering (QA) task in the Biomedical Domain. They used the weighted combination of word embedding terms by using word2vec [22] and measured the consine distances between the query terms and the passages. Finally they compare their results with the previous neural-net based models and reported improvements with their approach.

In previous research it has been identified that a particular search approach may vary considerably in it performance across different queries. There are many potential underlying problems that may cause this: variation in query quality (specific, unambiguous queries through to vague ambiguous ones), nature of the document set, aspects of the weighting scheme or preprocessing approaches. Rather than merely considering the mean average precision, it can be very informative to consider the performance of individual queries. Identifying difficult queries (those that the IR system produces low quality results) which could be the cause of decline MAP is an interesting problem. Mothe et al. [23] attempted to use the linguistic approaches in order to find the main reason of certain queries to become difficult. For each word, they computed the morphosyntactic category based on lexicons and a language model. They also calculated the semantic and syntactical features of each word by using wordnet and other analyzers. Looking at all these features they reported their correlation with the query difficulty. Similarly, He et al. [24] used a coherence-based approaches to measure the query difficulty. Their query based coherence scored illustrated the association with the average precision and they argued that this score can be used to anticipate the query difficulty.

3   Methodology

In traditional adhoc IR, a 'bag of words' model is adopted with no attention paid to word order or word position within a document. Weights are typically assigned to terms according to some heuristics, probability calculations or language model.

In this work, we view every document as being represented as passages or 'pseudo-documents' i.e. $d' = \{p_1, p_2, \ldots p_n\}$. We attempt to better estimate $sim(d, q)$ by estimating $sim(d', q)$. Different similarity functions are designed in a way that different characteristics of the passage level results can be used alone, or in combination with the document level results. We define $sim(d', q)$ as $f(sim(p_i, q), sim(d, q))$.

3.1   Similarity Functions

Following is a brief description of these similarity functions in which different characteristics were computed from the passage level evidence:

- {**SF1**} Max Passage: One way to compute the $sim(d', q)$ is to consider the similarity and ranking of the passage that has the highest similarity score to the query as a representative of the similarity of the document.

$$sim(d', q) = max(sim(p_i, q))$$

- {**SF2**} Sum of passages: It is similar to the max passage approach, but instead of taking only the top passage, the top k of the passages are taken and their similarity scores are combined by adding them together.

$$sim(d', q) = \sum_{i=1}^{k} [sim(p_i, q)]$$

- {**SF3**} Combination of document and passage similarity scores: In this case, the passage and document scores are combined and then the results are re-ranked based on the new score.

$$sim(d',q) = \alpha(max(sim(p_i,q))) + \beta(sim(d,q))$$

- {**SF4**} Inverse of rank: Rather than using the document or passage scores, the rank at which these passages are returned can also be used to find the similarity between the passages and the query. This can be calculated as follows:

$$sim(d',q) = (\frac{\sum_i \frac{1}{rankP_i}}{\#ofp_i}) \quad |p_i \in d'$$

- {**SF5**} Weighted Inverse of Rank: Another way to take the rank of these passages into account is to take the sum of the inverse ranks and pay less attention to lower ranks. Hence, the higher ranks will impact more on the results as compare to the lower values and will effect the overall ranking.

$$sim(d',q) = \sum_i (\frac{1}{rankP_i})^\alpha \quad |p_i \in d', \alpha > 1$$

3.2 Passage Boundaries

To run the experiments, all the documents and passages were first indexed in our IR system. We have used Solr 5.2.1[2] as a baseline system which is a high performance search server built using Apache Lucene Core. In this system, a vector space model is adopted with a weighting scheme based on the variation of tf-idf and Boolean model (BM) [25] is used.

We use two different test collections in the experiments. The WebAP test collection contains 6399 document and 150 queries in its dataset. We adopt overlapping windows for this collection and decompose each document into passages of length 250 words. This results in the creation of 140,000 passages for the WebAP collection. The second collection, the Ohsumed dataset, comprises 348,566 Medline abstracts as documents with 106 search queries. Given the relatively small document lengths, in defining passage boundaries, an overlapping window size of 30 words is used for this collection which creates a document set of passages of size 1.4 million pseudo-documents that gives 4–5 passages per document. We choose the half overlapping, fixed length window-size to index the documents, because these passages are more suitable computationally, convenient to use, and were proved to be very effective for document retrieval [5,10].

3.3 Evaluation

To evaluate the results and measure the quality of our approach, mean average precision (MAP) and precision@k are used as the evaluation metrics. The MAP

---

[2] http://lucene.apache.org/solr/5_2_1/index.html.

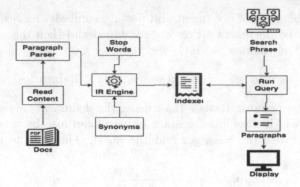

Fig. 1. Architectural diagram, extracted from [12].

value is used to give an overall view of the performance of the system with different similarity functions. Furthermore, precision@k was helpful in illustrating the behavior of the system with respect to correctly ranking relevant documents in the first k positions.

4   Experimental Setup

In this section, we present a brief explanation of the test collections we used, and also some detail of different parameters that we consider in our experiments. Lastly we will describe the brief overview of the evaluation measures that we used in the experiments.

Table 1. MAP(%) for WebAp and Ohsumed collection at k = 5 and k = 10, extracted from [12].

Similarity functions	MAP@5 (WebAP)	MAP@10 (WebAP)	MAP@5 (Ohsumed)	Map@10 (Ohsumed)
Document level (D)	9.52	18.60	2.97	4.75
Max passage (SF1)	9.43	18.56	3.23	4.96
Sum of passages (SF2)	9.42	18.54	3.19	**4.99**
Inverse of rank (SF4)	9.42	18.56	**3.27**	4.89
Weighted inverse of rank (SF5)	9.43	18.58	3.20	4.98
D+SF1	9.53	18.65	3.01	4.90
D+SF2	9.53	**18.67**	2.82	4.74
D+SF4	9.54	18.66	2.88	4.80
D+SF5	**9.55**	**18.67**	2.80	4.60

4.1   Test Collections

For our experiments we used the two different test collections that are freely available to use for experimental purposes.The following is a brief explanation of both datasets.

WebAp. Web Answer Passage (WebAP) is a test collection, which is obtained from the 2004 TREC Terabyte Track Gov2 collection. The dataset contains 6399 documents and 150 query topics and relevance judgment of top 50 documents per query topic. It is created mainly for the purpose of evaluating passage level retrieval results [26] but has been used in question answering (QA) task to retrieve sentence level answers as well [27,28]. The query topic section contains keyword based queries and the normal queries. We generated the results against both types and here we reported the performances that are based on the keyword based queries. On average, these results performed overall 2% better than the normal query ones across all similarity functions. Annotation at passage level (GOOD, FAIR, PERFECT etc.) is also included in this test collection that can be used to differentiate the different passages in term of their relevance to the query. The annotators found 8027 relevant answer passages to 82 TREC queries, which is 97 passages per query on average. From these annotated passages, 43% of them are perfect answers, 44% are excellent, 10% are good and the rest are fair answers. We have saved these passage annotations while indexing them in the system, but, we have not used them in our evaluation criteria. As the size of all the documents are fairly large compare to the other test collections we came across, therefore, we divided passages using overlapping window based approach of size 250 words.

Ohsumed. The Ohsumed collection consists of titles and abstracts from 270 Medline reference medical journals. It contains 348,566 articles along with 106 search queries. In total, there are 16,140 query-documents pairs upon which the relevance judgments were made. These relevance judgments are divided in three categories i.e. definitely relevant, possibly relevant, or not relevant. For experiments and evaluation, all the documents that are judged here as either possibly or definitely relevant were considered as relevant. Furthermore, only the documents to which the abstracts are available, were index and used for the retrieval task. Therefore, the experiments were conducted on the remaining set of 233,445 documents from the Ohsumed test collection. Also, to calculate the overall performance we considered only those queries, which had any relevant document(s) listed in the judgment file. Out of 106 queries in total, 97 of them were found to have relevant document(s) associated with it. This document collection is fairly large in terms document size but shorter in terms of document length as compare to the WebAP test collection. It does not include any annotation at passage level.

4.2   Assumptions and Experimental Parameters

For our experiments we used Solr-5.2.1 which is built on top of LUCENE[3]. Solr provided the functionality of removing the stop-words at indexing time. As shown in Fig. 1, we used that functionality to remove the stop words[4] from both collections. We have seen that the ranking after removing the stop-words is improved.

For different similarity measure functions, we used different parameters. For sum of passages (SF2) and inverse rank (SF4) function, we set the k value to be equal to 5 and the results were normalized having received the final score. Similarly, we gave twice the boost to the passage level score as compared to the document level score while combining the results together i.e $\alpha = 1, \beta = 2$. Giving the higher boost to passage level gives better performance to the inverse ranking functions, whereas higher boost at document level improved results for Max passage and Sum of passage results.

4.3   Evaluation Measures

In IR, different evaluation measures are used to measure how well the system is performing to satisfy the user's need in returning the relevant documents to a given query. In our case, to measure the quality and performance of our approach, we used Mean Average Precision (MAP) and precision@k. MAP value is used to give an overall performance overview of the system and different similarity functions across both test collections. On the other hand, precision@k was helpful in illustrating the user's experience and the behavior of relevant documents returned in terms of their ranking frequency with the different threshold values. We evaluated the precision value for top 40 unique documents, both at passage level and at document level.

5   Results

In this section we present the experimental results to show the performance of the different similarity functions at passage level and document level for both the WebAP and Ohsumed datasets.

In Fig. 2(a) and (b), a bar chart is used to compare the document-level score with the different similarity functions of passage level scores for WebAP and Ohsumed test collections.

Using the WebAP collection, the results show that combining the document level score with passage level score (SF3), gives an improvement in performance. The best results were found when the document level score was combined with the inverse rank functions (SF4, SF5) of the passage level ranking. The results show that, considering the rank of the documents instead of the similarity score gives better performance when document ranking is combined with the passage

---

[3] http://lucene.apache.org/.

[4] http://www.ranks.nl/stopwords.

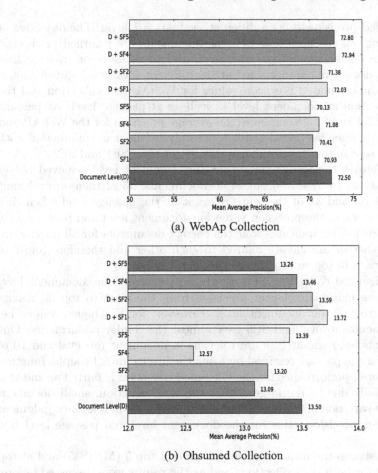

(a) WebAp Collection

(b) Ohsumed Collection

Fig. 2. Mean average precision for different similarity functions, extracted from [12].

level evidence. For the sum of passages (SF2) approach, only the top 5 (i.e. $k=5$) results were considered in calculating the query similarity score.

In contrast to WebAP, for the Oushmed collection the combination of document score with the max passage score performed better than the combination of inverse passage rank with document score. However, for functions not including the document level similarity, inverse rank by alpha (SF5) performed better than the other passage level similarity functions and give approximately similar performance in comparison to document level. Furthermore, the sum of passages (SF2) performed better here than the Max passage (SF1) score. The best results were observed for $k=2$. We have observed that the MAP values decrease as the k value increases, hence max passage similarity function performs better than the sum of passages function for WebAP test collection. However, in Ohsumed SF2 performed better than SF1 for $k=\{2,3,4\}$.

We also used precision@k as a different evaluation metric. The objective of this experiment was to check how well the documents are returned at the top k ranks at the document and passage level, and to measure on average how many relevant documents are returned at the different k values. Figure 3(a) and (b) illustrate the calculated precision values for WebAP test collection and the Ohsumed collection at document level as well as at passage level. At passage level we used SF4 and SF5 to measure the average precision for the WebAP and the Ohsumed, as when we considered it separately (without in conjunction with the document score), their performance was better than SF1 and SF2.

For the WebAP, the results show that the document level achieved better $p@k$ in comparison to SF4, and out of 40 documents, 33 of them are relevant in document level and 31 of them are relevant at the passage level when SF4 was used. On average, the precision value for document level and passage level was 90% and 86%. This indicates that the correct documents for all queries are clustered together or are closely related to each other and therefore, most of them are returned in top results, hence the high results.

For the Ohsumed collection, SF5 clearly outperformed the document level results and gave marginally better precision from the start to top 20 results (p@20) compared to the document level. However, for the higher values i.e. $k > 20$, the document level and SF5 gave almost the similar performance. Out of 40 documents approximately 9 are relevant in document retrieval and 10 of them are relevant in passage retrieval by using the inverse rank by alpha function (SF5). The overall performance for the Ohsumed collection is fairly low and this could be partially due to the large size of the test collection, small document length and the variation of relevant document information in relevance judgment file. On average, precision value for the document level and passage level was 24% and 25%.

Table 1 illustrates the mean average precision at top 5 (MAP@5) and at top 10 (MAP@10) for both test collections and as the results were discussed before, in the WebAP the combination of document level with passage level scores with different similarity functions give better results. The best results were obtained when the document score is combined with SF5. Whereas, for the Ohsumed, the functions that do not involve combining passage level and document level evidence gives better performance in both cases.

To get a better understanding on the statistical significance of the differences shown in the Table 1 for the test collections, we used the Student's t-test on paired samples for the top 50 MAP values with the difference of 5 (i.e. top 5, top 10, top 15, till top 50 etc). For the WebAP, we compared the document level results with the D+SF5 similarity function as it gave an overall better performance on the top results. The average MAP difference between both experiments was 0.18 with the standard deviation of 0.09 and the calculated p-value was 0.00024. Therefore, the performance shown by D+SF5 is statistically significant as compared to the normal document level results. Similarly, we performed the same t-test on the Ohsumed collection by comparing the document level results with D+SF4 due to its advantage over the performance on normal document

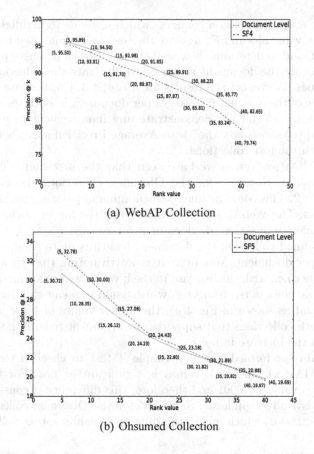

(a) WebAP Collection

(b) Ohsumed Collection

Fig. 3. Precision at K for different test collections, extracted from [12].

level results. For the Ohsumed, the average difference and standard deviation were 0.07 and 0.13 with the p-value of 0.069. Hence, for the Ohsumed, the results were not improved very significantly.

It is also seen that the value of α and β effects the overall results when the document level is combined with the passage level evidence (SF3). For both collections, giving the higher boost to passage level i.e. $\alpha <= \beta$, gave a better performance for the inverse ranking functions, whereas a higher boost at document level i.e. $\alpha > \beta$ improves the results for SF1 and SF2. We chose $\alpha = 1$ and $\beta = 2$ for the results shown in this paper because it gives an overall better performance for all the passage level similarity functions when combined with the document score.

5.1 Further Analysis of SF2

In the previous section, we used $k = 2$ to report the results for SF2 using the WebAp and the Oshumed test collection. We have seen that by varying the value of k, the average precision changes, which leads us to highlight the effect of changing the value of k in SF2 against the test collections used in this paper. To understand, and to determine how well the addition of passages performed in terms of improving the document ranking, we illustrate the behavior of SF2 at different k values. We report the results for $k = 1, 2, 3, 4, 5$, because considering the average size of the number of passages per document in both test collections, bigger k values i.e >5 did not demonstrate any improvement in performance. Figure 4(a) and (b) shows how the Mean Average Precision changes for different k values in both the test collections.

For the WebAP collection we have seen that the precision decreases with increasing k values. However, for the Ohsumed collections the best value is obtained for k = 2. This could be due to the number of passages per document in both collections. The WebAp has documents with the bigger document length, having more than 10 passages per document on average.

In the Ohsumed collection the document length is quite small with around 3–4 passages per document. Moreover, it is worth noting that by adding more passages together i.e., with the increase in the k value, we are losing the accuracy and adding more noise in the result set, which could be a cause of decrease in the MAP value. And as shown in Fig. 4(a), the higher values of k are giving lower precision in both collections that supports our argument regarding the decrease in efficacy and the increase in noise.

We have also performed the one sample T-test to check if the difference between the MAP at various k values is significant or not. For the WebAp collection, the p value <0.0001 and therefore, this difference is considered to be extremely statistically significant. Similarly, for the Ohsumed collection, the p values is also <0.0001, which makes the difference significant as well.

5.2 Query Difficulty

Oftentimes, information retrieval systems exhibit a substantial variance in accuracy across a set of queries. Systems may display a similar MAP, but quite a considerable variance in performance when considered in a query-by-query manner. A large body of work exists in predicting query performance; i.e. given a particular query, can one predict the expected MAP from a particular IR system? A range of techniques have been considered; these can be broadly categorised into two main categories: pre-retrieval and post-retrieval. Pre-retrieval techniques consider examining the query and looking at features of the query and the query term; these include linguistic approaches [23] and statistical approaches [24,29]. Post-retrieval, on the other hand, examines features of the returned answer and attempts to gauge the quality of the answer as a measure of the query difficulty. Researched approached include consider the distribution of similarity scores [30] and cohesion of the answer set [31].

In this work, we have explored a number of passage level approaches and demonstrated in some cases, a modest, yet significant improvement over the baseline adopting a classical document-level approach. However, it is not known if this improvement is due to a large number of slight improvements over a large range of queries or due to larger improvements over a small set of queries.

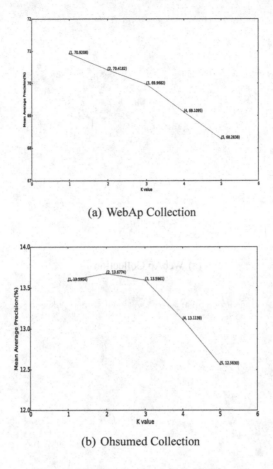

(a) WebAp Collection

(b) Ohsumed Collection

Fig. 4. SF2 results for top 5 K values.

Moreover, it is worth exploring if the best performing passage level approaches actually damage the performance for certain queries.

In this section, we present a query by query overview of the performance of the baseline and the best passage level ranking function in both the collections. In the WebAP collection, the SF4 approach performed best and in the Ohsumed collection, the SF5 approach gave the better performance. We use these similarity functions to compare their impact on all the queries in their respective test collections. We identify the queries for which there is a substantial change in performance between the two and attempt to provide an explanation for this change.

Figure 5(a) and (b) illustrate the average precision across all queries. As shown in Fig. 2(a) and (b), we compare the baseline results with the similarity functions that was giving the better performance at passage level i.e. SF4 in the WebAp and the SF5 for the Ohsumed collection. In the WebAP collection, we saw that for the difficult queries (queries which performed worst), the document

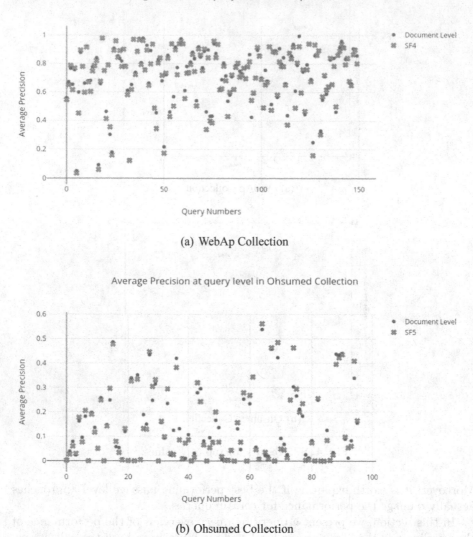

(a) WebAp Collection

(b) Ohsumed Collection

Fig. 5. Average precision of each query for different test collections.

level was giving better performance than the SF4 approach. We also measured the query length of bottom 10 queries against document level and SF4 and didn't find any significant difference between them. On average the query length of the document level results and SF4 was 3.3 and 3.1 words per query. Moreover, for the WebAP collection, we have seen that the SF4 performed better because of the substantial improvements in a small subset of the queries (easy and difficult ones) and not due to large number of slight improvements over a set of queries. Of the 150 queries in total, in SF4 performed better than the baseline in 38 of them.

It appears that, for the passage level technique (SF4), the worst-performing queries are damaged slightly and the those that perform well are boosted. For the poorly performing queries, the IR system has difficulty distinguishing the relevant from non-relevant documents (similar term frequency distributions). In incorporating passage level evidence we are possibly including evidence from weakly related passages. Rather than improving performance, we are merely hampering performance by incorporating information that does not improve our ability to make a useful similarity estimate.

For the Ohsumed collection, due to very low values of average precision, we considered the bottom 20 queries in order to get the better understanding of how well the difficult queries are performing against the document level and SF5. For difficult queries, SF5 gave better performance against the document level results and the average number of words per query noted for SF5 and document level was 6.5 and 6.4 words. Though the difference between them is not significant but SF5 slightly boosted the results for worst-performing queries. Among the total 96 queries in the Ohsumed collection, SF5 gave better accuracy for the 42 queries (including 25 difficult queries) compare to the document level results. Hence, we can say that the overall performance is increased due the small improvements in the large set of difficult queries.

An overall better approach would be to attempt to identify, in advance, which queries are likely to be improved by the passage level augmentation. To this end, we attempt to identify differences between those queries that are benefited by the passage level and those whose performance is damaged.

6   Conclusions and Future Work

In this paper, the main focus of our work was to see how effectively the passage level evidence affected the document retrieval. We explored several similarity measures that can be used to improve the document ranking. Though we saw that the rank of a passage is an effective measure, however the passage level evidence on its own is not ample to improve the document ranking significantly for the selected test collections. In addition to that, we undertook the detailed analysis of SF2 to understand its behavior on different k values. SF2 performed best when the value of k is smaller. For the WebAP collection, we notice that the precision decreases with increasing k values. However, for the Ohsumed collection, the best value is obtained for k = 2. Moreover, we investigated the idea of query difficulty with regards to its impact on our rank-based passage functions. For the WebAp, we compared the baseline results with SF4, and SF5 was used in the Ohsumed collection due to its higher performance. Final results reveal that for the passage level technique, the difficult queries are damaged slightly and the those that perform well are boosted for the WebAp collection. However, for the Ohsumed collection, SF5 promoted the performance of the worst-performing queries. Given the evidence that passage level evidence can improve the performance and given the results to show that the level of improvement often depends on the query difficulty, future work will explore other passage level evidence and also query difficulty estimation approaches to attempt to develop a more nuanced approached to ranking using passage level evidence in scenarios where the difficulty of the query can be estimated.

Acknowledgements. This work is supported by the Irish Research Council Employment Based Programme.

References

1. Robertson, S., Zaragoza, H., et al.: The probabilistic relevance framework: Bm25 and beyond. Found. Trends ® Inf. Retr. **3**, 333–389 (2009)
2. Roberts, I., Gaizauskas, R.: Evaluating passage retrieval approaches for question answering. In: McDonald, S., Tait, J. (eds.) ECIR 2004. LNCS, vol. 2997, pp. 72–84. Springer, Heidelberg (2004). https://doi.org/10.1007/978-3-540-24752-4_6
3. Sarwar, G., O'Riordan, C., Newell, J.: Passage level evidence for effective document level retrieval. In: Proceedings of the 9th International Joint Conference on Knowledge Discovery, Knowledge Engineering and Knowledge Management, pp. 83–90 (2017)
4. Hersh, W., Buckley, C., Leone, T., Hickam, D.: OHSUMED: an interactive retrieval evaluation and new large test collection for research. In: Croft, B.W., van Rijsbergen, C.J. (eds.) SIGIR 1994, pp. 192–201. Springer, London (1994). https://doi.org/10.1007/978-1-4471-2099-5_20
5. Callan, J.P.: Passage-level evidence in document retrieval. In: Croft, B.W., van Rijsbergen, C.J. (eds.) SIGIR 1994, pp. 302–310. Springer, London (1994). https://doi.org/10.1007/978-1-4471-2099-5_31
6. Hearst, M.A.: Texttiling: segmenting text into multi-paragraph subtopic passages. Comput. Linguist. **23**, 33–64 (1997)
7. Bendersky, M., Kurland, O.: Utilizing passage-based language models for document retrieval. In: Macdonald, C., Ounis, I., Plachouras, V., Ruthven, I., White, R.W. (eds.) ECIR 2008. LNCS, vol. 4956, pp. 162–174. Springer, Heidelberg (2008). https://doi.org/10.1007/978-3-540-78646-7_17
8. Kaszkiel, M., Zobel, J.: Effective ranking with arbitrary passages. J. Am. Soc. Inf. Sci. Technol. **52**, 344–364 (2001)
9. Clarke, C.L., Cormack, G.V., Lynam, T.R., Terra, E.L.: Question answering by passage selection. In: Strzalkowski, T., Harabagiu, S.M. (eds.) Advances in Open Domain Question Answering, pp. 259–283. Springer, Dordrecht (2008). https://doi.org/10.1007/978-1-4020-4746-6_8
10. Liu, X., Croft, W.B.: Passage retrieval based on language models. In: Proceedings of the Eleventh International Conference on Information and Knowledge Management, pp. 375–382. ACM (2002)
11. Jong, M.H., Ri, C.H., Choe, H.C., Hwang, C.J.: A method of passage-based document retrieval in question answering system. arXiv preprint arXiv:1512.05437 (2015)
12. Sarwar, G., O'Riordan, C., Newell, J.: Passage level evidence for effective document level retrieval (2017)
13. Buckley, C., Salton, G., Allan, J., Singhal, A.: Automatic query expansion using smart: TREC 3. NIST Special Publication SP, p. 69 (1995)
14. Hearst, M.A., Plaunt, C.: Subtopic structuring for full-length document access. In: Proceedings of the 16th Annual International ACM SIGIR Conference on Research and Development in Information Retrieval, pp. 59–68. ACM (1993)

15. Salton, G., Allan, J., Buckley, C.: Approaches to passage retrieval in full text information systems. In: Proceedings of the 16th Annual International ACM SIGIR Conference on Research and Development in Information Retrieval, pp. 49–58. ACM (1993)
16. Lavrenko, V., Croft, W.B.: Relevance based language models. In: Proceedings of the 24th Annual International ACM SIGIR Conference on Research and development in Information Retrieval, pp. 120–127. ACM (2001)
17. Krikon, E., Kurland, O., Bendersky, M.: Utilizing inter-passage and inter-document similarities for reranking search results. ACM Trans. Inf.Syst. (TOIS) **29**, 3 (2010)
18. Bendersky, M., Kurland, O.: Re-ranking search results using document-passage graphs. In: Proceedings of the 31st Annual International ACM SIGIR Conference on Research and Development in Information Retrieval, pp. 853–854. ACM (2008)
19. Ai, Q., O'Connor, B., Croft, W.B.: A neural passage model for ad-hoc document retrieval. In: Pasi, G., Piwowarski, B., Azzopardi, L., Hanbury, A. (eds.) ECIR 2018. LNCS, vol. 10772, pp. 537–543. Springer, Cham (2018). https://doi.org/10.1007/978-3-319-76941-7_41
20. Ponte, J.M., Croft, W.B.: A language modeling approach to information retrieval. In: Proceedings of the 21st Annual International ACM SIGIR Conference on Research and Development in Information Retrieval, pp. 275–281. ACM (1998)
21. Galkó, F., Eickhoff, C.: Biomedical question answering via weighted neural network passage retrieval. arXiv preprint arXiv:1801.02832 (2018)
22. Mikolov, T., Sutskever, I., Chen, K., Corrado, G.S., Dean, J.: Distributed representations of words and phrases and their compositionality. In: Advances in Neural Information Processing Systems, pp. 3111–3119 (2013)
23. Mothe, J., Tanguy, L.: Linguistic features to predict query difficulty
24. He, B., Ounis, I.: Inferring query performance using pre-retrieval predictors. In: Apostolico, A., Melucci, M. (eds.) SPIRE 2004. LNCS, vol. 3246, pp. 43–54. Springer, Heidelberg (2004). https://doi.org/10.1007/978-3-540-30213-1_5
25. Lashkari, A.H., Mahdavi, F., Ghomi, V.: A boolean model in information retrieval for search engines. In: International Conference on Information Management and Engineering, ICIME 2009, pp. 385–389. IEEE (2009)
26. Keikha, M., Park, J.H., Croft, W.B., Sanderson, M.: Retrieving passages and finding answers. In: Proceedings of the 2014 Australasian Document Computing Symposium, p. 81. ACM (2014)
27. Chen, R.C., Spina, D., Croft, W.B., Sanderson, M., Scholer, F.: Harnessing semantics for answer sentence retrieval. In: Proceedings of the Eighth Workshop on Exploiting Semantic Annotations in Information Retrieval, pp. 21–27. ACM (2015)
28. Yang, L., et al.: Beyond factoid QA: effective methods for non-factoid answer sentence retrieval. In: Ferro, N., et al. (eds.) ECIR 2016. LNCS, vol. 9626, pp. 115–128. Springer, Cham (2016). https://doi.org/10.1007/978-3-319-30671-1_9
29. He, J., Larson, M., de Rijke, M.: Using coherence-based measures to predict query difficulty. In: Macdonald, C., Ounis, I., Plachouras, V., Ruthven, I., White, R.W. (eds.) ECIR 2008. LNCS, vol. 4956, pp. 689–694. Springer, Heidelberg (2008). https://doi.org/10.1007/978-3-540-78646-7_80
30. Cummins, R., Jose, J., O'Riordan, C.: Improved query performance prediction using standard deviation. In: Proceedings of the 34th International ACM SIGIR Conference on Research and Development in Information Retrieval, SIGIR 2011, pp. 1089–1090. ACM, New York (2011)
31. Vinay, V., Cox, I.J., Milic-Frayling, N., Wood, K.: On ranking the effectiveness of searches. In: Proceedings of the 29th Annual International ACM SIGIR Conference on Research and Development in Information Retrieval, SIGIR 2006, pp. 398–404. ACM, New York (2006)

Robust Single-Document Summarizations and a Semantic Measurement of Quality

Liqun Shao$^{(\boxtimes)}$, Hao Zhang$^{(\boxtimes)}$, and Jie Wang$^{(\boxtimes)}$

Department of Computer Science, University of Massachusetts, Lowell, MA, USA
{Liqun_Shao,Hao_Zhang}@student.uml.edu, wang@cs.uml.edu

Abstract. The goal of this paper is to generate an effective summary for a given document with specific realtime requirements. We use the softplus function to enhance keyword rankings to favor important sentences, based on which we present a number of extractive summarization algorithms using various keyword extraction and topic clustering methods. We show that our algorithms not only meet the realtime requirements but also yield the best ROUGE scores on DUC-02 over all previously-known algorithms. We also evaluate our summarization methods over the SummBank dataset and other datasets to ensure that our methods are robust. Experiments show that summaries generated by our methods achieve higher or about the same ROUGE scores than extractive summaries generated by human evaluators. Moreover, we define a semantic measure based on word-embedding using Word Mover's Distance to evaluate the quality of summaries without human-generated benchmarks. We show that for our algorithms, the orderings of the ROUGE scores and the scores under the new measure are highly comparable, suggesting that this new measure may serve as a viable alternative for measuring the quality of a summary.

Keywords: Single-document summarizations · Keyword ranking · Topic clustering · Word embedding · SoftPlus function · Semantic similarity · Summarization evaluation · Realtime

1 Introduction

Text summarization algorithms have been studied intensively and extensively. An effective summary must convey the central meanings of the original document within a specific length boundary and must be readable. The common approach of unsupervised summarization algorithms extracts sentences based on importance rankings (e.g., see [8,14,17,24,29]), where a keyword may also be a phrase. A sentence with a larger number of keywords of higher ranking scores is considered more important for extraction. Supervised algorithms include CNN and RNN models for generating extractive and abstractive summaries (e.g., see [5,22,30]).

Our task is to construct a general-purpose text-automation tool to produce, among other things, an effective summary for a given document to meet the following realtime requirements for various text automation applications:

© Springer Nature Switzerland AG 2019
A. Fred et al. (Eds.): IC3K 2017, CCIS 976, pp. 118–138, 2019.
https://doi.org/10.1007/978-3-030-15640-4_7

1. Generate a summary instantly for a document of up to 2,000 words;
2. Generate a summary under 1 s for a document of around 5,000 words;
3. Generate a summary under 3 s for a very long document of around 10,000 words.

Moreover, we need to deal with documents of arbitrary topics without knowing what the topics will be. After investigating all existing summarization algorithms, we conclude that unsupervised single-document extractive summarization algorithms would be the best approach to meeting our requirements.

In particular, we use topic clusterings to obtain a strong and balanced topic coverage in the summary when extracting key sentences. We first determine which topic a sentence belongs to, and then extract key sentences to cover as many topics as possible within the given length boundary.

Human judgement is the best evaluation of the quality of a summarization algorithm. It is a standard practice to run an algorithm over DUC data and compute the ROUGE scores on a set of DUC benchmarks, which are human-generated summaries for articles of a moderate size. DUC-02 [8], in particular, is a small set of benchmarks for single-document abstractive summarizations. When dealing with a large number of documents of unknown topics and various sizes, human generated benchmarks may not be available and human judgement may be impractical, and so we would like to have an alternative mechanism to measure summarization quality without human involvement. Ideally, this mechanism should preserve the same ordering as ROUGE over DUC data; namely, if S_1 and S_2 are two summaries of the same DUC document produced by two algorithms, and the ROUGE score of S_1 is higher than that of S_2, then it should also be the case under the new measure.

Louis and Nenkova [15] devised an unsupervised method to evaluate summarization without human models using common similarity measures of Kullback-Leibler divergence, Jensen-Shannon divergence, and cosine similarity. These measures, as well as the information-theoretic similarity measure [1], are meant to measure lexical similarities, which are unsuitable for measuring semantic similarities.

Word embeddings such as Word2Vec can be used to fill this void. In particular, we devise a new measure called WESM (Word-Embedding Similarity Measure) based on Word Mover's Distance (WMD) [13] to measure word-embedding similarity of the summary and the original document. WESM is meant to evaluate summaries for new datasets when no human-generated benchmarks are available. WESM has an advantage that it can measure semantic similarities of documents. We show that WESM correlates well with ROUGE on DUC-02. Thus, we may use WESM as an alternative summarization evaluation method when benchmarks are unavailable.

The major contributions of this paper are summarized below:

1. We present a number of extractive summarization algorithms using topic clustering methods and enhanced keyword rankings using the softplus function, and show that they meet the imposed realtime requirements and outperform

all the previously-known summarization algorithms under the ROUGE measures over DUC-02.
2. We demonstrate the robustness of our summarization algorithms by evaluating them over various datasets. In particular, we show that, using the SummBank dataset, the summaries generated by our methods achieve higher ROUGE scores than summaries extracted by human evaluators presented in SummBank.
3. We propose a new mechanism WESM as an alternative measurement of summary quality when human-generated benchmarks are unavailable.

The rest of the paper is organized as follows: We survey in Sect. 2 unsupervised single-document summarization algorithms. We present in Sect. 3 the details of our summarization algorithms and describe WESM in Sect. 4. We report the results of extensive experiments in Sect. 5 and conclude the paper in Sect. 6.

2   Early Work

Early work on single-topic summarizations can be described in the following three categories: keyword extractions, coverage and diversity optimizations, and topic clusterings.

2.1   Keyword Extractions

To identify keywords in a document over a corpus of documents, the measure of term-frequency-inverse-document-frequency (TF-IDF) [31] is often used. When document corpora are unavailable, the measure of word co-occurrences (WCO) can produce a comparable performance to TF-IDF over a large corpus of documents [16]. The methods of TextRank [17] and RAKE (Rapid Automatic Keyword Extraction) [29] further refine the WCO method from different perspectives, which are also sufficiently fast to become candidates for meeting the real-time requirements.

TextRank computes the rank of a word in an undirected, weighted word-graph using a slightly modified PageRank algorithm [4]. To construct a word-graph for a given document, first remove stop words and represent each remaining word as a node, then link two words if they both appear in a sliding window of a small size. Finally, assign the number of co-occurrences of the endpoints of an edge as a weight to the edge.

RAKE first removes stop words using a stoplist, and then generates words (including phrases) using a set of word delimiters and a set of phrase delimiters. For each remaining word w, the degree of w is the frequency of w plus the number of co-occurrences of consecutive word pairs ww' and $w''w$ in the document, where w' and w'' are remaining words. The score of w is the degree of w divided by the frequency of w. We note that the quality of RAKE also depends on a properly-chosen stoplist, which is language dependent.

2.2   Coverage and Diversity Optimization

The general framework of selecting sentences gives rise to optimization problems with objective functions being monotone submodular [14] to promote coverage and diversity. Among them is an objective function in the form of $L(S) + \lambda R(S)$ with a summary S and a coefficient $\lambda \geq 0$, where $L(S)$ measures the coverage of the summary and $R(S)$ rewards diversity. We use SubmodularF to denote the algorithm computing this objective function. SubmodularF uses TF-IDF values of words in sentences to compute the cosine similarity of two sentences. While it is NP-hard to maximize a submodular objective function subject to a summary length constraint, the submodularity allows a greedy approximation with a proven approximation ratio of $1 - 1/\sqrt{e}$.

SubmodularF needs labeled data to train the parameters in the objective function to achieve a better summary and it is intended to work on multiple-document summarizations. While it is possible to work on a single document without a corpus, we note that the greedy algorithm has at least a quadratic-time complexity and it produces a summary with low ROUGE scores over DUC-02 (see Sect. 2.4), and so it would not be a good candidate to meet our needs. This also applies to a generalized objective function consisting of a submodular component and a non-submodular component [7].

2.3   Topic Clusterings

TextTiling [11] and LDA (Latent Dirichlet Allocation) [2] represent two different unsupervised approaches to topic clusterings for a given document. TextTiling represents a topic as a set of consecutive paragraphs in the document. It merges adjacent paragraphs that belong to the same topic. TextTiling identifies major topic-shifts based on patterns of lexical co-occurrences and distributions. LDA computes for each word a distribution under a pre-determined number of topics. LDA is a computation-heavy algorithm that incurs a runtime too high to meet our realtime requirements. TextTiling has a time complexity of almost being linear, which meets the requirements of efficiency.

2.4   Other Algorithms

Following the general framework of selecting sentences to meet the requirements of topic coverage and diversity, a number of unsupervised single-document summarization algorithms have been devised. The most notable is CP_3 [23], which produces the best ROUGE-1 (R-1), ROUGE-2 (R-2), and ROUGE-SU4 (R-SU4) scores on DUC-02 among all early algorithms, including Lead [24], DUC-02 Best, TextRank, LREG [5], Mead [26], ILP_{phrase} [36], URANK [34], UniformLink [35], Egraph + Coherence [25], Tgraph + Coherence (Topical Coherence for Graph-based Extractive Summarization) [24], NN-SE [5], and SubmodularF.

CP_3 maximizes importance, non-redundancy, and pattern-based coherence of sentences to generate a coherent summary using ILP. It computes the ranks of selected sentences for the summary by the Hubs and Authorities algorithm

(HITS) [12], and ensures that each selected sentence has unique information. It then uses mined patterns to extract sentences if the connectivity among nodes in the projection graph matches the connectivity among nodes in a coherence pattern. Because of space limitation, we omit the descriptions of the other algorithms.

Table 1 shows the comparison results, where R-1 represents ROUGE-1, R-2 represents ROUGE-2, and R-SU4 represents ROUGE-SU4. Note that the results for SubmodularF is obtained using the best parameters trained on DUC-03 [14], and for some of the algorithms, their R-SU4 scores are missing because the corresponding papers did not present R-SU4 results. We can see that CP_3 offers the best ROUGE scores over all previous algorithms. Thus, to demonstrate the effectiveness of our algorithms, we will compare our algorithms with only CP_3 over DUC-02.

Table 1. ROUGE scores (%) on DUC-02 data based from [33].

Methods	R-1	R-2	R-SU4
Lead	45.9	18.0	20.1
DUC 2002 best	48.0	22.8	
TextRank	47.0	19.5	21.7
LREG	43.8	20.7	
Mead	44.5	20.0	21.0
ILP_{phrase}	45.4	21.3	
URANK	48.5	21.5	
UniformLink	47.1	20.1	
Egraph + Coh.	48.5	23.0	25.3
Tgraph + Coh.	48.1	24.3	24.2
NN-SE	47.4	23.0	
SubmodularF	39.6	16.9	17.8
CP_3	**49.0**	**24.7**	**25.8**

Solving ILP, however, is time consuming even on documents of a moderate size, for ILP is NP-hard. Thus, CP_3 does not meet the requirements of time efficiency. We will need to investigate new methods.

3 Our Summarization Methods

We use TextRank and RAKE to obtain initial ranking scores of keywords, and use the softplus function [10]

$$sp(x) = \ln(1 + e^x) \tag{1}$$

to enhance keyword rankings to favor sentences that are more important.

3.1   Softplus Ranking

Assume that after filtering, a sentence s consists of k keywords $w_1, \cdots, w_k$, and w_i has a ranking score r_i produced by TextRank or RAKE. Following Shao and Wang [32], we use their central sentence extraction algorithm for ranking sentences by importance as Rank(s). We can rank s using one of the following two methods:

$$Rank(s) = \sum_{i=1}^{k} r_i \qquad (2)$$

$$Rank_{sp}(s) = \sum_{i=1}^{k} sp(r_i) \qquad (3)$$

Let DTRank (Direct TextRank) and ETRank (Enhanced TextRank) denote the methods of ranking sentences using, respectively, Rank(s) and Rank$_{sp}$(s) over TextRank keyword rankings, and DRAKE (Direct RAKE) and ERAKE (Enhanced RAKE) to denote the methods of ranking sentences using, respectively, Rank(s) and Rank$_{sp}$(s) over RAKE keyword rankings.

The softplus function is helpful because when x is a small positive number, $sp(x)$ increases the value of x significantly (see Fig. 1) and when x is large, $sp(x)$ is about the same as x, indicating that when x is large, the softplus function has little impact on the score. This is better than 2^x used in [32]. In particular, given two sentences s_1 and s_2, suppose that s_1 has a few keywords with high rankings and the rest of the keywords with low rankings, while s_2 has medium rankings for almost all the keywords. In this case, we would consider s_1 more important than s_2. However, we may end up with Rank(s_1) < Rank(s_2). To illustrate this using a numerical example, assume that s_1 and s_2 each consists of 5 keywords, with original scores (sc) and softplus scores (sp) given in the following Table 2.

Table 2. Numerical examples with given sc and sp scores based from [33].

s_1	w_{11}	w_{12}	w_{13}	w_{14}	w_{15}	Rank
sc	2.6	2.2	2.1	0.3	0.2	7.4
sp	2.67	2.31	2.22	0.85	0.80	**8.84**
s_2	w_{21}	w_{22}	w_{23}	w_{24}	w_{25}	
sc	1.6	1.5	1.5	1.5	1.4	**7.5**
sp	1.78	1.70	1.70	1.70	1.62	8.51

Sentence s_1 is more important than s_2 because it contains three keywords of much higher ranking scores than those of s_2. However, s_2 will be selected without using softplus. After using softplus, s_1 is selected as it should be.

For a real-life example, consider the following two sentences from an article in DUC-02:

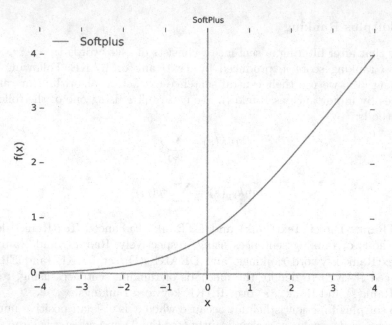

Fig. 1. Softplus function $\ln(1 + e^x)$ extracted from [33].

s_1: Hurricane Gilbert swept toward Jamaica yesterday with 100-mile-an-hour winds, and officials issued warnings to residents on the southern coasts of the Dominican Republic, Haiti and Cuba.

s_2: Forecasters said the hurricane was gaining strength as it passed over the ocean and would dump heavy rain on the Dominican Republic and Haiti as it moved south of Hispaniola, the Caribbean island they share, and headed west.

We consider s_1 more important as it specifies the name, strength, and direction of the hurricane, the places affected, and the official warnings. Using TextRank to compute keyword scores, we have $\mathrm{Rank}(s_1) = 1.538 < \mathrm{Rank}(s_2) = 1.603$, which returns a less important sentence s_2. After computing softplus, we have $\mathrm{Rank}_{sp}(s_1) = 8.430 > \mathrm{Rank}_{sp}(s_2) = 7.773$; the more important sentence s_1 is selected.

Note that not any exponential function would do the trick. What we want is a function to return roughly the same value as the input when the input is large, and a significantly larger value than the input when the input is much less than 1. The softplus function meets this requirement.

3.2   Topic Clustering Schemes

We consider four topic clustering schemes: TCS, TCP, TCTT, and TCLDA.

1. TCS selects sentences without checking topics.
2. TCP treats each paragraph as a separate topic.
3. TCTT partitions a document into a set of multi-paragraph segments using TextTiling.

4. TCLDA computes a topic distribution for each word using LDA. We set the number of topics from 5 to 8 depending on the length of the document. Assume that a document contains K topics ($5 \leq K \leq 8$) and the topic j consists of k_j words $w_{1j}, \cdots, w_{k_j,j}$, where $1 \leq j \leq K$ and w_{ij} has a probability $p_{ij} > 0$. For a document with n sentences $s_1, \cdots, s_n$, we use the following maximization to determine which topic t_z the sentence s_z belongs to ($1 \leq t \leq K$):

$$t_z = \operatorname*{argmax}_{1 \leq j \leq k} \left(\prod_{i:w_{ij} \in s_z} p_{ij} \right) \tag{4}$$

3.3   Summarization Algorithms

The length of a summary may be specified by users, either as a number of words or as a percentage of the number of characters of the original document. By a "30% summary" we mean that the number of characters of the summary does not exceed 30% of that of the original document.

Let L be the summary length (the total number of characters) specified by the user and S a summary. If S consist of m sentences $s_1, \cdots, s_m$, and the number of characters of s_i is ℓ_i, then the following inequality must hold:

$$\sum_{i=1}^{m} \ell_i \leq L.$$

Table 3. Description of all the Algorithms with different sentence-ranking (S-R) and topic-clustering (T-C) schemes based from [33].

Methods	S-R	T-C
ESTRank	ETRank	TCS
EPTRank	ETRank	TCP
ET3Rank	ETRank	TCTT
ELDATRank	ETRank	TCLDA
ESRAKE	ERAKE	TCS
EPRAKE	ERAKE	TCP
ET2RAKE	ERAKE	TCTT
ELDARAKE	ERAKE	TCLDA
STRank	DTRank	TCS
PTRank	DTRank	TCP
T3Rank	DTRank	TCTT
LDATRank	DTRank	TCLDA
SRAKE	DRAKE	TCS
PRAKE	DRAKE	TCP
T2RAKE	DRAKE	TCTT
LDARAKE	DRAKE	TCLDA

Depending on which sentence-ranking algorithm and which topic-clustering scheme to be used, we have eight combinations using ETRank and ERAKE, and similarly eight combinations using DTRank and DRAKE, shown in Table 3. For example, ET3Rank (Enhanced TextTiling TRank) means to use $\text{Rank}_{sp}(s)$ to rank sentences and TextTiling to compute topic clusterings, and T2RAKE (TextTiling RAKE) means to use $\text{Rank}(s)$ rank sentences over RAKE keywords and TextTiling to compute topic clusterings.

All algorithms follow the following procedure for selecting sentences (see Fig. 2):

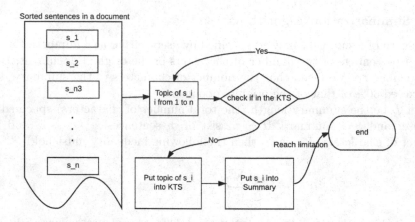

Fig. 2. The general procedure of selecting sentences.

1. Preprocessing phase
   (a) Identify keywords and compute the ranking of each keyword.
   (b) Compute the ranking of each sentence.
2. Sentence selection phase
   (a) Sort the sentences in descending order of their ranking scores.
   (b) Select sentences one at a time with a higher score to a lower score. Check if the selected sentence s belongs to the known-topic set (KTS) according to the underlying topic clustering scheme, where KTS is a set of topics from sentences placed in the summary so far. If s is in KTS, then discard it; otherwise, place s into the summary and its topic into KTS.
   (c) Continue this procedure until the summary reaches its length constraint.
   (d) If the number of topics contained in the KTS is equal to the number of topics in the document, empty KTS and repeat the procedure from Step 1.

Figure 3 shows an example of 30% summary generated by ET3Rank on an article in NewsIR-16.

The San Bernardino County Sheriff's Department said it was a matter of public safety when deputies opened fire from a helicopter on a wrong-way chase suspect on the 215 Freeway.

On Friday, a suspect led authorities on a dangerous high-speed chase through surface streets in Fontana and San Bernardino before he drove the wrong way in the northbound lanes of the freeway. He reached speeds as high as 100 mph and deputies deemed him a threat to public safety.

Lt. Mitch Datillo said there is a lot for deputies to take into account before firing from a helicopter.

"If you're near schools, if you're in residential areas. We have had times where we fully intended that it was getting to that level and we could not deploy, based on the backdrop and the public safety there," he said.

But when the suspect jumped out of his SUV after being shot, the car continued to move and slammed head-on into another SUV, injuring three people. A relative of that family told Eyewitness News that he questions the decision by deputies to open fire from the air.

While shooting from a helicopter is rare, it does happen. In 2004, a deputy with the Orange County Sheriff's Department opened fire from their helicopter on a suspect who was firing at deputies at a recycling plant near Irvine.

Eyewitness News spoke with use-of-force expert and Inyo County Sheriff's Deputy Ed. Obayashi, who said he agrees with the decision to shoot, based partly on the fact of the suspect's speed while heading in the wrong direction on the freeway.

"It could have been worse," he said. "That constitutes an immediate grave danger to the public and that justifies deadly force."

The Los Angeles County Sheriff's Special Enforcement Bureau is authorized and trains deputies to shoot from a helicopter. Ventura County sheriff's deputies are not trained, but after hearing about the deadly chase, officials said they may consider changing the policy and training deputies.

Summary:

The San Bernardino County Sheriff's Department said it was a matter of public safety when deputies opened fire from a helicopter on a wrong-way chase suspect on the 215 Freeway.

Lt. Mitch Datillo said there is a lot for deputies to take into account before firing from a helicopter.

In 2004, a deputy with the Orange County Sheriff's Department opened fire from their helicopter on a suspect who was firing at deputies at a recycling plant near Irvine.

The Los Angeles County Sheriff's Special Enforcement Bureau is authorized and trains deputies to shoot from a helicopter.

Fig. 3. An example of 30% summary of an article in NewsIR-16 by ET3Rank extracted from [33], where the original document is on the left and the summary is on the right.

4 A Word-Embedding Measurement of Quality

Word2vec [18,19] is an NN model that learns a vector representation for each word contained in a corpus of documents. The model consists of an input layer, a projection layer, and an output layer to predict nearby words in the context. In particular, a sequence of T words $w_1, \cdots, w_T$ are used to train a Word2Vec model for maximizing the probability of neighboring words:

$$\frac{1}{T} \sum_{t=1}^{T} \sum_{j \in b(t)} \log p(w_j | w_t) \tag{5}$$

where $b(t) = [t - c, t + c]$ is the set of center word w_t's neighboring words, c is the size of the training context, and $p(w_j | w_t)$ is defined by the softmax function. Word2Vec can learn complex word relationships if it trains on a very large data set.

4.1 Word Mover's Distance

Word Mover's Distance (WMD) [13] uses Word2Vec as a word embedding representation method. It measures the dissimilarity between two documents and calculates the minimum cumulative distance to "travel" from the embedded words of one document to the other. Although two documents may not share any words in common, WMD can still measure the semantical similarity by considering their word embeddings, while other bag-of-words or TF-IDF methods only measure the similarity by the appearance of words. A smaller value of WMD indicates that the two sentences are more similar.

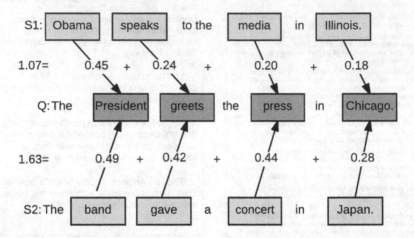

Fig. 4. The WMD metric on two sentences S1, S2 compared with the query sentence based on Q [13].

Fig. 4, extracted from [13], depicts an example of the WMD metric of two sentences S_1 and S_2 with a query sentence Q, respectively. Each directional edge represents the flow between two words, weighted with the corresponding distance, with stop words removed from each sentence. The WMD value of S_1 and Q is the summation of weights on the corresponding edges. The WMD value of S_2 and Q is similarly defined. Two sentences that are more similar semantically would have a smaller WMD value. Intuitively, traveling from *Illinois* to *Chicago* is much closer than from *Japan* to *Chicago*. Also, the word embedding vector for Illinois generated by Word2Vec, denoted by $v(Illinois)$, is closer to $v(Chicago)$ than $v(Japan)$. This concludes that sentence S_1 is more similar to query Q semantically than sentence S_2.

4.2 A Word-Embedding Similarity Measure

Motivated by WMD's ability of measuring semantic similarities of documents, we devise a summarization evaluation measure called WESM (Word-Embedding Similarity Measure). Given two documents D_1 and D_2, let WMD(D_1, D_2) denote the distance of D_1 and D_2. Given a document D, assume that it consists of ℓ paragraphs $P_1, \cdots, P_\ell$. Let S be a summary of D. We compare the word-embedding similarity of a summary S with D using WESM(S, D) as follows:

$$\text{WESM}(S, D) = \frac{1}{\ell} \sum_{i=1}^{\ell} \frac{1}{1 + \text{WMD}(S, P_i)} \tag{6}$$

The value of WESM(S, D) is between 0 and 1. Under this measure, a higher WESM(S, D) value indicates a higher semantic similarity of S and D.

5   Numerical Analysis

We evaluate the qualities of summarizations using the DUC-02 dataset [8] and the SummBank dataset [27]. DUC-02 consists of 60 reference sets, each of which consists of a number of documents, single-document summary benchmarks, and multi-document abstracts/extracts. The common ROUGE recall measures of ROUGE-1 (R-1), ROUGE-2 (R-2), and ROUGE-SU4 (R-SU4) are used to compare the quality of summarization algorithms over DUC data. Besides providing abstractive manual summaries like DUC02, SummBank also provides extractive summaries generated by human experts with different percentage of documents. Thus, evaluating extractive summarization algorithms over SummBank would make more sense than evaluations over DUC-02.

We evaluate our WESM evaluations over the DUC-02 dataset [8] and the NewsIR-16 dataset [6]. NewsIR-16 consists of 1 million articles from English news media sites and blogs.

We use various software packages to implement TextRank (with window size = 2) [20], RAKE [21], TexTiling [3], LDA and Word2Vec [28].

We use the existing Word2Vec model trained on English Wikipedia [9], which consists of 3.75 million articles formatted in XML. The reason to choose this dataset is for its large size and the diverse topics it covers.

5.1   ROUGE Evaluations over DUC-02

As mentioned before, it suffices to only consider CP_3 for the purpose of comparing the qualities of summaries, as CP_3 produces the best results among all previously known algorithms.

Among all the algorithms we devise, we only present those with at least one ROUGE score better than or equal to the corresponding score of CP_3, identified in bold (see Table 4). Also shown in the table is the average of the three ROUGE scores (R-AVG). We can see that ET3Rank is the winner, followed by T2RAKE; both are superior to CP_3. Moreover, ET2RAKE offers the highest ROUGE-1 score of 49.3.

Table 4. ROUGE scores (%) on DUC-02 data based from [33].

Methods	R-1	R-2	R-SU4	R-AVG
CP_3	49.0	24.7	25.8	33.17
ET3Rank	**49.2**	**25.6**	**27.5**	**34.10**
ESRAKE	**49.0**	23.6	**26.1**	32.90
ET2RAKE	**49.3**	21.4	24.5	31.73
PRAKE	**49.0**	24.5	25.3	32.93
T2RAKE	**49.1**	**25.4**	**25.8**	**33.43**

5.2   ROUGE Evaluations over SummBank

The SummBank dataset consists of about two-million extractive summaries of single documents and multi-documents created by manual and automatic methods, 40 news clusters in English and Chinese, and 360 multi-document, human-written non-extractive summaries. For our purpose, we evaluate our algorithms on single documents with extractive summaries. For each document, three human evaluators rank each sentence with a numerical score. Accordingly, three extractive summaries are generated for each given percentage by selecting sentences from the highest scores to lower scores until the given summary length is met.

Figure 5a shows the results of ROUGE1 scores (%) on summbank data with different percentage of sentence-based extraction methods. We can tell from the results that as the percentage goes up, the rouge1 score is incresing. ET2RAKE can achieve the best ROUGE1 score before 50% and after 50% ESRAKE can achieve best score. We can get similar results on ROUGE2 scores showing in Fig. 5b.

5.3   Softplus Function Revisit

The softplus function enhances sentence rankings for the following reasons: When x is a small positive number, $sp(x)$ increases the value of x with a significant impact and when x is large, $sp(x) \approx x$. We are curious whether the following generalization of the softplus function would provide further enhancement:

$$sp_k(x) = \ln(k + e^x), \tag{7}$$

where $k \geq 1$ is an integer. In other words, we would like to know if a larger value of k could help improve sentence rankings.

Figure 6a shows the ROUGE-1 scores on different values of k. We use the SummBank dataset on the 30% word-based extraction method. We can see that while ET3Rank achieves the highest ROUGE-1 score, the ROUGR-1 scores of ET3Rank, ESTRank, and EPTRank remain the same with different values of k. For ET2RAKE, when $k = 80$, it achieves the best ROUGE-1 scores, and after $k = 40$, their ROUGE-1 scores do not change much. The ROUGE-1 scores of ESPAKE and EPRAKE for $k > 1$ are worse than those when $k = 1$. Figure 6b depicts the ROUGE-2 scores of various algorithms on different values of k for the generalized softplus function sp_k, and the curves are similar to those of the ROUGE-1 scores. Thus, we conclude that using the generalized softplus function is only useful for ET2RAKE.

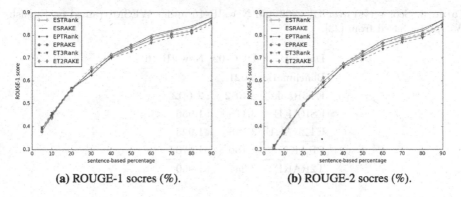

(a) ROUGE-1 socres (%).   **(b) ROUGE-2 socres (%).**

Fig. 5. ROUGE-1 and ROUGE-2 scores (%) on the summbank dataset with different percentages of sentence-based extraction methods.

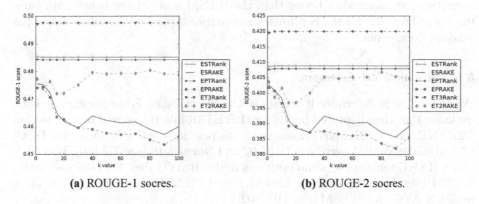

(a) ROUGE-1 socres.   **(b) ROUGE-2 socres.**

Fig. 6. ROUGE-1 and ROUGE-2 scores on the SummBank dataset with different values of k for the generalized softplus function sp_k.

5.4   WESM Evaluations over DUC-02 and NewsIR-16

Table 5 shows the evaluation results on DUC-02 and NewsIR-16 using WESM based on the Word2Vec model trained on English Wikipedia. The benchmark score in the second row is the average scores of the benchmark summaries against the original documents. The first number in the third row is the average score on all benchmark summaries in DUC-02. For the remaining rows, each number is the average score of summaries produced by the corresponding algorithm for all documents in DUC-02 and NewsIR-16. The size constraint of a summary on DUC-02 for each document is the same as that of the corresponding DUC-02 summary benchmark.

For NewsIR-16, we select at random 1,000 documents from NewsIR-16 and remove the title, references, and other unrelated content from each article. We observe that, in general, a 30% summary is sufficient to allow for a good summary. Thus, we compute 30% summaries of these articles using each algorithm.

Table 5. Scores (%) over DUC-02 and NewsIR-16 under WESM trained on English-Wikipedia based from [33].

Datasets	DUC-02	NewsIR-16
Benchmark	3.021	
ET3Rank	**3.382**	**2.002**
ESRAKE	3.175	1.956
ET2RAKE	3.148	1.923
PRAKE	3.150	1.970
T2RAKE	3.247	1.990

It is expected that the WESM scores of the summaries generated by our algorithms are somewhat better than the WESM score of the benchmark summaries in DUC-02, for the benchmark summaries often contain words not in the original documents.

5.5 Normalized L_1-norm

We would like to determine if WESM is a viable measure. From our experiments, we know that the all-around best algorithm ET3Rank, the second best algorithm T2RAKE, and ET2RAKE remain the same positions under R-AVG over DUC-02 and under WESM over both DUC-02 and NewsIR-16 (see Table 6), ESRAKE and PRAKE remain the same positions under R-AVG over DUC-02 and under WESM over NewsIR-16, while ESRAKE and PRAKE only differ by one place under R-AVG and WESM over DUC-02.

Table 6. Orderings of R-AVG scores over DUC-02 and WESM scores over DUC-02 and NewsIR-16 based from [33].

Methods	R-AVG	WESM	
	DUC-02	DUC-02	NewsIR-16
ET3Rank	1	1	1
ESRAKE	4	3	4
ET2RAKE	5	5	5
PRAKE	3	4	3
T2RAKE	2	2	2
	O_1	O_2	O_3

Next, we compare the ordering of the R-AVG scores and the WESM scores over DUC-02. For this purpose, we use the normalized L_1-norm to compare the distance of two orderings. Let $X = (x_1, x_2, \cdots, x_k)$ be a sequence of k objects, where each x_i has two values a_i and b_i such that $a_1, a_2, \ldots, a_k$ and $b_1, b_2, \ldots, b_k$ are, respectively, permutations of $1, 2, \ldots, k$. Let

$$D_k = \sum_{i=1}^{k} |(k - i + 1) - i|,$$

which is the maximum distance two permutations can possibly have. Then the normalized L_1-norm of $A = (a_1, a_2, \cdots, b_k)$ and $B = (b_1, b_2, \cdots, b_k)$ is defined by

$$\|A, B\|_1 = \frac{1}{D_k} \sum_{i=1}^{k} |a_i - b_i|.$$

Table 6 shows the orderings of the R-AVG scores over DUC-02 and WESM scores over DUC-02 and NewsIR-16 (from Tables 4 and 5).

It is straightforward to see that $D_5 = 12$, $\|O_1, O_2\|_1 = \|O_2, O_3\|_1 = 2/12 = 1/6$ and $\|O_1, O_3\|_1 = 0$. This indicates that WESM and ROUGE are highly comparable over DUC-02 and NewsIR-16, and the orderings of WESM on different datasets, while with larger spread, are still similar.

5.6   Runtime Analysis

We carried out runtime analysis through experiments on a computer with a 3.5 GHz Intel Xeon CPU E5-1620 v3. We used a Python implementation of our summarization algorithms. Since DUC-02 are short, all but LDA-based algorithms run in about the same time. To obtain a finer distinction, we ran our experiments on NewsIR-16. Since the average size of NewsIR-16 articles is 405 words, we selected at random a number of articles from NewsIR-16 and merged them to generate a new article. For each size from around 500 to around 10,000 words, with increments of 500 words, we selected at random 100 articles and computed the average runtime of different algorithms to produce 30% summary (see Fig. 7). We note that the time complexity of each of our algorithms incurs mainly in the preprocessing phase; the size of summaries in the sentence selection phase only incur minor fluctuations of computation time, and so it suffice to compare the runtime for producing 30% summaries.

We can see from Fig. 7 that ESRAKE and PRAKE incur about the same linear time and they are extremely fast. Also, ET3RANK, ET2RAKE, and T2RAKE incur about the same time. While the time is higher because of the use of TextTiling and is closed to being linear, it meets the realtime requirements. For example, for a document of up to 3,000 words, over 3,000 but less than 5,500 words, and 10,000 words, respectively, the runtime of ET3Rank is under 0.5, 1, and 2.75 s.

The runtime of SubmodularF is acceptable for documents of moderate sizes (not shown in the paper); but for a document of about 10,000 words, the runtime is close to 4 s. LDA-based algorithms is much higher. For example, LDARAKE incurs about 16 s for a document of about 2,000 words, about 41 s for a document of about 5,000 words, and about 79 s for a document of about 10,000 words.

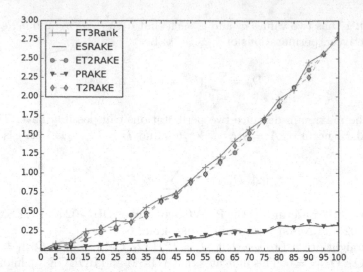

Fig. 7. Runtime analysis extracted from [33], where the unit on the x-axis is 100 words and the unit of the y-axis is seconds.

5.7   Comparisons with Human Evaluators

For each document, SummBank provides three summaries generated by, respectively, three human evaluators as references. In particular, given a document, a human evaluator assigns a numerical score to each sentence in the document. The forth reference assigns the average score of the three human evalutors' scores to each sentence. We sort the sentences in descending order in terms of their scores, and then select top sentences based on size requirements of summaries.

We seek to compare summarizations generated by our algorithms with those generated by human evaluators. In particular, we label each evaluator as Evaluator 1, Evaluator 2, and Evaluator 3. We compute the ROUGE-1 scores of, respectively, summaries generated by Evaluator 1 and our algorithms with those generated by the other two evalutors. That is, for each summary to be evaluated, we compute its ROUGE-1 scores with, respectively, Evaluator 2's summary and Evaluator 3's summary, and take the average of these two scores as the ROUGE-1 score.

In this case, the ROUGE-1 scores of Evaluator 1 is the baseline for comparisons. We repeat the same procedure using Evaluator 2 and Evaluator 3 as baselines. If the ROUGE-1 socres of our summarization algorithms are higher than or about the same as the baseline scores, then we can conclude that our algorithms are better or about the same as human extracted summaries. For the sake of comparisons, we also compare TextRank [17] with the three baselines.

Figure 8a depicts the ROUGE-1 scores of Evaluator 1 as the baseline, a set of our algorithms {ESTRank, ESRAKE, EPTRank, ET3Rank, ET2RAKE}, and TextRank. We can see that TextRank (represented by the green line) is in general worse than the baseline (represented by the red line), but better than the baseline when the sentence-based percentage is lower than 20%. The reason is that TextRank tends to select longer sentences as the summary, which takes advantages when the sentence-based percentage is low. EPTRAKE and ET2RAKE are better than TextRank above around 30%. EPTRAKE and ET2RAKE are better than the baseline below the 60% extractions, and above 60% extractions, our algorithms are very close to the baselines (see Fig. 8a and b). The results are a little bit lower than the baseline around 40% to 60% in Fig. 8c, but still close to the baseline. These results indicate that the summaries generated by our summarization algorithms are in general better than or about the same as human extracted summaries.

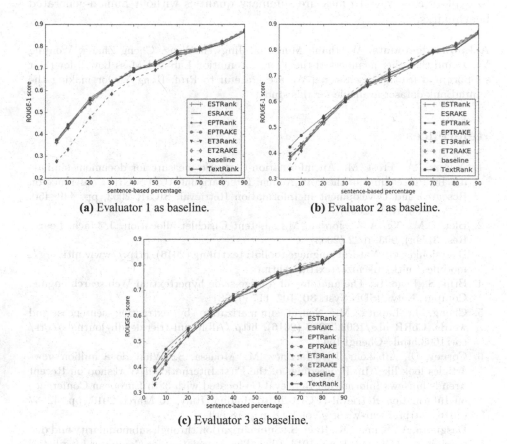

(a) Evaluator 1 as baseline.   (b) Evaluator 2 as baseline.

(c) Evaluator 3 as baseline.

Fig. 8. ROUGE-1 scores with Evaluator 1, Evaluator 2 and Evaluator 3 as baselines and other algorithms. (Color figure online)

6   Conclusions

We demonstrated the robustness of our summarization algorithms for generating effective summaries in realtime by evaluating them on various datasets. In particular, experiments on the SummBank dataset showed that summaries generated by our algorithms achieve higher or about the same ROUGE-1 scores than those extracted by human evaluators. We also presented a new semantic measure based on word-embedding similarities to evaluate the quality of a summary. We showed that ET3Rank is the best all-around algorithm. A web-based summarization tool using ET3Rank and T2RAKE is available at http://www.wsssumary.net.

To further obtain a better understanding of word-embedding similarity measures, we plan to compare WESM with human evaluation and other unsupervised methods including those devised by Louis and Nenkova [15]. We also plan to explore new ways to measure summary qualities without human-generated benchmarks.

Acknowledgements. We thank Ming Jia, Jingwen Wang, Cheng Zhang, Wenjing Yang, and the other members of the Text Automation Lab at UMass Lowell for their support and fruitful discussions. We are grateful to Prof. Hong Yu for making the SummBank dataset available for this study.

References

1. Aslam, J.A., Frost, M.: An information-theoretic measure for document similarity. In: Proceedings of the 26th Annual International ACM SIGIR Conference on Research and Development in Information Retrieval, SIGIR 2003, pp. 449–450. ACM, New York (2003)
2. Blei, D.M., Ng, A.Y., Jordan, M.I.: Latent Dirichlet allocation. J. Mach. Learn. Res. **3**(Jan), 993–1022 (2003)
3. Boutsioukis, G.: Natural language toolkit: texttiling (2016). http://www.nltk.org/_modules/-nltk/tokenize/texttiling.html
4. Brin, S., Page, L.: The anatomy of a large-scale hypertextual Web search engine. Comput. Netw. ISDN Syst. **30**, 107–117 (1998)
5. Cheng, J., Lapata, M.: Neural summarization by extracting sentences and words. CoRR abs/1603.07252 (2016). http://dblp.uni-trier.de/db/journals/corr/corr1603.html#ChengL16a
6. Corney, D., Albakour, D., Martinez, M., Moussa, S.: What do a million news articles look like? In: Proceedings of the First International Workshop on Recent Trends in News Information Retrieval Co-located with 38th European Conference on Information Retrieval (ECIR 2016), Padua, Italy, 20 March 2016, pp. 42–47 (2016). http://ceur-ws.org/Vol-1568/paper8.pdf
7. Dasgupta, A., Kumar, R., Ravi, S.: Summarization through submodularity and dispersion. In: ACL, vol. 1, pp. 1014–1022. The Association for Computer Linguistics (2013). http://dblp.uni-trier.de/db/conf/acl/acl2013-1.html#DasguptaKR13
8. DUC: Document understanding conference 2002 (2002). http://www-nlpir.nist.gov/projects/duc/guidelines/2002.html
9. Foundation, W.: Wikimedia downloads (2017). https://dumps.wikimedia.org/enwiki/latest/enwiki-latest-pages-articles.xml.bz2
10. Glorot, X., Bordes, A., Bengio, Y.: Deep sparse rectifier neural networks. In: AISTATS, vol. 15, p. 275 (2011)

11. Hearst, M.A.: TextTiling: segmenting text into multi-paragraph subtopic passages. Comput. Linguist. **23**(1), 33–64 (1997)
12. Kleinberg, J.M.: Authoritative sources in a hyperlinked environment. J. ACM (JACM) **46**(5), 604–632 (1999)
13. Kusner, M.J., Sun, Y., Kolkin, N.I., Weinberger, K.Q.: From word embeddings to document distances. In: Proceedings of the 32nd International Conference on Machine Learning (ICML 2015), pp. 957–966 (2015)
14. Lin, H., Bilmes, J.A.: A class of submodular functions for document summarization. In: Lin, D., Matsumoto, Y., Mihalcea, R. (eds.) ACL, pp. 510–520. The Association for Computer Linguistics (2011). http://dblp.uni-trier.de/db/conf/acl/acl2011.html#LinB11
15. Louis, A., Nenkova, A.: Automatically evaluating content selection in summarization without human models. In: Proceedings of the 2009 Conference on Empirical Methods in Natural Language Processing: Volume 1, vol. 1, pp. 306–314. EMNLP 2009. Association for Computational Linguistics, Stroudsburg (2009)
16. Matsuo, Y., Ishizuka, M.: Keyword extraction from a single document using word co-occurrence statistical information. In: Proceedings of the Sixteenth International Florida Artificial Intelligence Research Society Conference, pp. 392–396. AAAI Press (2003)
17. Mihalcea, R., Tarau, P.: TextRank: bringing order into texts. In: Proceedings of EMNLP-04 and the 2004 Conference on Empirical Methods in Natural Language Processing, July 2004
18. Mikolov, T., Chen, K., Corrado, G., Dean, J.: Efficient estimation of word representations in vector space. arXiv preprint arXiv:1301.3781 (2013)
19. Mikolov, T., Sutskever, I., Chen, K., Corrado, G.S., Dean, J.: Distributed representations of words and phrases and their compositionality. In: Advances in Neural Information Processing Systems, pp. 3111–3119 (2013)
20. MIT: TextRank implementation in python (2014). https://github.com/summanlp/textrank
21. MIT: A python implementation of the rapid automatic keyword extraction (2015). https://github.com/aneesha/RAKE
22. Nallapati, R., Zhou, B., dos Santos, C.N., Gülçehre, Ç., Xiang, B.: Abstractive text summarization using sequence-to-sequence RNNs and beyond. In: CoNLL, pp. 280–290. ACL (2016)
23. Parveen, D., Mesgar, M., Strube, M.: Generating coherent summaries of scientific articles using coherence patterns. In: Proceedings of the 2016 Conference on Empirical Methods in Natural Language Processing, pp. 772–783 (2016)
24. Parveen, D., Ramsl, H.M., Strube, M.: Topical coherence for graph-based extractive summarization. In: Márquez, L., Callison-Burch, C., Su, J., Pighin, D., Marton, Y. (eds.) EMNLP, pp. 1949–1954. The Association for Computational Linguistics (2015)
25. Parveen, D., Strube, M.: Integrating importance, non-redundancy and coherence in graph-based extractive summarization. In: Yang, Q., Wooldridge, M. (eds.) IJCAI, pp. 1298–1304. AAAI Press (2015). http://dblp.uni-trier.de/db/conf/ijcai/ijcai2015.html#Parveen015
26. Radev, D.R., et al.: Mead-a platform for multidocument multilingual text summarization. In: LREC (2004)
27. Radev, D., et al.: Summbank 1.0 LDC2003t16 (2003). https://catalog.ldc.upenn.edu/LDC2003T16
28. Rehurek, R.: Gensim 2.0.0 (2017). https://pypi.python.org/pypi/gensim

29. Rose, S., Engel, D., Cramer, N., Cowley, W.: Automatic keyword extraction from individual documents. In: Berry, M.W., Kogan, J. (eds.) Text Mining. Applications and Theory, pp. 1–20. Wiley (2010). https://doi.org/10.1002/9780470689646.ch1

30. Rush, A.M., Chopra, S., Weston, J.: A neural attention model for abstractive sentence summarization. CoRR abs/1509.00685 (2015). http://dblp.uni-trier.de/db/journals/corr/corr1509.html#RushCW15

31. Salton, G., Buckley, C.: Term weighting approaches in automatic text retrieval. Cornell University, Ithaca, NY, USA, Technical report (1987)

32. Shao, L., Wang, J.: DTATG: an automatic title generator based on dependency trees. In: Fred, A.L.N., Dietz, J.L.G., Aveiro, D., Liu, K., Bernardino, J., Filipe, J. (eds.) KDIR, pp. 166–173. SciTePress (2016). http://dblp.uni-trier.de/db/conf/ic3k/kdir2016.html#ShaoW16

33. Shao, L., Zhang, H., Jia, M., Wang, J.: Efficient and effective single-document summarizations and a word-embedding measurement of quality. In: Proceedings of the 9th International Joint Conference on Knowledge Discovery, Knowledge Engineering and Knowledge Management - (Volume 1), Funchal, Madeira, Portugal, 1–3 November 2017. pp. 114–122 (2017)

34. Wan, X.: Towards a unified approach to simultaneous single-document and multi-document summarizations. In: Proceedings of the 23rd International Conference on Computational Linguistics, pp. 1137–1145. Association for Computational Linguistics (2010)

35. Wan, X., Xiao, J.: Exploiting neighborhood knowledge for single document summarization and keyphrase extraction. ACM Trans. Inf. Syst. **28**(2) (2010). http://dblp.uni-trier.de/db/journals/tois/tois28.html#WanX10

36. Woodsend, K., Lapata, M.: Automatic generation of story highlights. In: Proceedings of the 48th Annual Meeting of the Association for Computational Linguistics, pp. 565–574. Association for Computational Linguistics (2010)

Adaptive Cluster Based Discovery of High Utility Itemsets

Piyush Lakhawat$^{(\boxtimes)}$ and Arun Somani

Iowa State University, Ames, IA 50011, USA
{piyush,arun}@iastate.edu
http://ecpe.ee.iastate.edu/dcnl

Abstract. Utility Itemset Mining (UIM) is a key analysis technique for data which is modeled by the Transactional data model. While improving the computational time and space efficiency of the mining of itemsets is important, it is also critically important to predict future itemsets accurately. In today's time, when both scientific and business competitive edge is commonly derived from first access to knowledge via advanced predictive ability, this problem becomes increasingly relevant. We established in our most recent work that having prior knowledge of approximate cluster structure of the dataset and using it implicitly in the mining process, can lend itself to accurate prediction of future itemsets. We evaluate the individual strength of each transaction while focusing on itemset prediction, and reshape the transaction utilities based on that. We extend our work by identifying that such reshaping of transaction utilities should be adaptive to the anticipated cluster structure, if there is a specific intended prediction window. We define novel concepts for making such an anticipation and integrate Time Series Forecasting into the evaluation. We perform additional illustrative experiments to demonstrate the application of our improved technique and also discuss future direction for this work.

Keywords: High utility itemset mining · Clustering ·
Adaptive itemset prediction · Time Series forecasting

1 Introduction

Itemset mining is searching for repeating patterns of significance in a transactional dataset. The main goal is to discover the frequently enough occurring patterns which have substantial (on the basis of a pre-defined threshold) collective importance (defined as utility) in a collection of transactions. It is one of the fields from data mining gaining rising popularity in the last several years [17]. This maybe attributed to two primary reasons. Firstly, that there is a key need to extract highly repetitive patterns from data in several data mining applications. Secondly, that data mining problems from many areas can be conveniently transformed into an itemset mining problem. Some of the noteworthy

© Springer Nature Switzerland AG 2019
A. Fred et al. (Eds.): IC3K 2017, CCIS 976, pp. 139–163, 2019.
https://doi.org/10.1007/978-3-030-15640-4_8

application areas include market basket analysis [20], bioinformatics [4,19], web-site click stream analysis [3,16] etc. which have seen increasing use of itemset mining techniques.

The inception [2] of itemset mining problem was on the basis of identifying patterns purely on their frequency of occurrence. Evolution of that led to subsequent models [9,18,24,25] where an additional utility value was given to the data objects on the basis of their relative utility(importance) in the analysis. The itemset mining criterion in this new model was a weighted combination sum of frequency and utility values of the data items. This work is an extension of our most recent work [14] where we have improved the effectiveness of Utility Itemset Mining model (UIM) by adding a prediction aspect to it by implicitly using the cluster structure. Building up on it, here we identify, define and incorporate an adaptive aspect into the prediction. Possessing reasonably accurate knowledge of possible future itemsets is of great value in all applications of Utility Itemset Mining where data is scarce or dynamic in nature and where discovery of knowledge sooner and with lesser amount of data adds much more value to them. A key intuition for our work has been inspired from the existence and knowledge of clusters present in the data. We established that prior knowledge of the clusters present in the data has a high potential in guiding the future itemsets discovery [14].

We now build upon that idea by defining a concept for anticipated "cluster contribution" for a future window of data, and evaluate it by using Time Series forecasting. We then integrate this knowledge into our Itemset Mining model [14] to predict itemsets specifically with the inclusion of this future window. Whenever there is the concept of prediction, the concept of an intended prediction window is implicitly present. Therefore, in case of itemsets as well there is a definite need to obtain predictions pertaining a specific window on time in the future. This work is a step in that direction.

The proposed prediction scheme here for high utility itemsets captures frequency, utility, cluster structure information and the dynamics of the cluster structure to predict the possible future itemsets with high accuracy. We have shown via experiments [14] on real datasets that we are able predict a good number of future itemsets with high accuracy over the baseline. With the addition of the adaptive aspect in this work, the application of our technique becomes richer. While Utility Itemset Mining is not a machine learning problem, but if it were, our model would be analogous to the Bayesian version of this problem with the cluster structure acting as the Prior.

Prior to getting into equation level analysis of our work, we will explain the main idea of our work with a toy example along with how this work adds to the current itemset mining framework. Itemset mining started as a formal problem called as Frequent Itemset Mining (FIM) from the field of market basket analysis [2]. In FIM, data objects are called transactions. Each of these transactions include a set of items and have a unique transaction ID. Items constituting these transactions are all part of a global set of item types. An itemset can be understood as a set of one or more item types. The main idea in FIM is to discover itemsets which can be found in more than a certain number (say Φ) of transactions.

To explain this, we employ a toy example of FIM as shown in Fig. 1 extracted from [14]. Let us assume Dataset D contains a set of transactions from a retail store. The set I represents a collection of various item types. Then the set of Frequent Itemsets would contain all itemsets which occur in two or more (as $\Phi =$ 2) transactions in D. In real world applications where the actual threshold values (Φ) are huge, a frequent itemset of kind (A, B) translates into an association rule of type A $\rightarrow$ B. The exact use of such an association rule varies from one application domain to another. For example, in market basket analysis it can simply mean that a customer buying item A is highly probable to buy item B too, therefore A and B should be advertised together.

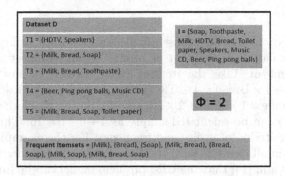

Fig. 1. Frequent itemset mining (extracted from [14]).

There is a certain key issue with the FIM problem. It does not have the ability to model the relative importance among the item types. Like in Fig. 1, a HDTV and a pack of soap have the same unit of importance. But in real life situations, the profit yield of a single unit sale of a HDTV will be much more than that of a soap. So for a threshold of two, the HDTV and Speakers will not be included in the list of frequent itemsets. An additional issue with this model is that it cannot model the occurrence frequency of items in the transactions. It is possible that in transaction T2 from Fig. 1 the customer bought one pack of bread, but in transaction T3 the customer bought two packs of bread. This model will not be able to distinguish between these two cases. To solve these issues Utility Itemset Mining (UIM) has been proposed as an evolved problem model of FIM.

This utility based version (UIM) of the problem from Fig. 1 is shown in Fig. 2 (extracted from [14]). In Fig. 2, adjacent to items in the transactions, the parenthesis contain the occurrence frequency for the item for that transaction. The right side of Fig. 2 shows the various item types. e(i) indicates the relative importance of each item type i. For this particular example they can be understood as the profit for the unit sale of the specific

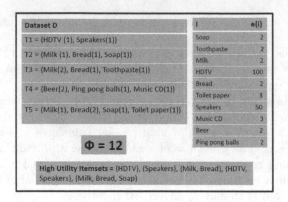

Fig. 2. Utility itemset mining (extracted from [14]).

item. Then the profit for an itemset (called as absolute utility of the item-set) is then calculated as the sum of profits of that itemset in all transactions it is present in. Like the itemset (milk, Bread) occurs in T2 (profit made $= 1 \times$ Milk $+ 1 \times$ Bread $= 4$), T3 (profit made $= 2 \times$ Milk $+ 1 \times$ Bread $= 6$) and T5 (profit made $= 1 \times$ Milk $+ 2 \times$ Bread $= 6$). So the absolute utility of itemset (Milk, Bread) can be calculated simply as $4 + 6 + 6 = 16$. Threshold (Φ) for UIM is a mixed criterion of utility and frequency. For the example in Fig. 2, the set of HUI contain all itemsets with total absolute utility higher than 12 (Φ).

We have shown in [14] that the UIM problem model can be further extended to add a prediction aspect to it. If we consider the problem in Fig. 2, let us assume we have high confidence that a college student customer is creating the transaction T4. In this case the information associated with T4 is more representative of a customer class of college students versus the population of all customers. Using this information smartly can allow us to predict a latent behavior of the class of college students if it exists in the data. But if we ignore this information it can potentially lead to an information loss owing to generalization. This has been the main motivation for us to explore ways for smartly using the information of clusters found in data in the UIM model. An added layer to this idea is that if transactions such as above show a higher rate of emergence as we progressively further analyze the dataset, then we can anticipate this group (college students) to have a higher impact on the future itemsets. This is the key idea of our predictive UIM model, proposed in this work and the previous one [14].

1.1 The Intuition for an Adaptive Prediction Enabled UIM Problem

To highlight the intuition behind predicting itemsets, let us understand the idea that datasets which can be modeled as transactional data have frequently occurring (repeating) patterns of interest in them (as a data signature). It is a vital piece of information which mining techniques look to obtain from these datasets. Like for the retail transactions data this means combination of actual products which are very frequently bought together. While on the same transactional data another analysis called clustering is also performed to understand the cluster structure present in the data (yet another data signature). In the analysis of retail transactions data this forms the backbone of customer segmentation analysis [20]. The key idea in performing customer segmentation analysis is to find clusters present in the transactions data, and then associate a customer type with each cluster.

Such clustering analysis of transactional data is done in many biomedical applications too. Gene expression study is one example area where the data types are studied using both itemset mining [4,19] and clustering analysis [5]. The implication of this is that itemset mining and clustering study different aspects of the same dataset. *While itemset mining abstracts the dataset in form of itemsets, clustering abstracts it in form of clusters of transactions.* We extract Fig. 3 from [14] which shows a visualization of this idea. Here we try to visualize the dataset as a solid cylinder. In this case a top view (if it corresponds to itemset mining) will project a circle (correspondingly itemsets). While a side view (if it corresponds to clustering) will project a rectangle (correspondingly clusters).

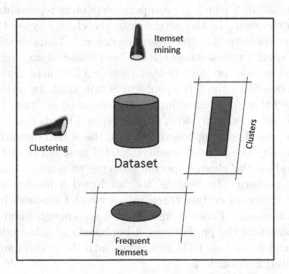

Fig. 3. Illustration of different abstractions of dataset (extracted from [14]).

Doing only clustering analysis or itemset mining analysis while ignoring the other creates a handicap because we do not use all available information which we have access to. Few of the recent transactional data clustering techniques are beginning to incorporate this idea. Like in a recent transactional clustering algorithm proposed in [26], the authors introduce a concept of weighted coverage density. It is a metric of cluster quality based on the itemset patterns present which is used to direct the clustering algorithm behavior. Based on the idea that frequently occurring patterns are an important characteristic of these datasets, the authors in [26] give the weights to items in this coverage density function based on their frequency of occurrence. It allows the clusters which are more practically useful to develop. We re-iterate two issues which we raised in [14], about the current UIM problem model:

1. If we divide the entire set of transactions into clusters and perform itemset mining in each cluster separately, we might miss an inter-cluster pattern.
2. If we perform itemset mining in the whole dataset disregarding clustering, a pattern highly specific to a cluster might be missed due to no support from any other cluster.

This informs us that we need to implicitly use knowledge the cluster structure while performing itemset mining.

1.2   Using the Cluster Structure Implicitly

Using the cluster structure implicitly in itemset mining can allow us to solve the above problems. The main idea is that knowledge of cluster structure can allow us to identify transactions which are comparatively more representative of cluster types present in the data. In the actual data the cluster types typically represent some real world entity (like the type of customer). Therefore the information present in these special transactions should be considered more characteristic of their cluster type instead of the whole dataset. So for these transactions using the common threshold in the UIM problem is not ideal. In order to solve this issue, we identified that some extra importance must be assigned to these special transactions associated strongly with cluster types. Our method of doing this is by introducing a new clustering based utility in the actual definition of the UIM problem model itself. This idea of modifying UIM problem model that we introduced in [14] enables the cluster specific patterns to emerge while still mining the inter-cluster patterns. In essence, we developed a mechanism to enhance the importance (utility) of certain transactions which translates into inflation in utility of certain itemsets. Those itemsets which are enough inflated to cross the threshold will constitute the predictions. A big benefit of this modification in the model is that it can fit into all UIM techniques as it does not change functioning of the itemset mining algorithms.

Going back to the example in Fig. 2, this new predictive UIM model will now provide extra importance/utility to the items in transaction T4 by identifying it as a special transaction (representative of a college student). Let us assume that the Music CD bought by this college student is of a current hit album. Then a hypothetical pattern of this Music CD bought along with some other common college student items is likely to repeat a lot. This should automatically lead to eventual discovery of this Music CD as a high utility item. The strength of the predictive UIM model is that it will cause a sooner (using less data) discovery of these patterns (itemsets).

1.3 Adaptivity Based on Anticipation of Cluster Structure

While the knowledge of cluster structure can potentially aid greatly in identifying future patterns, there is further temporal information which they can provide. The transactions are presented in timestamped order, and we intuitively understand that patterns emerging via incoming transactions will have a temporal aspect to them as well. In the same way, the cluster structure also has a dynamic temporal aspect to it. To understand it simply, in the example that we have been discussing above, it is quite possible that a particular cluster is showing higher propensity for increase in it utility contribution. What this exactly means will become clearer in the following sections. For now we can interpret it as, if a particular cluster (say the college students) shows a comparatively rapid increase in contribution to the population (number of purchases), it will also have greater contribution in future itemsets. If we can adapt to the rate of change of this contribution, we can improve our prediction quality and target it to a specific window in future. The definition of this future can be based on the interest of the analysis. The key to using this information effectively will depend on developing meaningful concepts which can capture it and also allow the use of predictive tools (like Time Series forecasting) on them.

In rest of the work, we first discuss the key works done on the itemset mining problem. Then we formally describe the itemset mining problem followed by the definition of our specifically defined clustering based utility which extended [14] the UIM model and its use in prediction. We then have a discussion on the use of clustering algorithm followed by the experiments on real data before we conclude.

2   Related Work

Fundamental problem of itemset mining was first established by Agrawal et al. in [2] as frequent itemset mining (FIM) in the market basket analysis domain. Their technique brought forth an important concept called downward closure property for creating the potential (candidate) frequent itemsets of size k by making use of the already discovered frequent itemsets of size k − 1. It is also popularly known as the apriori technique. It allows to significantly reduce the search space for the frequent itemsets which otherwise can easily become an exhaustive exponential problem. Following this many subsequent works extended this domain by introducing novel concepts like sampling techniques [23], dynamic itemset counting [8], parallel implementations [1] etc.

One limitation which eventually started to affect the analysis as data sizes got bigger was that "apriori" logic based solutions were sometimes generating an unmanageable set of candidate itemsets. As each candidate itemset does require a run over the entire data it immediately slows the itemset mining in a significant way. One strong solution to this problem was introduced in [12] called the FP-Growth. It does the itemset mining by creating a tree structure rather than candidate generation. Other techniques were also introduced like mining the dataset in vertical format (that is list items with sets of transactions) rather than the traditional horizontal format (list of transactions with items). One such work is proposed by Zaki in [27].

As discussed before FIM still lacked two key modeling capabilities, that of relative importance of various items (called utility) and the frequency of an item in a specific transaction. This led to the development of UIM in [9, 18, 24, 25] among others. In these the itemsets are mined on the basis of utility support in the dataset instead of only the occurrence frequency. It allowed the problem model to be of more practical significance.

The downward closure property for candidate generation does not work directly for the UIM problem. This developed the idea of a transaction weighted utility, which allowed the apriori type candidate generation again. This was the basis of the initial work done in utility mining with subsequent techniques proposed on various strategies for pruning the search space.

But the problem of a still very big candidate set was also present in these lines of solutions due to the use of "apriori" logic inherent within them. To solve this [25] proposed a tree based model called UP-Growth for Utility mining which goes over the dataset only twice and skips all the nested candidate generation.

Recently in [24] authors proposed Utility mining algorithms which use a closed set representation for itemsets which is very concise and yet captures all useful information.

3   Itemset Mining Problem Model

In this section we formally define the itemset mining problem. We first define the problem of Frequent itemset mining (FIM) followed by Utility itemset mining (UIM). These are generally accepted concepts throughout this domain, and the same problem setup can be seen in our previous work in [14].

$$I = \{a_1, a_2, \ldots, a_M\} = \text{Set of distinct item types} \tag{1}$$

$$D = \{T_1, T_2, \ldots, T_N\} = \text{Transaction dataset} \tag{2}$$

where each $T_i = \{x_1, x_2, \ldots\}, x_k \in I$

$$\text{itemset}(X) \text{ of size k} = \{x_1, x_2, \ldots, x_k\} \tag{3}$$

$$SC(X) = |\{T_i \text{ such that } X \in T_i \wedge T_i \in D\}| \tag{4}$$

$$\text{Frequent itemsets} = \{X \text{ such that } SC(X) \geq \Phi\} \tag{5}$$

The FIM lacks two key model aspects. It cannot model the frequency of an item type in a transaction and difference in relative importance of various item types. As shown earlier UIM overcomes these issues. UIM problem builds up on the FIM problem with additional information of external and internal utilities for items. Here is the external utility is a measure of unit importance of an item type. Of the two new concepts this one is a transaction independent utility. While the internal utility is a transaction specific utility. It is mostly the frequency or any other measure of quantity of an item in the transaction.

$$eu(a_i) = \text{ external utility of item type } a_i \tag{6}$$

$$iu(a_i, T_j) = \text{ internal utility of } a_i \text{ in } T_j \tag{7}$$

The absolute utility of an item in a transaction is defined as the product of its internal and external utility.

$$au(a_i, T_j) = eu(a_i) * iu(a_i, T_j) \tag{8}$$

Absolute utility of an itemset in a transaction is the sum of absolute utilities of its constituent items.

$$au(X, T_j) = \sum_{x_i \in X} au(x_i, T_j) \tag{9}$$

Absolute utility of a transaction (also called transaction utility) is the sum of absolute utilities of all its constituent items.

$$TU(T_j) = \sum_{x_i \in T_j} au(x_i, T_j) \tag{10}$$

Absolute utility of an itemset in the dataset D is the sum of absolute of that itemset in all transactions that it occurs in.

$$au(X, D) = \sum_{X \in T_j \wedge T_j \in D} au(X, T_j) \tag{11}$$

The set of HUI is the collection of all itemsets which have absolute utility more than or equal to in the dataset D.

$$\text{set of HUI} = \{X \text{ s.t. } au(X, D) \geq \Phi\} \tag{12}$$

The following three concepts are used in the solution techniques of UIM to achieve a downward closure property for efficient candidate generation similar to the FIM problem: Transaction weighted utility (TWU) of itemset X in dataset D is the sum of transaction utilities of transactions in which the itemset X occurs.

$$TWU(X, D) = \sum_{X \in T_j \wedge T_j \in D} TU(T_j) \tag{13}$$

Set of high transaction weighted utility itemsets (HTWUI) is a collection of all itemsets which have transaction weighted utility more than or equal to Φ in the dataset D.

$$\text{Set of HTWUI } = \{X \text{ s.t. } TWU(X) \geq \Phi\} \tag{14}$$

TWDC property [18,24]: "The transaction-weighted downward closure property states that for any itemset X that is not a HTWUI, all its supersets are low utility itemsets."

The goal of UIM is to find the set of all high utility itemsets for a given Φ. Here threshold Φ is a combination criterion of utility and frequency rather than a solely frequency based one in FIM. Figure 2 shows a small example illustrating UIM. The iu (internal utility) values for all items are written in parenthesis next to it in the example.

4   A Cluster Based Utility to Enhance the UIM Model

This section describes the cluster based UIM model developed by us [14] and how the adaptive itemset discovery is built by further enhancing it. We discussed in the first section that the goal is to extend the current UIM problem model to add prediction capability to it by implicitly using the cluster structure of data in itemset mining. *Certain transactions are more representative of a cluster type over others.* These special transactions include knowledge in them which is more representative of their cluster type than the whole data. So subjecting these transactions to the common population threshold in the UIM problem would not be ideal. In order to resolve this issue, we proposed a mechanism to assign some extra utility to these transactions. In order to do this we introduce a new clustering based utility in the definition of the UIM problem model. This addition introduces a prediction capability to the standard UIM problem model.

We call this new utility as the cluster utility of a transaction (and the items in it). This is also a transaction specific utility for items and is same for all the items present in the transaction. We also introduce the following two new concepts in the UIM model [14] before we define the cluster utility.

C as the set of all given clusters. Each cluster is defined as: $C_j = \{T_1, T_2, \ldots\}$. Cluster C_j is a subset of transactions from D.

We also introduce an affinity metric which represents the degree of similarity between a cluster C_j and a transaction T_i.

$$affinity(T_i, C_j) = \text{similarity between } T_i \text{ and } C_j \tag{15}$$

It should be understood that these additions to the UIM problem model assume that a fairly accurate cluster structure is given and an appropriate affinity metric is provided. The idea of accuracy here is of an attribute that a cluster structure portrays by capturing characteristics (repetitive patterns) of interest in the dataset. And by appropriateness of the affinity metric we mean a metric which captures the type of similarity (based on constituent items) between a cluster and a transaction that is of interest in the analysis. We claim that these assumptions are acceptable because the presence of these concepts is well established from the body of work containing transactional clustering techniques. These clustering techniques define subsets of transactions as clusters in the same way as we define them in our predictive UIM problem model. Also using some type of similarity metric is fairly common for these techniques [10,11,13]. The affinity metrics used in these techniques can be used in our extended UIM problem model by interpreting a unit transaction as a single element cluster.

$$cu(a, T_i) = 1 + k * max\{affinity(T_i, C_j) \forall C_j \in C\} \tag{16}$$

In Eq. 16, k is a tunable parameter and decides how aggressively the cluster information is used in the predictive UIM. Note that the cluster utility is same for all items in a transaction. The rationale behind this definition is to decide the cluster utility of a transaction based on the cluster which is most similar to it.

We integrated this new internal utility in the calculation of the absolute utilities. The new definition of absolute utility of an item a in a transaction T_i is given by the following:

$$au(a, T_i) = eu(a) * iu(a, T_i) * cu(a, T_i) \tag{17}$$

This implicitly changes the definitions of $au(X, T_i)$, $TU(T_i)$, $TWU(X, D)$, Set of HTWUI, $au(X, D)$ and the set of HUI. All techniques for UIM use the absolute utilities as the building blocks to search for high utility itemsets [9,18,24,25], so this predictive UIM problem model will integrate into all of them.

4.1 Resulting Effects of the Predictive Version of UIM Problem

The following were the impacts of making the above updates to the current UIM model (developed in [14]):

1. If we assume the affinity function has a range of $[0, 1]$, then the cluster utility of every item goes into the following range: $[1, 1 + k]$. It should be understood that cluster utility values close to 1 will mean that their associated transaction is very likely non-representative of any cluster type present in that data. Higher than "1" values will signal more similarity of the associated transaction with some given cluster in the data.
2. As the evolved definition of absolute utility of an item in a transaction is now the product of cluster utility, internal utility and external utility, all the other absolute utilities will either increase or remain same in the new predictive model.
3. In the case of same threshold Φ, the new predictive model will by definition find equal or more number of HUI than the standard UIM model. Besides this the set of HUI found by the current model will always a subset of the HUI found by the predictive model. This is again evident by the design of the new model.
4. Higher values of parameter k will aggressively use the cluster information and therefore produce more number of HUI. This is recommended when additional emphasis on cluster specific patterns is required.
5. In order to understand the additional itemsets (also can be called predicted itemsets) found, we should employ the following perspectives.
   - If additional data is arriving later in time, the predicted/additional itemsets found by the model at an earlier time are expected to be discovered in the list of HUI of the standard model at that time in the future. It should be understood in this way that certain pattern(s) are present in particular cluster(s), but with the present amount of data there is not enough utility support for them to appear in the list of HUI using the standard way. But with the numbers accumulating with time they are the very likely to next appear in the list of HUI according the flow on oncoming data. The trick of the predictive UIM model is to filter them and give them additional value to help in getting discovered earlier than the standard way.

- If we assume that the data is static i.e. new data will not be available at a later point in time, the additional HUI found in the predictive model are those itemsets which barely fell short of the cutoff to be in the list of HUI using the standard model. It might be owing to being specific to only one (or very few) cluster(s) present among many and as a result not being able to collect enough numbers to overcome the threshold. But these predicted/additional HUI will still have application specific value in various domains. Like in market basket analysis, a purchase pattern for a specific customer type can be used to create targeted advertisements for customers of that type.
6. It should be understood that this addition changes the calculations of various absolute utilities. But the idea of using absolute utilities to discover the set of HUI is identical. This allows the new predictive aspect to seamlessly integrate into all UIM algorithms.
7. The core concept emphasized here is that every cluster in the cluster structure of the data usually represents a real world entity. This has the following implications.
   - After achieving an acceptable cluster structure it can be re-used or extended to be kept using for same data source/set. It is acceptable to do this because the goal of cluster structure here is only to identify if a transaction is fairly representative of a cluster type or not. This saves the computing energy for calculating clusters from scratch every single time.
   - Another point to note is that the complete data is rarely needed to obtain a reasonable cluster structure for the purpose of this model. Randomly sampled fraction of a large dataset will me more often than not be sufficient to capture the cluster structure.

5   Choosing a Suitable Clustering Technique for the Model

An implicit part of the predictive UIM problem model is an assumption of the knowledge of a reasonably accurate cluster structure along with an appropriate similarity metric as discussed in the previous section. Therefore, it is vital to choose a suitable clustering technique. A lot of techniques are present which solve the problem of identifying clusters in categorical and transactional data. Each of those techniques develop the clusters in form of groups of transactions with similar transactions in each group. Most of these techniques [10,11,13] use a similarity metric between the clusters to conduct the clustering process using divisive, agglomerative or repartitioning algorithms. The respective affinity functions can be employed in our predictive UIM model by interpreting a transaction as a single element cluster. Therefore the choice of clustering technique to be used can sometimes be subjective based on the preferences and requirements of the application domain.

Our review suggested that multiple transactional clustering techniques conduct clustering using the idea of frequently occurring patterns in the transactions. These techniques can be suitable when the external utilities in the data are not present or are not very important. But from our perspective, in most real world applications, various item types have different relative importance in the analysis. In fact as discussed before, it has been the main reason for development of UIM as an evolved version of FIM. So in our opinion, a suitable clustering technique to be used in this predictive UIM model should use HUI's in the dataset as the basis rather frequent itemsets. A clustering technique developed by us which successfully captures the high utility patterns in the data [15] is employed. This clustering technique is a part of one of our previous works [15], and is a good choice according to us in the predictive model due to its strong applicability. We provide an overview of it in the Appendix at the end.

6   Adaptive Cluster Based Discovery of High Utility Itemsets

After understanding how this evolved UIM can have predictive capability for future itemsets, let us now understand how it can be done adaptively for a specific future window. We have identified that a metric of affinity is required for our model to function. This metric can be used interchangeably between transaction-transaction, cluster-cluster and cluster-transaction pairs. This specific affinity metric used here can be noted in the APPENDIX at the end of the paper. As we mentioned earlier in the paper, the key to achieving this adaptive discovery will be in capturing potential contribution of clusters in the future itemsets. In fact, if we have a numerical estimate of contributions of clusters relative to each other, that should suffice our need. This is because the implicit rationale behind our work is that most transactions are "emerging" from a cluster or a weighted combination of them. The affinity metric can help capture that.

Before we can start to anticipate such future contributions, we need to establish what the cluster contributions are up to the present moment in time. As we iterate through the transactions serially in the dataset, we can compute an affinity value for the transaction for each cluster. This can be interpreted as the contribution of the cluster in a particular transaction. If we normalize these values across all clusters, we can obtain the contributions of clusters relative to each other for a transaction. If we compute a running sum of these contributions for each cluster, then at any point in this run, a sorted list of normalized values of these contributions will also be the representation of cluster contributions to the dataset (and the itemsets in it).

Now these running sums will be in a timestamped ordered series, so we can estimate a future value at any point in time for these running sums. While these estimates will only be predictions, they will be based on the trends encountered in this "contribution metric" so far. Therefore if we calculate these estimates of cluster contributions, we can know how much of the itemsets to appear then will be "emerging" from each cluster relatively. Therefore, a sorted list of normalized values of these estimates will represent the "anticipated" contributions of clusters. For performing this estimation, Time Series forecasting techniques must be applied. Since the cluster development in each analysis can be unique, no one single Time Series model or set of parameters can be assigned which will guarantee performance in each case. However, certain traits will be there. As this metric is a rolling sum, and therefore monotonically increasing, the series is not stationary. Therefore, stationarity has to be induced each time. We suggest starting by differencing the series, and such trends will usually be captured well by that. Autocorrelations maybe be checked, but for most cases we suggest not using it as the transactions will be coming in a random order in terms of their being influenced by individual clusters. And finally, we suggest to keep a moving average component in the Time Series model, as there will some propagating baseline contribution for each cluster and this can help capture that.

The next step now would be transferring back the knowledge of these anticipated cluster contributions to the predictive UIM model which we described in the previous section. An intuitive way to do that would be selecting the clusters with the highest and the lowest anticipated contributions in the intended future window, and inflating the importance of the former and reverse for the latter in the analysis. This can be easily accomplished by reshaping the cluster utilities (as describe earlier) of each transaction. Each transaction has a cluster counterpart in that analysis which it is most affine to, and there is a tuneable parameter "k" which reflects how aggressively we wish to pursue the predictive aspect. So for the cluster with the highest anticipated contribution in the intended future window, we assign most aggressive values of "k" and for the cluster with the lowest anticipated contribution we assign most conservative values of "k". This is of course the most straightforward way of incorporating this "adaptive" aspect of our UIM model. Multiple clusters can be selected based on their anticipated contributions, and then a gradient of aggressive to conservative assignment of "k" can be performed while reshaping the cluster utilities for each transaction. Once the new cluster utilities are assigned, then it is just about generating the itemsets based on those using the same methodology we described in the previous section. The itemsets thus generated would include the predictions for the intended widow while adapting to the anticipated contributions for the cluster structure.

In the next section we present experiments on two real datasets from [14], where we evaluate results of the predictive UIM problem model. At the end we also show an illustration of how to perform an adaptive search based on the anticipated cluster contributions.

7   Experiments on Real Datasets

We first present an analysis of the results from the predictive UIM problem model followed by illustrating how to perform the adaptive search. We use two real datasets called BMSWebView1 (obtained from [6]) and Retail dataset (provided by [7] and obtained from [21]). BMSWebView1 is a real life dataset of website clickstream data with 59,601 transactions in it. Retail dataset contains 88,163 anonymized transactions from a Belgian retail store. The external utilities are randomly generated (between 1–50) by us for different item types in both the datasets by using a uniform random number generator. For performing evaluative experiments on UIM it is common to generate utility values [24]. In order to get the cluster structure to be used for the predictive UIM problem model, we use the utility based clustering algorithm discussed earlier and explained in the Appendix at the end. In order to do the actual mining process of the HUIs we implemented a popular UIM technique called the two-phase method [18]. It works by finding all the potential HUI's using the transaction weighted downward closure property that we discussed in an earlier section. Following that it iterates through the dataset to evaluate those potential HUI's and find the actual ones.

7.1 Experimental Design

We created the following experimental design to compare the effectiveness of our predictive UIM problem model with the current UIM problem model:

1. We create the following 4 versions of both the data sets:
   - Containing first 25% of the data.
   - Containing first 50% of the data.
   - Containing first 75% of the data.
   - Containing the complete data.

   Our interpretation of the complete dataset is as if it contains all the information which future holds. This setup is created so that it simulates a real application environment where as more data arrives with time it leads to more itemsets getting discovered.
2. In the analysis for each of these datasets we evaluate the set of HUI using the standard UIM model. For the retail dataset we use $\Phi = 50,000$ and for the BMSWebView1 dataset we use $\Phi = 20,000$. We choose these threshold values so that we work with a manageable number of HUI's. Higher values of Φ lead to fewer HUI and vice versa. The purpose of this step is to establish the checkpoints for the itemsets discovered by the standard UIM model for each version of both the datasets, and use it for comparisons with the predictive model.
3. Following that we generate two cluster structures for both the Retail dataset and the BMSWEbView1 dataset by using 1% and 5% of uniformly randomly sampled data using our clustering algorithm as described before. This results in 4 cluster structures in total which will be used to model the predictive UIM problem for each version of the two datasets. Rationale behind selecting two different fractions of datasets in doing the clustering is to observe the effect of this in the prediction of HUI's.
4. Following that we assign the cluster utility to each transaction and the constituent items in them based on the chosen cluster structure. This assignment is done in a conservative, moderate or aggressive manner based on the following criterion:

$$\text{conservative } k = \begin{cases} 0 \text{ if affinity}(T_i, C_j) < 0.25 \\ 1 \text{ otherwise} \end{cases} \tag{18}$$

$$\text{moderate } k = 1 \tag{19}$$

$$\text{aggressive } k = \begin{cases} 1 \text{ if affinity}(T_i, C_j) < 0.5 \\ 2 \text{ otherwise} \end{cases} \tag{20}$$

5. Once the cluster utilities are assigned we calculate the new values for all absolute utilities based on the predictive model. Then we evaluate the set of HUI for each of the above cases based on our predictive UIM problem model (for their respective Φ values) and do the comparisons with the ones found when using the standard UIM problem model on the same version of dataset. The key information pieces of interest are:

- **HUI Found:** The idea is to find the number of HUI discovered by the predictive UIM model for each version of both datasets for the two cluster structures. As discussed before this by definition should be equal to or more than the number HUI found using the standard way.
- **Additional HUI Found:** Here the goal is to evaluate the additional number of HUIs found by the predictive UIM problem model over the standard UIM problem model. This is actually the most important information we need, as it shows the additional information that the new model was able to predict using the knowledge of cluster structure of the dataset.
- **HUI not in Future Data:** This is also an important metric. It is the number of HUI found by the predictive UIM problem model which are not eventually discovered for the standard UIM model when using the complete dataset. The HUI in this category might represent patterns which are very cluster specific and could not find enough support from the complete data set to cross the threshold Φ. It should be understood that even though these itemsets cannot be called high utility itemsets (HUI) in the conventional sense, they do have "value" with respect to their specific cluster type(s) and they might also be very close to crossing the threshold for the standard UIM problem model.

These results from the above experiment are presented in Tables 1 and 2 (from [14]).

7.2   Important Points from the Experimental Analysis

The following inferences are drawn from the obtained results.

1. As we increase the fraction of transactions used in clustering, it results in an increase in number of HUI found and additional HUI found. This result is understandable, because with more transactions being used to create the cluster structure, it is expected that it will get closer to the true cluster structure of the dataset. This should result in more transactions developing higher affinity values with their respective clusters. Higher affinities will directly result in higher cluster based utilities, which further result in higher absolute utilities

Table 1. Experiment results: retail dataset (extracted from [14]).

Fraction of transactions used in clustering	Cluster utility assignment criterion	HUI found (in 25%, 50% and 75% data respectively)	Additional HUI found (in 25%, 50% and 75% data respectively)	HUI not in future data (in 25%, 50% and 75% data respectively)
0.01	Conservative	28, 53, 91	5, 14, 27	0, 0, 0
0.01	Moderate	30, 61, 99	7, 22, 35	0, 0, 0
0.01	Aggressive	32, 70, 107	9, 31, 43	0, 2, 6
0.05	Conservative	30, 64, 102	7, 25, 38	0, 1, 2
0.05	Moderate	31, 65, 110	8, 26, 46	0, 1, 5
0.05	Aggressive	33, 79, 126	10, 40, 62	0, 3, 19

Table 2. Experiment results: BMSWebView1 dataset (extracted from [14]).

Fraction of transactions used in clustering	Cluster utility assignment criterion	HUI found on 25%, 50% and 75% data respectively)	Additional HUI found (in 25%, 50% and 75% data respectively)	HUI not in future data (in 25%, 50% and 75% data respectively)
0.01	Conservative	15, 47, 105	7, 29, 64	0, 5, 23
0.01	Moderate	17, 54, 121	9, 36, 80	0, 6, 38
0.01	Aggressive	17, 57, 124	9, 39, 83	0, 6, 41
0.05	Conservative	15, 49, 107	7, 31, 66	0, 5, 25
0.05	Moderate	17, 54, 121	9, 36, 80	0, 6, 38
0.05	Aggressive	17, 57, 125	9, 39, 84	0, 6, 42

for itemsets. Higher absolute utilities directly translate into more itemsets crossing the threshold Φ.

Figures. 4, 5, 6 to 7 (from [14]) show the graphical illustrations. The Y-axis shows the HUI found in Figs. 4 and 5. Additional HUI found are shown on the Y-axis in Figs. 6 and 7. Four different predictive UIM problem models are shown in these figures based on two cluster structures and two cluster utility assignment criterion. The X-axis for these figures shows the dataset version used. Figures 4 and 5 also shows the HUI found when using the current UIM problem model.

2. Another observation from the experiment is that changing the cluster utility criterion from conservative to moderate to aggressive results in increase in the number of HUI found and additional HUI found. It is explainable as this graduated change directly causes increase in cluster utility for the transactions. Following the increase in cluster utility, increase in absolute utility for itemsets occurs. And increase in absolute utility for itemsets directly translates

into more itemsets crossing the threshold Φ. A graphical illustration is shown in Fig. 4. It should be noted that there are few HUI found (for the predictive model) which are not present in the list of HUI for the complete data (when using the standard model) particularly for cases of aggressive cluster utility assignment and especially when using 75% of data. This should be understood in a reasonable way. The reason for using Aggressive cluster utility assignment should be when the analysis is especially focused on discovering all possible cluster specific patterns along with the global patterns. Because the standard UIM problem model completely disregards the cluster structure, comparing it with that in this case becomes less relevant. Also it should be noted, when we use the 75% version of the data with the predictive UIM problem model, the complete data set can be called inadequate to verify the validity of the additional HUI discovered. This is because more data might be needed to claim one way or another.

3. The most significant point to note is that the predictive UIM problem model extracts quite a lot more (30% to 50% more for most cases in our experiments when being conservative or moderate in cluster utility assignment) actionable information (HUI) from the data when comparing to the standard UIM problem model. Most of additional HUI found by the new model are validated by the standard model when additional data becomes available. Few which are not found, can also hold value. These itemsets might represent patterns which are very specific to smaller cluster types and could not be found by the standard model due to the information loss issue discussed earlier.

7.3   Illustration of the Cluster Based Adaptive Itemset Discovery

We discussed in the previous section the methodology to perform adaptive Itemset discovery. This aspect of the model can be subjective in terms of the choice of the adaptive strategy (format of incorporation of the anticipated cluster contributions in doing the prediction). The Time Series model and parameters used to fit the series will also be data dependent. Therefore, instead of providing concrete guidelines we give an illustration of performing this adaptive itemset discovery. We do this in the following steps:

1. We create a cluster structure using 1% data of the BMSWebView1 dataset based on our clustering algorithm as described earlier.
2. We select the first 50% slice of the BMSWebView1 dataset, and evaluate the rolling cluster contribution sums for it.
3. We estimate the anticipated contributions for each cluster to the point in time where 75% of transactions will arrive, and normalize them. For fitting the time series we perform first order differencing. We also employ a moving average component of order 1. For computation, we used the statmodels library [22]. This model and parameters were picked based on trying various combination and selecting the one which is able to reasonably fit the series data. It should be noted that highly accurate estimations are not required here as we only need an idea of relative order among the estimates.

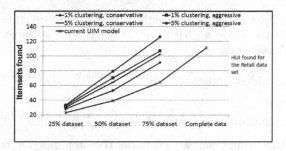

Fig. 4. HUI found for the Retail dataset (extracted from [14]).

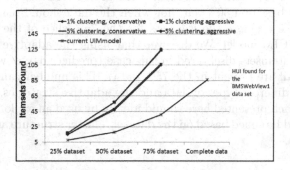

Fig. 5. HUI found for the BMSWebView1 dataset (extracted from [14]).

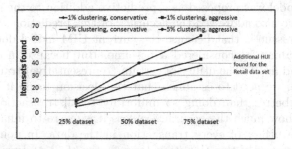

Fig. 6. Additional HUI found for the Retail dataset (extracted from [14]).

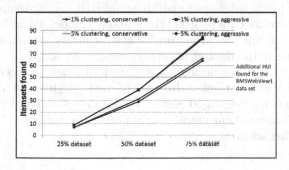

Fig. 7. Additional HUI found for the BMSWebView1 dataset (extracted from [14]).

4. We identify the cluster with the highest and the lowest anticipated contribution, and do the following with the transactions associated with them for cluster utility assignment:

$$\text{lowest anticipated, } k = \begin{cases} 0 & \text{if affinity}(T_i, C_j) < 0.25 \\ 1 & \text{otherwise} \end{cases} \tag{21}$$

$$\text{highest anticipated, } k = \begin{cases} 1 & \text{if affinity}(T_i, C_j) < 0.4 \\ 3 & \text{otherwise} \end{cases} \tag{22}$$

5. After doing this reshaping, we evaluate the itemsets for the 50%slice of BmsWebView1 dataset for $\Phi = 20{,}000$ using the updated utilities and the predictive UIM model. This would include the predictions based on the adaptive anticipations based on 50% data for when the data should reach 75%.

6. And lastly, we evaluate the itemsets for the 75% slice of the dataset using the classical UIM model. We discover that using the adaptive search results in 10% more itemsets discovered in this case (predictions), of which none are inaccurate (all are present in the 75% data). This number can however vary when we try different types of data and the adaptive strategies. The adaptive search approach presented here should ideally be used an exploratory analysis technique and be tuned based on the dataset, cluster structure and application requirements.

7.4   A Note on Prediction Accuracy

Because this model was proposed as a predictive addition to the standard UIM model in [14], we also addressed the accuracy of this prediction with respect to a baseline. The issue is that because the current UIM model does not do any prediction, it cannot be considered a baseline. But because in our model we are artificially adding to the utility of certain (representative) transactions (and hence itemsets), we need to establish that the decision to do it to the chosen transactions is better than doing so uniformly to all transactions. To say in simpler terms, how much the accuracy suffers if we were to inflate (artificially add to the) the utility of every transaction in the data. In doing an Itemset search by doing exactly this (inflation by a factor of 3) and we find that the accuracy suffers badly. We need to understand that accuracy here would mean how many of the predicted itemsets (Additionfal HUI found) are indeed found to be present in the future data by using the standard model. By inflating by factor of 3 we create a baseline for our aggressive cluster utility assignment model. We noted that for the Retail dataset accuracy dropped to 50.2% (from 96.2%) and 24.9% (from 84.9%) when working on 50% and 75% data respectively. For the case of BMSWebView1 dataset it dropped to a 44.7% (from 89.5%) and 19.6% (from 66.4%) when working on 50% and 75% data respectively. This proved that predictive performance of our model is significantly better (refer Tables 1 and 2) than these baseline schemes.

8 The Practical Benefits of Predictive UIM Problem Model

In today times data is used to guide planning, forecasting and decision making in almost all business and science applications. Actionable information is valued a lot and its early availability is valued even more. Reasons vary from creating more profit for businesses to early release of a drug. Faster processing of the data to achieve actionable information before the competition has been one of the approaches. But when availability of data itself is the bottleneck (which is happening for many applications in present times), it is most important to extract as much actionable information from the data as possible. Shown below is an illustration to demonstrate the benefit of the predictive UIM problem model to a business which depends on relevant advertising to push profits.

Let us assume that for a retail store with no advertising 1000 of items in each HUI are sold every month. Correct advertising leads to a X % increase in the sales. By correct advertising it is meant advertising based on discovered HUI. Therefore the sales achieved by the store in a month will be based on their choice of UIM problem model used in their analytics. For this analysis we use 50% of the Retail dataset with $\Phi = 50000$ and 10% of the transactions for clustering. The results are shown in Fig. 8.

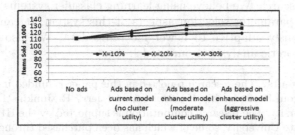

Fig. 8. Example impact of UIM model used (extracted from [14]).

9 Conclusion and Future Work

In this extended version of our previous work [14] we revisit that the current Utility Itemset Mining (UIM) problem model can be extended by including an important modeling capability of prediction, by identifying cluster specific patterns in the dataset. The idea is that all constituent transactions possess a unique predictive information in them to the degree to which they belong to a cluster of similar transactions in the whole data. Ignoring the presence of cluster structure and subjecting all transactions to the common threshold in the UIM problem leads this information loss.

Implicit use of cluster structure of data to solve this problem is highlighted. The use clustering based utility in the definition of the UIM problem model and modifying the definitions of absolute utilities based on it allows the cluster specific patterns to emerge while still mining the inter-cluster patterns. It also integrates well into all UIM techniques. Experiments results on two real datasets are presented to verify that the predictive UIM problem model extracts more useful information than the current classic UIM model. Significant revisions and extension in this work are:

1. We identify that there is a need of adaptive anticipation in our predictive Utility Itemset Mining model.
2. We develop and define concepts which can capture the idea of adaptive anticipation of the cluster structure.
3. We integrate these concepts into the predictive model by firstly discussing ways to analyze and evaluate the metrics associated with them, and then transferring that knowledge into our itemset mining model. A core part of this scheme involves fitting and forecasting Time Series models.
4. We conduct an illustrative experiment showing the way to perform adaptive cluster based discovery of High Utility Itemsets in a straightforward manner. We recommend an exploratory rationale to conduct such analysis.

For the future work, we plan to incorporate additional techniques which will aid in the adaptive search. We believe using learning classifier systems can automate the model and parameter selection aspects of this system. It can also make it more autonomously adaptive to newer incoming data. We also plan to do a information theoretic analysis of our model.

Acknowledgements. The research reported in this paper is funded in part by Philip and Virginia Sproul Professorship Endowment and Jerry R. Junkins Endowments at Iowa State University. The research computation is supported by the HPC@ISU equipment at Iowa State University, some of which has been purchased through funding provided by NSF under MRI grant number CNS 1229081 and CRI grant number 1205413. Any opinions, findings, and conclusions or recommendations expressed in this material are those of the author(s) and do not necessarily reflect the views of the funding agencies. We also thank Dr. Mayank Mishra, former Post Doctoral Fellow at Iowa State University for his contributions, suggestions and feedback during the intial phase of this work. He was also co-author on the conference paper [14] of which this work is an extension.

Appendix

```
Input: C ;
while max_aff ≥ min_aff do
    for C_i, C_j ∈ C do
        if affinity(C_i, C_j) > max_aff then
            max_aff = affinity(C_i, C_j);
            C_m1 = C_i;
            C_m2 = C_j;
    merge(C_m1, C_m2);
    update relevant affinities;
    for C_t ∈ C do
        if CU(C_t)/max(CU(C_k)∀C_k∈C) ≤ min_uty then
            delete C_t;
return C;
```
Algorithm 1. Clustering algorithm for categorical data with utility information.

C is the set of all given clusters. A cluster $C_k \in C$ is essentially a subset of transactions from D.

$$C_k = \{T_1, T_2 \ldots T_k | T_i \in D\} \tag{23}$$

$$I_{C_k} = \{a_i | a_i \in T_j \wedge T_j \in C_k\} = \text{item types in } C_k \tag{24}$$

Cluster utility (CU), relative utility (ru) of a category type in a cluster and the $affinity$ between clusters have the following definitions:

$$CU(C_k) = \sum_{T_j \in C_k} TU(T_j) = \text{Cluster utility of } C_k \tag{25}$$

CU is an overall measure of importance of a cluster, since it is the sum of utilities of all transactions in it.

$$\forall a_i \in I_{C_k}, ru(a_i, C_k) = \frac{\sum_{a_i \in I_{C_k} \wedge T_j \in C_k} au(a_i, T_j)}{CU(C_k)} \tag{26}$$

ru is the relative importance (since utility is a unit of importance) given to a_i among all I_{C_k} in C_k.

For clusters C_i and C_j:

$$affinity(C_i, C_j) = \sum_{a \in I_{C_k} \wedge a \in I_{C_j}} min(ru(a, C_i), ru(a, C_j)) \tag{27}$$

It is the sum of shared utility of common category types among two clusters. min_{aff} and min_{uty} are tunable parameters of the algorithm. min_{aff} decides the termination criterion of the clustering and min_{uty} decides the final selection criterion for the clusters.

References

1. Agrawal, R., Shafer, J.C.: Parallel mining of association rules. IEEE Trans. Knowl. Data Eng. **6**, 962–969 (1996)
2. Agrawal, R., Srikant, R., et al.: Fast algorithms for mining association rules. In: Proceedings of 20th International Conference on Very Large Data Bases, VLDB 1994, vol. 1215, pp. 487–499 (1994)
3. Ahmed, C.F., Tanbeer, S.K., Jeong, B.-S., Lee, Y.-K.: Efficient tree structures for high utility pattern mining in incremental databases. IEEE Trans. Knowl. Data Eng. **21**(12), 1708–1721 (2009)
4. Alves, R., Rodriguez-Baena, D.S., Aguilar-Ruiz, J.S.: Gene association analysis: a survey of frequent pattern mining from gene expression data. Brief. Bioinform. **11**(2), 210–224 (2009)
5. Andreopoulos, B., An, A., Wang, X., Schroeder, M.: A roadmap of clustering algorithms: finding a match for a biomedical application. Brief. Bioinform. **10**(3), 297–314 (2009)
6. BMSWebView1: SMPF: an open-source data mining library (2016). http://www.philippe-fournier-viger.com/spmf/index.php?link=datasets.php. Accessed 14 June 2016
7. Brijs, T., Swinnen, G., Vanhoof, K., Wets, G.: Using association rules for product assortment decisions: a case study. In: Knowledge Discovery and Data Mining, pp. 254–260 (1999)
8. Brin, S., Motwani, R., Ullman, J.D., Tsur, S.: Dynamic itemset counting and implication rules for market basket data. In: ACM SIGMOD Record, vol. 26, pp. 255–264. ACM (1997)
9. Chan, R.C., Yang, Q., Shen, Y.-D.: Mining high utility itemsets. In: Third IEEE International Conference on Data Mining, ICDM 2003, pp. 19–26. IEEE (2003)
10. Chen, K., Liu, L.: The "Best k" for entropy-based categorical data clustering (2005)
11. Guha, S., Rastogi, R., Shim, K.: ROCK: a robust clustering algorithm for categorical attributes. In: Proceedings of 15th International Conference on Data Engineering, pp. 512–521. IEEE (1999)
12. Han, J., Pei, J., Yin, Y.: Mining frequent patterns without candidate generation. In: ACM SIGMOD Record, vol. 29, pp. 1–12. ACM (2000)
13. Huang, Z.: Extensions to the k-means algorithm for clustering large data sets with categorical values. Data Min. Knowl. Discov. **2**(3), 283–304 (1998)
14. Lakhawat, P., Mishra, M., Somani, A.: A clustering based prediction scheme for high utility itemsets. In: Proceedings of the 9th International Joint Conference on Knowledge Discovery, Knowledge Engineering and Knowledge Management - Volume 1: KDIR, pp. 123–134. INSTICC, SciTePress (2017)
15. Lakhawat, P., Mishra, M., Somani, A.K.: A novel clustering algorithm to capture utility information in transactional data. In: KDIR, pp. 456–462 (2016)
16. Li, H.-F., Huang, H.-Y., Chen, Y.-C., Liu, Y.-J., Lee, S.-Y.: Fast and memory efficient mining of high utility itemsets in data streams. In: Eighth IEEE International Conference on Data Mining, ICDM 2008, pp. 881–886. IEEE (2008)
17. Liao, S.-H., Chu, P.-H., Hsiao, P.-Y.: Data mining techniques and applications-a decade review from 2000 to 2011. Expert. Syst. Appl. **39**(12), 11303–11311 (2012)
18. Liu, Y., Liao, W.-K., Choudhary, A.: A fast high utility itemsets mining algorithm. In: Proceedings of the 1st International Workshop on Utility-based Data Mining, pp. 90–99. ACM (2005)

19. Naulaerts, S., et al.: A primer to frequent itemset mining for bioinformatics. Brief. Bioinform. **16**(2), 216–231 (2015)
20. Ngai, E.W., Xiu, L., Chau, D.C.: Application of data mining techniques in customer relationship management: a literature review and classification. Expert. Syst. Appl. **36**(2), 2592–2602 (2009)
21. RetailDataset: Frequent itemset mining dataset repository (2016). http://fimi.ua.ac.be/data/. Accessed 14 June 2016
22. Seabold, S., Perktold, J.: StatsModels: econometric and statistical modeling with python. In: 9th Python in Science Conference (2010)
23. Toivonen, H., et al.: Sampling large databases for association rules. VLDB **96**, 134–145 (1996)
24. Tseng, V.S., Wu, C.-W., Fournier-Viger, P., Yu, P.S.: Efficient algorithms for mining the concise and lossless representation of high utility itemsets. IEEE Trans. Knowl. Data Eng. **27**(3), 726–739 (2015)
25. Tseng, V.S., Wu, C.-W., Shie, B.-E., Yu, P.S.: Up-growth: an efficient algorithm for high utility itemset mining. In: Proceedings of the 16th ACM SIGKDD International Conference on Knowledge Discovery and Data Mining, pp. 253–262. ACM (2010)
26. Yan, H., Chen, K., Liu, L., Yi, Z.: Scale: a scalable framework for efficiently clustering transactional data. Data Min. Knowl. Discov. **20**(1), 1–27 (2010)
27. Zaki, M.J.: Scalable algorithms for association mining. IEEE Trans. Knowl. Data Eng. **12**(3), 372–390 (2000)

Knowledge Based System for Composing Sentences to Summarize Documents

Andrey Timofeyev[⊠] and Ben Choi

Computer Science, Louisiana Tech University, Ruston, USA
andtimo@latech.edu, pro@benchoi.org

Abstract. This chapter provides the details on how to build a knowledge-based system that is capable of composing new sentences to summarize multiple documents. The system is also capable of identifying the main topics of the given documents and is able to derive new concepts based on the given text data. In order to process the documents conceptually to create abstractive summaries, the system makes use of the Cyc development platform that consists of the world's largest knowledge base and one of the most powerful inference engines. The resultant knowledge based system first uses natural language processing techniques to extracts syntactic structure of the documents and then maps the words of the sentences into related concepts in the knowledge base. It then uses the inference engine to generalize and fuse concepts to form more abstract concepts. Since a word can be mapped into multiple concepts, the system also includes new techniques to handle word-sense disambiguation by using concept weights. After the generalization, the system is able to identify the main topics and the key concepts of the documents. The system then composes new sentences based on the key concepts by linking subject concepts with their related predicate concepts. The syntactic structure of the newly created sentences extends beyond simple subject-predicate-object triplets by incorporating adjective and adverb modifiers. The final stage is then to map the linked concepts back to words to form the abstractive sentences. The system has been implemented and tested. The implementation encodes a process that consists of seven stages: syntactic analysis, words mapping, concept propagation, concept weights and relations accumulation, topic derivation, subject identification, and new sentence generation. The implementation has been tested on various documents and webpages. The test results showed that the system is capable of creating new sentences that include abstracted concepts not explicitly mentioned in the original documents and that contain information synthesized from different parts of the documents to compose a summary.

Keywords: Text summarization · Knowledge-based system ·
Natural language processing · Data mining · Artificial intelligence

1 Introduction

In this chapter, we describe in details how to build a knowledge based automatic summarization system [1] that is capable of creating abstractive summaries of the given documents by generalizing new concepts, deriving main topics, and composing new

© Springer Nature Switzerland AG 2019
A. Fred et al. (Eds.): IC3K 2017, CCIS 976, pp. 164–183, 2019.
https://doi.org/10.1007/978-3-030-15640-4_9

sentences. The system processes text data on documents and webpages and utilizes knowledge base and inference engine to produce an abstractive summary. It generates summaries by composing new sentences based on the semantics derived from the text.

The system uses both the syntactic structure provided by the given documents and the commonsense knowledge provided by a knowledge base. It performs deep syntactic analysis by using capabilities of advanced natural language processing techniques. It uses Cyc development platform as a source of background knowledge. The Cyc development platform consists of the world's largest ontology of commonsense knowledge and a reasoning engine that allows information comprehension and abstraction [2]. In addition, Cyc ontology serves as a backbone for semantic analysis, knowledge generalization, and natural language generation functionality of the system. The system is domain independent and unsupervised, being limited only by the commonsense ontology provided by the Cyc development platform.

Research in automatic text summarization has been conducted mostly by using extractive methods that extract parts of the given text as the summary. However, abstractive summarization that creates an abstract as the summary is considered more desirable. The task to create an abstract based on reading a document is considered complex from human reader and is more so for machine. When human readers perform document summarization they tend to use their commonsense and domain expertise about subject matter to merge information from various parts of the document and synthesize novel information that was not explicitly mentioned in the text [3]. Moreover, it is not a simple task for human readers to compose new sentences for the summary.

We attempt to develop a system that is capable of composing new sentences for the summary. Our system generalizes new abstract concepts based on the knowledge derived from the text. It automatically detects main topics described in the text. Moreover, it composes new English sentences for some of the most significant concepts. The created sentences form an abstractive summary, combining concepts from different parts of the input text.

The system conducts summarization process in three principal stages: knowledge acquisition, knowledge discovery, and knowledge representation. The knowledge acquisition stage derives syntactic structure of each sentence of the input document and maps words and their relations into Cyc knowledge base. Next, the knowledge discovery stage generalizes concepts upward in the Cyc ontology and detects main topics covered in the text. Finally, the knowledge representation stage composes new sentences for some of the most significant concepts defined in main topics. The syntactic structure of the newly created sentences follows an enhanced subject-predicate-object model, where adjective and adverb modifiers are used to produce more complex and informative sentences.

We have implemented our proposed system using modular and pipelined design framework. Modularity provides the ability to conveniently maintain parts of the system and to add new functionality as needed. The pipelined design framework allows comprehensible data flow between different modules. The system was tested on various documents and webpages. The test results show that the system is capable of identifying key concepts and discovering main topics comprised in the original text, generalizing new concept not explicitly mentioned in the text, and creating new sentences that contain information synthesized from various parts of the text. The newly created sentences have complex syntactic structures that enhance subject-predicate-object triplets with adjective and adverb modifiers. For example, the sentence "Colored grapefruit being sweet edible fruit" was automatically generated by the system analyzing encyclopedia articles describing grapefruits. Here, the subject concept "grapefruit" is modified by the adjective concept "colored" that was not explicitly mentioned in the text and the object concept "edible fruit" is modified by the adjective concept "sweet".

The sentence was created as the result of linked key concepts. The linked concepts is then mapped back to words to form the sentence. As we can see from the above example, the created sentence sound like made by a machine than by a human. Human reader might use the word "is" instead of "being" in the example sentence. In short, although our system is able to generate new abstractive sentences, there is much more research potential to further develop such a knowledge based system to compose new sentences as summary.

The rest of the paper is organized as follows. Section 2 outlines related work undertaken for automatic text summarization. Section 3 describes the summarization process workflow. Section 4 covers the system implementation in details. Section 5 provides detailed description of the system modules. Section 6 presents testing results. Section 7 provides the computational performance of the system. Section 8 discusses conclusions and directions of future work.

2 Related Work

Automatic text summarization seeks to compose a concise and coherent version of the original text preserving the most important information. Computational community has studied automatic text summarization problem since late 1950 s [4]. Studies in this area are generally divided into two main approaches – extractive and abstractive. Extractive text summarization aims to select the most important sentences from original text to form a summary. Such methods vary by different intermediate representations of the candidate sentences and different sentence scoring schemes [5]. Summaries created by extractive approach are highly relevant to the original text, but do not convey any new information. Most prominent methods in extractive text summarization use term frequency versus inverse document frequency (TF-IDF) metric [6, 7] and lexical chains for sentence representation [8, 9]. Statistical methods based on Latent Semantic Analysis (LSA), Bayesian topic modelling, Hidden Markov Model (HMM) and Conditional random field (CRF) derive underlying topics and use them as features for sentence selection [10, 11]. Despite significant advancements in the extractive text summarization, such approaches are not capable of semantic understanding and limited to the shallow knowledge contained in the text.

In contrast, abstractive text summarization aims to incorporate the meaning of the words and phrases and generalize knowledge not explicitly mentioned in the original text to form a summary. Phrase selection and merging methods in abstractive summarization aim to solve the problem of combining information from multiple sentences. Such methods construct clusters of phrases and then merge only informative ones to form summary sentences [12]. Graph transformation approaches convert original text into a form of sematic graph representation and then combine or reduce such representation with an aim of creating an abstractive summary [13, 14]. Summaries constructed by described methods consist of sentences not used in the original text, combining information from different parts, but such sentences do not convey new knowledge.

Several approaches attempt to incorporate semantic knowledge base into automatic text summarization by using WordNet lexical database [8, 15, 16]. Major drawback of WordNet system is the lack of domain-specific and common sense knowledge. Unlike Cyc, WordNet does not have reasoning engine and natural language generation capabilities.

Recent rapid development of deep learning contributes to the automatic text summarization, improving state-of-the-art performance. Deep learning methods applied to both extractive [17] and abstractive [18] summarization show promising results, but such approaches require vast amount of training data and powerful computational resources.

Our system extends to the one proposed in [19]. In the work, the structure of created sentences has simple subject-predicate-object pattern and new sentences are only created for clusters of compatible sentences found in the original text.

3 Knowledge-Based Abstractive Summarization Process

Our abstractive knowledge-based summarization system attempts to bring the machines one-step closer to the comprehension of the knowledge comprised in the text. The system performs text summarization in three principal stages: the knowledge acquisition, the knowledge discovery, and the knowledge representation. The overview of the summarization process is illustrated in Fig. 1.

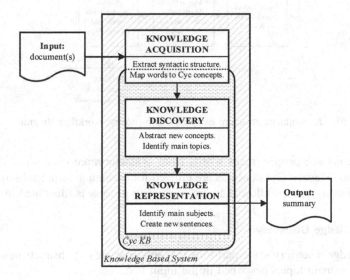

Fig. 1. System's workflow diagram [1].

During the knowledge acquisition stage, the algorithm receives text documents as an input, performs deep syntactic analysis, and maps the words with their syntactic relationships into the Cyc knowledge base. During the knowledge discovery stage, the system performs a generalization of new concepts by propagating the concepts that were mapped into Cyc knowledge base by the knowledge acquisition step. It also performs the task of the identification of the main topics of the text based on the mapped and generalized concepts. Finally, during the knowledge representation stage, the system generates new sentences using knowledge derived from the input text documents and the capabilities of the Cyc inference engine.

3.1   Knowledge Acquisition

The knowledge acquisition stage consists of two sub-processes. The first sub-process extracts the syntactic structures from the given documents. This sub-process serves as a data preprocessing and transformation step. It normalizes raw text data and transforms it into syntactic representation. The workflow diagram of the sub-process is outlined in Fig. 2.

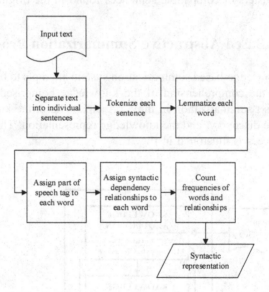

Fig. 2. Syntactic structure extraction sub-process workflow diagram.

The second sub-process maps words from syntactic representation of the text to Cyc concepts. Mapped Cyc concepts are utilized for reasoning during subsequent steps of the algorithm. The workflow diagram of the sub-process is illustrated in Fig. 3.

3.2   Knowledge Discovery

The knowledge discovery stage performs two sub-processes: it abstracts new concepts and identifies main topics described in the input text.

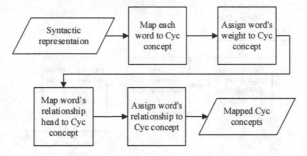

Fig. 3. Mapping words to Cyc concepts sub-process workflow diagram.

New concepts abstraction sub-process generalizes the information derived from the text. It finds the ancestors of mapped Cyc concepts and assigns the descendants' propagated weight and syntactic dependency relationships to the ancestors. It is an important part of the abstractive summarization process as it allows deriving concepts that are not explicitly mentioned in the input text. For example, concepts like "cat," "tiger," "jaguar," and "lion" are generalized into more abstract "feline" concept. The workflow diagram of the new concepts abstraction sub-process is illustrated in Fig. 4.

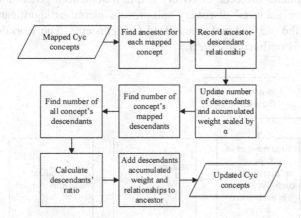

Fig. 4. New concepts abstraction sub-process workflow diagram.

The main topics identification sub-process detects topics described in the text with an assumption that they are represented by the most frequently used micro theories. Micro theories form the basis of the knowledge organization in Cyc ontology being the clusters of Cyc concepts and facts, typically representing one specific domain of knowledge. For example, #$BiologyMt is a micro theory containing biological knowledge, and #$MathMt is a micro theory containing concepts and facts describing the field of mathematics. Each Cyc concept is defined within a micro theory. The workflow diagram of the main topics identification sub-process is illustrated in Fig. 5.

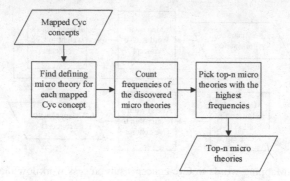

Fig. 5. Main topics identification sub-process workflow diagram.

3.3 Knowledge Representation

The knowledge representation stage utilizes powerful capabilities of the Cyc inference engine to generate new sentences based on the information discovered during knowledge acquisition and knowledge discovery steps. This stage uses mapped and generalized Cyc concepts, their syntactic dependency relationships, and the most frequent micro theories as inputs. The knowledge representation stage consists of two sub-processes – candidate subjects' discovery and new sentences generation.

The candidate subjects' discovery sub-process identifies significant subject concepts out of all the mapped and generalized Cyc concepts. The workflow diagram of the sub-process is outlined in Fig. 6.

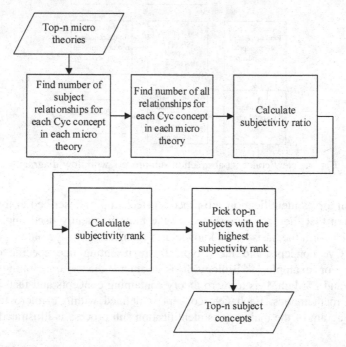

Fig. 6. Candidate subjects discovery sub-process workflow diagram.

The new sentences generation sub-process composes new sentences for each of the identified candidate subject concepts. The generated sentences serve as a final summary of the input text. The workflow diagram of the sub-process is outlined in Fig. 7.

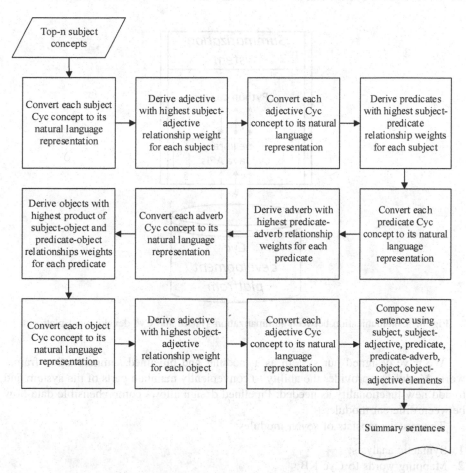

Fig. 7. New sentences generation sub-process workflow diagram.

4 Details of the System's Implementation

We chose Python as the implementation language to develop our system because of the advanced Natural Language Processing tools and libraries it supplies. Our system uses Cyc knowledge base and inference engine as a backbone for the semantic analysis. Cyc development platform supports communications with the knowledge base and utilization of the inference engine through the application programming interfaces (APIs) implemented in Java. We utilize Java-Python wrapper supported by JPype library to allow our system using Cyc Java API packages. JPype library is essentially an interface at a basic level of virtual machines [20]. It requires starting Java Virtual Machine with a path to the appropriate jar files before Java methods and classes can be accessible within Python code. Communication between our system and Cyc development platform is illustrated in Fig. 8. To the best of our knowledge, our developed system is the first Python-based system that allows communication with Cyc development platform.

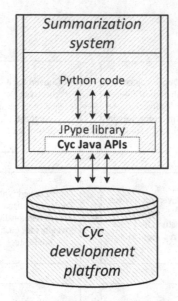

Fig. 8. Communication between summarization system and Cyc development platform.

We have designed our system as a modular and pipelined summarization framework. Modularity provides the ability to conveniently maintain parts of the system and to add new functionality as needed. Pipelined design allows comprehensible data flow between different modules.

The system consists of seven modules:

1. Syntactic analysis;
2. Mapping words to Cyc KB;
3. Concepts propagation;
4. Concepts' weights and relations accumulation;
5. Topics derivation;
6. Subjects identification;
7. New sentences generation.

Modules 1 and 2 together constitute the knowledge acquisition stage of the summarization process. Modules 3, 4 and 5 together make up the knowledge discovery stage of the summarization process. Modules 6 and 7 together form knowledge representation stage of the summarization process. System modules are illustrated in Fig. 9.

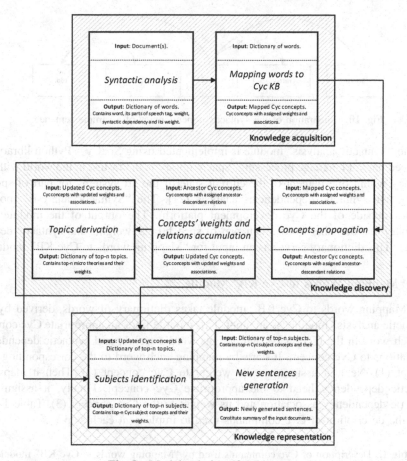

Fig. 9. Modular design of the system.

5 Description of the System's Modules

5.1 "Syntactic Analysis" Module

The first module in the system is the "Syntactic analysis" module. The role of this module is essentially a data preprocessing. The module takes documents as an input and transforms them into syntactic representations. It first performs text normalization by lemmatizing each word in each sentence. Then it derives part of speech tags, parses syntactic dependencies and counts word's weights. The syntactic dependencies are recorded in the following format: ("word" "type" "head"), where "word" is the dependent element, "type" is the type of the dependency, and "head" is the leading element. For example, applying syntactic parser on the following sentence: "John usually drinks strong coffee" produces the following syntactic dependencies between words: ("Steve" "nsubj" "drinks"), ("tea" "dobj" "drinks"), ("rarely" "advmod" "drinks"), ("black" "amod" "tea"). Syntactic dependencies of the example sentence are illustrated in Fig. 10.

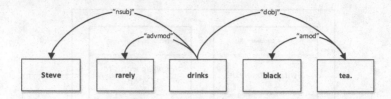

Fig. 10. Illustration of the syntactic dependencies of a sample sentence.

The "Syntactic analysis" module is implemented using SpaCy – Python library for advanced natural language processing. SpaCy library is the fastest in the world with the accuracy within one percent of the current state of the art systems for part of speech tagging and syntactic dependencies analysis [21]. The "Syntactic analysis" module operates outside of the Cyc development platform. The output of the module is a dictionary that contains words, their part of speech tags, weights and syntactic dependencies. This dictionary serves as an input for "Mapping words to Cyc KB" module.

5.2 "Mapping Words to Cyc KB" Module

The "Mapping words to Cyc KB" module takes dictionary of words, derived by the "Syntactic analysis" module, as an input. This module finds an appropriate Cyc concept for each word in the dictionary, and assigns word's weight and syntactic dependency associations to Cyc concept. It starts by mapping each word to the corresponding Cyc concept (1). Next, it assigns word's weight to Cyc concept (2). Then it maps the syntactic dependency head to the appropriate Cyc concept. Finally, it assigns the syntactic dependency association and its weight to the Cyc concept (3). Table 1 provides the description of Cyc commands used to implement each step.

Table 1. Description of Cyc commands used by "Mapping words to Cyc KB" module.

Step	Cyc command	Description
1	(#$and (#$denotation ?Word ?POS ?Num ?Concept) (#$wordForms ?Word ? WordForm "word") (#$genls ?POS ? POSTag))	Command uses built-in "#$denotation" Cyc predicate to relate a "word", its part of speech tag (?POS), and a sense number (? Num) to concept (?Concept). It also uses "# $wordForms" and "#$genls" predicates to accommodate for all variations of word's lexical forms
2	(#$conceptWeight ?Concept ?Weight)	Command uses user-defined "# $conceptWeight" Cyc predicate that assigns the weight (?Weight) to the concept (? Concept)
3	(#$conceptAssociation ?Concept ?Type ? HeadConcept ?Weight)	Command uses user-defined "# $conceptAssociation" Cyc predicate that assigns a specific type (?Type) of a syntactic dependency association, the leading element (?HeadConcept) and the weight (?Weight) to the concept (?Concept)

This module communicates with Cyc development platform and updates weight and syntactic dependency relations of Cyc concepts. The output of the module are mapped Cyc concepts with assigned weights and syntactic dependency relations. The mapped Cyc concepts serve as an input for "Concepts propagation" module. "Syntactic analysis" and "Mapping words to Cyc KB" modules together constitute the knowledge acquisition step of the summarization process.

5.3 "Concepts Propagation" Module

The "Concepts propagation" module takes Cyc concepts, mapped by "Mapping words to Cyc KB" module, as an input and finds their closest ancestor concepts. This module performs generalization and abstraction of new concepts that have not been mentioned in the text explicitly. It starts by querying Cyc knowledge base for all the concepts that have assigned weight (1). Then it finds an ancestor concept for each concept derived by the query (2). Next, it records the number of ancestor's descendant concepts and their weight (3). Finally, it assigns ancestor-descendant relation between ancestor and descendant concepts (4). Table 2 provides the description of Cyc commands used to implement each step.

Table 2. Description of Cyc commands used by "Concepts propagation" module.

Step	Cyc command	Description
1	(#$conceptWeight ?Concept ? Weight)	Command uses user-defined "#$conceptWeight" Cyc predicate to retrieve concepts (?Concept) that have assigned weights (?Weight)
2	(#$min-genls ?Concept)	Command uses built-in "min-genls" Cyc predicate to retrieve the closest ancestor concept for the given concept (?Concept)
3	(#$conceptDescendants ? Concept ?Weight ?Count)	Command uses user-defined "#$conceptDescendants" Cyc predicate to record the number of descendants (? Count) and their weight (?Weight) to the ancestor concept (?Concept)
4	(#$conceptAncestorOf ? Concept ?Descendant)	Command uses user-defined "#$conceptAncestorOf" predicate to assign ancestor-descendant relation between the ancestor concept (?Concept) and the descendant concept (?Descendant)

This module communicates with Cyc development platform to derive all mapped Cyc concepts, find closest ancestor concepts and update ancestor concepts' relations. The output of the module are ancestor Cyc concepts with assigned descendant concepts' weights and counts and ancestor-descendant relations. The ancestor Cyc concepts are used by "Concepts' weights and relations accumulation" module.

5.4   "Concepts' Weights and Relations Accumulation" Module

The "Concepts' weights and relations accumulation" module takes ancestor Cyc concepts as an input and adds descendants' accumulated weight and relations to ancestor concepts if the calculated descendant-ratio is higher than the threshold. The descendant-ratio is the number of mapped descendant concepts divided by the number of all descendant concepts of an ancestor concept. This module starts by querying Cyc knowledge base for all ancestor concepts (1). Then it calculates the descendant ratio for each ancestor concept (2.1, 2.2). Next, it adds propagated descendants' weight (3) and descendants' associations with their propagated weights (4) to ancestor concepts if the descendant-ratio is higher than the defined threshold. Table 3 provides the description of Cyc commands used to implement each step.

Table 3. Description of Cyc commands used by "Concepts' weights and relations accumulation" module.

Step	Cyc command	Description
1	(#$conceptDescendants ?Concept ?Weight ?Count)	Command uses user-defined "#$conceptDescendants" Cyc predicate to retrieve all concepts (?Concept) that have descendants
2.1	(#$conceptAncestorOf ?AncConcept ?MappedDesc)	Command uses user-defined "#$conceptAncestorOf" predicate to retrieve mapped descendant concepts (?MappedDesc) of the given ancestor concept (?AncConcept)
2.2	(#$genls ?AncConcept ?DescConcept)	Command uses built-in "#$genls" Cyc predicate to retrieve all descendant concepts (?DescConcept) of the given ancestor concept (?AncConcept)
3	(#$conceptWeight ?AncConcept ?DescWeight)	Command uses user-defined "#$conceptWeight" Cyc predicate to assigns the descendant concepts' propagated weight (?DescWeight) to the ancestor concept
4	(and (#$conceptAncestorOf ?AncConcept ?DescConcept) (#$conceptAssociation ?DescConcept ?Type ?HeadConcept ?Weight))	Command uses user-defined "#$conceptAncestorOf" and "#$conceptAssociation" Cyc predicates to assign descendant's association (?DescConcept) and its propagated weight (?Weight) to the ancestor concept (?AncConcept)

This module communicates with Cyc development platform to derive all ancestor Cyc concepts, find the number of ancestor's mapped descendants, find the number of all ancestor's descendants and update ancestor's weight and relations. The output of the module are the Cyc concepts with updated weights and syntactic dependency associations. Updated Cyc concepts are used by the "Topics derivation" and the "Subjects identification" modules.

5.5 "Topics Derivation" Module

The "Topics derivation" module takes updated Cyc concepts as an input and derives defining micro theory for each concept. Micro theories with the highest weights represent the main topics of the document. This module first derives defining micro theory for each Cyc concept that have assigned weight (1). Then it counts the weights of derived micro theories based on their frequencies and picks up top-n with the highest weights. Table 4 provides the description of Cyc command used to implement defining micro theory derivation.

Table 4. Description of Cyc command used by "Topics derivation" module.

Step	Cyc command	Description
1	(#$and (#$conceptWeight ?Concept ?Weight) (#$definingMt ?Concept ?MicroTheory))	Command uses user-defined "#$conceptWeight" Cyc predicate and built-in "definingMt" Cyc predicate to derive defining micro theory (?MicroTheory) for each concept (?Concept) that have assigned weight (?Weight)

This module communicates with Cyc development platform to derive defining micro theory for each mapped Cyc concept. Calculation of the derived micro theories' weights is handled outside of the Cyc development platform. The output of the module is the micro theories dictionary that contains top-n micro theories with highest weights. This dictionary serves as an input for the "Subjects identification" module. The "Concepts propagation", the "Concepts' weights and relations accumulation" and the "Topics derivation" modules together constitute knowledge discovery step of the summarization process.

5.6 "Subjects Identification" Module

The "Subjects identification" module uses updated Cyc concepts and the dictionary of top-n micro theories as an input to derive most informative subject concepts based on a subjectivity rank. Subjectivity ranks is the product of the concept's weight and the concept's subjectivity ratio. Subjectivity ratio is the number of concept's syntactic dependency associations labelled as "subject" relations divided by the total number of concept's syntactic dependency associations. Subjectivity rank allows identifying concepts with the strongest subject roles in the documents. The module start by querying Cyc knowledge base for all mapped Cyc concepts for each micro theory in top-n micro theories dictionary (1). Then it calculates subjectivity ratio and subjectivity rank for each derived Cyc concept (2.1, 2.2). Finally, it picks top-n subject concepts with the highest subjectivity rank. Table 5 provides the description of Cyc commands used to implement each step.

Table 5. Description of Cyc commands used by "Subjects identification" module.

Step	Cyc command	Description
1	(#$and (#$definingMt ?Concept ?MicroTheory) (#$conceptWeight ?Concept ?Weight))	Command uses built-in "#$definingMt" Cyc predicate and user-defined "conceptWeight" Cyc predicate to derive concepts (?Concept) that have assigned weight (?Weight) for each micro theory (?MicroTheory) in micro theories dictionary
2.1	(#$conceptAssociation ?Concept "nsubj" ?HeadConcept ?Weight)	Command uses user-defined "# $conceptAssociation" Cyc predicate with "nsubj" parameter to derive the concept's (?Concept) syntactic dependency associations labelled as "subject" relations
2.2	(#$conceptAssociation ?Concept ?Type ?HeadConcept ?Weight)	Command uses user-defined "# $conceptAssociation" Cyc predicate with no parameter specified (?Type) to derive all concept's (?Concept) syntactic dependency associations

This module communicates with Cyc development platform to derive mapped Cyc concepts for each defining micro theory in the input dictionary and to find the number of the concept's syntactic dependency associations labelled as "subject" relation and the number of all syntactic dependency associations of the concept. Calculations of the subjectivity ratio and the subjectivity rank are handled outside of the Cyc development platform. The output of the module is the dictionary that contains top-n subjects with the highest subjectivity rank. This dictionary serves as an input for the "New sentence generation" module.

5.7 "New Sentences Generation" Module

The "New sentences generation" module takes the dictionary of top-n most informative subjects as an input and produces new sentences for each of the subject to form a summary of the input documents. The module starts by deriving a natural language representation of each subject Cyc concept in the dictionary (1). Then it picks the adjective Cyc concept modifier with the highest subject-adjective syntactic dependency association weight (2) and derives its natural language representation. Next, it picks top-n predicate Cyc concepts with the highest subject-predicate syntactic dependency association weights (3) and derives their natural language representations. Then it picks the adverb Cyc concept modifier with the highest predicate-adverb syntactic dependency association weight (4) and derives its natural language representation. Next, it picks top-n object Cyc concepts with the highest product of subject-object and predicate-object syntactic dependency association weights (5.1, 5.2) and derives their natural language representations. Then, it picks the adjective Cyc concept modifier with the highest object-adjective syntactic dependency association weight and derives its natural language representation. Finally, it composes the new sentence using subject,

subject-adjective, predicate, predicate-adverb, object and object-adjective natural language representations. Table 6 provides the description of Cyc commands used to implement each step.

Table 6. Description of Cyc commands used by "New sentence generation" module.

Step	Cyc command	Description
1	(#$generate-phrase ?Concept)	Command uses built-in "#$generate-phrase" Cyc predicate to retrieve corresponding natural language representation for a Cyc concept (?Concept)
2	(#$conceptAssociation ?Concept "amod" ?HeadConcept ?Weight)	Command uses user-defined "#$conceptAssociation" Cyc predicate with "amod" parameter to derive Cyc concept (?Concept) associations labelled as adjective modifier syntactic dependency relation
3	(#$conceptAssociation ?Concept "pred" ?HeadConcept ?Weight)	Command uses user-defined "#$conceptAssociation" Cyc predicate with "pred" parameter to derive Cyc concept (?Concept) associations labelled as predicate syntactic dependency relation
4	(#$conceptAssociation ?Concept "advmod" ?HeadConcept ?Weight)	Command uses user-defined "#$conceptAssociation" Cyc predicate with "advmod" parameter to derive Cyc concept (?Concept) associations labelled as adverb modifier syntactic dependency relation
5.1	(#$conceptAssociation ?Concept "obj" ?HeadConcept ?Weight)	Command uses user-defined "#$conceptAssociation" Cyc predicate with "obj" parameter to derive Cyc concept (?Concept) associations labelled as object syntactic dependency relation
5.2	(#$conceptAssociation ?Concept "subj-obj" ?HeadConcept ?Weight)	Command uses user-defined "#$conceptAssociation" Cyc predicate with "subj-obj" parameter to derive Cyc concept (?Concept) associations labelled as subject-object syntactic dependency relation

This module communicates with Cyc development platform to derive appropriate Cyc concepts for each sentence element based on the weights of their syntactic dependency associations and derive their natural language representation. New sentences are composed outside of the Cyc development platform and serve as an output for the module and the whole summarization system. The "Subjects identification" and the "New sentences generation" modules together constitute the knowledge representation step of the summarization process.

6 Testing and Results

We have tested our system on various encyclopedia articles describing concepts from different domain. First, we conducted an experiment using multiple articles about grapefruits. In this experiment, we increased the number of analyzed articles on each run of the system, starting with a single article. Figure 11 illustrates new sentences created by the system. These results show the progression of sentence structure from simple subject-predicate-object triplet to more complex structure enhanced by the adjective and adverb modifiers when more articles were processed by the system.

> "Grapefruit being fruit." (a)
>
> "Grapefruit being colored edible fruit." (b)
>
> "Colored grapefruit being sweet edible fruit." (c)

Fig. 11. Test results of new sentences created for multiple articles about grapefruit; (a) – single article, (b) – two articles, (c) – three articles [1].

Next, we applied our system on five encyclopedia articles describing different types of felines, including cats, tigers, cougars, jaguars and lions. Figure 12 shows main topics and concepts extracted from the text and newly created sentences.

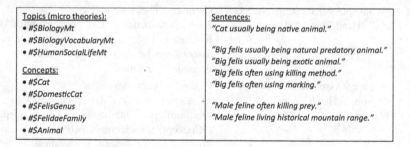

| Topics (micro theories):
• #$BiologyMt
• #$BiologyVocabularyMt
• #$HumanSocialLifeMt

Concepts:
• #$Cat
• #$DomesticCat
• #$FelisGenus
• #$FelidaeFamily
• #$Animal | Sentences:
"Cat usually being native animal."

"Big felis usually being natural predatory animal."
"Big felis usually being exotic animal."
"Big felis often using killing method."
"Big felis often using marking."

"Male feline often killing prey."
"Male feline living historical mountain range." |

Fig. 12. Test results of new sentences, concepts and main topics for encyclopedia articles about felines [1].

These results show that the system is able to abstract new concepts and create new sentences that contain information synthesized from different parts of the documents. Concepts like "canis", "mammal meat" and "felis" were derived by the generalization process and were not explicitly mentioned in the original documents. Our system yields better results compared to the reported in [19]. New sentences created by the system have structure that is more complex and contain information fused from various parts of the text. More testing results are reported in [1].

7 System's Performance

The computational complexity of our proposed system is upper bounded by the polynomial expression in the size of the vocabulary of the input documents and therefore, the system is considered to be of the polynomial time complexity. Vocabulary of the document is the number of the unique lemmas contained in the document. Table 7 illustrates the performance of the system when applied to the encyclopedia articles. The experiments were conducted on a machine with a 2.0 GHz Intel Xeon E5-2620 CPU and 32 GB of RAM.

Table 7. System performance scores using encyclopedia articles.

# of articles	Article name(s)	Source(s)	Vocabulary size (Lemmas)	CPU time (Seconds)
3	"Grapefruit"	Wikipedia, Morton, New world Encyclopedia	1988	2608
5	"Cat" "Tiger" "Cougar" "Jaguar" "Lion"	Wikipedia	5812	6974

8 Conclusions and Future Work

The task of producing an abstractive summary of a given text is considered challenging for humans and even more so for machines. Employing the semantic features and the syntactic structure of the text together with the world's largest knowledge base shows great potential in creating abstractive summaries. In this chapter, we thoroughly described the design and implementation of a knowledge-based abstractive summarization system that can automatically composes new sentences as the summary. Our knowledge-based system employs the Cyc knowledge base and its reasoning engine as a backbone for commonsense and inferencing ability. The system creates a summary of a given text by composing new sentences that contain the information aggregated from the various parts of the text. The structure of the summary sentences is enhanced from simple subject-predicate-object triplets to a more complex structure by adding adjective and adverb modifiers. Although our system is able to generate new abstractive sentences, there is much more research potential to further develop such a knowledge based system to compose new sentences as summary.

Future research potential includes enhancing the domain knowledge since the semantic knowledge and reasoning are limited to the functionality and performance of the underlining commonsense knowledge base. Our system is currently as knowledgeable as the capabilities of the Cyc knowledge base that is currently the largest ontology of commonsense knowledge. For future improvement, a system could use the information derived from the whole World Wide Web as a domain knowledge. This would possess challenging research questions such as information inconsistency and sense disambiguation. In addition, a robust inference engine would be required to process the information correctly and in a timely fashion. Another potential research is to improve the process and the structure of composing new sentences. Our system currently uses subject-predicate-object triplets enhanced by adjective and adverb modifiers. It does not yet resemble the structure of the sentences created by human. The structure of newly created sentences can be improved by using a more sophisticated representation of the syntactic structure of the sentence, such as graph representation. Moreover, another future research direction is to compose several connected sentences to form a coherent abstract. Currently, the sentences created by our system are not directly connected to each other. One possible enhancement is by representing the whole document as a graph of connected concepts with various relationships among them and then creating new sentences based on these relationships. Much more research is needed for a machine to create a coherent abstract to summarize documents.

References

1. Timofeyev, A., Choi, B.: Knowledge based automatic summarization. In: Proceedings of the 9th International Joint Conference on Knowledge Discovery, Knowledge Engineering and Knowledge Management (IC3 K 2017). pp. 350–356. SCITEPRESS (2017). https://doi.org/10.5220/0006580303500356
2. Cycorp – Cycorp Making Solutions Better. http://www.cyc.com
3. Cheung, J., Penn, G.: Towards robust abstractive multi-document summarization: a caseframe analysis of centrality and domain. In: Proceedings of the 51st Annual Meeting of the Association for Computational Linguistics, pp. 1233–1242. Association for Computational Linguistics (2013)
4. Luhn, H.: The automatic creation of literature abstracts. IBM J. Res. Dev. **2**, 159–165 (1958). https://doi.org/10.1147/Rd.22.0159
5. Nenkova, A., Mckeown, K.: A survey of text summarization techniques. In: Charu, A., Zhai, C. (eds.) Mining Text Data, pp. 43–76. Springer, Heidelberg (2012)
6. Hovy, E., Chin-Yew, L.: Automated text summarization and the SUMMARIST system. In: Proceedings of a Workshop Held at Baltimore, Maryland, 13–15 October 1998, pp. 197–214. Association for Computational Linguistics (1998). https://doi.org/10.3115/1119089.1119121
7. Radev, D., Jing, H., Styś, M., Tam, D.: Centroid-based summarization of multiple documents. Inf. Process. Manag. **40**, 919–938 (2004). https://doi.org/10.3115/1117575.1117578
8. Barzilay, R., Elhadad, M.: Using lexical chains for text summarization. Adv. Autom. Text Summ., 111–121 (1999). https://doi.org/10.7916/d85b09vz
9. Ye, S., Chua, T., Kan, M., Qiu, L.: Document concept lattice for text understanding and summarization. Inf. Process. & Manag. **43**, 1643–1662 (2007). https://doi.org/10.1016/J.Ipm.2007.03.010
10. Gong, Y., Liu, X.: Generic text summarization using relevance measure and latent semantic analysis. In: Proceedings of the 24th Annual International ACM SIGIR Conference on Research and Development in Information Retrieval, pp. 19–25. ACM (2001). https://doi.org/10.1145/383952.383955

11. Shen, D., Sun, J., Li, H., Yang, Q., Chen, Z.: Document summarization using conditional random fields. In: Proceedings of International Joint Conference on Artificial Intelligence, pp. 2862–2867. IJCAI (2007)
12. Bing, L., Li, P., Liao, Y., Lam, W., Guo, W., Passonneau, R.: Abstractive multi-document summarization via phrase selection and merging. In: Proceedings of the ACL-IJCNLP, pp. 1587–1597. Association for Computational Linguistics (2015)
13. Ganesan, K., Zhai, C., Han, J.: Opinosis: a graph-based approach to abstractive summarization of highly redundant opinions. In: Proceedings of the 23rd International Conference on Computational Linguistics, pp. 340–348. Association for Computational Linguistics (2010)
14. Moawad, I., Aref, M.: Semantic graph reduction approach for abstractive text summarization. In: 2012 Seventh International Conference Computer Engineering & Systems (ICCES), pp. 132–138. IEEE (2012). https://doi.org/10.1109/icces.2012.6408498
15. Bellare, K., Sharma, A.D., Loiwal, N., Mehta, V., Ramakrishnan, G., Bhattacharyya, P.: Generic text summarization using WordNet. In: Language Resources and Evaluation Conference, pp. 691–694. LREC (2004)
16. Pal, A., Saha, D.: An approach to automatic text summarization using WordNet. In: 2014 IEEE International Advance Computing Conference (IACC), pp. 1169–1173. IEEE (2014). https://doi.org/10.1109/iadcc.2014.6779492
17. Nallapati, R., Zhai, F., Zhou, B.: SummaRuNNer: a recurrent neural network based sequence model for extractive summarization of documents. In: Proceedings of the Thirty-First AAAI Conference on Artificial Intelligence (AAAI 2017). pp. 3075–3081. AAAI (2017)
18. Rush, A.M., Chopra, S., Wetson, J.: A neural attention model for abstractive sentence summarization. In: Proceedings of the 2015 Conference on Empirical Methods in Natural Language Processing, pp. 379–389. EMNLP (2015). https://doi.org/10.18653/v1/d15-1044
19. Choi, B., Huang, X.: Creating new sentences to summarize documents. In: The 10th IASTED International Conference on Artificial Intelligence and Application (AIA 2010), pp. 458–463. IASTED (2010)
20. Jpype - Java to Python Integration. http://jpype.sourceforge.net
21. Honnibal, M., Johnson, M.: An improved non-monotonic transition system for dependency parsing. In: Proceedings of the 2015 Conference on Empirical Methods in Natural Language Processing, pp. 1373–1378. EMNLP (2015). https://doi.org/10.18653/v1/d15-1162

A Modified Version of AlQuAnS: An Arabic Language Question Answering System

Ahmed Abdelmegied, Yasmin Ayman, Ahmad Eid,
Nagwa El-Makky, Ahmed Fathy, Ghada Khairy, Khaled Nagi,
Mohamed Nabil[✉], and Mohammed Yousri

Computer and Systems Engineering Department, Faculty of Engineering,
Alexandria University, Alexandria, Egypt
{ahmed.abdelmegied, yasmin.ayman, ahmad.eid, nagwamakky,
ahmed.fathy, ghada.khairy, khaled.nagi, mohamed.nabil,
mohamed.yousri}@alexu.edu.eg

Abstract. The challenges of the Arabic language and the lack of resources have made it difficult to provide Arabic Question Answering (QA) systems with high accuracy. These challenges motivated us to propose AlQuAnS-an Arabic Language Question Answering System that gives promising accuracy results. This paper proposes a modified version of AlQuAnS with a higher accuracy. The proposed system enhances the accuracy of the question classification, semantic interpreter and answer extraction modules. The provided performance evaluation study shows that our modified system outperforms other existing Arabic QA systems, especially with the newly introduced answer extraction module.

Keywords: Arabic question answering systems ·
Arabic morphological analysis · Question analysis · Question classification ·
Answer extraction · Semantic analysis · Question expansion

1 Introduction

Question Answering has gained great attention lately after the great progress in the field of Natural Language Processing (NLP), where Question Answering improves the search experience by suggesting an explicit answer for a user's provided question.

The process of question answering is as follows, when a user provides a question, this question is analyzed from a linguistic point of view, in attempt to predict the expected answer. Afterwards, related documents are searched to retrieve a valid answer for the provided question.

Great research efforts are made to provide reliable QA in different languages. unfortunately, Arabic QA doesn't gain great attention in these contributions although on 2016, 26 countries are using Arabic as their main language and 420 million people around the world talk Arabic which makes Arabic the 6th most spoken language.

The main reasons for the few attempts for building Arabic Question Answering systems are scarceness of Arabic datasets and the richness of Arabic morphology. The Arabic morphological richness imposes the need for intelligent morphological analyzer to process Arabic text.

© Springer Nature Switzerland AG 2019
A. Fred et al. (Eds.): IC3K 2017, CCIS 976, pp. 184–199, 2019.
https://doi.org/10.1007/978-3-030-15640-4_10

1.1 Arabic Morphology

Arabic is a rich morphological language which needs intelligent algorithms to analyze its text. Morphological analysis is a process of figuring out the word features; such as:

- root or stem,
- morphological pattern,
- part-of-speech (noun, verb or particle)
- number (singular, dual or plural)
- case or mood (nominative, accusative, genitive or jussive)

of the word. The root-patterned nonlinear morphology of Arabic makes both theoretical and computational processing for Arabic text extremely hard.

Since Arabic has a completely different orthography based on standard Arabic script going from right to left. Also, each letter has *three* different shapes depending on its position within the word, where each letter may have a diacritic sign above or below the letter. Changing the diacritic of one letter may change the meaning of the whole word. Printed and online text come usually *without* diacritics leaving plenty of room for word ambiguity.

Arabic is also a highly *derivational* language. It is a highly *inflectional* language as well.

$$Word = prefix(es) + lemma + suffix(es).$$

The prefixes can be articles, prepositions or conjunctions; whereas the suffixes are generally objects or personal/possessive anaphora. Both prefixes and suffixes can be combined, and thus a word can have zero or more affixes. Figure 1 shows an example of the composition of an Arabic word.

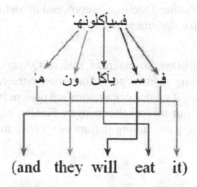

Fig. 1. Example Arabic inflection [1].

The absence of capital letters is another challenge in the Named Entity Recognition (NER) in Arabic [2, 3] Lots of Arabic names are adjectives; such as, "gameel" (handsome), "zaki" (intelligent), or "khaled" (immortal).

Last but not least, from a statistical viewpoint, if Arabic texts are compared to texts written in other languages which have a less complex morphology, Arabic texts look much sparser because of the inflectional characteristic of the language that we mentioned above. This specific characteristic of the language is the reason that makes it more difficult to handle each task in Natural Language Processing (NLP).

2 Motivation

Because of the mentioned challenges, we were motivated to propose AlQuAnS [4] – An Arabic Language Question Answering System that gives promising accuracy results. In this paper, we propose a modified version of AlQuAnS with improved accuracy of various modules. The overall performance results show that this modified version gives enhanced performance compared to past related work.

The rest of the paper is organized as follows. In Sect. 3, we give a short survey on the related standard work in the field of QA systems. Then, we focus on Arabic QA systems. Section 4 contains an overview of the system architecture of AlQuAnS and description of each system component. In Sect. 5 we show our modifications to AlQuAnS. The system evaluation is presented in Sect. 6. Section 7 concludes the paper and presents some ideas for our future work in this area.

3 Related Work

A Question Answering system is a system that takes an input question from the user, retrieves the related result sets to the question topic and then extracts an exact answer to the question to be returned to the user. A typical state-of-the-art Question Answering system, divides the Question Answering task into *three* core components:

- Question Analysis (including Question preprocessing and classification),
- Information Retrieval (or document retrieval),
- Answer Extraction.

Question classification plays an essential role in QA systems by classifying the submitted question according to its type. Information retrieval is very important for question answering, because if no correct answers are present in a document, no further processing can be carried out to find the answer. Finally, answer extraction aims at retrieving the correct passage containing the answer within the retrieved document.

3.1 Latin QA Systems

Kngine stands for *Knowledge Engine* (Kngine, n.d.) is a knowledge engine that is designed to give direct answers for questions. Kngine leverages natural language processing, machine learning, and data mining algorithms to build an extraction engine, that learns meaningful concepts, information and relationships from data. The authors claim that Kngine is the world's first multi-language question answering engine. Currently, Kngine supports English and other languages as Arabic, German and Spanish based on translation from the English language.

The authors of [5] propose an offline strategy for QA in which information is extracted automatically from electronic offline texts and stored for quick and easy access. The system extracts semantic relations (e.g., concept-instance relations) between lexical items using multiple Part-Of-Speech (POS) patterns. Then, it filters out the noise from the extracted relations using a machine-learned classifier. At the end, it tests the feasibility of this strategy on one semantic relation and a challenging subset of questions, which can be extended to include other types of questions.

LAMP [6] is a web-based QA system that takes advantage of the snippets in the search results returned by a search engine like Google. Asking a question such as "Who was the first American in space?", LAMP submits the question to Google and grabs its top 100 search results. Then, the system utilizes a Support Vector Machine (SVM) to classify the questions (e.g., this question asks for a person name). The system then extracts all information of the same type from the search result sets as *plausible answers*, using a Hidden Markov Model (HMM)-based named entity recognizer. For each plausible answer, the system constructs a snippet cluster which is composed of all the snippets containing that answer. For each plausible answer, the system constructs a snippet cluster which is composed of all the snippets containing that answer. Finally, the system uses cosine similarities between clusters and the question to get the best cluster that matches the question and returns the named entity that represents the best matching cluster.

The work of [7] addresses the problem where queries and relevant textual content significantly differ in their properties and are difficult to match with traditional information retrieval methods. A novel algorithm is presented that analyses the dependency structures of the known valid answer sentence. These acquired patterns are used to more precisely retrieve relevant text passages from the underlying document collection. The positions of key phrases in the answer sentence relative to the answer itself are analyzed and linked to a certain syntactic question type. The algorithm does not require a candidate sentence to be similar to the question in any respect.

IBM developed a statistical QA system for TREC 9 [8]. It is an application of maximum entropy classification for question and answer *type* prediction and named entity marking dealing only with *fact*-based questions. The system retrieves documents from a local encyclopedia. Then, it performs query expansion and, finally, does passage retrieval from the TREC collection. The paper also describes the answer selection algorithm. It determines the best sentence given the question and the occurrence of the expected answer type by minimizing various distance metrics applied over phrases or windows of text. For TREC 10 [9], IBM adapted the system to de with definition type questions and completed the trainability aspect of their QA system. The authors introduce the following:

- new and refined answer tag categories,
- query expansion lists,
- focus expansion using WordNet,
- dependency relationships using syntactic parsing, and
- a maximum-entropy formulation for answer selection.

For TREC 11, IBM collected a 4,000 question-answer corpus based on trivial questions for training and developed answer patterns for the TREC collection of documents [10]. The authors added three more features including:

- the occurrence of the answer candidate on the web,
- the re-ranking of answer candidate window using a statistical MT dictionary, and
- developed lexical patterns from supervised training pairs.

3.2 Arabic QA Systems

QARAB [11] is a QA system to support the Arabic language. The system is based on the *three*-module generic architecture:

- question analysis,
- passage retrieval, and
- answer extraction.

It extracts the answer from a collection of Arabic newspaper text. For that, it uses a keyword matching strategy along with matching simple structures extracted from both the question and the candidate documents selected by the information retrieval module using an existing tagger to identify proper names and other crucial lexical items. The system builds lexical entries for them on the fly. For system validation, four native Arabic speakers with university education presented 113 questions to the system and judged whether the answers of the system are correct or not.

The Arabic language was introduced for the first time in 2012 in the QA4MRE lab at CLEF [12]. The intension of the research is to ask questions which require a deep knowledge of individual short texts and in which systems are required to choose one answer from multiple answer choices. The work uses shallow information retrieval methods. Unfortunately, the overall accuracy of the system is 0.19 and the questions proposed by CLEF are suitable only for modern Arabic language.

ALQASIM [13] is an Arabic QA selection and validation system that answers multiple choice questions of QA4MRE @ CLEF 2013 test-set. It can be used as a part of the answer validation module of any ordinary Arabic QA system. It comes up with a new approach like the one used by human beings in reading tests. A person would normally read and understand a document thoroughly, and then begins to tackle the questions. So, the suggested approach divides the QA4MRE process into *three* phases:

- document analysis,
- locating questions and answers,
- answer selection.

ArabiQA [1] is a QA system that is fully oriented to the modern Arabic language. ArabiQA is obeying to the general norms reported at the CLEF conference. However, the system is not complete yet. The following points is a part of the researchers' investigation, as listed in their work:

- The adaptation of the JIRS passage retrieval system to retrieve passages from Arabic text.
- The development of the annotated ANERcorp to train the Named Entity Recognition (NER) system.

- The development of the ANERsys Named Entity Recognition system for modern Arabic text based on the maximum entropy approach.
- The development of an Answer Extraction module for Arabic text for *factoid* questions (Who, where and when questions).

DefArabicQA [14] presents a definitional QA system for the Arabic language. The system outperforms the use of web searching by two criteria. It permits the user to ask an ordinary question (e.g., *"What is X?"*) instead of typing in a keyword-based query. It then attempts to return an accurate answer instead of mining the web results for the expected information. The question topic is identified by using *two* lexical question patterns and the answer type expected is deduced from the *interrogative pronoun* of the question. Definition ranking is performed according to three scores: a pattern weight criterion, a snippet position criterion, and a word frequency criterion.

The IDRAAQ [15] system is another Arabic QA system based on *query expansion* and *passage retrieval*. It aims at enhancing the quality of retrieved passages with respect to a given question. In this system, a question analysis and classification module to extract the keywords, identify the structure of the expected answer and form the query to be passed to the Passage Retrieval (PR) module. The PR extracts a list of passages from an Information Retrieval process. Thereafter, this module performs a ranking process to improve the relevance of the candidate passages. Finally, the Answer Validation (AV) module validates an answer from a list of candidate answers.

Al-Bayan [16] is a *domain specific* Arabic QA system for the Holy Quran. It takes an Arabic question as input and retrieves semantically relevant verses as candidate passages. Then, an answer extraction module extracts the answer from verses obtained accompanied by their Tafseer (standard explanations of Quran). The system has *four* functionalities:

- It merges *two* Quranic ontologies and uses *two* Tafseer books.
- It applies a semantic search technique for information retrieval.
- It applies a state-of-the-art technique (SVM) for question classification.
- It builds Quranic-based training data sets for classification and Named Entities Recognition (NER).

4   System Architecture

4.1   Overview

Our proposed system is a modification of AlQuAnS – An Arabic Language Question Answering System [4]. We share the same architecture of AlQuAns except for some enhanced modules. Figure 2 shows the system architecture with modified modules highlighted.

AlQuAns is a QA system that works on an open domain and supports the Arabic language. The system consists of 4 main modules:

- Arabic pre-processor module: which preprocess input questions to make the data retrieval more accurate.
- Question analysis module: which includes 2 submodules; query expansion and question classification.

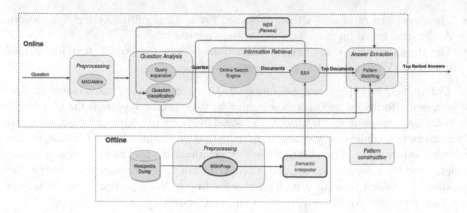

Fig. 2. The overall system architecture (adapted from [4]).

- Semantic information retrieval module: which can retrieve the semantically related documents.
- Answer extraction module: which extracts the ranked answers to the input questions from the retrieved documents with high accuracy.

Arabic Preprocessor. Text Preprocessing is done by applying morphological analysis software to identify the structure of the text. Typical operations include:

- normalization,
- stemming,
- Part-Of-Speech (POS) tagging, and
- stop words removal.

Morphologically, the Arabic language is one of the most complex and rich languages. Thus, morphological analysis of the Arabic language is one of the complex tasks that has been popular in recent research. The AlQuAnS relies on MADAMIRA [17]. MADAMIRA combines the best aspects of two previously commonly used systems for Arabic processing, MADA found in [18] and AMIRA found [19].

MADA is a system for Morphological Analysis and Disambiguation for Arabic. The primary purpose of MADA is to, given raw Arabic text, derive as much linguistic information as possible about each word in the text, thereby reducing or eliminating any ambiguity surrounding the word. MADAMIRA also includes TOKAN, a general tokenizer for MADA-disambiguated text [18]. TOKAN uses the information generated by the MADA component to tokenize each word according to a highly-customizable scheme. AMIRA is a system for tokenization, part-of-speech tagging, Base Phrase Chunking (BPC) and Named Entity Recognition (NER).

Question Analysis. The AlQuAnS divides this module to Query Expansion (QE) and Question Classification. For query expansion, the content and the semantic relations of the Arabic WordNet (AWN) ontology [20] are used. The AWN ontology is a free resource for modern standard Arabic. It is based on the design and the content of Princeton WordNet (PWN) [21]. It has a structure similar to wordnets and exists for approximately 40 languages. It is also connected to the Super Upper Merged Ontology (SUMO) [22]. SUMO is an upper level ontology which provides definitions for general purpose terms and acts as a foundation for more specific domain ontologies.

Our semantic QE approach uses *four* semantic relations among those existing between AWN synsets (items), words and forms. Therefore, the approach defines four sub-processes for the query expansion:

- QE by synonyms,
- QE by definitions,
- QE by subtypes, and
- QE by supertypes.

For question classification, The AlQuAnS uses the Support Vector Machines (SVM) classifier since it has shown to produce the best results during our experiments. Question classification needs a taxonomy to classify question types. AlQuAnS uses the work of Li and Roth [23]. which provides a hierarchical classifier, taxonomy and data to be used in English question classification. Since 2002, Li and Roth work has been used by all researchers who are interested in building QA systems. They propose a two-layered question taxonomy which contains six coarse grained categories and 50 fine grained categories. The coarse-grained categories are listed below.

- Abbreviation
- Description
- Entity
- Human
- Location
- Numeric value

In AlQuAnS we limit the taxonomy to LocationCity, LocationCountry, Human, Individual, NumericDate). With these *four* sub-categories, we focus more on a QA system that can answer questions that ask for cities, countries, humans individuals and different kind of dates (birthdays, event dates, etc.).

Information Retrieval. The Information Retrieval module consists of two submodules: The *Online Search Engine* and the *Passage Retrieval* submodules. Our system is designed to interface with common search engine modules. However, in our implementation, we choose the Yahoo API to be comparable to previous systems using the same API, e.g. [15]. For the *Passage Retrieval* submodule, AlQuAnS we construct a general Semantic Interpreter (SI) that can represent text meaning. The Semantic Interpreter depends on the Explicit Semantic Analysis (ESA) approach proposed in [24]. More details on this module are given in Sect. 5.1.

Answer Extraction. The purpose of the Answer Extraction (AE) module is to search for candidate answers within the relevant passages and extract the most likely answers. Using certain patterns for each type of question is the main approach. In general, patterns can be written by people or learnt from a training dataset. The type of the expected answers is always taken into consideration. The AlQuAns used a Named Entity Recognition system with the patterns extracted for each question type by adapting the approach proposed in [4].

The Answer Extraction module of AlQuAns is composed of *three* phases. The first and second phases are based on the approach in [4]. The *first* phase is to use the web documents retrieved by the Passage Retrieval module to construct a table of patterns for each question type. The *second* phase is to rank these patterns by calculating their corresponding precision. The *third* phase is to find the answer using the extracted answer patterns then filter the answers using the NER of MADAMIRA.

5   Proposed Modifications

In this paper, we enhanced the results of "AlQuAns" by modifying 2 modules, namely the Semantic Interpreter module and the Named Entity Recognition (NER) module. The NER module affects both the Answer Extraction module and the Question Classification module. The following subsections describe the modifications done in detail.

5.1   Semantic Interpreter

In AlQuAnS, we used the Explicit Semantic Approach (ESA) proposed in [24] with 11,000 Arabic Wikipedia documents to build the semantic interpreter. This leads to a short concept vector and hence less accuracy. In this paper, we use the whole Arabic Wikipedia dump of January 2018 which includes more than 1 million documents to build the semantic interpreter. This leads to a larger concept vector that enhances the accuracy of the semantic interpreter and the overall system performance. The following subsections describes in detail the Explicit Semantic Analysis approach and the way used in our system to compute the semantic relatedness between the question and the candidate answers.

Explicit Semantic Analysis. Given a set of concepts, C_1, ..., C_n, and a set of associated documents, d_1, ..., d_n, we build a sparse table T where each of the n columns corresponds to a concept, and each of the rows corresponds to a word that occurs in $\cup_{i=1...n} d_i$. An entry $T[i, j]$ in the table corresponds to the term frequency–inverse document frequency (tf-idf) value of term t_i in document d_j.

$$T[i,j] = tf(t_i, d_j) . log\frac{n}{df_i} \tag{1}$$

Where term frequency is defined as:

$$tf(t_i, d_j) = \{1 + log\ count(t_i, d_j)\ if\ count(t_i, d_j) > 0\ 0\ otherwise \tag{2}$$

and $df_i = |\{d_k: t_i \in d_k\}|$ is the number of documents in the collection that contains the term t_i (*document frequency*). Finally, cosine normalization is applied to each row to discard differences in document length:

$$T[i,j] \leftarrow \frac{T[i,j]}{\sqrt{\sum_{l=1}^{r} T[i,j]}} \tag{3}$$

where r is the number of terms.

The semantic interpretation of a word t_i is obtained as a row i of table T. In other words, the meaning of a word is given by a vector of concepts paired with their tf-idf scores, which reflects the relevance of each concept with respect to the word. The semantic interpretation of a text fragment, $\langle t_1, ..., t_k \rangle$, is the centroid of the vectors representing the individual words. This definition allows us to partially perform word sense disambiguation. Consider, for example, the interpretation vector for the term "mouse". It has two sets of strong components, which correspond to two possible meanings: "mouse (rodent)" and "mouse (computing)". Similarly, the interpretation vector of the word "screen" has strong components associated with "window screen" and "computer screen". In a text fragment such as "I purchased a mouse and a screen", summing the two interpretation vectors will boost the computer-related components, effectively disambiguating both words. Table T can also be viewed as an inverted index, which maps each word to a list of concepts where it appears. Inverted index provides a very efficient computation of distance between interpretation vectors.

Computing the Semantic Relatedness. ESA represents text as interpretation/concept vectors in the high-dimensional space of concepts. With this representation, computing semantic relatedness of text simply amounts to compare their vectors.

The user's question is passed to a search engine, e.g., Yahoo or Google, and the retrieved snippets are ranked using ESA. To determine the semantic relatedness between the question and the retrieved snippets, we compute the concept vectors of the question and the snippets using the Explicit Semantic Analysis module. Then, we compute the cosine similarity between the question concept vector and the concept vector of each snippet i. The result scores are used to select the top-scoring snippets that are relevant to the question. The more similar the snippets vector to the query vector is, the more likely it is related to the question as illustrated in Fig. 3.

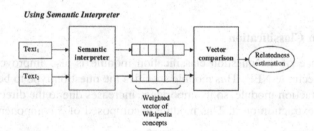

Fig. 3. The semantic relatedness between a question and a snippet (adapted from [25]).

5.2 Named Entity Recognition

The Answer Extraction module finds the matching patterns regardless of the answer word type, so it can extract irrelevant words as an answer like prepositions. Pattern <Name> <Answer> may give answer "In Pyramids" and considers the proposition "In" to be an answer. That is why we use a NER to filter the answer. Using the NER of MADAMIRA, we check the answers because we restrict ourselves to four types of questions: LocationCountry, LocationCity, HumanIndividual and NumericDate. NER of MADAMIRA can find the named entities of words in the three major categories: LOC, PERS and ORG. Other words that do not belong to these categories will not be added to the dictionary made for the word types. The answers of Loca-tionCountry and LocationCity questions are expected to be a location. For the NumericDate question type, we check its validity by checking if the word is a number or a month name. So, the system checks the words in the dictionary to make sure that these words are recognized to be entities. Our best approach is to check if these words are entities or not to be accepted as an answer.

The NER of Farasa [26] vs the NER of MADAMIRA. In AlQuAns we use the NER of MADAMIRA, that gives good results in general. But we found in our experiments that, for the Organization type, this NER fails in detecting English words that are translated to Arabic by just changing letters, (i.e., transliterated), e.g., UNICEF = . Farasa [26], which is a new alternative to MADAMIRA, claims to detect this type of words with a better accuracy due to the relatively small MADAMIRA's English/Arabic dictionary.

In addition, Farasa's performance regarding other categories of entities is also better than that of MADAMIRA. Table 1 shows the results of an experimental study that we conducted on the NER of Farasa and MADAMIRA, using Trec and Clef datasets [15].

Table 1. Accuracy comparison between the NER of MADAMIRA and Farasa.

	Precision		Recall		F-measure	
	MadaMira	Farasa	MadaMira	Farasa	MadaMira	Farasa
PERS	0.77	0.87	0.63	0.87	0.7	0.86
LOC	0.82	0.97	0.72	0.62	0.77	0.76
ORG	0.63	0.76	0.53	0.56	0.57	0.65
Total	0.79	0.89	0.66	0.68	0.71	0.78

5.3 Question Classification

The performance of the question classification module is also improved because of using a more accurate NER. This module specifies the question type to be used later in the answer extraction module, so its importance increases due to the direct dependency of the answer extraction on it. This module is composed of 3 components:

1. MADAMIRA as a stemmer and as a POS tagger
2. Farasa as an NER
3. SVM classifier, which takes a bag of words, the question term and the recognized named entities as features.

6   System Evaluation

We measure the performance improvements made to the new version of AlQuAnS using the standard metrics for QA evaluation, namely, *Accuracy, Mean Reciprocal Rank* (MRR) and *Answered* Questions (AQ). Also, we include previously established Arabic question answering systems result, such as [1, 15].

The definitions of these metrics are given below.

$$Accuracy = \frac{1}{N_s}\sum_{k \in S} V_{k,1} \tag{4}$$

$$MRR = Average_{k \in S}\left(\frac{1}{5}\sum_{j=1}^{5} V_{k,j}\right) \tag{5}$$

$$AQ = \frac{1}{N_s}\sum_{k \in S} max(V_{k,j}) \tag{6}$$

Where $V_{k,j}$ equals 1 if the answer to question k is found in the passage having the rank j, 0 otherwise.

The following subsections include the evaluation results of the question classification module, the answer extraction module and the overall modified system.

6.1 Question Classification

As stated previously, the NER affects the performance of the question classification module. Using the taxonomy of Li and Roth [23], Table 2 shows the results of the modified system and AlQuAns when applied on Clef and Trec dataset [15].

Table 2. Comparison between the first version of AlQuAnS and its modified version.

	Precision		Recall		F-measure	
	AlQuAns	Modified version	AlQuAns	Modified version	AlQuAns	Modified version
Entity	26.70%	26.70%	22.20%	22.20%	24.20%	24.20%
Human	70.80%	73.90%	86.30%	89.00%	77.80%	80.70%
Location	78.10%	81.30%	71.40%	74.30%	74.60%	77.60%
Number	97.80%	97.80%	84.60%	86.50%	90.70%	91.80%

6.2 Answer Extraction

Using the CLEF and TREC datasets used in evaluating the system in [15], we divide the datasets into training and testing sets. Together, they consist of 2,242 questions that pass through the Answer Extraction module. The results are shown in Table 3 which compares the accuracy of the Answer Extraction modules of the first version of AlQuAnS, its modified version and the corresponding module in Abouenour [15].

Table 3. Comparison between answer extraction accuracies.

	Abouenour	AlQuAns	Modified
Answer extraction	15.3%	50.9%	55.66%

6.3   Explicit Semantic Analysis Evaluation

In this subsection, we are going to compare the overall performance of the modified version of our system before and after enhancing the Explicit Semantic Analysis (ESA) component (by using the whole Arabic Wikipedia dump of January 2018 for building the semantic interpreter). Again, we benchmark the system against the work in [15]. For that, we managed to get the same training and benchmarking datasets. We update these datasets to adapt the answers since search engines deliver different; yet correct; results over time. For example, "How many Syrian refugees live in Jordan?". The answer changes each year.

As in the previous version of AlQuAnS, the ESA component provides a list of documents for each question ranked in decreasing order based on relatedness to the question.

As in AlQuAnS, we give the question and the set of documents to ESA module which process both to produce a list of most five related documents in decreasing order of relatedness to the given question. In AlQuAns, we proposed a method for ESA evaluation - which was used to get comparable results with the system in [15]. In this method, each document in the list is examined to check if there is an exact match with the answer or not. If this is true, then the document is considered a candidate that contains the question answer.

A criticism of this method is that if the answer is "١٠الاف سنويا" and the document contains "١٠الاف خلال السنة", this document will not be considered a candidate that contains the answer. To avoid false negative cases, like the one mentioned above, we propose another method, Method 2, where instead of searching for the whole text we verify that all terms of the answer exit in addition to more than 25% of the question terms.

Due to high Arabic inflection, we propose a third method, Method 3, in which we stem documents, questions and answers terms and then apply method 2. Also, we combine some question terms with answer terms which can give better results. For example, consider the question:

"كم تربح غوغل سنويا؟" and the answer which is just "١٠ مليون". If we depend only on the answer terms to judge whether a document is a candidate to contain the question's answer or not, this may produce a false positive result since the answer terms don't enforce to whom this 10 million belong.

Tables 4, 5 and 6 present the results of the overall system evaluation of AlQuAnS and its modified version (compared to [15]) for each of the proposed methods.

Table 4. Overall system evaluation using method 1.

	Accuracy	QA	MRR
Abouenour	20.20%	26.74%	9.22
AlQuAns	22.79%	47.67%	8.1
Modified version	23.32%	43.3%	7.8

Table 5. Overall system evaluation using method 2.

	Accuracy	QA	MRR
AlQuAns	22.2%	43%	4.4
Modified version	25.9%	49.2%	5.1

Table 6. Overall system evaluation using metric 3.

	Accuracy	QA	MRR
AlQuAns	31.69%	58%	6.3
Modified version	36.7%	58%	7.3

7 Conclusions and Future Work

Question answering is becoming more and more an essential part of our communication with the different devices and not only limited to search engines as it used to be. For example, chat bots are becoming the new way to communicate with computers. The importance of the question answering is increasing, to become a corner stone in the Natural Language Processing (NLP) field in the coming years.

In this paper, we propose a modified version of our Arabic Language Question Answering System (AlQuAnS). The proposed version enhances the accuracy of the question classification, semantic interpreter and answer extraction modules. We tried to push the currently existing components of the system to their limits to show that without introducing new components, just with more efforts with the current architecture and modules, we can reach a higher accuracy. The provided performance evaluation study shows that our modified version outperforms the previous version in addition to other existing Arabic QA systems.

Deep learning became one of the main components in many of the Natural Language Processing tasks, because of the impressive results it provides without the need to feature engineering. We intend to extend our work by applying deep learning techniques which are expected to give more enhancement to the overall performance of our system.

References

1. Benajiba, Y., Rosso, P.: Arabic Question Answering. Diploma of Advanced Studies. Technical University of Valencia, Spain (2007)
2. Benajiba, Y., Rosso, P.: Anersys 2.0: conquering the NER task for the Arabic language by combining the maximum entropy with pos-tag information. In: Proceedings of Workshop on Natural Language-Independent Engineering, IICAI-2007 (2007)
3. Benajiba, Y., Rosso, P., BenedíRuiz, J.M.: ANERsys: an Arabic named entity recognition system based on maximum entropy. In: Gelbukh, A. (ed.) CICLing 2007. LNCS, vol. 4394, pp. 143–153. Springer, Heidelberg (2007). https://doi.org/10.1007/978-3-540-70939-8_13

4. Nabil, M., et al.: AlQuAnS – an Arabic language question answering system. In: Proceedings of the 9th International Joint Conference on Knowledge Discovery, Knowledge Engineering and Knowledge Management - Volume 1: KDIR, pp. 144-154 (2017). https://doi.org/10.5220/0006602901440154. ISBN 978-989-758-271-4
5. Fleischman, M., Hovy, E., Echihabi, A.: Offline strategies for online question answering: answering questions before they are asked. In: Proceedings of the 41st Annual Meeting on Association for Computational Linguistics - Volume 1, Stroudsburg, PA, USA, pp. 1–7. ACL 2003. Association for Computational Linguistics (2003)
6. Zhang, D., Lee, W.S.: A web-based question answering system. In: Proceedings of the SMA Annual Symposium 2003. Singapore (2003)
7. Kaiser, M.: Answer sentence retrieval by matching dependency paths acquired from question/answer sentence pairs. In: Proceedings of the 13th Conference of the European Chapter of the Association for Computational Linguistics, EACL 2010, Stroudsburg, PA, USA, pp. 88–98. Association for Computational Linguistics (2012)
8. Ittycheriah, A., Franz, M., Zhu, W.-J., Ratnaparkhi, A., Mammone, R.J.: IBM's statistical question answering system. In: Proceedings of the Text Retrieval Conference. TREC-9 (2000)
9. Martin, A.I., Franz, M., Roukos, S.: IBM's statistical question answering system-TREC-10. In: Proceedings of the 10th Text Retrieval Conference. TREC-10 (2001)
10. Ittycheriah, A., Roukos, S.: IBM's statistical question answering system-TREC-11. IBM Thomas J Watson Research Center, Yorktown Heights, NY (2006)
11. Hammo, B., Abu-Salem, H., Lytinen, S.: QARAB: a question answering system to support the Arabic language. In: Proceedings of the ACL-02 Workshop on Computational Approaches to Semitic Languages, SEMITIC 2002, Stroudsburg, PA, USA, pp. 1–11. Association for Computational Linguistics (2002)
12. Trigui, O., Belguith, L.H., Rosso, P., Amor, H.B., Gafsaoui, B.: Arabic QA4MRE at CLEF 2012: Arabic question answering for machine reading evaluation. In: CLEF (Online Working Notes/Labs/Workshop) (2012)
13. Ezzeldin, A.M., Kholief, M.H., El-Sonbaty, Y.: ALQASIM: Arabic language question answer selection in machines. In: Forner, P., Müller, H., Paredes, R., Rosso, P., Stein, B. (eds.) CLEF 2013. LNCS, vol. 8138, pp. 100–103. Springer, Heidelberg (2013). https://doi.org/10.1007/978-3-642-40802-1_12
14. Trigui, O., Belguith, H., Rosso, P.: DefArabicQA: Arabic definition question answering system. In: Workshop on Language Resources and Human Language Technologies for Semitic Languages, 7th LREC, pp. 40–45. Valletta, Malta (2010)
15. Abouenour, L., Bouzouba, K., Rosso, P.: An evaluated semantic query expansion and structure-based approach for enhancing Arabic question/answering. Int. J. Inf. Commun. Technol. 3(3), 37–51 (2010)
16. Abdelnasser, H., et al.: Al-bayan: an Arabic question answering system for the holy Quran. In: Arabic Natural Language Processing Workshop, p. 57, Qatar (2014)
17. Pasha, A., et al.: MADAMIRA: a fast, comprehensive tool for morphological analysis and disambiguation of arabic. In: LREC, vol. 14, pp. 1094–1101 (2014)
18. Habash, N., Rambow, O., Roth, R.: MADA+TOKAN: a toolkit for Arabic tokenization, diacritization, morphological disambiguation, POS tagging, stemming and lemmatization. In: Proceedings of the 2nd International Conference on Arabic Language Resources and Tools (MEDAR), Cairo, Egypt, vol. 41, p. 62, April 2009
19. Diab, M.: Second generation AMIRA tools for Arabic processing: fast and robust tokenization, POS tagging, and base phrase chunking. In: 2nd International Conference on Arabic Language Resources and Tools, vol. 110 (2009)

20. Elkateb, S., et al.: Arabic WordNet and the challenges of Arabic. In: Proceedings of Arabic NLP/MT Conference, London, UK (2006)
21. Fellbaum, C.: WordNet and wordnets. In: Brown, K., et al. (eds.) Encyclopedia of Language and Linguistics, 2nd edn, pp. 665–670. Elsevier, Oxford (2005)
22. Niles, I., Pease, A.: Mapping WordNet to the sumo ontology. In: Proceedings of the IEEE International Knowledge Engineering Conference, pp. 23–26 (2003)
23. Li, X., Roth, D.: Learning question classifiers. In: Proceedings of the 19th International Conference on Computational Linguistics-Volume 1, pp. 1–7. Association for Computational Linguistics (2002)
24. Gabrilovich, E., Markovitch, S.: Computing semantic relatedness using wikipedia-based explicit semantic analysis. In: Proceedings of the 20th International Joint Conference on Artificial Intelligence, vol. 6, p. 12 (2007)
25. Gabrilovich, E., Markovitch, S.: Wikipedia-based semantic interpretation for natural language processing. J. Artif. Intell. Res. **34**, 443–498 (2009)
26. Abdelali, A., Darwish, K., Durrani, N., Mubarak, H.: Farasa: a fast and furious segmenter for Arabic. In: NAACL-2016 (2016)

Knowledge Engineering and Ontology Development

Ontology in Holonic Cooperative Manufacturing: A Solution to Share and Exchange the Knowledge

Ahmed R. Sadik[1,2(✉)] and Bodo Urban[1,2]

[1] University of Rostock, Universitätsplatz 1, 18055 Rostock, Germany
{ahmed.sadik,bodo.urban}@igd-r.fraunhofer.de
[2] Fraunhofer Institute for Computer Graphic Research IGD, Joachim-Jungius-Str. 11, 18059 Rostock, Germany

Abstract. Cooperative manufacturing is a new trend in industry, which depends on the existence of a collaborative robot. A collaborative robot is usually a light-weight robot which is capable of operating safely with a human co-worker in a shared work environment. During this cooperation, a vast amount of information is exchanged between the collaborative robot and the worker. This information constructs the cooperative manufacturing knowledge, which describes the production components and environment. In this research, we propose a holonic control solution, which uses the ontology concept to represent the cooperative manufacturing knowledge. The holonic control solution is implemented as an autonomous multi-agent system that exchanges the manufacturing knowledge based on an ontology model. Ultimately, the research illustrates and implements the proposed solution over a cooperative assembly scenario, which involves two workers and one collaborative robot, whom cooperate together to assemble a customized product.

Keywords: Ontology-based solution · Cooperative manufacturing · Holonic control · Multi-agent system

1 Introduction: Challenges in Cooperative Manufacturing

Cooperative and collaborative manufacturing are new terms in industry, which are usually mixed with each other. The reason behind this confusion is that both terms involve a cooperative/collaborative robot (cobot). However, a slight difference can distinguish between the two terms. In cooperative robotics, both the worker and the cobot are sequentially performing separate tasks over the same product in the same-shared workspace. But in collaborative robotics, they perform a shared task simultaneously [1]. The goal of the cooperative manufacturing is to combine the advantages of both the cobot and the worker at the same time, to afford a new intelligent manufacturing technique. However, with this new technique appears new challenges [2].

Figure 1 shows the challenges in cooperative robotics. These challenges are beyond the physical safety of the worker during the cooperation, which already gained a great focus in robotics research [3]. The first challenge after ensuring the worker physical safety, is to achieve the physical interaction between the cobot and the worker. The

© Springer Nature Switzerland AG 2019
A. Fred et al. (Eds.): IC3K 2017, CCIS 976, pp. 203–223, 2019.
https://doi.org/10.1007/978-3-030-15640-4_11

physical interaction can be achieved via a group of sensory and User Interface (UI) devices. The sensors and the UI convert the worker actions into input information. Exchanging this information with the cobot and the other manufacturing components is the second challenge in collaborative manufacturing. The third challenge is to build the manufacturing knowledge from this exchanged information. Thus, this knowledge is used to plan and control the manufacturing activities. Ultimately, comes the final challenge of collecting the knowledge from all the manufacturing components and reason it to provide collective decisions.

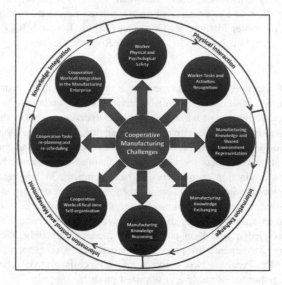

Fig. 1. Cooperative robotics challenges.

2 Problem Formulation

This article is focusing on two important challenges in cooperative manufacturing, which are discussed as below:

Manufacturing knowledge and environment representation: the abstract representation of the facts and the objects within the cooperative workcell is an essential necessity to establish a successful cooperation. Thus, in order to construct the cooperative manufacturing concept, a proper approach is required to describe the shared environment between the worker and the cobot including themselves. Also, the other production components such as the product parts and the manufacturing tools. Descriptive meta-data representation is essential to give a meaning of the objects, tasks, and operations within the cooperative workcell. Structural meta-data are required to structure bonds between the objects to compound new descriptive meta-objects, this also can be done by associating new attributes to an existing object. Also, the structure meta-data can be used to define the parent-child relation among the objects. Finally, administrative meta-data is required to control the cooperative task assignment and the cooperation planning, management, and execution.

Manufacturing knowledge exchanging: the knowledge is useless, unless it is exchanged and being used in reasoning. The knowledge cannot be shared unless a proper mean of communication allows its exchange. Due to the fundamentals of the Human-Robot Interaction (HRI), the information exchange is as much important as the physical safety. The manufacturing information and communication control system can be seen as the nervous system which connects the cobot and the worker together in one body. In the absence of the proper manufacturing control solution, the maximum usability of a cobot can never be reached, because it loses its real value as a smart tool. The challenge from the research point of view is to provide a communication language which can express the relations among the cooperative workcell components. Moreover, the actions and operations that can be performed by these components. Putting into consideration that this communication language should be human readable and in the same time can be processed by the machine (i.e., the cobot). The challenge from the technical point of view is to provide a communication mean that grantees the industrial connectivity (i.e., interoperability).

3   Solution Preliminaries

3.1   Autonomous Agent Communication

A software agent is a computer system situated in a specific environment that is capable of performing autonomous actions in this environment in order to meet its design objective. An agent is autonomous by nature; this means that an agent operates without a direct intervention of the humans, and has a high degree of controlling its actions and internal states [4]. In order to achieve this autonomy, an agent must be able to fulfil the following characteristics:

- Social: can interact with other artificial agents or humans within its environment in order to solve a problem.
- Responsive: capable of perceiving its environment and respond in a timely fashion to the changes occurring in it.
- Pro-active: able to exhibit opportunistic, goal directed behavior and take initiative.

Conceptually, an agent is a computing machine which is given a specific problem to solve. Therefore, it chooses certain set of actions and formulates the proper plans to accomplish the assigned task. The set of actions which are available to be performed by the agent are called a behaviour. The agent behaviours are mainly created by the agent programmer. An agent can execute one or more behaviour to reach its target. The selection of an execution behaviour among others would be based on a certain criteria which has been defined by the agent programmer. Building an execution plan is highly depending on the information which the agent infers from its environment including the other agents. A Multi-Agent System (MAS) is a collective system composed of a group of artificial agents, teaming together in a flexible distributed topology, to solve a problem beyond the capabilities of a single agent [5].

Java Agent DEvelopment (JADE) is a distributed middleware framework that can be used to develop an MAS as it is shown in Fig. 2 [6]. Each JADE instance is an independent thread which contains a set of containers. A container is a group of agents run under the same JADE runtime instance. Every platform must contain a main container.

A main container contains two necessary agents which are: an Agent Management System (AMS) and a Directory Facilitator (DF). AMS provides a unique Identifier (AID) for every agent under its platform to be used as an agent communication address. While the DF announces the services which agents can offer under its platform, to facilitate the agent services exchange, so that every agent can obtain its specific goal. JADE applies the reactive agent architecture which complies with the Foundation for Intelligent Physical Agent (FIPA) specifications [7]. FIPA is an IEEE Computer Society standards organization that promotes agent-based technology and the interoperability of its standards with other technologies. JADE agent use FIPA-Agent Communication Language (FIPA-ACL) to exchange messages either inside or outside its platform.

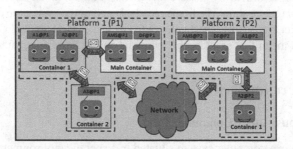

Fig. 2. JADE framework - an example.

JADE agent follows FIPA communication model stack which is very similar to the TCP/IP model as it can be seen in Fig. 3. Generally, a communication architecture model is a stack of layers, each layer specifies a set of data flow, information management, and communication control standard protocols. The purpose of a communication architecture model is to exchange the services and the information among the computing machines within a wired or a wireless network. FIPA communication model has in total 9 layers. The first 3 lower layers are exactly the same as in the TCP/IP model, while the upper 6 layers equal together to the application layer in the TCP/IP model. A brief description of FIPA communication model can be seen as below:

1   Physical Interaction Layer: this layer is linked directly to the actual network medium which is a part of the computing machine hardware. Standard IEEE 802.3-Ethernet and IEEE 802.11-Wireless Ethernet protocols are responsible for sending/receiving the network data packets.
2   Communication Interaction Layer: this layer uses the Internet Protocol (IP) to pack/unpacking the data into/from the IP datagrams. Also it provides the right network rout and IP-address for the datagrams.
3   Transport Layer: the transport layer makes sure that the IP datagrams are delivered from the source to the destination and vice-versa. Two famous communication control protocol can be used in this layer, which are Transmission Control Protocol (TCP) and User Datagram Protocol (UDP). TCP deploys a fixed length datagram via peer to peer connection with a reliable acknowledgment of packets delivery. While UDP deploys a variable length datagrams via peer to peer or broadcasting connection with no need of packets delivery acknowledgment.

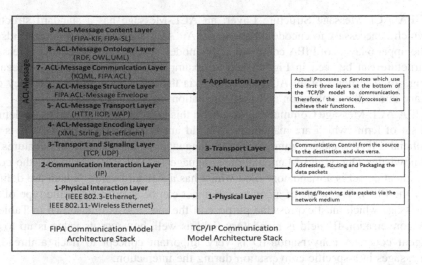

Fig. 3. An analogy between FIPA and TCP/IP communication model architectures.

4 FIPA ACL-Message Encoding Layer: this layer specify the message presentation standard format. Extensible Markup Language (XML) can be used to XML is the most famous standard to represent a structured electronic message. Other FIPA standard format such as String and bit-efficient can be also used to represent and ACL- Message.

5 FIPA ACL-Message Transport Layer: Message Transport Layer (MTP) is implementing standard application protocols which deal with the web applications such Hypertext Transfer Protocol (HTTP), Internet Inter-ORB Protocol (IIOP), and Wireless Application Protocol (WAP). These protocols are designed to facilitate the distributed collaborative information exchange via request-response interaction in client/server computer model.

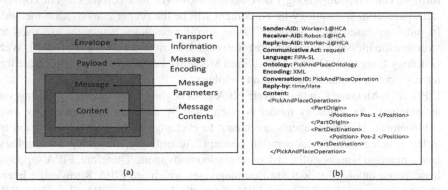

Fig. 4. (a) ACL-message structure [Fip15] – (b) ACL-message example.

6 FIPA ACL-Message Structure Layer: an ACL-Message has a standard structure which is necessary to encode the message. An ACL-Message structure depends on the upper 6 layers of FIPA communication model. A schematic of an ACL-Message structure can be seen in Fig. 4a and an example of the message can be seen in Fig. 4b. The fields of an ACL are coded via the agent programmer and they can vary due to the application and implementation approach.

7 FIPA ACL-Message Communication Layer: this layer is very important as it defines a set of terms which are mandatory to build an ACL-Message. FIPA-ACL is the official FIPA standard communication language which extends the features of Knowledge Query and Manipulation Language (KQML). For example, the communication act is a mandatory filed which has a standard values which are defined by the FIPA. The value of a commutation act can be seen as a specific type of the message which must express the purpose of the message as it is shown in Table 1. A conversation-ID field is mandatory field as well, however its value is up to the agent coder. A conversation-ID is very important concept to track a thread of messages in a specific conversation during the interaction.

Table 1. FIPA ACL communication acts.

Communication act	Purpose
Propose, accept-proposal, reject-proposal, cfp	Negotiation
Request, request-when, query-if, query-ref	Requesting information
Confirm, disconfirm, inform, inform-if, inform-ref	Passing information
Agree, refuse, cancel, subscribe	Performing actions
Not-understood, failure	Error handling
Propagate, proxy	Message referencing

8 FIPA ACL-Message Ontology Layer: an ACL-Message is flexible to afford different levels of conversation complexity. A String based massage is the simplest form of conversation among FIPA agents. However in a complex agent conversation scenario, an ontology-based content will be the proper conversation method. In ontology-based ACL-Message, some specific ontology languages are used to structure the message. FIPA support Resource Description Framework (RDF), Web Ontology Language (OWL), and Unified Modeling Language (UML) which are the most common languages to code an ontology.

9 FIPA ACL-Message Content Layer: FIPA goes beyond a conceptual modelling via an ontology. An ontology model is often used by an agent to represent its own environment. However, agents are meant to exchange and process information in order to achieve MAS cooperation concept. Accordingly, reasoning an ontology based message is an essential task of an autonomous agent. Therefore, FIPA supports logic based ontology model via two languages which are FIPA Knowledge Interchange Format (FIPA-KIF) and FIPA Semantic Language (FIPA-SL). FIPA-KIF and FIPA-SL languages allow to model the system knowledge based on first order logic and commonly used in AI. Therefore, using a logic based ontology model enables a reasoning software to process and analysis the knowledge of this model.

3.2 Ontology Concept in Cooperative Manufacturing

In philosophy, an ontology aims to study the nature of the existence and reality to form tight relations among the beings whom are part of this reality. The word ontology comes from combining two Greek words "Onto" which means a Being and "logia" which means a Divine Origin. Thus, ontology can be translated literally into the origin of the being. However, the concept of ontology has been frequently used in computer science in association with the AI to define the relation among the software objects. Although there is no a specific definition of the word ontology within the computer science filed, the following definitions shall draw a complete understadning of the meaning of ontology [8]:

- An ontology defines the basic terms and relations comprising the vocabulary of a topic area as well the rules for combining terms and relations to define extensions for this vocabulary [9].
- An ontology is a formal, explicit specification of a shared conceptualization [10].
- An ontology is a logical theory accounting for the intended meaning of a formal vocabulary [11]. i.e., "it is a commitment to a particular conceptualization of the world".
- An ontology provides the meta-information to describe the data semantics, represent knowledge, and communicate with various types of entities (e.g., software agents and humans) [12].
- An ontology can be described as the means of enabling communication and knowledge sharing by capturing a shared understanding of terms that can be used by both the humans and the machine software [13].

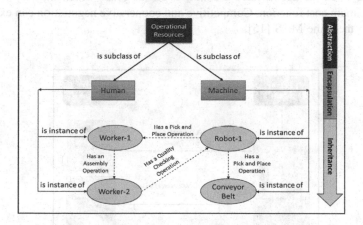

Fig. 5. An ontology example (cooperative operational resources).

The previous definitions of ontology can derive a precise definition of the ontology within the scope of cooperative manufacturing. Thus, an ontology is a conceptual tool to represent and create a common understanding for the manufacturing workcell entities. Furthermore, this common understanding would enable to exchange, reuse and extend the manufacturing knowledge. An ontology based model is extending the Object Oriented Programming (OOP) concepts by defining relations among the objects. Figure 5 illustrates an ontology example of a cooperative workcell which achieves the OOP concepts that can be summarized as the following:

- Abstraction: is a generalization process which can differ due to the context and the
- purpose of the code. In another words, abstraction is the process of exposing an object parameters which are general and can be used by all the other objects within the software domain.
- Encapsulation: can be seen as the opposite of abstraction. As it is simply means to hide an object parameters which can only be used by the object, to fit the context of the software domain.
- Inheritance: is the idea of having different instances of the same object with different parameters value.

3.3 Agent Ontology-Based Interaction

An ACL-Message is the main tool which an agent uses to interact among the other agents to achieve the cooperation goals. The power of an autonomous agent which distinguishes it from a software object locates in its ability to interact rather than applying static algorithms. An agent interaction is a form internal conversation where a group of agents negotiate to reach a mutual acceptable agreement on a certain matter [14]. An agent interaction can be based on cooperative or competitive negotiation. Competitive negotiation takes place when the agents have conflicted local goals, which every agent races to achieve with a minimum cost function. Cooperative negotiation takes place when the agents have a common global goals, which they try to achieve with a minimum cost function. Competitive and cooperative negotiation can exist along together in the same MAS [15].

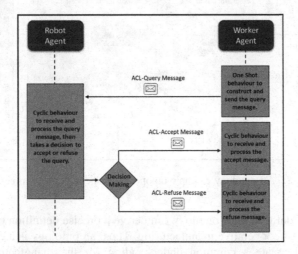

Fig. 6. Autonomous agents interaction pipe line example.

From a philosophical point of view, an agent is similar to the human being who has a group of behaviours and uses one or a group of them concurrently to respond to the environment situations. From the software point of view, a behaviour is an event handler routine which the agent uses to modify its parameters and negotiate with other agents. JADE offers different behaviours which are used to build an agent, the most common behaviours are discussed as below:

- One Shot Behaviour: is executed once when it is called by the agent, then it ends. It is very useful to trigger an event and to send an ACL-Message.
- Cyclic Behaviour: stays active as long as the agent is alive. It is very useful to receive a message with specific conversation-ID or communication act.

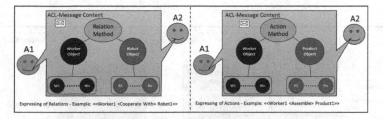

Fig. 7. Agents communication via ontology.

A software agent goes many steps farther than the software object by providing new concepts and tools such as the behaviours and the ACL-Message. One of the main roles of a behaviour is to control the follow of the ACL-Messages. The summation of an agent behaviour and an ACL-Message should infer the meaning of an agent interaction. The research in [16] states that "agent interaction is more powerful concept than ordinary algorithm". The main reason behind the previous statement that an interaction is providing the capability of learning from the input/output history tracking and changing the environment model based on this knowledge. While, algorithm is static and meant to produce an output due to a specific input [17]. Furthermore, using the concept of interaction via the agent behaviours and ACL-Messages, gives the agent the sense of intelligence by taking its own decisions based on the interaction context as it can be seen in Fig. 6.

XML Message Content	FIPA-SL Message Content

`<PickAndPlaceOperation>`
    `<PartOrigin>`
        `<Position> Pos-1 </Position>`
    `</PartOrigin>`
    `<PartDestination>`
        `<Position> Pos-2 </Position>`
    `</PartDestination>`
`</PickAndPlaceOperation>`
	`(PickAndPlaceOperation`
	    `(PartOrigin`
	        `:Position Pos-1)`
	    `(PartDestination`
	        `:Position Pos-2))`

Fig. 8. XML syntax versus FIPA-SL syntax.

The representation of the content field of an ACL-Message is String data type in case of simple agent conversation. However in a complex agent conversation, it is not only a must to representing the software objects, but also the relations among these object and the actions that they can perform as it is shown in the example in Fig. 7. Therefore, an ontology-based content will be the proper conversation method. XML or FIPA-SL languages are commonly used to represent an ACL-Message content. XML and FIPA-SL are slightly different in their syntax as it can be seen in Fig. 8. However, representing the ACL-Message in FIPA-SL is preferable in case of further reasoning of the message is needed based on logic theory. The representation of an ACL-Message can be also as a sequence of Bytes which is a light-weighted method from the programming point of view, but not perforable at all as it is non-human readable language, thus it cannot be debugged [18].

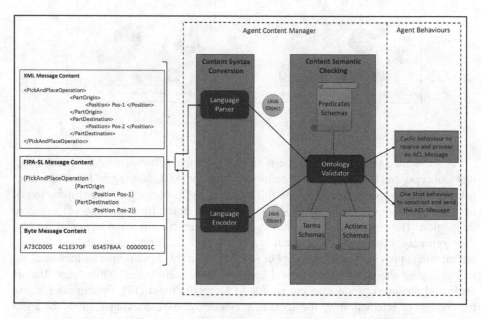

Fig. 9. Sending/Receiving mechanism of an ontology-based ACL-message.

One of the advantages of using the ontology is the mutual understanding among the software agent. In order to bring this mutual understanding among the agents, they should communicate via the same syntax and semantics. JADE agents are written as a JAVA code which obligate them to process JAVA objects. Therefore, during sending an ontology-based message, the sender must convert its internal representation of the message from JAVA syntax to the appropriate syntax of the corresponding content language (i.e. XML, FIPA-SL, Bytes). However, before the syntax conversion, semantic checking should be fulfilled. Thus, an agent must check and validate an ontology-based ACL-Message against the domain semantics before converting it to the proper syntax. Ontology schemas are the approach which an agent uses to express the domain semantics. JADE agents define three types of schemas which can be summarized as the following:

- Terms: a schema which contains expressions that indicate entities that exist in the agent domain and that agents may reason about. Terms can be seen as primitives which are atomic data types such as strings or integers, and concepts which are complex structure such as objects.
- Predicate: a schema which contains expressions that describe the status of the agent domain and the relationships between the concepts.
- Action: a schema which contains expressions that describe routines or operations which can be executed by an agent.

During an ontology-based ACL-Message reception, the opposite mechanism of the sending operation must be fulfilled. Therefore, the same schemas of the sender must be accessible by the receiver in order to interpret the message content. An illustration of an ontology-based ACL-Message interaction is shown in detail in Fig. 9.

4 Solution Concept: Holonic Control Architecture

In the late sixties, the term holon has been introduced for the first time by philosopher Koestler [19]. Koestler developed the term as a basic unit in his explanation of the evolution of the biological and social structures. Based on his observations that organisms (e.g., biological cells) are autonomous self-reliance units, which have a certain degree of independent control of their actions, yet they still subject to higher level of control instructions. His conclusion was that any organism is a whole "holos" and a part "on" in the same time, which derived the term holon [20]. The concept of holon has been adopted in the early nineties by the intelligent manufacturing systems (IMS) consortium, to define a new paradigm for the factory of the future. The following terminologies has been defined by the IMS to provide a better understanding of the Holonic Control Architecture (HCA):

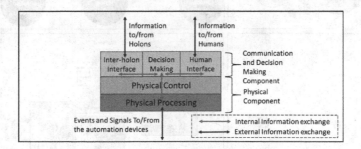

Fig. 10. Holon conceptual model.

- Holon: an autonomous cooperative building block of the manufacturing system that can be used to transform, transport, store and/or validate the information and the physical signals [21]. Figure 10 shows in detail the holon conceptual model.

- Autonomy: the capability of the holon to create and control the execution of its own plans and/or strategies.
- Cooperation: a process whereby a set of holons develop mutually acceptable plans and execute these plans together.
- Holarchy: a system of holons which cooperate to achieve a goal or objective. The holarchy defines the basic rules for cooperation of the holons and thereby limits their autonomy.

The HCA is basically a distributed control and communication topology which divides the manufacturing process tasks and responsibilities over three basic holon categories [22] which are as following:

- Product Holon (PH): is responsible for processing and storing the different production plans required to insure the correct manufacturing of a certain product.
- Order Holon (OH): is responsible for composing, managing the production orders. Furthermore, in a small-scale enterprise, it should assign the tasks to the present operating resources and monitor the execution status of the assigned tasks.
- Operational Resource Holon (ORH): is a physical entity within the manufacturing system, it can represent a robot, machine, worker, etc. The ORH is usually composed of two components. The first component is the physical component which represents the physical input/output (I/O) of a resource. The second component is the communication component which is responsible for translating the I/O events into information and conducting them to the other holons and vice-versa

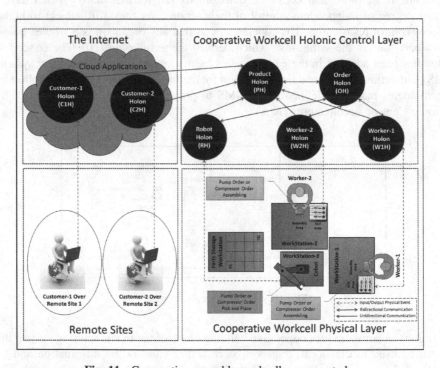

Fig. 11. Cooperative assembly workcell - a case study.

Figure 11 illustrates the idea of applying the HCA concept over a cooperative workcell which composes of two workers in cooperation with one cobot. The goal of the cooperative workcell is to assemble a family of a customized product. This case-study will be explained in details in the following section.

5 Case Study Implementation

5.1 Case Study Description

The goal of the case study is to implement the previously shown solution concept. Two Customer Holons (CHs) have been developed to customize the production orders as it can be seen in Fig. 12a. Both the CHs have a similar UI. The UI of the CH is providing a tool for ordering a specific product with certain features (i.e., parts). The customer selects the basic features and defines the needed amount of the product then sends the order to the PH [2].

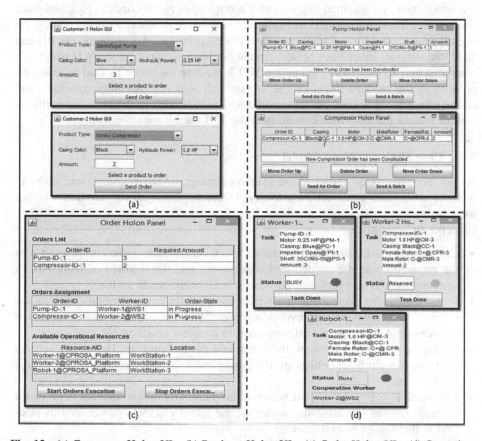

Fig. 12. (a) Customers Holon UI – (b) Products Holon UI – (c) Order Holon UI – (d) Operation resources Holon UI.

Two products can be manufactured in this case-study, the first is a centrifugal pump and the second is a screw compressor. The UIs of the pump and the compressor holons can be seen in Fig. 12b. The two products share some parts such as the casing and the electrical motor. The pump has two unique parts which are the impeller and the shaft, while the compressor has other two unique parts which are the male-rotor and the female-rotor. When a PH receives a product order from the CH, it constructs the building plans for this product order as it will be discussed later in details. The PH also has the ability to rearrange the orders or modify them before sending them to the OH. The OH is responsible for collecting the product orders from all the other PHs as it is shown in Fig. 12c. Simultaneously the OH discovers the existence of the operation resources. Furthermore, it starts and stops the production process. Two WHs (W1H, W2H) and one Robot Holon (RH) can be found as operation resources in this implementation as it is shown in Fig. 12d. The function of the workers within this case-study is to perform the assembly operation of the customized product orders, while the function of the cobot is to pick and place the customized parts of every production order to the proper worker workstation. As we do not have a robot hardware during this implementation, we assumed that the cobot always takes two seconds to pick and place one product. Therefore, the RH multiplies the number of products by two to obtain the overall time needed for the whole pick and place operations. Accordingly, the RH can have two statuses, either busy or free. Another status is required for the WH which is a reserve status. In the reserve status the WH is waiting the cobot to load at least one product to the worker, therefore the worker can start the assembly operation and subsequently the WH status turns to be busy. The WH stays in the busy status till the worker presses the task-done button, then the WH status would be free.

5.2   Case Study Ontology Model

As has been discussed earlier at the solution concept. JADE is using three different types of schemas to construct its ontology. Figure 13 shows all the required schemas used to build the case-study ontology. The first set of schemas are the terms (i.e., concepts and primitives):

- Compressor-Customer-Order: a schema which encapsulates some attributes such as the required color, the needed hydraulic power, and the required amount. Also it contains an AID as every customer-order is an agent needs an ID.
- Pump-Customer-Order: a schema which encapsulates some attributes such as the required color, the needed hydraulic power, and the required amount. Also it contains an AID as every customer-order is an agent needs an ID.
- Casing: a shared part between the pump and the compressor. The casing schema contains two attributes which are the casing color, and its position at the storage workstation.
- Electrical-Motor: a shared part between the pump and the compressor. The motor schema contains two attributes which are the motor electrical power, and its position at the storage workstation.
- Shaft: a unique part of the pump. The shaft schema contains two attributes which are the shaft material, and its position at the storage workstation.

- Impeller: a unique part of the pump. The impeller schema contains two attributes which are the impeller type, and its position at the storage workstation.
- Female-Rotor: a unique part of the compressor. The female-rotor schema contains two attributes which are the rotor size, and its position at the storage workstation.
- Male-Rotor: a unique part of the compressor. The male-rotor schema contains two attributes which are the rotor size, and its position at the storage workstation.
- Compressor: a concept schema which encapsulates many other schemas under it, those schemas are the casing, electrical-motor, female-rotor, and male-rotor. Every compressor is an agent; therefore, it must contain an AID.
- Pump: a concept schema which encapsulates many other schemas under it, those schemas are the casing, electrical-motor, shaft, and impeller. Every pump is an agent; therefore, it must contain an AID attribute.
- Compressor-Order: a schema which extends the compressor schema by adding the required amount of units.
- Pump-Order: a schema which extends the pump schema by adding the required amount of units.
- Operations-List: a schema which includes a list of operations which can be used to manufacture either a pump or a compressor. The schema can be used to manufacture a product which needs three operations or less.
- Compressor-Manufacturing-Order: a schema which combines a Compressor-Order schema and an Operations-List schema. Also it has an AID attribute as it acts as an agent.
- Pump-Manufacturing-Order: a schema which combines a Pump-Order schema and an Operations-List schema. Also it has an AID attribute as it acts as an agent.
- Worker: a schema which contains two attributes, the first one is the worker AID as it acts as a life agent, and the second is the worker location within the workcell (i.e., workstation). The worker agent is providing an UI for the worker for providing the assigned task and inquiring the task done event (see Fig. 12d). Two instances of the worker agent exist in this case-study scenario. The worker can have three statuses. A free status when there is no product orders or the production is not started. A reserve status when the worker is waiting the first product unit to be placed by the cobot. A busy status last while the cobot is handling the production orders till the worker triggers the task done event.
- Robot: a schema which contains one attribute, which is the robot AID as it acts as an agent. The robot schema does not have a workstation attribute because only there is only one cobot which is responsible for the pick and place. Therefore, the location of the cobot is not necessary required. However, in case of more than one cobot the cobot location attribute could be important. The robot agent provids an UI to show the assigned task and the status of the cobot (see Fig. 12d). The cobot can have two statuses. A free status when there is no product orders or the production is not started. A busy status last while the cobot is handling the production orders. A timer of two second has been assigned to every pick and place operation.

The second set of schemas which can be seen in Fig. 13 are the predicate schemas which are addressed as the following:

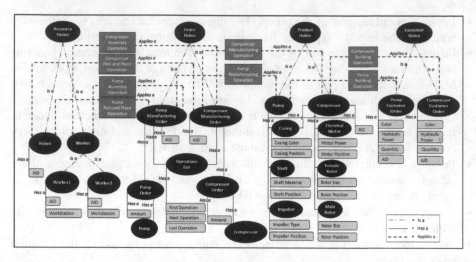

Fig. 13. Case-study ontology model.

- (concept-x) <Is-a> (concept-y): usually a relation between two concept schemas. This relation is similar to the object oriented abstraction. Thus, this predicate expression has been used to express the parent-child relationship between the concepts.
- (concept-x) <Has-a> (attribute-x): usually a relation between a concept and an attribute, an attribute can be a concept schema or a primitive. This relation is similar to object oriented inheritance. Thus, this predicate expression has been used to form sophisticated objects from simpler ones.
- (agent-x) <Applies-a> (action-x): usually a relation between a concept and an action schema. A concept uses this predicate expression to trigger one or more than one actions at the same time. The action schemas will be discussed below in details.

The third set of schemas which can be seen in Fig. 13 are the action schemas which are addressed as the following:

- Pump-Building-Operation: this action schema expects a Pump-Customer-Order concept schema as an input, and it is deployed either by customer-1 or customer-2 agents. An example of this operation can be seen at the ACL-Message content in Fig. 14a.
- Compressor-Building-Operation: this action schema expects a Compressor-Customer-Order concept schema as an input, and it is deployed by either customer-1 or customer-2 agents. An example of this operation can be seen at the ACL-Message content in Fig. 14b.
- Pump-Manufacturing-Operation: this action schema expects a Pump-Order and a Pump-Operations-List concept schemas as inputs, and it is deployed by the pump agent. A detailed example of this operation can be seen at the ACL-Message content in Fig. 14c.

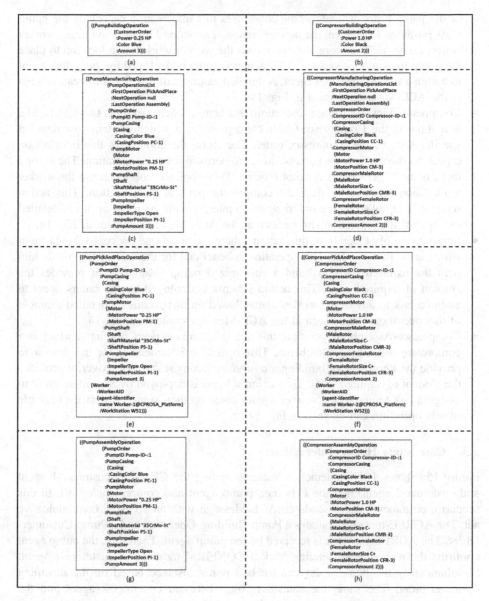

Fig. 14. Ontology-based ACL-messages used during the case-study.

- Compressor-Manufacturing-Operation: this action schema expects a Compressor-Order and a Compressor-Operations-List concept schemas as inputs, and it is deployed by the compressor agent. A detailed example of this operation can be seen at the ACL-Message content in Fig. 14d.
- Pump-Pick-And-Place-Operation: this action schema expects two inputs. The first input is the Pump-Order concept schema which contains the detailed specifications

of the pump order. Therefore, the cobot uses this information especially the pump parts positions to perform the pick operation. The second input is the target worker concept schema. Therefore, the cobot uses the worker workstation location to place the pump parts at this location. This action schema is deployed by the orders agent to assign a task to the robot agent. A detailed example of this operation can be seen at the ACL-Message content in Fig. 14e.

- Compressor-Pick-And-Place-Operation: this action schema expects two inputs. The first input is the Compressor-Order concept schema which contains the detailed specifications of the compressor order. Therefore, the cobot uses this information especially the compressor parts positions to perform the pick operation. The second input is the target worker concept schema. Therefore, the cobot can use the worker workstation location to place the compressor parts at this location. This action schema is deployed by the orders agent to interact with the robot agent. A detailed example of this operation can be seen at the ACL-Message content in Fig. 14f.
- Pump-Assembly-Operation: this action schema expects one concept schema input which is the pump-order. This operation is beneficial for the worker to provide him with the required parts to build a customized pump. Moreover, it provides the amount of required units. This action schema is deployed by the orders agent to assign a task to any of the worker agents based on their status. A detailed example of this operation can be seen at the ACL-Message content in Fig. 14g.
- Compressor-Assembly-Operation: this action schema expects one input which is a compressor-order concept schema. This operation is beneficial for the worker to provide the knowhow of building a customized compressor. Moreover, it provides the amount of required units. This action schema is deployed by the orders agent to assign a task to any of the worker agents based on their status. A detailed example of this operation can be seen in Fig. 14h.

5.3   Case Study Holons Interaction

Figure 15a shows JADE interaction scenario among the CHs (i.e., customer-1 agent and customer-2 agent) and the PHs (i.e., pump agent and compressor agent). In this scenario, customer-1 agent sends an ACL-Message with an AGREE communicative act. The AGREE-message contains a Pump-Building-Operation and a Pump-Customer-Order. The AGREE-message is received by the pump agent. Therefore, the pump agent confirms the receiving by sending back a CONFIRM-message to customer-1 agent. Simultaneously the pump agent constructs a pump instance based on the incoming customer-order. The same mechanism is used between cusomter-2 agent and the compressor agent to construct a new instance of a compressor associated with a customer-2 order. Figure 15b shows JADE interaction scenario between the PHs (i.e. pump agent and compressor agent) and the OH. This interaction is following the same mechanism used in before in Fig. 15a, except that it replaces the AGREE-messages with a PROPAGATE-messages.

Figure 15c shows JADE interaction scenario between the OH and the ORHs (i.e., worker-1 agent, worker-2 agent, and robot agent). During this interaction, the manufacturing operations are assigned to the operational resources based on their statuses. As it can be seen in lines 1, 2, 3, and 4 of Fig. 15c, the orders agent sends two

REQUEST-messages which are replied by two CONFIRM-messages. The first REQUEST-message assigns a Pump-Pick-And-Place-Operation to the robot agent. The second REQUEST-message assigns a Pump-Assembly-Operation to worker-1 agent. The reason that the pump-order has been processed first by the orders agent is that it is the first product order at the order list (refer to Fig. 12c). In line 5 of Fig. 15c, the robot agent sends an INFORM-REF-message to worker-1 agent to tell that it placed the first pump unit. Then, the robot agent sends two INFORM-IF-messages to the orders agent and worker-1 agent to tell that it finished handling all the required pump amounts (i.e., three pump units by referring to Fig. 12a, b, and d). The two INFORM-IF-messages can be seen in lines 6, and 7 of Fig. 15c. The same interaction mechanism can be seen in lines 9, 10, 11, 12, and 13 to assign the compressor-order manufacturing operations to the worker-2 agent and the robot agent. Lines 14, and 15 of Fig. 15c shows the INFORM-messages to express done-signals which are generated by worker-1 and worker-2 agents.

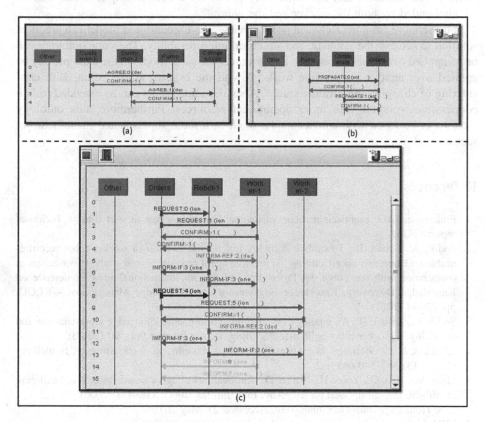

Fig. 15. Case-study interaction scenario.

6 Conclusion

This research has highlighted an important challenge in cooperative manufacturing. This challenge is the representation of the shared knowledge and the production entities in the cooperative workcell. Moreover, exchanging the represented manufacturing knowledge to obtain collective decisions. A holonic control concept has been purposed to solve this challenge. The implementation of this concept has been achieved via combining the autonomous agent communication with the ontology model. A case study of two workers in cooperation with one cobot has been chosen to verify the solution feasibility.

The conducted research presented the different approaches to implement an ontology model. Furthermore, implementing this model via the autonomous agent technology. The implementation showed that exchanging the manufacturing knowledge among the deployed agents supported the common understanding of the manufacturing environment and operations. By providing a natural language that can be comprehended by both the worker and the cobot.

Furthermore from the technical point of view, the implemented model is a practical solution to achieve the syntactic and structural interoperability. The same ontology can be re-applied over similar domains. For instance, the same model in the example can be applied over another cooperative workcell with the exact resource holon, with considering of changing the attribute values. Also, the same model can be extended to fit a cooperative workcell with more operational resources. Furthermore, this ontology model can be fused with another model to fit in a more sophisticated manufacturing scenario.

References

1. Fraunhofer IAO: Lightweight robots in manual assembly - best to start simply. Technical report (2016)
2. Sadik, A., Urban, B.: Towards a complex interaction scenario in worker-cobot reconfigurable collaborative manufacturing via reactive agent ontology - case-study: two workers in cooperation with one cobot. In: Proceedings of the 9th International Joint Conference on Knowledge Discovery, Knowledge Engineering and Knowledge Management - KEOD, pp. 27–38 (2017)
3. Sadik, A., Urban, B.: An ontology-based approach to enable knowledge representation and reasoning in worker-cobot agile manufacturing. Future Internet 9(4), 90 (2017)
4. Jennings, N., Wooldridge, M.: Agent Technology, 1st edn, pp. 3–28. Springer, Heidelberg (1998). ISBN 3-540-63591-2
5. Shen, W., Hao, Q., Yoon, H., Norrie, D.: Applications of agent-based systems in intelligent manufacturing: an updated review. Adv. Eng. Inform. 20(4), 415–431 (2006)
6. Jade Homepage. http://jade.tilab.com/. Accessed 21 May 2016
7. FIPA Homepage. http://www.fipa.org/. Accessed 10 July 2016
8. Rodrigues, N.: Development of an ontology for a multi-agent system controlling a production line. M.Sc. thesis, Instituto Politécnico de Bragança (2012)
9. Neches, R., et al.: Enabling technology for knowledge sharing. AI Mag. 12(3), 36–56 (1991)

10. Gruber, T.: Toward principles for the design of ontologies used for knowledge sharing. IN Int. J. Hum.-Comput. Stud. **43**(5), 907–928 (1995)
11. Wang, H., Gibbins, N., Payne, T., Redavid, D.: A formal model of the semantic web service ontology (WSMO). Inf. Syst. **37**(1), 33–60 (2012)
12. Fensel, D.: Ontology-based knowledge management. Computer **35**(11), 56–59 (2002)
13. Lai, L.: A knowledge engineering approach to knowledge management. Inf. Sci. **177**(19), 4072–4094 (2007)
14. Kumar, S.: Agent-Based Semantic Web Service Composition. Springer, Heidelberg (2012). ISBN 978-1-4614-4663-7
15. Bordini, R.H., Hübner, J.F., Wooldridge, M.: Programming Multi-agent Systems in AgentSpeak Using Jason. Wiley, Hoboken (2007). ISBN 978-0-470-02900-8
16. Goldin, D., Wegner, P.: Principles of interactive computation. In: Goldin, D., Smolka, S.A., Wegner, P. (eds.) Interactive Computation: The New Paradigm, pp. 25–37. Springer, Heidelberg (2006)
17. Teahan, W.: Artificial Intelligence – Agent Behaviour, 1st edn. BookBoon, London (2010). ISBN 978-87-7681-559-2
18. Bellifemine, F., Caire, G., Greenwood, D.: Developing Intelligent Agent Systems. Wiley, Hoboken (2007). ISBN 978-0-470-05747-6
19. Koestler, A.: The Ghost in the Machine. Hutchinson & Co., Ltd., London (1967). ISBN 0-14-019192-5
20. Botti, V., Boggino, A.G.: ANEMONA: A Multiagent Methodology for Holonic Manufacturing Systems. Springer Series in Advanced Manufacturing. Springer, Heidelberg (2010). https://doi.org/10.1007/978-1-84800-310-1. ISBN 13: 9781849967785
21. Babiceanu, R.F., Frank, F.: Development and applications of Holonic manufacturing systems: a survey. J. Intell. Manuf. **17**(1), 111–131 (2006)
22. Van Brussel, H., Wyns, J., Valckenaers, P., Bongaerts, L., Peeters, P.: Reference architecture for Holonic manufacturing systems: PROSA. Comput. Ind. **37**(3), 255–274 (1998)

Integrating Local and Global Data View for Bilingual Sense Correspondences

Fumiyo Fukumoto[1(✉)], Yoshimi Suzuki[1], Attaporn Wangpoonsarp[1],
and Meng Ji[2]

[1] Graduate Faculty of Interdisciplinary Research, University of Yamanashi,
Kofu, Japan
{fukumoto,ysuzuki,g16dhl01}@yamanashi.ac.jp
[2] University of Sydney, Sydney, Australia
Christine.ji@sydney.edu.au

Abstract. This paper presents a method of linking and creating bilingual sense correspondences between English and Japanese noun word dictionaries. We used local and global data views to identify bilingual sense correspondences. Locally, we extracted bilingual noun words by using simple sentence-based similarity. Globally, for each monolingual dictionary, we estimated domain-specific senses by using a textual corpus having category information. The extraction method is based on the sense similarities which are obtained by word embedding learning. We incorporated these data views. More precisely, we assigned a sense to each noun word of the extracted bilingual words keeping domain (category) consistency. We used the WordNet 3.0 and EDR Japanese dictionaries using Reuters and Mainichi Japanese newspaper corpora to evaluate our method. The results showed that the integration of local and global data views improved overall performance and we obtained 318 within the topmost 1,000 bilingual noun senses. Moreover, we found that the extracted bilingual noun senses can be used as a lexical resource for the machine translation as the translation results obtained by using our method was better than those obtained by a bilingual dictionary and slightly better than the results obtained by SYSTRANet.

Keywords: Bilingual sense correspondence ·
Domain specific senses · Word embeddings

1 Introduction

There has long been a great deal of interest in the retrieval of bilingual lexicons with the availability of a number of large-scale corpora. The extracted bilingual lexicon is widely used for cross-lingual NLP applications, such as machine translation (MT), cross-lingual information retrieval (CLIR), multilingual topic tracking, text classification and summarization. Much of the previous work on finding bilingual lexicons have focused on *word* correspondence, rather than *sense*. Interpretation of whether the extracted bilingual lexicon is correct relies on human

© Springer Nature Switzerland AG 2019
A. Fred et al. (Eds.): IC3K 2017, CCIS 976, pp. 224–241, 2019.
https://doi.org/10.1007/978-3-030-15640-4_12

intervention. For example, in most cases, we can accept a pair of English word "president" and Japanese word "大統領" as a bilingual lexicon, while the noun "president" has at least six different senses in WordNet including chairperson and university's president, and "大統領" has two senses in the EDR dictionary.

In this paper, we propose a method for bilingual noun word *sense* correspondence. We focused on manually constructed monolingual dictionaries in different languages because dictionaries such as WordNet [25, 26], ACQUILEX [3], COMLEX [12], and EDR Japanese dictionaries[1] are fine-grained and they are successfully utilized not only for NLP but also for their applications. We used them to make up the deficit of corpus statistics obtained from comparable corpora. We identified bilingual noun word senses based on local and global data views. Here, local data view indicates relevance between English and Japanese sentences. We extracted bilingual noun words by applying sentence-based similarity.

Global data view refers to domain/category information. The assumption behind this is that predominant sense of a word can depend on the domain or source of a document [9, 21]. We identified domain-specific senses using a corpus with category information. This method first identifies each sense of a word in the dictionary to its corresponding category. For each category, we created a graph, where each node refers to each sense of a word, and edges between nodes indicate similarity between two nodes. We applied a Markov Random Walk (MRW) model to the graph and ranked scores for each sense. Finally, we incorporated the local and global information, *i.e.*, we assigned a domain-specific sense to each noun word of the extracted bilingual words maintaining domain/category consistency.

The rest of the paper is organized as follows. The next section describes our approach, especially local and global data views. Section 3 reports some experiments with a discussion of evaluation. Finally, we summarize existing related work and conclude in Sect. 5.

2 System Design

The method consists of three steps: (1) bilingual noun word extraction, (2) identification of domain-specific senses, and (3) bilingual sense correspondence. Hereafter, we describe bilingual noun words as BN words and bilingual noun word senses as BNSs.

2.1 Local Data View

The first step is to extract BN words from the corpora. This process consists of two sub-steps: (i) retrieval of relevant documents, and (ii) BN word extraction based on sentence level similarity.

---

[1] www2.nict.go.jp/ipp/EDR/ENG/indexTop.html.

Table 1. Variables of χ^2 statistics [7].

	w_E	$\neg w_E$
w_J	$f(w_J, w_E) = a$	$f(w_J, \neg w_E) = b$
$\neg w_J$	$f(\neg w_J, w_E) = c$	$f(\neg w_J, \neg w_E) = d$

Retrieval of Relevant Documents. We used Reuters'96 and the Mainichi Japanese newspaper documents. Let $d_i^J (1 \leq i \leq s)$ and $d_j^E (1 \leq j \leq t)$ be a Mainichi document and a Reuters document, respectively. Each Reuters document d_j^E is translated into a Japanese document $d_j^{E\_mt}$ using English-Japanese MT software. We calculated similarity between two documents using BM25 [32], which is widely used in information retrieval studies[2]. BM25 is given by:

$$\text{BM25}(d_i^J, d_j^{E\_mt}) = \sum_{w \in d_j^{E\_mt}} w^{(1)} \frac{(k_1 + 1)tf_i}{K + tf_i} \frac{(k_3 + 1)qtf_j}{k_3 + qtf_j}, \tag{1}$$

where w is a word within $d_j^{E\_mt}$; $w^{(1)} = \log \frac{(t-n+0.5)}{(n+0.5)}$ is the weight of w; t is the number of Mainichi documents; n is the number of documents containing w; K refers to $k_1((1 - b) + b \frac{dl_i}{avdl})$; k_1, b, and k_3 are parameters set to 1, 1, and 1,000, respectively; dl_i is the document length of d_i^J; $avdl$ is the average document length in words; and tf_i and qtf_j are the frequencies of occurrence of the w ($\in d_j^{E\_mt}$) in d_i^J, and $d_j^{E\_mt}$, respectively. If the similarity value between d_i^J and $d_j^{E\_mt}$ is higher than the lower bound L_θ, these are regarded as relevant documents, and a document pair is created.

Bilingual Word Extraction. We assume that BN word correspondences obtained using relevant documents are unreliable as many noun words appear in a pair of relevant documents. Therefore, we applied sentence level retrieval. First, we applied simple χ^2 statistics to the extracted pairs of relevant documents and extracted Mainichi noun word w_J and Reuters noun word w_E pairs with χ^2 values greater than zero. The χ^2 statistic measures the lack of independence between w_J and w_E, and can be compared to the χ^2 distribution with one degree of freedom to judge extremeness [35]. It is defined by:

$$\chi^2(w_J, w_E) = \frac{(ad - bc)^2}{(a + b)(a + c)(b + d)(c + d)}. \tag{2}$$

a, b, c, and d in Eq. (2) are shown in Table 1. $f(x, y)$ in Table 1 refers to the co-occurrence frequencies of x and y on the Japanese and English sides, respectively. Next, for each w_J and w_E pair, we apply sentence level similarity given by:

---

[2] http://trec.nist.gov/.

$$S\_sim(w_J, w_E) =$$

$$\max_{S\_w_J \in Set_J, S\_w_E \in Set_E} sim(S\_w_J, S\_w_E),$$

where

$$sim(S\_w_J, S\_w_E) =$$

$$\frac{\mid S\_w_J \cap S^{mt}\_w_E \mid}{\mid S\_w_J \mid + \mid S^{mt}\_w_E \mid -2\times \mid S\_w_J \cap S^{mt}\_w_E \mid +2}. \tag{3}$$

Set_J and Set_E are sets of sentences that include w_J and w_E, respectively; $\mid X \mid$ is the number of noun words in a sentence X; $\mid S\_w_J \cap S^{mt}\_w_E \mid$ refers to the number of noun words that appear in both S_w_J and $S^{mt}\_w_E$; and $S^{mt}\_w_E$ is the translation result of S_w_E. The larger value of $sim(S\_w_J, S\_w_E)$ indicates the more similar these two sentences S_w_J and S_w_E. As shown in Eq. (4), we retrieved w_J and w_E as the BN word such that the similarity between w_J and $w'_E \in BP(w_J)$ are the largest value. Here, $BP(w_J)$ is a set of BN word pairs, each of which includes w_J on the Japanese side.

$$\langle w_J, w_E \rangle = \arg\max_{\langle w_J, w'_E \rangle \in BP(w_J)} S\_sim(w_J, w'_E). \tag{4}$$

2.2   Global Data View

The second step is to identify domain-specific senses for each noun word. Globally, we used bilingual category/domain correspondences, Reuters and Mainichi categories. The process is applied independently to the English (WordNet) and Japanese (EDR) dictionaries. We used the MRW model to ranking the senses. For each Reuter's category c_E and Mainichi category c_J such as "sports" and "economy" assigned to the Reuters (Mainichi) documents, we created a Graph $G = (S, E)$ that reflects the relationships between senses in a set S. S refers to a set of noun word senses in the Reuters (Mainichi) documents assigned to the category $c_E(c_J)$. Each sense $s_i \in S$ is represented by a vector. Each dimension of a vector corresponds to each word appearing in $syn \cup gloss$, where syn indicates a synset and $gloss$ refers to a gloss text in a dictionary. Each element of a dimension is a frequency count of the word in $syn \cup gloss$. E is a set of edges, which is a subset of $S * S$. Each edge $e_{ij} \in E$ is associated with an affinity weight $aw(i \rightarrow j)$. We used two affinity types between i and j. A directed relation is a hyponym relation, and an undirected relation is a synonym relation. The weight between two senses is computed using the WMD [17].

WMD measures the dissimilarity between two sentences as the minimum amount of distance that the embedded words of one sentence need to *travel* to reach the embedded words of another sentence. The word embedding is learned by using Word2Vec [24]. More precisely, Word2Vec learns vector representation of words from gloss text as the training documents. It is provided two models, a continuous bag-of-words, and skip-gram.

We used a skip-gram model as it gives better word representations when the data is small [24]. The skip-gram model's objective function L is to maximize the likelihood of the prediction of contextual words given the center word. Given a sequence of training words $w_1, w_2, \cdots, w_T$, the objective of the model is to maximized L:

$$L = \frac{1}{T} \sum_{t=1}^{T} \sum_{-k \leq j \leq k, j \neq 0} \log p(w_{t+j} \mid w_t)$$

where k is a hyperparameter defining the window of the training words. Every word w is associated with two learnable parameter vectors, input vector I_w and output vector O_w of the w. The probability of predicting the word w_i given the word w_j is defined as:

$$p(w_i \mid w_j) = \frac{\exp(I_{w_i}{}^\top O_{w_j})}{\sum_{l=1}^{V} \exp(I_l{}^\top O_{w_j})}$$

where V refers to the number of words in the vocabulary. For larger vocabulary size, it is not efficient for computation, as it is proportional to the number of words in the V. Word2vec uses the hierarchical softmax objective function to solve the problem.

Let $\mathbf{X} \in \mathbb{R}^{d \times n}$ be a Word2Vec embedding matrix for vocabulary size of n words. The ith column, $\mathbf{x_i} \in \mathbb{R}^d$ refers to the embedding of the ith word in d-dimensional space. We represent gloss text of each sense as normalized bag-of-words (nBOW) vector, $g \in \mathbb{R}^n$. The objective of the model is to minimize cumulative cost C of moving the gloss text g to g':

$$L = \sum_{i,j=1}^{n} \mathbf{T}_{i,j} \, c(i,j),$$

$$\text{subject to:} \sum_{j=1}^{n} \mathbf{T}_{ij} = g_i, \; \forall i \in \{1, \cdots, n\},$$

$$\sum_{i=1}^{n} \mathbf{T}_{ij} = g'_j. \; \forall j \in \{1, \cdots, n\}. \tag{5}$$

$\sum_{j=1}^{n} \mathbf{T}_{ij} = g_i$ indicates that outgoing flow from word i equals g_i. Similarly, $\sum_{i=1}^{n} \mathbf{T}_{ij} = g'_j$ shows that incoming flow to word j mush match g'_j. $c(i,j)$ in Eq. (5) refers to word travel cost which is defined by $c(i,j) = \| \mathbf{x}_i - \mathbf{x}_j \|_2$ [15].

The transition probability from s_i to s_j is then defined by normalizing the corresponding affinity weight:

$$p(i \rightarrow j) = \begin{cases} \dfrac{aw(i \rightarrow j)}{\sum\limits_{k=1}^{|S|} aw(i \rightarrow k)}, & \text{if } \Sigma aw \neq 0 \\[4mm] 0, & \text{otherwise.} \end{cases} \tag{6}$$

We used the row-normalized matrix $U = (U_{ij})_{|S|*|S|}$ to describe G with each sense corresponding to the transition probability, where $U_{ij} = p(i \rightarrow j)$. To make U a stochastic matrix, the rows with all zero elements are replaced by a smoothing vector with all elements set to $\frac{1}{|S|}$. The matrix form of the saliency score $Score(s_i)$ can be formulated in a recursive form as in the MRW model: $\lambda = \mu U^T \lambda + \frac{(1-\mu)}{|S|} e$, where $\lambda = [Score(s_i)]_{|S|*1}$ is a vector of saliency score for the senses. e is a column vector with all elements equal to 1. μ is a damping factor. We set μ to 0.85, as in the PageRank [2]. The final asymmetric transition matrix M is given by:

$$ M = \mu U^T + \frac{(1-\mu)}{|S|} ee^T \tag{7} $$

Each sense score in a specific category is obtained by the principal eigenvector of the new transition matrix M. We applied the algorithm for each category.[3] For implementation, we used the Eigen library.[4] We chose a vector with the largest eigenvalues. We normalized a vector and obtained rank scores of senses.

2.3 Bilingual Sense Correspondence

The final step is to retrieve BNSs using both results obtained by local and global data views. Let $\langle w_J, w_E \rangle \in Set_{\{w_J, w_E\}}$ be a pair of nouns obtained by the BN word extraction procedure where w_J has the number of m senses $w_{J\_s_i}(1 \leq i \leq m)$ and w_E has the n senses $w_{E\_s_j}(1 \leq j \leq n)$, respectively. We retrieved BNS pair $w_{J\_s_i}$ and $w_{E\_s_j}$:

$$ \langle w_{J\_s_i}, w_{E\_s_j} \rangle_{(c_J, c_E)} \text{ s.t. } w_{J\_s_i} \in Set_{c_J}, $$
$$ w_{E\_s_j} \in Set_{c_E}, $$
$$ \langle w_J, w_E \rangle \text{ satisfies RNN.} \tag{8} $$

We recall that the corpora used to identify domain-specific senses are Reuters and Mainichi documents, each of which has different categories. Therefore, we estimated the category correspondence according to the $\chi^2(c_J, c_E)$ statistics shown in Eq. (2). In Eq. (2), we simply replaced w_J by c_J and w_E by c_E as each document of relevant document pairs has category information. The subscript (c_J, c_E) of $\langle w_{J\_s_i}, w_{E\_s_j} \rangle_{(c_J, c_E)}$ in formula (8) refers to the result of category correspondence between Reuters and Mainichi obtained by Eq. (2). Set_{c_J} and Set_{c_E} show ranked sense lists for c_J, and c_E, respectively, obtained by the MRW model. RNN is the so-called Reciprocal Nearest Neighbors in that two noun senses are each other's most similar noun [14].

---

[3] The principal eigenvector is obtained by the power method and inverse iteration method.

[4] http://eigen.tuxfamily.org/index.php?title=Main_Page.

Table 2. Bilingual noun extraction [7].

	Pairs	Eng	Jap	# of bilingual nouns	# of nouns (top 1,000)	IRS (top 1,000)
Docs	196,368	133,854	20,882	172,895	162	2.32
Docs & Sent				115,918	329	4.83

3   Experiments

We evaluated each of the three procedures in the experiments, (1) BN extraction by using the results of relevant documents retrieval, (2) retrieving domain specific senses, and (3) BNS correspondences.

3.1   Local Data View

In this subsection, we report the results of BN extraction.

Experimental Setup. We used Reuters'96 and Mainichi Japanese newspaper corpora from 20 August 1996 to 19 August 1997. The Reuters'96 corpus consists of 806,792 documents organized into three types of coarse-grained categories, *i.e.*, topic, industry, and region. Each consists of 126, 870, and 366 categories. The Mainichi corpus consists of 119,051 documents organized into 16 categories. The difference in dates between Reuters and Mainichi documents is less than ± 3 days, *e.g.*, when the date of the Reuters document is 27 August, the corresponding Mainichi data is from 24 to 30 August. We set a small date difference because if some event occurred at some specific time period, the press of all countries reports it on one of these days. We used English-Japanese MT software (Internet Honyakuno-Ousama for Linux, Ver.5, IBM Corp.). Each Reuter's document was translated into a Japanese document, and BM25 was applied.

The training data for choosing the lower bound L_θ were Reuters 20 August 1996 and Mainichi from 17 to 23 August 1996. The total number of English and Japanese documents collected were 2,586 and 2,137, respectively, and the number of relevant documents collected manually for evaluation was 157. The classification was determined to be correct if the two human judges agreed on the evaluation. We used the F-score for evaluation of relevant document retrieval, which is a measure that balances precision (Prec) and recall (Rec). Let $cSet$ be a set of correct document pairs. The definitions of Prec and Rec are given by:

$$\text{Prec} = \frac{\mid \{(d_J, d_E) \mid (d_J, d_E) \in cSet, \text{BM25}(d_J, d_E) \geq L_\theta\} \mid}{\mid \{(d_J, d_E) \mid \text{BM25}(d_J, d_E) \geq L_\theta \mid}$$

$$\text{Rec} = \frac{\mid \{(d_J, d_E) \mid (d_J, d_E) \in cSet, \text{BM25}(d_J, d_E) \geq L_\theta\} \mid}{\mid \{(d_J, d_E) \mid (d_J, d_E) \in cSet \mid}$$

The best performance of F-score was 0.564 when the L_θ value was 150. We used the value ($L_\theta = 150$) to extract BN word pairs. We used one year of Reuters

Table 3. The results of sense assignments with and without word embedding (Word-Net).

Reu/SFC	Words	Senses	SFC	DSS	Wo Embedding			W Embedding		
					Correct S		IRS	Correct S		IRS
					DSS	D&S		DSS	D&S	
Economics/Economy	10,284	32,550	1,032	6,355	623	120	2.31	642	131	2.35
Sports/Sports	7,437	26,478	339	4,457	573	158	2.01	594	169	2.21
War/Military	7,681	26,831	913	4,366	510	68	1.41	531	73	1.50
Politics/Politics	10,349	32,536	793	5,981	612	103	2.21	624	112	2.30
Average	8,938	29,598	769	5,290	580	112	1.99	598	121	2.09

and Mainichi documents except for the training data that were used to estimate L_θ values. The difference in dates between them was less than ± 3 days.

Results. The results of BN words extraction are shown in Table 2. We compared the results obtained by our method, "Docs & Sent" with the results obtained by only applying χ^2 statistics to the results of relevant documents, "Docs" to examine how the sentence-based retrieval influences the performance. "Pairs" in Table 2 shows the number of bilingual document pairs. "Eng" and "Jap" show the numbers of Reuters and Mainichi documents within the pairs satisfying the similarity lower bound $L_\theta = 150$, respectively. "# of nouns" shows the number of correct BN in the topmost 1,000 according to the χ^2 statistics (Docs) and sentence-based similarity (Docs & Sent).

As shown in Table 2, sentence-based retrieval contributed to a reduction in the number of useless BN words without a decrease in accuracy, as about 67% (115,918/172,895) of the size obtained by "Docs" was retrieved, while about 2.03 (329/162) times the number of correct BN words were obtained in the topmost 1,000 nouns. "IRS" (Inverse Rank Score) is a measure of system performance by considering the rank of correct BN words within the candidate nouns; it is the sum of the inverse rank of each matching noun, *e.g.*, correct BN words by manual evaluation matches at ranks 2 and 4 give an IRS of $\frac{1}{2} + \frac{1}{4} = 0.75$. A higher IRS value indicates better system performance. Table 2 shows that sentence-based retrieval also contributes to ranking performance compared with the results obtained by applying χ^2 statistics only.

3.2 The Global Data View

Secondly, we report the results of retrieving domain specific senses from the WordNet and EDR dictionaries.

WordNet 3.0. We assigned the Reuters categories to each sense of words in WordNet. We selected 38 Reuters categories, each of which is assigned to more than 80,000 documents. For each category, we collected noun words with frequencies ≥ 5 within a document from the one-year Reuters corpus. There are no existing sense-tagged data for Reuter's categories that could be used for evaluation. Therefore, we selected a limited number of words and evaluated these words qualitatively. To do this, we used SFC resources [19], which annotate WordNet 2.0 synsets with domain labels. We selected 4 categories that are easy to manually identify corresponding Reuters and SFC categories. We used Reuters corpus to learn Word2Vec model. Statistics of data and the results are shown in Table 3. "Words" shows the number of different words with frequency ≥ 5 within a document assigned to the category shown in "Reu," and "Sense" shows their total number of senses. "SFC" refers to the number of senses appearing in the SFC resource. "DSS" (Domain-Specific Senses) is the number of senses assigned by our method. "Wo Embedding" and "W Embedding" indicate the method without word embedding, and with word embedding, respectively. "DSS of the # of Correct S" shows the number of correct senses in the topmost 1,000, and "D&S" refers to the number of correct senses appearing in both DSS and SFC.

As shown in Table 3, the numbers of correct senses obtained by "DSS" and "D&S" in both Wo Embedding and W Embedding did not exactly match. This is not surprising because our method using the Reuters corpus, while the SFC resource consists of 96% of the WordNet synsets, each of which is manually annotated using 115 different SFC. The IRS depends on the category, and the average IRS was 2.09 with word embedding method. It is interesting to note that some senses of words that were obtained correctly by our approach did not appear in the SFC resource. For example, the words "shot" and "strike" in the Sports category, and "liberty" and "military_hospital" in the war/military category were obtained by our approach but did not appear in the SFC. This is because we used WordNet 3.0, while SFC was based on WordNet 2.0. These observations clearly support the usefulness of our automated method.

In the WSD task, a first sense (FS) heuristic is often applied because of its power and lack of a requirement for expensive hand-annotated datasets [5, 21]. We compared the results obtained by DSS to those obtained by the FS heuristic. For each category, we randomly selected 10 words from the senses assigned by DSS and selected 10 sentences from the documents belonging to each corresponding category. As a result, we tested 100 sentences for each category. Table 4 shows the results. "Sense" refers to the number of average senses per word. The average precision (Avg) of our method was 0.69, while the results obtained by the method without word embedding and the FS were 0.68 and 0.59, respectively.

EDR Dictionary. We assigned categories from Mainichi Japanese documents to each sense of words in the EDR Japanese word dictionary[5]. We selected 11 out of 16 categories, each of which had a sufficient number of documents. All

---

[5] www2.nict.go.jp/out-promotion/techtransfer/EDR/index.html?.

Table 4. DSS against the FS heuristic (WordNet) [7].

Cat	Sense	DSS (Wo)	DSS (W)	FS
Economics	5.6	0.73	0.74	0.68
Sports	4.5	0.71	0.73	0.69
War	4.9	0.52	0.52	0.30
Politics	4.2	0.75	0.75	0.68
Average	4.8	0.68	0.69	0.59

Table 5. The results of sense assignments (EDR) [7].

Cat	Words	Senses	Wo Embedding		W Embedding	
			Cor	IRS	Cor	IRS
Economics	15,906	30,869	740	6.39	748	6.43
Sports	17,556	33,595	559	2.77	561	2.82
International	13,906	27,239	451	5.63	459	5.66
Average	15,789	30,568	583	4.93	589	4.97

documents were tagged by the morphological analyzer Chasen [20], and noun words were extracted. We used the corpus of Mainichi Japanese newspapers collected from 1991 to 2012 to learn Word2Vec model. We choose three categories for which it is easy to manually create correct data. Table 5 shows the statistics of the data and the results of the assignment. "Cor" shows the number of senses assigned by our approach correctly in the topmost 1,000 senses. The average IRS obtained by the EDR with word embedding was 4.97 and that of Reuters was 2.09. This is reasonable as the assignment task using EDR is easy compared to WordNet, *i.e.*, the average number of senses per word of the former is 1.93, while that of the latter is 3.31.

Table 6. DSS against the FS heuristic (EDR) [7].

Cat	Sense	DSS (Wo)	DSS (W)	FS
Economics	2.793	0.79	0.81	0.60
Sports	2.873	0.65	0.67	0.52
International	2.873	0.68	0.70	0.58
Average	2.846	0.70	0.73	0.57

In the WSD task, we randomly selected 30 words from the senses assigned by DSS. For each word, we selected 10 sentences from the documents belonging to each corresponding category. The FS in the EDR is determined based on the EDR corpus. Table 6 shows the results. As can be seen in Table 6, DSS was also

Table 7. The results of bilingual sense correspondences [7].

Approach	Candidates			Correct ext. (1,000)			RNN (1,071)			IRS		
	BN	BNS		BN	BNS		BN	BNS		BN	BNS	
		Wo	W		Wo	W		Wo	W		Wo	W
Local	171,895	—	—	329	—	—	431	—	—	2.32	—	—
Local & Global	171,895	115,918	115,920	437	312	318	679	580	589	4.10	4.35	4.37

better than the FS heuristics in Japanese data. The overall performance for the FS (0.57) was not better, similar to the case for the English data (0.59), while the number of senses per word in the Japanese resource was smaller than that in WordNet. There were many senses that did not occur in the EDR corpus, i.e., 62,460 nouns appeared in both EDR and Mainichi newspapers (from 1991 to 2000), 164,761 senses in all. Of these, 114,267 senses did not appear in the EDR corpus. This also demonstrates that automatic DSS with word embedding works well compared to the frequency-based FS heuristics.

3.3   Bilingual Sense Correspondence

Finally, we evaluated the performance of BNS correspondences.

Experimental Setup. The data for BNS correspondence was the Reuters and Mainichi corpora from the same period, i.e., 20 August 1996 to 19 August 1997. The total numbers of documents were 806,791, and 119,822, respectively. Locally, we extracted BN words using sentence-based similarity. We retrieved cross-lingually relevant Japanese documents with English documents. The difference in dates between them was less than ± 3 days. We used these documents to extract BN words. Globally, we assigned domain-specific senses for each of the 38 categories for WordNet 3.0 and 11 categories for EDR. We estimated category correspondences and retrieved BNSs according to their correspondences. We obtained 92 category correspondences in all with χ^2 values larger than zero. From these data, we extracted BNSs.

Results. Table 7 shows the results of BNS correspondences. "Local" indicates the results using only sentence-based similarity, and "Local & Global" shows the results obtained by our method. "Correct ext." refers to the number of correct extractions within the topmost 1,000, and "RNN" shows the number of correct extractions by applying RNN. "BN" refers to the number of BN words, and "BNS" is their senses. "Wo" and "W" show without word embedding and with word embedding, respectively.

As can be clearly seen in Table 7, the results with the integration of local and global data view improved overall performance of BN word extraction compared to local data only because 10.8% (437−329)/1,000 improvement within the topmost 1,000, and 23.1% (679−431)/1,071 improvement with RNN. We obtained

Table 8. Examples of bilingual noun senses [7].

Cat pair (Mai, Reu)	# of Pairs Cand	RNN	# of Correct senses(%)	Examples Sense_id (gloss text)	
(International, Government)	269	10	9 (90.0)	EDR:	ゲリラ_01 (an irregular group of soldiers given to sneak attacks)
				WordNet:	guerrilla_01 (a member of an irregular armed force)
(Economics, Economics)	4,964	58	44 (75.9)	EDR:	株_09 (stock, share)
				WordNet:	stock_01 (the capital raised by a corporation through the issue of shares)
(Sports, Sports)	6,560	68	48 (70.6)	EDR:	パー_02 (in golf, the average number of strokes for playing around a course)
				WordNet:	par_01 (the number of strokes set for each hole on a golf course)
(Local news, Crime)	2,903	34	23 (67.6)	EDR:	殺人_02 (the act of killing someone)
				WordNet:	killer_01 (someone who causes the death of a person)

318 BNSs within the topmost 1,000, although bilingual sense correspondence is a difficult task. Moreover, RNN is effective for BNS correspondences in both of with and without word embeddings. We obtained a total of 1,071 BNSs, which 580 were correct in word embeddings, while that without RNN was 318 within the topmost 1,000.

Table 8 lists examples of BNSs for each category correspondence. (x, y) of the category pair refers to the Mainichi and Reuters category correspondence. "Cand" denotes the number of extracted word pairs, and "RNN" shows word pairs obtained by RNN. "Sense_id" shows the sense and its order of appearance in each dictionary, WordNet, and EDR. Table 8 shows that the first three senses of words, "guerrilla," "stock," and "par" corresponded correctly. However, "the act of killing someone" in the EDR was incorrectly identified by "killer" (person) in WordNet. Our approach for identifying BNSs is based on term-based corpus statistics. It will be necessary to investigate other types of a lexicon, such as a verb and subjective/objective noun collocations, for further improvement. Our method for category correspondence is very simple as it is based on the χ^2 statistics. Much of the previous work on text categorization indicated that hierarchical structure (e.g., Amazon670K, MeSH, Yahoo!, LookSmart) improves the accuracy of text categorization, and it is worth attempting to use a hierarchical structure to determine corresponding categories with high accuracy.

Finally, we compared the results of bilingual sense correspondences with a machine-readable bilingual dictionary and two English-Japanese MT systems. We randomly choose 80 BNSs from 589 correct bilingual senses obtained by RNN. There were 40 different category pairs, and as shown in Table 9, the number of different English and Japanese words were 20, and 32, respectively. Table 10 shows examples of BNSs and its corresponding category pairs.

We choose titles of documents as a translation test data. Because they are short sentences, and hard to be affected by a syntactic analyzer in MT sys-

Table 9. Constituents of bilingual sense of words [7].

Eng	authority, board, budget, business, case coast, company deficit, finance, group, issue money, opposition people, power, president seat, space, state, trial
Jap	グループ, ビジネス, 宇宙, 沖, 会長, 海上 株, 幹部, 機関, 議席, 金, 国民, 最終, 財政 資金, 事業, 事件, 社長, 主義, 人, 政治, 政府 赤字, 大統領, 団体, 当局, 場合, 法廷, 本部 問題, 予算, 力

Table 10. Examples of bilingual senses [7].

Cat pair (Mai, Reu)	Sense pair (Mai, Reu)
(top news, industrial)	(権威_01, authority_01)
(international, international)	(当局_02, authority_05)
(top news, election)	(場合_02, case_01)
(top news, violence)	(事件_01, case_02)
(top news, funding)	(赤字_01, deficit_01)
(top news, politics)	(不足_02, deficit_02)

Table 11. Comparison against a dictionary and MT systems [7].

	# of correct senses (%)
Eijirou	329/800 (41.2)
Honyakuno-Ousama	521/800 (65.1)
SYSTRANet	550/800 (68.8)
RNN (Wo)	562/800 (70.3)
RNN (W)	566/800 (70.8)

tems which enable to approximate a fair comparison. For each of the 80 BNS pairs, we created translation test data. For example, in the word, "authority" of BNS pair (権威_01, authority_01) in Table 10, we randomly selected 10 titles sentences including "authority" from the Reuters documents assigned to the category "industrial". We translated these test data by using two MT systems[6], and compared the translation result of "authority". We also compared the results obtained by our method with an English-Japanese dictionary, Eijirou on the WEB[7]. In the English-Japanese dictionary, we used the first-sense heuristic (choosing the first sense of a word). The comparative results are shown in Table 11.

---

[6] We used Internet Honyakuno-Ousama and SYSTRANet English-Japanese MT software. www.systranet.com/translate.

[7] www.alc.co.jp.

As we can see from Table 11 that the results obtained by RNN with word embeddings were 70.8%, and it was better to the results obtained by bilingual dictionary (41.2%), and slightly better to the results obtained by RNN without word embeddings (70.3%) and SYSTRANet (68.8%). Moreover, it works well compared to the Honyakuno-Ousama (MT) that we used in the process of BN word extraction as local data view. It can be observed from these results that the extracted BNSs can be used as a lexical resource for MT system.

4   Related Work

Our approach to link bilingual word senses in dictionaries can be regarded as a type of ontology alignment. The earliest such attempts were Chimaera [22] and PROMPT [28]. Suchanek et al. developed an ontology alignment system called PARIS which relies on instance overlap-based cues to align instances, categories, and relations from two knowledge bases. They reported that the method is effective, although it remains insufficient to align ontologies that share few or no data entries in common. Wijaya et al. focused on the problem, and presented a method of aligning ontologies called PIDGIN that employs a very large natural language text as interlingua and graph-based self-supervised learning [34]. The use of corpora is similar to our method, although the target of integration is quite different, i.e., PIDGIN aimed at relation and category alignment, while our method aligned noun word senses.

In the context of bilingual lexicon extraction, much of the previous work used comparable corpora. One attempt involved directly retrieving bilingual lexicons from corpora [8,10]. The alternative approach consists of two steps: first, cross-lingual relevant documents are retrieved from comparable corpora, and then bilingual term correspondences within these relevant documents are estimated. Much of the previous work in finding relevant documents used MT systems or existing bilingual lexicons to translate one language into another [33]. Document pairs are then retrieved based on document similarity. Another approach to retrieving relevant documents involves the collection of relevant document URLs from the WWW [31]. Munteanu et al. proposed a method for extracting parallel sub-sentential fragments from very non-parallel bilingual corpora [27]. All of these methods successfully extracted bilingual lexicons but they ignored the meanings of words. One attempt to deal with the meaning of words is Kusner et al.'s method [17]. They presented the Word Mover's Distance (WMD) between text documents by utilizing word2vec embeddings [23,24]. Word2vec learns a vector representation for each word using a neural network architecture consisting of three layers, i.e. an input layer, a projecting layer, and an output layer to predict nearby words.

There also has been a lot of work where bilingual word vectors are induced using parallel corpora [4,6,13,16]. Dyer et al. presented an alignment model called FASTALIGN model which uses an alignment distribution defined by a single parameter that measures how close the alignment is to the diagonal [6].

Blunsem *et al.* extended Dyer *et al.*'s model for learning bilingual word representations. They marginalize out the alignments which enable to capture more bilingual semantic context [16]. Gouws *et al.* proposed a simple and computationally efficient model called BioBOWA (Bilingual Bag-of-Words without Alignments) for learning bilingual distributed representations of words which can scale to large monolingual datasets, and does not require word-aligned parallel training data [11]. The method requires monolingual data which trains directly and extracts a bilingual signal from a smaller set of raw-text sentence-aligned data. They evaluated the induced cross-lingual embeddings on the two tasks, *i.e.* document classification and lexical translation task, and the results showed that the method outperforms current state-of-the-art methods, especially it contributes to reducing computational cost.

In the context of domain-specific senses of a word, Magnini *et al.* presented a lexical resource where WordNet 2.0 synsets were annotated with Subject Field Codes (SFC) by a procedure that exploits the WordNet structure [1,19]. 96% of the WordNet synsets of the noun hierarchy could have been annotated using 115 different SFC, while identification of the domain labels for senses required a considerable amount of hand-labeling. McCarthy *et al.* presented a method to find domain-specific predominant noun senses automatically using a thesaurus acquired from raw textual corpora and the WordNet similarity package [21]. They tested two domains, "Sports" and "Finance."

To our knowledge, there have been only a few previous works on bilingual sense extraction [30]. One approach is word translation disambiguation presented by Li *et al.* [18]. Their method is based on one-to-many sense mapping. They used a machine learning technique that repeatedly constructs classifiers in the two languages in parallel. They reported that the approach significantly outperformed existing methods using two nouns [29], and seven of the twelve English words studied in WSD research by [36]. Their method requires a small number of sense-tagged training data in both of the two languages, while our method requires documents assigned to categories and a dictionary with gloss text which unfortunately hinders a direct and fair comparison between their system and ours.

Our method has three novel aspects. First, we propose a method to integrate different data views to improve the quality of bilingual sense correspondence. Especially, we make use of the distributed representation of words which captures large semantic context than by using only surface information of words. Second, from the perspective of existing knowledge-based integration, we propose a method for corresponding senses between two monolingual dictionaries via many-to-many sense mapping. Finally, from the perspective of robustness, the method is automated and requires only documents assigned to domains/categories and a dictionary with gloss text. It can be applied easily to a new domain, sense inventory, or different languages which are given sufficient documents.

5   Conclusion

We proposed an approach for linking and creating bilingual sense correspondences by combining local and global data views. The results of noun word senses from WordNet 3.0 and EDR Japanese dictionaries using Reuters and Mainichi Japanese newspaper corpora showed that local and global data views improved overall performance than using only local data view, especially, word embedding learning is effective to calculate the similarity of senses. Moreover, we found that the extracted bilingual noun senses can be used as a lexical resource for the machine translation as the translation results obtained by using our method was better than those obtained by a bilingual dictionary, and slightly better than the results obtained by SYSTRANet. Future work will include: (i) extending the method to use hierarchical structures of categories for category correspondence for further improvement, (ii) retrieving other parts of speech word senses for quantitative evaluation, and (iii) evaluation of the method using dictionaries other than English WordNet and Japanese EDR.

Acknowledgements. The authors would like to thank Bernardo Magnini for providing SFC resources, and the anonymous reviewers for their comments and suggestions. This work was supported by the Telecommunications Advancement Foundation, and Support Center for Advanced Telecommunications Technology Research, Foundation.

References

1. Bentivogli, L., Forner, P., Magnini, B., Pianta, E.: Revising the WordNet domains hierarchy: semantics, coverage and balancing. In: Proceedings of the Workshop on Multilingual Linguistic Resources, pp. 101–108 (2004)
2. Brin, S., Pagee, L.: Lexical issues in natural language processing. In: Proceedings of the 7th International Conference on World Wide Web, vol. 7, pp. 107–117 (1998)
3. Briscoe, E.J.: Lexical issues in natural language processing. In: Klein, E., Veltman, F. (eds.) Natural Language and Speech. ESPRIT Basic Research Series, pp. 39–68. Springer, Heidelberg (1991). https://doi.org/10.1007/978-3-642-77189-7_4
4. Brown, P.F., Pietra, V.J.D., Pietra, S.A.D., Mercer, R.L.: The mathematics of statistical machine translation: parameter estimation. Comput. Linguist. **19**(2), 263–311 (1993)
5. Cotton, S., Edmonds, P., Kilgarriff, A., Palmer, M.: SENSEVAL-2 (1998). http://www.sle.sharp.co.uk/senseval2/
6. Dyer, C., Chahuneau, V., Smith, N.A.: A simple, fast, and effective reparameterization of IBM model 2. In: Proceedings of the 2013 Conference of the North American Chapter of the Association for Computational Linguistics: Human Language Technologies, pp. 644–648 (2013)
7. Fukumoto, F., Suzuki, Y., Wangpoonsarp, A.: Is (president, 大統領) a correct sense pair? Linking and creating bilingual sense correspondences. In: Proceedings of the 9th International Conference on Knowledge Engineering and Ontology Development, pp. 39–48 (2017)
8. Fung, P., Cheung, P.: Mining very non-parallel corpora: parallel sentence and lexicon extraction via bootstrapping and EM. In: Proceedings of 2004 Conference on Empirical Methods in Natural Language Processing, pp. 57–63 (2004)

9. Gale, W.A., Church, K.W., Yarowsky, D.: One sense per discourse. In: Proceedings of Speech and Natural Language Workshop 1992, pp. 233–237 (1992)
10. Gaussier, E., Renders, H.M., Matveeva, I., Goutte, C., Déjean, H.: A geometric view on bilingual lexicon extraction from comparable corpora. In: Proceedings of the 42nd Annual Meeting of the Association for Computational Linguistics, pp. 527–534 (2004)
11. Gouws, S., Bengio, Y., Corrado, G.: BilBOWA: fast bilingual distributed representations without word alignments. In: Proceedings of the 32nd International Conference on Machine Learning, pp. 748–756 (2015)
12. Grishman, R., MacLeod, C., Meyers, A.: COMLEX syntax: building a computational lexicon. In: Proceedings of the 15th International Conference on Computational Linguistics, pp. 268–272 (1994)
13. Haghighi, A., Liang, P., Kirkpatrick, T.B., Klein, D.: Learning bilingual lexicons from monolingual corpora. In: Proceedings of 46th Annual Meeting of the Association for Computational Linguistics: Human Language Technologies, pp. 771–779 (2008)
14. Hindle, D.: Noun classification from predicate-argument structures. In: Proceedings of the 28th Annual Meeting of the Association for Computational Linguistics, pp. 268–275 (1990)
15. Hitchcock, F.L.: The distribution of a product from several sources to numerous localities. J. Math. Phys. 20, 224–230 (1941)
16. Kocisky, T., Hermann, K.M., Blunsom, P.: Learning bilingual word representations by marginalizing alignments. In: Proceedings of the 52nd Annual Meeting of the Association for Computational Linguistics, pp. 224–229 (2014)
17. Kusner, M.J., Sun, Y., Kolkin, N.I., Weinberger, K.Q.: From word embeddings to document distances. In: Proceedings of the 32nd International Conference on Machine Learning, pp. 957–966 (2015)
18. Li, H., Li, C.: Word translation disambiguation using bilingual bootstrapping. Comput. Linguist. 30, 1–22 (2004)
19. Magnini, B., Cavaglia, G.: Integrating subject field codes into WordNet. In: Proceedings of LREC-2000 (2000)
20. Matsumoto, Y., et al.: Japanese morphological analysis system ChaSen version 2.2.1. In: NAIST Technical report NAIST (2000)
21. McCarthy, D., Koeling, R., Weeds, J., Carroll, J.: Unsupervised acquisition of predominant word senses. Comput. Linguist. 33(4), 553–590 (2007)
22. McGuinness, D.L., Fikes, R., Rice, J., Wilder, S.: An environment for merging and testing large ontologies. In: Proceedings of the Conference on Principles of Knowledge Representation and Reasoning, pp. 483–493 (2000)
23. Mikolov, T., Sutskever, I., Chen, K., Corrado, G.S., Dean, J.: Distributed representations of words and phrases and their compositionality. In: Proceedings of NIPS, pp. 3111–3119 (2013)
24. Mikolov, T., Chen, K., Corrado, G., Dean, J.: Efficient estimation of word representations in vector space. CoRR abs/1301.3781 (2013)
25. Miller, G.A., Beckwith, R.T., Fellbaum, C.D., Gross, D., Miller, K.J.: WordNet: an on-line lexical database. Int. J. Lexicogr. 3(4), 235–244 (1990)
26. Miller, G.A.: Wordnet: a lexical database for English. Commun. ACM 38, 39–41 (1995)
27. Munteanu, D.S., Marcu, D.: Extracting parallel sub-sentential fragments from non-parallel corpora. In: Proceedings of the 21st International Conference on Computational Linguistics and 44th Annual Meeting of the Association for Computational Linguistics, pp. 81–88 (2006)

28. Noy, N.F., Musen, M.A.: PROMPT: algorithm and tool for automated ontology merging and alignment. In: Proceedings of the 17th National Conference on Artificial Intelligence, pp. 450–455 (2000)

29. Pedersen, T.: A simple approach to building ensembles of naive Bayesian classifiers for word sense disambiguation. In: Proceedings of the 2nd Conference on Empirical Methods in Natural Language Processing, pp. 197–207 (2000)

30. Plous, S., Ji, H.: A model for matching semantic maps between language (French/English, English/French). Comput. Linguist. **29**, 155–178 (2003)

31. Resnik, P., Smith, N.A.: The web as a parallel corpus. Computat. Linguist. **29**(3), 349–380 (2003)

32. Robertson, S.E., Walker, S.: Some simple effective approximations to the 2-poisson model for probabilistic weighted retrieval. In: Proceedings of the 17th Annual International ACM SIGIR Conference on Research and Development in Information Retrieval, pp. 232–241 (1994)

33. Utsuro, T., Horiuchi, T., Hamamoto, T., Hino, K., Nakayama, T.: Effect of cross-language IR in bilingual lexicon acquisition from comparable corpora. In: Proceedings of the 10th Conference of the European Chapter of the Association for Computational Linguistics, pp. 355–362 (2003)

34. Wijaya, D., Talukdar, P.P., Mitchell, T.: PIDGIN: ontology alignment using web text as interlingua. In: Proceedings of ACM Conference on Information and Knowledge Management, pp. 589–598 (2013)

35. Yang, Y., Pedersen, J.O.: A comparative study on feature selection in text categorization. In: Proceedings of the 14th International Conference on Machine Learning, pp. 412–420 (1997)

36. Yarowsky, D.: Unsupervised word sense disambiguation rivaling supervised methods. In: Proceedings of the 33rd Annual Meeting of the Association for Computational Linguistics, pp. 189–196 (1995)

Associative Representation and Processing of Databases Using DASNG and AVB+trees for Efficient Data Access

Adrian Horzyk[⊠]

AGH University of Science and Technology,
Mickiewicza Av. 30, 30-059 Krakow, Poland
horzyk@agh.edu.pl

Abstract. Today, we have to cope with a great amount of data – BIG data problems. The main issues concerned about BIG data are sparing representation, time efficiency of data access and processing, as well as data mining and knowledge discovery. When dealing with the big amount of data, time is crucial. The most of time for data processing in the contemporary computer science is lost for a various search operation to access appropriate data. This paper presents how data collected in relational databases can be transformed into the associative neuronal graph structures, and how searching operations can be accelerated thanks to the use of aggregation and association of the stored data. To achieve an extraordinary efficiency in data access, this paper introduces new AVB+trees which together with Deep Associative Semantic Neuronal Graphs which can typically allow for constant time access to the stored data. The presented solution allows representing horizontal and vertical relations between data and stored objects, expanding possibilities of relational databases and replacing various search operations by the specific graph structure. Another contribution is the expansion of the aggregation of the duplicates to all data tables which contain the same attributes. In such a way, the presented associative structures simplify and speed up all searching operations in comparison to the classic solutions.

Keywords: Deep neural network architectures · AVB-trees · AVB+trees ·
Big data representation and processing · Associative Graph Data Structures ·
Deep Associative Semantic Neuronal Graphs ·
Associative database transformation

1 Introduction

In computer science, we can use many various data structures to store data and some relations between them as well. Various data structures differ in their complexity, data access efficiency, construction speed, ability to self-organize and self-balance, memory usage and stored relations. The main focus of various data structure is usually put on the computational efficiency of typical operations like insert, remove, and update new elements, especially when dealing with big data [1, 21] processed by various data mining algorithms [7, 10, 23]. Moreover, the use of an appropriately chosen structure

© Springer Nature Switzerland AG 2019
A. Fred et al. (Eds.): IC3K 2017, CCIS 976, pp. 242–267, 2019.
https://doi.org/10.1007/978-3-030-15640-4_13

to the given task and data can allow for using more efficient algorithms than for other data structures. This paper draws attention to another aspect of data structures – on the representation of data relations and the richness and variety of these relations. The most simple data structures like one-dimensional arrays or lists cannot represent almost any data relations because of the linear order of the elements. They can only list elements in the order or without it, so they can be used to store data, but not relations. The use of tables consisting of various attributes enables representation of various objects modeled by a selected subset of the attributes and their values. In relational databases, the objects of various tables can be additionally related using primary and foreign keys, which enable to conclude about various relations between objects and their dependencies. However, when we want to draw conclusions about relations between objects of the same table, we have to use SQL to retrieve information about interesting relations, but it takes time and requires human activity to design appropriate SQL commands. Moreover, the results of such computations are typically not stored because when the stored data change, the results of previously computed results by executed SQL commands change as well, so we have to perform the same operations many times. That is why in computer science, we spend most of the computational time for searching for something in the data, executing many loops and nested loops on still greater amounts of data. Is that really necessary? Can we imagine computations without loops?

In this paper, a specific data structure is presented. This data structure is invented in such a way to store data in the very efficient form and quickly accessible way but to store data together with a possibly great variety of relations to avoid necessity search for them as in classic relational databases. Moreover, the way of storing data in the proposed data structure is invented to update the stored relations automatically during the insert, remove, or update operations, so the correct relations are always available and quickly accessible. This data structure is inspired by the human brain and biological neural networks [22, 24] which consist of very slow spiking neurons [8] in comparison to the very quickly clocked contemporary CPU and GPU processors. Why are biological neural networks so efficient in many computationally difficult tasks which can be hardly computed on contemporary computers? One of the reasons for it is related to the way how data are stored and organized inside the brain. Moreover, the brain structures not only store data but also process them, so they do not need to loop search for anything that is stored and related in their neuronal structures. That is why humans and animals can react so fast even in computationally very difficult situations.

This paper presents deep associatively-semantic neural graphs (DASNG) which are inspired by the human brain and biological neural networks and the way how real neurons work. The main focus of the DASNG neural networks is to apply neurons to store data from relational databases together with all relations which are represented inside the tables and between them using primary and foreign keys, but expanding them by extra relations which are useful and often searched using SQL commands. Thanks to the presented solution, it will not be necessary to use extra indices to sort data; to use complex and ineffective SQL commands to retrieve information about similarities and groups of similar objects (clusters); to loop many records of big data collections [1]; and [21, 26] to filter useful data or information because such kinds of information will be quickly available.

The presented neuronal data structure is self-organizing, self-balancing, self-sorting, and self-updating. It means that all the stored data are organized, balanced and sorted during the insert, remove and update operations, and this process is very efficient in comparison to the mechanisms used in the database. During this operations, all stored relations are also automatically updated, so we do not need to perform any extra operations on this structure or use any extra memory, e.g. for storing and updating indices.

2 Associations and Associative Structures and Relations

This paper gives a broad overview about associative processes and associative structures and defines associations on the basis of the processes that work in biological neural networks to apply them to various collections of data typically stored in relational and non-relational databases.

In the computer science, we used to use the dictionaries to associate pairs of values and retrieve the associated values using unique keys [5]. This process can be optimized using hash-tables, sorted arrays, or sorted lists and using the half-search algorithm.

In computational intelligence, we also use various associative structures as auto-associative memories (AAM), hetero-associative memories, bidirectional associative memories (BAM), multidirectional associative memories (MAM) and many others, but they are only intended to link one, two or more values together and address them by a content [2, 9, 19].

In biology, the association means not only binding the values or objects together but the possibility to recall information by a specific context which can be complex as well. The specific biologically-inspired associative relations have been introduced in [13]. According to this source, the associations have been divided to:

- Similarity associations (ASIM),
- Sequential associations (ASEQ),
- Contextual associations (ACON),
- Defining associations (ADEF),
- Suppression associations (ASUP).

The similarity associations are defined by the related values which are similar. When similar values are stored in close fields or connected nodes, then they are associated. The sequential and contextual associations are used to represent a sequence or chronology of stored objects or values. The defining and suppression associations are used to define objects as a combination of some features or objects with some possible restrictions or subtraction of some features or objects as well. Moreover, all these associations can be weighted using weighted connections. According to it, associations can be created between various combinations of values and objects and thanks to their weighting, they can be considered with different strength and importance. Such associations can naturally be represented by neurons which compute weighted sums of excitatory and inhibitory stimuli [9, 22]. The wealth of biological associations is not yet used and implemented enough in the structures and methods of contemporary computer science. The relations described above already where successfully implemented in many associative networks and memories described in [13–19], and [20]. This paper introduces this ability and applies it to represent relational databases enriched with extra vertical relations in the neuronal graph structure which associate them using the above-listed relations. The presented neuronal associative structures also weigh the relations what additionally enriches their inference capabilities. In comparison, primary-foreign key relations are not weighted in a relational database so we cannot easily reproduce the frequency, strength, or value of such relations without using extra attributes. The presented model allows us to do it and use in various inference processes on the data stored in the DASNG structures.

2.1   Associative Graph Data Structures

The Associative Graph Data Structures (AGDS) introduced in [13] can be used to represent data in an associative way using a graph structure as presented in Fig. 1. It can be noticed that in comparison to the classic table (Table 1), data presented in this graph form (Fig. 1) are sorted after all attributes, all duplicates for each attribute are aggregated and represented by the same nodes, and all objects are indirectly connected via values which define them. This form of data representation allows us to quickly move along the connections when searching for the most important relations instead of searching for these relations in nested loops when using classic database tables.

Thanks to the important properties of the AGDS structures, it is possible to substantially reduce the computational complexity of many often executed search operations on classic tabular structures. If any operation on a tabular structure has not constant computational complexity and we can achieve the constant computational complexity on an equivalent AGDS structure, we say that **the structure replaces the operation** as mentioned in [18]. For example, if we have to find all objects which attribute "sepal length" is 6.0 and "petal length" is 5.0, we usually need to loop all records stored in the table while we can go directly along the edges from the nodes representing values 6.0 and 5.0 of appropriate attributes in constant time and quickly computing the conjunction of these two conditions in the AGDS structure. The only difficulty is in ensuring effective access to value nodes representing unique values of data attributes. To solve this difficulty, it is possible to use hash-tables (maps) and sorted lists to make more efficient access to them. It is also possible to use modified B-trees and AVB-trees to speed up this access which can be reduced even to the constant computational complexity as proved in [17] and shown in [18] when we assume that there are many duplicates for each attribute in an equivalent tabular dataset. In this paper, an AVB+tree structure is presented which is even more efficient and functional than the AVB-tree structure presented in [18].

Table 1. Selected objects from the Iris dataset taken from UCI ML repository [31].

Objects	Attributes				
	Sepal length	Sepal width	Petal length	Petal width	Class
Object 1 (O1)	5.4	3.0	4.5	1.5	Versicolor
Object 1 (O2)	6.3	3.3	4.7	1.6	Versicolor
Object 1 (O3)	6.0	2.7	5.1	1.6	Versicolor
Object 1 (O4)	6.7	3.0	5.0	1.7	Versicolor
Object 1 (O5)	5.9	3.2	4.8	1.8	Versicolor
Object 1 (O6)	6.0	2.2	5.0	1.5	Virginica
Object 1 (O7)	6.0	3.0	4.8	1.8	Virginica
Object 1 (O8)	5.7	2.5	5.0	2.0	Virginica
Object 1 (O9)	6.5	3.2	5.1	2.0	Virginica

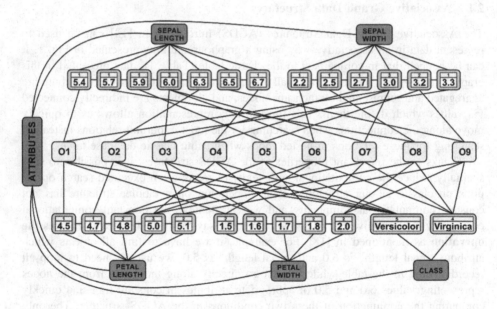

Fig. 1. An AGDS structure constructed on the basis of the data presented in Table 1.

2.2 Elements of the Associative Neural Networks Using Graph Structures

We used to the fact that each artificial neural network [9, 11] consists of artificial neurons and connections, and typically converted input data are directly put on the inputs of the first layer neurons, while outputs are directly read from the outputs of the last layer neurons. This model is not true from the biological point of view because bodies have plenty of receptors which transform input stimuli to the internal representation of the nervous system that converts the results on the stimulus of effectors (muscles, secretion of hormones etc.) which define the reaction and activities at the end of the processing. Thus, in the associative spiking and pulsing neurons (ASN and APN) defined in [17–19], and [20], receptors are also used to convert external data to the neural stimuli and effectors to produce results transferable to computer systems or various actuators. Receptors are organized using sensory input fields (SIF) [19], which represent data attributes and self-organize attribute values [18]. The associative spiking neurons (ASNs) [17] and associative pulsing neurons (APNs) [18] implement the time approach to all internal processes which take place inside these neurons. The time is crucial to define associative dependencies between data and objects represented in the associative structures described in the following sections. These neurons work asynchronously in parallel, and the results of inferences depend on the number of pulses (spikes) produced for a given input context defined by the combination of input data which may represent various search or filter criteria as described in [18, 19], and [20].

3   Self-organizing AVB+trees for Efficient Data Access

This paper introduced AVB+trees which further expand organization properties and data access speed of AVB-Trees presented in [18]. The AVB+trees in comparison to AVB-Trees contain extra connections which connect neighbor values in any defined linear order (e.g. numerical or lexicographical). These connections are called neighbor connections (shown in Fig. 2 in blue). These connections are created and updated automatically during the self-organizing and self-balancing algorithms implemented in AVB+trees. This paper describes how AVB+trees are constructed, how new values can be added, and existing values can be typically removed from these structures in less than logarithmic time assuming that they represent data in which rows some values are repeated (i.e. the data contains duplicates).

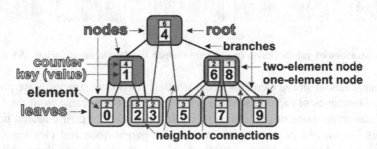

Fig. 2. Description of the AVB+tree structures consisting of nodes which can contain one or two elements that consist of keys (values) and counters, where elements are additionally connected using neighbor connections. (Color figure online)

AVB+trees can store one or two values (keys) in each node (Fig. 2), similarly to 3-degree B-trees or B+trees, however, the AVB+trees aggregate representation of duplicates and also store counters (in yellow boxes in Fig. 2) which count up the numbers of aggregated duplicates of keys (values) in each element. Moreover, in comparison to B-trees, all elements storing unique keys (values) are connected using neighbor connections (blue lines in Fig. 2) and thanks to them it is possible to move between always sorted values in order quickly. In comparison to B+trees, AVB+trees do not use extra nodes to organize access to the elements stored in leaves because AVB +trees store values in all nodes as B-trees and sort values as B+trees, additionally aggregating and counting duplicates, what substantially reduces the structure of AVB +trees and accelerate the access to all elements, especially for big data collections where are many duplicates. In results, AVB+trees are typically much smaller in size and height than B-trees and B+trees thanks to the aggregations of duplicates and not using any extra internal nodes as signposts as used in B+trees. The aggregation of duplicates also reduces the total number of self-balancing and reconstruction operations on the AVB+tree structures because duplicates only increment or decrement counters of elements according to performing an insert or remove operation on this structure. One AVB+tree always represents one data attribute (table column which is not a primary or foreign key).

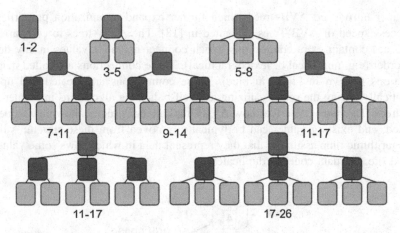

Fig. 3. Capacities of values (keys) or elements) which can be stored in various AVB+trees.

The capacities of stored elements in the smallest AVB+tree structures are presented in Fig. 3. The ranges of capacities of the presented AVB+trees came from the fact that each leaf can contain one or two elements, while the number of their children precisely determines the number of stored elements in each parent node and vice versa. If the node has two children, it stores a single element, and when it has three children, it stores two elements. We can also notice that various AVB+tree structures can sometimes contain the same number of elements. This feature makes possible to transform one tree structure to another one during insert and remove operations, but it also means that there is not a single structure that can store a given number of elements. It depends on the sequence in which elements are inserted into this structure or removed from it. The same collection of elements (e.g. 17 elements) can be stored in three different AVB +tree structures as shown in Fig. 3. This variety does not spoil anything, and the elements are correctly stored, sorted and available in any of the available structure for storing the given number of elements.

The AVB+trees is a collection of elements storing aggregated values (keys) in elements which counting up the numbers of aggregated and represented duplicates of these values (keys). Hence, the AVB+trees are especially dedicated to efficiently store big data collections where the same values are used to define many objects (rows, entities).

The AVB+trees provide a few common operations as other data structures: Insert, Remove, Update, GetMin, GetMax, and Search operations, however, we can also easily define other operations computing, e.g. Sum, Count, Average, or Median. These operations can calculate results faster than equivalent operations on classic tables, arrays, or lists because the total sum of all elements is computed going along neighbor connections multiplying the key values by the numbers of their occurrences (duplicates) stored in the AVB+tree elements.

3.1   Insert Operation on AVB+Trees

The Insert operation executed for a new key inserts a new element to the AVB+tree if any of the existing elements in this structure is not already representing this inserted key. A new AVB+tree element represents such a new key, and its counter is set to one (Fig. 4). In case, when an inserted key (value) is already represented by one of the existing elements in the AVB+tree structure, then no new element is added, but the counter of the existing element representing this value is incremented.

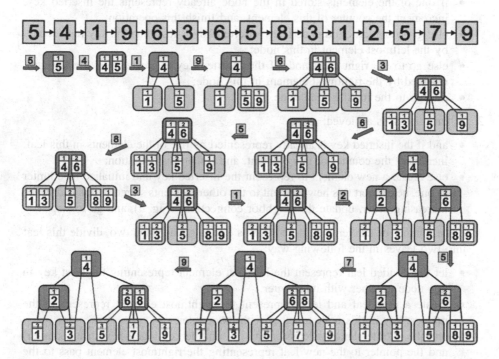

Fig. 4. A construction process of the AVB+tree presented for a sequence of 15 values (keys). (Color figure online)

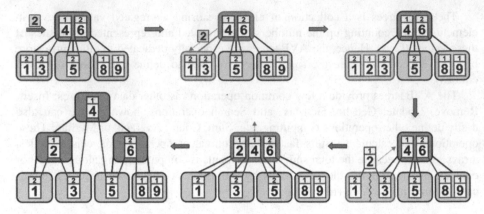

Fig. 5. A self-balancing mechanism of an AVB+tree during the Insert operation when adding key equal 2 to the current structure which must be reconstructed to be able to represent this new key. (Color figure online)

The Insert operation of the AVB+tree is processed as follows (Fig. 4):

1. Start from the root and go recursively down along the branches to the descendants until the leaf is not achieved after the following rules:

   - if one of the elements stored in the node already represents the inserted key, increment the counter of this element, and finish this operation;
   - else go to the left child node if the inserted key is less than the key represented by the leftmost element in this node;
   - else go to the right child node if the inserted key is greater than the key represented by the rightmost element in this node;
   - else go to the middle child node.

2. When the leaf is achieved:

   - and if the inserted key is already represented by one of the elements in this leaf, increment the counter of this element, and finish this operation;
   - else create a new element to represent the inserted key and initialize its counter to one, next insert this new element to the other elements stored in this leaf in the increasing order, update the neighbor connections (Fig. 5), and go to step 3.

3. If the number of all elements stored in this leaf is greater than two, divide this leaf into two leaves in the following way:

   - let the divided leaf represent the leftmost element representing the least key in this node together with its counter;
   - create a new leaf and let it represent the rightmost element representing the greatest key in this node together with its counter;
   - and the middle element (representing the middle key together with its counter) and the pointer to the new leaf representing the rightmost element pass to the parent node if it exists, and go to step 4;

- if the parent node does not exist, create it (a new root of the AVB+tree) and let it represent this middle element (representing the middle key together with its counter), and create new branches to the divided leaf representing the leftmost element and to the leaf pointed by the passed pointer to the new leaf representing the rightmost element (Fig. 5). Next, finish this operation.

4. Insert the passed element between the element(s) stored in this node in the key-increasing order after the following rules:

   - if the element has come from the left branch, insert it on the left side of the existing element(s) in this node;
   - if the element has come from the right branch, insert it on the right side of the existing element(s) in this node;
   - if the element has come from the middle branch, insert it between the existing element(s) in this node.

5. Create a new branch to the new node (or leaf) pointed by the passed pointer and insert this pointer to the child list of pointers immediately after the pointer representing the branch to the divided node (or leaf).

6. If the number of all elements stored in this node is greater than two, divide this node into two nodes in the following way:

   - let the existing node represent the leftmost element representing the least key in this node together with its counter;
   - create a new node and let it represent the rightmost element representing the greatest key in this node together with its counter;
   - the middle element (representing the middle key together with its counter) and the pointer to the new node representing the rightmost element pass to the parent node if it exists; and go back to step 4 (Fig. 5);
   - if the parent node does not exist, create it (a new root of the AVB+tree) and let it represent this middle element (representing the middle key together with its counter), and create new branches to the divided node representing the leftmost element and to the node pointed by the passed pointer to the new node representing the rightmost element (Fig. 5). Next, finish this operation.

In step 2, there is necessary to update the neighbor connections between subsequent elements (blue lines in Figs. 4 and 5). The neighbor connections are represented by pointers which are stored in the elements. When elements are moved between nodes of the AVB+tree, the pointers move inside elements together, not spoiling the representation of the element order. The update of neighbor connections is as easy as in the classic double-tied list of elements as shown in Fig. 5.

3.2 Remove Operation on AVB+Trees

The Remove operation allows to remove a key from the AVB+tree structure and next quickly rebalance and reorganize the structure automatically if necessary. If the removed key is duplicated in the current structure, then only the counter of the element which represents it is decremented. When the removed key is represented by the element which counter is equal one then the element is removed from the node. If this node is a leaf containing only a single element, then the leaf is removed as well, and a rebalancing operation of the AVB+tree is executed. Thus, the Remove operation is processed as follows (Figs. 6, 7 and 8):

1. Start from the root and go recursively down along the branches to the descendants until the removed key is found in one of the elements in the nodes after the following rules:

   - if one of the elements stored in the node represents the removed key go to step 2;
   - else if this node is a leaf, finish this operation without removing the key from the tree because this key was not found;
   - else go to the left child node if the removed key is less than the key represented by the leftmost element in this node;
   - else go to the right child node if the removed key is greater than the key represented by the rightmost element in this node;
   - else go to the middle child node.

2. Decrement the counter of the element representing the removed key and:

   - if the decremented counter is greater or equal one finish this operation successfully;
   - else remove the element from the node and go to step 3.

3. If the node where the element was removed is not a leaf go to step 12 else:

   - if there is still another element in this leaf after the reduction of the removed element then finish this operation successfully;
   - else remove the leaf and go to step 4.

4. If the parent node of the removed node has only a single element, go to step 5 else go to step 6.

5. If the second child of the parent node of the removed node also has only a single element (Fig. 6A) than join these two elements together and remove the second child as well, and go to step 7;
   else create the removed node again and move the parent element to this node and its neighbor connected element from its second child move to the parent node (Fig. 6B)

6. For the parent node of the removed element which contains two elements:

   - if the second neighbor element connected to the parent element which was connected to the removed element in the removed node is single in its node then move this parent element to this child joining them together in this child node (Fig. 6C);
   - else create the removed node again and move the parent element to this node and its neighbor connected element from its second child move to the parent node (Fig. 6D).

7. For the joined node, if the parent node has only a single element (Fig. 7E–H), go to step 8 else go to step 11.

8. If the second child of this parent node has only a single element; go to step 9 else go to step 10.

9. Join parent element with the second child element and move the joined element to the new joined parent (Fig. 7E) and go to step 7 until this parent is not a root of the tree. When the parent is the root finish this operation successfully.

10. For the second child containing two elements (Fig. 7F–H):

    - if the child of this child connected to the parent element is single in its node (Fig. 7F–G) move it to the parent and the node from the parent to the reconstructed branch where the nodes have been joined; next, go to step 6 balancing the second child of this parent.
    - else for the child of this child connected to the parent element is not alone in its node (Fig. 7H), move this child to this connected parent node and the parent element to the branch where the nodes have been joined. Next, finish this operation successfully.

11. For the second child containing two elements (Fig. 7I–J):

    - if one of the neighbor siblings of the joined node has a single element then move the parent element of the joined node to this neighbor sibling and move the joined node to the children of this neighbor siblings (Fig. 7I).
    - else move the connected parent element to the branch where the nodes have been joined, the first closest element from the two-element child to the node and its connected child to the child of the reconstructed branch (Fig. 7J).
    - Next, finish this operation successfully.

12. For elements removed from the non-leaf node (Fig. 8K–P):

    - if this node has only two children go to step 13;
    - else go to step 14.

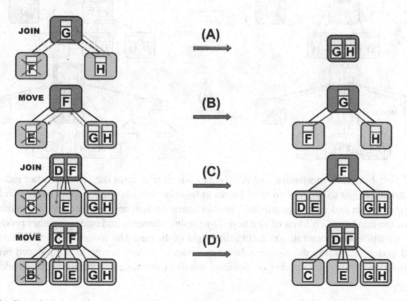

Fig. 6. Sample join and move operations used during the removal of elements from AVB+trees.

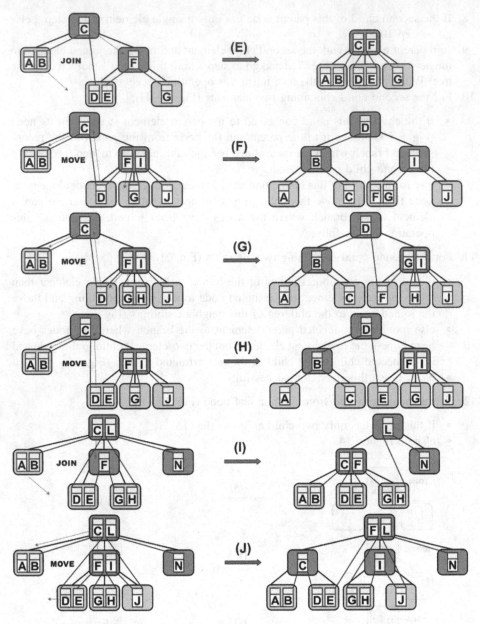

Fig. 7. Self-balancing mechanisms of AVB+trees which transform the structure after reduction of one branch height to self-organize all leaves to be only in the last layer again using two kinds of operations: join and move operations. The join operation reduces the structure (the number of nodes or the number of children of one node) by joining elements and nodes together producing simpler structures and sometimes reducing the height of the tree. The move operation restores the reduced nodes and moves the elements between nodes to restore leaves in the reduced branch. This operation reduces the number of elements stored in the nodes or the number of children.

13. If both two children have only a single element each then join them together in one node (Fig. 8K) and go to step 7;
     else move one element of the two-element child to the parent to replace the removed element (Fig. 8L–M). Next, finish this operation successfully.
14. If both two neighbor children have only a single element each then join them together in one node (Fig. 8N);
     else move one element of the two-element child to the parent to replace the removed element (Fig. 8O–P).

Next, finish this operation successfully.

3.3 Update Operation on AVB+Trees

The Update operation is a simple sequence of Remove and Insert operations because it is not possible to simply update a value in an element because of the structure

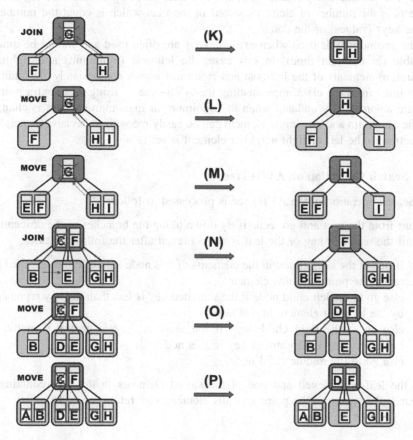

Fig. 8. Self-balancing mechanisms of AVB+trees for the elements removed from the nodes that are not leaves.

of AVB+trees which represent various relations. Data can be easily updated (a value can be changed) only in those structures which do not represent relations, e.g. unsorted arrays, lists, or tables. Hence, the Update operation on an AVB+tree removes the old key (value) from this structure using the Remove operation and inserts an updated one using the Insert operation.

3.4   GetMin and GetMax Operations on AVB+Trees

The GetMin and GetMax operations can be implemented in two different ways dependently on how often extreme elements are used in other computations using an AVB+tree structure.

The first way is used when extreme keys are not often used. In this case, it is necessary to start from the root node and always go along the left tree branches until the leaf is achieved and in its leftmost element (if there are two) is the minimum key (value) stored in this tree. Similarly, we go always along the right branches starting from the root node until the leaf is achieved and in its rightmost element (if there are two) is the maximum key (value) stored in this tree. These operations take log Ň time, where Ň is the number of elements stored in the tree, which is equal the number of unique keys (values) of the data.

The second way is used when extreme keys are often used and should be quickly available (in constant time). In this case, the leftmost (minimum) and rightmost (maximum) elements of the leftmost and rightmost leaves appropriately are additionally pointed from the class implementing the AVB+tree. If using these extra pointers they are automatically updated when the minimum or maximum element is changed, and the minimum and maximum element can be easily recognized because its neighbor connection to the left or right neighbor element is set to null.

3.5   Search Operation on AVB+Trees

The Search operation in the AVB+tree is processed as follows:

1. Start from the root and go recursively down along the branches to the descendants until the searched key or the leaf is not achieved after the following rules:

   - If one of the keys stored in the elements of this node equals to the searched key, return the pointer to this element;
   - else go to the left child node if the searched key is less than the key represented by the leftmost element in this node;
   - else go to the right child node if the searched key is greater than the key represented by the rightmost key in this node;
   - else go to the middle child node.

2. If the leaf is achieved and one of the stored elements in this leaf contains the searched key, return the pointer to this element, else return the null pointer.

3.6   Complexity and Efficiency of the Operations on AVB+trees

The complexity of all operations described above is at most logarithmic of the number (Ň) of unique attribute values $O(\log Ň)$, however, when $Ň \ll N$, where N is the total number of all attribute value in the collection (table), we can state that $O(\log N) \gg O(\log Ň) \approx O(1)$. Hence, when attributes contain many duplicates, we typically access data in constant time as well as perform all operations on AVB+trees in constant time.

4   Drawbacks of Relational Databases

Relational databases are the most commonly used databases today. They consist of tables which use primary and foreign keys to represent related entities. Peter Chen developed an entity-relational model (ER model) that describes interrelated things of interest in a specific domain of knowledge [3, 4]. The ER model is composed of entity types which classify the things of interests and specifies various horizontal relationships that can exist between instances of those entity types. This model is also an abstract data model that defines a data structure that can be implemented as a relational database. Entities may be characterized not only by relationships but also by additional properties (attributes), which include special identifies called primary keys. In the relational databases, each row of a table represents one instance of an entity type, and each field represents an attribute type, where a relationship between entities is implemented by storing a primary key of one entity as foreign keys in other entities of other tables (Fig. 9).

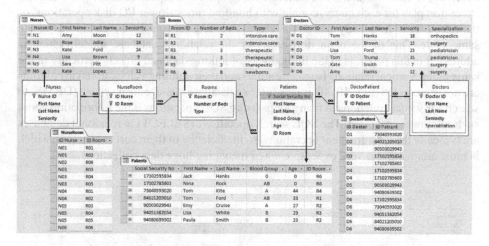

Fig. 9. A sample relational database Small Hospital consisting of 6 tables related patients to doctors and rooms and nurses which take care of the patients in these rooms.

In the relational database model, features are grouped in rows defining entities (tuples, records, objects) collected in tables. The rows of different tables can be horizontally linked together using primary and foreign keys. This kind of row linking allows defining more complex objects by other already represented objects in other tables. Primary keys must be unique and sorted to be quickly accessible. For sorting and indexing, we typically use B-trees or B+trees which can access data in logarithmic time [5, 12].

All modern databases use a Cost-Based Optimization (CBO) to optimize queries and to create an individual execution plan for each query. Execution plans can differ in computational cost and complexity depending on the number of rows and used indices. Execution plans can comprise dynamically created temporal indices for the current query if it improves the cost of the execution plan. Many times, heuristic or greedy algorithms are also used to quickly find a good-enough execution plan without brute force search which can be inefficient and too complex [12].

Moreover, we distinguish various join operations as nested loop-join, hash-join, and merge-join which can be more efficient in some specific situations. The join operations are frequently executed on every database, so their optimization is crucial. The nested loop-join operation takes $O(N * M)$ time, the hash-join operation is processed in $O(N + M)$ time, and the merge-join operation in $O(N + M)$ or $O(N * \log N + M * \log M)$ dependently on working on the sorted or unsorted data, where N and M are the numbers of merged records of two joined tables [12].

Statistics are also very useful and help to estimate the disk I/O and CPU operations and memory usage to find a good-enough execution plan, however, there is a certain cost of updating statistics as well. Hence, the I/O disk data access for reading and writing operations are bottlenecks of databases, especially when a database is huge and do not fit into memory because disk operations are typically at least hundreds of times slower than operations executed in the RAM.

Despite the many advantages of such a solution, we also come across many difficulties and bottlenecks, where the ER data model is not effective enough [12], e.g. the time necessary to update statistics and indices, sorting operations, quick finding a good-enough execution plan for each query, coping with hundred times slower I/O disk operations, or the necessity to frequently search for various vertical relations between entities of the same table. One of the main drawbacks of the relational database model, which is addressed in this paper, is in the limited way of linking data and objects vertically in the same table. Vertical relations between entities and their defining values stored in columns are not represented (Fig. 10). This lack forces a database management system (DBMS) to search for vertical relations in many loops using SQL operations if the information about such relations is required. The SQL search operations (SELECT) in relational databases are typically the most frequent operations, so inefficiency of them costs much time which is most annoying and very expensive when managing huge data collections.

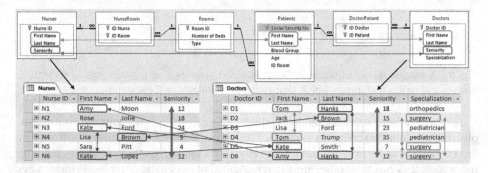

Fig. 10. Drawbacks of relational databases presented on a sample database Small Hospital.

Moreover, a few tables (here e.g. Nurses, Patients, and Doctors) can contain the same attributes (e.g. First Name and Last Name or Seniority in Fig. 10) very often, but such attributes are rarely aggregated and combined in relational databases together.

Furthermore, the objects can be naturally ordered only after a single selected attribute in each table. For sorting data after several attributes simultaneously, we use indices. The indices typically use B-trees, B+trees, or hash tables to sort and organize data in order to make them accessible in logarithmic time. The main drawback of using indices is an extra memory cost and the slowdown of addition, updating, and removal operations performed on the tables. In result, it is recommended to use indices only for data attributes which are frequently used in search operations. This paper presents how to overcome some of these drawbacks and organize data in such a way that both horizontal and vertical relations will be represented in the proposed deep associative neuronal graph data structure described in the following section.

In result of tabular representation of the data in relational databases and representation of only limited subset of relations (i.e. horizontal relations between entities between tables using primary and foreign keys), it is necessary to use many nested loops to search for interesting relations (especially various vertical relations between entities), filter, sort and join data and objects represented in this form. This form is still more inefficient when dealing with big data, and it is necessary to find better solutions which will allow representing more relations in new richer data structures that will replace various computationally inefficient operation by the structure and substantially decrease computational complexity of operations.

5 Deep Associative Semantic Neuronal Graphs

Deep Associative Semantic Neuronal Graphs (DASNG) first time introduced in [18] are based on the associative approach to computation and associative spiking or pulsing neurons presented in [13–19], and [20]. The DASNG networks can work as emergent cognitive neuronal systems [6, 25, 27, 30], and are similar to semantic networks that represent semantic relations between concepts that are linked together [29]. This kind of neural networks uses associative data structures mentioned in Sect. 2 of this paper which allow representing a much richer set of data and object relations. In many practical cases, this approach enables to conclude about the data directly instead of looping through the data. It increases the efficiency of many inference processes. Moreover, the DASNG use associative neurons (ASN or APN described in [17, 18], and [19]) instead of graph vertices. Such neurons automatically react to input stimuli and can produce spikes (pulses) which are interpreted as results of various inference process as a reaction to the input stimuli that define the context for search data, objects, or relations. This way of working is characteristic for the biological associative processes that take place in brains [22]. A human brain consists of many complex and very deep graph structures of connected neurons of various kinds [24] which use thousands of connections to represent our knowledge and make our intelligence work smartly, quickly, and context-sensitively. The DASNG structure enriches representation of data relations as mentioned in the previous section. The DASNG neural networks were designed to represent various kinds of databases, especially relational databases. Relational databases can be quickly transformed into the DASNG networks as shown in the following subsections.

5.1 Construction Backgrounds of Transformation of Relational Databases

Relational databases thanks to their structure and clear representation of internal relations between entities of various tables represented by primary and foreign keys can be easily transformed to the DASNG networks when applying a few important rules which determine the order of transformed elements. The rule which lets us easily select database tables that can be already transformed tells us to transform these tables for which the neurons in the DASNG network already represent all foreign keys. It practically means that we have to start from the tables which do not contain foreign keys, e.g. the tables marked by 1: Nurses, Rooms, and Doctors in Fig. 11. Next, the tables which contain foreign keys to the previously transformed tables can be transformed as well, e.g. the tables marked by 2: NurseRoom and Patients in Fig. 11. Finally, the tables with the most complex dependencies which foreign keys are represented later during this transformation process can be transformed at last, e.g. the table marked by 3: DoctorPatient in Fig. 11. The transformation process will be described and illustrated on the example database shown in Fig. 11 in the next subsection.

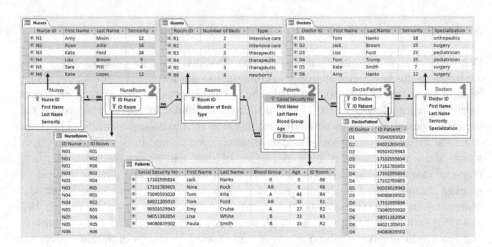

Fig. 11. The possible sequences of tables that can be transformed come from the already defined foreign keys by neurons in the DASNG network. The numbers from 1 to 3 show which tables can be transformed at first, which two can be transformed later, and which one can be transformed at last because of their foreign keys dependencies.

The transformation process has deterministic results. It means that we can start the transformation from any table without any foreign keys, and next transform other tables which foreign keys are already represented in the developed DASNG network in any possible order, but the finally created DASNG network will always be the same.

5.2   Transformation of a Sample Relational Database

The transformation process for the sample database (Fig. 11) can start from any table that does not contain any foreign keys (e.g. Nurses, Rooms, or Doctors). Here, we start from the Nurses table, and transform all its attributes (First Name, Last Name, and Seniority) into sensory input fields (grey rectangles in Fig. 12) containing AVB+trees which keys of elements represent receptors (green semicircles in Fig. 12) sensitive for all attribute values defined in this table as shown in Fig. 12. The receptors are connected to sensory neurons (white circles in Fig. 12) which can be charged by the receptors as well as other connected neurons of this network. The sensory neurons are connected to other sensory neurons that represent neighbor values of the same attribute. These neurons are also connected to object neurons representing entities of the Nurses table. There is usually no need to optimize access to object nodes by IDs representing primary keys (here: N1, N2, …, N6) because most of the primary keys in relational data tables are used only for the join operation, not for direct search. In such cases, primary keys are reducible as mentioned in the previous section and in [18]. However, when the primary keys represent real attributes of unique values which data must be stored and may be directly searched (non-reducible primary keys), then such values are represented in the same way as other attributes using SIFs, receptors, and sensory neurons. In the sample database mentioned in this paper, all primary of all tables are reducible and used only to relate the entities of the different tables.

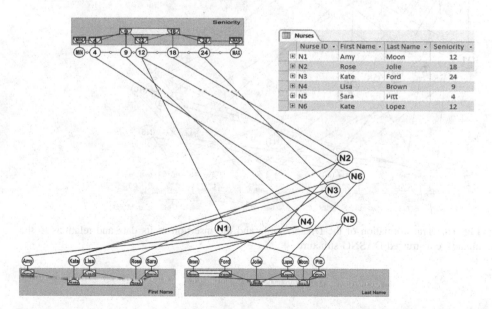

Fig. 12. Transformation of the Nurses table and the insertion of its data and relations to the already constructed DASNG structure. (Color figure online)

Figure 12 presents the result of the transformation of the Nurses table into the DASNG network created from scratch. It is noticeable that all duplicates are aggregated and represented by the same receptors inside the elements stored in the nodes of AVB +trees, e.g. the first name Kate or the seniority equal to 12 are represented only once. The orderable attribute Seniority was represented by the AVB+tree with additional receptors and neurons (MIN and MAX) sensitive for the extrema. In Fig. 12 and subsequent figures, the numbers of duplicates of the aggregated values are omitted in order to make these figures readable. In Fig. 13, the data from table Doctors were added to the previously created network from Fig. 12. The data representing the same attributes (First Name, Last Name, and Seniority) of the Nurses and Doctors tables were merged in the SIFs that aggregate duplicates not only in the scope of a single table but in the scope of all data tables which contain the same attributes. Such merges allow for faster and easier inferences about similarities, order, greatness, dependencies, groups, clusters, classes, and many important relations later. We can notice that the seniority of 12 years have one doctor and two nurses whose name and specialization can also be efficiently read going along the connections outgoing form neurons representing them. Figure 14 presents the next Rooms table which data are added to the DASNG network shown in Fig. 13.

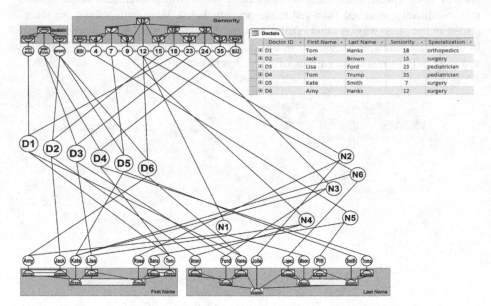

Fig. 13. Transformation of the Doctors table and the insertion of its data and relations to the already constructed DASNG structure.

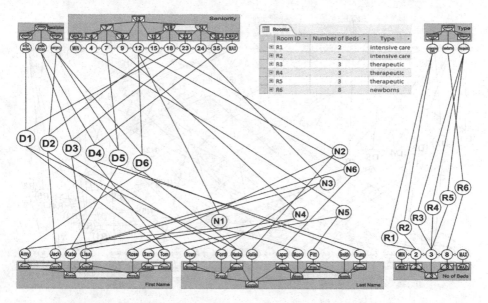

Fig. 14. Transformation of the Rooms table and the insertion of its data and relations to the already constructed DASNG structure.

The transformation of the next NurseRoom link-table links the neurons representing rooms and nurses together. It demonstrates how link-tables are transformed into the direct connections in the DASNG network (Fig. 15).

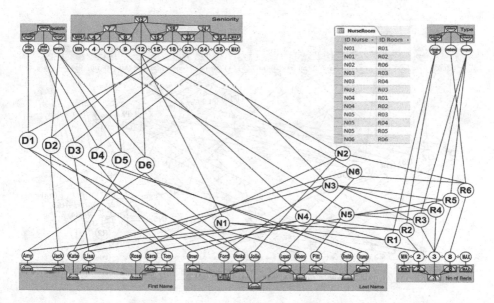

Fig. 15. Transformation of the NurseRoom table and the insertion of its data and relations to the already constructed DASNG structure.

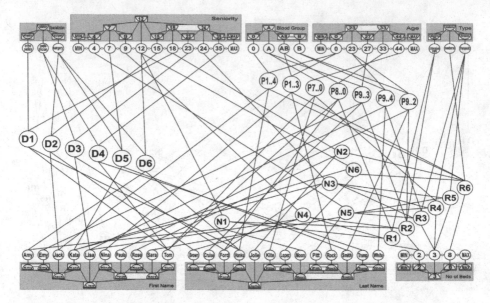

Fig. 16. Transformation of the Patients table and the insertion of its data and relations to the already constructed DASNG structure.

In Fig. 16, the data from table Patients are added, aggregated, and merged with the previously added data. Finally, the patients are linked to the doctors after the transformation of the DoctorPatient link-table as shown in Fig. 17.

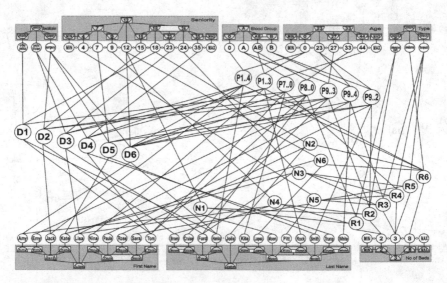

Fig. 17. Transformation of the DoctorPatient table and the insertion of its data and relations to the already constructed DASNG structure.

5.3   Complexity and Efficiency of the DASNG Operations Using
AVB+trees

The fundamental goal of any computations is to get correct results in acceptable time. Sometimes, we come across high computational complexities of various operations. Many times, the computational complexity is acceptable for small data collections, but when dealing with big data collections, those complexities might be even too high.

The efficiency of the operations inside the DASNG network were already described in [18], but the DASNG networks together with AVB+trees described in this paper allow for still more efficient access to all data, close values, similar or related objects and many other important relations. It is possible because the DASNG network represents additional direct and indirect relations between values and objects which are not available in relational databases without searching, filtering, or sorting.

The introduced AVB+trees allows for faster move to the neighbor values and process remove operations more efficiently than in AVB-trees or B-trees thanks to this direct connections to the neighbors which remove the need to move along parent branches to perform some operations.

The DASNG networks also allow proceeding computations in parallel as in biological neural networks. Hence, the computational complexity of the major part of operations can be reduced to constant or logarithmic dependently on how many duplicates are in the original data stored in the transformed data tables.

6   Conclusion and Final Remarks

This paper described the improvement of data access introducing and using AVB+trees instead of AVB-trees [17] implemented to self-organize and aggregate attribute values for the use together with the DASNG associative neural networks. The DASNG construction process was described and demonstrated on a sample database. The main contribution of AVB+trees is the ability to directly link neighbor values in a sorted order which allows for very fast access and makes the remove operations still more efficient than in AVB-trees. Moreover, the AVB+trees outperform classic B-trees and B +trees because they do not aggregate or count up duplicates and therefore they are much bigger than AVB+trees, especially for big data collections. Moreover, B-trees do not link neighbor values in sorted order and require to go through the tree structure to retrieve the next or previous value in logarithmic time. On the other hand, B+trees link neighbor values, but they use many internal nodes that represent keys which only show the way to the leaves where the objects are stored. Thus, they lose extra memory for data self-organization. The presented AVB+trees thanks to the aggregation and counting of duplicates are not only smaller but also require much less self-balancing and self-organizing operations in comparison to B-trees or B+trees because all duplicates require only increment or decrement the counters of the keys (values) stored in the elements in the tree nodes. In result, AVB+trees is more efficient than B-trees, B +trees, and AVB-trees, implementing beneficial features of these structures and removing their disadvantages.

Acknowledgements. This work was supported by AGH 11.11.120.612 and a grant from the National Science Centre DEC-2016/21/B/ST7/02220.

References

1. Apiletti, D., Baralis, E., Cerquitelli, T., Garza, P., Pulvirenti, F., Venturini, L.: Frequent itemsets mining for big data: a comparative analysis. Big Data Res. **9**, 67–83 (2017)
2. Agrawal, R., Imielinski, T., Swami, A.: Mining association rules between sets of items in large databases. In: ACM SIGMOND Conference on Management of Data, pp. 207–216 (1993)
3. Bagui, S., Earp, R.: Database Design Using Entity-Relationship Diagrams, 2nd edn. CRC Press, Boca Raton (2011)
4. Chen, P.: Entity-relationship modeling: historical events, future trends, and lessons learned. In: Broy, M., Denert, E. (eds.) Software Pioneers, pp. 296–310. Springer, Heidelberg (2002). https://doi.org/10.1007/978-3-642-59412-0_17
5. Cormen, T., Leiserson, Ch., Rivest, R., Stein, C.: Introduction to Algorithms, 2nd edn, pp. 434–454. MIT Press/McGraw-Hill, Cambridge/New York City (2001)
6. Duch, W., Dobosz, K.: Visualization for understanding of neurodynamical systems. Cogn. Neurodyn. **5**(2), 145–160 (2011)
7. Fayyad, U.P.-S.: From data mining to knowledge discovery in databases. In: Advances in Knowledge Discovery and Data Mining, vol. 17, pp. 37–54. MIT Press (1996)
8. Gerstner, W., Kistler, W.: Spiking Neuron Models: Single Neurons, Populations, Plasticity. Cambridge University Press, New York (2002)
9. Goodfellow, I., Bengio, Y., Courville, A.: Deep Learning. MIT Press, Cambridge (2016)
10. Han, J., Kamber, M.: Data Mining: Concepts and Techniques. Morgan Kaufmann, Burlington (2000)
11. Haykin, S.O.: Neural Networks and Learning Machines, 3rd edn. Prentice Hall, Upper Saddle River (2009)
12. Hellerstein, J.M., Stonebraker, M., Hamilton, J.: Architecture of a database system. Found. Trends Databases **1**(2), 141–259 (2007)
13. Horzyk, A.: Artificial Associative Systems and Associative Artificial Intelligence. Academic Publishing House EXIT, Warsaw (2013)
14. Horzyk, A., Starzyk, J.A., Graham, J.: Integration of semantic and episodic memories. IEEE Trans. Neural Netw. Learn. Syst. **28**(12), 3084–3095 (2017). https://doi.org/10.1109/tnnls.2017.2728203
15. Horzyk, A.: How does generalization and creativity come into being in neural associative systems and how does it form human-like knowledge? Neurocomputing **144**, 238–257 (2014). https://doi.org/10.1016/j.neucom.2014.04.046
16. Horzyk, A., Starzyk, J.A., Basawaraj: Emergent creativity in declarative memories. In: 2016 IEEE SSCI, pp. 1–8. IEEE Xplore, Curran Associates, Inc., Red Hook (2016). https://doi.org/10.1109/ssci.2016.7850029
17. Horzyk, A.: Neurons can sort data efficiently. In: Rutkowski, L., Korytkowski, M., Scherer, R., Tadeusiewicz, R., Zadeh, L.A., Zurada, J.M. (eds.) ICAISC 2017. LNCS (LNAI), vol. 10245, pp. 64–74. Springer, Cham (2017). https://doi.org/10.1007/978-3-319-59063-9_6
18. Horzyk, A.: Deep associative semantic neural graphs for knowledge representation and fast data exploration. In: Proceedings of KEOD 2017, pp. 67–79. SCITEPRESS Digital Library (2017)

19. Horzyk, A., Starzyk, J.A.: Fast neural network adaptation with associative pulsing neurons. In: 2017 IEEE Symposium Series on Computational Intelligence, pp. 339–346. IEEE Xplore (2017). https://doi.org/10.1109/ssci.2017.8285369

20. Horzyk, A., Starzyk, J.A.: Multi-class and multi-label classification using associative pulsing neural networks. In: 2018 IEEE World Congress on Computational Intelligence. IEEE Xplore (2018, in press)

21. Jin, X., Wah, B.W., Cheng, X., Wang, Y.: Significance and challenges of big data research. Big Data Res. 2(2), 59–64 (2015)

22. Kalat, J.W.: Biological Psychology. Wadsworth Publishing, Belmont (2012)

23. Linoff, G.S., Berry, M.A.: Data Mining Techniques: For Marketing, Sales, and Customer Relationship Management, 3rd edn. Wiley, Hoboken (2011)

24. Longstaff, A.: BIOS Instant Notes in Neuroscience. Garland Science, New York (2011)

25. Nuxoll, A., Laird, J.E.: A cognitive model of episodic memory integrated with a general cognitive architecture. In: International Conference on Cognitive Modelling, pp. 220–225 (2004)

26. Pääkkönen, P., Pakkala, D.: Reference architecture and classification of technologies, products and services for big data systems. Big Data Res. 2(4), 166–186 (2015)

27. Parisia, G.I., Tanib, J., Webera, C., Wermter, S.: Emergence of multimodal action representations from neural network self-organization. Cogn. Syst. Res. 43, 208–221 (2017)

28. Piatetsky-Shapiro, G., Frawley, W.J.: Knowledge Discovery in Databases. AAAI/MIT Press, Cambridge (1991)

29. Sowa, J.F.: Principles of Semantic Networks: Explorations in the Representation of Knowledge. Morgan Kaufmann, San Mateo (1991)

30. Starzyk, J.A., Graham, J.: MLECOG - motivated learning embodied cognitive architecture. IEEE Syst. J. PP(99), 1–12 (2015)

31. UCI Machine Learning Repository. http://archive.ics.uci.edu/ml/datasets/Iris. Accessed 04 Apr 2018

GeCoLan: A Constraint Language for Reasoning About Ecological Networks in the Semantic Web

Gianluca Torta[1(✉)], Liliana Ardissono[1], Marco Corona[1], Luigi La Riccia[2], Adriano Savoca[1], and Angioletta Voghera[2]

[1] Dipartimento di Informatica, Università di Torino, Turin, Italy
gianluca.torta@unito.it
[2] Dipartimento Interateneo di Scienze, Progetto e Politiche del Territorio, Turin, Italy
http://www.unito.it, http://www.polito.it

Abstract. Ecological Networks (ENs) describe the structure of existing real ecosystems and help planning their expansion, conservation and improvement. While various mathematical models of ENs have been defined, to our knowledge they focus on simulating ecosystems, but none of them deals with verifying whether any transformation proposals, as those collected in participatory decision-making processes for public policy making, are consistent with land usage restrictions.

As an attempt to fill this gap, we developed a model to represent the specifications for the local planning of ENs in a way that can support both the detection of constraint violations within new proposals of expansion, and the reasoning about improvements of the networks. In line with the GeoSpatial Semantic WEB, our model is based on an OWL ontology for the representation of ENs. Moreover, we define a language, GeCoLan, supporting constraint-based reasoning on semantic data. Even though this paper focuses on EN validation, our language can be employed to enable more complex tasks, such as the generation of proposals for improving ENs.

The present paper describes our ontological specification of ENs, the GeCoLan language for reasoning about specifications, and the tools we developed to support data acquisition and constraint verification on ENs.

Keywords: Geographic knowledge · Geographical constraints · GeoSPARQL · Ecological networks · Urban planning

1 Introduction

The process of fragmentation of nature and the consequent reduction of natural environments directly depend on the development of new urbanizations, infrastructural networks and intensive agriculture. Particular expressions of this fragmentation process are the endangering of plant varieties and the loss of habitats able to sustain the wild species and their migrations.

© Springer Nature Switzerland AG 2019
A. Fred et al. (Eds.): IC3K 2017, CCIS 976, pp. 268–293, 2019.
https://doi.org/10.1007/978-3-030-15640-4_14

The planning of Ecological Networks (ENs) has been proposed to model and simulate biotic and abiotic ecosystems and, therefore, understand their changes towards urban and territorial transformations: a way to overcome the isolation of protected natural areas due to the siege of wild urbanizations. The conservation of nature and the planning of ENs expansions are aimed to preserve biodiversity by reducing the process of fragmentation of nature especially in the most urbanized areas [1].

Although every sectoral approach, every point of view in urban planning maintains its value of knowledge and proposal, transversal and interdisciplinary studies have been encouraged, as far as they are able to restore the complexity of ecosystems. During the past years, several ENs have been implemented at different scales (from European down to municipality), resulting in the production of guidelines, planning documents and projects; e.g., [2–4]. Specifically, between 2014 and 2015 some of the authors of the present paper participated to an "Experimental activity of participatory elaboration of ecological network" [5] conducted by the Metropolitan City of Turin (Italy)[1] in collaboration with Polytechnic of Turin[2] and ENEA[3]. That project aimed at defining a proposal for the Ecological Network implementation at the local level in two pilot municipalities near Turin. The proposed approach was aimed at guiding local Public Administrations with measures to limit anthropogenic land use and, where possible, orient and qualify the conservation of ecosystem services.

We point out that describing ENs in informal ways, through linguistic guidelines, is useful for their presentation but challenges their management because it makes it difficult to compare specifications to one another, finding possible contradictions, and to integrate guidelines in order to obtain a single reference document for land planning. In fact, specifications are dispersed in multiple textual sources, that introduce different concepts and metrics to evaluate the properties of an EN.

We thus aim at providing formal approach to the representation of ENs, suitable for integrating heterogeneous information sources, and for automated analysis. For the specification of ENs, we adopt an ontology-based approach, in order to explicitly define the relations between entities and to formally characterize their attributes, supporting automated reasoning. This is in line with consolidated approaches to the representation of geographical knowledge (see the GeoSpatial Semantic WEB [6] and [7,8]) and provides a basis for a unified treatment of information in Geographical Information Systems (GIS). However, an important aspect of ENs is the specification and reasoning about constraints associated to the guidelines for land planning. Therefore, our work aims at integrating semantic knowledge representation with constraint-based reasoning [9] into a unified framework.

This paper presents an ontology for the description of ENs, and a constraint specification language supporting automatic reasoning about them:

---

[1] www.cittametropolitana.torino.it/.
[2] www.polito.it.
[3] www.enea.it.

- Our ontology is based on the outcome of the project [5]. We adopted OWL [10], augmented by the GeoSPARQL ontology [11], to describe the main entities and relations of ENs.
- Regarding the representation of EN specifications, we developed a new language, GeCoLan, guided by two main goals:
  - The expression of constraints on the EN domain in a simple and compact way, which simplifies reading and automated management of information.
  - The employment of specifications in other automatic tasks, which can't be implemented by simply querying an existing Knowledge Base (KB). For instance, checking the consistency of proposals for changes and additions to an existing EN, or automatically suggesting optimized changes and additions to it.

In line with recent research on geometric and geographic constraint reasoning, e.g., [12,13], *GeCoLan* abstracts from the details of the reasoning tasks that it supports and can thus be applied to other domains than the one in the focus of this paper.

GeCoLan is suitable to define complex arithmetic and geometric constraints, and supports constraint verification, as well as other rich types of reasoning, by exploiting the SPARQL query language [14] as a lower-level tool for constraint specification.

We developed a GeCoLan prototype reasoner and we tested it on a large dataset of geographic information derived from project [5]. Even though we obtained encouraging results regarding the applicability of our approach (see [15]), they were affected by the fact that the dataset included a certain amount of noise (e.g., overlapping geometries of structural elements that should have been disjoint) and extremely detailed geometries, composed of hundreds of vertexes. We thus decided to develop a data pre-processing tool that, before translating a source dataset (e.g., a set of ESRI shapefiles) to semantic data format (RDF [16] triples), pre-processes it by simplifying the geometries and some irregularities of its geographic objects.

In the following we describe the GeCoLan language, the prototype reasoner for checking its specifications on an EN, and our data pre-processing tool. The present paper extends the work described in [15] by providing more detail about our work, with examples, and with the description of the data pre-processing tool.

The remainder of this paper is organized as follows: Sect. 2 provides some background and positions our work in the related literature. Section 3 describes our representation of ENs specifications and provides details about the GeCoLan language. Section 4 describes the storage of information about an individual EN and the data pre-processing tool to acquire it. Section 5 presents our approach to the validation of ENs and the tool we developed for that purpose. Section 6 discusses the broader context of our work, outlining our future research directions. Section 7 concludes the paper.

2   Background and Related Work

Our work builds on existing literature about ENs and knowledge representation, and introduces a novel model for representing and managing constraints in ENs. The next subsections provide some background and position our work in the related research.

2.1   Ecological Networks and Their Representation

An Ecological Network is an interconnected system consisting of territorial areas that include natural and semi-natural habitats. As reported in [4], "although the way in which the model is elaborated and applied reflects certain conceptual and methodological variants and is subject to local and regional circumstances, ecological networks share two generic goals, namely (1) maintaining the functioning of ecosystems as a means of facilitating the conservation of species and habitats and (2) promoting the sustainable use of natural resources in order to reduce the impacts of new urbanizations on biodiversity and/or to increase the biodiversity value of managed landscapes". An EN is represented as a network including various types of elements, described below:

- Structural Elements are the *core areas* of the EN. They denote the areas having a primary ecological function, i.e., the areas with significant "natural-

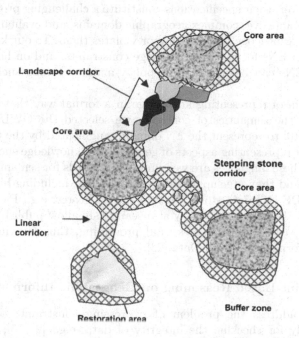

Fig. 1. Diagrammatic representation of the spatial configuration of an Ecological Network, from [4].

ness", that are relevant to preserve biodiversity. They are represented as as nodes of the EN.

– Adjoining Areas, also denoted as *buffers*, are the areas neighboring ($\geq$50 m) the Structural Elements. They represents the areas with the function to safeguard and increase the stability of the core areas.

– Connection Elements, alias *corridors*, are the areas with residual "naturalness" that connect the Structural Elements. They are represented as links of the EN.

Figure 1 depicts the general design of an Ecological Network.

So far, ENs have been largely studied and modeled in order to describe their dynamics. "Ecological network analysis (ENA) is a systems-oriented methodology to analyze within system interactions used to identify holistic properties that are otherwise not evident from the direct observations" [17]. Several mathematical models have been developed to analyze and predict the dynamics of ENs in terms of interactions between organisms in an ecosystem, starting from observational data; e.g., [17–21]. These models are aimed at modeling and simulating the dynamics of the relations among species, the existence of dynamical bottlenecks in the functioning of the ecosystems, etc., but they do not concern the verification or imposition of urban planning constraints on the ecosystems themselves, which is the objective of our work.

In the context of knowledge engineering, ENs provide a complex, inherently geographic domain that demands an expressive language to be conveniently represented. Moreover, their specifications constitute a challenging problem for representing constraints over complex geographic domains, and evaluating if a given (possibly large) knowledge base satisfies or violates them. To our knowledge, no existing work on ENs focuses on land-usage constraints, and on how the transformations of ENs can be regulated in policy-making, taking such constraints into account.

With the aim of representing knowledge in a formal way that supports the specification of the semantics of concepts, we selected the OWL Web Ontology Language [10] to represent the EN domain, augmented by the GeoSPARQL ontology [11] for representing aspects of geographical knowledge such as topological relations. These languages are well known standards for semantic knowledge representation and they are supported by many tools, including highly scalable and efficient RDF [16] data stores, such as Triple Stores; e.g., Parliament [22]. Being Semantic Web languages, they also seamlessly allow publishing the information on the Web for open access and processing, thus favoring knowledge sharing in the format of Linked Data [23].

2.2 Constraint-Based Reasoning on Geographic Information

Several works address the problem of expressing constraints on structured domains, mainly for checking the integrity of data, e.g., [24,25], and some of them specifically consider knowledge bases with geographic and geometric constraints. [26] introduces the High-Level Constraint Language (HLCL) to define geographic constraints on a conceptual model (i.e., Entity-Relationship) of a database, and proposes to translate them into SQL integrity constraints. Similarly, [13] exploits the Object-Constraint Language (OCL) on UML models. The main difference between the present work and these proposals stems from the fact that we assume that the domain is modeled as an OWL ontology, and that data is stored as RDF triples in a Triple Store.

A way to represent constraints in the Semantic Web, is through *rule languages*, such as SWRL (Semantic Web Rule Language) [27] and RuleML [28]. While the original expressiveness of those languages was not general enough to support constructs such as logic quantifiers, negation, disjunction, numeric and geometric expressions (all of which typically occur in EN specifications), subsequent extensions empowered them with the full expressiveness of First-Order Logic (FOL) [29,30]. Moreover, some work integrated SWRL with mathematical, geometrical, and other types of functions through built-ins; e.g., [31].

We introduce a new language, instead of extending an existing rule-based one, because of several syntactic aspects that make it particularly succinct and convenient for our needs. However, we don't exclude translating our language to a standard rule-based one in our future research, in order to exploit existing inference engines for those languages. Our language is named *GeCoLan* to recall *CoLan* [25], on which it is strongly based, with restrictions and extensions. CoLan is a language initially proposed for expressing integrity constraints in Object-Oriented Databases, and later used as the basis for the Constraint Interchange Format (CIF), an RDF schema for exchanging constraints on the Semantic Web [32].

The SPARQL [14,33] language has been used for expressing and checking constraints over OWL-based Triple Stores [34]. However, the direct adoption of SPARQL (or of other query languages) for the description of EN specifications fails to support reasoning tasks that cannot be implemented by simply querying an existing KB; e.g., suggesting changes to repair a constraint violation, possibly optimizing some desired measure. While our current work focuses on constraint verification, we introduce GeCoLan to provide a unified support to other proactive tasks, such as suggesting solutions to violation problems and exploring expansion possibilities for ENs.

3 Conceptual Representation of Ecological Networks

In the following we describe the OWL ontology we defined to represent the main concepts and relations concerning ENs, and the GeCoLan constraint specification language.

3.1 The Ecological Network Ontology

For the representation of Ecological Networks, we selected the OWL2 [35] language, which offers:

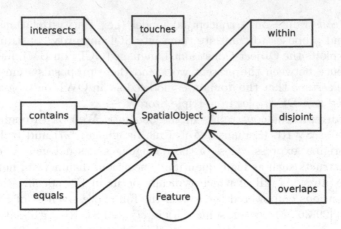

Fig. 2. A fragment of the GeoSPARQL ontology, from [15].

- IS-A relations to define *taxonomies* of concepts; e.g., hierarchies of land use types, of planned interventions, and so forth.
- Support to modeling and performing calculations with geographic/geometric shapes of concepts; e.g., elements of the EN and elements of land use maps.
- Specification of restrictions on concepts and on their relations. This is useful to formally represent definitions as the following one: "coppicing is a maintenance intervention that only applies to wooden areas".

Moreover, we imported the GeoSPARQL ontology [22,36], which defines geographic entities and relations:

- GeoSPARQL defines a *Feature* as a *SpatialObject* that has a *Geometry* on the 2D plane; a *Feature* can be either a *Point*, a *Curve* (in particular, a piecewise linear curve), or a *Polygon*.
- Moreover, GeoSPARQL defines a number of topologic geometric relations between *Features* that correspond to the basic relations identified in the literature about Geographic Information Systems: namely, the Simple Features relations [37], and the equivalent RCC8 [38], and Egenhofer relations [39]. Figure 2 shows the Simple Features topological properties, which relate objects of the *SpatialObject* class. For instance, the *touches* relation between two spatial objects *A* and *B* holds whenever the borders (but not the interiors) of *A* and *B* have a non-empty intersection. Moreover, the *overlaps* represents a non null intersection (but not an inclusion) between the areas of two spatial objects.

The EN ontology is defined around the *Feature* class. By specializing *Feature*, we define the four hierarchies of concepts representing the core of the EN domain:

- *EcologicalNetworkElement:* this is an element of the EN, i.e., either a Structural Element, or a Priority Expansion Element.[4] The latter is specialized to a Connection Element or Adjoining Area.
- *LandUseElement* represents a Land Use Element (LUE), i.e., a parcel of land defined in the Land Cover Piemonte (LCP) cartography [40], characterized by a specific type of land use; see below. The LCP structures Land Use Elements in 4 specification levels:
  - At level 1 the LCP defines 5 general types of land use: *WaterBody*, *WetLand*, *WoodenLand*, *AgriculturalLand*, and *ArtificialLand*, which we explicitly model as concepts of the EN ontology.
  - Moreover, the LCP includes 15 types of land use at level 2 of the taxonomy, 45 at level 3, and 97 at level 4. We specify the values of levels 2, 3, and 4 as properties of *LandUseElement*: *LCPlevel2*, *LCPlevel3*, and *LCPlevel4*.

Each *LandUseElement* is characterized by five evaluation criteria, which take values in $[1, 5]$, with 1 representing the maximum value and 5 the lowest one:

1. *naturality:* how close the element is to a natural environment;
2. *relevance:* how relevant it is for the conservation of the habitat;
3. *fragility:* how fragile it is with respect to the anthropogenic pressure;
4. *extroversion:* how much pressure it can exert on the neighboring areas;
5. *irreversibility:* how difficult it would be to change its use.

- *Intervention* represents an intervention for building, improving or conserving the EN.
- *Operation* represents a specific operation of elimination, construction or maintenance that is part of an intervention.

Figure 3 shows a portion of our EN ontology, with the *Feature* class depicted in dark grey and the roots of the *EcologicalNetworkElement* and *LandUseElement* in light grey. All of the concepts of the ontology inherit the topological relations defined by *Feature*. Thus, e.g., an individual *ConnectionElement* may *touch* a number of *LandUseElements*.

Figure 4 shows another portion of our EN ontology with the roots of the *Interventions* and *Operations* hierarchies in light grey.

In order to characterize the classes and properties used in our ontology, we exploit the powerful constructs of the OWL2 language (in particular, Class Expressions) in several places. For example:

- the *hasPlants* property applies to LUEs of types *WoodenLand* and *AgriLand*. The domain of *hasPlants* is therefore the following OWL Class Expression (in functional syntax):

```
ObjectUnionOf(WoodenLand AgriLand)
```

---

[4] The Priority Expansion Elements are the areas with residual ecological functionality where the priority is intervening to increase the functionality of the primary ecological network and implementing conservation measures.

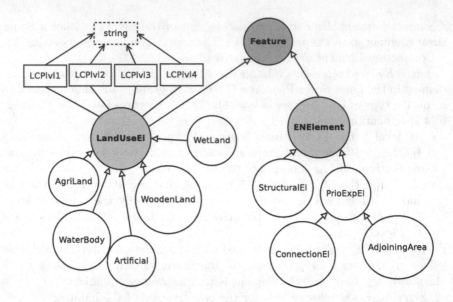

Fig. 3. A fragment of the EN ontology with EN elements and Land Use Elements.

– the *hasArea* property applies to *Features* whose geometry is a *Surface*. The domain of *hasArea* is thus:

$$\text{AllValuesFrom(hasGeometry Surface)}$$

– the *Coppicing* class (subclass of *Maintenance* operation) should have a linear geometry. Thus, Class *Coppicing* is also a subclass of the following Class Expression:

$$\text{AllValuesFrom(hasGeometry LineString)}$$

– the *Eradication* class (subclass of *Elimination* operation) should only *intersect* LUEs of type *WoodenLands*; moreover, such elements should have an *LCPlevel2* value of either "ShrubbyGrassyZone" or "OpenZone". Class *Eradication* is therefore also a subclass of the following Class Expression:

```
AllValuesFrom(sfIntersects
  (ObjectIntersectionOf(WoodenLand
  (DataAllValuesFrom(LCPlevel2
  DataOneOf("ShrubbyGrassyZone" "OpenZone")))))
```

It should be noticed that the above described specifications of ENs represent *integrity constraints* on the classes and properties defined by the ontology: they describe intrinsic properties of the EN. For instance, it would be meaningless to have an element of the *Coppicing* class with a non-linear geometry, or an *Eradication* operation over an urban area. Differently, the EN specifications described in the following section are meant to constrain the way we are *allowed to plan* an Ecological Network, and may possibly be violated by existing ENs that have

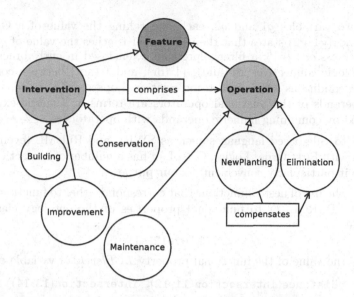

Fig. 4. Another fragment of the EN ontology with interventions and operations.

not been correctly planned. This is an important reason to encode the two types of constraints differently, besides the fact that OWL has limits on the logic constraints that it can express [41].

3.2 Constraints on EN Transformations

For the specification of constraints on the transformations of ENs we defined GeCoLan, having in mind the following requirements: first, the language must use the terms defined in the EN ontology (classes and properties) as its main vocabulary. Second, it must support the expression of *constraints* about the objects of the world modeled by the same ontology. Third, it must allow mixing logic, geometric, numeric, and time requirements into the constraints.

We named our language GeCoLan because it is intended to capture geometric and geographic constraints, beside more traditional types of constraints captured by the CoLan language [25] from which it derives. The terms of our language have one of the following types:

- literal values; e.g., numbers, strings, etc.;
- variables;
- function calls whose arguments are themselves terms.

GeCoLan offers the and, or, not, and implies connectives of First Order Logic to compose conditions. Moreover, the atoms can be:

- *property* predicates p(t1, t2), where p is the name of a property defined in the EN ontology, t_1 is a term representing an individual in the domain of p, and t_2 is a term that denotes an individual in the range of p. For example, given two variables $g1$ and $g2$, each one taking the value of a Geometry, sfTouches($g1, g2$) states that the value of $g1$ touches the value of $g2$.

- *filter expressions* $\{e\}^5$; a filter expression e, enclosed in curly brackets, can use the logic connectives && (and), || (or), and ! (not) between conditions. In turn, conditions are defined using relational operators >, <, <=, >=, =, !=. The operands of the relational operators are terms or numeric expressions obtained by combining numeric operands with operators +, -, /, *.

Compared to rule-based languages such as SWRL and RuleML (even in their extensions with First Order Logic), GeCoLan has a number of syntactic features that make it particularly convenient for our purposes:

- it allows the use of nested functions that correspond either to functions defined in (Geo)SPARQL, or to functional properties of the ontology classes. For example,

LCPlevel2(el)

denotes the value of the functional property *LCPlevel2* of variable el, while:

distance(intersection(l1,l2), intersection(l3,l4))

denotes the distance between the intersection area of $l1$ and $l2$, and the intersection area of $l3$ and $l4$. The $l1, \dots, l4$ variables are *Well Known Text* (WKT) literals, i.e., serializations of geometries.

- GeCoLan also allows the use of infix relational and arithmetic operators in expressions over complex terms. For example:

{distance(l1,l2) >= 2 * distance(l1,l3)}

means that the distance between the WKT literal values of variables $l1$ and $l2$ is at least twice as the distance between those of $l1$ and $l3$. Similarly,

{irreversibility(el) < 3 || extroversion(el) < 3)}

imposes that the values of functional properties *irreversibility* and *extroversion* of variable el are less than 3.

- moreover, it allows the quantifiers forall and exists with *range restricted* variables:

forall C(x)[s.t. $\psi(x)$]$\varphi(x)$
exists C(x)[s.t. $\psi(x)$]$\varphi(x)$

where C is an ontology concept, x is a variable that represents an individual, and $\psi(x)$ is an optional formula that further restricts the individuals of C. For example, "forall NewPlanting(np)" states that the value of variable np can be any instance of class *NewPlanting*. If we add a condition "s.t. compensates(np, el)", only individuals np that compensate some given elimination el will be considered.

As we aim at expressing constraints that can be either satisfied or violated by the knowledge base, we are only interested in closed formulas, in which all the variables are within the scope of a corresponding quantifier.

---

[5] Filter expressions correspond to whole constraints to be evaluated in the *FILTER* clause of SPARQL; see Sect. 5.1.

3.3   Example Specifications

In the following, we describe the representation of three sample specifications taken from the guidelines for the Local EN implementation devised in project [5].

Specification 1: Connection Elements. *Connection elements must avoid areas with maximum irreversibility and areas with maximum extroversion.*

This constraint is satisfied if a *ConnectionElement* does not *overlap* with any *LandUseElements* whose *irreversibility* or *extroversion* properties have the maximum value, i.e., a value >1. The specification can be encoded as follows:

```
forall ConnectionElement(ce)
forall LandUseElement(lue) such that sfOverlaps(ce,lue)
    {irreversibility(lue) > 1 && extroversion(lue) > 1}
```

The first universal quantifier restricts the range of variable *ce*, that must be a *ConnectionElement*. The second one restricts variable *lue*, that must be a *LandUseElement*, and must have a geometry G^6 that *overlaps* with the geometry of *ce*.[7]

The filter expression in curly brackets imposes that both the *irreversibility* and the *extroversion* of *lue* have a value >1. In the example we use several features of our ontology and language, e.g.:

- the geometric capabilities of GeoSPARQL enable to automatically find the *LandUseElements* that fall at least partially within a *ConnectionElement*;
- the filter expressions provide the ability to perform numeric comparisons between the values of some functional properties of *LandUseElements* and a numeric constant.

The second example constraints the creation of Buffer Zones to protect the elements of the EN:

Specification 2: Buffer Zones. *The creation of protection buffers is done, whenever possible, through interventions of restoration in areas surrounding the structural elements of the EN, with the goal of enhancing and protecting them. In case a structural element is surrounded by areas with maximum extroversion and/or maximum irreversibility, the buffers must be realized within the structural element (due to the impossibility of extending the element itself).*

Using the vocabulary of the EN ontology, a *BufferCreation* is an *Intervention* of *Conservation* that *touches* a *StructuralElement* of the EN, except when it

---

[6] We write G for short to denote functional property *hasGeometry* that applies to both *ConnectionElements* and *LandUseElements*.

[7] In GeoSPARQL, the topological relations such as *sfOverlaps* are computed on the geometries associated with the individuals in class *Feature* (*lue* and *ce* in our example) through the *defaultGeometry* property.

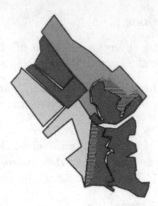

Fig. 5. Graphical representation of the two cases of the specification for Buffer Zones. The structural elements of the EN are colored in dark green, the Land Use Elements in light green are meadows (with low extroversion) while the LUEs in yellow are crops (with high extroversion). Buffers are depicted as shadowed areas. (Color figure online)

would *overlap* with one or more *LandUseElements* with maximum *irreversibility* or *extroversion*. In that case, the *BufferCreation* should be *within* the *StructuralElement*. Figure 5 shows the two cases: the lower buffer is within a *StructuralElement*, since otherwise it would overlap with a crop area of maximum extroversion. Differently, the upper buffer touches the *StructuralElement*, as it overlaps with a meadow of limited extroversion.

This specification can be encoded as follows:

```
forall BufferCreation(bc)
forall StructuralElement(sel)
forall LandUseElement(lue) such that (not sfWithin(lue,sel))
   ((sfTouches(bc,sel) and sfOverlaps(bc,lue))
      implies
      {(irreversibility(lue) > 1) and (extroversion(lue) > 1)})
    and
   ((sfWithin(bc,sel) and sfTouches(bc,lue))
      implies
      {(irreversibility(lue) = 1) or (extroversion(lue) = 1)})
```

The formula starts with universal quantifiers specifying the classes of variables *bc*, *sel*, and *lue*. The quantification of *lue* further restricts the attention to *LandUseElements* whose geometry is not *within* the geometry of *StructuralElement* *sel*. The body is the conjunction of two sub-specifications, corresponding to the two cases of Fig. 5: if (the geometry of) *bc* *touches* *sel*, then each *lue* that overlaps with *bc* must have non-maximum irreversibility and extroversion. Otherwise, if *bc* is *within sel*, then each *lue touched* by *bc* must have maximum irreversibility and/or extroversion.

The third example constrains eradication operations:

> **Specification 3: Eradication.** *Eradication in shrubby-grassy zones and open zones is generally forbidden. In case the eradication is unavoidable, it requires an authorization by the Municipality, and should be compensated by a new planting with an area at least twice as the eradicated area. For the new plantation, autochthonous plants and trees should be employed.*

The norm says that an *Eradication* is an *Operation* that must belong to an *Intervention* of *Improvement* that *isAuthorized*, and also *comprises* a *NewPlanting* operation that *compensates* the *Eradication*. The planting *hasArea* at least twice as that of the eradication. Finally, the *hasPlant* property of the *NewPlanting* must not contain any plant in the black-list **BL**: this is an individual of type *PlantsList* containing the forbidden exotic species. The norm can be encoded as follows:

```
forall Eradication(er)
exists NewPlanting(np) such that compensates(np, er)
forall Plant(pl) such that hasPlant(np, pl)
  (isAuthorized(interventionOf(er))
    implies
    ((not(hasPlant(BL, pl))) and {(area(np) ≥ 2 * area(er))}))
```

The formula mixes universal and existential quantifiers, in order to impose a combined restriction on each eradication *er*, the new planting *np* that compensates it (*np* must exist), and all the plants *pl* selected for *np*. The restriction applies only if the *Intervention* including *er* (obtained with functional property *interventionOf*) is authorized. It states that *pl* must not belong to **BL** and that the area of *np* must be at least twice as the area of *er*.

4 Acquisition and Storage of Geographic Information About ENs

4.1 Storage of the Information About an Individual EN

The ontological definition of ENs described in Sect. 3 supports the representation in RDF format [16] of data about an individual EN; i.e., which are the structural elements of a geographical area.

RDF is standard for knowledge representation in the Semantic Web and prescribes that each piece of information is represented as a <subject, predicate, object> triple. For instance, a specific Land Use Element is represented as follows:

lueid rdf : type	onto : LandUseElement
lueid rdf : type	geo : Feature
lueid geo : hasGeometry	*geoid*
lueid onto : area	1152.000000015134
lueid onto : perimeter	191.99999999289867
lueid onto : LCPlevel1	"2"
lueid onto : LCPlevel2	"2"
lueid onto : LCPlevel3	"2"
lueid onto : LCPlevel4	"2"
lueid onto : extroversion	2
lueid onto : irreversibility	4
lueid onto : fragility	4
lueid onto : naturality	2
lueid onto : relevance	3

where *lueid* is the unique URI of the Land Use Element, and *geoid* is the unique URI of its associated geometry. Note that the second triple, stating that *lueid* is a *Feature*, is automatically inferred by the Triple Store. This derives from the encoding of the ontology within the Triple Store itself, in particular from the following triple:

onto : LandUseElement rdfs : subClassOf geo : Feature

Being a standard, RDF is coupled with several tools for data interpretation and management. For instance, various Triple Stores are available to store and manage RDF triples in an efficient way, by answering SPARQL [14], and possibly GeoSPARQL [11], queries. In our experiments, we used the Parliament Triple Store [22] to memorize the data about the EN developed in project [5].

4.2 A Tool for Pre-processing and Acquiring Information About an EN

The process of acquisition of new geometries into the Triple Store is more complex than a simple mapping from their coordinates and (meta) attributes to a set of corresponding RDF triples. With the aim of creating an efficient and robust knowledge base, we introduce a preliminary phase of input processing within which we apply transformations to the geometries and synthesize new attributes from the attributes of the geometry and possibly from other knowledge already contained in the Triple Store.

The geometric transformations can be different depending on the quality and characteristics of the input data. One of such transformations consists in the simplification of a geometry obtained by reducing its number of vertexes. This reduction can yield significant computational benefits, because the time complexity of the algorithms behind the GeoSPARQL functions often directly depends on such a number. Clearly, reducing the vertexes leads to a distortion of the original geometries, and it is important to seek a trade-off between loss of precision and computational gains. Many algorithms for polygons simplification can be found in the literature, with different levels of efficiency and quality of the output; among these, we selected the very well known Douglas-Peucker algorithm [42]. This algorithm takes as input a polyline (in our case, a closed one) and a tolerance distance ϵ, and returns a similar polyline with a subset of the original points. Similarity means that the Hausdorff distance between the original and the computed polylines is less than the given tolerance. Suppose that we have a polyline described as a list of points; then, the algorithm recursively divides the list in two sublists choosing the split point such that it maximizes the distance d with the segment joining the end points of the list. If the distance d satisfies $d \leq \epsilon$, we can replace the polyline directly with that segment, otherwise the split point p is marked as a point to keep, and the split is recursively invoked on the two sublists determined by p.

Another useful pre-processing operation consists in filtering out all the polygons whose area is below a threshold. This can be done by computing the area of each input geometry with the help of a computational geometry library, skipping all the geometries that are too small for being of interest. When the number of such geometries is large, significant benefits can be obtained in terms of efficiency in the use of the system.

In order to get reliable results during the computation of the areas, in a desired unit of measure (e.g., square meters), it necessary that the Coordinate Reference System (CRS) used to describe the input geometries uses the same unit of measure; and, more importantly, it preserves the measure of areas when they are projected from the Earth surface to a Euclidean plane. Indeed, some projections preserve the topology of the area without giving any guarantee about the accuracy of their areas (e.g WGS84 projection); and vice-versa (e.g UTM* projections). This is just an example of the need to convert the input geometries from one CRS to another, for specific computations. As these operations are not supported by GeoSPARQL, it is necessary to pre-calculate them and possibly store them for later on-line use.

5   Validation of Ecological Networks

Intuitively, the validation of an individual EN against a set of constraints means analyzing the Triple Store describing the EN (i.e., the knowledge base) and checking that no RDF triple violates them. For instance, let us consider the task of checking the **Connection Elements** specification of Sect. 3.3. That means considering each *ConnectionElement ce* in the Triple Store, and verifying that all of the *LandUseElement*s overlapping with *ce* satisfy the given restrictions on the *extroversion* and *irreversibility* properties. We assume that all of the relevant facts are present in the store (*closed world* semantics). Therefore, if a required fact is missing, a violation is detected.

5.1   Translating Specifications to GeoSPARQL Queries

In order to check whether the EN specifications are satisfied by an existing knowledge base, we translate them to equivalent queries that can be executed by any engine that supports the GeoSPARQL standard. This approach enables us to exploit the engine to perform the reasoning tasks, instead of developing a GeCoLan interpreter from scratch. Given a closed GeCoLan formula ϕ, we translate it to a GeoSPARQL query q_ϕ such that:

$$KB \models \phi \leftrightarrow \begin{cases} [\![q_\phi]\!]^{KB} \neq \emptyset & \phi = \texttt{exists C(x)}\varphi\texttt{(x)} \\ [\![q_\phi]\!]^{KB} = \emptyset & \phi = \texttt{not exists C(x)}\varphi\texttt{(x)} \end{cases} \tag{1}$$

where ϕ is in one of the above forms, KB is the Triple Store against which we want to evaluate ϕ, and $[\![q_\phi]\!]^{KB}$ denotes the result of applying q_ϕ to KB.

Normalization of GeCoLan Constraints. Similar to [43,44], we define the translation inductively. Firstly, we consider some rewritings of ϕ into equivalent GeCoLan formulas to reduce the number of cases we have to explicitly translate:

forall C(x) s.t.ψ (φ)	T(forall x
	((C(x) and ψ) implies φ))
forall C(x) φ	T(not exists C(x) (not φ))
exists C(x) s.t.ψ (φ)	T(exists x
	(C(x) and ψ and φ)))
φ implies ψ	T(not φ or ψ)

After these rewritings, formula ϕ starts either with the "not exists C(x)", or with the "exists C(x)" prefix. It does not include any occurrences of the forall quantifier or of the implies connective.

Translation of Normalized Formulas to GeoSPARQL Queries. Before starting the translation of the normalized formulas to GeoSPARQL queries, we remove the prefix from ϕ, so that the values returned by the query are not completely projected out; see the example below. At this point, by translating ϕ to q_ϕ according to Eq. (1) and by applying q_ϕ to KB, we can check whether KB satisfies ϕ or not.

For finite domain classes $C_1, \ldots, C_k$, we define the cross product of their domains as follows:

$$ADom(x_1, \ldots, x_k) = \{x_1 \texttt{ rdf : type } C_1.$$
$$\ldots$$
$$x_k \texttt{ rdf : type } C_k.\}$$

We then define the following translations:

exists x φ	SELECT ($free(\varphi) - \{x\}$) WHERE $\{T(\varphi)\}$
φ or ψ	$T(\varphi)$ UNION $T(\psi)$
φ and ψ	$\{T(\varphi)\ T(\psi)\}$
$\neg\varphi$	$\{ADom(free(\varphi))$ FILTER NOT EXISTS $T(\varphi)\}$

The translation of exists involves the projection of variable x through a subquery, as x should no longer appear in outer formulas. The translations of or and **and** connectors are mapped, respectively, to the UNION clause of SPARQL and to a sequence of graph patterns. Finally, the negation of φ maps to a FILTER NOT EXISTS clause between the domains of the free variables and their assignments satisfying φ.

The atoms of GeCoLan formulas are translated as follows:

$$C(x) \qquad \{x\ \texttt{rdf : type }C.\}$$
$$p(t1, t2) \qquad \{\mathcal{T}(t1)\ \mathcal{T}(t2)\ \texttt{x1 p x2}.\}$$
$$\{e(t1, \ldots, tn)\} \quad \mathcal{T}(t1)\ \ldots \mathcal{T}(tn)\ \texttt{FILTER}\ e(\texttt{x1}, \ldots, \texttt{xn})$$

- The class C of a variable x is translated as a graph pattern with predicate rdf : type.
- Let us consider the translation of $p(t_1, t_2)$. First of all, we need to translate the terms t_1, t_2. For example, let the property atom be:

$$\texttt{member(hasPlants(lue), "Rudbekia")}$$

where t_1 is *hasPlants(lue)*, i.e., the application of a functional property *hasPlants* to a *LandUseElement lue*; the *hasPlants* property maps *lue* to a *Collection* element *col*. We need to introduce a new variable x_1 for representing the value of such property, and add the pattern {lue hasPlants x1} to the translation. Finally, we add the pattern {x1 member "Rudbekia"} to state that Rudbekia is a member of the $x1$ collection.
- The translation of filter expressions requires a similar approach to generate variables corresponding to applications of functional properties.

5.2 Example

We will now apply the above described translation method to the **Connection Elements** example of Sect. 3.3:

```
forall ConnectionElement(ce)
forall LandUseElement(lue) such that sfOverlaps(ce, lue)
    {irreversibility(lue) > 1 && extroversion(lue) > 1}
```

First, we remove the **forall** quantifiers:

```
not exists ConnectionElement(ce)
exists LandUseElement(lue)
    not (sfOverlaps(ce, lue) implies
            {irreversibility(lue) > 1 && extroversion(lue) > 1})
```

Then, we remove the **implies** connective:

```
not exists ConnectionElement(ce)
exists LandUseElement(lue)
    (sfOverlaps(ce, lue) and
        not{irreversibility(lue) > 1 && extroversion(lue) > 1})
```

Let us consider the translation of the filter expression:

$$\tau_0 = \{\{\texttt{lue irreversibility ir.}\}$$
$$\{\texttt{lue extroversion ex.}\}$$
$$\texttt{FILTER ((ir > 1) \&\& (ex > 1))}\}$$

Two new variables (named ir and ex for readability) have been added to hold the values of the *irreversibility* and *extroversion* properties of *lue*. Then, the filter expression (in which the property applications have been replaced with ir and ex) becomes the argument of a FILTER clause. The range expression for ce, lue is:

$$\tau_R = \{\texttt{ce rdf : type ConnectionElement.}$$
$$\texttt{lue rdf : type LandUseElement.}\}$$

Therefore, the translation of the negation (**not**) of the filter expression is:

$$\tau_1 = \{\tau_R \text{ FILTER NOT EXISTS } \tau_0\}$$

By applying the translation rules for the property predicates and conjunctions, we obtain the following translation for the body of the formula:

$$\tau_2 = \{\{\texttt{ce sfOverlaps lue.}\} \ \tau_1\}$$

Finally, we translate the existential quantifier on *lue* and class restrictions on *lue*, *ce* using the associated rules:

$$\tau_3 = \texttt{SELECT (ce) WHERE } \{\tau_R \ \tau_2\}$$

As already mentioned, we do not translate the first existential quantifier on ce, because this would leave no variables.

According to Eq. (1), given that the original formula started with **not exists**, it is satisfied if query τ_3 returns $\emptyset$.

5.3 A Tool for the Automated Translation and Execution of GeCoLan Formulas

We developed a translator from GeCoLan formulas to GeoSPARQL queries based on the ANTLR parser generator[8], which we selected because of its power and ease of use. Based on the formal specification of the GeCoLan grammar, ANTLR generated a generic parser based on the Visitor design pattern [45]. We then extended this parser to produce the correct GeoSPARQL fragments according to the grammar rules.

After translating a formula to GeoSPARQL, our tool submits it to the Parliament Triple Store through the Jena[9] library for execution. The result returned by the Triple Store is analyzed to determine whether the data satisfies the EN specification or not.

---

[8] www.antlr.org/.

[9] https://jena.apache.org/.

5.4 Experiment

We tested our translator on a portion of the dataset produced in project [5]. That dataset consisted of a set of ESRI shapefiles. We converted them to RDF using our pre-processing tool, which allows the user to define an appropriate mapping in order to associate shapefiles attributes to RDF properties.

Figure 6 shows a portion of the map we used. In the figure, land use elements are colored according to their first level Land Cover Piemonte type; e.g., artificial land is gray and water bodies are light blue.

Fig. 6. A portion of the map of the area covered by the Local EN proposal. (Color figure online)

We uploaded to Parliament the data located within a circle of 10 km diameter around a city in the neighborhood of Turin. Overall, the data consisted of 183,752 triples describing 5,162 *LandUseElements*, over which lay the elements of the EN: i.e., 579 *StructuralElements* and 1,054 *ConnectionElements*.

We first tested the **Connection Elements** example from Sect. 3.3. The query is challenging because it could require to consider all of the pairs formed by a *LandUseElement* and a *ConnectionElement*. Overall, the Triple Store contains almost 5.5M such pairs, and complex operations have to be performed on each one, such as checking whether the *LandUseElement* and *ConnectionElement* geometries overlap. The execution of the query took about 5.5 min on a medium-end laptop, pointing out that 595 *ConnectionElements* of the EN intersected at least a *LandUseElement* of maximum irreversibility or extroversion. Thus, in the project data, more than 55% of the *ConnectionElements* (595 out of 1,054) violate the EN specification.

We then tested the **Buffer Zones** example. The translation of the specification yields a GeoSPARQL query with four (partially nested) SELECTs and 44 lines. However, the execution took only a few seconds before answering that there are no violating *Buffer Creation*s in our data. We explain the efficiency of this query with the fact that the number of pending *Intervention*s of type *Buffer Creation* is usually small at a given time. For instance, in our dataset, there was only one intervention. The number of *LandUseElement*s and *StructuralElement*s that must be considered by the query is therefore strongly limited by the fact that they must be "close" to the *Buffer Creation*s; i.e., they touch, or overlap with them.

5.5   Beyond Constraint Verification

A natural extension of the EN validation task, which requires the full power of a language like GeCoLan, is the suggestion of how to fix the violations detected in a knowledge base. For example, it is quite plausible that the check of the **Connection Elements** specification may return a list of pairs (ce, lue) that indicate which *LandUseElement*s *lue* overlapping with some *ConnectionElement*s *ce* have invalid *extroversion* and/or *irreversibility*. Different actions could be identified to solve the problem; e.g., the *ConnectionElement ce* might be removed from the KB, or the geometry of *ce* could be reduced so that it no longer overlaps with the "bad" *LandUseElement lue*. However, in both cases, the proposed changes might generate new inconsistencies, caused by the fact that some elements of the EN become disconnected. Thus, in general, the identification of hypotheses of transformation of an EN have to be tightly integrated with the verification of their eligibility.

An even more challenging task would be to ask an automated reasoner to suggest how to connect a new *StructuralElement sel* to the rest of the EN, by proposing a path of new *ConnectionElement*s that lead from *sel* to an existing element of the EN.

The **Connection Elements** specification is relevant to all of the above tasks, but clearly not all of them can be solved by querying the KB through a language like SPARQL. Some tasks may require reasoning engines such as, e.g., Prolog [46], Answer Set Programming [47], and Constraint Programming [48], or even specialized libraries for 2D computational geometry [49,50]. For example, suppose that some EN specifications were translated to a Constraint Satisfaction Problem (CSP, [48]) for an EN containing a pair (ce, lue) which violates **Connection Elements**. If the following facts were retracted from the CSP:

```
ConnectionElement ce.
overlaps(ce, lue).
irreversibility(lue) = 1.
extroversion(lue) = 1.
```

a CSP solver might be able to suggest a change to the type of *ce*, and/or to its overlapping with *lue*, and/or to the attributes of *lue*, that satisfies the **Connection Elements** specification while preserving the connection of the EN elements (if this latter constraint is encoded in the CSP).

Of course, this is just an illustrative example. However, the point that we want to stress here, is that by adopting a higher-level language such as GeCoLan to encode the specifications, we can then (re-)use them as inputs to an appropriate combination of reasoners in order to solve more complex tasks.

6 Future Work

The study and implementation of further reasoning tasks based on GeCoLan represents one of the most important directions of our future work, in order to enable the interactive verification of the applicability of transformation proposals in a crowdsourcing context.

Whereas, at the current stage, we implemented EN validation as a standalone prototype, we aim at integrating it with a Participatory Geographical Information System (PGIS) to support online interaction with stakeholders in inclusive processes aimed at collecting feedback and project proposals for redesigning a geographical area. This would be a novel feature, as current Collaborative Web GIS (e.g., OnToMap [51–53], Ushahidi [54], PlanYourPlace [55] and other Collaborative Web GIS [56,57]) support a free introduction of geographic information, that has to be separately checked to evaluate the consistency and acceptability of user contributions. Basically, these applications only support feedback collection, and fail to provide validation functions to check the feasibility of the proposed actions.

In order to facilitate the convergence towards mutually agreed and feasible plans, it might be interesting to know how far the constraints on land usage are satisfied in a certain area, or whether any hypothetical actions, e.g., related to redevelopment project plans, are compatible with them. The present work is suitable for answering this kind of question by proposing a model for verifying the compliance of a set of geo-data with specifications concerning the related geographical area. Although in this paper we focus on the preservation and reconstruction of Ecological Networks, our model can be applied in rather different contexts, including the management of city plans, where detailed constraints have to be satisfied when building new elements or remodeling existing ones.

Another line of research we will pursue the improvement of the efficiency of validity checks. For instance, we plan to cache some types of pre-computed information (e.g., the intersections between elements of the EN), and to introduce an automatic optimization of the translations of GeCoLan formulas, in order to better exploit the operational semantics of GeoSPARQL and of its implementations.

7 Conclusions

This paper described an OWL ontology for the representation of Ecological Networks (ENs), and a semantic language (GeCoLan) for the specification and verification of EN transformation proposals. The language is aimed at enabling an automatic check of the consistency of transformation actions with the defined land usage restrictions, as well as at identifying existing inconsistencies in the

ENs. Moreover, the language is sufficiently expressive to support other reasoning tasks, such as the generation of proposals for amending inconsistencies in ENs, and the generation of optimized solution proposals.

We developed a prototype reasoner for the automatic validation of OWL-based representations of ENs: the reasoner automatically translates GeCoLan formulas to GeoSPARQL queries to efficiently implement the validation checks. A first test on the data collected in project [5] provided encouraging results; however, we observed that the noise present in the data affected performance. In order to support an efficient execution of reasoning tasks, we thus developed a data pre-processing tool that simplifies geographic datasets before translating them to the RDF representation needed for semantic reasoning. This paper describes both tools and their application to the dataset of project [5].

Acknowledgements. This work is partially funded by project MIMOSA (MultI-Modal Ontology-driven query system for the heterogeneous data of a SmArtcity, "Progetto di Ateneo Torino_call2014_L2_157", 2015–17), and by "Ricerca Locale" and "Ricerca Autofinanziata" of the University of Torino.

References

1. Jongman, R.: Nature conservation planning in Europe: developing ecological networks. Landsc. Urban Plan. **32**, 169–183 (1995)
2. Council of Europe: General guidelines for the development of the Pan-European Ecological Network. Nature and environment 107 (2000)
3. Bennett, G., Wit, P.: The development and application of ecological networks: a review of proposals, plans and programmes. AIDEnvironment (2001)
4. Bennett, G., Mulongoy, K.: Review of experience with ecological networks, corridors and buffer zones. Technical Series 23 (2006)
5. Città Metropolitana di Torino: Misura 323 del PSR 2007–2013 (in Italian) (2014). http://www.cittametropolitana.torino.it/cms/territorio-urbanistica/misura-323/misura-323-sperimentale
6. Janowicz, K., Scheider, S., Pehle, T., Ha, G.: Geospatial semantics and linked spatiotemporal data - past, present, and future. Semant. Web - Linked Spatiotemporal Data Geo-Ontol. **3**, 321–332 (2012)
7. Fonseca, F., Egenhofer, M., Davis Jr., C.A., Borges, K.: Ontologies and knowledge sharing in urban GIS. Comput. Environ. Urban Syst. **24**, 251–272 (2000)
8. Fonseca, F., Egenhofer, M., Agouris, P., Câmara, G.: Using ontologies for geographic information systems. Trans. GIS **3**, 231–257 (2002)
9. Dechter, R.: Constraint networks. In: Encyclopedia of Artificial Intelligence, 2nd ed. pp. 276–285 (1992)
10. W3C: Web ontology language (OWL) (2017). https://www.w3.org/OWL/
11. OCG: GeoSPARQL - a geographic query language for RDF data (2017). http://www.opengeospatial.org/standards/geosparql
12. Ajit, S., Sleeman, D., Fowler, D.W., Knott, D.: Constraint capture and maintenance in engineering design. Artif. Intell. Eng. Des. Anal. Manuf. **22**, 325–343 (2008)
13. Louwsma, J., Zlatanova, S., van Lammeren, R., van Oosterom, P.: Specifying and implementing constraints in GIS - with examples from a geo-virtual reality system. GeoInformatica **10**, 531–550 (2006)

14. W3C: SPARQL query language for RDF. https://www.w3.org/TR/rdf-sparql-query/
15. Torta, G., Ardissono, L., Savoca, A., Voghera, A., Riccia, L.L.: Representing ecological network specifications with semantic web techniques. In: Proceedings of 9th International Joint Conference on Knowledge Discovery, Knowledge Engineering and Knowledge Management (KEOD 2017), Funchal, Madeira, Portugal, pp. 86–97. SCITEPRESS (2017)
16. W3C: Resource description framework (RDF) (2017). https://www.w3.org/RDF/
17. Fath, B., Sharler, U., Ulanowicz, R., Hannon, B.: Ecological network analysis: network construction. Trends Ecol. Evol. **208**, 49–55 (2007)
18. Ulanowicz, R.: Quantitative methods for ecological network analysis. Comput. Biol. Chem. **28**, 321–339 (2004)
19. Lurgi, M., Robertson, D.: Automated experimentation in ecological networks. Autom. Exp. **3**, 1 (2011)
20. Gobluski, A., Westlund, E., Vandermeer, J., Pascual, M.: Ecological networks over the edge: hypergraph trait-mediated indirect interaction (TMII) structure. Trends Ecol. Evol. **31**, 344–354 (2016)
21. Pilosof, S., Porter, M., Pascual, M., Kefi, S.: The mulutilayer nature of ecological networks. Nat. Ecol. Evol. **1** (2017). Article No. 101
22. Battle, R., Kolas, D.: Enabling the geospatial semantic web with parliament and GeoSPARQL. Semant. Web **3**, 355–370 (2012)
23. W3C: Linked data (2018). https://www.w3.org/standards/semanticweb/data
24. Urban, S.: ALICE: an assertion language for integrity constraint expression. In: Proceedings of Computer Software and Applications Conference, pp. 292–299 (1989)
25. Bassiliades, N., Gray, P.: CoLan: a functional constraint language and its implementation. Data Knowl. Eng. **14**, 203–249 (1995)
26. Christensen, J.V., Johnsen, M.: Formalizing constraints for geographic information. In: Nilsson, A.G., Gustas, R., Wojtkowski, W., Wojtkowski, W.G., Wrycza, S., Zupančič, J. (eds.) Advances in Information Systems Development, pp. 657–667. Springer, Boston (2006). https://doi.org/10.1007/978-0-387-36402-5_57
27. Horrocks, I., Patel-Schneider, P., Boley, H., Tabet, S., Grosof, B., Dean, M.: SWRL: a semantic web rule language combining OWL and RuleML. W3C Member submission 21 (2004)
28. Boley, H., Tabet, S., Wagner, G.: Design rationale of RuleML: a markup language for semantic web rules. In: Proceedings of the First International Conference on Semantic Web Working, pp. 381–401, CEUR-WS.org (2001)
29. Boley, H., et al.: FOL RuleML: the first-order logic web language (2004). http://www.ruleml.org/fol
30. W3C: A Proposal for a SWRL Extension towards First-Order Logic (2005). https://www.w3.org/Submission/SWRL-FOL/
31. Keßler, C., Raubal, M., Wosniok, C.: Semantic rules for context-aware geographical information retrieval. In: Barnaghi, P., Moessner, K., Presser, M., Meissner, S. (eds.) EuroSSC 2009. LNCS, vol. 5741, pp. 77–92. Springer, Heidelberg (2009). https://doi.org/10.1007/978-3-642-04471-7_7
32. Gray, P., Hui, K., Preece, A.: An expressive constraint language for semantic web applications. In: E-Business and the Intelligent Web: Papers from the IJCAI 2001 Workshop, pp. 46–53 (2001)
33. Arenas, M., Gottlob, G., Pieris, A.: Expressive languages for querying the semantic web. In: Proceedings of the 33rd ACM SIGMOD-SIGACT-SIGART Symposium on Principles of Database Systems, pp. 14–26. ACM (2014)

34. Fürber, C., Hepp, M.: Using SPARQL and SPIN for data quality management on the semantic web. In: Abramowicz, W., Tolksdorf, R. (eds.) BIS 2010. LNBIP, vol. 47, pp. 35–46. Springer, Heidelberg (2010). https://doi.org/10.1007/978-3-642-12814-1_4

35. Grau, B., Horrocks, I., Motik, B., Parsia, B., Patel-Schneider, P., Sattler, U.: OWL 2: the next step for OWL. Web Semant.: Sci. Serv. Agents World Wide Web **6**, 309–322 (2008)

36. OGC: Geosparql vocabulary (2012). http://schemas.opengis.net/geosparql/1.0/geosparql_vocab_all.rdf

37. Open Geospatial Consortium, et al.: OpenGIS Implementation Standard for Geographic information-Simple feature access-Part 1: Common architecture (2011)

38. Cohn, A., Bennett, B., Gooday, J., Gotts, N.: Qualitative spatial representation and reasoning with the region connection calculus. GeoInformatica **1**, 275–316 (1997)

39. Egenhofer, M.J.: A formal definition of binary topological relationships. In: Litwin, W., Schek, H.-J. (eds.) FODO 1989. LNCS, vol. 367, pp. 457–472. Springer, Heidelberg (1989). https://doi.org/10.1007/3-540-51295-0_148

40. Provincia di Torino: Linee guida per le reti ecologiche (in Italian) (2014). http://www.provincia.torino.gov.it/territorio/file-storage/download/pdf/pian_territoriale/rete_ecologica/lgsv_lgre.pdf

41. Krötzsch, M.: Description Logic Rules. Studies on the Semantic Web, vol. 8. IOS Press, Amsterdam (2010)

42. Saalfeld, A.: Topologically consistent line simplification with the Douglas-Peucker algorithm. Cartogr. Geogr. Inf. Sci. **26**, 7–18 (1999)

43. Angles, R., Gutierrez, C.: The expressive power of SPARQL. In: Proceedings of International Semantic Web Conference, pp. 114–129 (2008)

44. Kostylev, E., Reutter, J., Ugarte, M.: Construct queries in SPARQL. In: LIPIcs-Leibniz International Proceedings in Informatics, vol. 31 (2015)

45. Gamma, E., Helm, R., Johnson, R., Vlissides, J.: Design Patterns: Elements of Reusable Object-Oriented Software. Addison-Wesley, Boston (1994)

46. Lloyd, J.W.: Foundations of Logic Programming. Springer, Heidelberg (2012). https://doi.org/10.1007/978-3-642-83189-8

47. Marek, V.W., Truszczyński, M.: Stable models and an alternative logic programming paradigm. In: Apt, K.R., Marek, V.W., Truszczynski, M., Warren, D.S. (eds.) The Logic Programming Paradigm, pp. 375–398. Springer, Heidelberg (1999). https://doi.org/10.1007/978-3-642-60085-2_17

48. Brailsford, S.C., Potts, C.N., Smith, B.M.: Constraint satisfaction problems: algorithms and applications. Eur. J. Oper. Res. **119**, 557–581 (1999)

49. Fabri, A., Giezeman, G.J., Kettner, L., Schirra, S., Schönherr, S.: On the design of CGAL a computational geometry algorithms library. Softw. Pract. Exp. **30**, 1167–1202 (2000)

50. Shekhar, S., Xiong, H.: Java Topology Suite (JTS). In: Shekhar, S., Xiong, H. (eds.) Encyclopedia of GIS, p. 601. Springer, Boston (2008). https://doi.org/10.1007/978-0-387-35973-1_664

51. Voghera, A., Crivello, R., Ardissono, L., Lucenteforte, M., Savoca, A., La Riccia, L.: Production of spatial representations through collaborative mapping. an experiment. In: Proceedings of 9th International Conference on Innovation in Urban and Regional Planning (INPUT 2016), pp. 356–361 (2016)

52. Ardissono, L., Lucenteforte, M., Mauro, N., Savoca, A., Voghera, A., La Riccia, L.: OnToMap - semantic community maps for knowledge sharing. In: Proceedings of Hypertext 2017, pp. 317–318. ACM (2017)

53. Ardissono, L., Ferrero, M., Petrone, G., Segnan, M.: Enhancing collaborative filtering with friendship information. In: Proceedings of the 25th Conference on User Modeling, Adaptation and Personalization, pp. 353–354. ACM (2017)
54. The Ushahidi Ecosystem: Ushahidi (2015). http://www.ushahidi.com/about
55. Hunter, A., et al.: PlanYourPlace - a geospatial infrastructure for sustainable community planning. Int. J. Geomat. Spat. Anal. **22**, 223–253 (2012)
56. Sun, Y., Li, S.: Real-time collaborative GIS: a technological review. ISPRS J. Photogramm. Remote Sens. **115**, 143–152 (2016)
57. Hu, Y., Lv, Z., Wu, J., Janowicz, K., Zhao, X., Yu, B.: A multistage collaborative 3D GIS to support public participation. Int. J. Digit. Earth **8**, 212–234 (2015)

The Linked Data Wiki: Leveraging Organizational Knowledge Bases with Linked Open Data

Matthias T. Frank[1][✉] and Stefan Zander[2]

[1] FZI Research Center for Information Technology,
Haid-und-Neu-Str. 10-14, Karlsruhe, Germany
frank@fzi.de
[2] Fachbereich Informatik, Hochschule Darmstadt, Darmstadt, Germany
stefan.zander@h-da.de

Abstract. Building meaningful knowledge bases for organizations like enterprises, NGOs or civil services is still a labor intensive and therefore expensive work, although semantic wiki approaches are already adopted in organizational contexts and corporate environments. One reason is that exploiting knowledge from external sources like other organizational knowledge bases or Linked Open Data as well as sharing knowledge in a meaningful way is difficult due to the lack of a common and shared schema definition. Therefore, redundant work has to be carried out for each new context. To overcome this issue, we introduce Linked Data Wiki, an approach that combines the power of Linked Open Vocabularies and -Data with established organizational semantic wiki systems for knowledge management in order to leverage the knowledge represented in organizational knowledge bases with Linked Open Data. Our approach includes a recommendation system to link concepts of an organizational context to openly published concepts and extract statements from that concepts that leverage the concept definition within the organizational context. The inclusion of potentially uncertain, incomplete, inconsistent or redundant public statements within an organization's knowledge base poses the challenge of interpreting such data correctly within the respective context.

1 Introduction

Within this work, we address the challenge of building meaningful knowledge bases for organizations like enterprises, NGOs or civil services while avoiding expensive redundant work for each new context. Our approach aims to leverage the knowledge represented in an organizational knowledge base with Linked Open Data (LOD). Preliminary studies for this work have been published in [1] and are further discussed in [2]. We complement the previous publications with additional literate review, a formalized representation of the Linked Data Wiki (LD-Wiki) approach and further proof of potential leverage that LOD can provide to organizational knowledge bases.

© Springer Nature Switzerland AG 2019
A. Fred et al. (Eds.): IC3K 2017, CCIS 976, pp. 294–319, 2019.
https://doi.org/10.1007/978-3-030-15640-4_15

This work is organized as follows: In Sect. 1, we define our understanding of knowledge as we use it for this work, show how this knowledge is currently managed in organizational contexts, which kind of public knowledge is available to leverage organizational knowledge bases, the challenges that develop for leveraging organizational knowledge and how we address these challenges in our approach. In Sect. 2, we discuss current semantic wiki approaches wrt. the implementation of semantic Web technology both on a syntactic and semantic level. In Sect. 3, we detail our approach of interlinking organizational knowledge bases with LOD. The implementation of the approach is described in Sect. 4. In Sect. 5, we discuss the potential of leverage by interlinking user created statements with Wikidata and DBpedia as two major resources for LOD. We conclude our work in Sect. 6 and discuss future work.

1.1 Definitions and Background

Definition of Knowledge. Within the scope of this work, we define knowledge as a theoretical understanding of a subject, formalized as explicit statements about this subject. It is not ensured whether these statements are true or false. Keeping in mind the triangle of reference[1] [3] shown in Fig. 1, we are also not able to draw

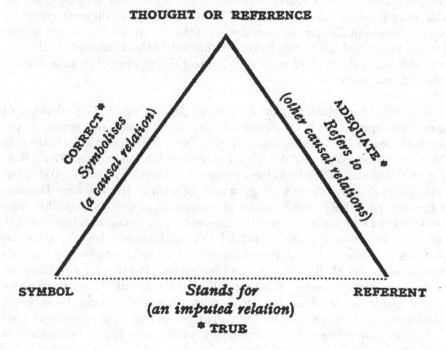

Fig. 1. Triangle of reference by Ogden and Richards [3]. symbol and referent have no direct connection.

---

[1] Also often referred to as triangle of signification.

a direct relation from a symbol to a real-world subject. We rather try to find symbols that represent the concept of a real-world subject at best. Neither does the formal representation of a concept modify the real-world subject, nor does the real-world subject influence the formal representation of its concept.

Formal Representation of Concepts. A concept is defined as the set of statements that every human associates with a real-world subject [3]. It is to be assumed that the set of statements associated with a real-world subject is varying for every human, wherefore no unique overall concept can be applied to a real-world subject. To still allow for a common understanding of real-world subjects, we have to find a formal representation that covers at least the most relevant statements commonly associated with that subject. Therefore, within the scope of this work, we define a concept as the subset of formal statements $\mathbb{RDF} = \{(s, p, o) : s \in Subject, p \in Predicate, o \in Object\}$ that are commonly shared within individual concepts of that subject. Further, we distinguish concepts that apply to the understanding of a subject within an organization including unpublished statements and concepts that are derived from openly available statements.

Identifier of Concepts. Technically, we use Uniform Resource Identifiers (URIs) to uniquely identify each concept. Using URIs rather than arbitrary textual labels, we can ensure that a unique URI does not represent different concepts. However, as concepts in contrast to real-world subjects are not necessarily unique and could be defined interdependently by different authors, multiple URIs may refer to the same subject. This leads to redundant definitions of the same concept among different sources.

Semantic Wiki for Organizational Knowledge Management. The adoption of semantic wiki approaches in organizational contexts and corporate environments has recently begun and is continuously growing [4–6]. This is particularly the case for Semantic MediaWiki (SMW) [7], an extension for the popular MediaWiki engine of Wikipedia, which introduces elements of the theWorldWideWeb Consortium (W3C)'s semantic technology stack[2] [8] such as the Resource Description Framework (RDF)'s triple model [9], semantic properties (so-called *roles* in Description Logic terms) as well as *Concepts*, i.e., dynamic categories that resemble the notion of domains in the RDF Schema language [10]. Those semantic features in conjunction with its collaborative knowledge engineering capabilities make semantic MediaWiki systems even more attractive for a deployment in professional environments (cf. listing *"Wiki of the Month"*[3]). SMW provides enhanced query construction capabilities with respect to organization-specific vocabularies and their specific contexts and allows to treat query results as first-class citizens and present them dynamically within wiki pages. Organizations

---

[2] A newer version of the semantic Web technology can be accessed at: https://smiy.wordpress.com/2011/01/10/the-common-layered-semantic-web-technology-stack/.

[3] https://www.semantic-mediawiki.org/wiki/Wiki_of_the_Month.

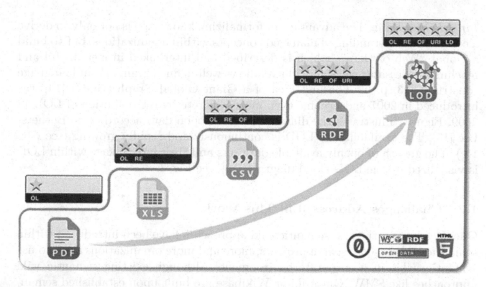

Fig. 2. Levels of Open Data [15]: 5-star data has to be machine processable and inter-linked with other resources.

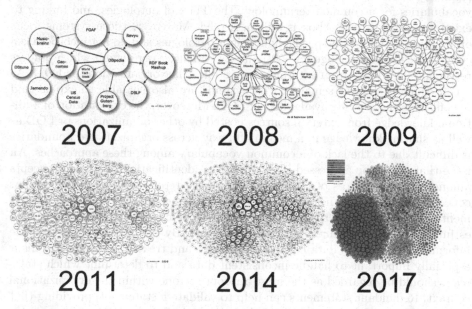

Fig. 3. Growth of Linked Open Data since 2007 [19]: The amount of data sets published as LOD have increased from 12 in 2007 to more than a thousand in 2017.

like enterprises, NGOs or civil services can benefit from such features, which enable query construction, query expansion, and filtering using a lightweight set of ontological semantics [11,12].

Linked Open Data. The advantage of formalizing knowledge is not only to derive a common understanding of managed concepts within organizations, but to build a global "Web of Data", which is described and interlinked in meaningful and machine-processable ways and which follows well-defined grammar and language constructs [13, p. 5]. The first idea of a Giant Global Graph (GGG) [14] was introduced in 2007 and become even more concrete by the definition of LOD in 2009. Figure 2 illustrates the different levels of open data according to Berners-Lee [15]. The availability of LOD is continuously and rapidly growing (see [16–18]). The growth of openly available data sets and their interlinkage within LOD is visualized by the LOD cloud diagram [19], see Fig. 3.

1.2   Challenges Addressed in This Work

One decade after the first semantic wiki approaches have been introduced within semantic Web-based research projects, more and more organizations start to use semantic wikis in a corporate environment. Although existing semantic wiki approaches like SMW, Ontowiki or Wikibase are built upon established semantic Web technologies, their utilization in wiki-based representation frameworks is primarily bound to a syntactic level. Support for wiki user in reusing established vocabularies for a common terminology, the Tbox of ontologies, and linking to existing entities in the Abox is still neglected. Moreover, those systems focus on building organization-specific lightweight ontologies and do not incorporate a common schema knowledge (cf. [20]) and its semantics per default which hinders retrieving knowledge from external sources like other organizations or LOD. As a consequence, current semantic wiki systems are also not able to exploit and benefit from the growing availability of LOD. Moreover, the exploitation of additional knowledge from external sources hosted by other organizations or LOD as well as sharing knowledge in a meaningful way across organizational boundaries is difficult due to the lack of a common vocabulary among these approaches. An issue that has to be addressed is therefore the identification of similar concepts among multiple sources of formalized knowledge representations. Once similar concepts are identified and interlinked, the provenance information of each statement retrieved from interlinked concepts has to be carefully tracked in order to estimate the trustworthiness of these statements. By evaluation the provenance information, uncertain data has to be identified and treated accordingly. This is especially important to handle inconsistent data and to determine which statement should be regarded as the most appropriate one within the organizational context. Redundant statements can help to validate a statement, providing that the provenance of each statement is independent of each other and not just a mirrored information which may also mirror a false statement. To handle incomplete data, we have to learn the schema of other instances of the same category and identify statements that are likely missing.

1.3   Contributions

The proposed approach aims to overcome the limitation of a common schema knowledge or aligned ontology in organizational knowledge bases[4] by supporting the annotation of organization-specific schema knowledge with the common and well-established terminology of Linked Open Vocabularies [20], hence extending the schema knowledge by interlinking modelled entities with Linked Open Data entities. Based on the resulting extended and interlinked schema knowledge, the so-called *TBox* in description logics [21], additional information can be provided for given entities[5]. The retrieved statements help users in maintaining attributes of individuals described in the wiki system so that their correctness and validity can be evaluated on the basis of acquired externally hosted data where a common and shared agreement is prevalent. The approach includes a *recommendation system* to link concepts of an organizational context to openly published concepts and *extract statements* from that concepts that leverage the concept definition within the organizational context. The inclusion of potentially uncertain, incomplete, inconsistent or redundant public statements within an organization's knowledge base poses the challenge of interpreting such data correctly within the respective context. We contribute to this challenge by *maintaining provenance information* for each statement. As a consequence, our work elaborates around the following research questions:

- RQ1: How can users of organizational wikis be supported in establishing meaningful links to concepts in Linked Open Data?
- RQ2: What is the potential leverage of Linked Open Data for organizational knowledge bases?

We hypothesize that the information value of organizational knowledge bases will increase with the integration of LOD.

2   Related Work

The review of related works is separated in three parts: In Sect. 2.1, existing semantic wiki software is reviewed where special emphasis is given to their *openness* towards a semantic technology stack. In Sect. 2.2, approaches for linked data management are introduced to show their strengths and limitations. The findings of both previous aspects are then summarized in Sect. 2.3 and close this section.

2.1   Semantic Wiki Software

In the following part, we introduce different approaches for organizational knowledge management using semantic wiki software.

---

[4] We use the terms *'knowledge base'* and *'semantic wiki'* interchangeably throughout this work as a semantic wiki resembles a collaboratively created knowledge base.

[5] I.e., data or facts hosted internally in a local knowledge base.

Semantic MediaWiki. Software applications for creating semantic wikis already exist; one of the best-known applications is SMW [7]. As many other wiki approaches, SMW is based on the MediaWiki engine, the technical base for Wikipedia. The latest release[6] of SMW supports the development of organization-specific knowledge bases and enables the querying of contained data (so-called facts) within the wiki in structured and well-defined ways. It is also possible to export semantically described facts to an external RDF store, which allows to use the W3C standardized query language SPARQL Protocol and RDF Query Language (SPARQL) for extended query capabilities. More extensions for SMW exist that provide better syntactical linkage of data modelled in SMW and RDF data like the Triple Store Connector (ontoprise GmbH, discontinued), the SparqlExtension[7], or the RDFIO[8] extension. All these approaches have in common that they provide semantic web technology merely on a syntactical layer rather than a full-fledged integration on a semantic layer. Only the LinkedWiki[9] extension focuses on exploiting LOD for organizational knowledge bases which are built on top of the MediaWiki engine.

WikiBase. In contrast to SMW, where data is managed and presented within the same application, Wikibase[10] splits the semantic wiki application into a repository and an independent client. Both parts are implemented as extensions for the MediaWiki engine. The central repository provides capabilities to collaboratively store and manage structured, non-relational data. One ore more clients can retrieve and embed structured data from the central repository into the respective organizational wiki system.

Cargo. Koren [22] presents the MediaWiki extension Cargo, since (according to his words) most semantic wiki applications are just used to structure and query data within an organizational wiki rather than integrating data on a semantic level or providing facilities of addressing semantic heterogeneity. The Cargo extension also provides functionality for structuring and querying data, however without employing any semantic Web technology. Cargo instead provides a wrapper around relational databases and exploits the well-established functionality of SQL including the limitation that entailment regime computations are hardly possible. The Cargo approach is therefore limited to concepts that are known within an organization and does not aim for including shared concepts like in LOD.

OntoWiki. One example for a non-MediaWiki based semantic wiki applications is OntoWiki, see [23]. OntoWiki focuses on modelling a machine readable knowledge base without providing a knowledge presentation for human readers like free text and natural language. Although the introduced semantic wiki software

---

[6] https://github.com/SemanticMediaWiki/SemanticMediaWiki/releases.
[7] https://www.mediawiki.org/wiki/Extension:SparqlExtension.
[8] https://www.mediawiki.org/wiki/Extension:RDFIO.
[9] https://www.mediawiki.org/wiki/Extension:LinkedWiki.
[10] http://wikiba.se/.

applications support semantic Web technology like RDF or even SPARQL on a syntactic level, the data integration across multiple data sources still requires a lot of manual effort due to the establishment of a common data scheme on a semantic level. OntoWiki [24] follows a different approach by providing an authoring, publication and visualization interface for the Data Web. OntoWiki supports navigation through RDF knowledge bases using SPARQL-generated lists, tables and trees. However, the authors do not mention the support for creating new links as they focus on accessing existing links only. The implemented RDFauthor approach builds on RDFa by preserving provenance information in RDFa representations following the named-graph paradigm and by establishing a mapping from RDFa view representations to authoring widgets. A number of tools in addition to OntoWiki are discussed that focus on data linking, quality improvement, enrichment, evolution and visualization. The advantage of the OntoWiki approach is the comprehensive user interface for arbitrary RDF knowledge graphs. However, there is a risk of overloading the user interface with more features which may decrease the usability.

Summarization of Semantic Wiki Software. A summarization of the previously discussed characteristics of semantic wiki applications is presented in Table 1.

Table 1. Characteristics of semantic Wiki applications [2].

Approach	Underlying engine	Internal data storage	Data export format	Query construction	Integration of LOV/LOD
Semantic MW	MediaWiki	Relational (RDF mirror possible)[a]	RDF (OWL only)	#ask: (SPARQL)	Manual import of single terms
Cargo	MediaWiki	Relational	CSV	#cargo_query (SQL-like)	-
WikiBase	MediaWiki	Relational	JSON or RDF	WB-Client (SPARQL)	WikiData-scheme
OntoWiki	-	Relational or RDF	RDF	SPARQL	Publish ontol-ogy with LOV

[a]https://www.semantic-mediawiki.org/wiki/Help:Using_SPARQL_and_RDF_stores

The overview in Table 1 points out that the introduced semantic wiki systems do either lack in native support of RDF knowledge management like SMW, Cargo, or WikiBase or managing unstructured content like OntoWiki. Furthermore, the introduced semantic wiki systems do not support linkage from concepts within an organizational knowledge base to LOD, e.g. by providing adequate recommendations, nor do they track provenance information of derived statements.

2.2 Linked Data Management

In this part, we introduce different approaches for managing linked data.

WikiData. Although the semantic wiki software applications introduced in Sect. 2.1 support semantic web technology like RDF or even SPARQL on a syntactical level, the data integration across multiple data sources is still hard due to a common data scheme on a semantical level. Vrandecic and Krötzsch [25] describe the collaborative data scheme in WikiData as one possible solution for a common data scheme in order to extend schema knowledge in other wikis, especially Wikipedia. However, this approach does also define a data schema which is independent from Linked Open Vocabulary (LOV). WikiData employs WikiBase as the underlying semantic data management system.

Versioning and Evolution Framework. The Versioning and Evolution Framework for RDF Knowledge Bases [26] provides a compatibility concept between ontologies and an assistant for changes which involves the user in the decision whether or not to accept a change. The authors use ontology versioning to keep track of different versions of an ontology and provide the possibility to allow branching and merging operations. The approach is based on atomic changes like additions or deletions of statements to or from an RDF graph which are aggregated to a hierarchy of changes and facilitate the human reviewing process on various levels of detail. The changes can be annotated with meta-information and classified as ontology evolution patterns. The advantage of this approach is that it is similar to well-known versioning approaches as they are widely used in software development like the popular GIT-system. However, the work on this framework has been discontinued in favour of OntoWiki.

SoftWiki. The SoftWiki approach [23] provides semantic wiki representations for building an enterprise knowledge base. SoftWiki enables users to create, enrich, and manage defined requirements. It provides web-based accessibility for ease of use. No installation is required on the user side and collaborators can be invited through a weblink. Provenance information are not implemented in SoftWiki. The approach provides traceability of changes and optional comments and discussions for every single part of the requirements engineering knowledge base. The advantage of the SoftWiki approach is that is has already been applied to a real business context. However, the approach is still on an early stage and further evaluation is needed. Especially the cloud based approach may not fit the security policies of organizations.

Linked Data Washing Machine. The Linked Data Washing Machine approach [27] aims on creating knowledge out of interlinked data. Adaptive user interfaces and interaction paradigms to empower users to formulate expressive queries for exploiting the rich structure of linked data. Users are able to give feedback on the automatically obtained suggestions in order to improve them. User interaction has to preserve privacy, ensure provenance, and be regulated using access control. Authoring tools should hide technicalities of the RDF, RDFS, or OWL data models and assist the user through what-you-see-is-what-you-get (WYSIWYG). Different information structures need to be seamlessly combinable in a provenance preserving way in a single visualization or authoring environment even if the information to be visualised or authored is obtained or stored in various linked data sources. The authors investigate unsupervised and supervised machine learning techniques to enable knowledge base maintainers to produce high quality mappings. They also use a semi-automatic repair method to increase the quality of Linked Data. Users have to be enabled to effortlessly give feedback to improve quality of Linked Data. Tools and services should be deployed to classify and interlink datasets automatically, to assess their information quality, and suggest enrichments and repairs to the published datasets. The advantage of the Linked Data Washing Machine is the integrative approach which combines the individual challenges rather than regarding them isolated. However, this approach still lacks on practicality of the discussed solution and remains on a theoretical stage.

WYSIWYM Approach. The what-you-see-is-what-you-mean (WYSIWYM) approach [28] aims on authoring of structured content based on Schema.org. The authors describe the manual composition process aiming at the creation of documents which use semantic knowledge representation formalism. The manual composition is supported by a graphical user interface. The work does not focus on provenance, origin or source if LOD. The approach provides a set of quality attributes for semantic content authoring (SCA) systems with corresponding user interfaces for their realization. Those include usability, automation, generalizability, collaboration, customizability, and evaluability. The paper provides a consolidated literate review of existing approaches including in-depth review of four SCA-systems. The crowdsourcing quality assessment methodology [29] aims on improving the quality of Linked Data in general. Although this approach focuses on quality improvement of existing LOD in DBpedia only, rather than supporting the interlinkage of new organizational specific entities, the approach provides a valuable contribution by using a list of data quality dimensions (criteria). The authors discuss four quality dimensions: Accuracy, relevancy, representational consistency, and interlinking.

DBpedia Concepts for Wikidata. Another approach makes use of the statements of Wikidata by using DBpedia concepts in order to exploit the benefits of both approaches [30]. The approach used the human-readable Wikipedia article identifiers to create IRIs for concepts in each Wikipedia language edition, use RDF and Named Graphs as its original data model, and provide http://wikidata. dbpedia.org/ as a Linked Data interface and SPARQL endpoint. Wikidata uses language-independent numeric identifiers and developed its own data model, which provides better means for capturing provenance information. Wikidata has a smaller dataset than DBpedia but higher quality and provenance information due to manual curation. Provenance extractors can be used to export as much knowledge as possible. Extractors can get labels, aliases, descriptions, different types of sitelinks, references, statements, and qualifiers.

LODFlow. Rautenberg et al. [31] discuss a workflow management system for linked data processing called LODFlow. They use LODFlow to create and manage the execution of workflows which interact with workflow participants. In addition, they provide visual programming frontends to enable users to construct their applications as a visual graph by connecting nodes together. LODFlow can help to preserve provenance by adding comprehensive metadata such as the version, invocation, and configuration of the tool execution in a concrete workflow instantiation. The authors plan workflows for Linked Data datasets maintenance to enable provenance extraction and reproducibility over time. LODFlow engine supports the interpretation of resources from the Linked Data Workflow Project Ontology and the invocation additional tools. They employ Luzzu for quality analysis. The advantage of LODFlow is that it is tested and applied to a large-scale real-world use case. However, the complexity of a full workflow management system for linked data aims to data scientists and cannot be used without special training. Therefore it does not fit to our intended use as an organizational wiki system which can easy be used by any employee.

OpenAnno. In contrast to the WikiData approach, the OpenAnno approach [32] focuses on mapping individually created ontologies to LOV in order to support the interlinkage of local knowledge bases with existing LOD sources in a semi-automated fashion.

X-Link. Fafalios et al introduce X-Link [33] to support the exploitation of LOD for open and configurable Named Entity Extraction (NEE). This approach aims on identifying entities in texts and linking them to related (Web) resources. The authors also propose an extension of Open Annotation Data Model (OADM) for relating the output of the NEE process. X-Link allows users to define categories of entities and exploiting one or more semantic knowledge bases. However, the approach does not consider any other statement about a concepts within an organizational context besides the label of this entity.

2.3   Discussion

In Sect. 2.1 we have shown that current semantic wiki applications provide technical integration of semantic Web technology on a syntactic level. In Sect. 2.2 we have outlined first approaches for enriching organizational knowledge bases with addition information from LOD. However, the introduced semantic wiki approaches do not support the annotation and interlinkage of organizational knowledge with LOD on a semantic level while considering the formal, model-theoretic semantics of the underlying ontology language, i.e., a vocabulary's formal semantics. Such a recommendation system is provided by Open-Anno, but it is not integrated in any of the introduced semantic wiki applications. The statements maintained by one of these semantic wiki applications cannot be updated by external services as the statements contained within a wiki are always considered as master data. When importing statements from external sources into an organizational wiki, none of the introduced semantic wiki applications consider the context or the linkage of the data. Both is important in order to evaluate given statements, especially when they are inconsistent, redundant or ambiguous. To overcome these limitations, we introduce our Linked Data Wiki approach in Sect. 3.

3 Approach

In this section, we introduce the LD-Wiki, an approach that aims at leveraging semantic organizational knowledge bases with LOD. The approach is separated in three parts: In Sect. 3.1, we define the initial state of organizational knowledge management systems and the target state we want to reach with the LD-Wiki approach. The challenges that have to be addressed by the approach are stated in Sect. 3.2. In Sect. 3.3, we propose the architecture for the LD-Wiki approach.

3.1 Initial and Target State

To specify the requirements for the LD-Wiki approach, we define the initial state of organizational knowledge management systems and available public knowledge, describe the intended target state of the organizational knowledge base and formalize the requirements to transform the initial state to the target state.

Organizational Knowledge. In the initial state, we assume that a given organizational knowledge base with a set of statements exists; however, these statements are not linked to public concept definition yet. Therefore, let $OKB = \{(s, p, o) \in RDF\}$ be the set of RDF statements in an organizational knowledge base. In terms of an organization, statements in OKB are characterized as reliable per default because they are maintained by the organization in controlled and well-defined ways. These statements are also more specialized regarding the demand of the organization. However, this reliability and specialization requires high maintenance effort and can only be applied to a limited subset of statements. We therefore regard statements in OKB as trusted.

Public Knowledge. On the other hand, there is a large body of formalized public knowledge represented as statements in LOD. Let $LOD = \{(s, p, o) \in RDF\}$ be the set of RDF statements in LOD. In terms of an organization, statements in LOD are characterized as a freely available, extensive but general description of common concepts with varying provenance that could be uncertain, incomplete, inconsistent or redundant. We therefore regard statements in LOD as initially untrusted.

Leveraged Organizational Knowledge. The target state represents an organizational knowledge base OKB' that contains all statements of OKB, complemented with the following sets of RDF statements:

- $LS = \{(s, p, o) \in \mathbb{RDF}\}$ that *link* concepts of OKB to concepts in LOD by a semantic relationship
- $DS = \{(s, p, o) \in \mathbb{RDF}\}$ *derived* from LOD concepts in LS
- $PS = \{(s, p, o) \in \mathbb{RDF}\}$ that state the *provenance* of statements in LS and DS.

We therefore define the target state as $OKB' = OKB \cup LS \cup DS \cup PS$.

3.2   Challenges

In contrast to providing only statements of OKB within an organizational wiki, our approach does also include external statements from multiple sources of LOD, which are linked to OKB by statements in LS. The inclusion of external statements in DS causes issues when the same concept is described in multiple sources. One of these issues is potentially redundant or inconsistent data. We address this issue by exploiting the gathered provenance information and evaluate the statements in DS based on a ranking derived from contained provenance statements in PS. To reach the defined target state, we have to address the following challenges:

Provenance of Statements. When including initially untrusted statements from LOD to trusted statements in OKB, we have to keep track of the provenance of each statement and make it transparent to consumers of OKB' in order to gain trust. Tracking the provenance information is particularity essential for statements in LS and DS. For LS, relevant information includes at first the author of the statement and the role the author embodies within the organization. Authors of statements in LS can be software agents that assume a link of a concept in OKB to LOD based on similarity algorithms, members of the organization that are in charge of OKB or other persons who have access to the system. Taking into account the trustworthiness of an author, it can be estimated whether to include statements about the linked concept in LOD to OKB' or not. As concepts in OKB as well as in LOD may change over time, it is also important to track the point in time when a link between a concept in OKB to a concept in LOD was created. If a link is not confirmed to be still valid for a long time period, it becomes less trustworthy compared to a recently confirmed link. However, if links are not confirmed but recently changed, a high update rate of links related to a concept might also indicate that facts hold only for a short time, making assertions less trustworthy since they might already be outdated. The trust of statements in LS is crucial for the derived statements in DS. Relevant provenance information for statements in DS therefore include the level of trust of the respective statement in LS at the time of inclusion in OKB'. All statements about the provenance in LS and DS are included in PS.

Uncertain Statements. Subject to the level of trust of a statement in DS, this statement has to be regarded as uncertain within the organizational context. Uncertain statements can help for a better understanding of a concept, but can not be used as proof for other statements. To increase trust of uncertain statements in DS, these statements could be verified by an author trusted by the organization.

Redundant Statements. As of the nature of LOD outlined in Sect. 1, redundant statements may exist among different sources of LOD. Redundant statements may appear between statements in OKB and DS but also within DS. Although redundant statements do no lead to a knowledge gain, these statements can increase trust of statements in OKB', provided that a redundant statement has a trusted provenance and the provenance of redundant statements is independent to prevent improper trust due to error propagation. The aspect of error propagation requires additional supervision and is not addressed in detail within this work.

Inconsistent Statements. Like redundant statements, inconsistent statements might appear between statements in OKB and DS and also within DS. In contrast to redundant statements, inconsistent statements can decrease the trust of statements in DS. To decide which statement in DS should be included in OKB', threshold values for trust in provenance in conjunction with the time of the last update of a statement can be defined and evaluated to decide for the most appropriate statement. If this decision can not be made by formalized provenance information, it should to be made by curators of OKB'.

Missing Statements. Another issue outlined in Sect. 1 is that formalized concept representation can never cover all statements that are associated with a real-world subject. Statements in OKB or different sources of LOD may therefore cover different aspects of a subject and real-world tests indicate that it is valid to assume that some statements are always missing. To highlight at least the most relevant missing statements commonly associated with that subject, common statements of similar concepts in LOD can be exploited. If most of the concepts within a specific class of concepts contain statements using the same predicate, a statement using that predicate is likely missing for the rest of the concepts within that class. For example, if most concepts within the class of "cities" contain statements using the predicate "has major", statements using this predicate are potentially missing for the other concepts within the class of "cities" and can be suggested for supervision in order to derive a more complete definition of that concept.

Transparent Provenance. The potential amount of provenance information in PS could also raise lead to problems. Although this provenance information is necessary in order to evaluate the trustworthiness of statements in DS, it would be confusing for the consumers of OKB' to show all available provenance information in PS for each statement in DS. We address this challenge by evaluation the provenance information in the background and just showing the resulting statement to the user with an option to expand the underlying provenance-based derivation of the statement.

3.3 Architecture

One characteristic of our approach is the strict separation of statements in the RDF store maintained by an dedicated knowledge management module and the non-semantic part of the wiki, like free text, place-holders for the semantic statements of OKB', and wiki markup syntax, which are still maintained by the semantic wiki software. The technical architecture for our approach consists of a knowledge management layer and a knowledge representation layer as illustrated in Fig. 4. By separating the semantic statements from the non-semantic part of the wiki, we avoid the issue of syncing statements between the wiki and the knowledge base. Additionally, we are able to maintain and curate the semantic statements outside of the wiki without causing inconsistent data. This separation of semantic and non-semantic data is therefore a prerequisite for the transparent integration of statements in OKB managed by the wiki itself and external statements from LOD. The main contribution is thus not on a technical layer, but aims at supporting the schema integration on a semantic layer. We provide a set of established LOV to encourage the reuse of these vocabularies in organizational wikis.

Knowledge Management. The Linked Data Management Module (LDaMM) is the stand-alone business logic module for the knowledge management layer which queries LOD on demand, updates the local RDF knowledge graph in OKB' and serves the semantic wiki software with curated statements. The LDaMM is also responsible for reasoning and rule execution, which help to curate the local knowledge graph. The resulting organizational knowledge base OKB' using LOV is the foundation for further recommendations of annotations in LS from OKB to LOD. These annotations allow to enrich the organizational knowledge base with additional information in DS. In order to distinguish organization-specific statements originated from OKB and statements gathered from DS within OKB', we track the provenance information of each statement in PS. The provenance information is stored using named graphs in the RDF-store, which extend the default triple model consisting of subject, predicate and object to quadruples, containing an ID for each statement. This ID allows us to attach provenance information to each statement. Using the provenance information in PS, we can also handle uncertain or inconsistent statements in DS and provide consumers of OKB' with the latest and most suitable information.

Knowledge Representation. As business logic module for the human friendly representation layer, the LD-Wiki approach involves a semantic wiki software to collaboratively modify unstructured content, statements in OKB by invoking LDaMM and also the structure of the wiki pages using a simplified markup language. For the knowledge representation, the semantic wiki software relies on the statements of OKB' provided by LDaMM, rather than relying on statements

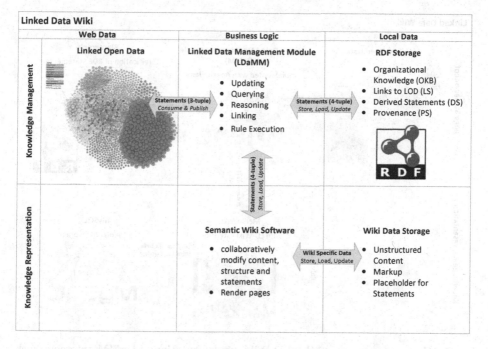

Fig. 4. Architecture of the LD-Wiki approach: knowledge management layer for enriching the local RDF-graph with Web knowledge and curating it, representation layer for a user friendly representation of RDF-data enriched and formatted using locally stored unstructured content and wiki markup.

in OKB managed by semantic wiki software itself as it is done by e.g. SMW. Avoiding redundant management of knowledge in the representation layer, we ensure that the organizational knowledge management is always in a consistent state. However, the semantic wiki software has to provide additional unstructured content for a human friendly presentation like free text and markup information which is stored in a separate local data storage to manage the data for the representation layer.

4   Implementation

For the implementation of the LD-Wiki approach, we build on the open source framework of MediaWiki. In contrast to other MediaWiki-based approaches discussed in Sect. 2.1, we implement the knowledge management with LDaMM as a stand-alone module that controls storing, querying, updating, reasoning and rule execution of RDF-statements, rather than integrating the knowledge management in MediaWiki itself. This allows for a lightweight MediaWiki extension that triggers LDaMM for rendering wiki pages (Sect. 4.1) and also if a user creates new wiki pages for the terminology (Sect. 4.2) or individual concepts (Sect. 4.3) of the organization knowledge base. An overview of the core components of the implementation of LD-Wiki is given in Fig. 5.

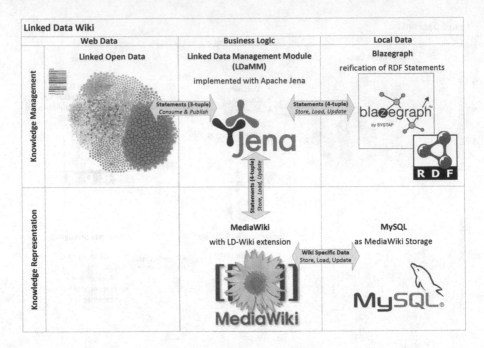

Fig. 5. Core components of the LD-Wiki implementation: LDaMM interacts with MediaWiki and stores statements retrieved from LOD to Blazegraph RDF store

4.1   Rendering Wiki Pages

The Wiki pages in LD-Wiki consist of free text for a human readable presentation, placeholder for data from LDaMM and MediaWiki syntax as a simplified markup language to format the style of the page. When a page is requested, the according parser function[11] of the LD-Wiki extension requests the necessary data from LDaMM and replaces each place holder with the according value from the knowledge base OKB'.

4.2   New Terminological Box (TBox) Pages

The key factor to let the LD-Wiki approach work well and build a TBox which can be interpreted in the context of LOD, it is necessary to interlink new classes of concepts in OKB with classes from LOV. Classes are represented as categories in MediaWiki. Therefore, whenever a new category is created within the wiki, LDaMM is triggered to query for existing classes in LOV with the same label as the label for the new category. If one or more classes are found, users of LD-Wiki can select the classes that represent the intended category at the best.

Figure 6 shows how this looks like in LD-Wiki. For creating new classes within the local knowledge management OKB, the user opens the special page for creating a new category in MediaWiki and provides the string that labels that new

---

[11] https://www.mediawiki.org/wiki/Parser_functions.

class of concepts. When submitting this string, MediaWiki sends it to LDaMM in the knowledge management layer. LDaMM invokes SPARQL queries to search for classes in LOD that are labeled with the same string. If, for example, the user would like to create a new category of cities for a German-language terminology, he would probably enter the string "Stadt" for this category. To find classes related to that string in LOD, LDaMM produces a query string as shown in Listing 1.1 to discover classes that have the label "Stadt" with a German language tag. This query string is then executed at available public SPARQL endpoints to discover adequate classes of concepts. Expected results would be for example http://schema.org/City, http://dbpedia.org/ontology/City or http://www.wikidata.org/entity/Q515. LDaMM returns these results to MediaWiki where the user can select the adequate concepts. On creation of the new category in MediaWiki including the interlinked concepts, the information of the new category and the linked concepts are send back to LDAMM and stored to the local knowledge graph OKB', including provenance information.

Listing 1.1. Query classes with German label "Stadt".

```
1   SELECT * WHERE {
2       ?category rdf:type rdf:Class;
3           rdfs:label "Stadt"@de. }'
```

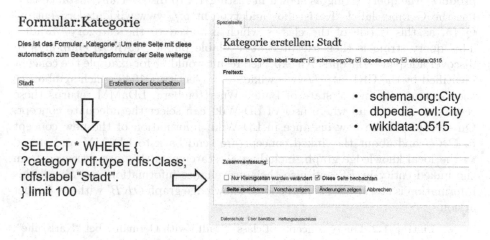

Fig. 6. Interlink new category in LD-Wiki with existing class in LOV [2]: classes of concepts in schema.org, DBpedia and WikiData are recommended for a new category with the label "Stadt".

4.3   New Assertional Box (ABox) Pages

Assuming that the categories of LD-Wiki are linked to the according classes in LOV as discussed in Sect. 4.2, we can assist the user on creating new concepts for the ABox in the wiki. Instances of a class are represented as pages within the category that represents that class in the wiki. Therefore, whenever a page is created, LDaMM is triggered to query for existing concepts in LOD with the same label as the new page and the same class as the category of the new wiki page. If one or more concepts are found, users of the wiki can select the concept that represent the intended subject for the new wiki page. The benefit for this kind of interlinkage is that we can query directly for properties of these concept in LOD or retrieve a summary of entity data using entity summarization tools like LinkSUM [34].

Figure 7 shows how this is done in LD-Wiki. For creating a new instance within OKB, users of LD-Wiki open the special page for creating new instances in MediaWiki, provide the string that labels that new instance and selects the category of which the new page should be an instance of. When submitting this string, MediaWiki again sends it to LDaMM in the knowledge management layer together with the identifier of the selected category. LDaMM invokes SPARQL queries to search for concepts in LOD that are labeled with the same string and are instances of any of the classes that the given category is linked to. If, for example, the user would like to create a new instance of the category "Stadt" for the German-language terminology in our example, he or she would enter the name of this city as string, e.g. "Karlsruhe", and select the category "Stadt" for it. To find instances related to that string and category in LOD, LDaMM produces the query string as shown in Listing 1.2 to discover any instance that has the German label "Karlsruhe" and type http://www.wikidata.org/entity/Q515, as this is one of the classes which is linked to the category "Stadt". This query string is then executed at available public SPARQL endpoints to discover adequate concepts. An expected result would be for example the concept identified by the URI http://www.wikidata.org/entity/Q1040 which symbolizes the German city in the state of Baden-Wuerttemberg. LDaMM returns these results to MediaWiki where user of LD-Wiki can select the adequate concept. On creation of the new instance in LD-Wiki, information of the new concept in OKB and about the linked concept are send back to LDaMM and stored to the local knowledge graph, including all statements that are retrieved from the linked entity in LS and also their provenance information in PS. All this information is now available in the local knowledge graph OKB' without further action.

Listing 1.2. Query concepts of class "Stadt" with German label "Karlsruhe".

```
1   SELECT * WHERE {
2           ?instance
3           rdf:type
4           <http://www.wikidata.org/entity/Q515> ;
5           rdfs:label "Karlsruhe" . }
```

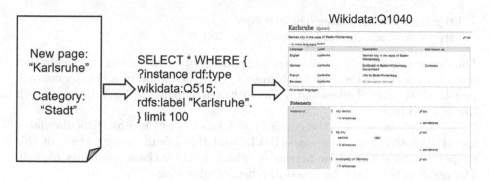

Fig. 7. Interlink new instance in LD-Wiki with concept from LOD [2]: Statements about the concept are retrieved from WikiData.

5   Proof of Concept

To proof the LD-Wiki approach, we use the SPARQL endpoints of DBpedia[12] and Wikidata[13] as two major instances of LOD resources. Due to the different implementation of these endpoints, the query string has to be mapped to meet the individual characteristics. The proof of concept covers the aspects of the research questions raised in Sect. 1.3 using the implementation of LD-Wiki described in Sect. 4 and is therefore separated in two parts: In Sect. 5.1, we evaluate the research question how users of organizational wikis can be supported in establishing meaningful links to concepts in LOD and in Sect. 5.2 we evaluate the potential leverage of LOD for organizational knowledge bases.

5.1   Meaningful Links to Concepts in LOD

New TBox Pages. The first step is to run the query described in Listing 1.1 on endpoints of DBpedia and Wikidata in order to discover relevant classes of concepts. Wikidata uses the property http://www.wikidata.org/prop/direct/ P279 (subclass of) to describe subclasses of other classes. We therefore map the property-value pair "rdf:type rdf:Class" to this wikidata property which results in the query described in Listing 1.3:

Listing 1.3. Query classes with German label "Stadt" in Wikidata.

```
1   SELECT * WHERE {
2       ?category
3           <http://www.wikidata.org/prop/direct/P279>
4           ?class ;
5           rdfs:label "Stadt"@de .}
```

When executing this query at the SPARQL endpoint of Wikidata, we receive two classes:

---

[12] http://dbpedia.org/sparql.
[13] https://query.wikidata.org.

- http://www.wikidata.org/entity/Q515
- http://www.wikidata.org/entity/Q15253706

The first result describes a city as a large and permanent human settlement and the second result is the class for a more specific definition of a city by country that holds the size of cities and towns in Korea, Japan, the USA, China, North Korea and France.

For DBpedia, we map the class of rdfs:Class to owl:Class as DBpedia makes use of Web Ontology Language (OWL) and the default configuration of this endpoint does not imply superclasses which would include rdfs:Class as well. The result is the query described in reflstadt@dbpedia:

Listing 1.4. Query classes with German label "Stadt" in DBpedia.

```
1   SELECT * WHERE {
2          ?category rdf:type owl:Class ;
3          rdfs:label "Stadt"@de .}
```

When executing this query at the SPARQL endpoint of DBpedia, we receive again two classes:

- http://dbpedia.org/ontology/City
- http://dbpedia.org/ontology/Town

New ABox Pages. Next, we test the retrieval of instance data for a given concept. In our example, we want to execute the query shown in Listing 1.5 on the SPARQL endpoints of DBpedia and Wikidata.

Listing 1.5. Example Query.

```
1   SELECT * WHERE {
2          ?instance
3          rdf:type
4          <http://www.wikidata.org/entity/Q515>;
5          rdfs:label "Karlsruhe"@de. }
```

Wikidata uses the property http://www.wikidata.org/prop/direct/P31 (instance of) to indicate that an instance belongs to a specific category. We therefore map the property rdf:type to the Wikidata-specific term:

Listing 1.6. Query concepts of class "Stadt" with German label "Karlsruhe" in DBpedia.

```
1   SELECT * WHERE {
2          ?instance
3          <http://www.wikidata.org/prop/direct/P31>
4          <http://www.wikidata.org/entity/Q515> ;
5          rdfs:label "Karlsruhe"@de .}
```

For this query, we get two matching instances:

- http://www.wikidata.org/entity/Q1040
- http://www.wikidata.org/entity/Q1026577

The first result refers to the German city in the state of Baden-Wuerttemberg, the second result refers to a city in North Dacota. Depending on the instance the user wants to refer to, he or she has to select the appropriate one. This example does also show that a completely automatic information retrieval is difficult to control and therefore human supervision of this process is still reasonable. If we run the query with the more strict definition of a city by country using the query string shown in Listing 1.7, we do not get any result.

Listing 1.7. Query concepts of class "Stadt" with German label "Karlsruhe" in DBpedia.

```
1  SELECT * WHERE {
2          ?instance
3          <http://www.wikidata.org/prop/direct/P31>
4          <http://www.wikidata.org/entity/Q15253706>;
5          rdfs:label "Karlsruhe"@de .}
```

For DBpedia, we run the query for instances of http://dbpedia.org/ontology/City or http://dbpedia.org/ontology/Town:

Listing 1.8. Query concepts of class "Stadt" with German label "Karlsruhe" in DBpedia.

```
1  SELECT * WHERE {
2          ?instance rdf:type
                 <http://dbpedia.org/ontology/Town> ;
3          rdfs:label "Karlsruhe"@de .}
```

The single result of this query is the instance of http://dbpedia.org/resource/Karlsruhe.

5.2   Leverage of LOD for Organizational Knowledge Bases

To evaluate the number of subclasses that currently exist in WikiData as the potential leverage of LOD for organizational knowledge bases, we query the amount of formalized classes in WikiData as shown in Listing 1.9:

Listing 1.9. Number of formally described subclasses in WikiData.

```
1  SELECT * WHERE {
2          ?category
3          <http://www.wikidata.org/prop/direct/P279>
4          ?class .}
```

For the number of instances of a given class, e.g. the class of cities, we use the query described in Listing 1.10 which returns a number of 20.867 results:

Listing 1.10. Number of formally described instances of class Q515 ("city") in Wiki-Data.

```
1  SELECT * WHERE {
2         ?instance
3         <http://www.wikidata.org/prop/direct/P31>
4         <http://www.wikidata.org/entity/Q515> .}
```

In our use case, we could leverage the concept of "Karlsruhe" in OKB with the statements in DS retrieved from the linked concept in LOD using the query described in Listing 1.11. This query returns a number of 485 statements that can be included in OKB' to leverage the concept of "Karlsruhe". For comparison, using the WikiData concept of "New York City" (Q60), the query returns 831 statements.

Listing 1.11. Number of statements for Q1040 ("Karlsruhe") in WikiData.

```
1  SELECT * WHERE {
2         <http://www.wikidata.org/entity/Q1040>
3         ?p
4         ?o .}
```

5.3 Discussion of Results

By executing queries on general concepts like instances of cities, we have shown that adequate LOD records exist to leverage organizational knowledge bases. These concepts provide hundreds of statements that refer to a subject and can be employed for a common understanding of subjects across the boundaries of an organization.

6 Conclusion

In this work, whe have introduced LD-Wiki approach to assist users of organizational wikis in establishing and curating meaningful relations to LOD concepts by building adequate SPARQL queries based on the user's input and the given context. In Sect. 1, we have motivated our research with the demand of building meaningful knowledge bases for organizations while avoiding expensive redundant work for each new context. We discussed related work in Sect. 2 and pointed out the missing support for leveraging organizational knowledge bases with LOD. To overcome this limitation, we introduced the LD-Wiki approach in Sect. 3 which aims to separate knowledge management and knowledge representation in order to gain a consistent knowledge base that also covers statements from LOD while keeping track of the provenance of each statement. The implementation of the LD-Wiki approach using primarily open source frameworks is described in Sect. 4. In Sect. 5, we have shown queries adopted to WikiData and DBpedia and the results we got from these sources.

With the implementation of the LD-Wiki approach we have shown how we can assist users of organizational wikis with creating new links to LOD entities. By executing queries on general concepts like instances of cities, we have shown that adequate LOD records exist to leverage organizational knowledge bases. To track the provenance of statements DS derived from LOD, we have introduced the additional set of statements PS. Statements in DS leverage an organizational knowledge base OKB to OKB' without affecting the knowledge representation. By evaluating the provenance information in PS, software agents can take the provenance of statements into account for reasoning the trustworthiness of statements in OKB'. Exploiting the gathered provenance information for semantic reasoning is a precondition to increase the informative value of an organizational knowledge base.

Further research has to be carried out and have to prove that the LD-Wiki approach can also be applied to other knowledge domains. Open issues for future work include the privacy for confidential data on the one hand while publishing parts of the corporate knowledge base as LOD on the other hand. This requires a proper implementation of Access Control Lists (ACLs) with carefully designed access roles for each statement in the knowledge base.

References

1. Frank, M., Zander, S.: Linked open data for organizational knowledge bases: towards a linked data Wiki. In: Bleimann, U., Humm, B., Loew, R., Regier, S., Stengel, I., Walsh, P. (eds.) Collaborative European Research Conference, pp. 50–57 (2017)
2. Frank, M., Zander, S.: Exploiting linked open data for enhancing MediaWiki-based semantic organizational knowledge bases. In: SciTePress (ed.) KEOD (2017)
3. Ogden, C.K., Richards, I.A.: The Meaning of Meaning: A Study of the Influence of Language upon Thought and of the Science of Symbolism. 10th edn, 4th impr. edn. International Library of Psychology, Philosophy and Scientific Method. Routledge and Kegan Paul, London (1956)
4. Ghidini, C., et al.: Collaborative knowledge engineering via semantic MediaWiki. In: Auer, S., Schaffert, S., Pellegrini, T. (eds.) International Conference on Semantic Systems (I-SEMANTICS 2008), Graz, Austria, pp. 134–141 (2008)
5. Kleiner, F., Abecker, A.: Semantic MediaWiki as an integration platform for IT service management. LNI **176**, 73–78 (2010)
6. Aveiro, D., Pinto, D.: Implementing organizational self awareness - a semantic MediaWiki based enterprise ontology management approach, pp. 453–461 (2013)
7. Krötzsch, M., Vrandečić, D., Völkel, M.: Semantic MediaWiki. In: Cruz, I., et al. (eds.) ISWC 2006. LNCS, vol. 4273, pp. 935–942. Springer, Heidelberg (2006). https://doi.org/10.1007/11926078_68
8. W3C: Semantic web stack (2007)
9. Klyne, G., Carroll, J.J.: Resource description framework (RDF): concepts and abstract syntax: W3C recommendation, 10 February 2004 (2004)

10. Brickley, D., Guha, R.V.: RDF vocabulary description language 1.0: RDF schema (2004)
11. Vrandecic, D., Krötzsch, M.: Reusing ontological background knowledge in semantic wikis. CEUR Workshop Proceedings, vol. 206 (2006)
12. Zander, S., Swertz, C., Verdú, E., Pérez, M.J.V., Henning, P.: A semantic MediaWiki-based approach for the collaborative development of pedagogically meaningful learning content annotations. In: Molli, P., Breslin, J.G., Vidal, M.-E. (eds.) SWCS 2013-2014. LNCS, vol. 9507, pp. 73–111. Springer, Cham (2016). https://doi.org/10.1007/978-3-319-32667-2_5
13. Hebeler, J.: Semantic Web programming. Wiley, Indianapolis (2009)
14. Berners-Lee, T.: Giant global graph (2007)
15. Berners-Lee, T.: Linked-data design issues (2009)
16. Bizer, C., Heath, T., Berners-Lee, T.: Linked data - the story so far. Int. J. Semant. Web Inf. Syst. 5, 1–22 (2009)
17. Hausenblas, M.: Exploiting linked data to build web applications. IEEE Internet Comput. 13, 68–73 (2009)
18. Heath, T., Bizer, C.: Linked Data: Evolving the Web into a Global Data Space. Synthesis Lectures on the Semantic Web. Morgan & Claypool Publishers, San Rafael (2011)
19. Abele, A., McCrae, J.P., Buitelaar, P., Jentzsch, A., Cyganiak, R.: Linking open data cloud diagram (2017)
20. Janowicz, K., Hitzler, P., Adams, B., Kolas, D., Vardeman, C.: Five stars of linked data vocabulary use. Semant. Web 5, 173–176 (2014)
21. Baader, F., Calvanese, D., McGuinness, D., Nardi, D., Patel-Schneider, P.: The Description Logic Handbook: Theory, Implementation and Applications. Cambridge University Press, Cambridge (2003)
22. Koren, Y.: Cargo and the future of semantic MediaWiki. In: SMWCon Spring 2015. St. Louis, MO, USA (2015)
23. Auer, S., Jungmann, B., Schönefeld, F.: Semantic Wiki representations for building an enterprise knowledge base. In: Antoniou, G., et al. (eds.) Reasoning Web 2007. LNCS, vol. 4636, pp. 330–333. Springer, Heidelberg (2007). https://doi.org/10.1007/978-3-540-74615-7_7
24. Frischmuth, P., Martin, M., Tramp, S., Riechert, T., Auer, S.: OntoWiki - an authoring, publication and visualization interface for the data web. Semant. Web 6, 215–240 (2015)
25. Vrandecic, D., Krötzsch, M.: Wikidata: a free collaborative knowledgebase. Commun. ACM 57, 78–85 (2014)
26. Auer, S., Herre, H.: A versioning and evolution framework for RDF knowledge bases. In: Virbitskaite, I., Voronkov, A. (eds.) PSI 2006. LNCS, vol. 4378, pp. 55–69. Springer, Heidelberg (2007). https://doi.org/10.1007/978-3-540-70881-0_8
27. Auer, S.: Creating knowledge out of interlinked data: making the web a data washing machine (2011)
28. Khalili, A., Auer, S.: WYSIWYM authoring of structured content based on Schema.org. In: Lin, X., Manolopoulos, Y., Srivastava, D., Huang, G. (eds.) WISE 2013. LNCS, vol. 8181, pp. 425–438. Springer, Heidelberg (2013). https://doi.org/10.1007/978-3-642-41154-0_32
29. Acosta, M., Zaveri, A., Simperl, E., Kontokostas, D., Auer, S., Lehmann, J.: Crowdsourcing linked data quality assessment. In: Alani, H., et al. (eds.) ISWC 2013. LNCS, vol. 8219, pp. 260–276. Springer, Heidelberg (2013). https://doi.org/10.1007/978-3-642-41338-4_17

30. Ismayilov, A., Kontokostas, D., Auer, S., Lehmann, J., Hellmann, S.: Wikidata through the eyes of DBPedia. CoRR abs/1507.04180 (2015)
31. Rautenberg, S., Ermilov, I., Marx, E., Auer, S., Ngomo, A.C.N.: LodFlow: a workflow management system for linked data processing semantics 2015, Vienna, Austria, 15–17 September 2015. In: Polleres, A., Pellegrini, T., Hellmann, S., Parreira, J.X. (eds.) Proceedings of the 11th International Conference on Semantic Systems, SEMANTICS 2015, Vienna, Austria, 15–17 September 2015, pp. 137–144. ACM (2015)
32. Frank, M., Zander, S.: Pushing the CIDOC-conceptual reference model towards LOD by open annotations. In: Oberweis, A., Reussner, R.H. (eds.) Modellierung 2016, 2–4 März 2016, Karlsruhe. LNI, GI, pp. 13–28 (2016)
33. Fafalios, P., Baritakis, M., Tzitzikas, Y.: Exploiting linked data for open and configurable named entity extraction. Int. J. Artif. Intell. Tools 24, 1540012 (2015)
34. Thalhammer, A., Lasierra, N., Rettinger, A.: LinkSUM: using link analysis to summarize entity data. In: Bozzon, A., Cudre-Maroux, P., Pautasso, C. (eds.) ICWE 2016. LNCS, vol. 9671, pp. 244–261. Springer, Cham (2016). https://doi.org/10.1007/978-3-319-38791-8_14

Social and Community Related Themes in Ontology Evaluation: Findings from an Interview Study

Marzieh Talebpour[(✉)], Martin Sykora, and Tom Jackson

School of Business and Economics,
Loughborough University, Loughborough, UK
{m.talebpour, m.d.Sykora, t.w.Jackson}@lboro.ac.uk

Abstract. A deep exploration of what the term "quality" implicates in the field of ontology selection and reuse takes us much further than what the literature has mostly focused on, that is the internal characteristics of ontologies. A qualitative study with interviews of ontologists and knowledge engineers in different domains, ranging from biomedical field to manufacturing industry reveals novel social and community related themes, that have long been neglected. These themes include responsiveness of the developer team or organization, knowing and trusting the developer team, regular updates and maintenance, and many others. This paper explores such connections, arguing that community and social aspects of ontologies are generally linked to their quality. We believe that this work represents a significant contribution to the field of ontology evaluation, with the hope that the research community can further draw on these initial findings in developing relevant social quality metrics for ontology evaluation and selection.

Keywords: Ontology quality · Social quality metrics · Ontology reuse

1 Introduction

Ontologies play a major role in the field of knowledge and information management by furnishing the semantics to heterogeneous systems and [1], bridging multiple domains and enabling linked data [2]. They are also employed in different domains for various purposes. Ontologies provide many benefits, no matter in which domain they are used. They not only facilitate communication and knowledge transfer between systems, between humans, and between humans and systems [3], by uniquely identifying the meaning of different concepts in any domain, but they can also avoid the costs associated with new developments of knowledge models.

Despite the significant role that ontologies play in the semantic web, there is still little understanding about the way they should be built and developed [4]. Some believe that the cost of building and maintaining ontologies in certain domains can outweigh the potential benefits gained by using them [2, 5]. To deal with this concern, some have suggested reusing previously built ontologies, since this will help in achieving one of the main goals of ontology construction, that is to share and reuse

© Springer Nature Switzerland AG 2019
A. Fred et al. (Eds.): IC3K 2017, CCIS 976, pp. 320–336, 2019.
https://doi.org/10.1007/978-3-030-15640-4_16

semantics [6], and will also save significant amount of time and financial resources. [7] believe that the future of construction of large-scale knowledge-based systems is highly dependent on reusing the components built by others, while such issues are still at the forefront of ontology engineering [8].

Regardless of all the advantages of reusing ontologies and the availability of different ontologies, ontology reuse has always been a challenging task [7]. Methods for building ontologies are usually blamed for lack of reuse strategies and some argue that these methodologies are not explicitly concerned with ontology reuse [9]. Others consider the first steps of ontology reuse, that is the identification and evaluation of the knowledge sources which can be useful for an application domain [10], as the hardest step in the process of ontology reuse. Researchers not only have to find the most appropriate ontologies for their search query, but they should also be able to evaluate those ontologies according to different implicit or explicit criteria.

This study aims to address some of the challenges faced in the first steps of the general process of reusing ontologies, which is to evaluate and then select the right ontology for reuse. This study contributes with qualitative data and findings to this ongoing challenge by documenting the process of selecting an ontology for reuse. It differs from previous studies, which focused purely on evaluating different pre-selected metrics. In this study, our focus was to qualitatively understand the process and reasoning behind ontology selection and reuse, with a particular focus on the under-researched social and community aspects of ontology quality. Interviews were used to understand how ontologists and knowledge engineers in different domains search for, evaluate and select an ontology for reuse. This paper is an extended version of [11] and aims to study and explore (1) the main characteristics of a reusable ontology, (2) the main metrics used to evaluate the quality of an ontology before selecting it for reuse, and (3) the link between community related metrics e.g. who has built the ontology, who has used the ontology, etc. and ontology evaluation for selection and reuse.

2 Background

Ontology evaluation is one of the most popular topics in the field of ontology engineering. It is used to refer to several different activities including detecting faults in an ontology, assessing an ontology's quality, measuring its fitness for a specific purpose, etc. There are many different ways of defining ontology evaluation; one of the most popular and also the earliest definitions was provided by [12] where the term evaluation was used to refer to the technical judgment of an ontology, considering different aspects of it, such as the definitions of its components, documentation and software environment. According to this definition, evaluation encompasses validation and verification; ontology validation is mainly concerned with the correctness of an ontology whereas ontology verification is more concerned with determining how well an ontology corresponds to what it should represent [13]. In the other word, ontology validation focuses on building the correct ontology whereas ontology verification is about building an ontology correctly [14].

Ontology evaluation has also been widely defined as the process of determining the adequacy and quality of an ontology for being used for a specific goal and in a specific context [15]. This definition is used to link the process of ontology evaluation to ontology selection. The aim of ontology selection is to identify an ontology, an ontology module or a set of ontologies that satisfy a certain set of criteria or selection requirements [16]. Some consider ontology evaluation as the core to ontology selection and argue that ontology evaluation is influenced by different components of the selection process e.g. selection criteria, type of output, the libraries that the selection is based on, etc. [15]. The term "assessment" is also used to refer to this particular definition of ontology evaluation and is commonly defined as the activity of checking and judging an ontology against different user requirements like usability, usefulness, etc. [17]. Unlike the first definition of the ontology evaluation [12], in which the developer team is responsible for validating and verifying an ontology, ontology assessment and evaluation for selection is done by the end users.

Ontology evaluation can also refer to a function or an activity that aims to map an ontology or a component of an ontology e.g. its concepts to a score or a number, e.g. usually in range of 0 to 1 [18]. The main aim of these types of processes/functions is to measure and assess the quality of an ontology with regards to a set of predefined metrics or requirements [19]. This definition is somehow similar to what [17] define as ontology quality assurance that refers to the activity of examining every process carried out and every product built during the ontology development process and making sure that the level of their quality is satisfactory. Moreover, and according to the literature, the expressions "Ontology Evaluation" and "Ontology Ranking" are sometimes used interchangeably. While they both tend to refer to a set of similar criteria, for us, ontology ranking is the process of sorting ontologies in a descending order of quality, according to the score that is assigned to them in the evaluation process.

There are many different reasons why ontologies are evaluated. The main goals can be categorized as either for quality assessment, for tracking progress in ontology evolution, or for ranking, each of these are briefly described next.

Evaluation for correctness; refers to those approaches that aim to measure the logical and formal correctness of an ontology content [20, 21]. One of the most well-known applications for evaluating the correctness of ontologies is OntOlogy Pitfall Scanner (OOPS) [22]. OOPS is based on a catalogue of 40 bad practices or pitfalls that can happen in ontology development and it is able to automatically detect them [22]. ODEval is also developed by [23] to evaluate knowledge representation of RDF(S), OWL, and DAML + OIL concept taxonomies by capturing different circularity and redundancy problems as well as partition errors.

Evaluation for quality assessment; assessing the quality of ontologies is another main reason for evaluating them. This type of evaluation is mostly done by end users and helps in the process of ontology selection for reuse. Ontology assessment is a very challenging task both because of lack of generic quality evaluation solution and metric and also because determining the right elements of quality to evaluate is difficult [24].

Evaluation for tracking progress in ontology evolution [19, 25]; the aim of this type of evaluation is to track different characteristics and changes of ontologies over time and over different versions [26]. ONTO-EVOAL approach, for example, uses patter modelling to make sure that consistency and quality is maintained in the process of ontology evolution [27].

Evaluation for Ranking [21]; search and selection systems in the field of ontology engineering usually show a ranked list of ontologies in output. To do that, they should first be able to evaluate ontologies according to different query-dependent and query independent criteria, then assign some score to the ontologies based on how well they are covering or meeting those criteria, and finally rank ontologies based on their score. In Swoogle, for example, a PageRank [28] like algorithm is used to calculate the rank of each ontology based on the number of link from and to those ontologies [29].

Ontology evaluation is important in the ontology development process, whether it is built from scratch, automatically or by reusing other ontologies [30]. While building an ontology from scratch, developers need to evaluate the outcome ontology, to measure its quality [31], to check if it meets their application requirements [30] and also to identify the potential refinement steps [32]. Evaluation is also helpful in checking the homogeneity and consistency of an ontology when it is automatically populated from different resources [26, 30]. Building an ontology from scratch is a very costly as well as a time-consuming task [33, 34]; therefore, ontologists are urged to consider reusing exiting ontologies before building a new one [35]. Ontology evaluation is and has always been a major concept when it comes ontology reuse [36]. Some argue that ontology evaluation is one of the main issues that should be addressed if ontologies are to become widely adopted and reused by the community [32, 33, 36, 37].

Moreover, the number of ontologies on the web has been increasing rapidly [30] and users usually face multiple ontologies when they need to choose or use one in their everyday activities [19, 32, 38]. Before using an ontology in an application or selecting it for reuse, ontologists have to assess its quality and correctness and also compare it with the other available ones in the domain. This is when ontology evaluation comes into the picture; ontology evaluation is believed to be the core to the ontology selection process [16] and is used to select the best or the most appropriate ontology among many other candidates in a domain [32]. Evaluating an ontology is considered as a complicated process [19, 39]; it is believed that failure to evaluate ontologies and to choose the right ontology might lead to using the ones with a lower quality [19].

There are various ontology evaluation methods and several ways of classifying them in the literature. According to [32], ontology evaluation can be done in four major ways: (1) evaluating an ontology by comparing it to a "golden standard", (2) evaluating an ontology by comparing it to a source of data, (3) evaluating an ontology by running it in an application as part of a system and evaluating the resulting performance, and (4) asking human experts to evaluate an ontology against a set of predefined quality criteria.

Beside the above-mentioned methods, that are very popular in the literature, there are some other ways of classifying ontology evaluation approaches. For example, they can be classified based on the type of the metrics they use to assess ontologies. Some approaches are based on qualitative metrics and tend to rely on expert users' judgement and ratings about an ontology or a module in an ontology [40]. Qualitative approaches can also be used to evaluate an ontology based on the principles that are/were used in its construction [35]. Other evaluation approaches in the literature are based on different quantitative criteria about different aspects of ontologies such as its structure, content, etc. These approaches, that are also known as formal rational approaches, are usually concerned with technical and economic aspects of ontologies and use different goal based strategies [33].

Moreover, ontology evaluation approaches can be glass-box or black-box. Glass-box approaches tend to evaluate the internal content and structure of ontologies [36]; they are blamed for not predicting how ontology might perform in an application. In contrast, black-box approaches do not explicitly use knowledge of the internal structure of ontologies and focus on the quality of an ontology performance and results [36]. Ontologies can also be evaluated as a whole or according to their different layers e.g. data level, taxonomy level, application level, etc. [34] has divided the concept of ontology quality to two broad types: "Total Quality" and "Partial Quality". Some believe that evaluating an ontology as a whole, specially automatically, is not possible or practical, especially considering the complex structure of ontologies [32].

From all the methods, metric-based approaches (4) are very popular and different researchers have attempted to introduce various metrics and measures that can be used to evaluate ontologies and help in the decision-making process for ontology selection. The aim of this method, that is also called featured-based approach, is to offer a quantitative perspective of evaluating ontologies by gathering data and meta-data on different aspect of the ontology [26].

Ontometric [41], as one of the most popular examples of this approach, consists of a detailed set of 160 criteria to examine different dimensions of ontologies namely content, language, ontology construction methodologies, costs, and tools. While many of the criteria in metric-based evaluation approaches aim to measure different internal components of an ontology e.g. structure, content, coverage, etc., some of these have focused on non-ontological and social aspects [39] of ontologies like popularity [42–44].

Besides how ontologies are built and what they are covering or even not covering, how they are used by communities is one of the dimensions and important aspects of ontologies that can be used to evaluate or select them. [14] define user-based ontology evaluation as the process of evaluating an ontology though users' experiences and by capturing different subjective information about ontologies. The term "Social Quality" has also been used to reflect the existence of ontologies as well as agents and users in communities [24] and refers to the level of agreement about an ontology and among different participants or members of a community [39]. [39] argue that there is a link between the quality of an ontology and community approval and participation in its evolution.

Popularity or acceptance are two of the most popular and used terms in the literature to refer to the social aspects of ontologies' quality; however, there is still no consensus on the definition of these terms. Popularity and acceptance tend to be mostly used to refer to the number of times an ontology has been viewed or used in a specific repository. NCBO Ontology Recommender [45] for example, calculates the popularity of an ontology by checking the presence of the ontology in well-known repositories as well as looking into the number of visits or pageviews to an ontology in ontology repositories in a recent specific period [45]. In the paper by [24] the authors also refer to the term history to indicate the number of times an ontology has been used.

The second definition of popularity is based on applying the PageRank algorithm [28] to ontology engineering field and focuses on the import feature of ontologies. [43] for example has defined the term "direct popularity" as the number of ontologies importing a given ontology. [44] used the same definition to define what they call popularity, that for them is measured by considering how much an ontology is referenced by others. As a part of the authority metric in [46], authors have mentioned a metric called citation and have defined it as the number of occurrence of daml:sameClassAs, rdfs:seeAlso, owl:imports in a given ontology.

Social quality plays an important role in ontology evaluation for selection and reuse. According to a study that was conducted by [47], relying on the experiences of other users for evaluating ontologies will lessen the efforts needed to assess an ontology and reduce the problems that users face while selecting an ontology. [39] also highlight the importance of relying on the wisdom of crowd in ontology evaluation and believe that improving the overall quality of ontological content on the web is a shared responsibility within a community.

3 Methodology

Semi-structured interviews with ontologists and knowledge engineers were conducted to investigate the thinking behind and the processes commonly involved in evaluating ontologies for their reuse. Purposive sampling was used to find the experts in the field of ontology engineering [48]. Different sampling strategy namely intensity sampling was applied to find the ontologies that have been reused and then to interview the individuals who had built or had reused those ontologies [49]. Moreover, homogenous sampling was used to find different ontology related research groups in different organizations and universities working in different domains.

Table 1. Domain expertise of ontologists and knowledge engineers interviewed.

Code	Domain, organization, or project
NBI1	Ontologist/IBM, Smarter Planet Project
NBI2	Professor, Manufacturing Informatics
NBI3	Ontology engineer/Semantic Web
NBI4	Researcher/Laboratory for Applied Ontology
NBI5	Researcher/Smart Cities, Geo Ontologies
SB1	Ontology developer/Industry, W3C, NHS
SB2	Researcher/BioPortal
SB3	CEO and ontology developer/Bioinformatics
SB4	Lecturer/Computing Science and Biology
SB5	Research scientist/Protégé group
NBI6	Researcher/Industrial ontologies
BI1	Group leader/Bioinformatics, Gene ontology
BI2	Researcher/BioPortal
BI3	Ontology Developer/Bioinformatics, Gene ontology
BI4	Researcher/Biomedical Informatics

The suitability of the interview questions was tested in a pilot phase to establish the relevance of the interview questions to the research. Five ontologists and knowledge experts took part in this first pilot round of interviews. All these interviews were recorded, with permission, and were transcribed and thematically analyzed. The pilot phase was also helpful in determining the time it takes to conduct the interview as well as the flow and order of the interview questions.

15 researchers with different levels of expertise and knowledge engineering backgrounds were interviewed. As it is seen in the Table 1, four out of the fifteen interviewees had only worked in the biomedical field, five had some biomedical experience but had also worked in other fields such as computer science, and the rest of the interviewees were mostly involved in manufacturing, smart cities, etc. The semi-structured interview protocol focused on how each individual (i) built, (ii) searched for, (iii) evaluated and (iv) reused ontologies. Interviews ranged from 20 to 60 min, all of which were conducted via Skype. Interviews were recorded, and the interviewer took field notes during the interview. Field notes and transcriptions were coded using NVivo.

Interviews were conducted until no new information or theme was found [50] and the conceptual saturation was reached. The sample size can also be justified by some of the previous similar research on ontology evaluation for example the survey that was conducted by [51], which had 10 participants. Based upon the research questions, we began by coding for the following themes:

1. Building a reusable ontology
2. Characteristics of a reusable ontology
3. Finding a reusable ontology
4. Evaluating/trusting/selecting ontologies
5. The importance of community.

4 Findings

According to the interview findings, metrics for evaluating the quality of an ontology for reuse can be classified into the following categories:

- Metrics based on different internal components of ontologies including content, structure, coverage, etc.
- Metrics related to different metadata about an ontology such as methodology used, availability of documentation, language, etc.
- Metrics based on the social aspects of ontologies like community, popularity, ontology developer team, etc.

The following parts of this paper moves on to describe in detail different metrics that were considered and used by the participants of this study in the evaluation process as well as how they referred to the community to search for, find and evaluate an ontology for reuse.

4.1   Evaluation Based on Internal Aspects of Ontologies

As it is seen in the literature, many of the evaluation methods are based on different internal components of ontologies such as content, structure, etc. When asked about the quality of ontologies and ontology evaluation, some of the interviewees made a link between ontology content and definitions and their quality. SB3 and SB4 for example pointed out that they check the correctness of an ontology's content before selecting it for reuse. Ontologists and knowledge engineers not only care about the content of an ontology, but they consider other content related metrics such as consistency, correctness, coverage, etc. NBI1 for example mentioned coverage and the relationship between concepts as two of the metrics that he uses for ontology evaluation. Some of the interviewees mentioned being "well-structured" as one of the characteristics of a good, reusable ontology. According to them, a well-structured ontology can be defined as an ontology that has some rich (NBI4) and correct (SB1) connections between its categories. Ontology syntax, clear definitions and scope were among the other internal characteristics of ontologies that can be used for evaluating them.

4.2   Evaluation Based on Metadata About Ontologies

Besides the internal components of ontologies, wide range of metadata and additional elements of information about different aspects of ontologies can also be used for their evaluation. Many of the respondents found having access to additional information on ontologies, both in form of labels and comments for/on different ontology components or as external documentation, to be very helpful. Moreover, some of the interviewees mentioned that before selecting an ontology for reuse, they would like to know if the ontology is based on any standard, methodology or a common framework. Respondents also emphasized the importance of reusing other ontologies while building a new one and said that before selecting an ontology for reuse, they will check and see if the ontology has reused other ontologies and if it is based on upper level ontologies. Language that an ontology is built in and its size were among the other metadata about ontologies that can be used for their evaluation.

4.3   Evaluation Based on Community and Social Aspects

Communities can affect different aspects of the process of ontology selection for reuse, from how users search for and find reusable ontologies to how they evaluate those ontologies before selecting them for reuse. This section will first discuss how community and social aspects of ontologies help in the ontology search and discovery process and will then move on in exploring how different social related metrics can be used in the evaluation process.

Community and Ontology Search. One of the fundamental objectives of the interviews was to explore how ontologists and knowledge engineers search for reusable ontologies? Consequently, the question "how do you find the ontology you want to reuse?" was asked and while the researcher was expecting to hear about some of the popular search engines in ontology engineering domain like Swoogle, BioPortal, etc., literature and published papers were mentioned by many of the interviewees as one of their main sources of finding the ontologies they need.

Interviewee NBI4 for example, blamed his domain for lack of good and well-established repositories for ontologies and said that "I go to the literature". Another interviewee, SB3, also emphasized the significant role of literature in the process of searching for ontologies and mentioned that "reading publications around the ontology" is a very good method to help find the ontology, especially if someone is new to the field.

Besides helping to find a reusable ontology, some of the other interviewees stated that they use the literature and research papers as a tool to evaluate the quality of an ontology. Respondent NBI4 pointed out:

"If an ontology is good and is used, you find a cite in the literature."

Being based on published research papers will not only affect the quality of an ontology, but according to some of the respondents, will also affect the popularity of an ontology; BI4 for example stated:

"Popular ontologies are better ontologies, people are just familiar with popular ontologies so whenever you go to any ontology related conference, you will always have a workshop or a paper that talks about the ontology."

Community and Ontology Evaluation. As was highlighted in Sect. 2, various work has looked at the quality and evaluation of ontologies, however while some of the papers have attempted to cover the social aspects of ontology evaluation, none have gone further than measuring popularity, authority, and history of ontologies and almost all of them have neglected the other interactions in the community that can affect the way ontologies are evaluated, selected, and reused. Hence to explore the role of community in ontology sharing and reuse, participants were asked how interactions with people in their domain may affect the way they tend to evaluate an ontology for reuse. According to the interviews, participants not only use the community to evaluate an ontology before selecting it for reuse, but some of them also evaluate the ontologies they are building by the feedback they receive from the community.

Build Related Information. Several researchers mentioned the importance of different types of build related information such as who/which organization has built the ontology, what the ontology has been built for e.g. the use case, who are the different stakeholders of the ontology, how the ontology was built (e.g. in collaboration), etc. Interestingly, one of the first things interviewees would say was that to evaluate an ontology, they will ask themselves if they know the developer of the ontology?

Interviewee BI3 for example emphasized the importance of knowing the developer team and its effect on the reuse process:

"I have to say, in reusing thing, there is often politics and connections are as important as anything else. So, it is not always the best one that wins."

He also added, quality of an ontology may sometimes come second:

"You know there might be constraint in terms of I may not like a particular ontology but because a bunch of other people are using it and I want to standardize with them, I might use it anyway."

Respondent SB4 also brought up the issue of trusting the developer team:

"Science is a social enterprise, I mean this is how everything works in science, you know if you look at a paper, do you trust the paper? you look at the authors first and then you read the paper and then you pick about what they have done but yes I mean it is a major criteria, major quality criteria, it may or may not right; it is a bit of old boys club but yes that is how people make decision. I normally read the definitions and then go to other things; do I trust the people who are making it?"

Besides the information about the developer team or organization, some of the respondents would consider the reasons that ontology was built and used for before selecting an ontology. They were also interested in having some information about the stakeholders of the ontologies. Interviewee SB3 said:

"Completely separated from the people developing it, are there other people who uses this ontology beyond just that group, that tells you something about it. I think also finding out how they are using it, is also important, you know what data is being annotated with those ontology is also important question, but I have some data and I know I want to integrate with something done in another institute, what is the ontology there they are using, that is also important, so I think there is a list of the things you want to check!"

Regular Updates and Maintenance. Ontology maintainability is one of the significant metrics while evaluating the quality of an ontology and before selecting it for reuse. In the interviews, there were numerous examples of linking the quality of an ontology to how regularly it is updated and maintained. For some participants like NBI3, regularity of updates was the first thing that they would look at when evaluating a particular ontology:

"Somebody build ontology during his research in 1998 and he stored it on the web and then he left it, it is available but not updated, things will get obsolete very soon so we make sure to use the ontologies which are regularly updated, it is the first thing."

Some of the respondents like SB3 compared maintenance with some of the very popular quality metrics in the literature like coverage and said:

"Does it have my terms? I think is important but there are many others that you need to consider when you are picking an ontology beyond just does it have the words in ontology, about maintenance, do they update regularly, do they release regularly? do they have a record of doing that? How responsive they are to updates when you need new terms? all that sort of stuff. If they are publishing it once every two years it is probably not a good ontology."

Other participants like BI1 firmly believed that updates and maintenance play a very important role in their domain and said:

"No way that an ontology is keeping on in biology not getting updated, biology is changing too fast so all the relevant ontologies in biology are getting updated."

Interviewee NBI2 also made a link between the nature of the domain that he is working in and the necessity of regular updates:

"It is about flexibility, if you want to, in manufacturing business things are changing all the time, so you need solutions that are easy and flexible to stay in, to stay relevant to what you are doing tomorrow as well as what you are trying to do today."

Interviewee BI3 compared the ontology engineering with software engineering and said:

"If you are going to reuse a piece of open source software you will do the same thing, you will open the GitHub website and say you know if you looked in it and nobody updated it or anything in three years, you might think no; whereas if it looks like there is an active ongoing community, you will think yes, if I have problems I can ask people and I can get bugs fixed."

BI4 believed that there is a link between the popularity of an ontology and the regularity of updating it and said:

"It might be useful to use popular ones because there are the ones that are mostly updated so gene ontology has a release I think every day or every 12 h, so the popular ontologies are the ones that are most updated."

Not only the regularity of updates is important, but also how people deal with it is the other important issue. Respondent SB3 talked about the importance of having an update mechanism and said:

"I think in the field that I am working, there are other challenges, one of which is how you deal with update mechanism of ontologies, if you annotate data to ontology which is typically use case for how you keep up-to-date with the fact that ontologies change reasonably often, you might have a big database of data, that you used the data in, new ontologies come along, the effect the way the data has been represented in your database, gotta have a update mechanisms for dealing with that and that can be tricky actually, it is not as simple often as swapping things out when something gets made obsolete, it is replaced with other things, you have to deal with."

Responsiveness. Responsiveness of the ontology developer team was among one of the other widely mentioned criteria when evaluating the quality of ontologies for reuse. Some of the respondents argued that not only knowing the developer team or organization is important, but also having an active ongoing community and their willingness to collaborate, evolve and develop the ontology further is an important factor when assessing an ontology. Interviewee BI3 put it in this way when he was asked about the importance of responsiveness:

"I would say it is definitely high up; I mean having someone at the other end of line that you feel that you can trust is definitely very important. If it looks like there is an active ongoing community, you will think yes if I have problems I can ask people and I can get bugs fixed."

SB5 used one of the popular ontologies in her field as an example and added:

"For example, the fact that the Gene ontology has a huge community behind it is important because it means that they have a curation process in place and quality assurance and so on; so that kind of gives more confidence that the ontology is as good as it can be, it is not perfect for sure but I mean that it is vetted by the community."

Respondent BI1 chose responsiveness as the first quality metric he would consider for evaluating an ontology and compared it with one of the very popular ontology evaluation metrics, that is availability of documentation:

"I would say the responsive of the team obviously is the top-quality metric for me, because nothing is perfect but if something gets improved then it will get good like if you have a question, you need to add a term, something does not make sense, you contact them, they answer and they answer in a constructive way; this is good because all the ontologies are work in progress, there is no finished ontology in my domain."

Popularity. When asked about the link between popularity of an ontology and its quality, participants had interesting thoughts and responses. Most of the interviewees defined popularity as the number of times an ontology has been viewed or used in a repository. However, some of the interviewees doubted the importance of this metric. The responses can be classified into the following groups: (1) those who were against this metric, (2) those who liked popularity as a quality metric for ontology evaluation but did not agree with the way it was being computed and (3) those who found this metric useful.

The first group of respondents believed that the popularity of an ontology or the number of times it has been used is not that important. As interviewee BI1 would put it:

"To me it would not be very important except if two ontologies are really very equal in everything else, I will take the most used ones, but I do not think, it is not really relevant to me, if it is the right tool for the job, it is the right tool!"

It was also believed that the number of times an ontology is used depends on different factors such as its size, level of specialization and the domain that it is built in and cannot be considered as a metric to measure its quality. According to interviewee BI1:

"Some ontologies are more specialized, so less people use them because it corresponds to a very special need, but may this people, are the right people and are using it well."

Interviewee SB3 also linked the use of an ontology to its size and added:

"If there is a small ontology but really focused on representing an area that has not been done before but it is correct, it is absolutely correct, I think that is perfectly reasonable, even if it is not widely used."

Some other interviewees like NBI5 found popularity a helpful metric, but believed that it is highly dependent on the domain that the ontology is used in:

"It depends on the domain that it has been reused in, if it is just medical domain, it is difficult to say that it is a reusable ontology!"

The second group agreed on the necessity of having such a metric to identify the more popular ontologies in different domains but were not sure about the usefulness of the current methods that are used to measure the popularity. As interviewee NBI3 would put it:

"How many times an ontology is viewed will not help you, I may click just for exploration, and I will say it is not my thing and I don't want it; it shows how catchy the term is or how important, how regularly, how often this term is chosen, but it does not mean the use of the ontology; so, I think there should be some other way."

BI4 used a very interesting personal experience to prove the inaccuracy of the current techniques of measuring the popularity:

"When we were visualizing all the user exploration on ontologies on BioPortal, and we found that gene ontology is not accessed that much using BioPortal and I thought that it was very surprising because the gene ontology is very famous and then I found out because there is a gene ontology browser called AmiGo, and their visualizer tool is much better than BioPortal visualization of gene ontology, so people generally go to gene ontology website and lunch the AmiGo browser and go to gene ontology there, so you can say that gene ontology is much more accepted but if you just look at the clicks (in BioPortal) and you might say that gene ontology is not that much famous."

Interviewee SB3 also thought that having a quality metric like popularity is a step in the right direction but believed that it might be misleading by causing a snowball effect; according to him:

"I can see that you can also putting a little metric for usage or browsing or how many people read these things, that is a kind of useful but it does not tell you the whole picture, you know you can end up with a false signal there; you recommended an ontology because it is useful because someone uses it and then you recommend it so someone else uses it and so on and so on, what I mean, so you are getting in that cycle of, it grows and grows!"

The last and also the minority group were those who thought it worth having a metric like popularity and highlighted the importance of community acceptance. According to interviewee NBI4:

"If a community is using the ontology and is happy with it, I take thing to account, so I try to reuse or to do something to extend it or maybe very careful on changing it. I need to have motivations because after all ontologies should have people working in the domain and so if they are happy with that one and I see things that are no good, I point it out and I may suggest an extension, whatever but I try to reuse what I have."

The other definition of this metric that focuses on the link between popularity and the number of imported ontologies was also brought up by some of the respondents. NBI5 for example, made a link between the quality of an ontology and the fact that the ontology has reused other ontologies and said:

"The quality of an ontology depends on the relation between the ontology to upper level ontologies; the more 'same-as', 'equivalent-as' links I can find in an ontology. It also can be seen as a sign or a feature of the ontology that can be reused because if it is 'same -as' a concept that we already know, then it can be replaced."

NBI6 also believed that reusing some of the ontologies are inevitable and not importing will seem as a negative impression:

"Whenever I have an ontology where there is a person, I will never ever create my own person class, I will always reuse FOAF. I think it would be ridiculous to create my own class and some of those are very very strong class definition, so it will always worth reusing and I think it will be even mistake by ontology engineer to develop their own class and for me, if I see an ontology doing that, I will get a negative impression."

5 Discussion

The notion of ontology quality and the process of evaluating it is one of the most significant and also complicated components in the field of ontology engineering. The challenge of choosing the right or best ontology for a task or reuse is what ontologists and knowledge engineers face on a daily basis. Despite the importance of this matter and the widespread research on this topic, there are still many unanswered questions and challenges in ontology evaluation. Interviewees have shown a range of different responses when they were asked about the ontology evaluation process; some of them mentioned the different well-known internal quality metrics such as ontology content, structure, and others; however, and surprisingly, the main focus of most of the responses was on different metadata and social aspects related to ontologies. The scope of this study has particularly focused on the ways communities can help in the process of ontology selection and evaluation.

As it was discussed before, community related factors such as reputation of the developer team or organization in the domain and regularity of updates were highlighted as some very important metrics to be considered when evaluating and selecting an ontology for reuse. The results of this study have also found that the quality of ontologies is generally considered to be limited; ontologists and knowledge engineers have pointed out that either way there isn't such a thing as a complete or finished ontology, hence ontologists often need to count on the responsiveness of the ontology developer team and organization as well as their attitude toward the requests for changes. However, this has not previously been described and most of the existing studies have failed to cover and analyze the association between ontology quality and evaluation and the role of the community in that process.

Ontology popularity [42] is one of the most commonly defined and used social quality metric in the literature and many of the prior studies have noted the importance of this metric. However, some of the interviewees doubted the link between the quality of an ontology and its popularity. According to the interviews, respondents care more about the projects that the ontology has been or is being used in, compared to the number of times it was used. Regarding the second definition of popularity, that is more about the linkage and the citation between ontologies [46], it seems that further research should be undertaken to investigate the importance of this factor and the way it can be employed to calculate popularity of an ontology.

Overall, the evidence from this exploratory study suggests that there is a clear interest for community-based ontology evaluation and the need for relevant metrics. Further research is needed to confirm the quality metrics suggested in these research interviews and what their relative importance may be, whether there are differences in ontology engineering domains, or other important idiosyncrasies deserving further attention. To provide more generalizable findings for this research, the next stage of our research agenda will be to conduct large scale data collection via a survey targeting ontology engineers from heterogeneous domains. The expected outcome would be to introduce a community-based quality metrics as well as to design and implement suggestions and guidelines that will help in designing and implementing ontologies that can be more easily found and reused, based on community measures identified through this ongoing research work.

6 Conclusion

The main goal of the current study was to determine and explore the set of steps that ontologists and knowledge engineers tend to take in different phases of ontology selection process, from ontology search and discovery to ontology evaluation and selection. The study has found that while internal characteristics of ontologies like content, structure and consistency are considered in the evaluation process, ontology evaluation is mostly focused on non-ontological features of ontologies such as metadata about ontologies, social and community related quality metrics. It was also shown that ontologies are usually considered as incomplete ongoing projects; therefore, it is important to know and also to trust the ontology developer and maintenance team or organization before selecting it for reuse. These findings enhance understanding of the metrics used in the evaluation process and it is hoped that they can be of help to the community in the ontology selection process. A natural progression of this work would be a framework of non-ontological quality metrics for ontology evaluation and selection.

References

1. Shadbolt, N., Berners-Lee, T., Hall, W.: The semantic web revisited. IEEE Intell. Syst. **21** (3), 96 (2006)
2. El Kadiri, S., Kiritsis, D.: Ontologies in the context of product lifecycle management: state of the art literature review. Int. J. Prod. Res. **53**(18), 5657–5668 (2015)
3. Bürger, T., Simperl, E.: Measuring the benefits of ontologies. In: Meersman, R., Tari, Z., Herrero, P. (eds.) OTM 2008. LNCS, vol. 5333, pp. 584–594. Springer, Heidelberg (2008). https://doi.org/10.1007/978-3-540-88875-8_82
4. Ding, Y., Foo, S.: Ontology research and development. Part 2 - a review of ontology mapping and evolving. J. Inf. Sci. **28**(5), 375–388 (2002)
5. Alani, H., Brewster, C., Shadbolt, N.: Ranking ontologies with AKTiveRank. In: Cruz, I., et al. (eds.) ISWC 2006. LNCS, vol. 4273, pp. 1–15. Springer, Heidelberg (2006). https://doi.org/10.1007/11926078_1
6. Simperl, E.: Reusing ontologies on the semantic web: a feasibility study. Data Knowl. Eng. **68**(10), 905–925 (2009)
7. Uschold, M., et al.: Ontology reuse and application. Form. Ontol. Inf. Syst. **179**, 192 (1998)
8. Presutti, V., Lodi, G., Nuzzolese, A., Gangemi, A., Peroni, S., Asprino, L.: The role of ontology design patterns in linked data projects. In: Comyn-Wattiau, I., Tanaka, K., Song, I.-Y., Yamamoto, S., Saeki, M. (eds.) ER 2016. LNCS, vol. 9974, pp. 113–121. Springer, Cham (2016). https://doi.org/10.1007/978-3-319-46397-1_9
9. Annamalai, M., Sterling, L.: Guidelines for constructing reusable domain ontologies. In: 3rd Workshop on Ontologies in Agent Systems Sofitel, no. July, pp. 71–74 (2003)
10. Bontas, E.P., Mochol, M., Tolksdorf, R.: Case studies on ontology reuse. In: Proceedings of IKNOW05 International Conference on Knowledge Management, vol. 74, pp. 345–353 (2005)
11. Talebpour, M., Sykora, M.D., Jackson, T.W.: The role of community and social metrics in ontology evaluation: an interview study of ontology reuse. In: 9th International Joint Conference on Knowledge Discovery, Knowledge Engineering and Knowledge Management, pp. 119–127 (2017)
12. Gómez-Pérez, A.: Some ideas and examples to evaluate ontologies. In: CAIA, p. 299 (1995)
13. Gómez-Pérez, A.: Evaluation of taxonomic knowledge in ontologies and knowledge bases (1999)
14. Hlomani, H., Stacey, D.: Approaches, methods, metrics, measures, and subjectivity in ontology evaluation: a survey. Semant. Web J. **1**, 1–11 (2014)
15. Fernández, M., Cantador, I., Castells, P.: CORE: a tool for collaborative ontology reuse and evaluation. In: CEUR Workshop Proceedings, vol. 179 (2006)
16. Sabou, M., Lopez, V., Motta, E., Uren, V.: Ontology selection: ontology evaluation on the real semantic web. In: 4th International EON Workshop, Evaluation of Ontologies for the Web, EON 2006, vol. 179 (2006)

17. Suarez-Figueroa, M.C., Gómez-Pérez, A.: First attempt towards a standard glossary of ontology engineering terminology. In: 8th International Conference on Terminology and Knowledge Engineering, TKE 2008, pp. 1–15 (2008)
18. Brank, J., Mladenic, D., Grobelnik, M.: Gold standard based ontology evaluation using instance assignment. In: Proceedings of EON 2006 Workshop (2006)
19. Yu, J., Thom, J.A., Tam, A.: Requirements-oriented methodology for evaluating ontologies. Inf. Syst. **34**(8), 686–711 (2009)
20. Jonquet, C., Musen, M.A., Shah, N.H.: Building a biomedical ontology recommender web service. Biomed. Seman. **1**, S1 (2010)
21. Duque-Ramos, A., et al.: Evaluation of the OQuaRE framework for ontology quality. Expert Syst. Appl. **40**(7), 2696–2703 (2013)
22. Poveda-Villalón, M., Gómez-Pérez, A., Suárez-Figueroa, M.C.: Oops!(ontology pitfall scanner!): an on-line tool for ontology evaluation. Semant. Web Inf. Syst. **10**(2), 7–24 (2014)
23. Corcho, Ó., Gómez-Pérez, A., González-Cabero, R., Suárez-Figueroa, M.C.: ODEval: a tool for evaluating RDF(S), DAML+OIL, and OWL concept taxonomies. In: Bramer, M., Devedzic, V. (eds.) AIAI 2004. IIFIP, vol. 154, pp. 369–382. Springer, Boston, MA (2004). https://doi.org/10.1007/1-4020-8151-0_32
24. Burton-Jones, A., Storey, V.C., Sugumaran, V., Ahluwalia, P.: A semiotic metrics suite for assessing the quality of ontologies. Data Knowl. Eng. **55**(1), 84–102 (2005)
25. Yang, Z., Zhang, D., Ye, C.: Evaluation metrics for ontology complexity and evolution analysis. In: Proceedings - IEEE International Conference on E-Business Engineering, ICEBE 2006, no. 90204010, pp. 162–169 (2006)
26. Arpinar, I.B., Giriloganathan, K, Aleman-Meza, B.: Ontology quality by detection of conflicts in metadata. In: CEUR Workshop Proceedings, vol. 179 (2006)
27. Djedidi, R., Aufaure, M.A.: ONTO-EVOAL an ontology evolution approach guided by pattern modeling and quality evaluation. In: Proceedings of 6th International Symposium, Sofia, Bulgaria, 15–19 February 2010, FoIKS 2010, vol. 6 (2010)
28. Page, L., Brin, S., Motwani, R., Winograd, T.: The PageRank citation ranking: bringing order to the web. World Wide Web Internet Web Inf. Syst. **54**(1999-66), 1–17 (1998)
29. Ding, L., Finin, T., Reddivari, P., Cost, R.S., Sachs, J.: Swoogle : a search and metadata engine for the semantic web. In: ACM Conference on Information and Knowledge Management, pp. 652–659 (2004)
30. Tartir, S., Arpinar, I.B., Sheth, A.P.: Ontological evaluation and validation. In: Poli, R., Healy, M., Kameas, A. (eds.) Theory and Applications of Ontology: Computer Applications, pp. 115–130. Springer, Dordrecht (2010). https://doi.org/10.1007/978-90-481-8847-5_5
31. Ning, H.N.H., Shihan, D.S.D.: Structure-based ontology evaluation. In: 2006 EEE International Conference on E-Business Engineering, ICEBE 2006, pp. 2–7 (2006)
32. Brank, J., Grobelnik, M., Mladenic, D.: A survey of ontology evaluation techniques. In: Conference on Data Mining and Data Warehouses, SiKDD 2005, p. 4 (2005)
33. Maiga, G., Ddembe, W.: A flexible biomedical ontology selection tool. In: Kizza, M., Lynch, K., Nath, R., Aisbett, J., Vir, P. (eds.) Strengthening the Role of ICT in Development, vol. 5, pp. 171–189. Fountain Publishers (2009)
34. Bandeira, J., Bittencourt, I.I., Espinheira, P., Isotani, S.: FOCA: a methodology for ontology evaluation, vol. 3, pp. 1–3 (2016)
35. Brewster, C., Alani, H., Dasmahapatra, S., Wilks, Y.: Data driven ontology evaluation. In: 4th International Conference on Language Resources and Evaluation, LREC 2004, p. 4 (2004)
36. Gangemi, A., Catenacci, C., Ciaramita, M., Lehmann, J.: Qood grid: a metaontology-based framework for ontology evaluation and selection. In: Proceedings of EON 2006, vol. 4011, pp. 140–154 (2006)

37. Obrst, L., Ceusters, W., Mani, I., Ray, S., Smith, B.: The evaluation of ontologies. Seman. Web, 139–158 (2007)
38. Yu, J., Thom, J.A., Tam, A.: Ontology evaluation using Wikipedia categories for browsing. In: Proceedings of the Sixteenth ACM Conference on Information and Knowledge Management, CIKM 2007, p. 223 (2007)
39. McDaniel, M., Storey, V.C., Sugumaran, V.: The role of community acceptance in assessing ontology quality. In: Métais, E., Meziane, F., Saraee, M., Sugumaran, V., Vadera, S. (eds.) NLDB 2016. LNCS, vol. 9612, pp. 24–36. Springer, Cham (2016). https://doi.org/10.1007/978-3-319-41754-7_3
40. Porzel, R., Malaka, R.: A Task-based approach for ontology evaluation. Biomed. Semant. (2004)
41. Lozano-Tello, A., Gomez-Perez, A.: ONTOMETRIC: a method to choose the appropriate ontology. Database Manag. 15(2), 1–18 (2004)
42. Martínez-Romero, M., Vázquez-Naya, J.M., Pereira, J., Pazos, A.: BiOSS: a system for biomedical ontology selection. Comput. Methods Programs Biomed. 114(1), 125–140 (2014)
43. Fernández, M., Overbeeke, C., Sabou, M., Motta, E.: What makes a good ontology? A case-study in fine-grained knowledge reuse. In: Gómez-Pérez, A., Yu, Y., Ding, Y. (eds.) ASWC 2009. LNCS, vol. 5926, pp. 61–75. Springer, Heidelberg (2009). https://doi.org/10.1007/978-3-642-10871-6_5
44. Wang, X., Guo, L., Fang, J.: Automated ontology selection based on description logic. In: Proceedings of 2008 12th International Conference on Computer Supported Cooperative Work in Design, CSCWD, vol. 1, pp. 482–487 (2008)
45. Martínez-Romero, M., Jonquet, C., O'connor, M.J., Graybeal, J., Pazos, A., Musen, M.A.: NCBO ontology recommender 2.0: an enhanced approach for biomedical ontology recommendation. J. Biomed. Seman. 8(1), 21 (2017)
46. Supekar, K., Patel, C., Lee, Y.: Characterizing quality of knowledge on semantic web. In: 7th International Florida Artificial Intelligence Research Society Conference, pp. 220–228 (2004)
47. Lewen, H., d'Aquin, M.: Extending open rating systems for ontology ranking and reuse. In: Cimiano, P., Pinto, H.S. (eds.) EKAW 2010. LNCS (LNAI), vol. 6317, pp. 441–450. Springer, Heidelberg (2010). https://doi.org/10.1007/978-3-642-16438-5_34
48. Palinkas, L.A., Horwitz, S.M., Green, C.A., Wisdom, J.P., Duan, N., Hoagwood, K.: Purposeful sampling for qualitative data collection and analysis in mixed method implementation research. Adm. Policy Ment. Health 42(5), 2–4 (2015)
49. Suri, H.: Purposeful sampling in qualitative research synthesis. Qual. Res. J. 11(2), 63–75 (2011)
50. Guest, G., Bunce, A., Johnson, L.: How many interviews are enough? An experiment with data saturation and variability. Field Methods 18(1), 59–82 (2006)
51. Tello, A.J.: Métrica de idoneidad de ontologías. Universidad de Extremadura (2002)

Knowledge Management and Information Sharing

Empowering IT Organizations Through a Confluence of Knowledge for Value Integration into the IT Services Firm's Business Model

Nabil Georges Badr(✉)

Grenoble Graduate School of Business, Grenoble, France
nabil.badr@alumni.grenoble-em.com

Abstract. Challenges in operationalizing business innovation based on information technology (i.e. advancing new technology from the lab to the business operations) affect the ability of IT organizations to implement and effectively exploit these technologies. In IT services firms, these challenges are often linked to conflicting priorities, integration issues, inadequate infrastructure capabilities and the availability of the required knowledge/skills. Sometimes insurmountable these challenges leave the firm incapable to incorporate emerging information technologies into their business model. At the intersection of knowledge-based theory of the firm and the theory of dynamic capabilities, the study draws insight from the two cases in IT services companies. We seek to understand mechanism required to manage the flow knowledge assets for successful integration of innovation, while assimilating the tacit knowledge of the customer as a major component in the value integration. The study has far-reaching implications for practice and produces interesting opportunities for further research.

Keywords: Knowledge transfer · Knowledge acquisition ·
Technology innovation integration · IT organizational learning

1 Introduction

Business models that align strategies, processes, capabilities and resources drive the competitive success of a firm [1]. Companies in IT services gain their competitiveness via their digital business model; i.e. how they offer digital services to their customers. These companies have to improve their computing platforms in order to optimize their digital business models [2] and they often do it with the use of emerging technologies. Emerging technologies in IT are technologies such as cloud, business process automation and customer facing innovations that have the potential to innovate the way business is conducted. This translates into increased value propositions to customers internal and/or external to the firm.

IT based business model innovations introduce emerging technologies in IT into the infrastructure and drive change into the IT organization. The function of the IT organization and the related managerial influences must motivate emerging technology adoption through skill building and knowledge acquisition [3]. In a dynamically

© Springer Nature Switzerland AG 2019
A. Fred et al. (Eds.): IC3K 2017, CCIS 976, pp. 339–359, 2019.
https://doi.org/10.1007/978-3-030-15640-4_17

competitive knowledge economy [4], this is a clear challenge for the IT operation consisting of both tacit (knowledge and management competence) and explicit elements (operational procedures and standards) to effectively support and bring value to a firm's strategically relevant capabilities [5]. While the resistance to take risks in a fast decision making environment impacts the firm's ability to implement technological innovation [6], the continuous need for IT assessment of technology introduction practices [7] changes the implementation strategy roadmaps challenging the IT leadership and the organizational competence [8].

Managers consistently emphasize the importance of organizational mechanisms that positively influence the transformation of new knowledge through initiating new ideas, insights, and opportunities [9]. Practitioners want to prepare their organization for the new technology [10] in order to reduce the reluctance of IT organizations to integrate emerging technologies: training, education and knowledge acquisition constitute a predominant theme among what practitioners consider as investments to drive innovation while maintaining the delivery of a continuous IT service [11].

The paper treats these challenges in the context of IT organizations of IT services companies. For these companies, emerging IT is not just a tool to support business processes or to enable business model innovation, but for both. These organizations are often called upon to be the internal IT provider for the internal customers (i.e. employees) and external solutions and service providers for IT clients (i.e. customers).

What transformations based on Knowledge Management practices should IT organizations apply in order to embrace innovations based on emerging IT to better integrate the technological value proposition into the firm's business model?

Our paper is organized as follows. A background section reviews the literature and sets the theoretical foundation for our study through an overview of dynamic capability and learning capability of IT. The methodology section presents the research design and introduces our empirical setting. Findings are shared in the next section with a discussion on the value incorporated into the knowledge exchange between the exploitative and explorative capabilities of the IT organization, while assimilating the tacit knowledge of the customer as a major component in the value integration. The final section introduces mechanisms for knowledge acquisition and transfer enabling IT organization's capability for innovation and emphasizing the confluence of knowledge that is essential to the value integration into the firm's business model [12].

2 Background

When innovating a business model, IT leadership and IT organizations, endure multidimensional challenges, especially in IT services companies. These IT organizations must participate in the success of their host companies in an effort to lead IT based innovation, internally and externally. This requires IT organizational capabilities that dynamically adapt through the proficient collaboration of people, processes and technology [13]. IT organizations in IT service companies have two customers: IT is not only a cornerstone for the internal business model with internal users of the company, but also the core business in providing customer-facing services [14]. This puts a burden on the IT organization stretching its abilities to cover users' issues internal and external to the company context with a persisting conundrum of providing a reliable service to existing customers or creating new customers through innovation integration [15]. For instance, obstacles to knowledge acquisition and training demands, product procurement dilemmas, implementation and support prevail [16].

Theory has not yet addressed the potential obstacles to business model innovation based on emerging IT integration that may constrain the knowledge management, transfer capabilities of the IT organization, and hinder IT from building on organizational knowledge [15].

2.1 IT Organization Dynamic Capability

Largely, IT organizational capabilities have received a fair share of attention in various context. IS research on resource based views (RBV) delineates resources as physical capital (e.g. property, plant, etc.), human capital (e.g. people, experience, relationships, etc.) and organizational capital (e.g. organizational structure and processes, etc.) [18]. Although resources and capabilities may be considered part of a firm's total assets, a capability is the organizational ability to coordinate a set of resources (human, financial, organizational or data, etc.) to create a certain outcome [19].

Leadership capabilities in fostering business to IT communication and governance as well as the readiness of IT and the level of stakeholder participation are critical success factors [20]. Handoff and communication best practices between advance technology groups and operations groups help drive knowledge diffusion into the organizational structure [21]. This competence with its explicit (operational procedures and standards) and tacit (knowledge and management competence) elements [5] is fundamental for the decision making capabilities of what technology should be implemented by the Information Management strategy [6].

. Closer to the technology implementation function, IT capability was described as the ability to diffuse or support a wide variety of hardware and software [22]; ultimately using enterprise management systems of IT integration [6], for knowledge and work-flow management [23].

Knowledge management and assimilation constitute an essential organizational dynamic capability. Researchers position knowledge as a *"baseline for the service-ability and the maintainability"* [24, 25] of the components and systems involved in providing IT services in continuity that is in line with the current and planned business requirements. Teece et al. [26] define *"dynamic capabilities"* as *"the firm's ability to integrate, build, and reconfigure internal and external competencies to address rapidly changing environments"* (p. 516).

Focused inward on IT organizational capabilities, this study distinguishes IT organizations' ability to deploy and operate IT platforms, i.e. capabilities of exploitation and their ability to learn and innovate IT solutions, i.e. capabilities of exploration [27].

For the background of this research, exploitation capabilities are operational level capabilities that reflect an ability to perform routine and required activities within the IT function [28]. These capabilities include fundamental processes of operation with the required key resources such as applications, information, infrastructure and people. Empirical studies [29, 30] showed that firms or business units with stronger exploration and exploitation capabilities outperform others. Though both capabilities could be conceived as theories for learning [30], exploration capabilities are aimed at discovering new possibilities for innovation while capabilities of exploitation are intended to invest acquired knowledge for value creation [31].

2.2 Knowledge Based Theory of the Firm

Knowledge-based theory conceptualizes the firm as an institution for integrating knowledge [32]. The primary contribution of this theory is in exploring the coordination mechanisms through which firms integrate the specialist (tacit) knowledge of their members as the basis of organizational capability. Knowledge transfer within an organization as essential organizational capability.

In close connection to these capabilities, Nonaka's broad contribution to the theory of organizational knowledge creation [33] emphasizes that organizational knowledge is created through a continuous cycle of dialogue and transformation between tacit and explicit knowledge [34]. The SECI model introduced by Nonaka and Takeuchi [35: 71–72, 89], exhibits the cyclic nature of creating new organizational knowledge. Tacit knowledge is normally acquired through shared experience (Socialization) that typically occurs in a traditional apprenticeship mode. Next, the transformation of knowledge from of tacit into explicit could be carried on through publishing examples, concepts, images, and written documents that articulate knowledge and presents it to others (Externalization); the cycle continues as explicit knowledge is then collected, combined, then edited or processed to form new knowledge that is available to everyone (Combination). Explicit to tacit knowledge transformation as exemplified by the principle of learning by doing, comes to be part of an individual's knowledge and will become assets for an organization (Internalization). However, such models can be highly theoretical with empirical shortcomings of information divergence into inadequate knowledge creation that may overlook concepts of culture, context and objectives for this transformation [36].

2.3 IT Organizational Learning Capability

Certain organizations are able to acquire and assimilate new external knowledge [37], but are not able to transform and exploit it successfully in order to create value from their absorptive capacity [38]. The literature reviewed has identified organizational learning capabilities of experimentation [39], and the interaction with the external environment [40] was shown to positively associate with the introduction of novel product innovations in firms. A moderating effect of knowledge complexity on the relationship between organizational learning capability and technological innovation implementation was indicated [41], and related to organizational attributes [42].

In organizational learning contexts, the organization's capability to take on the associated learning curve was related to the organization's absorptive capacity [39]. The organizational capability to take on the associated learning curve was related to the absorptive capacity [17]. Zahra and George [43, 44] suggested a dynamic capability attribute for the absorptive capacity pointing out the existence of two subsets or components of absorptive capacity: potential absorptive capacity (knowledge acquisition and assimilation) and realized absorptive capacity (transformation and exploitation of knowledge). Organizational units operating in a dynamic setting improve their performance by increasing their skills, expertise, and potential absorptive capacity [39].

Exploitation capabilities rely fundamentally on the organization's absorptive capacity and build on prior development of its constituent, individual absorptive capacities [45]. Thus, the potential absorptive capacity drives the exploration capabilities. Mechanisms associated with the coordination capabilities (i.e. cross-functional interfaces, participation, and job rotation) primarily enhance potential absorptive capacity increasing the acquisition, assimilation and transformation of new external knowledge. Other organizational mechanisms associated with socialization capabilities (connectedness and socialization tactics) primarily strengthen realized absorptive capacity [46]. The realized absorptive capacity empowers the organization to extract value through their capability of exploitation and an effective timing of knowledge deployment [26].

Research has posited that organizations acquire information and transform it into collective knowledge assets [47] often with knowledge management systems (KMS) [48] with a strong dependency on IT leadership communication and governance practices. Esteva et al. [21] prescribed a handoff of knowledge between advance technology groups and operations groups. External knowledge transfer was identified as a key factor in integrating technology [49] and an antecedent to innovation integration [50]. Outsourcing activities [51, 52] often including a strategic partner [53] were identified to facilitate the knowledge transfer into the organization.

Knowledge infrastructures are known to enable dynamic organizational capabilities [54]. This paper presents empirical evidence on mechanisms for empowering IT organizations through for value integration through the agile management of their technology assets.

3 Methodology

This exploratory research into practice levers two in-depth qualitative case studies [55]. Case study methodology has been used to study knowledge transfer practices in similar contexts [56–58]. Research activities followed a case study protocol, conducted in three stages, on location with IT organizations in a telecom services Company A, and in an application hosting services Company B, selected purposefully [59] for this study.

Data collection and analysis were performed as data was acquired [60] as more information and a better understanding of the relevant data is developed. Case reports were written immediately after the data collection exercise in order to maintain the required details. The timely and detailed transcripts from the research activity recorded participants inputs captured during the interviews and workshops and immediately heightened the accuracy of what was reported, supporting the *descriptive validity* [61]. Lincoln and Guba [62] articulated principles of *consistency* and *dependability* as concepts of reliability in quantitative research and argued that because reliability is a necessary condition for validity, demonstrating validity in qualitative research is sufficient to establish reliability.

The study's reliability is reinforced through the use of a *case study protocol*, the consistent review of the data, observations, and discussions and a systematic case study methodology [63, 64].

The data analysis technique is designed a priori [65], in order to systematically consider all the data that would be collected in relevance to the research. Throughout the field activities, data collection and analysis, systematic procedures are followed in a rigorous process in order to capture the detail [60]. Multiple interviews, workshops and date collection methods improved the *dependability* of the research [66].

The construct of validity is supported by employing multiple data collection methods [55] through interviews and brainstorming sessions [67], with data gathered from other [68], such as company websites, documents, and organization charts.

An initial coding (sorting based on seed concepts) was performed during the discovery workshop. This allowed for the participants to contribute to the coding process reducing researcher potential bias. Care is taken to self-disclose the role of the researcher [69], revealing assumptions, beliefs, and biases if present in the research process and the analysis exercise in order to maintain the distance from potentially perceived biases and strengthen the validity of the research [70]. Case study transcripts are taken back to the participants in the study in a form of member checking [71], in order to assess the usefulness of the study. This validation by the participants and their related feedback in the discussion workshop enriched the *credibility* [72] and the *interpretive validity* [61] of the research. In the discussion, the findings are strengthened by triangulation [73] from the literature and from practitioners.

3.1 Site Selection

Two in-depth case explorations were conducted, on location, with IT organizations in Telecom **Company A**, and in Application Hosting Services **Company B**, selected purposefully [74] for this research (Table 1).

Company A is a leading internet services provider and hosting solutions, established in 1995 with 130+ employees. The IT organization is composed of 15 members managing security credentials, moves and changes of the internal users; planning of new technology deployment; internal and external customers.

Over a 2.5 year project launched in the beginning of 2010, Company A implemented a new business process management application based on emerging BPM (Business Process Management) technology to support the operational activities of the company in delivering these new services and reporting on the related activities. Leveraging BPM, **Company A** adapted the way of doing business and changed the operational systems, organizational structures and pricing models, to support the integration of the new mobile services in the market. The disruption to the IT organization and the business organization was substantial. The IT management team faced a user base resisting change and reluctance from the IT staff to adopt and adapt the new application. In addition to the barriers of cost and knowledge acquisition, **Company A**, also confronted challenges of planning and timing of decision to deploy and prepare the IT and the business organization.

Table 1. Our case study setting – site selection.

	Company A	Company B
Company background	Leading internet services provider and hosting solutions, established in 1995 (130+ employees)	Hosting and cloud services, re-established in 2006 (42 employees)
IT organization	15 members managing security credentials, internal moves and changes; planning of new technology deployment; internal and external customers	12 employees in charge of planning, implementation and support of internal infrastructure with a service desk attending to escalated customer calls
Emerging IT integration objectives	Service automation for self-provisioning OSS delivering 3G/4G services to subscribers	Provide a turnkey IT solution based on software as a service (SAAS)
Risk mitigation measures	Clear definition of risks on IT and the business to leverage company resources and accomplish the business objectives	Informed on the challenges and risks, customers participated in creating the solution to mitigate the risks

Company B's business, on the other hand, is in hosting and cloud services, re-established in 2006 with 42 employees in total. Twelve employees form the IT organization in charge of the planning, implementation and support of the internal infrastructure with a service desk attending to escalated customer calls. With a challenge to serve the internal IT needs and the needs of external customers, such as onsite support, the IT organization of **Company B** was reluctant to use the emerging cloud technologies even for their internal systems. IT leadership had to manoeuvre their IT organization to support a public cloud service.

Additionally, in order to support this new service, **Company B** needed to setup a service desk and implement a portal to be integrated into their application hosting services support platform in order to provide the customer required service levels. This presented yet another disruption and exposed the already burdened IT organization supporting the customer facing services to undertake an internal project. The IT management team with an organization of 12 employees, had to meet the trials of strict maintenance windows and space limitations with resource constraints.

Similarities in the sites selected reinforce the findings by adding depth into the discovery; similarities to note are of industry context [75], culture [76], and international presence [77], IT organization setting: centralized management model [78] with a collective decision making [79].

These sites also present complementarities where by **Company A** implemented an internally facing solution to enable an external service and **Company B** deployed a solution that is used by both internal and external customers. The sites differ in organization size [80], maturity [81] and the scope of their project implementation [82]. The choice of these sites aimed to uncover potential cross case observations further enriching the empirical study. The IT resources in these companies tend to pool fulfilling both, customer facing and internal IT duties. This was stated to effect a specific set of constraints on the involved IT resources and the IT organization such that reduced maintenance windows, and potentially shift coverage and skill distribution.

3.2   Data Collection and Analysis

Data Collection instruments were developed to capture input from the activities (Table 2). A preparation meeting set the stage for the activities and helped identify key informants that could represent a cross section of institutional knowledge.

Discovery workshops followed with data collection activities that combined interviews and brainstorming sessions [83]. Focus group workshops were conducted due to the nature of the topic that requires stimulation and interaction [84]. These workshops recorded all the participants' input while probing for details; where possible, using illustrative examples to help establish neutrality in the process [59]. In total data collection involved 15 informants chosen from the two companies. Saturation interviews were subsequently conducted with senior managers from each company.

Case summaries and cross-case comparison were compiled in a tabular summary [85], in the form of interview transcripts, field notes from observations, and relevant exhibits (e.g. organizational structures, web sites of each company, company presentations material).

The data analysis investigated the data correlation through a predefined coding system [86] in order to organize the data and provide a means to introduce the interpretations [87]. A step by step 'Key Point' coding technique [88] was applied to the interview transcripts [89], and relevant concepts are identified (Table 2).

Finally, an open discussion forum was conducted among all participant at each company separately in order to deepen the concepts.

Table 2. Key Codes for the Key Point Coding technique.

Concept:	Key Code
Knowledge acquisition	Acquire new knowledge [37]
	Seek external knowledge [91]
Knowledge transfer	Transfer acquired knowledge [48, 92]
	Training activities [16, 37]
	Participation in decision making [9, 93]
Emerging concept	Explore the tacit knowledge of the customer

This paper is part of a more developed study [11] and it further extends a short paper that was introduced at conference on knowledge management [90] into the value integration realized into the firm's business model through the IT organizational capability to manage the flow knowledge assets. It focuses on one Key Concepts of the larger study: knowledge acquisition and transfer that is isolated by the coding technique to support the findings and focus on significant observations in accordance with the research question (Table 3).

One Key Code captures "knowledge acquisition mechanisms" into concepts of acquiring new knowledge (such as through training sessions, conferences, labs for in-house training) [37] and seeking external knowledge from knowledge networks [91] (subject matter experts, joint R&D efforts, external consultants, and other implementations).

A second Key Code helps extract practices in transferring acquired knowledge [48, 92] internally through research and collaboration (through users' manuals, knowledge sharing sessions, training materials [16, 37] and knowledge management systems [48, 92] and participative decision making [9, 93]. From the coding technique, a concept of "exploring the tacit knowledge of the customer" was allowed to emerge. The coding results were then shared in a discussion with the participants is focus group sessions for validation and additional input.

4 Findings and Discussion

Our study uncovered knowledge management mechanisms for enabling IT organization's capability for innovation (Table 3) and introduces them in a summative form, excerpt from the interview transcripts to enrich the conversation. This section presents practices of knowledge acquisition (acquiring new knowledge and seeking external knowledge contributions), and knowledge transfer tactics (such as training and participative decision-making).

Special attention is given to a concept of knowledge acquisition, through exploring the tacit knowledge of the customer, which emerged from the coding process.

Table 3. Knowledge management mechanisms enabling IT organization's capability for innovation.

Objectives	Mechanisms
Knowledge acquisition practices	– Attending conferences: Network with peers "gain the confidence with the technology and come and convey the knowledge internally" – Build awareness about alternative solutions through research and library searches – Engage an external consultant to provide workshops – Architectural review session (external consultants) to insource the required knowledge – R&D efforts with peer organizations, key partners and suppliers
Knowledge transfer tactics	– Training and cross training of technical staff (train the trainer, labs, champions, etc.) – Establish regular (bi-weekly) knowledge sharing sessions – Setup a database of training materials (user manuals) – Setup knowledge management systems (sorting & categorization) – Establish cross functional share IT knowledge across the IT organization – Participation of IT and business in decision making
Exploiting the tacit knowledge of the customer	– Collaborate with peer organizations in a form of knowledge networks – Internal and customer facing IT teams engaged in knowledge sharing – Share the lessons learned from solving customer issues with the business (possibly drive a new service offering) – Educate the customer to increase their appetite for innovation (scouting for opportunities)

4.1   Knowledge Acquisition Practices

Indeed, knowledge acquisition practices were identified as key enablers to IT organizational capabilities. Both companies suggested that IT organizations could be better prepared for the integration of emerging IT primarily through Knowledge Acquisition mechanisms of training, seeking external knowledge and sharing it internally.

At **Company A**, the IT organization's learning capabilities were enhanced by attending conferences: an opportunity to network with peers and learn then disseminate the knowledge within the organization. *"First we send them to conference. They will then have a chance to network with peers and learn, gain the confidence with the technology and come and convey the knowledge internally"* indicated the operations manager of **Company A**.

The degree of tacit-ness of newly acquired knowledge necessitated richer organizational information processing mechanisms. An integration working group made up of cross organizational members and representations of IT in the business led the knowledge transfer in **Company A**. Job rotations enhanced knowledge redistribution among the technical IT team members. In order to address the architectural implications and learn about potential system interaction with existing systems (e.g. Active Directory support), **Company A** started architectural review session emphasizing the role of external consultants in order to insource the required knowledge.

On the other hand, organizational dynamics of socialization (the perspective of a group rather than an individual) practiced by the IT organization stimulated **Company B**'s sales team to increase the organization's business-IT knowledge. The participation of IT in the process of decision making primarily strengthened the realized absorptive capacity [9] of the IT organization and elevated the organization's capability to strengthen their business-IT knowledge.

Company B conducted research of other implementations in peer organizations in a form of knowledge networks with the objective of insourcing the required knowledge. Thus, external knowledge was sought through the engagement of consultants and joint R&D activities with key providers and partners. Testing and R&D activities enriched the individual skills of the IT employees. Their accumulated experience increased the levels of organizational knowledge. *"… We setup R&D efforts with peer organizations, key partners and suppliers and review and research other implementations in peer organizations"* (**Company B**). Learning capability of experimentation [39], and interaction with external environments [40] were shown by research studies to positively associate with the introduction of novel product innovations in firms.

4.2   Knowledge Transfer Tactics

Collaboration and brainstorming sessions helped disseminate the acquired knowledge. Investments were required to, in face of this disruption, supplement the resources and transition the knowledge. From reallocating budgets to hiring qualified consultants, the IT organization of **Company B** had to leverage the company resources properly and provide extensive employee training through knowledge building programs.

Extending outside the boundaries of the firm, for **Company B**, continual training plans empowered the IT organization to become more effective in supporting the customer base. Training sessions were carried in-house; selected team members were assigned and trained on specific technologies to form subject matter experts. Further, IT teams attended conferences to stay ahead of the learning curve and setup labs and databases of training materials for in-house training activities. In-house training facilitated the spread of knowledge and reduced the corresponding knowledge acquisition costs.

4.3 Deployment of Knowledge Management Tools

Case management and monitoring tools provided feedback from the customer into the business planning to drive alignment of the objectives of the business. Such tools enabled the IT organization of **Company A** to gain visibility into the customer experience and to measure the service health (metrics) through related monitoring and reporting functions. This awareness incentivized the IT organization to handle the implementation of EIT with the knowledge of the impacts it had on the customer. In addition to the benefits received from collaboration tools, **Company B** included knowledge management systems in their toolset as part of their knowledge sharing strategy.

Knowledge management systems consolidated this knowledge in to an information base on internal and external customers. **Company B** used this convergence of information to participate in delivering the vision internally with an enthusiasm to contribute input. The operations executive of **Company B** described, "*Knowledge transfer tactics between the teams were applied. They involve the sorting and categorization of information with knowledge management systems in order to leave time for the internal functionality empowering the front lines. Through communication between these teams, the internal team is aware of the customer issues. This was fruitful in the ability of IT to participate in delivering the vision internally with an excitement, progress and ability to participate effectively in the input*".

4.4 Exploiting the Tacit Knowledge of the Customer

Emerging from the analysis is a concept that depicts the phenomenon of exploring the tacit knowledge of the customer. This study shows a potential added value for IT organizations that collaborate with the customer of their services, especially in mitigating risks and improving eventual outcomes. **Company B** reported that the IT reluctance phenomena extending to their customers hindered their ability to provide their services to these customers. Learning workshops held with the customers, increased the awareness of the customer issues and reduced the customer reluctance to adopt the technology. To close the loop, IT shared lessons learned from solving customer issues with the business as they brought forth recommendation to drive more business through new products and services. This approach stimulated the creativity of the IT team, as a motivation to start driving the innovative ideas through to the business strategy [95].

The transfer of knowledge to internal customers (i.e. employees of the company) was accomplished through carefully designed user training sessions and detailed users' manuals. The task for the IT organization was then also to participate in "*educating the customer to increase the enthusiasm at the customer level*". This helped **Company A** overcome users' resistance to adopting the new business process management

(BPM) platform and eased the task on the IT organization. This approach was also observed at **Company B** where the employees, the internal customers of the solutions we consulted in the deployment of hosting projects. The IT organization established biweekly knowledge sharing sessions with internal customers (employees) in order to discover the challenges and help reduce adoption issues.

Facing the external customer base, **Company B** reportedly focused on enhancing the consultancy skills of the engineers. The "IT organization was a consultant to the customer … the IT team scouted for opportunities at the customers' base, and feedback is brought back to the business" clarified the operations manager. Their exposure as a consultant with the external customer motivated their creativity as they started driving the innovative ideas through to the business strategy.

On the operations side, and in close communication with the customer-facing support teams, the IT organization was aware of the customer issues. The IT support team (customer facing) in **Company B** meets with the IT infrastructure team (Internal team) regularly to review the customer issues, build the knowledge base and solicit the collaboration of ideas across the technical team internal and external. Meanwhile, the customer facing support teams, share the lessons learned from solving customer issues with the business. This works as a feedback into the business of the issues facing IT which may in turn drive a business solution or a new service. By combining the knowledge of the customer facing technical teams and the internally facing IT infrastructure teams, these knowledge management and transfer capabilities built on the organizational knowledge to improve the operational/functional competences of **Company B**.

5 Conclusion and Guidance for Practice

The case study has revealed that through training of IT in both technology and in the related business aspects, IT organizations in the IT services industry were able to shape their technical and analytical capability (i.e. analysis of the business requirements, ROI, business value of technology) and become enablers of innovation.

IT organizations previewed the business and technical benefits of potential solutions. This was an opportunity to embed visionary and forward looking IT solutions into the firm. The IT Director of **Company A** explicated that "*This tactic has fueled the enthusiasm of the IT organization and raised the confidence of the business in the IT organization and elevated the value of the IT organization to the business.*" The IT organization became part of the strategic trend setting capacity of the organization, which encouraged the members of the IT organization to embrace the new deployment.

The opportunity to lead internally reportedly raised the "confidence" of the business in IT organizational capabilities and encourages the IT organization to embrace the new technology. IT became an agent of change, elevating the value of IT in the organization and innovating the business. The IT organization was then empowered to drive the next phases of the implementation of the IT based business innovation. For instance, the IT team of **Company A** was involved in all new systems introductions and the IT organization, in the case of the BPM implementation, was able to introduce process automation initiatives and be a leader in the company's business model innovation.

The IT leadership was able to *push other concepts that were originally outside the scope of the current project such as shopping carts, self-service and collection activities, and integration of handhelds, [...]. Thus, enabling the POS platforms and other mobile applications "*. Added the Director of IT, explaining how such approaches expanded the innovative aspect of the solution and helped drive a niche service offering to the market.

Building upon the theory of organizational knowledge creation, these findings are reminders of Nonaka's model of spiral of organizational knowledge creation [33] through combining tacit and explicit knowledge into a cyclic process of organizational knowledge building. Our study could be considered as an empirical extension of this theory. Mechanisms for knowledge acquisition and knowledge transfer explored maybe framed reciprocally, by the two dimension of organizational knowledge creation lens: (1) mechanisms for the acquisition of knowledge that relate to the type of knowledge (tacit vs. explicit) and (2) knowledge transfer tactics that depend on level of social interaction to convert this knowledge into organizational assets.

5.1   Mechanisms for Knowledge Acquisition and Transfer

The site selection proved helpful in highlighting the different mechanisms of knowledge acquisition and transfer, however analogous, they seem nuanced relative to project scope.

In the case of **Company A**, a heightened focus was clear on building the organizational learning capabilities that addresses the internal customer needs, as the project's scope was mostly internal in scope. Job rotations were instrumental in building a deep knowledge bench. IT team members attended conferences and networked with peers to seek external knowledge. Resorting to external resource augmentation the IT team insourced required new knowledge, conducting training sessions to transition knowledge to users and reduce adoption resistance. Tools deployed were case management and monitoring that gathered information and converted it into organizational knowledge.

Company B's project on the other hand, was more pervasive in scope. The customer base was preliminarily external to the firm. The IT organization had to reach outside the firm's boundary to seek new knowledge through the engagement of consultants and joint R&D activities with key providers and partners, researching other implementations in peer organizations in a form of knowledge networks with the objective of insourcing the required knowledge. Collaboration and brainstorming sessions among members of the IT organization the acquired knowledge and knowledge management systems consolidated this knowledge in to an information base on internal and external customers. Continual training plans empowered the IT organization to become more effective in supporting the customer base and learning workshops held with the customers, increased the awareness of the customer issues and reduced customer reluctance to adopt the technology. They also included knowledge management systems in their toolset as part of their knowledge sharing strategy.

5.2   Enabling IT Organization's Capability for Innovation

In either case, the empirical statements explicate that IT organization embrace innovation integration by reinforcing knowledge acquisition practices through training, collaborations with key partners and suppliers, testing and R&D. IT organizations reportedly gained confidence with emerging technology integration by capitalizing upon learning opportunities from peer networks, consultants and conducting joint R&D activities with key providers and partners. Acquired knowledge is shared internally in cooperation with the business and other team members through the integration of new ideas with the use of knowledge management tools, research and testing practices. Tools for knowledge management consolidated this knowledge into an information base on external and external customers.

In both cases, the customer was an integral part of the knowledge institutionalization process. In one case (**Company A**), internal testing and R&D activities enriched the individual skills of the employees. The participation of IT in the process of decision making elevated the organization's capability to strengthen their business-IT knowledge and job rotations enhanced knowledge redistribution among the technical IT team members. Acquired knowledge is mutualized in a collaborative approach with customers. The IT organization learns about the customer issues (supporting them more effectively) and about their needs and requirements, which reinforced the ability of IT to support the vision of the business. A suggestion that customer collaboration would likely ease of adoption of the new service (especially for the internal customer of the IT organization), and prepare the IT organization for the potential risk induced by the emerging technologies to the external customer. Integration working groups connect with the business to gain insight into the business requirements from IT and gauge the business readiness for the IT innovation. Then cooperating with customers (i.e. internal customer of IT and external customer of the business and IT) in testing, planning, and risk assessment, IT organizations could influence the customer's readiness for integrating innovation. Furthermore, collaboration and brainstorming sessions helped disseminate the acquired knowledge.

Integration working groups made up of cross-organizational members and representations of IT in the business lead the transfer of knowledge. Integration working groups connect with the business to gain insight into the business requirements from IT and gauge the business readiness for the IT innovation.

5.3   Emphasizing the Confluence of Knowledge

This study shows that IT organizations must continually build, adapt, and reconfigure their competences to succeed in a changing environment through knowledge acquisition and transfer mechanisms.

The IT organization is faced with a trade-off between exploration and exploitation, between mustering resources to support an operation or reallocating them to leverage their knowledge to address immediate needs versus acquiring new knowledge to innovate and address potentially new challenges. They develop dynamic organizational capabilities of exploration and exploitation, emphasizing the confluence of knowledge.

Investments are required to build IT skills and competence, muster key resources, and formalize key activities. Innovative IT organizations develop key partnership with suppliers and peers, and exploit the tacit knowledge of the customer. IT leadership of confident organizations drive their organizational capabilities to become levers for business model innovation. They motivate their IT organizational learning capabilities, and demonstrate leadership competence; encourage the adoption of standards through networking with peers.

Customer participation in the learning process has started to interest researchers [96]. Alliances between producers of services and consumers of these services have the potential to bolster the value proposition of the firm [97]. Acquired knowledge is shared externally in a collaborative approach with customers. The IT organization is aligned with the customer and about their needs and requirements (supporting them more effectively), which reinforced the ability of IT to support the vision of the business. This duality of function for IT organizations presents some advantages: practitioners report benefits of lessons learned and correlation of the effect of internal outages on the customer services could influence the ability to effectively dissemination knowledge.

Findings of this study supplement extant literature on the role of knowledge flows in product innovation [94] with rigor in identifying knowledge management mechanisms for innovation integration. These mechanisms underscore the development of dynamic organizational capabilities of exploration and exploitation, emphasizing the confluence of knowledge (Fig. 1). This confluence of knowledge becomes a cyclic process of exploration and exploitation of knowledge assets in a perpetual knowledge-sharing ecosystem that yields to a continuous organizational learning with significant value to organizational capability building. Knowledge flow between the exploratory and the exploitative IT teams converges into a potential for innovation integration.

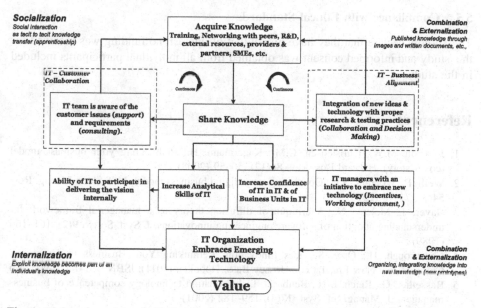

Fig. 1. Value proposition in innovation integration through the lens of Nonaka's knowledge creation model.

Learnings from this study highlight a confluence of knowledge from the customer base, the business, peer organizations, standards and best practices, that has the potential of increasing the exploratory and exploitative capabilities, raising the awareness, analytical skills and the confidence of IT organizations to "integrate new ideas and embrace emerging technologies".

5.4 Limitations and Opportunities for Further Research

This paper is part of a larger research effort exploring mechanisms of innovation integration employed by IT organizations [98, 99]. The specific topic of this paper treats those mechanisms of knowledge management adopted to prepare IT organizations for innovation integration. Findings of this study corroborate evidence that tacit knowledge transfer is often supported by open communication, peer-trust and unrestricted sharing of knowledge [56]. Although the research has reached its aim, some unavoidable limitations can be noted. The study was conducted in two companies, hence limits the generalizability of the findings. Limitations related to case study research the research and other contexts such as culture and industry can be recognized [100].

The indicated limitations of this study could offer opportunities for follow on research. For instance, additional fieldwork, possibly in the form of wider focus groups, with chief information officers, IS professionals and consultants [101] would examine the applicability of the framework in other cultural, organizational and other contexts, in order to strengthen the practice implications of the concepts introduced by this study [102]. Academic researchers in IT innovation, MIS, organizational dynamic capabilities and resource-based views would find the opportunity to exploit the findings of this study into interesting quantitative and qualitative projects.

5.5 Compliance with Ethical Standards

The authors declare that they have no conflict of interest, no funding was received for this study and informed consent was obtained from all individual participants included in the study.

References

1. Johnson, M.W., Christensen, C.M., Kagermann, H.: Reinventing your business model (cover story). Harvard Bus. Rev. **86**(12), 50–59 (2008)
2. Weill, P., Woerner, S.L.: Optimizing your digital business model. MIT Sloan Manag. Rev. **54**(3), 71–78 (2013)
3. Bayer, J., Melone, N.: A critique of diffusion theory as a managerial framework for understanding adoption of software engineering innovations. J. Syst. Softw. **9**(2), 161–166 (1989)
4. Chesbrough, H.: Open Services Innovation: Rethinking Your Business to Grow and Compete in a New Era, 1st edn. Jossey-Bass, Hoboken (2011). ISBN 978-0-470-90574-6
5. Bassellier, G., Reich, B.H., Benbasat, I.: Information technology competence of business managers. J. Manag. Inf. Syst. **17**(4), 159–182 (2001)

6. Galliers, R.D., Leidner, D.E. (eds.): Strategic Information Management: Challenges and Strategies in Managing Information Systems. Routledge, Abingdon (2014)
7. Cash, J.I., Earl, M.J., Morison, R.: Teaming up to crack innovation and enterprise integration. Harvard Bus. Rev. **86**(11), 90–100 (2008)
8. Duncan, N.B.: Capturing flexibility of information technology infrastructure: a study of resource characteristics and their measure. J. Manag. Inf. Syst. **12**(2), 37–57 (1995)
9. Jansen, J.J., Van den Bosch, F.A.J., Volberda, H.W.: Managing potential and realized absorptive capacity: how do organizational antecedents matter? AOM J. **48**(6), 999–1015 (2005)
10. Cooper, R.B., Zmud, R.W.: Information technology implementation research: a technological diffusion approach. Manag. Sci. **36**(2), 123–139 (1990)
11. Badr, N.: Integration of IT based business model innovation: potential challenges in integrating emerging technologies. Business Leadership Review DBA Special Issue: Impact & Practice: Making the DBA Count. Issue 12: Vol. 1 (DBA) 1 June 2014
12. Hacklin, F., Björkdahl, J., Wallin, M.W.: Strategies for business model innovation: how firms reel in migrating value. Long Range Plan. **51**(1), 82–110 (2018). ISSN 0024-6301
13. Mocker, M., Teubner, A.: Towards a comprehensive model of information strategy. In: Proceedings of ECIS 2005. Paper 62 (2005)
14. Keel, A.J., Orr, M.A., Hernandez, R.R., Patrocinio, E.A., Bouchard, J.: From a technology-oriented to a service-oriented approach to IT management. IBM Syst. J. **46**(3), 549–564 (2007)
15. Berthon, P., Hulbert, J.M., Pitt, L.F.: To serve or create? Strategic orientations toward customers and innovation. Calif. Manag. Rev. **42**(1), 37–58 (1999)
16. Edwards, C., Peppard, J.: Operationalizing strategy through process. Long Range Plan. **30**, 753–767 (1997)
17. Lane, P.J., Lubatkin, M.: Relative absorptive capacity and inter-organizational learning. Strat. Manag. J. **19**, 461–477 (1998)
18. Barney, J.B.: Firm resources and sustained competitive advantage. J. Manag. **17**(1), 99–120 (1991)
19. Grant, R.M.: The resource-based theory of competitive advantage: implications for strategy formulation. Calif. Manag. Rev. **33**(3), 114–135 (1991)
20. Rau, K.: Effective governance of IT: design, objectives roles and relationships. Comput. J. Inf. Syst. Manag. **21**(2), 21–40 (2004)
21. Esteva, J., Smith-Sharp, W., Gangeddula, S.: A formal technology introduction process. J. Am. Acad. Bus. Camb. **9**(1), 40–46 (2006)
22. Byrd, T.A., Turner, E.D.: An exploratory analysis of the information technology infrastructure flexibility construct. J. MIS **17**(1), 167–208 (2000)
23. Mulligan, P.: Specification of a capability-based it classification framework. Inf. Manag. **39**(8), 647–658 (2002)
24. Blanchard, S.B.: Maintainability: A Key to Effective Serviceability and Maintenance Management. Wiley, New York (1995)
25. Lim, J., Stratopoulos, T.C., Wirjanto, T. S.: Path dependence of dynamic information technology capability: an empirical investigation. J. Manag. Inf. Syst. **28**(3), 45–84. Winter (2011–2012)
26. Teece, D.J., Pisano, G., Shuen, A.: Dynamic capabilities and strategic management. Strat. Manag. J. **18**(7), 509–533 (1997)
27. Lavie, D., Stettner, U., Tushman, M.L.: Exploration and exploitation within and across organizations. Acad. Manag. Ann. **4**, 109–155 (2010)
28. Collis, D.J.: Research note: how valuable are organizational capabilities? Strat. Manag. J. **15**, 143–152 (1994)

29. Gibson, C., Birkinshaw, J.: The antecedents, consequences, and mediating role of organizational ambidexterity. Acad. Manag. J. **47**(2), 209–226 (2004)
30. He, Z.L., Wong, P.K.: Exploration vs exploitation: an empirical test of the ambidexterity hypothesis. Organ. Sci. **15**, 481–494 (2004)
31. March, J.G.: Exploration and exploitation in organizational learning. Organ. Sci. **2**, 71–87 (1991)
32. Grant, R.M.: Toward a knowledge-based theory of the firm. Strat. Manag. J. **17**(S2), 109–122 (1996)
33. Nonaka, I.: A dynamic theory of organizational knowledge creation. Organ. Sci. **5**(1), 14–37 (1994)
34. Nonaka, L., Takeuchi, H., Umemoto, K.: A theory of organizational knowledge creation. Int. J. Technol. Manag. **11**(7–8), 833–845 (1996)
35. Nonaka, I., Takeuchi, H.: The Knowledge-Creating Company: How Japanese Companies Create the Dynamics of Innovation. Oxford University Press, Oxford (1995)
36. Gourlay, S.: The SECI model of knowledge creation: some empirical shortcomings, pp. 377–385 (2003)
37. Roberts, N., Galluch, P.S., Dinger, M., Grover, V.: Absorptive capacity and information systems research: review synthesis, and direction for future research. MIS Q. **36**(2), 625–648 (2012)
38. Kranz, J.J., Hanelt, A., Kolbe, L.M.: Understanding the influence of absorptive capacity and ambidexterity on the process of business model change–the case of on-premise and cloud-computing software. Inf. Syst. J. **26**, 477–517 (2016)
39. Cohen, W.M., Levinthal, D.: Absorptive capacity: a new perspective on learning and innovation. Adm. Sci. Q. **35**, 128–152 (1990)
40. Varis, M., Littunen, H.: Types of innovation, sources of information and performance in entrepreneurial SMEs. Eur. J. Innov. Manag. **13**(2), 128–154 (2010)
41. Mat, A., Razak, R.: The influence of organizational learning capability on success of technological innovation (product) implementation with moderating effect of knowledge complexity. Int. J. Bus. Soc. Sci. **2**(17), 217–225 (2011)
42. Forés, B., Camisón, C.: Does incremental and radical innovation performance depend on different types of knowledge accumulation capabilities and organizational size? J. Bus. Res. **69**(2), 831–848 (2016)
43. Zahra, S.A., George, G.: The net-enabled business innovation cycle and the evolution of dynamic capabilities. Inf. Syst. Res. **13**(2), 147–150 (2002)
44. Zahra, S.A., George, G.: Absorptive capacity: a review, reconceptualization, and extension. Acad. Manag. Rev. **27**, 185–203 (2002)
45. Lane, P.J., Koka, B.R., Pathak, S.: The reification of absorptive capacity: a critical review and rejuvenation of the construct. Acad. Manag. Rev. **31**(4), 833–863 (2006)
46. Tsai, W.: Knowledge transfer in intra-organizational networks: effects of network position and absorptive capacity on business-unit innovation and performance. AOM J. **44**, 996–1004 (2001)
47. Legris, P., Collerette, P.: A roadmap for IT project implementation: integrating stakeholders and change management issues. Proj. Manag. J. **37**(5), 64–75 (2006)
48. Alavi, M., Leidner, D.: Review: knowledge management systems: conceptual foundation and research issues. MIS Q. **25**(1), 107–136 (2001)
49. Frank, A.G., Ribeiro, J.L.D.: An integrative model for knowledge transfer between new product development project teams. Knowl. Manag. Res. Pract. **12**(2), 215–225 (2014)
50. Teo, T.S., Bhattacherjee, A.: Knowledge transfer and utilization in IT outsourcing partnerships: a preliminary model of antecedents and outcomes. Inf. Manag. **51**(2), 177–186 (2014)

51. Willcocks, L., Feeny, D., Olson, N.: Implementing core IS capabilities: Feeny-Willcocks IT governance and management framework revisited. Eur. Manag. J. **24**(1), 28–37 (2006)
52. Naghavi, A., Ottaviano, I.P.G.: Outsourcing, complementary innovations, and growth. Ind. Corp. Change **19**(4), 1009–1035 (2010). Advance Access Published 21 January
53. Palmer, J.W., Markus, M.L.: The performance impacts of quick response and strategic alignment in specialty retailing. Inf. Syst. Res. **11**(3), 241–259 (2000)
54. Easterby-Smith, M., Prieto, I.M.: Dynamic capabilities and knowledge management: an integrative role for learning? Br. J. Manag. **19**(3), 235–249 (2008)
55. Yin, R.K.: Case Study Research: Design and Methods, 4th edn. Sage, Newbury Park (2009). ISBN: 978-1-4129-6099-1
56. Chugh R.: Do Australian Universities encourage tacit knowledge transfer? In: Proceedings of the 7th International Joint Conference on Knowledge Discovery, Knowledge Engineering and Knowledge Management - Volume 1: KMIS, (IC3K 2015), pp. 128–135 (2015). ISBN 978-989-758-158-8
57. Rottman, J.W.: Successful knowledge transfer within offshore supplier networks: a case study exploring social capital in strategic alliances. J. Inf. Technol. **23**(1), 31–43 (2008)
58. Lee, Z., Lee, J.: An ERP implementation case study from a knowledge transfer perspective. J. Inf. Technol. **15**(4), 281–288 (2000)
59. Patton, M.Q.: Qualitative Evaluation and Research Methods. Sage Publications, Thousand Oaks (2002)
60. Glaser, B.G., Strauss, A.: The Discovery of Grounded Theory: Strategies for Qualitative Research. Aldine Publishing Co., Chicago (1967). The seminal work in grounded theory
61. Maxwell, J.A.: Understanding and validity in qualitative research. Harvard Educ. Rev. **62** (3), 279–300 (1992)
62. Lincoln, Y.S., Guba, E.G.: Naturalistic Inquiry, pp. 313–316. Sage, Newbury Park (1985)
63. Eisenhardt, K.M.: Building theories from case study research. Acad. Manag. Rev. **14**(4), 532–550 (1989)
64. Eisenhardt, K.M., Graebner, M.E.: Theory building from cases: opportunities and challenges. Acad. Manag. J. **50**(1), 25–32 (2007)
65. Miles, M.B., Huberman, A.M.: Qualitative Data Analysis: An Expanded Source Book, 2nd edn. Sage Publications Inc., California (1994)
66. Denzin, N.K.: The art and politics of interpretation. In: Denzin, N.K., Lincoln, Y.S. (eds.) Handbook of Qualitative Research, pp. 500–515. Sage, Thousand Oaks (1994)
67. King, N., Horrocks, C.: Interviews in Qualitative Research. Sage, Hokoben (2010)
68. Neuman, W.L.: Social Research Methods: Qualitative and Quantitative Approaches, 4th edn. Allyn and Bacon, Boston (2000)
69. Moustakas, C.: Phenomenological Research Methods. Sage, Thousand Oaks (1994)
70. Creswell, J.W., Miller, D.L.: Determining validity in qualitative inquiry. Theory Pract. **39** (3), 124 (2000)
71. Lincoln, Y.S., Guba, E.G.: Judging the quality of case study reports. Int. J. Qual. Stud. Educ. **3**(1), 53–59 (1990)
72. Lincoln, Y.S., Guba, E.G.: Paradigmatic Controversies, Contradictions, and Emerging Confluences. In: Denzin, N.K., Lincoln, Y.S. (eds.) Handbook of Qualitative Research, pp. 163–188. Sage, Thousand Oaks (2000)
73. Denzin, N.: The Research Act. Prentice Hall, Englewood Cliffs (1984)
74. Patton, M.Q.: Qualitative Evaluation and Research Methods, 2nd edn. Sage, Newbury Park, CA (1990)
75. Miles, R.E., Snow, C.C., Miles, G.: TheFuture.org. Long Range Plan. **33**(3), 300–321 (1990)

76. Lyytinen, K., Damsgaard, J.: What's wrong with the diffusion of innovation theory? In: Ardis, M.A., Marcolin, B.L. (eds.) Working Conference on Diffusing Software Product and Process Innovations. IFIP — The International Federation for Information Processing, vol. 59, pp. 173–190. Springer, Boston (2001). https://doi.org/10.1007/978-0-387-35404-0_11

77. Zmud, R.W.: Diffusion of modern software practices: influence of centralization and formalization. Manag. Sci. **28**(12), 1421–1431 (1982)

78. Damanpour, F.: Organizational innovation: a meta-analysis of effects of determinants and moderators. AOM J. **34**(3), 555–590 (1991)

79. Rogers, E.M.: Diffusion of Innovations. Free Press, New York (1962)

80. Kwon, T.H.A.: Diffusion of innovation approach to MIS infusion: conceptualization, methodology, and management strategies. In: Proceedings of the 10th International Conference on IS, Copenhagen, Denmark, pp. 139–146 (1990)

81. Fichman, R.G., Kemerer, C.F.: The assimilation of software process innovations: an organizational learning perspective. Manag. Sci. **43**(10), 1345–1363 (1997)

82. Grover, V., Goslar, M.D.: The initiation, adoption, and implementation of telecommunications technologies in U.S. organizations. J. MIS **10**(1), 141–163 (1993)

83. Hargadon, A.B., Sutton, R.I.: Technology brokering and innovation in a product development firm. Adm. Sci. Q. **42**, 716–749 (1997)

84. Stewart, D.W., Shamdasani, P.N., Rook, D.W.: Focus Groups: Theory and Practice. Sage Publications, Thousand Oaks (2007)

85. Creswell, J.W.: Qualitative Inquiry and Research Design: Choosing Among Five Traditions. Sage, Thousand Oaks (1998)

86. Miles, M., Huberman, A.M.: Qualitative Data Analysis: A Sourcebook of New Methods. Sage Publications, Newbury Park (1991)

87. Strauss, A., Corbin, J.: Basics of Qualitative Research. Sage Publications, Newbury Park (1990)

88. Allan, G.: A critique of using grounded theory as a research method. Electron. J. Bus. Res. Methods **2**(1), 1–10 (2003)

89. Douglas, D.: Inductive theory generation: a grounded approach to business inquiry. Electron. J. Bus. Res. Methods **2**(1), 47–54 (2003). Article 4, Academic Conferences International Limited

90. Badr, N.: Empowering capability for innovation in IT organizations - a confluence of knowledge for continual organizational learning. In: Proceedings of the 9th International Joint Conference on Knowledge Discovery, Knowledge Engineering and Knowledge Management (IC3K 2017) - Volume 3: KMIS, pp. 17–28. ISBN: 978-989-758-273-8 (2017)

91. Pugh, K., Prusak, L.: Designing effective knowledge networks. MIT Sloan Manag. Rev. **55**(1), 79–88 (2013)

92. Gatewood, B.: Clouds on the information Horizon: how to avoid the storm. Inf. Manag. J. **43**(4), 32–36 (2009)

93. Xue, Y., Huigang, L., Bolton, W.R.: Information technology governance in information technology investment decision processes: the impact of investment characteristics, external environment, and internal context. MIS Q. **32**(1), 67–96 (2008)

94. Lai, J., Lui, S.S., Tsang, E.W.: Intrafirm knowledge transfer and employee innovative behavior: the role of total and balanced knowledge flows. J. Prod. Innov. Manag. **33**(1), 90–103 (2016)

95. Lumpkin, G.T., Lichtenstein, B.B.: The role of organizational learning in the opportunity-recognition process. Entrep. Theory Pract. **29**(4), 451–472 (2005)

96. Morgan, T., Obal, M., Anokhin, S.: Customer participation and new product performance: towards the understanding of the mechanisms and key contingencies. Res. Policy 47(2), 498–510 (2018)

97. Kavusan, K., Noorderhaven, N.G., Duysters, G.M.: Knowledge acquisition and complementary specialization in alliances: the impact of technological overlap and alliance experience. Res. Policy 45(10), 2153–2165 (2016)

98. Badr, N.G.: Empowering IT organizations' capabilities of emerging technology integration through user participation in innovations based on IT. In: Caporarello, L., Cesaroni, F., Giesecke, R., Missikoff, M. (eds.) Digitally Supported Innovation. LNISO, vol. 18, pp. 11–33. Springer, Cham (2016). https://doi.org/10.1007/978-3-319-40265-9_2

99. Badr, N.G.: Integrating emerging technologies in IT services companies: the "Driver" CIO. In: 22nd Americas Conference on Information Systems, San Diego. Manuscript ID AMCIS-0127-2016. R2 (2016)

100. Al-Ammary, J.: The strategic alignment between knowledge management and information systems strategy: the impact of contextual and cultural factors. J. Inf. Knowl. Manag. 13 (01), 1450006 (2014)

101. Rosemann, M., Vessey, I.: Linking theory and practice: performing a reality check on a model of is success. In: Bartmann, D., et al. (eds.) Proceedings of the 13th European Conference on Information Systems, 26–28 May, Regensburg, Germany (2005)

102. Rosemann, M., Vessey, I.: Toward improving the relevance of information systems research to practice: the role of applicability checks. MIS Q. 32(1), 1–22 (2008)

How Do Japanese SMEs Generate Digital Business Value from SMACIT Technologies with Knowledge Creation?

Christian Riera[✉] and Junichi Iijima

Tokyo Institute of Technology,
Ookayama 2-12-1-W9-66, Meguro, Tokyo, Japan
{riera.c.aa,iijima.j.aa}@m.titech.ac.jp

Abstract. This study provides further evidence from Japanese Small and Medium Enterprises (SME) on the capabilities organizations need in order to take advantage of the opportunities that digital technologies (such as Social, Mobile, Analytics, Cloud and IoT or SMACIT) offer. Quantitative data is used to validate and expand previous findings on the relationship between IT, Digital Business Value and Knowledge Creation Capabilities (KCC). KCC is explored as an organizational capability that moderates the value obtained from IT and digital technologies. The level of achievement of business objectives by IT and digital technologies was analyzed using four categories of business objectives from the Balanced Scorecard. The evidence shows that organizations that are able to efficiently apply IT to achieve business objectives can also experience similar results on digital technologies. This implies that in order to be successful with digital technologies, a foundation would be the successful delivery of IT. A deeper analysis was conducted on Knowledge Creation Process as a preliminary study yielded to inconclusive findings suggesting that KCC had a negative impact on business objectives in opposition to what Knowledge-based view may consider and; in opposite to the characteristic that SMACIT technologies are highly dependent on information and could be considered to go hand in hand with how new information and knowledge is combined in order to create new products and services.

Keywords: Knowledge Creating Capabilities · Digital Business Value · IT Business Value

1 Introduction

The opportunities that digital technologies like SMACIT (Social, Mobile, Analytics, Cloud and Internet of Things) [20] bring to organizations are currently a major focus for both academia and industry. Since such technologies become available to a wider public, their simple usage or replication is not sufficient to provide a source of competitive advantage [18, 19]. The challenge that organizations face is how to gain competitive advantage from digital technologies and stay relevant in the market [18, 19]. Available research suggests that how digital technologies are combined with organizations' capabilities is a key for success in the Digital arena. Studies already have pointed out that having a clear digital strategy focusing either on Customer Engagement or Digitized Services & Products in one hand; together with a Digital Services Platform supporting Agility & Innovation and; an Operational Backbone delivering Operational Excellence is how companies address the challenges and opportunities that digital technologies bring [18].

The quest to create competitive advantage from digital technologies applies to any size of organizations. While large organizations usually have more resources than Small and Medium Enterprises (SME), SME have some advantages such as a simpler decision process supported by fewer levels of hierarchy [3]. We focus on Japanese SMEs due to their economic relevance. It is reported by the Ministry of Economy, Trade and Industry in Japan that they account for 99.7% of all enterprises from Japanese economy [22]. This fact creates the need to understand how to use IT and digital technologies.

SMACIT technologies like Social, Mobile, Analytics or Internet or Things are highly dependent on data, information and knowledge. Since such technologies either generate data, use data or both; a preliminary research [16] aimed to explore the relationship between Knowledge Creation Capabilities (KCC), IT and Digital Business Value. Knowledge Creation Capabilities [15] refers to the balance of the four knowledge creation processes from Nonaka and Takeuchi's SECI model [13]. KCC concept acknowledges that there could be a bottleneck in the knowledge creation process when an organization either over-focuses or has a lack-of focus on a particular SECI process. IT Business value was defined as the achievement of business objectives by the use of IT. Similarly, Digital Business Value was defined as the achievement of business objectives by the use of digital technologies [16]. Following the Balance Scorecard categorization [9], four categories of business objectives were used: Customer, Financial, Business Process and Learning & Growth. Such categorization enabled the study to address the individuality of the organizations as each one has their own objectives when they invest or engage on IT and digital technologies.

IT and its impact on business performance have been deeply explored over decades. Initially the term IT Productivity Paradox was used as a challenging statement regarding the contribution that IT provided to the productivity statistics [2]. Over the years this challenge was addressed first by measuring the direct impact of IT investment on business performance results. Later on the exploration identified that the results were different according to the type of IT asset [24, 25]. After that the focus turned onto the business processes on which IT was being utilized [21]. Finally, the exploration looked into organizational capabilities as a way to explain why some organizations were more successful than others even if they invested on similar type of technology [2, 14, 16, 25].

On the other hand, the utilization of digital technologies and in particular how companies go under Digital Transformation is the subject of recent studies [17–19]. This paper is aligned with studies focusing on organizational capabilities and aims to apply the learnings from IT Productivity Paradox and how its research has evolved over the years onto the Digital arena.

The preliminary research [16] identified that IT Business Value was highly related to Digital Business value, suggesting that the organizations that were able to achieve IT Business Value (achievement of business objectives by the use of IT) most likely also were able to achieve Digital Business Value (achievement of business objectives by the application of digital technologies). That research did not yield conclusive results for KCC and even suggested a negative impact of that relationship. Considering the inconclusive results for the impact of KCC to IT and Digital Business Value as well as other limitations such as the small number of observations from the preliminary study; this time a further exploration is done over the four knowledge creation processes from SECI model: Socialization, Externalization, Combination and Internalization.

This study contributes to the literature by first validating the relationship between IT Business Value and Digital Business Value. Secondly, it provides further insights on the positive relationship between KCC and IT Business Value; identifying in particular which type of objectives KCC support and which Knowledge Conversion Processes from SECI Model contributed to that relationship.

Section 2 describes the framework and hypotheses. Measurements and methodology are described in Sect. 3. Section 4 includes analysis and findings. Finally, Discussion and Conclusions are included in Sects. 5 and 6.

2   Framework and Hypotheses

2.1   IT Business Value

The debate on the contribution that IT brings to organizations was formally defined when the IT Productivity Paradox term was raised. While some researchers found this relationship to be positive, others found negative and even neutral relationships as included in Table 1 [16]. The research focus evolved from seeing IT investment as independent assets to the consideration of organizational characteristics or capabilities that moderate the results that organizations obtain from IT.

Table 1. Key studies exploring IT, firm performance and other firm capabilities (adapted from [7 on 16])

Research focus	Studies	Findings
IT and organizational performance	Mahmood et al. (1993), Weill (1992), Wilson (1993), Loveman (1994)	None or negative
	Weill (1992), Wilson (1993), Loveman (1994), Brynjolfsson and Hitt (1995), Brynjolfsson and Hitt (1996), Hitt and Brynjolfsson (1996), Brynjolfsson et al.(1998), Greenan et al. (2001)	Positive
IT, organizational performance and organizational capabilities	Bresnahan et al. (2002), Brynjolfsson et al. (1998), Ramirez et al.(2001), Francalanci and Galal (1998), Devaraj and Kohli (2002), Tallon et al. (2000), Weill et al. (2004, 2005)	Positive

The term IT Business Value has been considered to address the concerns raised by the IT Productivity Paradox but from a positive perspective. Productivity or profitability improvement, cost reduction, revenue and sales increase are some of the financial contributions where IT has been linked to [11]. At the same time, other measures that derive in organizational performance such as developing competitive advantage, increasing customer proximity or improving customer satisfaction are also areas where IT can contribute. An early study proposed IT Business Value Model based on the Resource-based view where the combination of IT resources (Technology and HR) with complementary organizational resources enabled business processes and, then business processes performance was actually perceived as Organizational Performance [11].

Dynamic capabilities theory was developed in response to the dynamic nature of the market and its changes over time. The changes on the market require organizations to modify its resources in order to stay relevant [23]. Dynamic capabilities can also be seen as the foundation that makes managers acquire and combine resources in order to generate value-creating strategies [8].

Based on these concepts, IT Business Value was defined as the contribution that IT resources and capabilities make to help an organization to achieve its objectives [16].

In order to address the different objectives that organizations pursue, the study used the four categories defined by the Balance Scorecard [9]: Customer, Financial, Business Process and Learning & Growth. This approach offered a simple but concrete way to address the individuality of the organizations.

2.2 Digital Business Value

The research on digital technologies has been taking place over the recent years with focus on identifying best practices from organizations that have been successful in the transformation to the digital environment [18–20]. In a similar manner than IT Business Value, the definition of Digital Business Value is described as the contribution that digital technologies make to help an organization achieve its objectives [16].

2.3 Difference Between Digitized and Digital

The terms Digitized, Digital, Digitalization and Digital Transformation among others have been heavily used over recent years without a shared definition. During the data collection this study avoided using such terms and instead referred to digital technologies or SMACIT in order to avoid any misconception of the terms.

We are aligned with the definition provided by the Centre for Information Systems Research from Massachusetts Institute of Technology in which Digitized is seen as an operational necessity requiring standardizing business process, with benefits mainly on the operational excellence. Digital referring to a customer-centric value proposition or creation of new customer value delivered in the form of digital offerings [17]. Digitized may include digital technologies but it may not necessarily translate onto new digital offerings or new value for the customers. The same study suggests that successful companies in the digital economy will have both characteristics: Digital to provide customer value and Digitized to provide scale and efficiency.

This study inquired on business objectives where digital technologies like SMACIT contributed. We consider the data collected may include both business objectives searching Digitization (Digitize) and Digitalization (Digital) objectives. Nevertheless the main assumption is that the majority of the SMEs from the target population may be still on the Digitized stage. This cannot be verified as the study didn't collect information on digital strategy or specific value created for customers based on digital offerings.

2.4 Knowledge Creating Capabilities and SECI Process

Knowledge is considered as a strategic asset to the organizations by the Knowledge-based view [8]. Business improvement is considered also a key motivation for organizations to engage in knowledge management initiatives [5]. Knowledge Creation is generally accepted to be part of Knowledge Management process [1, 4, 6] and by itself is an important strategic asset of the organization [8 cited in 10].

In the area of Knowledge Creation, Nonaka and Takeuchi contributed with the Knowledge Creation theory [13]. In their theory they acknowledged two types of knowledge: tacit and explicit. They proposed the SECI Model process where knowledge was created through the interaction and transformation of tacit and explicit knowledge. Such interaction is considered the spiral of knowledge creation where knowledge increases after each cycle [13].

The concern of a bottleneck in this spiral was captured by Knowledge Creating Capabilities or "Balanced SECI" [15]. KCC was defined as the level in which all four SECI Processes can act together and its measurement has been also done previously in the SME context [15].

Since the study of the relationship between KCC, IT Business Value and Digital Business Value in the preliminary research led to inconclusive findings; the current study added the exploration at each of the four SECI processes to understand the relationship IT and Digital Business Value.

2.5 Research Framework and Hypotheses

The main hypothesis in this study is defined as: "there is a positive relationship between Knowledge Creating Capabilities, IT Business and Digital Business Value". The detailed hypotheses are:

- H1: The achievement of business objectives by digital technologies (Digital Business Value) is related to the achievement or business objectives by IT (IT Business Value).
- H2: Knowledge Creating Capabilities are present in organizations that achieve business value from IT (IT Business Value).
- H3: Knowledge Creating Capabilities are present in organizations that achieve business value from digital technologies (Digital Business Value).

The research framework is adapted from [16] (see Figs. 1 and 2).

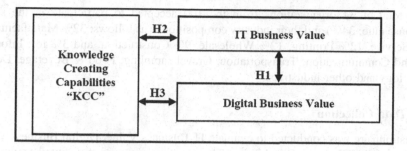

Fig. 1. Research framework (adapted from [16])

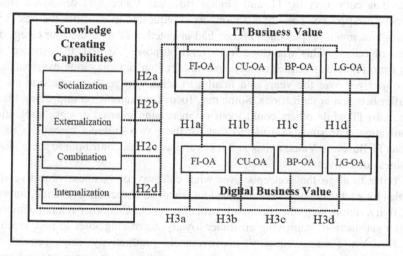

Fig. 2. Research framework at component level (adapted from [16])

3 Measurements and Methodology

3.1 Target Population

One hundred Japanese SMEs selected by the Japanese Ministry of Economy, Trade and Industry in the list of "Competitive IT Strategy SME Selection 100" from 2015, 2016 and 2017 [12] are selected as the target for this research. The SMEs are in principle self-nominated but they needed to include a case or sample of effective utilization of IT and demonstrated good business performance for the selection. This data set was selected precisely due to the characteristic of having evidence showing an effective use of technology. This was expected to facilitate testing of the relationship between IT Business Value, Digital Business Value and with KCC. Previous studies have also used a similar population [14–16].

A total of 34 organizations from the 100 accepted to participate in the study (response ratio: 34%) and their industry composition is as follows: 32% Manufacturing, 18% Service, 12% Printing, 12% Wholesale, 9% Construction, and 3% for: Information and Communication, Transportation, Gravel sampling, Food & Beverage, Dental technology and other industries.

3.2   Data Collection

A questionnaire was conducted to evaluate IT Business Value, Digital Business Value and Knowledge Creation Capabilities. The questionnaire was distributed to the 100 companies mailbox address and follow up calls were done to increase the response rate. As mentioned in previous section the response ratio obtained was 34%.

The data collection for IT and Digital Business Value was organized from an investment perspective. The organizations were requested to consider the past 3 years and asses how much (in percentage) they had invested in IT over the four categories of business objectives. This was done for several purposes. At first, to consider lagged results from IT investment. Secondly, to consider that organizations may pursue different objectives over the years and finally, to acknowledge that organizations focus may differ between organizations. Some may focus for example on improving financial outcomes by IT while others could focus on increasing internal process integration or harmonization. The study considered that for these two different categories of organizations IT Business Value exists and it is valid as IT can contribute to the realization of business objectives.

In order to align the concepts over what category of business objective meant, examples for each category were included as Financial (expanding revenue, improving productivity, improving the financial structure, etc.), Customer-related (improving customer satisfaction, improving customer loyalty, increasing sales to new customers, etc.), Business Process (quality improvement, productivity improvement, etc.), Learning and growth (securing human resources, human resources education, creativity, development capability, etc.).

The level of contribution used a Likert scale: Not Achieved, Partially Achieved, Highly Achieved and Fully Achieved and it was applied for the 4 categories of business objectives. This was used for both measuring IT Business Value as well as Digital Business Value.

To align the understanding of the organizations on which digital technologies were addressed in the questionnaire, a list of digital technologies with a brief explanation was included including Mobile, Cloud, SNS (Social Networking Service), Big Data and Analytics, Internet of Things (IoT), Artificial Intelligence (AI) and 3D printing technology.

Knowledge Creation Capabilities were evaluated using a questionnaire that measured each of the SECI processes. The instrument has been used in previous studies [15] and listed six items or behaviors related to each of the four SECI Model processes. Organizations needed to select 12 out of 24 behaviors that reflected their employees' behaviors. KCC was calculated as the minimum score from the 4 SECI Model processes.

4 Analysis and Findings

Both correlation and analysis of variance were applied in order to identify the relationship between IT Business Value, Digital Business Value and KCC. The exploration included both an overall level between the variables as well as between their internal components. For instance the score of each of the 4 SECI Processes in KCC, the achievement level in each of the 4 business objectives types (Financial, Customer, Business Process and Learning & Growth) for both IT BV and Digital BV.

The variables used in the study are included in Table 2.

The level of objective achievement used for both IT Business Value and Digital Business value measures is represented in the Y-Axis for the figures in this paper. The scale use is as follows: 1 - Not Achieved, 2 - Partially Achieved, 3 - Highly Achieved, 4 - Fully Achieved).

Table 2. List of variables used in the study.

Knowledge Creation Capabilities	IT Business Value (achievement of business objectives using IT)	Digital Business Value (achievement of business objectives using digital technologies)
KCC (minimum of SECI process score)	IT BV (average of the achievement of 4 types)	Digital BV (average of the achievement of 4 types)
KCC L/M/H groups according to KCC	IT FI-OA (achievement of financial objectives)	DI FI-OA (achievement of financial objectives)
SECI Socialization and L/M/H groups	IT CU-OA (achievement of customer objectives)	DI CU-OA (achievement of customer objectives)
SECI Externalization and L/M/H groups	IT BP-OA (achievement of business processes objectives)	DI BP-OA (achievement of business processes objectives)
SECI Combination and L/M/H groups	IT LG-OA (achievement of learning & growth objectives)	DI LG-OA (achievement of learning & growth objectives)
SECI Internalization and L/M/H groups		

4.1 Relationship Between IT Business Value and Digital Business Value

The correlation analysis identified below relationships:

- Positive relationship [r = 0.810, n = 27, p = 0.000] between overall IT Business Value and overall Digital Business Value (compound achievement of 4 types of business objectives by the use of digital technologies) (see Fig. 3).

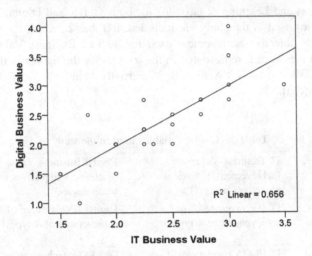

Fig. 3. IT Business Value and Digital Business Value.

- Positive relationships between IT Business Value per each of the 4 types of business objectives and their pair on Digital Business Value.
  - Achievement of Financial related objectives by IT and by digital technologies [r = 0.813, n = 23, p = 0.000] (see Fig. 4).

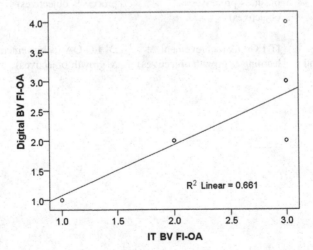

Fig. 4. Achievement of Financial related objectives using IT and digital technologies.

– Achievement of Customer related objectives by IT and by digital technologies [r = 0.792, n = 24, p = 0.000] (see Fig. 5).

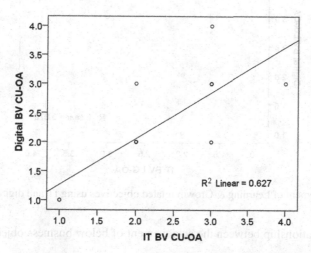

Fig. 5. Achievement of Customer related objectives using IT and digital technologies.

– Achievement of Business Process related objectives by IT and by digital technologies [r = 0.707, n = 24, p = 0.000] (see Fig. 6).

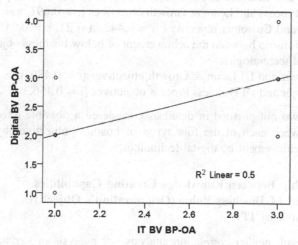

Fig. 6. Achievement of Business Process related objectives using IT and digital technologies.

– Achievement of Learning & Growth related objectives by IT and by digital technologies [r = 0.937, n = 18, p = 0.000] (see Fig. 7).

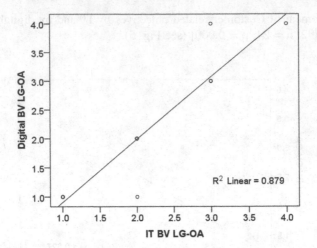

Fig. 7. Achievement of Learning & Growth related objectives using IT and digital technologies.

- Positive relationship between the achievement of below business objective types by using IT:
  - Business Process and Learning & Growth objectives by IT [r = 0.574, n = 22, p = 0.005]
- Positive relationship between the achievement of the following business objective types by using digital technologies:
  - Customer and Business Process objectives [r = 0.623, n = 22, p = 0.002]
  - Customer and Learn & Growth objectives [r = 0.476, n = 18, p = 0.046]
  - Business Process and Learn & Growth objectives [r = 0.691, n = 18, p = 0.002]
  - Financial and Customer objectives [r = 0.442, n = 21, p = 0.045]
- Positive relationship between the achievement of below business objective types by IT and digital technologies:
  - IT Customer and DI Learn & Growth objectives [r = 0.489, n = 18, p = 0.040]
  - IT Customer and DI Business Process objectives [r = 0.456, n = 24, p = 0.025].

The above two not pursued in detail as considered a possible effect of the other correlations between each of the four types of business objectives by IT and their correspondent achievement by digital technologies.

4.2 Relationship Between Knowledge Creating Capabilities (KCC) and IT Business Value (Organization's Objectives Achievement by IT)

At an overall level, neither correlation analysis nor analysis of variance identified a direct relationship between KCC and the aggregated measure of IT Business Value (average achievement of the four types of business objectives by the use of IT). In the same way as the preliminary study suggested, the impact of KCC level seemed to affect the level of achieved IT Business value in a negative way although it was not verified statistically (see Fig. 8).

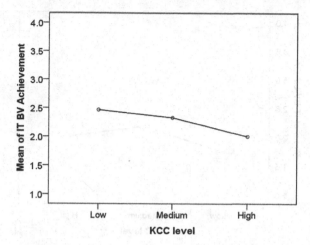

Fig. 8. KCC level and IT Business Value (objectives achievement using IT), not statistically significant.

From the exploration on the four types of business objectives identified a positive relation [r = 0.435, n = 23, p = 0.038] between KCC and the achievement of Learning & Growth business objectives by the use of IT (see Fig. 9).

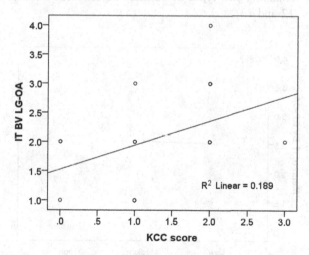

Fig. 9. KCC score and achievement of Learning & Growth objectives using IT.

The analysis of variance using the KCC score itself confirmed the relationship statistically [F(3, 19) = 3.369, p = 0.040]. These findings were observed only as trend without statistically significant results when the Low, Medium and High KCC categorization was used (see Fig. 10).

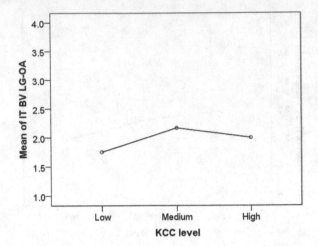

Fig. 10. KCC level and achievement of Learning & Growth related objectives using IT, not statistically significant.

At the same time, although no significant relationship was found, a positive trend was observed for the level of KCC and the achievement of Business Process objectives by the use of IT (see Fig. 11). In addition, a negative trend was observed for the level of KCC and the remaining two types of business objectives: Financial and Customer related (see Figs. 12 and 13).

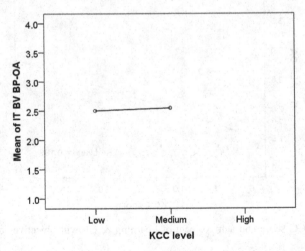

Fig. 11. KCC level and achievement of Business Process related objectives using IT.

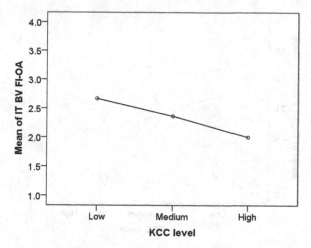

Fig. 12. KCC level and achievement of Financial related objectives using IT, not statistically significant.

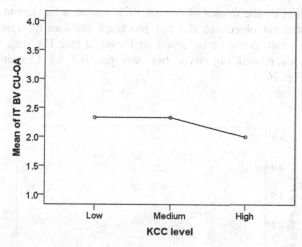

Fig. 13. KCC level and achievement of Customer related objectives using IT, not statistically significant.

4.3 Relationship Between KCC and Digital Business Value (Organization's Objectives Achievement by Digital Technologies)

The correlation analysis did not identify a direct relationship between KCC and overall Digital Business Value (compound achievement of 4 types of business objectives by the use of digital technologies). The analysis of variance suggested a negative relation but it was not verified statistically [$F(1, 25) = 2.124$, $p = 0.157$] either (see Fig. 14).

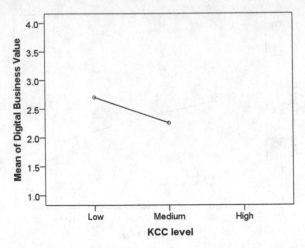

Fig. 14. KCC level and Digital Business Value (objectives achievement using digital technologies), not statistically significant.

The exploration on the impact of overall KCC on the achievement of any of the four types of business objectives did not produced statistically significant results. Similar negative trends could be observed on Financial (see Fig. 15), Customer and Business Processes related objectives but was positive for Learning & Growth objectives (see Fig. 16).

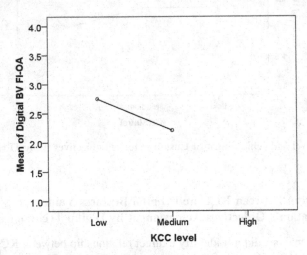

Fig. 15. KCC level and achievement of Financial related objectives using digital technologies, not statistically significant.

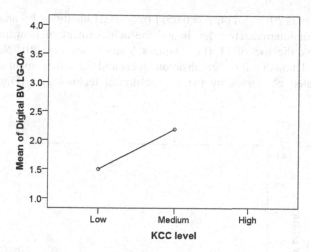

Fig. 16. KCC level and achievement of Learning & Growth related objectives using digital technologies, not statistically significant.

4.4   Relationship of SECI Processes with IT Business Value and Digital Business Value

A deeper look on each of the four SECI Processes (Socialization, Externalization, Socialization and Combination) in KCC and their relationship with IT Business Value as well as with Digital Business Value was conducted. The main motivation for this analysis was the initial findings in this study of a positive relationship between KCC and the achievement of Learning & Growth objectives by the use of IT on previous section (see Figs. 9 and 10).

This exploration yielded below results:

- No statistically significant relationship identified for Socialization or Externalization and IT Business value. Neither Digital Business Value at overall level nor at business objectives categories.
- Positive relationship for Combination and the achievement of Learning & Growth objectives by the use of IT (IT Business Value) [r = 0.606, n = 23, p = 0.002] (see Fig. 17). Such results were also verified with analysis of variance [F (2, 20) = 4.738, p = 0.021] (see Fig. 18). No statistically significant relationship for Combination and the achievement of Learning & Growth objectives by the use of digital technologies (Digital Business Value).
- Difference [F(2, 21) = 5.707, p = 0.010] identified by analysis of variance between Combination levels and the achievement of Customer objectives by the use of digital technologies (Digital Business Value) (see Fig. 19). No statistically significant relationship for Combination levels and the achievement of Customer related objectives by the use of IT (IT Business Value).

- Difference [$F(2, 20) = 3.474$, $p = 0.051$] ($p > 0.05$) identified by analysis of variance between Internalization levels and the achievement of Learning & Growth objectives by the use of IT (IT Business Value) (see Fig. 20). No statistically significant relationship for Internalization levels and the achievement of Learning & Growth related objectives by the use of digital technologies (Digital Business Value).

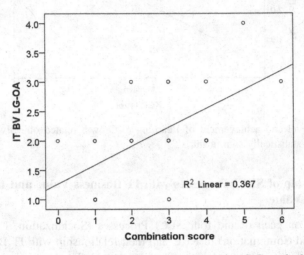

Fig. 17. SECI Combination process and achievement of Learning & Growth objectives using IT

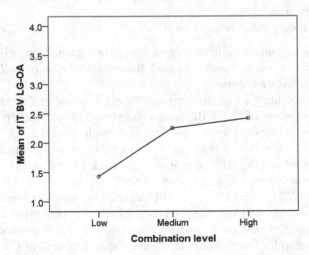

Fig. 18. SECI Combination process level and achievement of Learning & Growth objectives using IT.

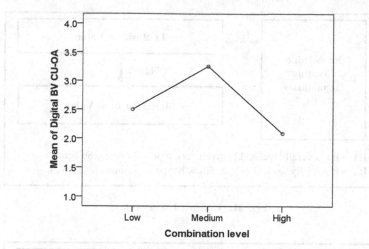

Fig. 19. SECI Combination process level and achievement of Customer objectives using digital technologies (High and Medium groups difference at sig. 0.008).

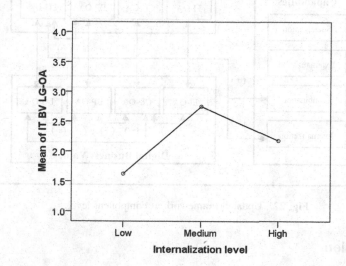

Fig. 20. SECI Internalization process level and achievement of Learning & Growth objectives using IT (statistically significant at p = 0.051. Low and Medium groups difference at 0.047).

4.5 Relationship Between SECI Processes

The correlation analysis identified below relationships between SECI Processes:

– Socialization and Externalization [r = 0.358, n = 33, p = 0.041]
– Combination and Internalization [r = 0.356, n = 33, p = 0.042].

The Updated Framework is described as below (see Figs. 21 and 22).

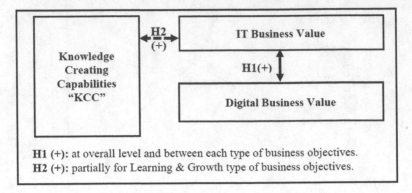

Fig. 21. Updated Framework.

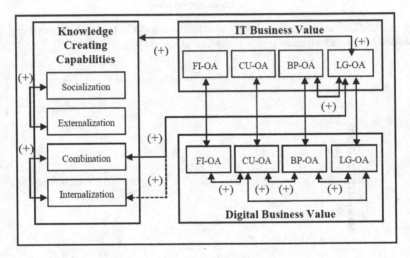

Fig. 22. Updated Framework at component level.

5   Discussion

This research used a flexible but at the same time concrete way to measure the impact that IT and digital technologies had on organizations. Flexibility was provided as it did not try to align all organizations to a specific measure like revenue or productivity. Concreteness was ensured as organizations were requested to classify IT and digital technologies investment across four categories of business objectives they were supporting and, then evaluate the level of objective achievement.

The results from the exploration of Hypothesis 1 confirmed the relationship between IT Business Value and Digital Business Value. In other words, the level of achievement of business objectives by the utilization of IT was identified to be related to the level of achievement of business objectives by the utilization of digital technologies and vice versa. This was observed not only at an overall level between IT

Business Value and Digital Business Value but also was between each of the four types of business objectives: Customer related, Financial related, Business Process and Learning & Growth. For instance, the level or achievement of Customer related business objectives by IT was related with the level of achievement Customer related business objectives by digital technologies. All these relationships were positive.

We consider there could be several explanations for such relationship. The first and simplest would be that organizations see digital technologies only as technological tools which belong to IT and as such did not differentiate. A second -and the one we consider more appropriate- is aligned with dynamic capabilities. In this case the observed relationship may reflect that some organizations have mastered (developed or enhanced their capabilities) how to use IT for delivering business value and, such capabilities are also useful for delivering business value with digital technologies. Additionally, it may be considered that since the experience that organizations have dealing with IT spans over decades, succeeding with new technologies may be partially moderated by the success organizations face with IT (or traditional IT).

A relationship was also identified between the achievement of Business Process objectives and the achievement of Learning & Growth objectives supported by IT.

The relationship between the four types of business objectives was stronger on Digital Business Value. The multiple relationships identified between Customer, Business Process and Learning & Growth objectives, together with the relationship between Customer and Finance type of business objectives supported by digital technologies suggested that the organizations that are able to benefit from digital technologies have some capabilities that allow them to succeed in any of the type of business objectives.

These results are aligned with the preliminary study [16] where this relationship between IT Business Value and Digital Business Value was also observed.

Hypothesis 2 clarified the impact that Knowledge Creating Capabilities have on the achievement of business objectives by IT. In specific with the achievement of Learning & Growth related business objectives by IT. The deeper exploration at SECI Processes level allowed to identify that Combination process ($p < 0.05$) and Internalization process ($p = 0.051$) were related to the achievement of Learning & Growth business objectives by IT. Combination being the process where the explicit knowledge that was gathered both internally and externally is combined into new knowledge. Internalization is the process where the explicit knowledge generated by Internalization is integrated onto individual's tacit knowledge by learning and doing. Hypothesis 2 suggests that the organizations that were able to achieve Learning & Growth objectives by the utilization of IT had strong Combination and Internalization processes. A reason for this could be that organizations where knowledge creation is considered valuable may reflect such focus on Learning & Growth objectives. Such organizational focus may also influence on actually using IT to achieve such objectives.

These results provided empirical and statistically significant evidence to initial observations from the preliminary study [16].

Hypothesis 3 explored the relationship that Knowledge Creating Capabilities (KCC) had with the achievement of business objectives by the use of digital technologies. Without statistically significant results, the negative relationship observed suggests that the stronger the organizations focus on the creation of new knowledge, they may see a decrease in the level of achievement of business objectives in general. The negative trend was observed for three of the business objectives types (Financial, Customer and Business Processes) but positive for Learning & Growth objectives. This also can be interpreted together with Hypothesis 2 findings as it shows a positive relationship between the focus on knowledge creation by the organizations and the achievement of Learning & Growth objectives, either it is by IT or by the use of digital technologies. Although not validated by the statistical analysis the perceived negative relationship between KCC and the remaining three types of business objectives may actually remind us that the organizational resources are limited, therefore the more an organization pursues for knowledge creation and devotes its resources to such objectives then they risk of not paying attention to other business objectives categories.

These results are aligned with previous study [16].

The study provides some insights on how organizations that are looking to apply digital technologies (SMACIT) or even further planning to engage in Digitalization (Digital or Digital Transformation) may refer to. In particular, how the capabilities that allow organizations to effectively deliver IT in a way that it supports their business objectives may also help to deliver digital technologies in the same manner.

It is important to acknowledge that the organizations in this study belong to a specific population with particular characteristics. First they were awarded by the Japanese Government due to their effective use of IT to support and improve their business. Another characteristic is that the organizations were Japanese SME, and culture aspects may have influenced the self-evaluation of the level of achievement of business objectives.

6   Conclusions

This study served to verify the contribution that IT and digital technologies (SMACIT) have on the achievement of business objectives. Hypothesis 1 verified the close relationship between the achievement of objectives using IT and by digital technologies. The relationship was observed at an overall level and also between each of the four types of business objectives. These results contribute with evidence of the close relationship between success on implementation of IT and success implementing digital technologies.

Hypothesis 2 evaluated the relationship between Knowledge Creating Capabilities and the achievement of business objectives supported by IT. The results indicated that the relationship exists with the Learning & Growth business objectives type. Additionally, the results confirmed that Combination and Internalization processes were the contributors to the achievement of Learning & Growth objectives.

Hypothesis 3 tested the relationship between Knowledge Creating Capabilities and the achievement of business objectives by the use of digital technologies. The exploration didn't yield statistically significant results but some trends were observed. They were negative for Financial, Customer and Business Processes objective achievement and positive for Learning & Growth objectives.

We consider this study contributes with empirical evidence suggesting that organizations that are able to efficiently apply IT towards the achievement of business objectives can also experience similar results while applying digital technologies. Another way to interpret the results is also to consider that in order to be successful for the implementation of digital technologies; an initial foundation would be the successful delivery of IT to achieve business objectives. Organizations need to identify the capabilities that will allow them to successfully deliver IT and implement digital technologies in a way they support business objectives. This study explored if Knowledge Creation Capabilities were part of such enabling capabilities. The analysis yielded results indicating that the achievement of Learning & Growth business objectives by the use of IT was indeed related to Knowledge Creation Capabilities. At the same time, a clear relationship between how IT supported the achievement of Learning & Growth objectives and how it was related to the achievement of the same objective types by the use of digital technologies.

We recommend the future work to continue pursuing the identification of the capabilities that organizations need in order to benefit from digital technologies or SMACIT. A first answer to this was identified by this study providing empirical evidence that having capabilities to successfully deploy IT in a way that generates Business Value may be foundation for achieving similar results with digital technologies. Acknowledging such relationship is important but we consider the exploration is not over as there could be other organization capabilities that could contribute to achieving further business value from digital technologies. Some studies have already pointed out that having a clear digital strategy focusing either on Customer Engagement or Digitized Services & Products in one hand, together with a Digital Services Platform supporting Agility & Innovation and, last but not least, an Operational Backbone delivering Operational Excellence are how organizations address the challenges and opportunities that the Digital Age brings.

References

1. Benbya, H., Passiante, G., Belbaly, N.A.: Corporate portal: a tool for knowledge management synchronization. Int. J. Inf. Manag. **24**(3), 201–220 (2004)
2. Brynjolfsson, E., Hitt, M.: Beyond the productivity paradox. Commun. ACM **41**(8), 49–55 (1998)
3. Carcary, M., Doherty, E., Conway, G.: The adoption of cloud computing by Irish SMEs – an exploratory study. Electron. J. Inf. Syst. Eval. **17**(1), 003–014 (2014)
4. Chen, M., Chen, A.: Knowledge management performance evaluation: a decade review from 1995 to 2004. J. Inf. Sci. **32**(1), 17–38 (2006)
5. Choi, B., Lee, S.: An empirical investigation of KM styles and their effect on corporate performance. Inf. Manag. **40**, 403–417 (2003)
6. Davenport, T.H., Prusak, L.: Working Knowledge: How Organizations Manage What They Know. Harvard Business School Press, Boston (2000)
7. Dedrick, J., Gurbaxani, V., Kraemer, K.L.: Information technology and economic performance: a critical review of the empirical evidence. ACM Comput. Surv. **35**(1), 1–28 (2003)
8. Grant, R.M.: Prospering in dynamically-competitive environments: organizational capability as knowledge integration. Organ. Sci. **7**(4), 375–387 (1996)

9. Kaplan, R., Norton, D.: The Balanced Scorecard - Translating Strategy into Action. Harvard Business Review Press, Boston (1996)
10. Lewin, A., Massini, S.: Knowledge creation and organizational capabilities of innovating and imitating firms. In: Tsoukas, H., Mylonopoulos, N. (eds.) Organizations as Knowledge Systems, pp. 209–237. Palgrave Macmillan, London (2004). https://doi.org/10.1057/9780230524545_10
11. Melville, N., Kraemer, K., Gurbaxani, V.: Review: information technology and organizational performance: an integrative model of IT business value. MIS Q. **28**(2), 283–322 (2004)
12. Ministry of Economy, Trade and Industry of Japan: Competitive IT Strategy SME Selection 100. http://www.meti.go.jp/english/press/2017/0531_003.html (English), http://www.meti.go.jp/policy/it_policy/investment/it_keiei/100sen.html (Japanese). Accessed 17 Feb 2018
13. Nonaka, I., Takeuchi, H.: The Knowledge-Creating Company. Oxford University Press, New York (1995)
14. Riera, C., Iijima, J.: A study of the effect of organizational IQ on IT investment and productivity. In: International Conference on Wireless Communications, Networking and Mobile Computing, Shanghai, pp. 4185–4188 (2007)
15. Riera, C., Senoo, D., Iijima, J.: A study of the effect of knowledge creating capabilities on corporate performance. Int. J. Knowl. Manag. Stud. **3**(1/2), 116–133 (2009)
16. Riera, C., Iijima, J.: Linking knowledge creating capabilities, IT business value and digital business value: an exploratory study in Japanese SMEs. In: Proceedings of the 9th International Joint Conference on Knowledge Discovery, Knowledge Engineering and Knowledge Management (IC3 K 2017 KMIS), Funchal, Madeira, Portugal, vol. 3, pp. 29–40 (2017)
17. Ross, J., Beath, C., Sebastian, I.: Digital ≠ Digital. Research Briefing, vol. XVII, no. 10. MIT Sloan Center for Information Systems Research, Cambridge, MA (2017)
18. Ross, J., Sebastian, I., Beath, C., Mocker, M., Moloney, K., Fonstad, N.: Designing and executing digital strategies. In: Thirty Seventh International Conference on Information Systems, ICIS 2016, Dublin (2016)
19. Ross, J., et al.: The Technology Advantage Practice of The Boston Consulting Group: Designing digital organizations. Working paper no. 406. Centre for Information Systems Research, Massachusetts Institute of Technology, Cambridge, MA (2016)
20. Sebastian, I., Ross, J., Beath, C., Mocker, M., Moloney, K., Fonstad, N.: How big old companies navigate digital transformation. MIS Q. Exec. **16**(3), 197–213 (2017)
21. Sandulli, F.D., Lopez-Sanchez, J.I., Rodriguez-Duarte, A., Fernandez-Mendez, J.: Analysing the IT Paradox in the Supply Chain (2007). https://ssrn.com/abstract=1105687. Accessed 20 May 2017
22. SME Agency: White Paper on Small and Medium Enterprises in Japan (2016). http://www.chusho.meti.go.jp/pamflet/hakusyo/H28/download/2016hakushopanflet_eng.pdf. Accessed 20 May 2017
23. Teece, D.J., Pisano, G., Shuen, A.: Dynamic capabilities and strategic management. Strateg. Manag. J. **18**(7), 509–534 (1997)
24. Weill, P.: The relationship between investment in information technology and firm performance: a study of the value manufacturing sector. Inf. Syst. Res. **3**(4), 307–333 (1992)
25. Weill, P., Aral, S.: IT assets, organizational capabilities and firm performance: how resource allocations and organizational differences explain performance variation. Organ. Sci. **18**(5), 763–780 (2007)

Common Information Systems Maturity Validation Resilience Readiness Levels (ResRLs)

Rauno Pirinen[1,2(✉)]

[1] The National Defense University, Helsinki, Finland
[2] Laurea University of Applied Sciences, Espoo, Finland
rauno.pirinen@laurea.fi

Abstract. This revised study expands a series of investigations of the resilience readiness levels (ResRLs) of information systems, including their aspects, factors, definitions, criteria, references, and questionnaires. The aim is to contribute to the combined total maturity measures approach and the pre-operational validation of shared and adaptive information services and systems. The overall research question is followed: How can ResRLs be understood in the domain of shared operative information systems and services? The purpose of the study to improve the manner of information systems acceptance, operational validation, pre-order validation, risk assessment, the development of adaptive mechanisms, and the integration of information systems and services by actors and authorities across national borders. The main contribution of the study is in the validation of the maturity of operative information systems regarding their resilience, including the examination of several factors and descriptions of technical resilience. In addition to the validation of maturity, the study expands the revised compatibility of maturity levels by upgrading the ResRLs seven-layer model to the nine-level model according to technological readiness levels (TRLs) and integration readiness levels (IRLs) to improve the responsiveness of the European Operational Concept Validation framework.

Keywords: Common information sharing · Resilience ·
Resilience readiness level · Maturity model · Operational validation ·
Technical resilience

1 Introduction

The aim of this study is to contribute to the maturity validation and resilience metrics of operative information systems. The study focuses on the factors and descriptions of technical resilience and validation maturity. It provides a revision of the compatibility upgrade from the seven-level resilience readiness level (ResRL) model [1] to the nine-level model based on a white paper on technological readiness levels (TRL) [2], integration readiness levels (IRL), and descriptions of the nine levels descriptions [3] for consistency with the European Operational Concept Validation Methodology [4].

In this study, the research questions were formulated to guide the examination of the ways in which the descriptions and definitions of existing TRLs, IRLs, and new ResRLs

© Springer Nature Switzerland AG 2019
A. Fred et al. (Eds.): IC3K 2017, CCIS 976, pp. 383–403, 2019.
https://doi.org/10.1007/978-3-030-15640-4_19

as well as their criteria, references, and questionnaires can be employed to realize and validate the integration, communication, and adaptive dynamic resilient functionalities in operative information systems and information sharing. This study analyses the cases of operative maritime and data fusion systems and focuses on the descriptions, factors, initiators, and drivers of resilience readiness in order to contribute to future discussions about maturity validation processes and pre-validation processes with regard to research and innovation action funding by the European Commission H2020.

Standardization is an essential element in sharing information, information systems resilience, and effectiveness. It requires going beyond the syntactic nature of information technology and delving into the human functions at the semantic, pragmatic, critical realist, and social levels of organizational functions. As shown in Fig. 1, the research themes of this study prioritize improvements in the resilience approach of a complex service or system as well as the descriptions and factors of TRLs and IRLs for progress of the European Operational Concept Validation Methodology [4].

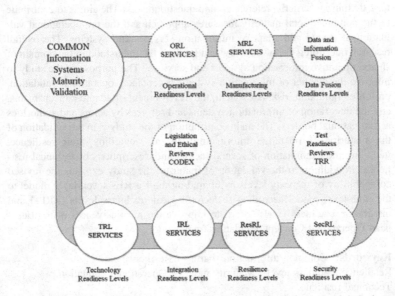

Fig. 1. Common information systems maturity validation approach [1] which is here further addressed to the European Operational Concept Validation Methodology [4].

In this study, the term "external validity" refers to establishing an expanded domain in which the study's findings and conclusions can be generalized to the progress of European Operational Concept Validation framework. The study adopts the method of increasing understanding through information systems research and maturity-integration facilities, such as utility and communication, resilience readiness, networked data fusion realization capability. The focus of validation standardization is regarded by the following: European Committee for Standardization and European Committee for Electro-technical Standardization (CEN-CENELEC); CEN/TC391 on Societal and Citizen Security; and the International Organization for Standardization (ISO) Standard 16290 Space Systems.

This study is based on an ongoing and cumulative data collection and the expansion of three (n = 3) preliminary research and development (R&D) projects: (1) European Union's Common Information Sharing Environment (EU_CISE_2020), including R&D-related research on work packages (n = 8) of the EU_CISE research consortium and research agenda targets related to the public authority in Finland; (2) Maritime Integrated Surveillance Awareness (MARISA), including eight work packages (n = 8) in the current H2020 project and EU_CISE continuum; and (3) the Academy of Finland Strategic Research Council's project From Failand to Winland, which is an ongoing National Critical Research Project (#WINLandFI), which includes five (n = 5) work packages.

The multiple case study approach is used. The method is described in previous studies that addressed "the case research strategy in studies of information systems" [5]; "building theories from case study research" [6]; "case studies and theory development in the social sciences" [7]; "qualitative data analysis" [8]; "real world research" [9]; and "case study research design and methods" [10]. The multiple case study followed replication logic, and the selected cases serve in a manner that is similar to multiple experiments, and they show similar results. The cases of externally funded projects (n = 3) emphasize the detailed contextual analysis of a limited number of events or conditions and their relationships when the relevant behavior is not manipulated and the role of the researcher is that of an "objective outsider" [11]. The selected cases of three preliminary research and development (R&D) projects (n = 3) are described in the following paragraphs.

EU_CISE_2020 Project: [Project ID 608385; Funded Under FP7-SECURITY]. The project's mandate is to examine common information sharing environments (CISE) that foster cross-sectorial and cross-border collaborations among public authorities and the dissemination of the EU_CISE initiative and steps along the Maritime EU_CISE roadmap. The EU_CISE project entails the widest possible experimental environment, encompassing innovative and collaborative services and processes between European institutions. Its reference points comprise a broad spectrum of factors in the field of European integrated services, which arise from the European legal framework as well as collaborative studies and related pilot projects.

MARISA Project: [Project ID 740698; Funded Under H2020]. The goal of the MARISA project is to provide security communities that operate at sea with a data fusion toolkit, which includes a suite of methods, techniques, and software modules for correlating and fusing various heterogeneous and homogeneous data and information from different sources, including the Internet and social networks, with the aim of improving information exchange, situational awareness, decision-making, reaction capabilities, and resilience. The expected solution will provide mechanisms for obtaining insights from big data sources, performing analyses of a variety of data based on geographical and spatial representation, using techniques to search for typical and new patterns that identify connections between events, and exploring predictive analysis models to represent the effects of relationships of observed objects and phenomena.

#WINLandFI Project: [Funding ID 303623; from April 2016 to March 2019]. The #WINLandFI research project moves from a Failand (i.e., a failed future Finland) to a Winland, such as Finland where resilient policy-making has been used to respond to key security threats. What kinds of security risks and threats could paralyze Finland such that our country would become Failand? The project data include the argument that Failand would become a reality if two of the most fundamental elements of a functioning society failed—food security and energy security. Both are closely linked to water security. In addition, these research data include reasons for setting resilience such that failure is likely to result from the sum of three key components: long-term pressures, shocks and surprises, decision-making, and policy responses.

In this operative domain, there is no single agreed definition of the term "resilience." In this study, the keyword "resilience," which is derived from the Latin *resilier* refers to the study of technical resilience and the ability to rebound, recover, or jump back in the critical fields of systems and decision-making processes. In this study, the term "resilience" refers mainly to the ability of critical, institutional, organizational, hardware, software, or operative service systems to mitigate the severity and likelihood of failures or losses, to adapt to changing conditions, and to respond appropriately after the evidence of failure, fact finding, consideration of response, scenario-based alignment, and progressive action competencies. The relevant literature on the technical perspective of "resilience" includes the following: on resilience engineering [12]; on viewpoints of robustness, persistence, and resilience [13]; on genealogies of resilience [14].

In addition, the term resilience encompasses several recent and related aspects in the social sciences. The term is also used in discussions of international finance and economic policy, corporate risk analysis, the psychology of trauma, policy-regulation development, urban, regional, and national planning, public health care, and national security. The term "ecological resilience" refers to the ability of the ecosystem to regenerate after stress and overloading. "Social resilience" was understood as the ability of communities to withstand external shocks to their social infrastructure [15, p. 361]. Social resilience can be observed in the positive and negative aspects of social exclusion, marginalization, and social capital [15, p. 352]. Social resilience is understood as important in forming relationships and the mutual trust of others, such as citizens' attitudes and responsibility.

In information systems, "resilience" is understood as a complex process that involves multiple overlapping and iterative tasks that concern design theory and system theory. The term also refers to a multi-methodological approach that involves thinking, building, improving, and evaluating a successful information system and its communication regarding its suitability to the applied domain, and information sharing. In the present study, the term applies to resilient systems [16] and resilience engineering [12]. The aim is to contribute to the information sharing and technical resilience that are related to the ontology of information technology, data additivity capabilities, parallel communication protocols, nexus management, and adaptive dynamic factors and effects of high-value technological artifacts, digital infrastructures, and critical systems.

There are many reasons for the progress of resilience, such as the increasing number of systems, interconnections, and transaction elements over time. The system's complexity increases, and the resulting interactions become challenging to maintain, such as the number of updates, difficulties in use and facilitation, life cycles, continuity management, and understanding emergent relations and causalities between the terms "resilience," "elastic," "robustness," "complexity," and "persistence." In this operative environment, the term "resilience" is first related to the term "robustness." In this setting, the term "robustness" refers to "the degree to which a system is able to withstand an unexpected internal or external event or change without degradation of in system's performance." The term "robustness" indicates "the degree to which system operates correctly in the presence of exceptional conditions." The term "resilience" refers to the system's ability to recover, retrieve, restore, or regenerate its performance after unexpected events that decrease its performance [13].

The study of resilience is further challenged by the adaptive nature of networked systems. They become increasingly difficult to understand, predict, and control. However, although there is no single agreed definition of the term resilience, there are numerous middle-range theories that explain resilience and its sources, paths, and effects, such as the following: the resilience and stability of ecological systems [17]; toward common information sharing: a study of integration readiness levels [18]; resilience in globalization and transitional pathways [19]; from systems ecology to the political economy of crisis adaptation and management [20]. In this study, the rationality and motivation for a further description of resilience factors is based on the usefulness of these theories and categories for data collection, data fusion, knowledge fusion, analysis, and triangulation in real R&D cases, research consortiums, and the co-creation of validation for externally funded R&D activities, especially the design and implementation of thematic studies, regional-global configurations, and integration strategies.

In this operative environment, knowledge management is understood as a discipline that is concerned with the analysis and technical support of the practices used in an authority-related organization and in decision-making to identify, create, represent, distribute, and enable the adoption and leveraging of the real-world practices used in collaborative authority settings, particularly public authority organizational processes. Effective knowledge management and information sharing are increasingly imperative in shared source of collaboration and rationale advantages. They are key in the ability of successful public authority organizations to bolster the collective, shared expertise of employees, actors, and partners. In this context, the term resilience refers to the knowledge gained by adaptive changes. The term resilience needs on demand refers to several aspects of resilience, such as planning and preparation; absorbing disturbance; recovering; and adapting according to known or unknown threats.

At the macro level of this study, the research questions are formulated to guide the examination of how existing TRLs, IRLs, and new ResRLs descriptions and their factors, definition, criteria, references, and questionnaires can be usefully employed to realize and validate integration, communication, and dynamic functionalities in information systems and information sharing. At the micro level, this study examines shared information systems in the cases of shared maritime and data fusion systems by focusing on the following resilience readiness factors, initiators, and drivers: (i) realization, such as the usefulness, sharing, and dissemination of an information system as a common digital service, product or solution involving shared information across appropriate borders of applied domains; (ii) validation, that is, pre-operational validation, pre-order validation for procurements, internal and external validity, which can, for example, be useful in national and global deployment and dissemination processes, operational validation of information systems, improving integration success, achieving common ontological coherence, and improving information systems' adaptive capabilities, integration, and service sharing.

The main objective of this research is to address the issue of increasing trustworthiness such that related studies are comprehensible for EU Horizon audiences and innovation funding in EC H2020. The study design is based on a thorough understanding of the theoretical framework and the relevant literature. The experiential knowledge of collaborative integration is used to answer the research questions as well as to determine the learning processes and their meanings. In this study, validity refers to the establishment of casual relationships such as nexus impacts. Causal relationships are interactions among shared readiness measures and information systems, realizations from the perspective of readiness levels, information sharing across borders of various domains, and the use of commonly shared information systems. For example, information is shared and education is collaborative and disseminated across national borders, which was undertaken by maritime universities throughout the European Union by utilizing data fusion (i.e., collective interactions by owners of data), such as through the Maritime Data Fusion User Community.

The expected contributions of this study are the operational and pre-operational validation (POV) and utility of standardization and interconnections: (1) improvement in metrics for information systems and services dynamics and integration; (2) advances in global procurement management and pre-order validation; (3) pre-operational validation in information system investigations; (4) progress in the operational validation of information system implementation; (5) the implications of the findings for the compliance of TRLs, IRLs, and improved ResRLs; (6) usefulness of information system sharing and interconnections; (7) expansion of large and networked information-intensive services that can extend shared solutions and routes of shared information utilization and common global information and information system sharing; (8) educational competence-related advances in R&D-related functions in higher education institutions, which in this case can be shared across national borders.

2   Continuum of Research

The path dependency of ResRLs and related knowledge are investigated by triangulation with the relevant literature. Examples are computer networks [21], system engineering [22], systems readiness levels [23] and the development of an integration readiness level [3]. This study focuses on factors of ResRLs, understanding readiness levels, realizing them in operative environments, using mid-range metrics and models of validation, reasons for extending the maturity validation process, which are examined in the following continuum of previous studies: "Toward common information systems maturity validation: resilience readiness levels (ResRL)" [1]; "Toward common information sharing: study of integration readiness levels" [18]; "Studies of integration readiness levels: Case shared maritime situational awareness system" [24]; "Samples of externally funded research and development projects in higher education: Case integration readiness levels" [25].

2.1   Technology Readiness Levels (TRL)

The first widely well-known model used to investigate the validation of TRLs, IRLs, and ResRLs was described in the early literature on computer networks [21]. The open system interconnection (OSI) model was developed by [26]. Here, the OSI model is embedded in the internal factors of TRLs, IRLs, and ResRLs. Subsequently, the OSI model was used [23] as the starting point in the development of maturity readiness levels. The OSI model has been widely used in computer networking to structure data transmitted on a network. The model allows for the integration of various technologies on the same network, networking themes [27], and system approaches to computer networks [28]. The reflective view of technology readiness (TRLs) assessments theme was presented in a white paper [2] and a subsequent retrospective description [29]. In the continuum of TRLs–IRLs development, this development path was described as follows: "it was necessary to develop an index that could indicate how integration occurs" [23, p. 6]. This index "considered not only physical properties of integration, such as interfaces or standards, but also interaction, compatibility, reliability, quality, performance and consistent ontology when two pieces are being integrated."

The TRLs includes nine levels [2]. The TRL metric was developed to assess technology and research interventions, and it was included in numerous efforts by the National Aeronautics and Space Administration and United States Department of Defense. Many early works in this field included definitions of the risks and costs associated with various TRLs. The literature indicates that TRLs were used to validate the readiness levels and maturity of an individual technology. Hence, TRLs adopt a given technology from the basic principles as well as concept evaluation, validation, prototype demonstration, completion, and successful operations [23].

Table 1. Technology readiness levels (TRL).

TRLs	Descriptions
TRL (9)	**Actual system proven in operational environment** | competitive manufacturing in the case of key enabling technologies or in space | last mile research | high value impacts | action research | field study | dissemination strategy | realization of canvas
TRL (8)	**System complete and qualified** | networking and integration services | infrastructure providing a framework for dealing with data having characteristics such as variety, volume, velocity and complexity | components and modules with the right capabilities to quickly and concurrently access and process data in the storage | external data sources and legacy systems functions | tools for the user | action research | organizational adaptions and changes
TRL (7)	**System prototype demonstration in operational environment** | systems functions and objects | multilingual information | entities, relations, temporal and spatial parameters | contextual information | system-to-system interfaces | communication measures | external systems demonstration | authorization issues | operational validation | identity and access mgmt. | action research | design science research
TRL (6)	**Technology demonstrated in relevant environment** | industrially relevant environment in the case of key enabling technologies | adapters and gateways for the integration | user refinement technology | field study | feasibility study | design science research

(*continued*)

Table 1. (*continued*)

TRLs	Descriptions
TRL (5)	**Technology validated in relevant environment** | industrially relevant environment in the case of key enabling technologies | the basic technological components are integrated so they can be tested in a simulated environment | supporting elements in a simulated operational environment | pre-operational technological artifacts | design science research | development research | field study | feasibility study
TRL (4)	**Technology validated in lab** | following successful proof-of-concept work | components are integrated | test results and estimations of differences between validation and expected system goals | technological artifacts | laboratory accounting | development research
TRL (3)	**Experimental proof-of-concept** | laboratory tests | measure parameters | test environment | active R&D initiated | experimental critical functions | components availability and stability | technology transition | development research | scenario analysis | strategy analytic and canvas
TRL (2)	**Technology concept formulated** | application articulated | basic principles | design of artifact | practical applications can be invented | publications or other references | limited to analytic studies | analysis to support the concept | case study analysis | design science research | development research | canvas
TRL (1)	**Basic principles observed** | applied research and development | studies of a technology's basic properties | scenario and proactive studies | case study analysis | studies of a technology's basic properties | scientific research begins to be translated into applied R&D | co-creation drivers | idea alignments | proposals | scope

These characterizations TRLs are useful in technology development. In this study, they refer to how a technology is implemented and developed further according to "needed on-demand adaptive changes" (resilience) within complete information-intensive systems and applied services. In addition, it was recognized that, currently, many complex systems fail in the integration phase and especially in case of "if emergent adaptive change is needed as on demand" as the resilience phase. With regard to this study, the readiness factors, functionalities, and capabilities of resilience are investigated for the further development of maturity aspects, questionnaires, validation capabilities, and metrics. Examples are the nexus of mutual causalities and the impacts of integration processes due to the increasing speed of technological development, the effects of new updates, and the need for increasingly adaptive and resilient systems [30]. In this context, TRLs can be used in a systematic metric and measurement system that supports the assessment of the maturity of a particular technology and the consistent comparison of the maturity of different types of technologies, such as CISE Information Sharing and MARISA Data Fusion technologies.

The TRL guidelines for the Horizon 2020 Work Program TRLs have been referenced widely and used in H2020 proposals, evaluations, and validations. The guidelines include the following: TRL 1 basic principles observed; TRL 2 technology concept formulated; TRL 3 experimental proof-of-concept; TRL 4 technology validated in the laboratory; TRL 5 technology validated in a relevant environment (an industrially relevant environment in the case of key enabling technologies); TRL 6 technology demonstrated in relevant environment (an industrially relevant environment in the case of key enabling technologies); TRL 7 system prototype demonstration in operational environment; TRL 8 system complete and qualified; TRL 9 actual system proven in operational environment (competitive manufacturing in the case of key enabling technologies or in space). Table 1 provides descriptions of the TRL metrics and applied methodologies in the context of this study. However, the following sources may also be consulted: U.S. Department of Defense (DoD) TRL definition; NASA TRL definition; European Space Agency (ESA) TRL definition; European Commission TRL definition; and The United States Department of Energy (DOE) TRL definition in TRL Wikipedia.

2.2   Integration Readiness Levels (IRL)

IRL metrics were introduced by the Systems Development and Maturity Laboratory at the Stevens Institute of Technology. They were developed to assess the progress of information system integration and communication in the engineering field. The study aimed at realizing and validating IRL metrics in the extended context of the ISO DIS 16290 standard development framework that was established by the International Standards Organization. IRL metrics have been defined as a "systematic measurement of the interfacing of compatible interactions for various technologies and the consistent comparison of the maturity between integration points" [3, p. 5]. IRLs were used to describe and understand the integration maturity of a developing technology by using another technology or a mature information system.

IRLs contribute to TRLs by checking the location of a technology on an integration readiness scale and offering suggestions to improve integration with other technologies. In general, similar to TRLs, IRLs were designed to assess the risk and development needs of information systems integration. The rationale for the present IRLs research is that TRLs do not accurately capture the risk involved in adopting a new technology, and technology can differ architecturally according to integration readiness and system integration. In this environment, because the complexity of a system or information could increase, and a practical situation often involves a service-oriented network and shared systems, it is reasonable to employ a reliable method and ontology to achieve integration readiness. Hence, other readiness levels can be combined in the development of complex information-intensive systems of information sharing and the integration of systems in a shared system.

Described IRLs development path dependency [23] was based on the OSI model as follows: "a generic integration index required first examining what each layer really meant in the context of networking and then extrapolating that to general integration terms" [p. 6]. In this description, which is shown in Table 2, IRLs were defined as the increasing maturity of the integration between any two technologies between 2006 and 2010 through the development of an integration readiness level [3] by using a system maturity assessment approach [30]. In Table 2, IRL metrics are described in the context of this continuum of study.

As shown in Table 2, IRL layer 1 represents an interface level because integration is not possible without selecting the medium, which can affect the properties and performance of a system. Layer 2 represents interaction, that is, the ability of two technologies to influence each other over a given medium, which can be understood as the proof-of-concept of integration, such as facilitating bandwidth, error correction, and data flow control. Layer 3 represents compatibility. If two integrating technologies do not use the same interpretable data constructs or a common language, then they cannot exchange information and data fusion is difficult. Layer 4 represents a data integrity check. There is sufficient detail in the quality and assurance of the integration between technologies, which means that the data sent are received, and a checking mechanism exists. In addition, the data could be changed if part of their route were on an unsecured medium (cf. realizations [27] and understanding of layers [3]).

Table 2. Integration readiness levels (IRL).

IRLs	Descriptions
IRL (9)	**Integration is mission-proven through successful operations, e.g., harmonized operative and industrial realizations.** Integration of the information system and its sustainable maturity management is achieved; information system sharing and information sharing is realized
IRL (8)	**Integration completed and mission qualified though tests and demonstrations.** Examples are test bed, living lab, and final validation. Integration of service-based sharing level; integration of the information system is realized, implemented, and described, and actor-specific services are activated
IRL (7)	**The integration and technologies have been verified and validated with sufficient detail to be actionable.** Integration of communication and interaction; readiness for completing the information system integration is achieved and actor-specific services are validated
IRL (6)	**The integration technologies can accept, translate, and structure information for its intended application.** Readiness of technological functionalities for completing an integration is realized
IRL (5)	**There is sufficient control between the technologies necessary to establish, manage, and terminate the integration.** Integration process of management facilities is validated and implemented. Quality system for integration management is activated
IRL (4)	**There is sufficient detail in the quality and assurance of the integration between technologies.** Readiness of technology for integration management functions is achieved
IRL (3)	**There is compatibility between technologies for orderly and efficiently integration and interaction, such as a common language.** Compatibility in the infrastructure, architecture level, and ontology is achieved
IRL (2)	**There is some level of specificity that characterizes the interaction between technologies through their interface.** Infrastructure and architecture outlines are planned and agreed; integration of "proof-o-concept" is activated
IRL (1)	**An interface between technologies has been identified with sufficient detail to allow characterization of the relationship.** Usefulness, scope, and need for integration are understood, and the medium is described

In Table 2, IRL layer 5 represents integration control, which includes establishing, maintaining, and terminating integration, for example, it is possible to establish integration with other nodes for the high availability or performance pressures. Layer 6 represents the interpretation and translation of data, specifying the information to be exchanged and the information itself, as well as the ability to translate from a foreign data structure to a used one. Layer 7 represents the verified and validated integration of two technologies, such as the integration of performance, throughput, and reliability requirements. Layers 8 and 9 describe operational support and proven integration with a system environment, which corresponds to levels 8 and 9 of the TRL [3]. In layer 8 of the IRLs, a system-level demonstration in the relevant environment can be performed (the system is proven in a laboratory test). Level 9 denotes that the integrated technologies are successfully used both in the system environment and in operations (see also [30]).

3 Methodology

First, it was decided whether to conduct a case analysis or cross-case analysis [31]. The first two pilot studies [25] were conducted on integration projects in the context of industrial solutions and operative systems: "Industrial system projects" [32] and "Operative systems" [33]. We begin with a case analysis, which involves a case study of each integrated unit.

These results comprise a research data continuum (cf. The Art of Case Study Research [34] and the description of multiple cases in [10]). The methodological continuum was extended in "Toward common information sharing: Study of integration readiness levels" [18], which was a complementary case analysis. "Toward common information systems maturity validation: Resilience readiness levels (ResRL)" [4] and the present study are multiple case studies that include triangulation [31].

As part of the research continuum, the present study employs a complementary multiple case analysis, in which answers to various common questions are grouped, and different perspectives on central issues are analyzed [6]. In the descriptive setting, formal and open-ended interviews were conducted [3]. In the cross-analysis, the case study fits a cross case of each interview question with a guided approach. The data collected in the interviews are grouped by topic according to relevant data from the guide, which will not be found in the same place in each note and open-ended segment of the interviews [9]. The selection of interviews constitutes descriptive analytics, as mentioned in [31, p. 376]. In this operative environment, the pre-operational validation processes are similar to the methodological validation used in a grounded approach [35], especially in triangulation [36].

In this study, the collected data were cumulative, and they were applied in a qualitative-descriptive analysis and triangulation between January 2010 and February 2018. In this study, the data were collected according to externally funded R&D projects (n = 3), which were analyzed as multiple case studies, including triangulation. The data were placed in the following sub-categories: management data, (n = 95) files, which include strategies, drafts of visions, legislation, papers with a regional focus, scoreboards and indicators; data of meetings, development days, and reviews, (n = 94) files, which include data displays, evaluations, reviews, learning diaries, development proposals, and reports. Beginning in June 2017, the MARISA strategy canvas data were included and analyzed (n = 38 participants and n = 4 parallel sessions). Graphical canvas representations produced (n = 4) high-value elements of authorities and stakeholders that were connected to the determination of development targets, purchase choices, and continuums for the utilization of innovative data fusion functionalities, products, and services.

In this study, a summary list of research attributes was compiled to validate and describe the methodological rigor in the performed case studies [37]. Although methodological rigor was used in different cases with respect to specific attributes, the overall assessed rigor could be extended and improved (cf. [38]). The list of included attributes was extended from [37].

In this study, the main research attributes are as follows: (1) title of the study: Common information systems maturity validation: Resilience readiness levels (ResRLs); (2) research question: How can ResRL metrics be understood and described in the domain of shared information systems and services?; (3) unit of analysis: samples of resilience aspects of information systems integration and data fusion cases that are implemented, well documented and experienced; (4) importance of the study: contributes to research on information systems maturity, ResRL metrics and related development of the ISO/DIS 16290 standard series, the European Committee for Standardization (CEN-CENELE), the European Committee for Electro-technical Standardization, and CEN/TC391 on Societal and Citizen Security; (5) methodological focus: continuum of case study analysis, including triangulation and cross-analysis; (6) methodology: qualitative analysis, saturation, and triangulation; (7) research target: information service-system validation, standardization, and dissemination; (8) data collection methods: the collected cumulative project data between 2008 and 2018; the questions and interviewee were recorded, coded, reduced, archived, and translated from Finnish to English; (9) LimeSurvey questionnaires by ISDEFE were used to assess the integration activities on a system maturity scale; (questionnaires and comparison of research findings were based on [3]); (10) MARISA strategy canvas and graphical canvas representations were used.

4   Research Findings

The term resilience is used in many fields, such as engineering, infrastructure, organization, psychology, ethics, law, and socio-ecology. In this study, the scope was the technical and human-based realization of resilience readiness and decision-making. The factors and descriptions of future development were in compliance with nine levels of TRLs, IRLs, and ResRLs. The study focused on resilience in a domain where operative actors and civilian decision-makers collectively utilize analysis in cross-national border operations.

In this study, the term resilience is related to maturity and capabilities as well as the ability to recover from adverse events. It refers to the decision-making ability related to absorption and adaption, including the following themes: (1) readiness of clean data for adaptive changes; (2) resilience initiators, resilience drivers, resilience enablers, and resilience aspects of national and global pipelines; (3) modular design and dynamic strategy, and human action competence; (4) additive and dynamic capabilities and mechanisms, such as hardware, software, services, and humans in a loop; (5) clusters, high availability, parallel options, disaster control functionalities, collective activities, and safety networks; (6) mutability of configurable mechanisms, causalities, entities, services, and learning by resilience, adaptive operational resources, cognitive capabilities, and information sharing; (7) action-based situational intelligence; (8) domain intelligence, nexus management of various actors and stakeholders; (9) global intelligence, responsibility, international interactions, global pipelines, sustainability, global data sharing, and continuity.

The findings revealed that in this operative environment, "information systems maturity validation" was approached in individual institutions with respect to a specific validation depending on, for example, the rules, guidance, literature, regulation, standards, agreements, best practices, and characteristics of the system, which was then validated. The validation processes were used to determine whether the improved or developed service or product (artifact) met the requirements of the activity and whether the service or product satisfied its intended use and collectively agreed needs. The starting point in the development process was the identification of relevant stakeholders' and users' needs. The outcomes were mature and validated artifacts typically in the form of capability, which was the readiness for implementation.

Similarities were found between the activities performed in practical validation and the type of documented information produced for the validation of integrated information systems. One way of understanding the resilience-related practices in the analyzed cases was to examine the canonical documents and data standards accumulated in the practices of the stakeholders in question, their actor networks, and implementations with regard to factors of resilience.

Followed functionalities of ResRLs for nine level categories setting founded: (1) basic resilience principles and relevant user needs-based requirements for trials (e.g., dynamic and adaptive requirements, and a resilience-threat risk study of critical aspects (critical assets and aspects of cyber and hybrid threads)); (2) concept of operations and field-domain related regulations (e.g., asset, risk and vulnerability factors); (3) planned pre-operational validation, designed analytics, designed experimental critical functionalities, conducted a vulnerability study, and established proof-of-concept; (4) dynamic capabilities and modularity validation in a laboratory environment (e.g., security and resilience measures); (5) capabilities and modularity validation in a relevant operative environment (e.g., process, human and technical factors); (6) trial demonstration in a relevant operative environment (actionable resilience and concept of operations); (7) demonstration of resiliency in a shared operative environment (e.g., dynamic, adaptive and resilience factors in nexus); (8) validation of resilience functionalities completed and through test and demonstration; (9) harmonization of resilient system operations through successful mission operations, implementation of risk-threat-vulnerability assessments, performance qualification, emergency and cyber and hybrid threats response sharing, and resilience in action competence.

The findings also showed that the use of the terms resilience readiness, functionalities of resilience, and resilient learning depended on the case and the evolution domain, cultural and development paths, event mechanisms, integration, and applied technology. "Resilience readiness" referred to the proactive achievements of surviving capabilities in unexpected changes and ways of enhancing capabilities at all levels of operation and the event mechanism to create adaptive decision-making paths that were both robust and flexible. Table 3 provides a description of the first level of the combined ResRL factors in event mechanisms.

The operative focus of the term resilience was the monitoring and revising of risk models and the proactive use of resources in the face of disruption or the pressure of ongoing activities, such as control, operations, production, resilient learning, service, or trade-industry interactions. "Resilience" referred to the ability to recover from or build new positions from misfortune or adaption to mandatory change. "Resilience" included four abilities: (1) plan and prepare; (2) absorb disturbance; (3) recover; (4) adapt to known or unknown threats. The outcomes of the genealogies of the term resilience were as follows: the empirical and multidisciplinary R&D results contributed to practical operations and necessitated revisions to middle-range theories, such as modular strategy. Table 3 shows the second level of the ResRL factors proposed for modularity.

"Functionalities of resilience" can be understood as a combination of relevant responses, purposes, and factors that an authority or stakeholder chooses with respect to necessary adaptive responses to the mutability of information-intensive systems. Operative response and decision-making were path dependent on national and global rules, testing validation readiness, legislation, regulation, standards, agreements, best practices, trust management, risks, an ethical codex, and ethical effects, such as privacy, confidence, and the adaptive and dynamic characteristics of the system and networked architectures. Table 3 shows the third level of ResRLs as aspects of mutability.

In addition, the findings showed that mutual impacts and causalities, such as nexus and responsibility aspects, were significantly related to operational processes, concepts of operations, and resilience functionalities. The focus was on determining whether the "needed changes on demand" and "adapted, improved or developed system" met all requirements of the shared operational validation concepts and whether the service or product satisfied its intended use and proofs in the collective cross-border operative context. Table 3 shows the fourth level of ResRL descriptions as the proposed factors of operation resources.

"Resilient learning" referred to a pedagogical outcome when faced with inevitable difficulties and challenges, such as learning by those described frequently in national strategic research agendas and H2020 calls. In the context of this study, "resilience" referred to survival capabilities by the "realization of needed changes on demand" using appropriate situational intelligence. This finding indicated new possibilities for novel learning designs and new curriculums by adapting learning to adaptive-learning processes, such as in collective higher education institutions. Table 3 shows the fifth level of ResRL descriptions as aspects of situational intelligence.

A methodological example of canvas stakeholders-centered work on furthering high-value impact-based learning and value-based learning is the following: the goals of MARISA canvas workshops were to benefit the participants by expanding their understanding of the contribution of data fusion and how it could be achieved and represented by strategic reasoning. The participants worked in groups of six to seven stakeholders to discuss and improve their ideas of research and development (R&D), learning, and their work-in-progress. They completed a canvas as a proposal (CaaP) in collaboration with the developers.

The findings showed that in the shared system, ResRLs led to a common language and a method that furthered the organizational communication of scientists, engineers, management, and other decision-making stakeholders in systems engineering guidance, overall response, and confidence. However, a primary difficulty was that the proposed ResRLs criteria and integration factors were interpreted in multiple ways. Hence, it would be easier if the expressions were more formal and more elaborate, such as the types of operational activities needed and the concept of operations. However, the resilience and integration functions included diversity. The findings indicated that the descriptions should include a greater amount of case-sensitive data. In addition, there should be a place for the criteria inserted by users and user communities. Table 3 shows the sixth level of ResRL descriptions as factors and aspects of mutual impacts.

Table 3. Resilience readiness levels (ResRL).

ResRLs	Descriptions
ResRL (9)	**Responsibility:** social and ethical; actor engagement; shared roles; attitude; action competence and capability; education in organizations and higher education; responsibility of citizens, actors, and authorities; mutual trust; action formats; path dependency; cultural dependency; knowledge management; trust-based information sharing; transparency; confidence; sustainability; proactive views; scenario quality
ResRL (8)	**Mutual impacts:** nexus and interactions; cooperation validation; regulation; standards; collective resources; ontological alignment; hybrid and cyber systems; external actors mgmt.; collective training and awareness; network updates; collective R&D and I activities; cognitive maps and tools; impact animation; proactive activities; global databases and services; capability sharing management; expertise community
ResRL (7)	**Situational intelligence:** situational awareness and analytic system; cognitive computing; guidance services; resilient learning; machine learning; action competence and skills; recovery automation; belief-false-bias recognizance; pre-operational validation; priorities and decisions; adaption strategy; tensor analysis and applications; continuous belief functions; graphical models; simulation; rationale for target
ResRL (6)	**Activation: resilience demonstrated in relevant environment:** industrially relevant environment in the case of key enabling technologies; parallel adapters and gateways for the integration; user refinement technology; field study; feasibility study; design science research
ResRL (5)	**Dynamic and adaptive operation resources:** adaptive capabilities in concept of operations; human in loop; situation analytic an data fusion tools; reaction capabilities; response design and logic; performance and adaption indicators; data mgmt.; network management; resource management; disaster recovery; replication management; priorities; asset management; control management; configuration and change management; vulnerability management; incident management; risk management; value management

(*continued*)

Table 3. (*continued*)

ResRLs	Descriptions
ResRL (4)	**Resilience validated in lab:** following successful proof-of-concept work; components integrated; test results and estimations of differences between validation and expected system goals; technological artifacts; laboratory accounting; development research
ResRL (3)	**Mutability:** modular strategy; configurable mechanisms-entities-services; adaption models; dynamic systems; divergent communication routes and methods; encryption management; mean time between failures; manual disaster control functions; socio-technological interactions; task and sharing management; location and time management; situational information functions; modular compatibility; disruption identification; independent networks; adaptive, dynamic, and resilient systems engineering
ResRL (2)	**Modularity:** compatibility; parallel functions; clustering; high availability; data and information refinement; manual-automation redundancy functions; diagnostic structures; renewable components; component availability; replicative providers; reimbursable management; modularity design; device data and modular structure control; configuration settings and mutability control
ResRL (1)	**Events and Mechanisms:** components; devices; drivers; kernel functions; technological compatibility; parallel options and devices; serialization and transactions; pool of interfaces; routing paths and network functionalities; manual modes; attributes; parameters; sensors; logs

The findings also showed that the current form of the proposed ResRLs was useful for the realization of integration and adaptation in general. However, the proposed ResRL descriptions were not understood as a complete solution to the realization of resilience and integration maturity but as a specific operational validation path and tool for communication among all parties in a critical project, including their mutual confidence and trust in pre-order validation. One outcome was that the collective responsibility included citizens, actors, and authorities. Other aspects and factors of responsibility are shown in Table 3.

5 Discussion

This study was based on a continuum of levels of technological readiness (TRL), integration readiness (IRL), and resilience readiness (ResRLs), which are the elements in the thinking about, building, improving, and testing of information systems, networked and distributed integration, and its domain ontology (see Fig. 1). However, this view was furthered by combined system readiness levels (SRL), which were described as a combination of the TRL functions of technologies and IRL integrations, which were introduced by [23] and extended by [39].

The concept of SRL metrics is recognized as the collector of data fusion-ready metrics represented by a single SRL metric that is defined based on the amalgamation of other existing readiness levels, thus providing a method for linking different readiness level metrics. One aspect of SRL's significance is that it contributes credibility to the quantitative collection of readiness levels, and it opens possibilities for expanding SRLs by incorporating other readiness and validity metrics, such as the manufacturing readiness level, software readiness level, SRLs, and information systems maturity as well as validation on a general scale [1] and [30].

In the contexts of EU CISE 2020 information sharing and MARISA data fusion, it is noteworthy that the review of the literature on readiness metrics yielded similarities to a combination of decision-making items, a component of pre-operational or pre-order validation, and procurement management activities. Integration and data fusion could also be related to a modular implementation strategy, which is an approach to challenges related to the mobilization, steering, and organization of multiple stake-holders in wide-scale R&D collaboration. Here, the focus was on the challenges to realizing large-scale technological and information-intensive systems, which were understood not as standalone entities but as integrated with other information systems, communication technologies, and technical and non-technical elements in the domain of national and global information sharing, and integrated infrastructures as well as data and information fusion. This finding also showed that an integrated system could be a shared system in a network of shared information (cf. building nationwide information infrastructures [40] and the case of building the Internet [41]). Figure 1 shows a slightly revised proposal by [1] to extend the Common Information Systems Maturity Services Validation Approach to the European Commission.

The findings of this study showed both advantages of and challenges to the standardization and maturity development related to the ISO DIS 16290 and authority-based decision-making interconnectedness of the CEN-CENELEC and the European Committee for Electro-technical Standardization and CEN/TC391 on Societal and Citizen Security. However, ResRLs are a promising area R&D on maturity, which could make an expanded contribution to the overall scale of maturity metrics for information systems and the understanding of information system maturity.

The descriptions and factors of the proposed ResRLs present a challenge to global procurement management, such as national–international agreements and descriptions of work. Fine-grained descriptions and shared understandings of the pre-operational validation of ResRLs and resilience functionalities are needed, such as the development of terminology settings in a web ontology language. The proposed ResRLs descriptions require further testing in operational validation contexts and information systems development-realization phases. Further descriptions of the analyzed categories and questionnaires for ResRLs are also required.

The proposed ResRLs are useful where collective adaptive and dynamic functionalities are required. The findings of this study showed that data and information fusion could increase resilience and adaptive reasoning in decision-making and cross-border interactions. Relations among and the causalities of ResRLs dimensions of data fusion and decision-making also require future research. Further research is also required to understand resilience functionalities in expanded, large, networked information-intensive services that extend the shared solutions and routes of big data utilization as well as global information sharing. Resilience and nexus are mutual effects that could be focused learning themes in research on higher education, especially in shared university networks across national borders in the European Union.

The study has significant implications for further discussions of information sharing and future readiness levels. The results of the TRLs, IRLs, and ResRLs did not address enough to sub-levels and utility levels, such as user interfaces or security readiness (e.g., cyber and hybrid threat-related aspects) or action competency. Successful integration is highly dependent on users' and actors' experiences and understanding, such as the amount of work needed for successful and sustainable integration, including all necessary sub-solutions, especially regarding cyber security resilience to hybrid threats.

Thus, questionnaires about maturity should be complemented by an expanded checklist that would allow for the removal of the subjectivity of many maturity metrics. The findings also indicated that the participants may have interpreted each maturity related metric differently and that some decision-making criteria may have belonged to a different scale, thereby altering their criticality. The findings indicated that some presented criteria belonged in a test laboratory environment, which could be improved by adding their descriptions to the questionnaire or creating a sheet for the test laboratory to avoid conflicts in moving integration to production. The findings also indicated that the scale of the pre-operational validation concept depends on the case, development path, and system architecture. The use of a modular strategy and the alignment of attributes for operational validation were considered because the speed and diversity of applied technological development are increasingly high even on a three-year scale.

The mutability category included high-level system interface diagrams that were completed in an integration project, in which interface requirements and an inventory of external interfaces were defined at the concept level. The proof of the functional interactions phase was obtained by testing individual modules to verify that the module component functions worked in combination, and the software components, the operating system, middleware, loaded applications, subassemblies, cross-technology issue measurement, and performance characteristic validations were completed. The evaluation of prototype compatibility could be based on the best option of a system or prototype for testing operability and usefulness is collectively designed.

As shown in Tables 2 and 3, the final systems readiness validation between layers five and seven and activation followed [3]. The OSI model as included part of this view, including an evaluation of the artifacts, such as the service or information system; an evaluation of the efficiency, utility, performance and better, faster, cheaper factors and functions of innovation; the analytical validation of artifacts, such as the service or information system (e.g., technical performance, efficiency, simulation, formal verification, socio-technical outcomes, and organizational impacts); the activation of artifacts, such as service or information systems and integration (e.g., proof of production, value returns, proof of commercialization, and real-world and high-value impacts).

Finally, in the harmonization category, the findings showed that the operational effectiveness and suitability for the operational environment is relative challenging, measuring integration-related failure rates, and recovery from failure are fully characterized. Then, the realization is consistent with the integration and resilience requirements, and the sustainable maturity functions are activated for continuity management. Information technology and systems or services are evaluated daily for real-world, high-value impacts by practitioners and researchers of harmonization and realization.

Maturity (Tables 2 and 3) comprised the IRLs and ResRLs related to maturity, as described in [3] and [4]. In information systems, the continuous management of maturity was based on appropriate requirements. A model was proposed to improve the continuity of information systems and services. This proposal extends to the management of solutions when the failure rate increases over time. For example, the model could be useful in system recovery in the case of disruptions and interruptions in production process-related systems.

As shown in Tables 2 and 3, quality assurance concerned the procedures, processes and systems used to guarantee and improve the quality of operations. In this study, quality assurance was used to define operation-enhancing and appropriate procedures, methods, and tools as well as to monitor and develop operations in a systematic manner. In this study, quality referred to the suitability of procedures, processes, and systems in relation to strategic objectives such as the integration strategy. Quality assurance and related systems combine knowledge-based structures with the body of knowledge.

The continuums of IRLs and ResRLs explored in this study still have major challenges: human subjectivity, confidence, and trust building in data estimates. However, both IRLs and ResRLs could be needed increasingly to measure project and system integration and resilience as well as demonstrate the magnitude of achieved performance and integration level while allowing for the successful evaluation of integration and systems harmonization. Development requirements of integration are clearly increasing because: (1) operational and managerial independence of operations; (2) increasing commercial value of data; (3) challenges of borders and cultures; (4) emergent strategies and behavior (terror, cyber and hybrid aspects); (5) difficulties in mutual trust building; (6) evolutionary and development path dependency.

References

1. Pirinen, R.: Towards common information systems maturity validation - resilience readiness levels (ResRL). In: Proceedings of the 9th International Joint Conference on Knowledge Discovery, Knowledge Engineering and Knowledge Management, pp. 259–266. Scitepress, Madeira (2017)
2. Mankins, J.: Technology Readiness Levels. A White Paper. NASA, Washington (1995)
3. Sauser, B., Gove, R., Forbes, E., Ramirez-Marquez, J.: Integration maturity metrics: development of an integration readiness level. Inf. Knowl. Syst. Manag. 9(1), 17–46 (2010)
4. European Organisation for the Safety of Air Navigation (EUROCONTROL): European Operational Concept Validation Methodology Homepage. https://www.eurocontrol.int/sites/default/files/publication/files/e-ocvm3-vol-1-022010.pdf. Accessed 10 Apr 2018
5. Benbasat, I., Goldstein, D.K., Mead, M.: The case research strategy in studies of information systems. MIS Q. 11(3), 369–386 (1987)
6. Eisenhardt, K.M.: Building theories from case study research. Acad. Manag. Rev. 14(1), 532–550 (1989)
7. George, A.L., Bennett, A.: Case Studies and Theory Development in the Social Sciences, 4th edn. MIT Press, Cambridge (2005)
8. Miles, M.B., Huberman, A.M.: Qualitative Data Analysis: An Expanded Sourcebook, 2nd edn. Sage Publications, Thousand Oaks (1994)

9. Robson, C.: Real World Research, 2nd edn. Blackwell Publishing, Oxford (2002)
10. Yin, R.K.: Case Study Research Design and Methods, 4th edn. Sage Publications, Thousand Oaks (2009)
11. Herr, K., Anderson, G.L.: The action research dissertation: a guide for students and faculty, 2nd edn. Sage Publications, Thousand Oaks (2005)
12. Atooh-Okine, N.O.: Resilience Engineering Models and Analysis, 1st edn. Cambridge University Press, New York (2016)
13. Kott, A., Abdelzaher, T.: Resiliency and robustness of complex systems and networks. In: Suri, N., Cabri, G. (eds.) Adaptive, Dynamic and Resilient Systems, pp. 67–85. Taylor & Francis, Boca Raton (2014)
14. Walker, J., Cooper, M.: Genealogies of resilience: from systems ecology to the political economy of crisis adaptation. Secur. Dialogue **42**, 143–160 (2011)
15. Adger, N.W.: Social and ecological resilience: are they related. Prog. Hum. Geogr. **24**(3), 347–364 (2000)
16. Suri, N., Cabri, G.: Adaptive, Dynamic and Resilient Systems, 1st edn. Taylor & Francis, Boca Raton (2014)
17. Holling, C.S.: Resilience and stability of ecological systems. Annu. Rev. Ecol. Syst. **4**, 1–23 (1973)
18. Pirinen, R.: Towards common information sharing: study of integration readiness levels. In: Proceedings of the 7th International Joint Conference on Knowledge Discovery, Knowledge Engineering and Knowledge Management, pp. 355–364. Scitepress, Lisbon (2015)
19. Wilson, G.: Community resilience, globalization, and transitional pathways. Geoforum **43** (6), 1218–1231 (2012)
20. Brassett, J., Vaughan-Williams, N.: Security and the performative politics of resilience: critical infrastructure protection and humanitarian emergency preparedness. Secur. Dialogue **46**(1), 32–50 (2015)
21. Tanenbaum, A.S.: Computer Networks, 4th edn. Prentice Hall, Upper Saddle River (1988)
22. Eisner, H.: Systems Engineering: Building Successful Systems, 1st edn. Morgan & Claypools, San Rafael (2011)
23. Sauser, B., Verma, D., Ramirez-Marquez, J., Gove, R.: From TRL to SRL: the concept of systems readiness levels. In: Proceedings of the Conference on Systems Engineering Research, Los Angeles, paper #126, pp. 1–10 (2006)
24. Pirinen, R.: Studies of integration readiness levels: case shared maritime situational awareness system. In: Proceedings of the Joint Intelligence and Security Informatics Conference, pp. 212–215. IEEE, The Hague (2014)
25. Pirinen, R., Sivlén, E., Mantere, E.: Samples of externally funded research and development projects in higher education: case integration readiness levels. In: Proceedings of the IEEE World Engineering Education Forum, Dubai, United Arab Emirate, pp. 691–700 (2014)
26. Zimmermann, H.: OSI reference model: the ISO model of architecture for open systems interconnection. IEEE Trans. Commun. **24**(4), 425–432 (1980)
27. Beasley, J.S.: Networking, 2nd edn. Pearson Education, Boston (2009)
28. Peterson, L.L., Davie, B.S.: Computer Networks: A System Approach, 5th edn. Elsevier, Burlington (2012)
29. Mankins, J.: Technology readiness assessments: a retrospective. Acta Astronaut. **65**, 1216–1223 (2009)
30. Tan, W., Ramirez-Marquez, J., Sauser, B.: A probabilistic approach to system maturity assessment. Syst. Eng. **14**(3), 279–293 (2011)
31. Patton, M.: Qualitative Evaluation and Research Methods, 2nd edn. Sage Publications, London (1990)

32. Sivlén, E., Pirinen, R.: Utilization of the integration readiness level in the context of industrial system projects. In: Proceedings of the IEEE World Engineering Education Forum (WEEF-2014), Dubai, United Arab Emirates, pp. 701–710 (2014)
33. Mantere, E., Pirinen, R.: Utilization of the integration readiness level in operative systems. In: Proceedings of the IEEE World Engineering Education Forum (WEEF-2014), Dubai, United Arab Emirates, pp. 726–735 (2014)
34. Stake, R.: The Art of Case Study Research, 1st edn. Sage Publications, Thousand Oaks (1995)
35. Corbin, J., Strauss, A.: Basics of Qualitative Research: Techniques and Procedures for Developing Grounded Theory, 3rd edn. Sage Publications, Los Angeles (2008)
36. Campbell, D.T., Fiske, D.W.: Convergent and discriminant validation by the multitrait-multimethod matrix. Psychol. Bull. **56**, 81–105 (1959)
37. Dubé, L., Paré, G.: Rigor in information systems positivist case research: current practices, trends and recommendation. MIS Q. **27**(4), 597–635 (2003)
38. Davison, R.M., Martinsons, M.G., Kock, N.: Principles of canonical action research. Inf. Syst. J. **14**, 65–86 (2004)
39. Luna, S., Lopes, A., Tao, H., Zapata, F., Pineda, R.: Integration, verification, validation, test, and evaluation (IVVT&E) framework for system of systems (SoS). Procedia Comput. Sci. **20**, 298–305 (2013)
40. Aanestad, M., Jensen, T.B.: Building nation-wide information infrastructures in healthcare through modular implementation strategies. J. Strateg. Inf. Syst. **20**, 161–176 (2011)
41. Hanseth, O., Lyytinen, K.: Design theory for dynamic complexity in information infrastructures: the case of building internet. J. Inf. Technol. **28**, 1–19 (2010)

Author Index

Printed in the United States
By Bookmasters